Contemplating Courts

Contemplating Courts

Lee Epstein, *Editor*

Washington University in St. Louis

PRESS

A Division of Congressional Quarterly Inc.
Washington, D.C.

Copyright © 1995 Congressional Quarterly Inc.
1414 22nd Street, N.W., Washington, D.C. 20037

Printed and bound in the United States of America.

Art director, cover: Anne Masters Design, Inc.

Original painting, cover: James Yang

Library of Congress Cataloging-in-Publication Data

Contemplating courts / Lee Epstein, editor.
    p.   cm.
   Includes bibliographical references and index.
   ISBN 0-87187-983-2 (cloth : alk. paper). — ISBN 0-87187-982-4
(pbk. : alk. paper)
    1. Judicial process—United States.   2. Justice, Administration
of—United States.   3. Courts—United States.   I. Epstein, Lee,
1958-
KF8700.C66   1995
347.73'1—dc20
[347.3071]   95-6649
                                               CIP

For Harold

Contents

Preface

A few years ago, one of my former doctoral students asked me if I knew of any good readers for an undergraduate course on the judicial process. He was just getting settled in a new academic position and realized that he would need to order books for the coming semester. I responded with a few suggestions but, in the end, none of the current offerings satisfied either of us.

What we both wanted was something akin to Lawrence C. Dodd and Bruce I. Oppenheimer's *Congress Reconsidered*—a book of original, thought-provoking, and timely essays tailored to the needs of political science students; a book that would give students a compelling sample of our discipline's scholarship without the unnecessary jargon; a book whose contents could be appreciated by scholars and students alike. Unfortunately, nothing like that existed for the study of the judicial process; there was no *Courts Reconsidered*.

When conversations with others confirmed this void, I resolved to fill it by bringing the equivalent of *Congress Reconsidered* to law and courts-oriented classes. This meant, for one thing, aiming at something short of comprehensiveness. Just as *Congress Reconsidered* does not cover every aspect of legislative politics, *Contemplating Courts* does not provide an in-depth look at every dimension of judicial politics. That is because instructors typically use these kinds of books in conjunction with other texts or readings. By the same token, just as *Congress Reconsidered* presents many approaches to the study of legislative politics, I wanted the book to reflect the pluralism of the field of law and courts. Scholars of judicial politics are a varied lot, focusing on diverse substantive topics and invoking myriad research strategies. So I thought it especially important that the book convey to students the wide array of contemporary thinking on judicial processes.

With these goals in mind, *Contemplating Courts* was developed. The scope of the resulting book is revealed in its part titles—"Actors in the Legal System," "Trial Courts," "Lower Appellate Courts," "The U.S. Supreme Court," and "The Impact of Courts." These are subjects covered in virtually every judicial politics course, and instructors will be able to integrate the essays from each of the parts, in any order they choose, into their syllabi. One of the advantages of a book of readings, of course, is the flexibility it provides.

The choice of essayists also reflects my goals about the scope of the volume, for they are as varied as the field itself. Some of the contributors use numerical data to make their points; others take more contextual and historical routes. What is more, because the contributors range from Harold J. Spaeth—a founder of the modern-day study of judicial politics—to Lauren Bowen—a young but impressive Ph.D.—the chapters reflect the thinking of more than just a generation of legal analysts. They encapsulate older perspectives that have withstood the test of time and newer ones that seem quite promising.

My suggestions to the essayists were simple. First, their chapters needed to be accessible to college students. Although graduate students will find the book useful, I did not want the contributors to lose sight of the fact that undergraduates were a primary audience. As they mapped out their chapters, then, I hoped that they would consider how upper-division students would react to their work. I also asked them to avoid long literature reviews or other information that textbooks often provide.

Second, I advised the authors to use statistics or mathematics if their work required them. After all, it is important to show students how political scientists go about answering interesting substantive questions; and many scholars use abstract formalizations to represent political processes mathematically, invoke statistical techniques to test their expectations against data, and so forth. I did, however, ask the authors who used statistics or mathematics in their chapters to take great care to explain their procedures clearly.

The chapters more than exceeded my expectations. The authors raise interesting research questions, use appropriate analytic strategies, and convey their messages in accessible prose without jargon. In the end, I had to make only two adjustments to the original plan. First, I supplemented the essays with a chapter on research design. "Studying Law and Courts" (Chapter 1) provides students with an overview of the key elements contained in most sociolegal research and defines important terms used in other chapters, such as "variables," "statistical significance," and so forth. Second, I added methodological appendices that specifically address the logic of regression, probit, and logit models. Statistically speaking, these are the most sophisticated tools used in the book. And, while the essayists who rely on them provide excellent explanations, I thought it best to set them out clearly and uniformly in an appendix so that interested students could develop further intuitions about the way they worked.

In the end, my greatest hope is that Contemplating Courts has as long an academic life as *Congress Reconsidered,* now in its fifth edition. The contributors and I have tried to produce a book that will accomplish that end. Please let me know where we have succeeded and where we have not so that any necessary adjustments can be made in future editions.

In editing this volume, I have accrued many, many debts. Now is the time to pay off at least some of them. First and foremost, I thank the people at CQ Press. This is the fourth book I have published with them, and I will keep coming back as long as they will have me. As far as I'm concerned, they run the most professional shop in the business, never sacrificing integrity for profit. Brenda Carter, CQ Press acquisitions editor, deserves special recognition. Despite her job title, Brenda did more than "acquire" this volume; she guided it through every stage of the process and offered many constructive suggestions. She was never shy about letting me know when and where I had gone astray—the most fundamentally important task an editor can perform. I am also grateful to Nancy Lammers, a director at Congressional Quarterly, who commissioned the wonderful cover art, among other things. Our copy editor, Joanne Ainsworth, too, deserves kudos. Joanne faced the daunting task of making sense out of seventeen chapters, written by scholars with significantly different theoretical, methodological, and substantive concerns. And she came through splendidly. I know I speak for all the contributors in acknowledging her efforts on our behalf. Finally, to Ann O'Malley I offer my sincere thanks for considerably smoothing the production process.

This brings me to the essayists, who all worked hard to produce their chapters. Without their outstanding contributions this book would not have been as strong, or even possible. I am especially indebted to Lawrence Baum, Gregory A. Caldeira, Joseph F. Kobylka, Lynn Mather, and Thomas G. Walker—all of whom provided valuable moral support and concrete suggestions as the project progressed. Jeffrey A. Segal was, as always, a constant source of inspiration. He never begged off debating even the most minor of points, and more often than not he forced me to reconsider my position. Throughout this project, indeed throughout my entire professional life, he has been my biggest fan and my harshest critic. I am grateful for both.

My third set of debts is to the members of the Department of Political Science at Washington University. I can hardly imagine a better set of colleagues. They are intellectually engaging and congenial—an unbeatable combination. It is hard to know how to thank two of them, in particular. As chair of the department, John Sprague has supported all my efforts with more force than I could possibly deserve. As a colleague with an interest in public law issues, Jack Knight has done much to reshape my thinking about judicial politics; he is always ready to read the roughest of drafts and listen to even my most half-baked ideas.

Finally, a few personal acknowledgments. My parents, Ann and Ken Spole, have supported my career with genuine enthusiasm, as has my husband, Jay (although occasionally with less enthusiasm, especially after long days at the office). My professional life would have been far different had the personal side been any less. Last but surely not least is Harold J. Spaeth, to whom I dedicate this book. What can I say about a man whose work I so admire, whose professional life I seek to emulate? He is one of the true heroes of my generation of scholars, and I am proud to count him among my closest friends. Harold, this one's for you.

Lee Epstein
Washington University in St. Louis

Contributors

Lawrence Baum is professor of political science at Ohio State University. He is the author of *American Courts* (1994) and *The Supreme Court* (1995). His research has dealt with issues such as the sources of change in Supreme Court policy and interactions between the Supreme Court and lower courts. He is currently engaged in research on assessment of explanations for the behavior of judges.

Lauren Bowen is an assistant professor of political science at John Carroll University. She received her Ph.D. from the University of Kentucky in 1992, writing a dissertation entitled, "Attorney Advertising in the Wake of *Bates v. State Bar of Arizona* (1977): A Study of Judicial Impact." The major findings of the dissertation are forthcoming in *American Politics Quarterly*. She is currently researching the impact of sexual harassment decisions by the U.S. Supreme Court on all affected populations.

Gregory A. Caldeira is a professor of political science at Ohio State University. He received a Ph.D. from Princeton University in 1978. He has published articles on the courts and American politics in the *American Political Science Review*, the *American Journal of Political Science*, the *Journal of Politics*, the *Law and Society Review*, the *British Journal of Political Science*, and many other journals. Currently he is engaged in programs of research on the role and effect of organized interests in the formation of the Supreme Court's agenda; the relationship between interest groups and the Senate in the selection of federal judges, especially on the Supreme Court; and public attitudes toward the European Court of Justice and national high courts in the European Union.

Charles M. Cameron received his Ph.D. from Princeton University and is now assistant professor of political science at Columbia University. A former Brookings Fellow and recipient of grants from the National Science Foundation, his work has appeared in leading journals of political science. He is a specialist in applied formal theory, who, with Jeffrey Segal and Donald Songer, is writing a book on the judicial hierarchy.

Thomas W. Church is professor and chair of the Political Science Department at the State University of New York, Albany. He received his B.A. from Whitman College and his

Ph.D. from Cornell University. His research has focused on the operation of civil and criminal trial courts and, more generally, on issues relating to the intersection of law and public policy. His most recent work is a comparative study of environmental law and policy in the United States and northern Europe.

Lee Epstein is professor of political science and resident fellow of the Business, Law, and Economics Center at Washington University in Saint Louis, Missouri. She received her Ph.D. from Emory University in 1983. She is the author of *Conservatives in Court* (1985), and the coauthor of several books, including *The Supreme Court and Legal Change* (1992) with Joseph F. Kobylka, and *Constitutional Law for a Changing America* (1995) with Thomas G. Walker. Her articles on the Supreme Court, interest groups, and related topics have appeared in political science and law journals, including the *American Political Science Review*, the *American Journal of Political Science*, and the *Journal of Politics*. Her current research invokes game theory to study judicial decision making.

Charles H. Franklin is associate professor of political science at the University of Wisconsin, Madison. In addition to work on public opinion and the Supreme Court, he has written on U.S. Senate campaigns and party identification. His articles have appeared in the *American Political Science Review* and the *American Journal of Political Science*.

Leslie Friedman Goldstein is the author of *Constitutional Rights of Women* (1988), *In Defense of the Text* (1991), and *Contemporary Cases in Women's Rights* (1994) and is the editor of *Feminist Jurisprudence: The Difference Debate* (1992). She is professor of political science at the University of Delaware and former chair of the Law and Courts Section of the American Political Science Association.

Christine B. Harrington is the director of the Institute for Law and Society and associate professor of politics at New York University. She has published articles on the politics of court reform, dispute processing and alternative dispute resolution, regulatory litigation, legal ideology, constitutive and interpretive sociolegal theory, and the American legal profession. She is the author of *Shadow Justice: The Ideology and Institutionalization of Alternatives to Court* (1985); the coauthor, with Lief Carter, of *Administrative Law and Politics* (1991); and the coeditor, with Paul Brace and Gary King, of *The Presidency in American Politics* (1989), and, with Maureen Cain, of *Lawyers in the Postmodern World: Translation and Transgression* (1994).

Joseph F. Kobylka is associate professor of political science at Southern Methodist University. He received his Ph.D. from the University of Minnesota. He is the author of *The*

Politics of Obscenity (1991) and the coauthor of *The Supreme Court and Legal Change* (1992) and *Public Interest Law* (1992), both with Lee Epstein. He has also published articles in a variety of law and political science journals. He is finishing a judicial biography of Justice Harry A. Blackmun and beginning a study of the judicial manifestations of the modern controversy surrounding church-state relations.

Liane C. Kosaki received her Ph.D. from the University of Michigan, Ann Arbor. She is currently visiting assistant professor of political science at Beloit College. She has written numerous papers on public opinion and the Supreme Court and is currently working on a book, with Charles H. Franklin, on the subject.

Kevin T. McGuire is assistant professor of political science at the University of Minnesota. He received his Ph.D. from Ohio State University. His publications include *The Supreme Court Bar: Legal Elites in the Washington Community* (1993) and several articles on decision making in the U.S. Supreme Court.

Lynn Mather is professor of government at Dartmouth College. Her research has focused on trial courts in the United States. She has published *Plea Bargaining or Trial?* and *Empirical Theories about Courts*, as well as various journal articles. Her current research addresses the role of lawyers in divorce cases, exploring issues of lawyer-client interaction, gender difference among divorce lawyers, the effect of mediation on lawyers, and the nature of legal negotiation. Professor Mather has served as chair of the Law and Courts Section of the American Political Science Association (1993-1994) and treasurer of the Law and Society Association (1983-1987).

David C. Nixon is a graduate student in political science at Washington University in St. Louis. He specializes in American politics and political methodology and is currently completing his doctoral dissertation on relations between legislators and bureaucrats.

Richard L. Pacelle, Jr., is assistant professor of political science at the University of Missouri, St. Louis. He did his graduate work at Ohio State University and is the author of *The Transformation of the Supreme Court's Agenda: From the New Deal to the Reagan Administration*. His current research is concerned with the notion of issue evolution in the Supreme Court.

Gerald N. Rosenberg is associate professor in the Department of Political Science and lecturer in law at the University of Chicago. He earned a master's degree in politics and philosophy from Oxford University, a doctor of law degree from the University of Michigan, and a doctorate in political science from Yale University. A member of the Washington, D.C., bar, he is the author of *The Hollow Hope: Can Courts Bring about Social Change?* (1991).

Kim Lane Scheppele is Arthur F. Thurnau Associate Professor of Political Science and Public Policy and adjunct associate professor of law at the University of Michigan. She received her doctoral degree in sociology in 1985 from the University of Chicago. She is the author of *Legal Secrets: Equality and Efficiency in the Common Law* and has written extensively about rape, domestic violence, abortion, and legal theory. She is currently working on a new book about the development of constitutional consciousness in a post-communist society, having spent the 1994-1995 academic year working at the Hungarian Constitutional Court.

Jeffrey A. Segal is professor of political science at the State University of New York at Stony Brook. He received his doctoral degree from Michigan State University in 1983. His books include *The Supreme Court and the Attitudinal Model* (1993) with Harold J. Spaeth, and *The Supreme Court Compendium* (1994) with Lee Epstein, Harold J. Spaeth, and Thomas G. Walker. His articles on the Supreme Court have appeared in the *American Political Science Review*, the *American Journal of Political Science*, the *Journal of Politics*, and elsewhere.

Donald R. Songer is professor of political science at the University of South Carolina. He received his doctorate from the University of North Carolina in 1975. He is currently directing a project funded by the National Science Foundation to create a multi-user database on the decisions of the U.S. courts of appeals from 1925 to 1988. His work on appellate court decision making and judicial impact has appeared in a number of journals, including the *American Political Science Review*, the *American Journal of Political Science*, the *Journal of Politics*, and *Judicature*.

Harold J. Spaeth is professor of political science at Michigan State University. He received his Ph.D. from the University of Cincinnati and his J.D. from the University of Michigan. He is the author or coauthor of more than ten books, including *Supreme Court Decision Making* (1976) and *The Supreme Court and the Attitudinal Model* (1993). Professor Spaeth is also principal investigator of the United States Supreme Court Judicial Database.

Thomas G. Walker is professor of political science at Emory University. He received his Ph.D. from the University of Kentucky. He is the author or coauthor of ten books, including *A Court Divided* (1988), which won the prestigious V. O. Key, Jr., Award for the best book on southern politics. Currently he is engaged, with Lee Epstein and William Dixon, in a study of U.S. Supreme Court decision making in times of international crises.

Daniel S. Ward is assistant professor of political science at Rice University. He received his Ph.D. from New York University in 1989. His research has focused on political institutions and legislative behavior. Among his publications are articles in the *Journal of Politics, Legislative Studies Quarterly, Comparative Politics,* and *Party Politics.*

John R. Wright is professor of political science at George Washington University. His research on interest groups and various aspects of American politics has been published in the *American Political Science Review,* the *American Journal of Political Science,* the *Journal of Politics,* and other specialized journals.

1 Studying Law and Courts

Lee Epstein

In the 1963 case of *School District of Abington Township v. Schempp,* the U.S. Supreme Court ruled that the First Amendment to the Constitution prohibits prayer and Bible-reading exercises in public school. This ruling was immensely controversial. Many public schools throughout the United States—but especially in the South—had historically engaged in some form of prayer in school. The public outcry against *Schempp* was so great that members of Congress immediately introduced nearly 150 proposals to overturn the decision.

Given the hostile political environment surrounding the Court's pronouncement, a natural question arises: Did school districts comply with *Schempp?* In his textbook *The Supreme Court,* the political scientist Lawrence Baum (1992b, 214) provides one answer when he writes that "[w]ithin three years . . . the frequency of school prayer and Bible readings had declined by about one-half; . . . this decline is noteworthy. But equally striking is the continuation in so many schools of practices that the Supreme Court had declared to be unconstitutional."

Although Baum's statement provides useful information about public response to *Schempp,* it points to an interesting question: How does Baum know that only about one-half of all schools complied with the Court's rulings? To put the question more generally, from where do the authors of textbooks obtain the facts and figures that populate their works? The answer to these questions is quite simple. Usually textbook writers rely on studies conducted by other researchers working in their field. In making the claim about the effect of the school prayer decisions, for example, Baum cited a study by H. Frank Way, Jr. (1968), who surveyed school districts and found that compliance was occurring in only about half.

From this perspective we can begin to understand the importance of research. The most obvious benefit is the useful information that scholarly studies provide to society. The

Brenda Carter, Jack Knight, Lynn Mather, Jeffrey A. Segal, and Thomas G. Walker made very useful comments on an earlier version of this chapter. Segal also drafted several sections, and I am most grateful for his help.

results of Way's survey, for instance, highlight the Supreme Court's lack of power to enforce its decisions; it may be unable to generate compliance with its rulings if we—the people—reject them. Somewhat less obvious, though, is the role played by research and how it influences what instructors teach and what students learn. It was Way's study of prayer in school that enabled Baum to write about compliance with the Court's decision. And it is Baum's textbook, not necessarily Way's study, that instructors assign to their students to read.

This point—that an intimate link exists between research and teaching—is often obscured in debates that pit one against the other. We have all heard the voices of the commentators who complain that professors spend too much time conducting research and too little teaching students. Without denying the validity of these claims, I would say that at the very least they set up a false and unfair dichotomy. As the Way-Baum connection illustrates, much of what scholars teach and students learn comes from research. The converse is true as well. Students, through their questions, often generate research ideas. My own experience bears this out. While I was teaching a course on defendants' rights, a student asked me a penetrating question about the death penalty. When I found I could not supply a definitive answer, I asked one of my colleagues the question. He, in turn, suggested that we conduct some research to derive a solution. We did, and a book that I now use in that very class (Epstein and Kobylka 1992) resulted.[1]

As readers can probably tell, I have strong feelings about the relation between teaching and research, feelings that occasionally run counter to fashionable commentary. The purpose of this book, however, is not to provide an abstract response to those who set teaching against research. Rather, by example it lends support to their interrelatedness. In each chapter, authors raise significant substantive questions and address them through appropriate analytic research strategies. One of the goals of the book is to bring the research process to students and instructors *directly,* not by the usual route of researcher to textbook writer to student (for example, Way to Baum to student).

A second and related objective is to give students some sense of the mechanics behind conducting research. Undergraduates, in particular, often see their professors furiously typing something into a computer or sifting through various collections in the library. But they have little idea about what they are up to or about the research process.

The contributors to this book provide a window to this process by exploring specific topics related to law and courts. Jeffrey A. Segal, Donald R. Songer, and Charles M. Cameron, for example, consider the relation between lower and upper appellate courts; Richard Pacelle examines the marked change in the Supreme Court's agenda; and so on. In what follows, I take a more general course. I outline the research process, leaving the details up to the essayists to fill in.

Figure 1-1 The Research Process

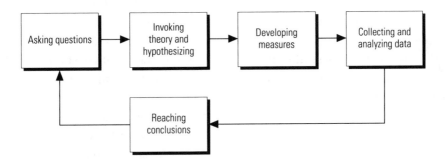

Sources: Bernstein and Dyer 1984, 3: Williamson et al., 1982, 7.

An Outline of the Research Process

The social-scientific research process is not a monolith; instead, it reflects the diversity of theoretical and substantive interests of the various disciplines. Consider the contributions to this volume. All the authors are concerned with issues relating to law and courts, but a mere glance at their essays attests to the pluralism of approaches. For example, although the contributions of Harold J. Spaeth and Leslie Friedman Goldstein both concentrate on judicial decision making, they ask very different questions. Spaeth considers how judges decide cases; Goldstein asks how they *should* decide cases. The subtle but crucial difference in the wording of their questions gives rise to divergent research strategies: Spaeth takes a data-intense approach, and Goldstein takes a more contextual one.

For all the differences, however, patterns exist. Virtually all research on law and courts—and, for that matter, on political and social phenomena more generally—shares some common features. Studies tend to (1) focus on specific research questions, (2) invoke theories to provide initial answers (or predictions), (3) develop ways (or measures) to turn predictions into testable hypotheses, and (4) examine the hypotheses against observable facts to reach some conclusions. Figure 1-1 provides a visual description of this process; below, I consider each of these features, with emphasis on their relation to legal social scientific scholarship.[2]

Asking the Question

Almost all research starts with a basic question or set of questions to which the scholar wants to learn the answer. In the field of law and courts, questions can be as broad in scope as, What factors generate crime in the United States? to ones more narrowly focused, such as, Does the death penalty serve to deter murder? They can center on aggregates (Why does the Supreme Court vote the way it does?) or individuals (Why does Chief Justice Rehnquist vote the way he does?). And they may be focused on events occurring at a specific point in time (What explains the senators' votes in the confirmation proceedings for Robert Bork in 1987?) or over time (What explains senators' votes in confirmation proceedings between 1900 and 1994?).

How do scholars select their research questions? An important factor is interest. Scholars, like all people, are interested in some topics more than others. And since research questions are a way to narrow a topic, it is not too surprising that scholars focus on things that interest them. Suppose I am intrigued by the relationship between international crises and judicial decision making in cases concerning civil liberties. If that is my interest, I might then narrow my question to something along these lines: Are jurists more likely to repress rights and liberties during times of war?

Another, related factor is curiosity. Many things can lead scholars to become curious about particular phenomenon. When my student asked me the question about the death penalty that I could not answer, I became curious—almost insatiably so—about the appropriate response. Curiosity can also emerge from discrepancies between what scholars think they know and what they observe. To return to the issue of war and liberties, I thought I knew the answer to the question posed above: according to research by Jeffrey A. Segal and Harold J. Spaeth (1993), external events, such as wars and international crises, should not influence judicial rulings unless the litigation itself deals with such events. That is because justices base their decisions on the facts of cases in light of their own ideological attitudes and values. They are "single-minded seekers of legal policy" whose ideology dictates their votes. Or, as Segal and Spaeth (1993, 65) put it, "Rehnquist votes the way he does because he is extremely conservative; Marshall voted the way he did because he is extremely liberal." Thus, this view—what Segal and Spaeth label an *attitudinal* approach— leaves no room for external events, such as wars, that are not explicitly part of the facts of the case; in general, Rehnquist will take the conservative position and Marshall will take the liberal one, regardless of whether or not a war is occurring.[3]

Although the logic invoked by Segal and Spaeth seems to make sense, I became troubled by the presence of certain "facts" that do not sit comfortably with their explanation. For one thing, the justices have implied that they, like "all citizens . . . both in and out of uniform, feel the impact of war in greater or lesser measure" (*Korematsu v. United States* 1944). According to some scholars (for example, Emerson 1970), this kind of statement is suggestive. It implies that the Court thinks of cases—even those unrelated to the war effort—differently during times of war and peace. There is yet another piece of the puzzle that did not add up to me. That is, analysts (for example, Dahl 1957) have long argued that as part of the ruling regime, the Court usually upholds the interests of the majority, a phenomenon that may be even more attenuated during times of crisis or when national security interests are at stake. Under this view, the initiation of crisis conditions jolts the

Court into the necessity of being more sensitive to the interests and wishes of the public and other government institutions. The discrepancy between the explanation of Segal and Spaeth and these "facts" only heightened my curiosity; I became genuinely puzzled.

Theorizing about Possible Answers

Once scholars hit upon questions they find interesting or about which they are curious, the next step is to think about possible answers, which can be used to generate predictions or expectations. Where do scholars find these potential answers?

Sometimes they discover them in the scholarly literature; they scrutinize the results of past research and apply them to their problem. That is why most academic publications, including many of the chapters in this book, include reviews of the relevant literature. For example, in thinking about decision making during times of war, I would want to know if any other scholar had attempted to answer precisely the same question. And, in fact, a search I conducted of journals and books turned up several studies directly on point. *The System of Freedom of Expression*, by Emerson (1970), for one, provides a descriptive analysis of cases decided before and after periods of threat to the nation's external security. Emerson finds that the Court is more likely to repress rights and liberties when the United States is at war, even in cases unrelated to the particular international crisis.

Emerson's work provides me with valuable leverage on my *specific* research problem. And I certainly would mention the study in my literature review. But since social scientists strive to produce *general* explanations, more often than not they seek broader answers to their research questions. That is why we turn to "theories." In the context of social science research, theories are sets of "principles" that provide us insight into why actors behave the way they do (see Williamson et al. 1982). Scholars often use these insights to develop crisp expectations about the relations that intrigue them.

By way of illustration, reconsider the object of my interest: the relation between war and judicial decision making. How might I use theory to inform my research? I would start by identifying appropriate theories, those that speak to the issue of political decision making. Then, I would use those theories to generate expectations about the relationship between war and judicial decisions in civil liberties cases. For my research, I would have no trouble in finding such theories, since scholars in political science have paid a good deal of attention to the subject of decision making. We already know about one such theory—the attitudinal approach offered by Segal and Spaeth—and the expectations about the relationship between war and judicial decision making that it would generate (that is, there would be *no* relation independent of the facts of the case). But there are others. Many *rational choice* theories of judicial decision making, for example, begin with the same assumption as Segal and Spaeth—that justices are goal-directed, single-minded seekers of legal policy (Eskridge 1991a and 1991b). But, unlike Segal and Spaeth, choice theories of judicial decisions emphasize that these goal-directed actors operate in strategic or independent decision-making context: the justices know that their "fates" depend on the preferences of other actors—such as Congress, the president, and their colleagues—and choices they expect these other actors to make, not just on their own actions (Ordeshook 1992, chap. 1).[4] This notion of interdependent choice is important for the following reason. If justices really are single-minded seekers of legal policy, then they necessarily care about the "law," broadly defined. And if they care about the ultimate state of the law—about generating policy that other institutions will not overturn—then they must act strategically, taking into account the preferences of others and the actions they expect others to take. Occasionally, such calculations will lead them to act in a sophisticated fashion (that is, in a way that does not reflect their sincere or true preferences) so as to avoid the possibility of seeing their most preferred policy rejected by their colleagues in favor of their least preferred one, of Congress replacing their preference with its own, of political noncompliance, and so forth (Murphy 1964; Rodriguez 1994).

If we adopt this rational choice theory, then we would obtain a prediction about the relationship between war and judicial decision making very different from the one generated by Segal and Spaeth. Suppose Justice X were to select among three possible outcomes in an ordinary criminal case, unrelated to any war effort. Further suppose that Justice X preferred outcome 1 to 2 and outcome 2 to 3. In such a case, we would posit that the attitudinal Justice X would always choose outcome 1, regardless of whether or not America was fighting a war, while the strategic Justice X might choose outcome 2 if—depending on the political context (for example, a time of war), the preferences of the political actors involved (for example, Congress), and the actions those actors are expected to take—that would allow her to avoid outcome 3. In other words, while Segal and Spaeth's attitudinal theory posits that no relation will exist between judicial decisions and wars (unless, of course, the war is part of the case facts), the rational choice view of the Court suggests that a relationship could emerge, depending on the preferences of the key political actors and the actions they are expected to take.

In the pages that follow, students will see how other researchers invoke various theories to guide their research, to help them to formulate expectations about the relations under investigation. In many of these chapters, however, students will find that essayists use the term *model* instead of *theory*. Indeed, in his essay, Spaeth refers to the attitudinal approach as a model, not a theory. What are the differences between these two terms?[5]

The answer to this question, as Figure 1-2 suggests, depends on the nature of the model. As we can see, the two parts of Figure 1-2 are models in the sense that they are "visual depiction[s] of how something works" (Williamson et al. 1982, 20); yet, they provide us with very different kinds of information. The first part of the Figure *describes* how cases proceed through the U.S. Supreme Court, but it does not explain much about that process.

Figure 1-2 Descriptive and Explanatory Models

Descriptive Model: The Processing of Supreme Court Cases Placed on the Plenary Docket

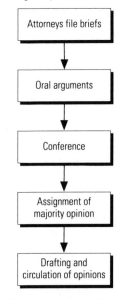

Explanatory Model: The Attitudinal Model of Judicial Decision Making

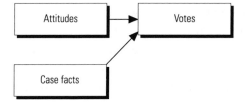

From this picture we could not, for example, say why the Court affirms some cases and reverses others; all we learn from the diagram is that the Court makes decisions on the merits of cases after it hears oral arguments, holds conferences, and so forth. The attitudinal model depicted in the second part of Figure 1-2 is quite different. It shows that a justice's decision in a given case is influenced by the facts of that case in relation to the justice's ideology. To put it differently, attitudinalists assert that two factors—case facts and ideology—*explain* judicial decisions.

Seen in this way, the first part of Figure 1-2 is a descriptive model, and the second part is an explanatory one. Undeniably, both are useful for scholars conducting research on law and courts. But descriptive models can only help us to build theory, whereas explanatory models possess all of the attributes of theory. Hence, for our purposes, when models—such as Segal and Spaeth's attitudinal model—seek to explain some phenomenon, *models* and *theories* are synonymous. It is only those models that seek to describe phenomenon that are wholly distinct from theory.

The chapters to come serve to reinforce the significance of theories and models (from this point on, I use the terms *theories* and *models* interchangeably with the understanding that I am talking about explanatory models).[6] The essays also serve to shore up an important point: however useful theories and models may be, they have their limits. In particular, students should keep in mind that they are simplified versions of reality, much like an airplane model is a simplified version of a real airplane (Schrodt 1991, 294). Just as an expertly constructed model airplane may look—though not act—exactly like the real thing, models in social science are not meant to constitute reality. To the contrary, they are purposefully designed to ignore certain aspects of the real world and focus instead on a crucial set of explanatory factors. In seeking to explain the relation between war and judicial decision making, for example, I might be able to list dozens of reasons why a given justice in a given case during a given war would, say, repress rights and liberties: the justice served in the military, the justice admired the president who was serving as commander in chief, and so forth. But suppose I could identify one major underlying explanation, such as the one proposed by the attitudinal model, and I could deploy that model to show that 80 percent of all judicial votes cast during all wars conducted during our nation's history could be explained by the case facts and political ideology. If this was the case, then the attitudinal model would provide us with an extraordinarily useful tool for explaining and understanding not just one justice's vote but most votes cast by most justices.

This example reflects both the disadvantages and advantages of theory. When we try to make generalizations about a phenomenon—say, judicial decision making—we lose the specifics that are part of reality (those specifics may form the 20 percent of the votes left unexplained by ideology and case facts in my illustration above). Yet, the simplifications inherent in models provide social scientists with useful handles for understanding the real world and for reaching general conclusions about the way that world works.

Operationally Defining Concepts

As I noted earlier, theories and models also provide us with ways to develop expectations about the relation we are seeking to explain. If I were to invoke the attitudinal model to explore the relation between judicial decision making in civil liberties cases and wars, I would expect to find that such external events—unless they were part of the case facts—had no effect on judicial voting; justices would simply vote their attitudes. In contrast, if I were to adopt a rational choice approach, I would predict that wars may have some effect on the vote, depending on the preferences of other actors, such as Congress and the president.

We often refer to these kinds of predictions—ones that our models and theories generate—as hypotheses. Hypotheses are claims about the relationships between variables. By *variables*, I mean "observable characteristics" of some phenomenon that, as the name suggests, vary. Sex is a variable: it can take on one of two values, male or female. We can also think of judicial decisions as a variable. Depending on the nature of the study, for example, decisions can take on the value of liberal or conservative, important or unimportant to the public, repressive or tolerant, and so forth. In social science research, we often talk about two kinds of variables, *independent* and *dependent* variables. *Dependent* variables are the things we are trying to explain; *independent* variables are those properties that we think cause the variation in our dependent variables. Hence, in my example about the relationship between war and judicial decision making, the political environment (whether we are engaged in a war or not) would constitute my independent variable, and judicial outcomes (whether the Court decided for or against the civil liberties claim), the dependent variable.

But hypotheses do more than state the variables under examination; they also posit a relationship between the dependent and independent variables. To return to my example, the attitudinal model would lead to the following hypothesis: judicial outcomes (the dependent variable) will not necessarily be any more or less supportive of civil liberties during times of war than in times of peace; only attitudes and case facts will determine outcomes. The strategic component of rational choice theories would suggest a very different kind of prediction: even after we consider (or control for) case facts and attitudes, judicial outcomes will be less supportive of civil liberties during times of war than during times of peace if that is the preference of other key political actors, and if the justices expect them to act on their preference (that is, override decisions to the contrary).

Making predictions or hypothesizing about, in my case, judicial decisions is one thing; determining the accuracy of those predictions is quite another. Indeed, in systematic sociolegal research, as in all social science work, scholars face particularly acute problems in testing their predictions. One of the most severe problems concerns measurement. Think about it this way. Suppose I was a chemist who wanted to determine the relation between water and temperature. Theory leads me to the prediction that when water freezes it turns to ice. Measurement is no obstacle: we can simply define *water* as H_2O and *freezing* as 32 degrees Fahrenheit. These are "operational" definitions on which all chemists and even schoolchildren would agree. Now reconsider the topic of judicial decision making in civil liberties cases during times of war. Unlike chemists, who enjoy consensus over the definitions of terms like *water*, legal scholars do not necessarily agree on what constitutes "civil liberties" cases. Should we define them strictly with regard to the First Amendment or should we consider cases involving criminal justice and equality, as well? What about wars? Are "wars" only those declared by Congress, or do they include long-term, but undeclared, military efforts, such as those that took place in Korea and Vietnam?

Because reasonable people might disagree over how to define operationally the concepts of civil liberties or wars, these are decisions I, as the researcher, must make. Making choices about appropriate measures, thus, constitutes part of the research process. But the decisions scholars make are not unfettered; in fact, their colleagues will judge them by two criteria, *reliability* and *validity*. A *reliable* measure "is one that can be used over and over again with comparable results," regardless of who does the measuring (Williamson et al. 1982, 70). Say I classified President Reagan's air strike on Libya as a war, but another researcher, *using my measurement procedure,* did not classify the same air strike as a war. That would provide some evidence that my measure was unreliable and, hence, should not be used.[7]

Why are some measures unreliable? The most common reason is that they are vague. As Bernstein and Dyer (1984, 60) note, "All too often in the political science literature, measurement procedures are not described or are only vaguely noted.... Fellow scientists cannot tell how the original researcher obtained his results, nor can they replicate (repeat) the work to check its accuracy." To put it another way, if I classified the Libyan air strike as a war and the next researchers, using my procedures, did not, the problem is mine, not theirs. I failed to describe adequately my operational definition or measure of war. To prevent this problem, I would be best off to use a crisp definition, such as, "Wars are those military efforts that have been declared by Congress." Since Congress never declared war against Libya, there would be no reason why I or the researchers seeking to replicate my work would classify Reagan's air strike as a war.

In addition to reliability, scholars look for measures that are *valid.* A measure is valid if it "measures a property as it was defined" (Bernstein and Dyer 1984, 61). Operationally defining war by the criteria of congressional declaration is a valid measure of war: few would disagree that a war is occurring when Congress declares one.[8] But suppose I define a state of war as the condition that exists each day on which 500 or more people die in the United States. This would not be a valid measure of war because U.S. deaths come about from many factors—murders, heart attacks, suicides—and not necessarily from wars. If I defined *war* in this way, then, other researchers could attack my work—and rightfully so— on the ground that I would be testing the Court's response to deaths, not wars.

When reading the chapters to come or, for that matter, any social scientific research, keep these points in mind. It is not enough for researchers to ask interesting questions and to invoke appropriate theories; they must also develop measures that reliably and validly tap the concepts that make up the posited relationships.

Testing Expectations against Data

The next stage in the research process is one of the most delicate: it involves amassing evidence to explore expectations generated by models and then analyzing that evidence.[9] As students will see, virtually all the chapters in this volume have such an *empirical* component, meaning that the writers seek to evaluate their hypotheses against observations in the real world. But there is great variety in the kinds of evidence they bring to bear on their research questions and in the types of analyses they invoke.

To clarify these points, let us return to the question of war and judicial decision making. Suppose I wanted to test the attitudinal model's prediction that only facts and ideology—and not external events on issues unrelated to the case, such as wars—affect the votes of the justices. What kinds of evidence or data could I collect? And how might I analyze that evidence? One approach would be to examine contextually specific Court decisions. For example, I could select a few cases that occurred, say, directly before the onset of World War II and a few cases decided during the war in which the same set of justices participated. Then, I might closely read the opinions in those cases to determine whether the war had any effect. If I followed this approach, my test would take the form of a descriptive comparison of the opinions handed down before and during the war.

Another approach would be to examine Court outcomes systematically. For example, on the basis of some clear criteria, I could classify the outcome of every Court decision handed down, say, during the past sixty years, as pro-liberties or anti-liberties. These outcomes, thus, would constitute my dependent variable, or the property I was trying to explain. I would also note certain attributes of the outcomes I was classifying, such as whether or not the cases occurred during a time of war; whether they involved religion, free speech, or free press; whether the Court was a liberal or conservative one; whether the case facts centered on a war-related issue; and so forth. These attributes are my independent variables, or those properties that I think cause variation in my dependent variable. Naturally, the independent variables emanate from the model under analysis. For example, to explore (that is, test) the attitudinal model's prediction that only the facts of the case and the ideology of the Court affect judicial decisions, I must have knowledge of those independent variables—case facts and court ideology.

This last step—testing the model—I might accomplish by invoking a statistical procedure—one that would allow me to determine whether war had any effect on Court outcomes after I considered (or controlled for) those variables that the attitudinal model considers critical: Court ideology and case facts. In other words, I would want to employ statistical tools to probe the relation between judicial outcomes and the political environment (times of war or not), ideology, and case facts. Such statistical tools come in many forms, but all center on an important concept in social science research: *probability*. Scholars use this term in much the same way as laypersons, to refer to the likelihood that something will occur. But to scholars, probability means more than simply *guessing* about whether something will or will not happen. It is often used to establish—with some degree of precision—"the likelihood of a given set of data emerging by chance" (Hoover 1988, 98). To see this usage of probability, think about jurors examining blood on a murder weapon. Suppose a medical expert told them that the chance of a random relationship between the blood found on the weapon and the defendant's blood was only one in a hundred. The jurors would surely feel a good deal more confident in making the inference that the defendant wielded the murder weapon than if the expert had told them that there were fifty chances out of a hundred. The same is true of social scientists. Quite typically, we consider data important at a *level of significance* of .05 or less (represented in tables throughout this book as $p \leq .05$), which means that there are only—at maximum—five chances in a hundred that the relation would occur by chance. To put it another way, we want to believe that there is a 95 percent chance or better that our dependent variable is related to our independent variable (or, conversely, that there is a 5 percent chance or less that the independent variable is unrelated to the dependent variable). Statistics allow us to make these kinds of claims.

In the appendixes to this book, David Nixon and I provide information on the statistical approaches commonly used in the field of law and courts (Appendixes A and B) and on where students can find data used in the field (Appendix C). For now it is enough to note that the two research strategies outlined above—the contextual and the systematic—are quite distinct, with each having its assets and deficits. On the one hand, the detailed analysis of case opinions does not necessarily lend itself well to generalizations. In other words, after conducting this kind of analysis, I might be able to make some claims about the attitudinal model's ability to account for certain judicial decisions during certain periods of time. But those claims would be limited in time and scope and would be largely descriptive in nature. On the other hand, the more systematic examination of case outcomes would provide me with little information about the policies enunciated by the Court and about the ways in which the justices themselves constructed and interpreted the facts and law in cases. In the end, I would be able to explain something about judicial decision making and, perhaps, reach some generalizations. But I would miss nuances in that process; nor would I capture specific statements on the part of the Court that might have some bearing on my theory.

What is more (and what is probably obvious by now), different approaches can occasionally lead to different conclusions. To return to my research interest, it is quite possible that an in-depth investigation of Court opinions would lead me to question the attitudinal model, while my systematic classification of Court outcomes would lead me to accept its premises. Or vice versa. The general point is that students should take note of the approaches used by authors and realize that their results may be dependent on the kinds of evidence they amass and the analytic tools they invoke. To see why this is so, students could conjure up different ways to conduct the very same research and explore their ideas with the kinds of data identified in Appendix C.

Discussion

In the final analysis, then, the research process confronts the scholar with a series of choices: On what question should I focus? What model should I invoke? How should I go about measuring key concepts? What kinds of evidence should I amass and how should I examine that evidence? To these questions, as we have seen, there are no necessarily "right" answers; only possibilities.

That, though, is what makes the social scientific research process both challenging and, at times, frustrating. As scholars, we know that it is very difficult to get at the "truth," at the answers to the questions we seek to address. Yet, we also know that the results of our work are important, for they can structure the way society views its political institutions and the way in which students—our future scholars, teachers, and leaders—think about political phenomena. So, as the essays in this volume reveal, we trudge on, using the research process in the hope that we will uncover the truth of whatever it is we study.

Notes

1. The question had to do with U.S. Supreme Court decisions in two death penalty cases, *Furman v. Georgia* (1972) and *Gregg v. Georgia* (1976). In *Furman,* five justices struck down as unconstitutional the procedure used by most states for imposing capital punishment; but four years later (in *Gregg*) seven justices reasserted the constitutionality of the death penalty, upholding a newly devised schema for its execution. The question the student asked was, Why did the law experience such an abrupt change in only a few short years? At the time, I didn't have a particularly good answer. In *The Supreme Court and Legal Change* (1992), Joseph F. Kobylka and I try to provide one.

2. My goal here is to point out some of the general thinking behind the research process, rather than provide an in-depth perspective. Interested students might consult Hoover (1988), which treats the logic of the scientific method lucidly. Manheim and Rich (1991) and Babbie (1992) are excellent textbooks on the subject.

3. This point deserves some clarification. Suppose the Supreme Court heard two criminal cases during World War II, one involving a criminal conviction for treason against the U.S. government and the other an ordinary burglary case, unrelated to the war effort. According to attitudinalists, the existence of a war would be relevant to the Court's decision in the first case because it would be part of the facts; but it would not influence the vote in the second example.

4. In rational choice models of judicial decisions, thus, it is not enough to say, as the attitudinal model does, that Justice X chose action 1 over 2 because she preferred 1 to 2. Rather, the strategic assumption suggests the following proposition: Justice X chose 1 because X believed that the other relevant actors—perhaps Justice Y or Senator Z—would choose 2, 3, or another action, and given these choices, action 1 led to a better outcome for Justice X than did other alternative actions (see Ordeshook 1992, 8).

5. I adapt this discussion from Williamson et al. 1982, 20-21.

6. I thank Jeffrey A. Segal for his help in writing this paragraph.

7. I adapt this example from Bernstein and Dyer 1984, 60.

8. Still, we might question the validity of this measure because it would exclude military efforts, such as those in Korea and Vietnam, that many analysts consider wars.

9. The logic in this paragraph comes from Manheim and Rich 1991, 28.

Part I Actors in the Legal System

When journalists write about judicial proceedings, they often refer to a *"court,"* as in "The court ruled for the defendant," or "The court dismissed the case." Such terminology gives the lie to two beliefs. The first is that courts are themselves useful explanatory concepts.[1] This is typically not the case, because, as we all know, courts cannot rule for defendants or dismiss cases: only individuals can do these things. To be sure, it may be convenient and even important for journalists and scholars to talk about collectivities (such as courts) making choices (such as ruling for defendants or dismissing cases). But when we do so, we must realize that it is individuals who make choices, have preferences, learn, and so forth. Accordingly, complete explanations of collectivities should be grounded in terms of individual choice. To understand courts we must understand the preferences of and choices confronting individuals within that collectivity.[2]

This brings me to a second concern with journalistic accounts invoking *"courts."* Because they so often equate the term "courts" with judges, these accounts cannot possibly convey the breadth of actors involved in judicial proceedings. As anyone who has observed a judicial proceeding knows, numerous actors are involved in addition to the judge. Lawyers present cases; sometimes jurors decide them. Attorneys representing interest groups even get into the act, especially at the appellate level. Occasionally they sponsor cases, meaning that they represent a particular litigant; they also file amicus curiae (friend of the court) briefs in support of one party over the other. Behind the scenes, too, many actors labor to influence the process. In most states, citizens have some say in selecting their judiciary; and, of course, at the federal level the process of judicial selection formally lies in the hands of the president and the Senate.

The chapters contained in this part of the book shore up these and other distinctions between the way journalists think about legal actors and the way scholars do. The authors of the first two essays, chapters 2 and 3, consider the selection of judges and demonstrate that actors external to judicial proceedings—voters, organized interests, government officials—play a critical role in determining who sits on our nation's bench. But they focus on very different selection systems and use divergent data. Lawrence Baum studies election systems—the predominant method used by states to select their judges—and asks how voters choose between candidates for judgeships and why they make the choices they do. To address these questions, Baum invokes an unusually rich database: a set of surveys that followed the same citizens (residents of Ohio) through three "waves," two conducted prior to the November general election in 1990 and one shortly afterward. These data lead him to intriguing conclusions about the factors that influence voters in judicial contests (and, for that matter, other kinds of contests, in which voters possess little information about specific candidates). He found, first, that voters did not know much about the judicial candidates; second, that those voters who did recognize one candidate's name but not the other, almost always voted for the candidate they knew; and, finally, that, beyond name recognition, voters seized on whatever information they could gather: political party affiliations, gender, and race. These and other findings allow Baum to join an important debate about the selection of judges: Should states allow voters—who often cannot make meaningful distinctions between judicial candidates—to elect judges? Or should they switch to systems that give elected institutions a dominant role in the process?

Gregory A. Caldeira and John R. Wright also consider the selection of judges, but they focus on the federal judiciary, whose members are appointed—not elected. The questions they explore are of immense importance to understanding the contemporary confirmation process: Why has organized conflict about federal judgeships arisen? Why has such conflict become part of the game of choosing federal judges in the last decade or so? By carefully examining some of the most heated confirmation battles in American history, they provide answers to these and other questions about the role of lobbyists and their effectiveness. In particular, they ascribe the institutionalization of organized conflict to the growth in breadth and depth of the pressure group environment, the existence of divided government during the 1980s, the increased importance of the federal courts, and the lack of information possessed by key decision makers, to name just a few of the many reasons. These findings, as Caldeira and Wright demonstrate, have important implications for future confirmation proceedings and for the strategies adopted by presidents in naming federal judges.

Kevin T. McGuire, too, explores the world of lobbyists, although his emphasis is different from that of Caldeira and Wright. His focus is on lawyers specializing in advocacy before the U.S. Supreme Court. McGuire's primary argument is that these lawyers are akin to the sophisticated interest group representatives in Washington, D.C., who regularly lobby Congress and the executive. To develop this claim, McGuire contrasts the Supreme Court lawyers who work in Washington, D.C., with those who work outside the capital. Data collected from an impressive range of sources lead him to conclude that not only do more of the Supreme Court's lawyers work in Washington but their expertise in Supreme Court litigation is far greater. No matter who these veterans represent, they tend to succeed at greater rates than their nonexperienced counterparts.

Finally, in Chapter 5, Joseph F. Kobylka picks up on topics explored throughout this part of the book. He focuses on the relationship between interest groups and the process of legal change. Specifically, he asks whether group representatives can direct, alter, or inhibit doctrinal shifts in constitutional interpretation. To address this question, he turns his sights on the First Amendment's Religious Establishment Clause. This is a long-contested and fascinating area of law, and one that—given membership changes on the U.S. Supreme Court and pressures from the administrations of Ronald Reagan and George Bush—should have experienced abrupt legal change during the 1980s but did not. On the basis of a careful examination of Court opinions, organizational briefs, public opinion polls, and transcripts of oral arguments, Kobylka attributes the relative stability in Establishment Clause jurisprudence to the strategic exploitation of legal arguments by attorneys representing particular kinds of organized interests.

Taken together, these essays are a diverse lot. Even from this brief description, we can see that they focus on different substantive topics, from federal and state judges to attorneys to interest groups. They invoke different kinds of data, from voter surveys to historical records to court cases to attorneys' briefs. Still, they share some important features. First, these chapters demonstrate that courts are about more than judges. They are about the voters who elect judges and the organized interests that participate in Senate confirmation battles—both of which have an important voice in determining who sits on our nation's judiciary. They are also about those who provide the grist for the judicial mill— the attorneys who argue the cases and the interest group representatives who craft arguments. Without all these actors, our judiciary would look and function very differently.

Second, the authors endeavor to understand why actors make the choices they do, regardless of whether those individuals are voters selecting judges, lobbyists mobilizing for a Senate confirmation battle, litigants hiring attorneys, or interest group lawyers honing their arguments. They carefully lay out the preferences of the various actors—preferences about who sits on our courts, whom to hire for legal representation, and what arguments courts adopt—and detail how those preferences lead to decisions between judicial candidates in elections, between participating or not in Senate confirmation battles, between competing attorneys, and among arguments to integrate into legal briefs. Accordingly, the authors move us away from journalistic and descriptive accounts and toward explanations about the behavior of the actors who populate our nation's judicial system.

Notes

1. I adapt this discussion of courts from Ordeshook 1986, 1-2.
2. It bears emphasis that scholars too often treat *Congress, interest groups, political parties,* and so forth as unitary actors. But in so doing, they are usually mindful of the microlevel foundations of their work. That is, they recognize that political institutions and collectivities don't have preferences; only individuals do.

2 Electing Judges

Lawrence Baum

Across the fifty states, more than twenty-eight thousand people serve as judges (Court Statistics Project 1992). Each had to be chosen for that position in some way.

The process of choosing judges is significant. One reason is that the prestige and power of judgeships make them attractive positions, and the selection process determines who wins these prizes. More important, the selection of judges affects the policies that courts make. Judges are the primary decision makers in the judicial branch, and they hold a good deal of freedom to make decisions as they see fit.

This freedom is not absolute: judges are constrained by the legal rules they are called on to apply, by other participants in the courts, and by their political environments. But they have considerable room to follow their own preferences and predilections. Clarence Thomas holds the same position on the U.S. Supreme Court that Thurgood Marshall did, but the conservative Thomas casts votes and writes opinions that are quite different from those of the liberal Marshall. In the same way, the policies of state courts reflect the membership of those courts.

The states use a variety of procedures to select their judges, but most states give voters a role in the selection process. There has been considerable debate about the desirability of elections as a means to choose judges, and that debate makes it especially important to understand how these elections work in practice. In this chapter, I examine the process of electing judges, focusing on the 1990 election of two justices to the Ohio Supreme Court. A close look at one pair of contests can provide a sense of how judicial elections work as a means to select judges.

The survey research presented in this chapter was funded by the National Science Foundation under award SES-9010956. I appreciate the foundation's support, the work of Ohio State University's Polimetrics Laboratory in conducting the surveys, and the collaborative efforts of Paul Allen Beck, Aage Clausen, and Charles Smith on the larger project from which this chapter draws. I am also grateful for valuable comments on earlier versions of this chapter by Aage Clausen and Carol Mock, for technical help from Christopher Zorn, and for extensive research assistance from Rorie Spill.

Selection Systems

The fifty states use a variety of formal systems to select their judges, and often there are heated battles about alternative systems. These battles reflect a widespread belief that formal rules make a difference and disagreement about which set of rules produces the most desirable results (Champagne and Haydel 1993).

Much of the disagreement about formal selection systems concerns the role of the general public in choosing judges (see Dubois 1980). Some people argue that judges, as powerful policy makers, should be accountable to the public for their decisions. If state judges rule on issues as fundamental as the death penalty and abortion, people should have a right to decide which people make those rulings. Others contend that public accountability is undesirable for judges, whose decisions should be based on their reading of the law rather than the views of their constituents. Opponents of judicial elections also argue that the public cannot identify the best-qualified candidates for judgeships.

When the United States was founded, the prevailing view among writers of state constitutions was that the public should have no direct role in selecting judges. But the Jacksonian revolution of the early nineteenth century brought demands for popular election of judges, and since then the option of excluding the public altogether has had little support. In this century those who seek to limit the role of the public favor the Missouri Plan, sometimes called merit selection. In this system a judge is initially chosen by the governor from a commission's list of nominees, and the public periodically can vote for or against retention of that judge in office. The Missouri Plan is intended to satisfy public demands for some role in selection of judges while keeping most of the power in other hands (Ashman and Alfini 1974, 7-11; Haynes 1944, chaps. 2-4).

Even today, most of the original thirteen states (and Maine as well) give their governor or legislature the power to choose judges. But other states—a total of forty-one—employ either the standard form of election or, in somewhat fewer states, the Missouri Plan retention election (*Book of the States* 1992, 233-235).

The institution of judicial elections gives voters in most states a great deal of potential power over the membership of their courts. But nowhere does the public have full control. Where the Missouri Plan is used, voters can do no more than reject a sitting judge, difficult to accomplish when there is no opposing candidate and rarely achieved in practice (Hall and Aspin 1987). In Missouri, which has used the Missouri Plan for its appellate courts and big-city trial courts for more than fifty years, only two judges have ever been rejected (Lhotka and Bryant 1992). And in the event of a rejection, it is the nominating commission and governor who then choose a new judge.

In states that allow contests between candidates, it is common for a candidate to run without opposition (Baum 1983; Dubois 1980, chap. 4; Hannah 1978). In turn, that candidate may be an incumbent who became a judge through a governor's interim appointment. For many years prior to 1992 this combination of appointment and an absence of challengers meant that Minnesota voters effectively were excluded from selecting supreme court justices (Abramowicz 1992). This was an extreme situation, but in many states frequent interim appointments and limited electoral competition severely narrow voters' power to choose judges.

Of course, voters are in a better position when they choose between competing candidates, and for many courts this is the standard situation. For instance, every contest for the Ohio Supreme Court since 1972 has been contested. How meaningful this choice is depends largely on who the candidates are and what the voters know about them. The first matter is obvious: people can choose only between the options they are given. But just as important is what voters are able to learn about the candidates from whom they can choose.

Information and the Vote in Judicial Elections

Voting can be understood as a process of gathering and using information about candidates (Converse 1962; Hinckley, Hofstetter, and Kessel 1974; Moon 1990). In presidential elections, the typical voter's task is to sort out a substantial body of conflicting information. Voters differ in how much they know about presidential candidates, and those voters who know a great deal and those who know less may make their choices in somewhat different ways (Sniderman, Glaser, and Griffin 1990; but see Rahn et al. 1990). Relatively few voters, however, suffer from a paucity of information.

The picture is somewhat different for offices a step or two below the presidency—the U.S. Senate, the House of Representatives, and state governorships (Abramowitz and Segal 1992; Hinckley 1980). Especially in elections to the House, voters are provided with less information than they receive in presidential elections. As a result, the average voter's decision is based on much less evidence. In particular, because of minimal media coverage and limited campaign funds, candidates who challenge House incumbents often find it difficult to convey much information about themselves to the voters. But even in House elections, voters are likely to know something about the incumbent. And the voter who has managed to learn nothing at all about the candidates still can choose between candidates on the basis of their political party affiliations, conveniently listed on the ballot.

Contests for less visible offices, such as state auditor or county coroner, present greater difficulties for voters. Information about the candidates typically is scarce, and the ballot often contains a long list of electoral contests. Thus, voters are in a difficult position: they are required to gather and sort out what little can be discerned about the candidates in each contest from the large body of information they are receiving about the whole array of contests. To make a truly informed judgment in every contest might require a full-time commitment in the weeks before election day. The great majority of people, busy with their lives and limited in their concern about politics, spend much less time gathering information about candidates. Thus, the typical voter learns little about the candidates in these "low-information contests" below the top levels.

One option for the beleaguered citizen is not to vote at all. That is a common choice in the current era. In 1990, for instance, only a minority of eligible Ohioans turned out at the polls (U.S. Bureau of the Census 1991). People who do go to the polls can cast votes in the more visible contests and then skip those for which they have less information, and this "roll-off" in voting from higher to lower offices is common. Yet once people appear at the polls, they are inclined to vote in all the contests on the ballot. In Hamilton County (Cincinnati, Ohio) in 1992, for instance, 87 percent of the people who went to the polls chose one of the candidates for county coroner, and 85 percent voted in the contest for county engineer, even though most voters probably knew little about the candidates for those positions. More voters skipped the various judicial contests, but the average level of participation in contested judicial races was 80 percent (Taft 1993).

In low-information contests the ballot is the one universal source of information. Voters can make choices on the basis of their familiarity with the candidates' names. The names also allow inferences about gender and ethnicity. Where occupations are listed, voters can react to incumbency or to the occupations themselves. In partisan contests the ballot also supplies the candidates' party affiliations; in nonpartisan contests, voters can try to infer those affiliations from candidates' names.

In addition to the ballot, some voters use lists of endorsed candidates that may be provided by political party organizations, interest groups, or newspapers. Some recall information from news stories or campaign advertising. And some voters have direct knowledge about the candidates from acquaintanceship, a campaign event, or other sources.

Where political parties are listed on the ballot, partisanship is probably the most powerful consideration for voters in low-information contests. The great majority of voters feel some identification with the Republican or Democratic parties, an identification that structures their choices even in presidential contests. If voters possess little information about the candidates, as they generally do in partisan judicial elections (McKnight, Schaefer, and Johnson 1978), Democratic and Republican voters tend to choose the candidate affiliated with their own party. Thus, even though they may know very little about the candidates, voters can base their decision on a quite meaningful criterion—albeit one that some people think is inappropriate for choosing judges.

But most judicial elections in the states are not formally partisan: voters choose between candidates whose party affiliations are not listed on the ballot, or they decide whether to vote for or against a Missouri Plan judge who is not identified by party. How do they make choices in that situation?

Studies of nonpartisan elections for judgeships and other offices suggest that voters do what they can with the information they possess, especially information gleaned from the ballot itself, but that they suffer from the absence of more extensive and more reliable information (Byrne and Pueschel 1974; Dubois 1980 and 1984; Mueller 1970; Nakanishi, Cooper, and Kassarjian 1974; Pomper 1966; Welch and Bledsoe 1986). As a result, the choices of many voters are neither firmly based nor highly meaningful.

This reality is illustrated by a study of voting on the basis of political party affiliations. Dubois (1980) analyzed the county-level correlations between voting for governor and for the supreme court in the states that elect supreme court justices. Positive correlations would mean that a party's supreme court candidates tended to do better in the counties where the party's gubernatorial candidate did better; the higher the positive correlation, the stronger this tendency. Dubois found a pattern of high positive correlations in states that used a partisan ballot for judicial contests, indicating that many voters made their choices on a partisan basis. Where Democrats and Republicans ran against each other in states with a nonpartisan ballot, the average correlation was positive but much lower, and the variation in correlations from one election to the next was high. This pattern suggests that many voters in these states wanted to choose supreme court justices on a partisan basis but that their ability to identify the candidates' parties correctly varied a good deal from election to election (see also Squire and Smith 1988).

Relying on limited and sometimes misleading information, voters can produce surprising outcomes. One example is the defeat in 1990 of the chief justice of the Washington Supreme Court (Bone 1990; London 1990). There was no apparent discontent with the chief justice, and his opponent was a lawyer who did not actually campaign. But the opponent's name was Charles Johnson, a name also held by a Seattle trial judge and one with a familiar look, while the chief justice had the less pleasing name of Keith Callow and apparently was known to few voters.

Some circumstances allow voters to obtain more information about their choices in nonpartisan contests. In local elections large numbers of voters may learn a good deal from personal contact with the candidates and campaign workers and from interaction with other citizens (Raymond 1992). On the whole, voters are likely to be best informed about judicial candidates in contests conducted for local judgeships in rural areas, where personal knowledge of the candidates is highest and there are relatively few contests competing for voters' attention (see Raymond and Paluch 1994).

In unusual circumstances campaigns and the mass media distribute a great deal of information about the candidates, putting voters in a good position to make meaningful choices. One classic example was California's retention elections for state supreme court justices in 1986. Elections in which voters can vote only yes or no on an incumbent put them at an even greater disadvantage than nonpartisan contests (see Griffin and Horan 1983). But three of the incumbent California justices had received enormous publicity, chiefly because of their votes to overturn death sentences, and interest groups ran massive campaigns against them. As a result, the voters who participated in those retention elections possessed a level of information more typical of the highest partisan offices, and the defeat of the three justices reflected a widespread judgment by voters about a major judicial issue (Wold and Culver 1987).

Of course, these kinds of contests are fairly rare, and the standard situation in judicial elections is one of limited information. In light of this reality, many people argue that the Missouri Plan should be adopted to limit the role of the general public in selecting judges. If voters cannot make meaningful choices between judicial candidates, why should they be allowed to choose? That question provides a backdrop for examination of one year's contests for seats on the Ohio Supreme Court.

The Election Setting

Ohio voters choose between supreme court candidates in a setting that reflects formal election rules and the conduct and coverage of election campaigns. Both create conditions that limit the information available to voters. Thus, elections to the Ohio Supreme Court are a good example of low-information electoral contests.

Formal Rules

Ohio elects its seven supreme court justices to six-year staggered terms, so that every two years at least two justices are chosen. For its judicial elections the state uses the unique combination of partisan primaries and nonpartisan general elections, a product of historical circumstances rather than deliberate design (Aumann 1931). This means that competing candidates in the general election ordinarily are a Republican and a Democrat, but they are not labeled by party on the ballot.

Supreme court justices are elected on the regular general election days in even-numbered years. The same ballot includes contests for a variety of other offices, including the U.S. House of Representatives, either president or governor, and (two-thirds of the time) the U.S. Senate—all of which interest the average voter much more than the state supreme court.

The ballot includes no information on supreme court candidates other than their names. Not only are their political party affiliations absent, but Ohio does not indicate incumbency or occupation. Except for what they can infer from names, voters must obtain information about candidates from other sources.

Supreme Court Elections

Traditionally, contests for seats on the Ohio Supreme Court featured small campaigns and little attention from the mass media (Barber 1971 and 1972). Provided with little information, voters made use of what they did know. Candidates with recognizable names had a clear advantage, even if the recognition was false. One familiar name in Ohio politics was "Brown," and lawyers fortunate enough to hold this name flocked to run for the supreme court in order to take advantage of this fact. In two instances both parties' candidates were named Brown.

Voting patterns followed partisan lines to the extent that candidates generally did better in counties where their party's candidate for governor also did better. One reason is that some voters had direct knowledge of candidates' party affiliations. Other voters could try to guess candidates' parties from their names, on the basis of ethnicity or the party affiliations of other political figures with the same names. It appears that many voters did make such guesses, because the correlation between the success of a party's gubernatorial and supreme court candidates at the county level increased when candidates had names that allowed the correct inference about their political party affiliation (Dubois 1980, 81-84). For instance, voters guessed correctly that candidates named Taft, like the Ohio senator and president in earlier eras, were Republicans. But in 1970 a Republican with a Democratic-sounding name ran against a Democrat with a Republican-sounding name, and the Democratic candidate fared better in the counties where the party's candidate for governor did worse. This result underlined the paucity of information that voters received before they entered the voting booth.

Supreme court elections grew in scale and received more media coverage in the 1980s (Tarr and Porter 1988, chap. 4). One source of this change was the court's increased liberalism on economic issues, which attracted attention and opposition from business groups. Chief Justice Frank Celebrezze, a Democrat, attracted even more attention as an individual: allegations were made that he created serious conflict within the court and that he had been hostile and vindictive toward the state bar association, the leading group of lawyers. Economic issues attracted campaign contributions and thus gave candidates a better opportunity to reach the voters, while the allegations about Celebrezze were good fodder for newspaper and television stories.

As a result, more voters participated in the supreme court contests. And surveys of voters during the 1984 and 1986 elections showed that the relatively large volume of information provided to them had an effect, especially in making voters aware of the charges against the chief justice (Baum 1987 and 1988-1989). That awareness helped to defeat Celebrezze in 1986 and worked against another Democratic candidate in 1984. And the contest for chief justice in 1986 showed that under unusual conditions voters can know a good deal about their choices in a judicial election. In the elections after 1986, however, media interest and levels of campaigning gradually declined, bringing supreme court elections closer to their traditional low-key character.

The 1990 Contests

Two seats on the court were at stake in 1990. Both had first-term Republican incumbents, Andrew Douglas and Craig Wright. Douglas had been a city council member in Toledo for nineteen years and served on the state court of appeals for four years before his 1984 election to the supreme court. His opponent was Stuart Banks, a lawyer with a private practice in the medium-sized city of Youngstown. Wright had been a trial judge in Columbus for fourteen years before his election to the supreme court. His Democratic opponent was Stephanie Tubbs Jones, a Cleveland trial judge for nine years. As an African American and a woman, Jones stood out from the other three candidates. Also in the Wright-Jones race was J. Ross Haffey, a lawyer from the Cleveland area. Haffey ultimately won 10 percent of the vote, a respectable level, but I concentrate on the two major candidates. None of the candidates had a name that would sound Republican or Democratic to voters.

There was little publicity about the supreme court contests prior to the unofficial beginning of the campaign season in early September. None of the candidates had faced an opponent in the May primary election. Jones, chosen by the state Democratic organization to replace a candidate in ill health, had not even run in the primary. Jones's service as a judge undoubtedly gave her some recognition in Cleveland. Banks, chosen by the Democratic organization to run in a race that most people saw as unwinnable, was essentially unknown. Indeed, Douglas did defeat Banks by a large margin, while Wright defeated Jones in a close contest. Table 2-1 summarizes relevant information about the two races.

In examining voters' behavior in these contests, I rely primarily on a set of surveys dealing with the 1990 contests for statewide office in Ohio. The surveys followed the same Ohioans through three "waves," two conducted prior to the November general election and one shortly afterward (see Beck et al. 1992).[1] That set of surveys provides an opportunity to study how and why voters made their choices in the two contests for the Ohio Supreme Court—a special opportunity, since detailed surveys of voters in judicial contests are unusual.

It is important, however, to recognize the problems involved in using surveys to understand voting behavior. One problem is the difficulty of getting responses from a representative sample of the population, a difficulty that has increased as more and more people refuse to participate in surveys. Because those who do not participate in surveys differ somewhat from those who do, it has become more difficult to make inferences about the electorate as a whole from survey responses (Brehm 1993).

More fundamental are problems concerning participants' responses to survey questions (see Zaller and Feldman 1992). People may not respond accurately to questions, chiefly

Table 2-1 Summary Information on Electoral Contests for the Ohio Supreme Court, 1990

Candidate	Party	Vote No.	%
		Contest 1	
Stuart J. Banks	Democratic	756,481	27.3
Andrew Douglas[a]	Republican	2,013,630	72.7
		Contest 2	
Stephanie Tubbs Jones	Democratic	1,255,556	43.9
Craig Wright[a]	Republican	1,319,422	46.2
J. Ross Haffey[b]	Independent	283,883	9.9

Source: Data for vote totals from Taft 1991, 89.

[a] The incumbent.   [b] Haffey had been associated with the Democratic party.

because of limitations in their ability to recall relevant information. And survey questions may elicit "false" responses from people, especially from those who want to demonstrate their knowledge or interest or simply to assist the interviewer.

The problems of survey responses are exacerbated when participants are asked about low-information contests, such as the typical judicial election. Because voters usually know so little about these contests, and because the contests are not highly salient to them, they may be able to provide little information about their choices—or, worse, much of what they say may have little to do with their actual behavior.

The 1990 Ohio surveys illustrate this problem. In the postelection survey, respondents were asked if they turned out to vote and if they made a choice in each of the statewide contests. The questions were designed to address the problem of limited recall: people who said they had turned out were told the candidates' names in each contest and given the options of indicating the candidate for whom they had voted, of indicating that they voted in that race but could not recall for whom they had voted, or of saying that they *might* have voted. Even so, the responses suggest that many people who actually voted in the supreme court contests were sure that they had not.[2] The responses are shown in Table 2-2.

All this does not mean that we cannot learn anything from the set of surveys. On the contrary, they provide a wealth of information about supreme court voters in 1990. But the responses have to be interpreted with care—and with considerable caution. Most important, the inability of many respondents to remember how they voted and other limita-

Table 2-2 Actual and Recollected Participation in Supreme Court Contests, among Voters Who Turned Out at the Polls (percent)

	Actual	Survey respondents		
		Measure 1 [a]	Measure 2 [b]	Measure 3 [c]
Contest 1	76.5	45.2	58.2	62.9
Contest 2	79.0	37.3	54.0	57.6

Source: Data for actual vote from Taft 1991, 89, 93.

[a] Respondents who recalled which candidate they voted for when provided with their names.

[b] Respondents in measure 1 plus respondents who said they voted but who did not know for which candidate they voted.

[c] Respondents in measure 2 plus respondents who did not know whether they voted in this contest (thus, all respondents except those who said they definitely did not vote).

tions in what they could recall about the candidates rule out complex analyses of the factors that shaped their voting choices: the surveys simply could not elicit enough information about the considerations that shaped votes or even about what those votes were.

Contests and Voters

Ohio's potential voters began the campaign period with little knowledge of the supreme court candidates. In the first wave of the survey, conducted in early September, respondents were asked if they recognized each candidate's name and, if so, whether they could rate the candidate on a "thermometer," from 0 (very negative) to 100 (very positive), with 50 as the neutral point.

The results are shown in Table 2-3. Douglas was the only candidate recognized by more than 6 percent of the respondents and the only one rated by more than 4 percent. Moreover, a high proportion of the ratings for each candidate were at the neutral 50 point, suggesting a lack of substantial information about them. Less than 6 percent of the respondents had positive or negative feelings about Douglas, and no other candidate elicited such feelings from as many as 3 percent of the respondents.

Those who recognized the candidates were asked to identify the candidates' party affiliations, perhaps the most relevant piece of information about them. Among these small groups of respondents, the proportions providing the correct affiliation ranged from 47 percent for Jones and Wright to 16 percent for Banks. The others said they did not know the candidates' parties or gave the wrong answer.

Table 2-3 Recognition and Rating of Supreme Court Candidates,
Survey Wave 1, All Respondents (percent)

Candidate	Recognized	Rated	Gave nonneutral rating
Banks	5.4	3.9	1.9
Douglas	11.2	8.4	5.7
Jones	4.6	3.8	2.6
Wright	4.2	3.2	2.1

Note: Percentages in each cell are percentages of respondents who met the criteria listed above. Only those who recognized a candidate were asked to rate that candidate. A non-neutral rating is something other than 50.

Clearly, the level of voter knowledge about the candidates at the beginning of the fall campaigns was low. Given the very limited information available to voters up to that time, the results for the Democratic challengers are not surprising. Yet it is noteworthy that so few voters even recognized the two Republicans who had sat on the Ohio Supreme Court for six years.

The state's news media do give attention to the supreme court's work, primarily in stories about major decisions, but the positions of individual justices seldom are highlighted. Justices get far more attention when improper behavior or interpersonal conflicts are alleged. For example, a reported physical scuffle between Justices Douglas and Wright in 1991 was given considerable space in the press (Snell 1991). Douglas and Wright received attention in 1985 and 1986 for their involvement in partisan conflicts within the court. But the three years preceding the 1990 contests had been fairly quiet in that respect, so it is understandable that few voters were familiar with the incumbents. The question was how much they would learn about them during the campaigns.

Information Providers

Candidates for the Ohio Supreme Court attempt to get information to the voters. Their success in communicating information depends largely on the assistance they get from political parties and interest groups and on the coverage of their campaigns by the mass media.

Ohio's political party leaders care about winning supreme court elections. Aside from the general value of holding high offices, occasionally there are cases in which the parties have high stakes, such as those involving disputes about election rules. Because Ohio's supreme court justices tend to vote for the interests of their own party, the party that has a majority of justices gains a considerable advantage. Partisan control of the court often is at stake, as it was in 1990: four Republicans and three Democrats sat on the supreme court, so defeat of either Wright or Douglas would give the Democrats a majority. For this reason the party organizations play an active part in selecting candidates, and they provide some financial assistance to campaigns.

But the supreme court is only one of many offices that concern the parties, and it is not their first priority. In 1990, for example, Ohio voters were selecting a new governor, and the governorship is the office that party officials care most about. In addition, the contests for state auditor and secretary of state were unusually significant, because these officials would sit on the board that drew up state legislative districts after the 1990 census was completed.

Even when their other involvement in the supreme court campaigns is limited, the parties play an important part by including judicial candidates on their slate cards, lists of the party's candidates that they send to voters prior to the election. For voters who receive and use these cards, they compensate for the ballot's lack of information on the party affiliations of supreme court candidates.

Many interest groups care about the Ohio Supreme Court. The court makes significant decisions on many policy issues, and its rulings on economic matters, such as workers' compensation, can have considerable financial impact on Ohioans. Groups representing business, labor, and professions such as medicine involve themselves in supreme court contests, primarily by contributing money. In the 1986 contest for chief justice, contributions by economic interest groups had fueled an unprecedented level of spending for a supreme court race—nearly $3 million. Labor unions also seek to build support for their favored candidates within their sizable memberships, and in 1986 and 1988 that support seemed to win votes for union-endorsed supreme court candidates (Hojnacki and Baum 1992).

Interest groups had some interest in the 1990 supreme court contests. One unusual feature of these contests was that most Ohio labor unions supported Douglas, a Republican whose positions on the court generally coincided with those of the labor movement, along with Jones, a Democrat. The American Federation of Labor and Congress of Industrial Organizations (AFL-CIO) and individual unions gave more than $100,000 to Jones and more than $200,000 to Douglas. Wright received contributions from public utilities and other business groups.[3] But because the stakes did not seem as high, interest groups gave the supreme court a lower priority than they had four years earlier.

The limited commitment of parties and interest groups to supreme court campaigns in most election years, including 1990, limits the scale of those campaigns. In 1990, Ohio's gubernatorial candidates spent $13 million on their campaigns. In three of the other four campaigns for statewide executive-branch offices, more than $3 million was spent (Johnson 1990). The candidates for the supreme court spent far less. Wright spent $634,000 in his close win over Jones, who spent $281,000. Douglas overwhelmed Banks in spending, by a margin of $386,000 to $12,000. All the candidates except Banks could run meaningful campaigns with the amounts they spent, but they had only a moderate ability to reach voters—particularly through television commercials, the most expensive and probably the most effective mechanism.

Judicial candidates face an additional limitation: the rule of legal ethics that prohibits them from making "pledges or promises of conduct in office other than the faithful and impartial performance of the duties of the office" or announcing their "views on disputed legal or political issues" (American Bar Association 1989, 150). Despite this provision, intended to prevent candidates from taking positions on issues that might come before them, Ohio candidates sometimes indicate their policy positions in general terms. Candidates for trial judgeships occasionally say that they would take tough stands against crime. In the 1986 contest for chief justice, Frank Celebrezze, the Democratic incumbent, emphasized the court's support of worker and consumer interests as a reason to keep him in office. But the rule still constrains what candidates can say about their positions on legal issues.

The mass media could compensate for the limited scale of supreme court campaigns with heavy coverage of those campaigns, but they typically do not. Political campaigns have to compete for time and space with a wide array of nonpolitical news, and contests for the supreme court have to compete with other contests that interest reporters and editors more. As a result, coverage of races for the supreme court is spotty.

The extent of the 1990 coverage is illustrated by the *Cleveland Plain Dealer,* the newspaper with the largest circulation in the state and one that devotes more coverage to state politics than most others. In the period between Labor Day and election day, the *Plain Dealer* had only one extensive story on each of the two supreme court contests, both published in late October. The paper also published reports of its own endorsements and those by legal groups, a mid-October story on a charge related to a fund-raising event for Douglas, and a report of the Republicans' advantage in fund-raising. The supreme court contests never reached the first section of the *Plain Dealer* or—with one exception—even the front page of a back section. (A story about financial contributions to the candidates, focusing on the incumbents, did get printed on the front page of the newspaper in July.) The accurate perception that Douglas would win easily might explain the lack of media interest in his contest with Banks, but the closely contested race between Wright and Jones did not receive much more attention.

What Voters Learned

Because the campaigns and media coverage were limited, the average Ohioan was unlikely to become an expert on the supreme court contests by election day. Yet the campaign

Table 2-4 Recognition and Rating of Supreme Court Candidates, Survey Wave 3 (percent)

Candidate	All respondents			Voters and possible voters [a]		
	Recognized	Rated	Nonneutral rating	Recognized	Rated	Nonneutral rating
Banks	60.5	34.4	14.1	80.5	54.4	25.2
Douglas	63.7	38.0	20.3	82.9	62.3	41.3
Jones	57.5	32.7	17.5	79.4	53.3	35.0
Wright	55.4	30.1	14.3	76.8	50.3	30.4

[a] Includes respondents who said they voted or might have voted in that contest, whether or not they indicated their choice.

period did expose the voters to some information about the candidates. What was the result?

We can begin by returning to the thermometers as a measure of familiarity with the candidates. Table 2-4 is a presentation of the distribution of thermometer ratings among all respondents in the postelection wave of the survey, a group comparable to those included in Table 2-3, and the distribution for respondents who said they voted or might have voted in the contest in question.

The results show striking increases in citizens' knowledge of the candidates. Not surprisingly, the proportions in each category are considerably higher for respondents identified as voters in the judicial contests. Yet even among voters, significant numbers of people could not recognize the candidates or could not rate them.

The limited differences among candidates suggest that respondents exaggerated their awareness of at least the lesser-known candidates. Still, in a situation in which little information is available, the ability to recognize and rate a candidate may indicate that a voter possesses real knowledge about the candidate (see Clausen et al. 1992, 10). The largest differences among candidates were in the proportions of voters who gave them nonneutral ratings. These differences, particularly those between Douglas and Banks, probably provide the most accurate picture of variation in voters' knowledge of the candidates.

Other questions reinforce the impression that voters knew little about the candidates. One set of questions asked about the candidates' positions on government regulation of abortion on a scale from complete prohibition to no prohibition. A year earlier the U.S. Supreme Court had decided the case of *Webster v. Reproductive Health Services* (1989), granting the states greater power to regulate abortion and—many people thought at the time—preparing to overturn *Roe v. Wade* (1973) and thus to allow the states near-total control over abortion policy. The Ohio legislature was widely expected to use this new power to establish substantial restrictions on abortion. If it did so, the state supreme court would determine whether the Ohio Constitution limited the legislature's power over abortion. Given the importance of abortion as an issue, there was perhaps no more critical question about the judicial candidates than their positions on that issue.

But voters faced enormous difficulty in learning the candidates' positions about abortion. Restricted by the rules against discussion of issues, the candidates apparently said nothing about abortion. A highly committed voter might have gleaned something about the candidates' positions from past statements or from some of the incumbents' votes and opinions in cases, but the task would have been difficult, time-consuming, and subject to error.

The survey results reflect this difficulty. The question about abortion was asked only of voters who recalled which candidate they chose in each contest, the most knowledgeable group of voters. Yet for each candidate only about one in five voters offered a judgment about where the candidate stood on abortion, and it is doubtful that many of those voters actually knew the candidate's position. (Larger numbers of voters ascribed positions to the supreme court candidates on other issues, such as limits on fund-raising by public officials, on which it is doubtful that *anyone* really knew their views.) Told nothing about the candidates' positions on regulation of abortion, the voters could hardly know much about those positions.

Voters also were asked to place the candidates on an ideological scale and to indicate how well adjectives such as *honest* and *hard-working* applied to them. On each of these questions for each candidate, only a minority of voters offered a judgment. Again, it is very difficult to fault people for an inability to assess the candidates, because the necessary information was not readily available.

There were a few pieces of information that an alert voter might have been expected to gather. One was the unusual support from the state's labor movement for the Republican Douglas, support that received some attention in the news media before and during the 1990 campaign. Voters were asked whether the candidates were "close" to a series of groups. Only 17 percent identified Douglas as close to labor unions, while 23 percent thought he was close to business. Clearly, Douglas's labor ties did not stand out.

The candidates' political party affiliations also were reported in the media. Respondents were not asked to identify those affiliations in the postelection wave of the survey, but part of the second wave was conducted in the days just prior to the election, a time when citizens were receiving the largest volume of information. Among the respondents who ultimately voted, most still did not recognize the candidates' names and thus were not asked about their party affiliations. Among those who *were* asked about candidates' parties, altogether 26 percent of the responses identified a candidate's party correctly, 9 percent answered incorrectly, and 64 percent said that they did not know.

Thus the Ohioans who voted in the contests for supreme court justice typically could provide very limited information about the candidates from whom they chose. A highly attentive voter would have known more than did most of the respondents. But the fundamental source of their limited knowledge was the limited information provided to them.

How Voters Explained Their Choices

Respondents who reported that they had voted for a particular supreme court candidate were asked, "Was there anything in particular about [that candidate] that made you want to vote for him [or her]?" Follow-up questions about additional considerations in voters' decisions were asked in order to elicit as much information as possible. The respondents were then asked a comparable question about reasons for voting against the opposing candidate. In this way voters were given an opportunity to explain their choices.

Their responses need to be interpreted with particular care. Although psychologists disagree about this point (Ericsson and Simon 1984; Smith and Miller 1978), there is considerable evidence to suggest that people's verbal explanations of their behavior are far from perfect (Nisbett and Wilson 1977; Wilson and Nisbett 1978). People who reach conclusions based on quite meaningful considerations may have difficulty recalling those considerations. Further, voters often feel a need to provide good reasons for those choices, so they may offer "false" responses to the kind of question posed to them in this survey. Still, their responses tell us something about the kinds of considerations that they took into account, and analyzing them provides an initial perspective on voting decisions in the supreme court contests. Respondents were far more likely to offer positive than negative reasons, and the negative reasons frequently were just the other side of the positive ones, so I will focus on the positive reasons.

Combining voters in the two contests, a substantial minority of those who recalled voting for a candidate did not offer any reasons for their choices, even with a fairly broad definition of what constitutes a "reason." Voters who did provide reasons for their votes were categorized according to the first or primary reason they cited, and the results are shown in Table 2-5. (The percentages for Banks should be read with caution, because of the small number of respondents who provided reasons for choosing him.) As shown in the table, voters mentioned a variety of considerations.

Many people—16 percent of the total—cited their candidate's political party affiliation. Thus, a significant minority of voters saw the candidates' affiliations as an important basis for their choices. About one-quarter of the voters who referred to Douglas's party affiliation inaccurately called him a Democrat, undoubtedly because of his links with organized labor and his reputation as a liberal. There were no errors in references to other candidates' party affiliations.

Table 2-5 Attributes of Supreme Court Candidates That Voters Cited as Reasons for Voting for Them (percent)

Category	Banks	Douglas	Jones	Wright	Total
Political party	20	15	9	27	16
Issues	13	6	5	5	6
General	13	2	3	0	3
Specific[a]	0	4	2	5	3
Incumbency and incumbent's record	13	19	2	27	15
Personal qualities and qualifications	0	8	15	10	10
Gender and race	0	0	38[b]	0	11
Name familiarity	0	6	3	10	5
Sources of support	0	4	2	5	3
Interest groups	0	1	2	0	1
Other endorsements	0	3	0	5	2
Sources of information[c]	20	24	20	15	21
Mass media	7	5	2	0	3
Campaigns[d]	13	10	14	12	12
Acquaintances	0	1	3	2	2
Personal knowledge	0	7	2	0	4
Localism[e]	7	12	2	0	6
Job performance	0	6	2	0	3
General	7	6	0	0	3
General	27	5	6	2	6
Favorable to one candidate	13	1	6	2	4
Comparison of candidates	13	4	0	0	3
Number of voters providing reasons	15	97	66	41	219

Note: Voters who cited more than one reason are classified by the first or dominant reason they cited. Percentages for main categories do not necessarily add up to 100 and percentages for subcategories do not necessarily add up to totals for categories because of rounding. Percentages are based only on the responses of voters who provided reasons. Responses were obtained from the original forms used by the interviewers, and a small proportion of those forms were unavailable.

[a] Includes references to ideology.

[b] Does not include voters who cited both party and gender or those who cited gender as a secondary reason; if these were included, the proportion for Jones would be 45 percent.

[c] Includes voters who cited only a source of information and not the substance of the information they received. Voters who cited the substance of information are in another category.

[d] Includes references to candidates' advertisements and commercials.

[e] Includes all references to a candidate's past or present area of residence.

Only 6 percent of the voters referred to the candidates' stands on issues in even the most general way. This is hardly a surprising result. With the partial exception of Douglas's liberal position on some economic issues, voters had very little opportunity to learn what the candidates stood for.

Incumbency seemed to provide a substantial advantage to Douglas and Wright, because a large minority of those who voted for them cited their status as incumbents or referred to their good performance in office. Few of the voters for Banks and Jones cited the bad record of the incumbents or the need for a change. This, too, is unsurprising in light of the lack of controversy concerning the supreme court in the preceding four years. Douglas and Wright also benefited from incumbency through name recognition and familiarity. The many years that Douglas held office in Toledo added to his familiarity and support. Many Douglas voters had personal knowledge of him or reacted favorably to his residence and job performance in Toledo. Among the relatively few voters who offered reasons to vote against a candidate, several referred to their unfamiliarity with Jones, and far more said that they knew nothing about Banks. Undoubtedly that lack of knowledge worked against both candidates, especially Banks.

The most distinctive pattern of reasons was offered by those who voted for Jones. As their only or primary reason for choosing her, 38 percent offered that she was a woman, a member of a racial minority group, or both. The great majority of these respondents referred only to her gender, and just one referred only to her race.

If references to both political party and gender and citations of gender as a secondary reason are added in, 44 percent of the voters for Jones referred to gender. Only one voter cited it as a reason to vote against her. The fact that nearly all references to Jones as a woman were favorable suggests that gender benefited her substantially. It may be, however, that respondents who voted against Jones because she was a woman were reluctant to offer that explanation to an interviewer.

About 15 percent of the voters cited the campaigns (primarily television commercials) or mass media as the basis for their choices without specifying what they had learned from these sources. These responses are not necessarily accurate; one scholar has called voters "pack rats" who gather and store pieces of political information and cannot recall clearly where that information came from (Jamieson 1992, 17). But the responses suggest that at least some voters were reached by the campaigns and media coverage, and voters citing other reasons could well have gathered the relevant information from those sources.

Many of the reasons cited by voters demonstrated little substantive knowledge of the candidates. Indeed, the general lack of depth to the reasons that voters offered is striking. It is true that even a statement with as little content as the judgment that one candidate was better than the other may be based on a meaningful comparison between the qualities that each would bring to the supreme court. Yet in a situation where knowledge was so difficult to obtain, it is unlikely that many voters knew a great deal about the candidates. In this respect, the large number of voters who offered no reasons for their votes is noteworthy.

Correlates of the Vote

Political scientists who study voting behavior typically test statistical models in which the choice between candidates is the dependent variable to be explained and a variety of voter characteristics and attitudes are treated as independent variables to explain the vote. These tests can estimate the absolute and relative importance of possible determinants of the vote.

This approach is quite appropriate to contests in which voters have received and can remember a good deal of information about the candidates. It is less appropriate for the two supreme court contests I am examining. One reason is the high proportion of voters who could not recall which candidate they chose—or, in many instances, whether they voted for any candidate. This means that even if we wanted to explain the votes only of those people who did recall which candidate they chose, the results would be distorted statistically (Berk 1983).[4] And because voters knew so little about the candidates, many variables that scholars usually put into models of the vote, such as perceptions of candidates' positions on issues, are largely irrelevant.

But we do have some evidence about the considerations that might have influenced the voters, and we can examine that evidence in conjunction with the patterns of actual votes in the two supreme court contests. The reasons that voters offered for those choices point to some variables that might explain their choices.

One such variable is knowledge of the candidates. If voters have some familiarity with one candidate but not the other, they are likely to vote for the candidate they know. And despite voters' claims about their recognition of the candidates, shown in Table 2-4, it is likely that Andrew Douglas had a powerful advantage over Stuart Banks because he was far better known.

To assess this possibility, we can look directly at the relationship between knowledge of the candidates and the vote, shown in Table 2-6. In the Banks-Douglas contest, Douglas did very well among voters who could recognize and rate both candidates or who could recognize and rate neither. But his advantage was even greater among those voters who could recognize and rate only him. (Not surprisingly, there were almost no voters who knew Banks but not Douglas.) In the Jones-Wright contest, the results are quite stark. The candidates split the vote almost evenly when both or neither were known, but each won all the votes among respondents with whom they had a knowledge advantage.

Another way to assess the effect of information is through the phenomenon of "friends and neighbors" voting. Especially in nonpartisan contests, candidates tend to be successful in garnering votes from their home areas (Aspin and Hall 1989). The primary reason is

Table 2-6 Vote for Supreme Court Candidates by Ability to Recognize and Rate Candidates (percent)

Candidate	Ability to recognize and rate candidates			
	Both candidates [a]	Neither candidate [b]	Banks or Jones only [c]	Douglas or Wright only [d]
Banks	19.3	25.0	—	3.7
Douglas	80.7	75.0	—	96.3
Jones	52.8	50.9	100.0	0.0
Wright	47.2	49.1	0.0	100.0

Note: Dash=number of voters was too small to be meaningful. Respondents who reported votes for other candidates are excluded.

[a] Number of respondents for Banks-Douglas contest=150; for Jones-Wright contest=106.

[b] Number of respondents for Banks-Douglas contest=60; for Jones-Wright contest=53.

[c] Number of respondents for Banks-Douglas contest=2; for Jones-Wright contest=21.

[d] Number of respondents for Banks-Douglas contest=27; for Jones-Wright contest=14.

name recognition. Thus, by looking at the candidates' success in their home counties, we can get a sense of the advantage that name recognition provided to them. The voting patterns are shown in Table 2-7, in which I calculated a home-county advantage for each candidate directly and then controlled for the electoral strength of the candidate's political party in that county. The second figure is the better measure of the home-county advantage, since any candidate could expect to do better in counties where the candidate's party is stronger.[5]

The data in the table show that all candidates except for Banks did better in their home counties than would be expected from the pattern of party strength in that county. Douglas had the largest "friends and neighbors" advantage. This result makes sense, because Douglas had the longest and most visible officeholding experience in his home county, and Banks had none. These results provide further evidence that name recognition made a difference.

Familiarity aside, how can we explain differences among voters in their choices? The place to begin is with political party identification. Even a few days before the election, relatively few voters could identify the candidates' party affiliations. But other voters learned those affiliations from the parties' slate cards, which listed their candidates, and many voters cited party as the primary basis for their choices.

In Table 2-8 the strong relationship in both contests between party identification and

Table 2-7 Proportions of Vote Won by Democratic Supreme Court Candidates Statewide and in Candidates' Home Counties (percent)

Candidate (home county)	Candidate's percent of the vote		Home-county advantage	
	Home county	Statewide	Simple [a]	Controlling for party strength [b]
Banks (Mahoning)	30.6	27.3	3.3	−10.4
Douglas (Lucas)	79.0	72.7	6.3	11.7
Jones (Cuyahoga)	61.8	48.8	13.0	5.3
Wright (Franklin)	62.9	51.2	11.7	8.2

Source: Data for vote by county from Taft 1991, 92-99.

Note: Voters who chose other candidates are excluded.

[a] The difference between the candidate's percentage of the vote in the home county and statewide.

[b] The figure controlling for party strength takes into account the success of the party's candidates in the nonjudicial statewide contests in that county. For instance, on average, Democratic nonjudicial candidates did 7.3 percent better in Cuyahoga County than they did statewide. That 7.3 percent was treated as a correction for party strength and subtracted from Jones's 13.0 simple advantage to produce an advantage of 5.7 percent controlling for party strength.

the vote is shown. Democratic voters were more likely to choose the Democratic candidates than were Republicans, and strong Republicans and Democrats were more likely to choose their own party's candidate than were people with weaker party affiliations. The measures of statistical significance show that in each contest the relationships between party identification and voting almost surely were real rather than a result of chance.

The strength of the relationship differed between the two contests. In the Banks-Douglas contest it was decidedly weaker than in any other statewide race in 1990, and Douglas had so much of an advantage over Banks that he won more votes even from respondents who called themselves strong Democrats. Party identification had a stronger link with voting in the Jones-Wright contest—about as strong as in the partisan contests for state treasurer and auditor.

To what extent did use of a party organization's slate card facilitate party voting? The answer differs for the two races. Among voters who reported using a slate card in voting, about one-fifth of those who voted in the supreme court contests, there was a 57 percent difference between Democratic and Republican voters in the Jones-Wright contest; that is, the proportion of Democrats who voted for the Democrat Jones was 57 percentage points higher than the proportion of Republicans who chose her. For voters who did not report using a slate card, the difference was somewhat smaller, 46 percent. The slate card had a greater impact in the Banks-Douglas contest; among those using the list, the difference

Table 2-8 Vote for Supreme Court Candidates by Voters' Party Identifications (percent)

| | Democrats | | | | Republicans | | |
Vote	Strong	Weak	Leaning	Independents	Leaning	Weak	Strong
Banks	40.6	25.5	8.3	19.0	22.7	19.6	2.0
Douglas	59.4	74.5	91.7	81.0	77.3	80.4	98.0
Jones	91.2	66.7	73.7	68.8	43.5	32.3	15.8
Wright	8.8	33.3	26.3	31.2	56.5	67.7	84.2

Note: Voters who reported votes for other candidates are excluded. For the Banks-Douglas contest, tau-c=.224, $p < .01$; for the Jones-Wright contest tau-c=.581, $p < .001$. Tau-c is a measure of the strength of the relationship between two variables in this type of table; the higher it is, the stronger the relationship. p, a measure of statistical significance, is the likelihood that the relationship between two variables occurred as a matter of chance in this sample of voters rather than because the relationship really existed among all voters. Thus, $p < .01$ means that the likelihood was less than 1 in 100 that the relationship occurred as a matter of chance. Because this sample of voters was not entirely random, however, the level of statistical significance could be at least slightly different. Tau-c's in the other statewide contests were as follows: .685 for governor, .694 for secretary of state, .676 for attorney general, .511 for auditor, and .595 for treasurer.

between Democrats and Republicans was 32 percent, while it was only 9 percent for other voters. Thus, as badly as Banks fared, the use of slate cards by Democratic voters helped him to win votes.

Most voters could not place the candidates on an ideological scale, but those who did tended to define the candidates' positions by political party—the Republicans as moderate to conservative, the Democrats as moderate to liberal. (In light of the media's depiction of the Republican Douglas as a liberal on economic issues, it is interesting that three voters placed him on the conservative side of the spectrum for every voter who placed him on the liberal side.)

We might expect voters' own ideological positions to have an impact on their choices, with liberals inclined toward the Democrats and conservatives toward the Republicans. In fact, liberals were far more likely to support Jones than were conservatives. But this relationship simply reflected the tendency for liberals to identify with the Democratic party and conservatives with the Republicans; with a statistical control for party identification, the relationship between ideology and votes disappeared. This result is not surprising, because so few voters referred to ideology or specific policy issues in explaining their choices.

The most meaningful piece of information disclosed by the ballot itself was gender, and the large number of positive references to Jones as a female candidate suggests that gender affected the vote. Indeed, it had a strong effect: among our respondents, 62 percent of the women and 43 percent of the men voted for Jones, a difference of 19 percent. In part, this difference may have reflected the "gender gap," the current tendency for women to vote more Democratic than men. All the other statewide races pitted men against men or women against women, so they provide a good comparison with the Jones-Wright contest. In four of those six other races women voted for Democrats at a higher rate than men, but the largest difference was only 7 percent. When voters' party identifications were taken into account as a statistical control, the relationship between gender and the vote remained substantial and very significant statistically in the Jones-Wright contest, far stronger than in any of the other contests. Clearly, many voters responded to Jones and Wright in terms of gender.

The ballot did not identify the candidates by race, of course, but undoubtedly many people in Cleveland knew of Jones's race prior to the campaign, and voters who saw her commercials or other campaign coverage in the media might well have recalled when they went to the polls that she was an African American. Voters have some tendency to polarize along racial lines; did that tendency appear in the Jones-Wright contest? The results were dramatic: among the respondents who recalled their votes, 47 percent of the white voters and 100 percent of the black voters chose Jones.[6] Some of this difference reflected differences in the party identifications of white and black voters: every Democratic candidate for statewide office did better among black voters than among whites. But the differences were largest in the Jones-Wright contest. And although these differences nearly disappeared in the other contests when political party identifications were controlled, they remained substantial and statistically significant in the Jones-Wright contest.

As in some earlier supreme court elections, Ohio's labor unions might have influenced their members to support candidates endorsed by the labor movement. An especially interesting question is whether the endorsement of the Republican Douglas by most labor unions, which contrasted with unions' usual practice of endorsing Democrats, induced union members to support Douglas. The results are ambiguous (see also Asher, Ripley, and Snyder 1991). Because union members tend to be Democrats, every Democratic candidate for statewide office did better among union members than among other voters. This union advantage for the Democrats was lowest in the Douglas-Banks contest, at 4 percent. But the advantage was essentially the same in the contest for attorney general and only a little higher, at 7 percent, in the Jones-Wright contest. And Democrats who belonged to a union were considerably more likely to vote for Banks than were nonunion Democrats.

In any case, the impact of unions on their members' voting choices was less important than the decisions by unions to contribute money to Douglas rather than to Banks. Those decisions enhanced Douglas's capacity to run an effective campaign and helped limit Banks to a small-scale campaign.

Summarizing the Evidence

Taken together, the survey data do not point to definitive conclusions about how voters chose supreme court candidates. They do, however, provide some sense of those choices. Clearly, most voters knew little about the candidates. Voters who knew at least something about one candidate and nothing about the other almost always chose the candidate they knew. Beyond name recognition in itself, voters seized on whatever information they could glean: political party affiliations, gender, race. As a result, there are meaningful patterns of votes in the two contests. The Democratic candidates received more support from Democratic voters. Stephanie Tubbs Jones received an extra measure of votes from women and from black voters.

We should not ascribe too much meaning to voters' choices, however. Large numbers of people who voted in the supreme court contests could not recall which candidate they chose or, in many instances, whether they voted at all. Most of those voters probably had little basis for their choices. Even among the respondents who did recall how they voted, many could not articulate any reasons for their choices and many others offered reasons that had little substance. The victories of the incumbents Andrew Douglas and Craig Wright hardly reflected approval of their skills in legal analysis or of the legal policies they supported. In light of the paucity of information available to voters, such an interpretation of their votes would be highly unreasonable.

Conclusion

Judicial elections differ from each other in important characteristics, such as the amount of information provided to voters. For this reason no single set of elections can be regarded as typical. But the picture of the voters that emerges from Ohio's supreme court contests in 1990 is consistent with what we know about "ordinary" statewide judicial elections, those without special circumstances that increase candidates' visibility to voters. What are the implications about elections as a means to select judges?

Supporters of the Missouri Plan would point to the findings as additional evidence for adoption of that system, which allows voters only to retain or remove judges who are already in office. If voters' choices are not very meaningful, they would argue, most of the power to select judges should go to commissioners, who can assess candidates' qualifications, and governors, who can make informed choices among commission nominees.

This argument has considerable force. It applies especially well to the system used in Ohio, whose ballot provides no information other than the candidates' names and which does not distribute information pamphlets to voters. But states are hesitant to change their rules for electing public officials. The widespread adoption of the Missouri Plan is an exception to this tendency, but the rate of adoptions has slowed considerably as voters in states such as Ohio resist giving up their right to elect judges (Felice and Kilwein 1992). Most states continue to use judicial elections, and this is likely to remain true in the future.

Moreover, an argument can be made that judicial elections are desirable. Judges are major public officials, more important than many others that we elect, and giving the voters a chance to choose them enhances popular control of government. This chance is more useful where more information is readily available to voters through the ballot, particularly political party affiliations (see Dubois 1980), but even a system like that in Ohio provides some basis for popular control.

It should be noted as well that an election can be meaningful even if many voters choose candidates on the basis of very little information. In a close contest, a minority of knowledgeable voters can determine the result. This appears to be what happened in two of the contests for the Ohio Supreme Court in 1984 and 1986, where voters who had reached negative judgments about the performance of incumbents seemed to tip the balance against them.

This may not have been true of the close Jones-Wright contest in 1990, in which substantive information about the candidates was difficult to obtain. And scarcity of information has led to some outcomes in judicial elections across the country that seemed to have little or no meaningful basis. That kind of scarcity leads many voters to express a desire for more information to guide their choices of judges (Sheldon and Lovrich 1983), and efforts could be made to increase the supply of information to voters.

Despite the heated debate about how to select judges, it is not clear that formal systems make an enormous difference. For one thing, the various systems differ less in practice than they do on paper. In each system, for instance, the governor plays a major role in choosing judges. And every system draws from the same pool of potential judges: lawyers who have achieved the visibility and political support that make them serious candidates for selection. For these reasons, studies have not found dramatic differences among the various formal systems in the characteristics of the state supreme court justices they produce (Glick and Emmert 1987). This is not to say that the same seven people would sit on the Ohio Supreme Court if Ohio used gubernatorial appointment or the Missouri Plan to choose its judges. But, on the whole, the same *kinds* of people would serve.

Nor do formal systems for selecting judges necessarily produce systematic differences in the policies that courts adopt. They have some effect on judicial policies, simply because they help determine which specific people are chosen to serve as judges. If Ohio used the Missouri Plan, its current supreme court might have more conservative policies on personal injury law or more liberal policies on criminal procedure. But such differences may be more random than systematic, because the same kinds of people serve under different systems and because they are influenced by the same social and political environment in their state.

This does not mean that we should abandon the debate about formal selection systems for judges, because those systems do have some consequences—although more limited and more complicated than many people have thought. Formal systems aside, the selection of judges deserves continuing attention, because the process of choosing judges determines which people make judicial policies on major public issues. Thus, even if it were impossible to change the formal rules for selection of judges, it is important that people who are interested in the courts seek a better understanding of how those rules work to give us the judges we have.

Notes

1. There were 1,277 respondents in the first wave. In the second wave, designed to have fewer respondents, 492 of the first-wave respondents were reinterviewed. The third wave included 1,033 of the first-wave respondents.

2. Another possibility is that respondents exaggerated their turnout at the polls and their voting in nonjudicial contests and that the recall of participation in the supreme court contests is essentially accurate. But the more straightforward interpretation, one consistent with two Wisconsin studies (Adamany and Dubois 1975; Adamany and Shelley 1980), is that many voters simply forgot that they had chosen supreme court candidates. On inability to recall judicial votes, see also Griffin and Horan (1979).

3. Information on contributions and spending in the supreme court contests was obtained from the financial reports that candidates filed with the Ohio secretary of state's office. These reports provide only a partial picture of campaign finances; for instance, they do not identify the interest group affiliations of individual contributors.

4. Statistical methods exist to correct for this distortion, but they work imperfectly, and it might not be possible to use them effectively with these survey data.

5. This expectation generally is not as strong in nonpartisan contests, where party voting is weaker. Still, the "corrected" measure of advantage is probably more accurate than the simple measure.

6. The number of black respondents in this category, however, was only twenty-four. This number reflects the fact that most respondents, regardless of race, did not recall and report votes in the supreme court contests.

3 Lobbying for Justice: The Rise of Organized Conflict in the Politics of Federal Judgeships

Gregory A. Caldeira and John R. Wright

Under Article II of the U.S. Constitution, the president and Senate share the work of staffing the federal judiciary, one of the many "invitations to conflict" built into our charter. Typically, they have declined this invitation: throughout most of our nation's history, presidents have nominated and senators confirmed judges without overt conflict. Yet conflict has occasionally erupted, sometimes in short episodes, sometimes for an extended period. During the past decade, in particular, Americans have sat glued to their television sets as senators parlayed with Robert Bork and grilled Clarence Thomas.

These and other sensational political fights also engaged scholars, rekindling their interest in the politics of selecting judges. During the 1990s, analysts considered numerous questions relating to the confirmation process, including why presidents nominate particular individuals, why senators vote the way they do, and why the public supports or opposes particular candidates. In this chapter, we explore yet another intriguing dimension of federal judicial selection—organized conflict over federal judicial nominations.

Until recently, the active participation of a diverse set of organized interests in the selection of federal judges had not been a regular feature of our politics, or had not been, in the parlance of political science, "institutionalized." This changed during the 1980s. As Republican judges chosen by Ronald Reagan took their seats alongside the liberal appointees of Jimmy Carter, organized interests clashed again and again in the Senate Judiciary Committee and on the floor of the Senate, fighting for control of the federal bench. As a result, the selection of federal judges—once a "cozy triangle" of senators, the executive branch, and the bar—became a major arena for the participation of interest groups. Senators and presidents came to expect interest groups to stake out positions and work on judicial nominations; organized conflict became part of the political calculus of participants. What is more, despite changes in administration, the broad participation of orga-

We thank the National Science Foundation, through its Law and Social Science Program, for financial support of the project from which this research derives. We also thank the numerous staff members in interest groups and archivists at several institutions for their patience.

nized interests and the battle lines drawn in the 1980s over the politics of judicial nominations have persisted in the 1990s.

Here we offer a theoretical model and an explanation, actually a set of explanations, for the changes in the political activities of organized interests on federal judicial nominations and for the Senate's response. Why, given the large amounts of money and time it takes to oppose candidates for a federal judgeship, would organized interests engage in this form of participation? And, why, in light of the seeming lack of incentives, would senators respond in kind to the calls of organized interests for more careful screening of federal judges? Why, more generally, has organized conflict about federal judgeships arisen and become institutionalized?

The Actors and Their Goals

Occasionally when political actors make decisions, they know that a given course of action will produce a particular outcome. The selection of federal judges, though, does not fall into that category; rather it poses a problem of decision making under uncertainty (for a similar conception of the role of organized interests, see Caldeira and Wright 1994; Hansen 1991). For any particular nomination, the legislature and executive, theoretically, have the option of choosing from among hundreds of lawyers who meet the formal qualifications. Presidents and senators want to know how a candidate stands on the fundamental legal and political issues of the day. Yet neither has the time to do the homework required to make a reliable determination of the professional quality and the policy views of all of the potential candidates. This is where interest groups come in. In our theoretical formulation, we argue for the informational role of organized interests in the selection of federal judges.[1] That is, legislators and the executive use the participation of interest groups as an aid in the location and selection of nominees. Interest groups provide senators with information about the views of crucial constituencies toward particular candidates for the bench, information not otherwise easily available to them. Groups inform senators about the "politics" of nominations.

We ground this argument in a general assumption about the actors involved in the confirmation process: judges, senators, and interest groups have goals and pursue them instrumentally. More specifically, we assume, first, that judges seek to maximize their policy preferences by etching them into law. In other words, judges with liberal inclinations seek to push case outcomes in that direction, whereas their conservative counterparts wish it to move the other way. If federal judges did not pursue ideological agendas, organized interests on both sides of the spectrum would show less concern about who sits on the federal courts than they in fact do.

Second, we assume that senators wish to maximize their chances for reelection. Senators pursue other goals, such as "good public policy," but they do so constrained by the goal of reelection. Unless senators can see a connection between the concerns of their electoral constituencies and the politics of federal judicial candidacies, they do not attempt to influence the outcome of individual nominations. Policy-oriented arguments for or against a judicial nominee, then, must be accompanied by those that stress how senators' constituents will react (for empirical treatments of roll-call voting, see Cameron, Cover, and Segal 1990; Segal, Cameron, and Cover 1992). Indeed, in the absence of electoral pressure, senators treat positions on the federal bench as patronage and simply support each other's candidates (otherwise known as logrolling, the practice of vote trading among legislators to gain support for bills or candidates of benefit to each other's electoral fortunes).

Third, we assume that an organized interest seeks to achieve two primary goals (see Clark and Wilson 1961; Wilson 1973): to influence public policy and to retain members. If a group hopes to attain these twin objectives, it should not waste time and money on participating in confirmation battles unless two conditions obtain: first, that its leaders believe that the nomination touches an issue of high concern to the members of the organization, and second, that its leaders think that they could win the battle or, at least, suspect that their participation would help accomplish other organizational goals.

Even if these conditions exist, organizations may think twice about involving themselves in a confirmation battle, for they know that effective participation is an expensive proposition. It requires significant effort from staff; displaces other issues on an organization's agenda; taxes the relations between an organization and the Senate; can strain relations with political allies and financial supporters; and costs a great deal of money if an organization tries to influence public opinion with paid advertisements or tries to tap national sentiment through polls. If the venture bears no fruit, it can undermine an organization's reputation for credibility. Still, when groups do participate, they send a strong signal to senators that some segment of the population is concerned about a nomination. Given legislators' concerns about reelection and constituent opinion, these are signals they can hardly afford to ignore.

Interest Groups and Federal Judicial Selection

Having laid out our theoretical argument, we turn to the development of organized conflict and seek to understand how it became an institutionalized or regular part of the confirmation process. Through a historical discussion of the role of organized interests in the controversial nominations to the federal courts, we develop a picture of the confirmation process, the environment within which it operates, the circumstances under which it shifted, and the role of organized interests. In the final section of the chapter, we use this historical material to answer our primary research question, Why has organized conflict about federal judgeships arisen and become institutionalized?

Judicial Nominations in the Nineteenth Century

During much of the nineteenth century, political partisanship, regional splits, the relative weakness of the president in comparison to the Senate, and the comparatively low status of the Court characterized the politics of choosing federal judges (Friedman 1983, 1986; Hall 1979, 1980). The U.S. Supreme Court figured as an important issue in at least one presidential campaign (Westin 1951); but we have no evidence of any direct electoral consequences for individual senators based on the positions they took on nominations to the high bench. For the most part, staffing of the Court involved a small set of political actors—the president, the Senate, and, on occasion, local elites if a particular state had a good claim on a particular seat (Shapiro 1990; but see Ainsworth and Maltese 1992).

We would not, therefore, anticipate much participation from organized interests in the selection of federal judges until the twentieth century. And, in fact, this was the case: although thousands of individuals, some of them members of organizations, pressured the president or senators, organized interests as interests did not participate in the process (Ross 1990, 5). Even if they had participated, senators probably would not have responded, since direct election of the Senate did not become part of the Constitution until 1913; and not until the late nineteenth century did members seek reelection as a matter of course and see the job as a career.

Judicial Nominations from Taft through Eisenhower

These trends continued into the twentieth century. Apart from occasional flare-ups of organized conflict, during most of the century the key actors—the Senate Judiciary Committee, the administration, and the bar associations—made appointments in relative isolation (see, for example, Solomon 1984). Even on those rare occasions when organized interests mobilized and played a major role in the rejection or near defeat of a nominee to the federal courts, the basic system of choosing federal judges—a triangle of the executive, the Senate and its Judiciary Committee, and the bar—would soon reassert itself.

This was so because most groups (and there were not many during this period) had little interest in the federal courts, and those that had some could not mobilize in a credible way. The problem was that until a rule change in the late 1920s the Senate debated and voted on federal judicial nominations in executive session (Harris 1951, 253-255). So even if an organization engaged in lobbying efforts, individual senators could avoid responsibility for positions on the nomination. The Senate leaked information, of course, but still, an organization had no reliable means of monitoring the behavior of individual senators. Our model requires that if there is to be strong and organized conflict the legislators must have reelection as a primary goal, organizations must be capable of sending a strong signal about electoral chances, and organizations must have an opportunity to observe the behavior of legislators.

Yet there were a few instances of real, organized conflict, and they are worthy of note. During the administration of William Howard Taft, for example, organized labor opposed Horace H. Lurton's nomination to the Supreme Court (Ross 1990, 6 n. 6). Several organizations—the American Federation of Labor (AFL), the Order of Railroad Telegraphers, and the Brotherhood of Locomotive Firemen and Engineers—wrote letters to President Taft in opposition to Lurton. President Taft went ahead with the nomination, but the leader of the AFL, Samuel Gompers, continued to oppose Lurton. Several liberal organizations and trade unions opposed President Taft's choice of Mahlon Pitney in 1912 (Bickel and Schmidt 1984, 326-332). Organized interests failed to invest substantial resources on either of these nominations and failed to influence their outcome.

The nomination of Louis D. Brandeis to the Supreme Court in 1916 was the source of even greater controversy (see Mason 1946, 465-508; Todd 1965; United States 1916). Interestingly, although opposition to Brandeis was well-organized and orchestrated, none of those who spoke out did so as an official representative of an organization. Opponents acted formally or informally as proxies for corporate interests. Lawyers from Wall Street urged members of the American Bar Association to contact senators. Leaders of many liberal organizations signed a petition in support of Brandeis, but none claimed to stand for the views of the membership. Supporters launched a campaign in the mass media to counter the charges of conservative critics. The effort on both sides was impressive; and it represented the first of the modern episodes in organized conflict.

The nomination of Charles Evans Hughes as chief justice was also interesting. No organizations opposed Hughes, yet his nomination drew, surprisingly, thirty negative votes in the Senate. Because the Senate acted promptly on the nomination, organizations had little chance to act. The opposition to the nomination was partly because of the rift between conservative and progressive members of the Republican party and partly because the progressives among Republicans and Democrats disliked his representation of corporate interests (Pusey 1951, 648-667; Ross 1990, 10).

What is important in the Hughes nomination is that the Senate, in dividing so sharply in its vote, showed a willingness to cross the executive and to take on a tough issue. Perhaps that willingness encouraged organized interests to mobilize just a month later when President Herbert Hoover sent up the nomination of John J. Parker of the U.S. Court of Appeals for the Fourth Circuit (see Burris 1987; Fish 1988-1989; Goings 1990; Grossman and Wasby 1972; Hine 1977; United States 1930; and Watson 1963). Soon after President Hoover announced the nomination, both the AFL and the National Association for the Advancement of Colored People (NAACP) announced opposition to Judge Parker. Organized labor opposed Parker for what its leaders considered an antilabor decision in *United Mine Workers v. Red Jacket Consolidated Coal and Coke Company* (1927).[2] The NAACP sought the defeat of Parker because of racial comments he made in the gubernatorial campaign of 1920 and because of his failure to take issue with the North Carolina Constitution's denial of voting rights to blacks (see Lisio 1985). This pair of organizations launched a lobbying effort in Washington and at the grass roots that was impressive, especially in comparison with previous fights. Members and officers of the NAACP generated thousands of letters and telegrams to senators and newspaper editors around the nation. The NAACP made particularly good use of local chapters. The AFL also mobilized its local affiliates, although not on the same scale, generating many additional letters and editorials.

For members of the NAACP, participation in the fight against Parker, especially in the South but elsewhere as well, must have sent a strong and credible signal to senators, given the high cost of visible political activity for blacks. Changes in the Senate's rules permitted labor and blacks to hold individual senators to account. The electoral threat was very real for Republicans in the Senate; and the NAACP made it an issue in the fall of 1930, targeting Republicans with significant black constituencies who had voted for Parker (Goings 1990, 54-74; Hine 1977). Other than the NAACP and the AFL, few of the national organizations with a reason to oppose Parker had the capacity to sustain a lobbying effort in Washington and at the grass roots.

Between Parker in 1930 and the next major battle, over Clement Haynsworth in 1969, a wide variety of organizations participated in the consideration of nominations to the Supreme Court—writing letters, taking positions, and generating publicity—but none seems to have made much of a mark or invested much of its resources (see Grossman 1965). Organized labor—the AFL and the United Automobile Workers (UAW)—supported the Supreme Court nominee Hugo Black (Dunne 1977, 50-56; Ross 1990, 15). A scattering of individual right-wingers opposed Felix Frankfurter in 1938 (United States 1939). Many organizations on the left—for example, the National Lawyers' Guild—opposed the nomination of Tom C. Clark in 1949, presumably because of the role he had played as attorney general in enforcing federal rules on loyalty (Ross 1990, 14). These interests did not, however, possess significant electoral clout or credibility as Washington lobbyists. And, for organizations with significant grass-roots support, fighting a nomination to the Supreme Court was not a good investment of resources during this long period of Democratic dominance.

During the 1950s and 1960s, some conservative individuals and organizations objected to the nominations of Earl Warren, John M. Harlan, Potter Stewart, and Thurgood Marshall. None of those who opposed these nominations had much credibility in the Senate. During most of the period between Parker and Haynsworth, Democrats dominated Congress and the executive. Those who might have opposed liberal or moderate nominees could not call on a conservative counterpart of the NAACP, AFL, UAW, and United Mine Workers (UMW). That is, groups with the ability to reduce senatorial uncertainty about the political effect of a nomination did not have sufficient reason to become active in opposition; and those who did engage in opposition could not provide reliable signals about the views of constituents.

The Elevation of Abe Fortas

Before turning to the Haynsworth battle, we must mention an intervening event—the controversial defeat of Abe Fortas's elevation to the chief justiceship and Homer Thornberry's nomination to be associate justice in 1968. Several conservative organizations testified in opposition to Fortas's elevation (United States 1968) and engaged in grass-roots lobbying.[3] Elite members of the bar rallied in support of Fortas, at the urging of the White House and friends of Fortas. For Fortas, as for the nominations of the 1950s and 1960s, institutional conflict figured more prominently in the calculus of senators than did organized opposition. Sen. Robert P. Griffin (R-Mich.) orchestrated opposition to Fortas and Thornberry, first on the Republican side of the aisle and then among southern Democrats.

President Lyndon B. Johnson put up an impressive fight in support of Fortas and Thornberry. During a period of two and a half months, his lobbyists took the pulse of the Senate in more than a dozen separate head counts. Legislative liaison in the executive branch worked in tandem with Andrew Biemiller, the lobbyist of the AFL-CIO (Congress of Industrial Organizations) and Clarence Mitchell, the lobbyist of the NAACP. For blacks and organized labor, the federal courts constituted a critical part of their political strategies, so they had a strong motivation to take part. Justice Fortas possessed superb credentials in the corporate world, and the White House used pressure from executives of strategically placed corporations to lobby senators in a number of states. Similarly, the administration called upon Fortas's friends in the organized Jewish community for assistance in creating pressure on crucial senators. Finally, a former law partner of Fortas's— Paul Porter—created a group to conduct a public relations campaign and to organize the support of elite lawyers. This group, the AFL-CIO, NAACP, and President Johnson's corporate contacts generated a substantial amount of activity at the grass-roots level.

In the controversy over Fortas and Thornberry, we see several features for the first time—features that later reappeared as organized conflict became a part of the process. For the first time, the White House had invested substantial resources in a sophisticated effort to confirm a nominee. For the first time, the president and loyal organizations engaged in "cooperative lobbying." For other nominations, supporters and opponents had rallied the elite bar and law professors, but Paul Porter's group fine-tuned and used this method on a much larger scale. Last but not least, that group waged a systematic battle for the attention of newspapers, magazines, and radio.

The Defeats of Clement Haynsworth and G. Harold Carswell

Much enmity from the Fortas controversy carried over into the consideration of Clement Haynsworth. But the constellation of forces in conflict over Haynsworth in 1969 was far greater than that involved in the Fortas proceedings.[4] By the time of the Haynsworth battle, dozens of organizations, representing "new" constituencies, had arisen that possessed significant strength at the grass roots. They and liberals in the Senate saw the nomination as an opportunity to test President Richard M. Nixon's commitment to placing conservative jurists in the courts.

Organized labor, which declared against the nomination only a few days after President Nixon named Haynsworth, led the coalition in opposition. The AFL-CIO pulled out all the stops. It mobilized the leadership of the 50 state federations and 120 affiliated unions. And it asked rank-and-file members to contact senators. The message from labor to senators: the vote on Haynsworth would figure in the AFL-CIO's decisions on financial and electoral support in the elections of 1970 and 1972. Organized labor employed a crew of forty lobbyists on Capitol Hill at the height of the battle over Haynsworth. The Leadership Conference on Civil Rights—a permanent coalition of labor, civil rights, and liberal organizations, 125 strong at that point—opposed Haynsworth for his lack of sensitivity to the concerns of blacks in his tenure on the Fourth Circuit. It lobbied extensively in Washington and at the grass roots. At the hearings, nearly thirty organizations testified or submitted a memorandum for the record in opposition to Haynsworth. Between the members of the Leadership Conference and the AFL-CIO and the chapters, locals, and affiliates of these members, hundreds and hundreds of organizations stood against this nomination.

President Nixon launched a major initiative in behalf of Haynsworth in response to the organized opposition (Maltese 1990). The efforts of the administration included a campaign of public relations; mobilization of the state parties to put pressure on senators; direct lobbying by the White House in the Senate; cooperative efforts with friendly interest groups; and the targeting of the big financial supporters of swing senators. But the effort was not enough: the Senate turned down Haynsworth by a vote of 45 to 55.

In the wake of the defeat of Haynsworth, President Nixon sent up the name of Judge G. Harold Carswell of the Fifth Circuit (see Harris 1970; U.S. Congress 1970; and Wasby and Grossman 1972). Ultimately, Carswell ran into as much, probably more, opposition than had Judge Haynsworth in the fall of 1969. The charge: insensitivity as a lawyer and judge to the civil rights of blacks. Nearly the same coalition of organized interests came out against Carswell, but during the hearings few—less than ten—organizations testified against him. Hundreds of lawyers and many law professors signed letters and petitions in opposition to

Carswell. Labor, which had led the fight against Haynsworth, opted for a subsidiary role. Instead, given the centrality of race as an issue, the Leadership Conference stood front and center on this nomination. Senators resisted another fight so soon after Haynsworth, and organizations undoubtedly had to push the limits of available resources. Opposition to Carswell crystallized slowly. In the wake of the hearings, several liberal senators, especially Birch Bayh (D-Ind.), became convinced of the danger Carswell posed and so worked alongside organized labor and the Leadership Conference to mobilize grass-roots concern and to put pressure on the undecided and swing members of the Senate. Through the Leadership Conference on Civil Rights, liberals launched a massive effort at the grass roots. It culminated in a "fly-in" of important constituents from the memberships of organizations in the Leadership Conference. These constituents moved from office to office of the senators from their states or regions as the day of reckoning approached. Lobbying of the more traditional kind buttressed the efforts at the grass roots. The record suggests a sophisticated campaign of lobbying. The extraordinary effort on the part of the Leadership Conference and organized labor, particularly after a recent battle, undoubtedly sent a strong signal of the concerns of this set of constituencies.

President Nixon rose to the challenge and took advantage of most of the tools he had used in the battle over Haynsworth (see Massaro 1990, 105-134). He did not, however, mobilize the support of organized interests on the conservative side in cooperative lobbying. Instead, he relied on the efforts of staff in the White House and at the Department of Justice. Indeed, this lack of organized support among lawyers, bar associations, and conservative organizations constituted one of the administration's chief problems in selling Carswell's nomination to the Senate. In the absence of concern from organized interests, senators of the president's party could afford to deviate on this issue. Not surprisingly, the nominee went down in defeat.

Some elements of the coalitions in opposition to Haynsworth and Carswell came together again in response to Nixon's nomination of William H. Rehnquist in 1971. Thus, for example, the leadership of labor unions and liberal civil rights groups opposed Rehnquist in testimony before the Senate (United States 1971). But neither the Leadership Conference nor the AFL-CIO seems to have engaged in an intense campaign of lobbying in Washington or at the grass roots. Despite a substantial number of negative votes, the nomination of Rehnquist ultimately carried.

By the middle of the 1970s, then, organized participation in nominations had become institutionalized. Even the well-received nomination of John Paul Stevens to the Supreme Court drew a significant amount of organizational response and the opposition of a small number of organized interests.

The Carter Years

Not surprisingly, conflict over judges persisted in the Carter years. Indeed, warfare between conservatives and liberals intensified. This was so, in part, because the Democratic Congress created more than 150 new judicial seats for the president to fill, thereby raising the stakes considerably. It was also true that Carter vowed to choose judges on merit and to diversify the federal bench. To implement these objectives, the president created the United States Circuit Judge Nominating Commission. These commissions would, he argued, yield more openness, candidates of higher quality, and a more representative set of judges. In his words, "Each panel is encouraged to make special efforts to seek out and identify well-qualified women and members of minority groups as potential nominees." President Carter also ordered the attorney general, before recommending a candidate, to "consider whether an affirmative effort has been made . . . to identify candidates, including women and members of minority groups." Officials on occasion made statements interpretable as a commitment to quotas of women and minorities on the bench.

Carter's plans sat comfortably with liberal organized interests, which sought to undermine traditional criteria (such as length of experience in practice)—criteria that worked against blacks, Hispanics, and women. But they worried conservative interests, for these groups viewed "affirmative action" criteria as a buzzword for "liberalism." They, in other words, were deeply concerned that Carter would stack the judiciary—and keep in mind that the president had the opportunity to appoint 150 or so new judges—with jurists adverse to their policy interests.

Compounding matters for conservative interests were changes in the Senate (Slotnick 1979). Under the chairmanship of Sen. Edward Kennedy in 1979, the Judiciary Committee created a detailed questionnaire; it asked whether the nominee had "demonstrated a commitment to equal justice," devoted time to "serving the disadvantaged," and belonged "to an organization or club which excludes persons or discriminates on the basis of race, sex, or religion." Conservative senators and organized interests criticized the intrusiveness and ideological character of these questions. The written questionnaire required a comprehensive list of organizational memberships, an obvious set of ideological clues. And, in interviews, members of the panels in a significant number of instances asked a candidate about his or her views on affirmative action, the Equal Rights Amendment, the rights of defendants, and freedom of expression (Berkson 1979). Conservatives complained of the interactions of the Standing Committee on the Judiciary of the American Bar Association (ABA) with liberal groups. They rankled as well at the deference of the majority of the Senate Judiciary Committee to the reviews of nominees conducted by the Judicial Screening Panel of the Federation of Women Lawyers and the National Bar Association.

Liberals and conservatives in the Senate, aided and abetted by organized interests, jousted over a long list of nominations, often in hearings, most of the time behind closed doors, and on occasion during votes in committee and the floor. Two of the instances of open and organized conflict revolved around nominations to the U.S. Court of Appeals for the District of Columbia. One of the nominees—Representative Abner Mikva of Chicago, long a vocal advocate of liberal causes—ran into vociferous opposition from the National Rifle Association and the gun lobby. The Senate in time confirmed Mikva, but thirty-one senators cast their votes against him. The second, Patricia Wald—long an activist in the public interest movement and at the time an assistant attorney general in the Department of Justice—faced conservative opposition and drew twenty-one negative votes in the Senate.

The Reagan Years

Soon after his inauguration President Reagan rescinded the executive order by which President Carter had created judicial nominating panels; and, on March 6, 1981, Attorney General William French Smith announced new procedures.[5] The administration invited Republican senators, or other officeholders in states in which the Republicans did not hold a seat, to submit three to five names for each vacancy on the district court. For the courts of appeals, the administration would seek suggestions from a broad range of sources. Each Tuesday, Attorney General Smith, Deputy Attorney General Edward C. Schmults, and Jonathan C. Rose (assistant attorney general in the Office of Legal Policy) would meet with aides to review the credentials of candidates for vacancies. Then, on Thursdays, Smith, Schmults, and Rose would take the names of candidates they had chosen, usually one or two, to the White House for a meeting with the Federal Judicial Selection Committee. It included Chief of Staff James A. Baker III; Deputy Chief Michael Deaver; Counselor Edwin Meese III; Counsel Fred Fielding, who served as chair of the group; E. Pendleton James, of the Office of Personnel Administration; and M. G. Oglesby, a White House assistant for legislative affairs. The name of the individual who received the committee's blessing would go to the president for approval—after a clean bill of health from the Federal Bureau of Investigation (FBI) and the ABA's Standing Committee on the Judiciary.

The purpose of this process was to ferret out conservatives committed to the principles of the Reagan administration. This the committee accomplished well. In the first term, President Reagan appointed to the federal courts of appeals many strong conservatives who shared varying combinations of youth, brilliance, and academic credentials: Richard A. Posner (Seventh Circuit), Frank Easterbrook (Seventh Circuit), J. Harvie Wilkinson (Fourth Circuit), Kenneth Starr (District of Columbia Circuit), Edith Jones (Fifth Circuit), Ralph Winter (Second Circuit), and Pasco Bowman (Eighth Circuit). These nominees ran into surprisingly little opposition.[6] During the early years, liberal interest groups had a long list of battles to fight (proposals in Congress to ban abortion, return prayer to school, and so forth), so judgeships ranked as a low priority.

In fact, in Reagan's first administration, his nominees probably faced more frequent opposition from conservative organizations than from liberals—especially if we take into account skirmishes in the phase prior to submission of the nomination to the Senate. For a seat on the Eighth Circuit, organized interests derailed the candidacy of Judith Whittaker, a lawyer for Hallmark Cards, on account of her support for the Equal Rights Amendment (ERA) and alleged feminist sympathies. In the late part of the first and early part of the second term, conservatives in the Senate and conservative groups quashed a number of nominations, including that of Andrew Frey. President Reagan had nominated Frey, then a deputy solicitor general, for a seat on the District of Columbia Circuit in the summer of 1984. When Frey's contributions to Planned Parenthood and a gun-control organization came to light, the National Rifle Association and pro-life organizations lobbied the White House in opposition to the nomination. Soon after Reagan received a strong letter in opposition from thirteen conservative members of the Senate, he withdrew the nomination.

In short, it was conservative, not liberal, organizations that showed their muscle during the first few years of the Reagan presidency. Liberals did little to counter the administration's judicial strategy. Even the most conservative nominations, such as Robert Bork for the District of Columbia Circuit, flew through the Senate with no organized opposition. This changed immediately after the defeat of the Democratic presidential ticket in November of 1984. With the prospect of Reagan filling eighty-five new judgeships, representatives of various public interest and civil rights groups met to consider a strategy to cope with a new wave of conservative nominations. This meeting of organizations resulted in the formation of the Judicial Selection Project under the umbrella of the Alliance for Justice, which itself was founded in the early 1980s to represent twenty-five or so organizations in the areas of legal services, regulatory reform, and restrictions on lobbying and advocacy. The project would have its own staff, conduct and disseminate research on nominations, and try to form coalitions. In recognition of the limitations on resources, its leaders agreed to concentrate on the candidates whose professional credentials or commitment to "equal justice under law" had raised doubts. Ultimately, nearly thirty organizations joined the Judicial Selection Project, including the AFL-CIO and the liberal public interest group, People for the American Way (PFAW).

Members of the Judicial Selection Project met regularly to consider candidates for the bench, before and after presidential announcements. For each candidate, the staff of members of the project would make between twenty and thirty calls to members and relevant people located in the circuit or district of the seat. A standard list of contacts would include public defenders, public interest lawyers, lawyers for the American Civil Liberties Union

(ACLU), cooperative attorneys for the NAACP Legal Defense and Education Fund, and lawyers for legal services. By the late 1980s, several of the members had added permanent staff to monitor judicial nominations. Thus, for example, People for the American Way, which had concentrated on nominations since 1985, created a "Nominations Network" in 1988, a set of active members who would inform the staff of PFAW about candidates. If a candidacy raised serious questions for the Judicial Selection Project, staff members would do further research and submit a report for the consideration of the Senate Judiciary Committee. It would also seek broadly based organizational support for the report. In the most extreme cases, in which the project took a position against a nomination, the staff would attempt to coax its organizational members to allocate resources for inside and grass-roots lobbying and advertising.

Earlier in the decade, conservatives had formed a similar organization—the Judicial Reform Project, under the aegis of the Free Congress Research and Education Foundation—to help the administration recruit conservatives, to perform and publicize research, and to seek changes in the field of law enforcement. Patrick McGuigan, a member of the staff of Free Congress, served as director of the Judicial Reform Project. Coalitions for America—similarly located at Free Congress—became an umbrella for the lobbying efforts of many organizations in behalf of conservative nominees and against moderates and liberals. More than one hundred organizations, virtually all the conservative groups in the Washington, D.C., area, became members of Coalitions for America. It focuses on a range of issues; on each, a set of the members of Coalitions for America comes together. On judgeships, a subset known as the "Library Court" coalition was formed. It includes a vast array of conservative interest groups (for example, the National Right to Life Committee, the American Conservative Union, the National Rifle Association, Concerned Women for America, the National Association of Evangelicals, and the Conservative Caucus). In effect, Coalitions for America serves on the conservative side as the functional equivalent of the Leadership Conference on Civil Rights. In coalition building on nominations, the Library Court Group comes into conflict with the Alliance for Justice. The Judicial Reform Project squares off against the Judicial Selection Project in executing and publicizing research.

It was only inevitable, then, that the Senate would become a battlefield. The first shots were fired in late 1985 over the nomination of Alex Kozinski for a seat on the Ninth Circuit. Controversy surrounded Kozinski's tenure during the Reagan administration at the Merit Systems Protection Board; critics saw him as hostile to "whistle blowers," the intended beneficiaries of the board. Nevertheless, Kozinski's nomination passed through the Judiciary Committee without objection. The Government Accountability Project (GAP), a "good government" group, had testified against Kozinski, but no senators took action. Soon after the hearing, another watchdog organization, Common Cause, raised questions about the nomination. GAP prevailed on Sen. Carl Levin of the Government

Affairs Committee, which oversees the board, to hold an investigation of Kozinski's tenure. But the Library Court Group of Coalitions for America orchestrated a last-minute effort to help the Reagan administration win approval for Kozinski. The Senate ended up confirming him by a vote of 54 to 43.

Three battles followed in quick succession in the spring of 1986. Liberal organizations, under the leadership of the Judicial Selection Project, launched major campaigns against the nominations of Sidney Fitzwater (district judge, Texas), Jefferson Sessions (district judge, Alabama), and Daniel Manion (judge in the Seventh Circuit). Liberal organizations accused Fitzwater, a state judge, of engaging in intimidation of black and Hispanic voters in Dallas. The coalition against Fitzwater, led by Ann Lewis of the Americans for Democratic Action, consisted of black and Hispanic organizations in a campaign of inside and grass-roots lobbying. Despite the organizational mobilization, Fitzwater cleared the committee by a vote of 10 to 5 and the Senate by 52 to 43. Sessions, a U.S. attorney in Alabama, had roused the ire of black organizations because of prosecutions against civil rights activists for voting fraud and because he had made some controversial comments about the NAACP. On this nomination, the NAACP Legal Defense and Education Fund led the fight. The Committee on the Judiciary rejected Sessions on a 10-to-5 vote.

The battle over Daniel Manion in 1986, in a sense, constituted a dress rehearsal for the fight over Judge Bork's nomination to the Supreme Court in 1987. Manion's nomination ran into trouble because of his familial ties to the John Birch Society, his activity as a legislator on behalf of the right-to-life movement, and modest legal credentials. Both sides mobilized thousands of activists and conducted an intense inside lobbying campaign. People for the American Way, on the liberal side, purchased advertisements against Manion in newspapers and on radio and television. Two hundred law professors and nearly fifty deans of law schools came out against Manion; some, but not many, lawyers, academics, and deans spoke in behalf of the nomination. In the wake of parliamentary maneuvering, Manion gained confirmation—but by only one vote.

Behind the scenes the Judicial Selection Project had fended off at least four and perhaps more candidacies for seats on the courts of appeals during 1985 and 1986. We mention three. William Harvey, a law professor at Indiana University, had served a controversial tenure as chairman of the Board of Directors of the Legal Services Corporation and had made highly critical statements about the federal courts. The Judicial Selection Project provided information on Harvey's record to the ABA's Standing Committee on the Judiciary. Subsequently, the ABA accorded Harvey a rating of "not qualified." Michael Horowitz, formerly general counsel of the Office of Management and Budget, had gained the enmity of liberal organizations when he attempted to use regulatory reforms as a means of decreasing the effectiveness of lobbying in the public interest sector. The report of the Judicial Selection Project gave a bill of particulars against Horowitz. This strong hint of a battle apparently led Horowitz to withdraw his name. Lino Graglia, a law professor at the University of Texas, had written books and articles against judicial review and busing for school desegregation. The Reagan administration sent his name to the ABA for a seat on the Fifth Circuit. Once again, the Judicial Selection Project devoted a great deal of effort to relaying information about Graglia and his writings to the administration and then to the ABA committee. The ABA found Graglia not qualified.

The biggest battle, however, was yet to come. Organizational participation in the nomination of Judge Robert Bork in July 1987 broke all records. Liberals spoke of more than three hundred organizations in the anti-Bork coalition; conservatives, of more than one hundred in support. Every part of the liberal interest group community participated in some manner: environmentalists, consumers, civil rights activists, nonprofit organizations, mental health associations, the handicapped, women, gays and lesbians, and unions. This coalition used a wide variety of tactics, including advertising and grass-roots events, informed by focus groups, and polling. President Reagan's staff resisted, but, eventually, conservative organizations drew upon elements of Coalitions for America. The White House sought and received the support of big business and some trade associations. The nomination of Judge Bork brought out an epic amount of organized activity, which the candidate himself blames for his eventual defeat (see Bork 1990).

The Bush Administration

Conservatives criticized President Bush on many counts, but most approved of his judicial nominations. The Bush White House, like Reagan's, took care in its ideological screening of candidates. Moreover, because the government remained divided along partisan lines (the Congress was Democratic; the president, Republican), the federal courts remained an important battleground for the left and right. The institutionalization of conflict proceeded apace, and many Bush nominees became the subject of public conflict between organized interests. Five nominations ended with roll-call votes, either in committee or on the floor, but on only one, that of Judge Kenneth Ryskamp to the Eleventh Circuit, did the Senate reject the nominee.[7] President Bush initially nominated Judge Ryskamp of Florida in 1990, but because of the complaints of civil rights organizations about insensitivity to minorities and membership in a private club, the Judiciary Committee took no action in the 101st Congress. Then, in the 102d Congress, Bush resubmitted his name. This time around, People for the American Way attacked Judge Ryskamp for bias in his rulings against plaintiffs in civil rights cases. Organizations in Florida representing blacks, women, Cubans, and Jews engaged in tough lobbying against Ryskamp with a crucial player, Sen. Bob Graham (D-Fla.). Senator Graham decided to oppose the nomination, and the Judiciary Committee killed it on a 6-to-8 vote.

Bush's nomination of Clarence Thomas to the Supreme Court, of course, engendered a tremendous outpouring of organizational activity on both sides, although probably not nearly as much as the Bork nomination (see Brock 1993; Caldeira and Smith 1993; Overby et al. 1992; Phelps and Winternitz 1992). Because Judge Thomas was an African American, black interest groups split and it was difficult for liberal organizations to mobilize against the nomination. Nevertheless, parts of the anti-Bork coalition came together and lobbied hard against the Thomas nomination. By the end of the initial hearings, more than forty senators had declared their opposition to the nomination; and, then, Professor Anita Hill's allegations of sexual harassment by Thomas led to a second set of hearings, which nearly buried Thomas. Ultimately, the nomination carried the day, 52 to 48, probably surviving because Thomas's race neutralized the opposition of black constituencies and because of the failure of liberals to organize early and broadly, as they had done so effectively in the fight over Judge Bork. Like the Bork battle, however, the Thomas nomination involved a large number of organizations, a highly public controversy, a wide variety of tactics, and attempts by interest groups to indicate to senators the electoral consequences of their votes. Seen in this way, the Thomas nomination is, perhaps, a classic illustration of how organized interests play an informational role for senators in an environment of political uncertainty.

The Clinton Administration

So far, President Clinton has avoided a clash on the scale of Bork, Thomas, or Ryskamp; but many of his nominations have run into organized opposition, from both liberals and conservatives. Even on consensual nominations such as Ruth Bader Ginsburg and Stephen Breyer to the Supreme Court, organized interests have taken positions, testified, done re-search, and lobbied in Washington and at the grass-roots level. For example, some pro-life organizations, the National Home Schooling Association, the consumer advocate Ralph Nader, and activists in antitrust policy testified against the nomination of Breyer; and the Alliance for Justice and Coalitions for America, the two main monitoring organizations, delivered lengthy written analyses of his record. Thus, the institutional apparatus for large-scale organizational conflicts remains in place; and presumably, should President Clinton nominate someone outside of the middle of the spectrum, fireworks would ensue.

Explanations for the Rise of Organized Conflict

In the previous section we have offered a broad outline of the confirmation process—emphasizing the environment within which it operates, the circumstances under which it shifted, and the role of organized interests. In what follows, we use the historical material to shed light on the question, Why has organized conflict become a regular part of the game of choosing federal judges? The reasons, as suggested in our historical discussion, center on changes occurring within (1) the interest group environment, (2) Congress, (3) the Courts, and (4) the Executive Branch.

The Interest Group Environment

In explaining the rise and institutionalization of organized conflict, surely we should consider how interest group politics have changed during the past few decades. Below we highlight five of those changes and explain how they help us to address our research question.

The Mobilization of Interests. The mobilization of organized interests on federal judgeships derives in part from three broader trends in the pressure group environment. The first is the explosion of organizations of every sort during the 1960s and 1970s (Berry 1989a; Walker 1983). Prior to the 1960s, there were simply not that many organized interest groups. And those that did exist tended to represent commercial or private interests (such as business, trade, and professional associations). These commercial-type interests used litigation where appropriate, but they did not see the courts as a central forum for the vindication of their interests—largely because New Deal Democrats (that is, economic liberals) dominated the federal judiciary from the onset of the Roosevelt presidency (Epstein 1985; Twiss 1942). Accordingly, existing groups had little incentive to involve themselves in judicial confirmations. Beginning in the 1960s and continuing through the 1980s, however, that changed radically. Numerous (liberal) public interest groups formed to represent the interests of disadvantaged segments of society. Since these new organizations often used the courts to achieve their objectives, it is hardly a surprise that they took an interest in judicial nominees.

Second, representation in Washington, D.C., has grown tremendously. Every conceivable organized interest now has some presence there. Those who took part in the nominating fights of the last couple of decades, most of whom maintain an office in the capital, simply reflect the national trend. Obviously, being situated in the Washington, D.C., area greatly reduces organizational costs: groups need not expend funds on costly hotel rooms and airfare to engage in lobbying.

Finally, organized interests now have the tools to do the job. They can send flyers to target groups, mobilize constituents important to senators, take out advertisements in newspapers, conduct polls, and so forth. All of these tools facilitate their efforts to influence key decision makers in the executive and legislative branches.

Conservative Counter-Mobilization. Once upon a time, cozy triangles made up of unified interest groups, members of congressional committees, and bureaucrats made policy with little guidance from Congress or the executive. They were able to do so because they agreed on the direction that policy should take. But the entry of diverse and divisive interests has brought conflict where once harmony reigned. Now, instead of cozy triangles, organized interests come into conflict with one another and complicate the lives of those who make decisions (Berry 1989b; Salisbury 1990).

The rise of organized conflict came about as two movements sought to counterbalance liberal public interest groups that had arisen during the 1960s and 1970s. The first was the "New Right," which was dissatisfied with a wide range of federal policies, including those on civil rights, law enforcement, welfare, school prayer, abortion, the Equal Rights Amendment, and gay rights. To challenge these policies, dozens of politically conservative organizations sprang up in the 1970s and early 1980s: Concerned Women for America and the Eagle Forum, for conservative women; the National Right to Life Committee and the American Life League, for antiabortion advocates; the Moral Majority and the Christian Action Council, for supporters of traditional family values. Conservatives emulated liberals and established a network of "public interest" law firms (for example, the Washington Legal Foundation) around the nation (Epstein 1985). Older organizations—such as the American Conservative Union and the National Rifle Association—gained new vigor in this period.

At the same time as the New Right was attracting supporters, big business began to challenge liberal public interest groups, which had been quite successful in obtaining passage of legislation—at the expense of the business community—that protected consumers and the environment. Beginning in the 1970s, big business attempted to educate the American public about the wonders of free enterprise; corporations advertised in newspapers and magazines.

Still—and much to the chagrin of their New Right counterparts—corporate interests were not major players in judicial confirmation proceedings. This was so even though corporations had met innumerable defeats in the federal courts at the hands of consumers, environmentalists, and the federal government in the Carter years. Presumably, then, business had an interest in a judiciary of the sort President Reagan had in mind. Yet, it was the New Right—and not corporations—that led the march against, and in favor of, particular judicial candidates.

Organizational Membership and Fundraising. If organized interests took action only to further policy goals in the federal courts, we should anticipate a significant allocation of resources if and only if opposition to a nomination had a reasonable probability of success. Organized interests would not, therefore, take up hopeless causes. Yet organized interests pursue multiple goals. For some of the organizations we have studied, taking a position on a nomination helped them to achieve other goals—maintaining or increasing membership or raising funds. Thus, for example, in 1991, more than thirty women's organizations, along with the ACLU and Planned Parenthood, took out advertisements in the *New York Times* and other places in order to seek support for the close questioning of Judge Souter's views on the right to privacy. The advertisement advised readers to write to and telephone senators and the president and, of course, to write a check to support the coalition. Direct mail, advertisements, and grass-roots organizing against Judge Souter did not go to waste; these efforts contributed to the mobilization of women concerned about abortion rights.

Learning and the Institutionalization of Conflict. Prior to the early 1980s, few organized interests would have contemplated opposition to a nominee for the federal courts. The leadership of many organizations saw the opposing of nominations as a hopeless task; after all, only a handful of nominees had met defeat through the early 1980s. For those active in litigation, the leadership feared reprisals by those against whom it might have taken a position. Furthermore, since only a handful of organizations had taken a position against a judicial nominee, organized interests lacked the cover of a large coalition. By the early 1990s, hundreds of organizations on both sides had adopted positions on and worked for or against nominees to all levels of the federal courts. A position once unthinkable is today within the realm of options for hundreds of organizations at the national level and thousands at the state and local levels. Each time an organization takes a position on a nomination, the next decision is just a little bit easier.

As our earlier discussion revealed, liberal organizations have strong links to past fights over nominations. With each fight, from the late 1960s through the mid-1980s, liberal groups picked up strategies and tactics. These included the use of distinguished members of the bar, law professors, coalitional lobbying, advertising and polling, grass-roots lobbying, and so on. Similarly, after several close calls and defeats, conservatives refined tactics and borrowed some tools from their opponents.

The Rise of the Grand Coalition against Bork. It may have been during confirmation battles of the late 1960s that organized interests began developing their strategies and tactics, but it was during the Bork proceedings that they perfected them—particularly the art of building coalitions. In fact, this single nomination, perhaps more than any other, helps us to understand why conflict is now such a regular part of the confirmation scene.

To be sure, the fight over the Bork nomination has blessed us with a number of lively and well-written books about the formation of the giant coalition against Judge Bork (Bronner 1989; McGuigan and Weyrich 1990; and Pertschuk and Schaetzel 1989). These books do not, however, give one a proper sense of perspective about how many years the coalition was in the making and the many battles through which the eventual partners had suffered together and oftentimes alone during the early years of the Reagan administration. The coalition against Judge Bork did not come together by accident; it was the product of a series of skirmishes during the 1980s. It represented, in a sense, a great reprisal against the Reagan administration for the blows that the parts of the coalition had taken at its hands during the earlier part of the decade. The uprisings on a smaller scale against a series of nominations before and after Bork brought together parts of this gigantic coalition. We lack the space to recount the story of the growth of the "grand coalition," so we provide brief sketches of two of the issues on which subsets of the coalition had done battle during the 1980s.[8]

Early in his first administration, President Reagan took on the entire "civil rights establishment." These actions galvanized the opposition of the more than 180 organizations in the Leadership Conference on Civil Rights. He removed several members of the Commission on Civil Rights and Equal Employment Opportunity Commission and made a series of "recess appointments" to fill the vacancies. These actions drew strong opposition in Congress and among organized interests (Fagin 1983). Many in the Civil Rights Division of the Department of Justice as well as litigators in civil rights organizations charged that proceedings against federal contractors for racial discrimination had been deliberately slowed down. Changes in regulations figured in the strategy of the Reagan administration; it sought to modify rules to limit the application of laws barring discrimination against minorities, women, and the handicapped (Clark 1981; Wines 1982).

From the beginning, the Reagan administration targeted the Legal Services Corporation for drastic de-fanging and perhaps abolition (Boyd 1983; MacKerron 1981; Pierce 1981). A diverse coalition of individuals and organizations opposed the proposed changes in the Legal Services Corporation. It included public welfare, legal aid, and consumer groups; the American Civil Liberties Union; Common Cause; the American Bar Association; state and local bar associations; the League of Women Voters; the UAW; the American Association of Retired Persons; the National Council of Churches of Christ; the NAACP; the Conference of Mayors; the Gray Panthers; and the National Council of La Raza. A much smaller number of organizations worked for these changes: the American Farm Bureau Federation, the Conservative Caucus, the Moral Majority, the Chamber of Commerce, and the National Conservative Political Action Committee. In the first wave of proposals, the administration attempted to redirect funds for the Legal Services Corporation from a line item to a "block grant" for state governments to allocate on a discretionary basis. Then, in a second series of blows, the president made a number of recess appointments of people who, for the most part, had shown hostility to the Legal Services Corporation. One of the chief goals of the Reagan administration was to prevent lawyers funded by the Legal Services Corporation from filing broad lawsuits against government and corporations.

Congress

Pressure group politics is not the only thing that has changed during the past two decades. The congressional political climate has undergone alterations as well. In what follows we consider two aspects of that climate and explain how they helped to contribute to the institutionalization of organized conflict surrounding judicial nominations.

Changes in the Electoral Environment of the Senate. In the 1980s and even in the 1970s, members of the Senate faced an electoral environment markedly different from the politics of the 1950s and 1960s. The extraordinary mobilization of interests has translated into the empowerment of a diverse array of new constituencies in the electoral arena. These "new" constituencies include women, blacks, Hispanics, the mentally ill, the disabled, senior citizens, Christians, and homosexuals. Demonstrated electoral clout provided good reason for members of the Senate to listen carefully to the entreaties of organized interests for or against particular nominees to the federal bench. These newly mobilized interests—together with persistent older ones—are ingredients in the constituencies of many senators; and the new mix has changed the calculus on judicial nominations for many senators, especially in the South but elsewhere as well.

To put it another way, many organized interests can back up the entreaties of Washington lobbyists with a credible, if unspoken, threat of electoral reprisal. Surely, this is a lesson many senators learned in the wake of Clarence Thomas's confirmation. Several of those who voted for Thomas were defeated by candidates who made a point of the incumbent's support. And those challengers received the backing of the organized interests that had worked for Thomas's defeat.

Nominating Politics in an Environment of Scarce Information. Staffing the federal government constitutes one of the most difficult and intractable problems any administration faces (Heclo 1977; Mackenzie 1981). Lack of experienced people, weak or unestablished networks of communication, and rapid turnover of staff plague the executive branch. Those in the executive and legislative branches who select federal judges confront a similar lack of relevant and reliable information about potential candidates. Only recently has the Senate Judiciary Committee hired a significant number of people to investigate nominees; and, even now, most nominees receive only the most cursory review. Not until the chairmanship of Sen. Edward Kennedy (D-Mass.) in 1979 did the committee hire any investigators to check into the backgrounds and qualifications of candidates.[9] In an environment of little information, the ability of organized interests to present sound information about candidates gives them distinctive advantages. Credibility as providers of information about the candidates and preferences of constituencies may permit organized interests to force the hands of those senators who do not wish to cause a disturbance over a nomination. The Judicial Selection Project of the Alliance for Justice and the Judicial Reform Project of the Free Congress Foundation, along with other groups, serve as proxies for the staff that the Senate Judiciary Committee and the Department of Justice should hire to do a reasonable job of investigating potential judges. Increased staffing on the Judiciary Committee does not vitiate the informational role of organized interests; staffers become a source of allies for outside groups and may actually provide additional incentives for participation.

Divided Government. From 1969 to 1977 and again from 1981 to 1993, divided government presided over national policy making. Until the waning days of the Bush administration, most observers thought divided government a likely feature of national government: Democrats would hold the House and usually the Senate; the Republicans would control the executive branch.

Divided government makes compromise and the building of coalitions more difficult than under government controlled by one party (Fiorina 1992; Shafer 1988, 108-147; Smith 1988, chap. 17). It dramatically raises the costs of making decisions, in the politics of appointments as elsewhere. The president cannot sit down with the leaders of his party within Congress and come to a meeting of minds; he must consider the preferences of the leaders of the opposition, who control one or more houses. Historically, nominees to the Supreme Court have met with defeat more often under divided government (Segal 1987; but see Mayhew 1990). If, as in much of the Reagan and Bush administrations, the opposing party controls one or more houses of the legislature, the chief executive must reckon with the independent power of often-hostile committee chairs. The political conflict inherent in divided government provides a welcome haven for the thrusts of organized interests eager to shape the federal bench.

The dramatic increase in the number of important constitutional cases on the doctrine of "separation of powers" and the extent of legislative and executive power is, we think, a consequence of the prolonged period of divided government. Many of these cases, incidentally, were brought by some of the organized interests who launched into the fight over judicial nominations in the 1980s. In time, structural issues become tightly linked to ongoing political coalitions.[10] Traditionally, Republicans have evinced skepticism of executive power and jealously guarded the authority of the national legislature. By the 1980s, conservatives and the leaders of the Republican party had begun to view the executive branch as a franchise and, accordingly, to bemoan the loss of presidential powers to the micromanagement of Congress (for example, Rabkin 1988). By the same token, Democrats and liberals, once eager aggrandizers of presidential power, began to see the wisdom of strong legislative checks on the executive branch (Shapiro 1983). Few foresaw change in the composition of the legislature and executive.

The Courts

The courts too contributed to the institutionalization of organized conflict but in ways that were very different from those of Congress. As we describe below, because the federal judiciary manifested a relatively even partisan balance, it took on new importance in the ensuing ideological battles over seats on the federal courts.

The Partisan and Ideological Balance in the Federal Courts. The Supreme Court, at the departure of Justice Lewis F. Powell, Jr., in 1987, stood evenly divided on many issues; the courts of appeals, in some circuits, stood in a similar situation at various points during the 1980s. The closer the balance, perceived or actual, the greater the incentive for organized interests to take part in the monitoring of and fights against nominations. In a number of fights during the Reagan era, opponents of a nominee used partisan and ideological balance as an argument against the appointment of a committed conservative; the fight over Judge Bork was only the most salient example. By the end of President Reagan's first term, he had not yet appointed half of the sitting federal judges (see Goldman 1985, 1990).

Thus, President Reagan's reelection in 1984 was a major impetus to the organization of effective opposition against the administration's judicial strategy. Reagan's second term and Bush's single term finished the work; conservatives now dominate the federal bench. As the ideological balance has tipped more and more in favor of conservatives, liberal organizations have not spent as much capital in this arena, but, as would be anticipated, they have continued monitoring and opposing nominations, if only to act as a limit on the influence of the new right.

The Increased Importance of the Federal Courts. Conservatives realized much later than did liberals the strategic importance of the federal courts (but see Twiss 1942). This changed in the 1970s, as conservatives organized and began to use strategies and tactics in the federal courts on which liberals had relied for decades (for example, Epstein 1985). The reason why conservatives began to litigate is not difficult to discern: they believed that the Supreme Court of the 1960s, then under the leadership of Earl Warren, had damaged their causes and that liberal interests had engineered some of the more devastating of those rulings (such as *Brown v. Board of Education,* 1954, 1955, and *Miranda v. Arizona,* 1966). Conservatives, thus, went into court to counterbalance their ideological opponents, the result being that the federal judiciary took on new importance. It became a battlefield in the ensuing ideological war.

Part and parcel of the increased importance of the federal courts are dramatic changes in American administrative law (Shapiro 1988; Stewart 1975). This shift in orientation makes the lower federal courts of great strategic importance in the making of policy. Until the 1960s, the federal courts of appeals as a matter of course deferred to the judgments of agency officials, just as Congress had intended in the Administrative Procedure Act of 1946. In the late 1960s and throughout the 1970s, the courts of appeals, with the District of Columbia Circuit leading the way, took a much more aggressive stance toward administrative decisions. No longer would federal appellate judges roll over for administrative agencies; indeed, they designated themselves "partners" with administrators in rule making. Even after the Supreme Court cut back on the more expansive doctrines of judicial review of administrative action, the federal courts of appeals continued to play a critical role in the making of administrative law. In many of the battles over nominations in the 1980s, administrative law figured as an important issue.

Consider the American Farm Bureau Federation. It became involved in judicial nominations in large part because of the importance of administrative law and the appellate courts to its policy agenda. The Farm Bureau showed a sophisticated awareness of the crucial linkage between the federal appellate courts and decision making in the executive branch and independent agencies. Under both Republicans and Democrats, the Department of Agriculture favors farmers and agribusiness and other clients and allies; it tries to carry out deals struck in committee and subcommittee in the making of agricultural legislation. Environmental and consumer organizations normally do not receive that sort of attention in the Department of Agriculture. Thus, environmentalists and consumers use the federal courts to challenge the legality of the Department of Agriculture's rules and regulations. Agricultural organizations would, naturally, prefer to have friendly federal judges who defer, after the fashion of the Administrative Procedures Act of the 1940s and 1950s, to the decisions of agencies. They do not favor aggressive review of administrative action by the federal bench. For farmers and other business interests, the lower federal courts may actually prove more important than the Supreme Court. After all, the Supreme Court reviews very few of the decisions in the federal trial and appellate courts. For both traditional and "new right" conservatives, the federal courts may seem like safe havens in light of some of the successes in Congress of have-nots—as in the Civil Rights Act of 1990.

The Executive Branch

No account of the institutionalization of organized conflict, as our historical discussion reveals, would be complete without consideration of the president's role and the changing partisan landscape under which the presidential office has operated. In what follows, we consider three ways in which changes in the executive branch contributed to the conflict that now characterizes judicial nominations.

Success of the Republicans at the Presidential Level. Until the 1968 election, Democrats could hope to make many nominations to the federal courts as the parties naturally alternated in the presidency, for the two major political parties competed on an equal basis for control of the executive. But from 1968 through 1992, the electoral map made a Democratic presidency a long-shot. Reagan's election, in particular, dramatically worsened the fortunes of liberals. Neither Congress nor the executive showed much sympathy to the causes of the liberal interest groups; and the Supreme Court of the late 1970s and early 1980s was no longer the reliable partner of liberal interest groups it had been during the 1960s. By the mid-1980s, many organizations on the left attempted to avoid the Supreme Court whenever possible and, instead, sought to keep their claims in the lower courts (especially the District of Columbia Circuit, where they attempted to force administrative agencies to adopt their preferred positions, and the Ninth Circuit, where they could challenge loose environmental policies). Thus, nominations to the lower federal courts looked very important (especially in the District of Columbia and Ninth circuits) even as early as 1982. The aggressiveness of early Reagan appointees did nothing to ease the concerns of liberals.

Change in the Presidential Policy Agenda. Unlike Carter and Ford and even Nixon, President Reagan made a serious attempt to push forward an agenda of many controversial social issues (see Goldman 1989). President Reagan's emphasis gave organized interests in opposition strong incentives to worry about the outcome of these issues. The items on President Reagan's legislative agenda—opposition to abortion and busing, support for prayer in school, and so on—called into question many of the decisions closest to the heart of those in organized interests of the liberal stripe. This legislative agenda would have overturned, via statutory or constitutional means, a wide variety of decisions made in the federal courts over a period of three decades. Ultimately, President Reagan failed to gain legislative acceptance for this agenda—some conservatives and liberals would say, for lack of real effort—but, at the outset, no one could predict the outcome with any degree of certainty. President Reagan, after all, dominated Congress during the first part of his first term, and the Republicans did control the Senate. The threat of legislative overruling of judicial decisions and stripping of some areas from the purview of the federal courts made the federal courts even more central to the agenda of liberal organized interests.

The Sophisticated Picking of Judges. President Carter had placed a high priority on affirmative action for women, blacks, and Hispanics in the selection of federal judges, and that infuriated the "new right" and motivated it to begin the systematic monitoring of nominations to the federal courts. In response, President Reagan, and to a lesser extent President Bush, made the picking of judges a high priority (Murphy 1990; O'Brien 1988).

The boldness and sophistication of the Reagan judge pickers infuriated organized interests on the liberal side. Officials in the Reagan administration showed little aversion to risk, unlike past and subsequent administrations; tough battles were simply the price one had to pay for "good" judges. Decision makers in the White House and the Department of Justice knew in advance of most of the "problems" that turned up concerning nominees; in some cases what the liberals saw as troubling problems, the conservatives in the administration perceived as attractive qualities. Reaganites, at any rate, pushed forward on controversial nominations despite the threat of a fight from liberal interests. In turn, leaders of liberal interest groups saw the systematic nature of Reagan's judicial strategy as a severe threat to the gains made in the federal courts through the years. It provided a powerful incentive to organize the monitoring of nominations and to engage in direct and grass-roots lobbying in opposition to candidates found unacceptable.

Conclusion

We have shown the rise and institutionalization of a new regime in the politics of federal judicial selection. Organized interests now figure as central actors. Signs of this new regime became apparent at various times from the 1930s through the early 1970s. In the 1970s, more and more organizations began to focus on federal judicial nominations. The new system then came into full bloom in a series of highly charged conflicts in the 1980s. Today, in a period once again of divided government, organized conflict is likely to re-emerge.

In the last two years, we have not witnessed a fight on anything near the scale of the controversy over Judge Bork. Yet it is a mistake, we think, to see the lack of fights of that magnitude as indicative of the absence of serious, organized conflict. The contending organizations and coalitions possess a wide range of options short of all-out mobilization. In this respect, the organization of interests in the politics of federal judicial selection resembles other areas of public policy, in which visible conflict is the exception rather than the norm. Interest groups do not go to war often; they spend most of their time in monitoring events, doing research, talking to key contacts, and communicating with members.

Does the organizational activity of which we have written really make much of a difference? Some commentators do not think so. The new conventional wisdom—more groups, less clout—does not, however, take into account the more subtle forms of influence. If organized interests face other organizations in the selection of federal judges, we might at first glance decide that there was no net effect. Yet it is quite possible to imagine both organizations influencing the shape of federal judicial selections. That is our reading of President Bush's nomination of David Souter. He could not nominate a moderate, or someone whose views on privacy could be determined, for fear of an uprising among a coalition of conservative organizations. And he could not nominate a known conservative, because of the difficulties President Reagan had encountered from liberal organizations with essentially the same Senate in several fights in the late 1980s. Thus, Bush adopted a strategy of ambiguity. No one on either side of the political spectrum can be sure of Souter's location, even though most have a clear guess. The institutionalization of organized pressure from both the left and the right limited President Bush's options. Accordingly, both sets of organized interests made a difference. The same sort of pressures might account for President Clinton's nominations of Ruth Bader Ginsburg and Stephen Breyer to the Supreme Court.

Ideological and partisan balance on the federal bench increases the incentives for organized interests to put pressure on senators. Two or three years ago, we might have predicted a withdrawal from the field by liberal organizations after Reagan and Bush had packed the federal courts with conservatives. But it has not happened. Even if an organization on the right or left sees little positive result from fights over nominations, it cannot afford to withdraw from the arena for fear of greater influence on the part of its opponents.

Notes

1. The debates about the Constitution and discussions in *The Federalist* show an acute awareness of the informational problem the president would face in the selection of judges and other personnel. A senator, it was thought, would possess knowledge—unavailable to the president—of the people and conditions in his or her state. The president had virtually no one to help him in the choice of judges and of personnel for the executive branch. Thus, from an informational point of view, it made good sense to require the advice and consent of the Senate. So, for that matter, did the practice of presidential deference to a senator's candidate for a position on the federal trial bench within his jurisdiction. Senators acted, in effect, as talent scouts for the president. In the nineteenth century, a senator might well have an intimate knowledge of the professionally qualified and politically correct candidates for the federal bench; today such a situation is no longer plausible. Organized interests, in our informational model, at least part of the time perform the function once filled by members of the Senate.

2. In this case, Parker affirmed a lower-court decision upholding "yellow-dog" contracts, which were used by employers to keep their employees from joining labor unions.

3. We have reviewed information on the fight over Fortas and Thornberry in the Lyndon Baines Johnson Library at the University of Texas. Here, we make no direct references to documents in the collection, but our research there generally informs our analysis. For some of the works on the Fortas nomination, see Kalman 1990; Massaro 1990; Murphy 1988; and Shogan 1972.

4. On Haynsworth, see Frank 1991; Maltese 1990; Massaro 1990, 78-104; Steele 1970; and U.S. Congress 1969. For evidence of organized activity, we have extensively searched the archives of the Leadership Conference on Civil Rights at the Library of Congress.

5. This description comes from personal interviews and a variety of printed sources, including Brownstein 1984, 2338; Cohen 1981, 1171.

6. We cannot determine how often and with what effect the opponents of the Reagan administration opposed candidates in the stage prior to the president's recommendation and the ABA Standing Committee's investigation. For a candidate rejected at this earlier stage, see Toledano 1990, 33-37.

7. Several more became mired in controversy and never came to a hearing in the Senate Judiciary Committee. In an early skirmish, the Alliance for Justice, the NAACP, other civil rights orga-

nizations, and groups working for the rights of the disabled put pressure on the Judiciary Committee to question the nomination of Clarence Thomas to the District of Columbia Circuit. These organizations sought not so much to defeat Thomas as to build a record should he receive a nomination to the Supreme Court; others worked hard for Thomas. On the nomination of Judge David H. Souter to the Supreme Court in the summer of 1990, the future of *Roe v. Wade* was the primary issue; and this, of course, had direct electoral implications for many senators. Many liberal women's organizations took a position, engaged in grass-roots activities, and lobbied against him in the Senate.

8. In a complete reckoning, we would discuss legislation to weaken the antitrust laws and to codify the administration's permissiveness toward mergers, fights over the environment, consumer issues, proposals to restrict attorneys' fees, voting rights, access to justice, administration of the Social Security Act, the Human Life Amendment and related statutes, and many other issues on which liberal interests mobilized against the Reagan administration. Ultimately, the fight about the nomination of Judge Bork brought into combat virtually every organization that had participated in one or more of the battles over these issues.

9. Under the leadership of Sen. James O. Eastland (D-Miss.) in the 1960s and early 1970s, the committee built up an enormous staff, but, apparently, few of them had anything to do with nominations. Eastland used the allocation of staff to keep liberals on the committee in line (see Aberbach 1990, 280). The assignments he made for subcommittees on federal judicial nominations make clear Chairman Eastland's strategy of keeping liberals as far away as possible from controversial candidates for seats in the southern and border states.

10. Some of these skirmishes have featured strange bedfellows. We think, for example, of the alliance of the Public Citizen Litigation Group and the Washington Legal Foundation in the recent controversy about whether the Federal Advisory Act covers the functions of the American Bar Association's Standing Committee on the Judiciary and thus comes under the Freedom of Information Act.

4 Capital Investments in the U.S. Supreme Court: Winning with Washington Representation

Kevin T. McGuire

The tobacco industry is widely considered to be one of the most influential players in Washington's power game. Whether policy making emanates from administrative agencies within the executive branch or from committees within the legislative branch, the tobacco lobby enjoys favorable relations with decision makers. Thus, despite increased concerns about the health risks associated with smoking, critical coverage by the mass media, and much negative public opinion, cigarette manufacturers have lobbied successfully against many proposed federal policies targeted at their industry. The success of the tobacco industry, like the success of so many large corporate interests, can be attributed in part to those whom they hire to represent them: experienced members of Washington's community of representatives. Philip Morris, Inc., for example, the nation's largest cigarette company, retains the services of at least two of Washington's largest and most prestigious law firms, Arnold & Porter and Covington & Burling (Close, Steele, and Buckner 1993), both of which have substantial numbers of experienced lawyer-lobbyists, skilled in advocating the interests of their clients before the federal government (Berry 1989, 90-94). The selection by Philip Morris of such notable counsel is indicative of a more general pattern of behavior; Washington lawyers with expertise are, quite often, sought out by sophisticated clients for representation before congressional and executive decision makers.

What happens, however, when the tobacco industry needs a lawyer in the U.S. Supreme Court? Are there lawyers in Washington who are veterans of litigating before the justices to whom the industry can turn? Even if there are such lawyers, does that mean that cigarette manufacturers are more likely to win because they retain them? The case of *Cipollone v. Liggett Group* (1992) is instructive.[1] Indeed, it provides some interesting clues to answering these questions.

Cipollone has its genesis within the 1965 Federal Cigarette Labeling and Advertising Act. Among its provisions was the requirement that cigarette manufacturers place the following warning on all packages of cigarettes, "Caution: Cigarette Smoking May Be Haz-

I am grateful to Kim Seidl, who collected many of the data for this chapter.

ardous to Your Health." The law went into effect on January 1, 1966, but by this time Rose Cipollone, a forty-one-year-old New Jersey woman, had been smoking for more than twenty years. During that time, medical research began to link cigarette smoking to a variety of health problems, and in 1964 the Surgeon General's Advisory Committee on Smoking and Health released its report, which stated that cigarettes posed a significant health threat. Mrs. Cipollone, though, was skeptical. She reasoned that "if there was anything that dangerous . . . the tobacco people wouldn't allow it and the government wouldn't let them do that." [2] So she continued to smoke; after all, a good many studies, sponsored by the tobacco industry, cast doubt on the surgeon general's findings.

Smoking several packs a day, Mrs. Cipollone eventually developed lung cancer. After her cancer was diagnosed, she sued the manufacturers of the cigarettes she had smoked, including Philip Morris, accusing them of, among other things, misrepresenting the dangers of smoking and conspiring to withhold scientific evidence of those dangers. Still, she remained a smoker—even after one of her lungs was removed—and died in October 1984. Her husband and her son continued to litigate on her behalf.

The tobacco companies, in contrast, turned to the Labeling and Advertising Act, the law that required the warning labels. As they interpreted the law, Congress had intended to prohibit the kind of product liability claim that the Cipollone's were pursuing. In their view, given that the federal government was undertaking complete regulation of the tobacco industry's advertising, any claims against tobacco companies that were based on state law—such as Mrs. Cipollone's, which relied on New Jersey's product liability law—were preempted. In other words, because the federal law requiring the warning labels established national regulations for cigarette companies, it precluded similar actions by the states in the same area; the Cipollones' claims against the tobacco industry, therefore, conflicted with the federal policy.

Although the legal question involved was fairly narrow, the stakes in the case were very high indeed. A ruling by the Supreme Court against Philip Morris and the other cigarette manufacturers could lead to countless other claims against them and, consequently, potentially staggering costs. The tobacco companies would need the best counsel they could find, not neophytes to litigating in the Court, but experienced lawyers who would ably advocate their interests before the justices. To whom, then, did they turn for representation? A small law firm in Washington, D.C.—Klein, Farr, Smith & Taranto—with a very specialized practice, Supreme Court litigation. The reasons for this firm's emphasis were obvious enough: its partners were all Ivy League graduates and members of the law reviews at schools such as Harvard and Yale; each of them had served as a law clerk on the United States Supreme Court; two were former members of the Office of the Solicitor General and had considerable experience practicing before the justices. Clearly, this was a firm rich with Supreme Court talent.

Their expertise was fairly plain, but their influence on the outcome in *Cipollone v. Liggett Group* was less clear. As is often the case, the Court's decision was mixed. On the one hand, the justices ruled that smokers could sue cigarette manufacturers; on the other hand, the Court limited those suits to the claims of conspiracy and fraud, claims that can be very difficult to prove.

What does this case imply about who represents whom in the Supreme Court and with what effect? It would seem to suggest that, just as there are sophisticated representatives within Washington who regularly lobby Congress and the executive, so too are there lawyers in the capital who emphasize advocacy in the Supreme Court. Furthermore, large organizations, such as cigarette manufacturers, take advantage of the credentials of these lawyers and benefit from their abilities. Do these assumptions withstand close scrutiny?

In this chapter, I address three related questions. First, is there a high concentration of Supreme Court lawyers in Washington from which litigants tend to draw? Second, to the extent that there are a substantial number of such practitioners, who are the most likely consumers of their services? And, finally, what benefits—if any—are enjoyed by those who turn to the Washington legal community for counsel when their cases are before the high court? Here, I pose these questions for decisions on the merits by analyzing data on orally argued cases from the 1982 term of the Court. Much of the data that I employ are drawn from the *United States Supreme Court Judicial Database,* which contains a wealth of information on the issues, parties, and decisions of the Court.[3] In addition, by consulting various editions of the *U.S. Reports,* the *Martindale-Hubbell Law Directory,* and the online database *Supreme Court Briefs,* I collected data on the lawyers who participated in each case argued during the 1982 term. Naturally, studying decisions on the merits for only a single term provides but a snapshot of the Court's docket, but any term is likely to feature interesting and important differences that persist from one year to the next.

In many significant respects, I contrast the Supreme Court's lawyers who work in Washington, D.C., with those who work outside the capital. As we will see, not only do more of the Supreme Court's lawyers work in Washington, but their expertise is far greater and, notably, has consequences for the justices' decision making—no matter whom they represent.

Lawyers Inside and Outside the Beltway

A good starting point for considering the importance of Washington representation in the Supreme Court is to examine the overall geographic distribution of both the bar of the Court and the American bar as a whole. After all, cases come to the Court from any number of lower state and federal appellate courts, and consequently one might expect to find lawyers appearing in the Supreme Court in more or less the same proportions in which

Figure 4-1 Relationship between National Bar and Supreme Court Bar

State percentage of Supreme Court bar

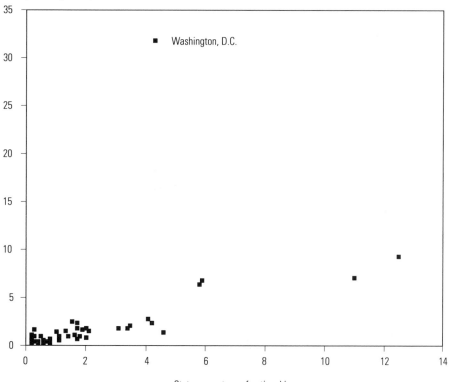

State percentage of national bar

they are found in the states. Thus, whether the lawyers within the capital command a disproportionate share of the justices' attention must be judged in relation to their numbers within the overall population of lawyers. Figure 4-1 provides a graphic depiction of this relation.

The most reasonable interpretation of these data is that, proportionally speaking, the lawyers who appear before the Supreme Court generally reflect the states in which they practice. In fact, the percentage of the national bar in a state provides a fairly accurate estimate of its contribution to the ranks of practicing Supreme Court counsel: these two percentages differ by less than 1.5 percent, on average. One might logically conclude, therefore, that there are no systematic differences between the lawyers who appear in the Supreme Court and the total population of American lawyers. Note, however, that there is one significant outlier to this general linear trend—the District of Columbia, which has a substantially greater share of the Court's counsel; indeed, the proportion of the Court's bar

Figure 4-2   Relationship between National Bar and Supreme Court Bar, Private Practitioners Only

State percentage of Supreme Court bar

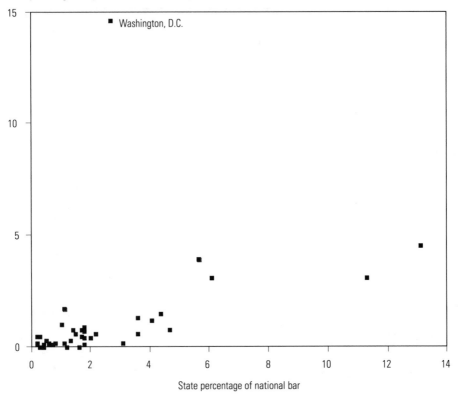

State percentage of national bar

that is found in Washington—32 percent—is roughly seven times its percentage of the total lawyer population.

Of course, the U.S. government is party to a great many cases (for example, in all federal prosecutions, the U.S. government is a party), and this might naturally help to account for the capital's leading role. In 1982, for instance, some 49 percent of the Court's lawyers in Washington represented the federal government. Still, Figure 4-2 demonstrates quite convincingly that the percentage of lawyers who represent the government tells only part of the story. In this figure, I control for the effects of this high percentage by restricting the data to the single largest group of nongovernment lawyers (that is, lawyers in private practice), and these parallel percentages make the point in an equally striking fashion. Washington's share of private practitioners who appear in the Supreme Court outpaces that city's percentage of all private lawyers at a rate of five to one. What this means is that when parties to litigation in the Supreme Court begin to shop for counsel, they are more likely to

Table 4-1 Ratio of Supreme Court Lawyers to Lawyer Populations

Lawyer population	Lawyers located in Washington	Lawyers located outside Washington
All lawyers	1:94	1:966
Private practitioners	1:91	1:1,425

Source: Data on Supreme Court lawyers collected by the author; data on all U.S. lawyers drawn from Curran et al. 1986.

choose those lawyers who work in close proximity to the Court itself. To put it another way, the Supreme Court bar within Washington is uncharacteristically large in relation to its national counterparts.

Why would this be? One hundred fifty years ago, when Washington's lawyers also swelled the ranks of the Supreme Court bar, the explanation would have centered on the difficulties associated with traveling to Washington to argue a case. Prior to the advent of modern modes of transportation, lawyers from the hinterlands would often forgo the rigors of journeying to the capital and simply refer their cases to members of the local Washington bar (Warren 1939; White 1988). Today, with Washington only a plane ride away from even the most distant states, the reasons for its prominence lie elsewhere. First, the legal profession has become increasingly specialized, allowing lawyers to emphasize particular areas of substantive or procedural expertise (Heinz and Laumann 1982). Hence, it is scarcely surprising to find law firms that, like Klein, Farr, Smith & Taranto, emphasize appellate litigation. Second, the number of individuals in Washington who are in the business of formally representing interests before government—many of whom are lawyers (Schlozman and Tierney 1986)—has soared during the last thirty years (Walker 1983). The confluence of these two forces has allowed many within the Washington community to focus some of their efforts on Supreme Court practice.

Just how many lawyers are apt to practice in the high court in a given year can be gauged quite readily by the data in Table 4-1. Here, I present the ratio of Supreme Court lawyers to the larger pools of counsel from which they are drawn. Even the most conservative assessment of these data would lead to the conclusion that the Washington bar contributes far more Supreme Court practitioners than do its counterparts outside the federal city. Within Washington, for example, 1 of every 94 lawyers has litigated at least one case in the Supreme Court. In contrast, lawyers outside the Beltway appear at the much lower rate of 1 to 966. The differences that exist within the private bar tell a similar tale: the Washington ratio remains roughly the same, at 1 to 91; for all other private practitioners, however, the ratio decreases to 1 to 1,425.

Table 4-2 Employment of Supreme Court Lawyers (percent)

Employment	Lawyers located in Washington	Lawyers located outside Washington
Federal government	48.5	0.0
State and local government	0.0	32.6
Private practice	46.2	48.3
Organized interest group	4.3	6.7
Corporate in-house counsel	0.0	6.0
Legal aid and public defense	1.0	4.3
Academic law	0.0	2.1
N	301	652

Source: Data collected by the author.

These differences are all the more glaring when one considers that few lawyers in Washington are actually litigators. Unlike the lawyers in most other locations, a great many work for the federal government in any of numerous administrative capacities, and even among those in private practice, energies are frequently aimed outside the courtroom at such activities as congressional lobbying or public relations (see, for example, Nelson et al. 1988). If one were to restrict the populations, for instance, to those lawyers for whom litigation was a part of their work, the ratios for the Washington bar would no doubt be even greater.

By now it should be clear that the Washington, D.C., bar—in both a relative and an absolute sense—is a dominant force in the environment of the Court. Knowing that these lawyers, in the aggregate, are a commanding presence in the Court, however, does not reveal anything about who they are, the kind of work they do, or how they compare with those outside of the federal city. Table 4-2, in which is shown the employment setting of the Supreme Court lawyers both in and out of Washington, helps to disentangle such issues. Among other things, these data reveal that, in some respects, the two groups are not all that different from one another. A significant number of both groups consist of lawyers who represent the interests of a government; in Washington, 49 percent litigate on behalf of the federal government, whereas about one-third of the non-Washington bar are counsel to state and local governments.[4] Likewise, private practitioners and lawyers for organized interests constitute similar proportions across categories.

Beyond that, however, there is some noteworthy occupational variability. The Supreme Court's lawyers who work outside of the capital evidence a bit more diversity in their working environments. Whereas corporate attorneys and law professors make up nearly 10 percent of the lawyers outside of Washington, none of the practitioners in the capital are found in these categories. The reasons for such differences are not difficult to discern. Most in-house counsel have specific administrative responsibilities within a corporation and rarely appear in court, and usually, but by no means always, the academics who appear before the justices come from the nation's prestigious law schools, most of which are found outside Washington (see McGuire 1993, 30-34).

The larger, more significant feature that these differences underscore is the homogeneity of the Supreme Court's Washington bar. Unlike their contemporaries beyond the Beltway, almost all of the Court's lawyers in Washington work in one of two settings—the federal government and private practice. What is more, they assume almost identical proportions; in fact, there are just about as many Supreme Court practitioners within the law firms along the streets of the capital as there are within the halls of the federal government. In short, Washington's Supreme Court bar is highly concentrated.[5]

Still, one should be cautious about inferring too much from these data. Delineating the concentration of lawyers in Washington is certainly an important first step in this analysis, but that concentration by itself reveals little, if anything, about the work they do. After all, a much more interesting question is whether the lawyers in Washington are different, *qualitatively*, from other Supreme Court counsel. Now, we do know, of course, that at least one category of the Washington bar—the lawyers in the solicitor general's office—are more able litigators than most. The Office of the Solicitor General, located within the Department of Justice, exists for the purpose of representing the interests of the federal government before the Supreme Court. The expertise of its members is attributable, in no small measure, to their appearing before the justices in case after case, year after year (Caplan 1987; Salokar 1992), not to mention that their client, the United States, wields considerable institutional credibility in the Court. In the absence of additional data, though, the same cannot be said of the balance of the bar. Are Washington's Supreme Court practitioners any more experienced at litigating in the high court than other lawyers?

One obvious way to address this question is to compare the litigation experience of both groups. If the appellate practitioners in Washington are truly distinctive, then they should have, on average, a larger number of Supreme Court cases to their credit. To deal with this issue, I determined, for each lawyer who appeared as counsel on the merits during the 1982 term of the Court, whether that lawyer had served in a similar capacity in at least one other case during the preceding five years. To be sure, this is hardly an ideal measure of expertise, yet it does provide a fair indication of the likely practice patterns of any given lawyer.[6] With these data in hand, the percentage of veteran litigators—both overall and within the large subset of private practitioners—can be easily calculated and contrasted. These percentages are presented in Table 4-3.

What is immediately apparent is that the Washington bar has noticeably higher levels of experience in the Supreme Court. Taking the Court's bar in toto, more than 40 percent of

Table 4-3 Percentage of Supreme Court Lawyers with Prior Experience in the Supreme Court

Population of Supreme Court lawyers	Lawyers located in Washington	Lawyers located outside Washington	t score [a]
All lawyers	41.2	19.6	7.20
Private practitioners	25.9	8.6	5.05

Source: Data collected by the author.

[a] Differences between both groups are significant at $p < .001$.

those in the capital can boast of being veterans of litigation in the high court. By comparison, less than half as many lawyers outside of Washington can advance similar claims. Experience is also a conspicuous factor for those in private practice in Washington, as well. Their expertise runs at a rate three times greater than the private lawyers outside the capital. Neither of these differences is trivial; both are significant in a statistical sense, and dramatically so.

It is a safe bet then that one out of every four private practitioners in the capital who appears before the Supreme Court justices will do so again. Among the remainder of the lawyers in private practice, however, not even one in ten is likely to have another case in the Supreme Court. In sum, not only do more private practitioners in Washington appear in the Court, but they also appear in the Court more regularly.

Bear in mind that these Washington lawyers are but a modest segment of all lawyers in the country, and yet their rate of participation in cases before the Court is much higher. These data imply that a small number of lawyers (that is, those in Washington) are handling a larger percentage of cases, whereas a much larger number of lawyers (that is, those outside Washington) are counsel in a smaller portion; in relative terms, Washington lawyers have an inordinate quantity of litigation expertise.

Whether parties to Supreme Court litigation regard this experience as valuable and attempt to capitalize on it remains to be seen. Obviously, some parties seek representation by members of the Washington legal community; otherwise, the Court's bar in the capital would not be as large or as experienced as it is. The significance of representation by members of the Washington bar, however, depends on whether discernible patterns can be seen in their work. If well-heeled political actors seek their counsel, and likewise if less sophisticated litigants do not, such representation could influence judicial outcomes.

Who Works with Whom?

A prevailing theme in judicial politics is that representation matters. Scholars of judicial decision making have demonstrated, over and over again, that certain parties tend to prevail more often than others, and among the reasons cited for their different rates of success is the litigation expertise of their counsel (see, for example, Caldeira and Wright 1988; Songer and Sheehan 1992; Wheeler et al. 1987). Repeat players—organizational litigants such as governments, big corporations, unions, and the like—enjoy numerous advantages, including the ability to muster superior legal talent; those who are involved in litigation only rarely, or one-shotters—individual litigants such as indigents, small businesses, and social or political minorities—typically do not command such representational resources (Galanter 1974). Empirically, the different success rates of these two types of litigants are often rather marked. So most studies have concluded that repeat players prevail because of the host of benefits—including legal expertise—that attend that status. The problem, however, is that one rarely knows anything about the litigation experience of the lawyers who practice in the Court: legal expertise is, instead, simply assumed to exist as a function of litigant status. Repeat players win, and their (presumably better) lawyers are thought to pave the road to success. But do sophisticated litigants such as tobacco companies, automobile manufacturers, airlines, or the telecommunications industry actually turn to experienced members of the Washington legal community for representation in the high court? There is ample reason to believe that they do, but no one has yet presented data on the use of experienced lawyers—to say nothing of experienced Washington lawyers—by different parties for cases on the merits.[7] Clearly, a good many lawyers are veterans of Supreme Court litigation, especially in the capital; who employs them?

Here, I choose to focus on the lawyers whom parties tap to appear before the justices during oral argument. Of course, by the time the justices are making decisions on the merits, most parties are represented by several attorneys, not one. My research strategy, then, ignores potentially important information about which litigants use which lawyers. Still, since defending the interests of the client directly before the Court is the one prominent role that is common to each party in every case, comparing counsel between parties becomes a relatively easy matter.[8] If the repeat players rely disproportionately on litigation expertise (that is, the Washington bar and the veteran litigators within it), that would serve to validate some of the common assumptions about who works with whom.

Combining petitioners and respondents in Table 4-4, I calculated, for each of the six largest categories of litigants, the percentage employing three different types of counsel: experienced Supreme Court practitioners, lawyers within the capital, and the intersection of these two groups—the seasoned appellate advocates who work in Washington.[9] In each instance, the results are enlightening. Almost without exception, repeat players use all

Table 4-4 Parties Using Experienced Lawyers and Washington Lawyers in the Supreme Court (percent)

Type of party	Experienced lawyer [a]	Washington lawyer [a]	Experienced Washington lawyer [a]	N
Federal government	78.6	98.6	78.6	73
Union	54.6	54.6	45.5	11
Corporation	33.0	42.1	21.6	53
Business	15.1	22.6	9.4	44
Individual	26.0	12.3	8.2	83
State and local government	34.3	7.2	4.2	70

Source: Data on lawyers collected by the author; data on parties drawn from Harold J. Spaeth, *United States Supreme Court Judicial Database* (Ann Arbor, Mich.: ICPSR, 1993).

[a] Differences between parties are significant at $p < .001$.

three types, one-shotters do not. On close inspection, it is apparent that the nature of legal representation closely tracks litigant status.

Organizational litigants recruit to their teams Supreme Court counsel with greater expertise than their individual counterparts. The most obvious example is the federal government. In most cases in which it participates, the government's lawyer has been actively involved in recent cases. Likewise, more than half of all unions prefer lawyers with expertise. The frequency with which this class of litigant uses veteran representation is simply a manifestation of a more general tendency; organized interests, such as the American Federation of Labor and Congress of Industrial Organizations, the American Civil Liberties Union, and other groups that litigate regularly, are represented by very able practitioners who appear in the Supreme Court again and again (see, for example, Epstein 1985; Sorauf 1976).

Many states are frequent parties to cases in the Court—some annually—and the likelihood of their cases being argued by experienced counsel is also quite high. Unlike states, however, corporations generally do not routinely appear before the Court, and yet fully one-third of them engage experienced representation. Conversely, less experienced counsel is normally the lot of the one-shotters: the vast majority of businesses and individuals are represented by newcomers to the Court.

The savvy of organizational litigants is further reinforced by their proclivity for Washington-based counsel. In substantial numbers, these parties seek the assistance of the lawyers closest to the daily workings of the Court. The logic that drives these selections is not difficult to divine. Such political players, accustomed to looking within the system of

Washington representation for support in the pressure politics of Congress or the administrative agencies probably follow their same basic instincts when they are in the Supreme Court: needing someone to advocate their interests before a group of decision makers in the federal government, they might reason that it is probably wise to get someone in Washington to do it. Thus, for example, fully 40 percent of all major corporations seek their representation from lawyers inside the Beltway, whereas only half as many of the smaller, individual businesses look to Washington for counsel.

Unions and individuals also underscore this divergence. Suppose, for the sake of argument, two cases before the Court involved a dispute between labor and management concerning the same provision of federal labor law. If the party representing labor in one case was an individual worker, the chances are slim that he or she would be backed by a Washington lawyer. If, in the other case, a union was the labor litigant, the odds would be that the lawyer for the union practiced in Washington.

Since the solicitor general's office is, practically speaking, the sole representative of the federal government in the Supreme Court, the most common consumer of the capital's counsel is the federal government.[10] At the state and local levels, however, attorneys general seldom relinquish an opportunity to appear in the Court, so yielding the argument to a Washington lawyer is rare.

The most forceful illustration of the relationship between the status of a party and the type of representation it selects can be seen by surveying the use of experienced lawyers in Washington. With the exception of state and local governments, the differences between the repeat players and one-shotters are striking, to say the least. For obvious reasons, the federal government's percentage remains at the same high level. In addition, a good number of unions and corporations—some 46 percent and 22 percent, respectively—demand that their lawyers be established practitioners within Washington's legal circles. Those who do not find these numbers significant would do well to put them into perspective; that nearly one of every four corporations goes before the Supreme Court represented by an experienced Washingtonian is not likely to be a function of chance. Actually, the corporate appetite for veteran Washington lawyers is genuinely pronounced, particularly in light of the much lower levels of such expertise among litigants of lesser status. A large and important category of litigant regularly turns to the same group of lawyers for representation. This situation is all the more significant, given that these corporations are making their selections from what is a fairly small group of attorneys.

What explains these choices? The answer is, I think, that the repeat players have a wealth of practical political know-how and recognize the potential benefits of having genuine specialists on their side. Absent such intelligence and resources, litigants do not turn to the Washington legal community for support. This is fairly persuasive evidence that the assumptions about the quality of counsel among different types of litigants are correct.

What we cannot know from these data is whether these litigants actually benefit from their specialized representation. Having an established Supreme Court practitioner from Washington representing you before the Court is one thing; winning is quite another. Whether the investment in these lawyers actually pays substantial dividends is the question to which I now turn.

Litigants, Lawyers, and Outcomes

With a bit of clever detective work, one might piece together the various clues to the story thus far and conclude that the case has been solved: The Supreme Court's lawyers are concentrated in Washington, D.C., and those in Washington have significant expertise. Sophisticated litigants know who these lawyers are, retaining them to represent their interests in the high court. These parties win more often than not, so their success, consequently, must be a function of their having better lawyers. That conclusion may not be wrong, but so far I have presented no direct evidence to support it. To see why more evidence is needed, permit me to illustrate the problem by analogy.

Suppose I were interested in predicting the outcomes of major league baseball games. My intention would be to develop a model that would enable me to estimate (with, it is hoped, a fair degree of accuracy) who would win any given game, the home team or the visitors. Assuming a home-field advantage, I could posit a rather crude model, simply guessing that the home team would win every game, and I might be correct in a majority of instances. But predicting that baseball teams win just because they have the home-field advantage would be rather naive and, quite often, wrong. What would be a more reliable indicator of success?

One plausible explanation would be that good pitching has a significant effect on the outcome of a game. For example, my hypothesis could be that veteran pitchers are, all else being equal, better than rookies. In any game in which a seasoned hurler faces a pitcher new to the big leagues, then, I would expect the team with the more experienced pitcher to win. Such a prediction rule might prove fruitful. Still, there are two problems with this strategy. A minor problem is that many games will not involve such a match-up; there will be games in which both pitchers are either rookies or veterans, and my decision rule gives little guidance. A more serious problem is that pitching, although no doubt important to the outcome of any game, is not the sole determinant of who wins and loses: the team with the more experienced pitcher may win, but that team might have won anyway because of some combination of hitting, fielding, management, and so on. My predictions might be very satisfying, in a statistical sense, but substantively, my single-factor explanation would be somewhat far afield.

This is precisely the situation that must be confronted when attempting to assess the effect of experienced lawyers on the decision making of the Supreme Court. It may well be that the parties who select their representation from within the Washington community win a larger percentage of their cases than those litigants whose counsel come from other locations. Similarly, the parties who engage knowledgeable Supreme Court practitioners may be treated more favorably on average than those with unseasoned lawyers. Absent further information, however, one could not say with certainty that their judicial successes could be attributed to those who represented them. The cases may have been decided the same way by the Court, even without those lawyers. What, then, is the solution?

If I were still trying to predict baseball winners, the solution would be obvious enough. I could gather additional data—batting averages, runs-batted-in, fielding percentages, errors committed, and so on—for each individual team. With these data, I could more easily sort out the effects of each and speak with greater confidence about the influence of different types of pitchers. In trying to predict outcomes in the Supreme Court, however, the task is considerably more complicated. Although the types of parties in the Court are generally obvious, their characteristics that might affect who wins and loses—relative wealth, legal expertise, and litigation strategy, for example—are difficult to discern. Fortunately, I have information on one of these factors, legal expertise; however, I have no comparable data to reflect the other kinds of systematic differences that are believed to exist between the repeat players and the one-shotters. How could I measure them?

Imagine that, in my baseball illustration, no such data were available. One way to deal with the problem would be to assume that a team's standing was a useful, albeit imperfect, indicator of the more specific qualities on which I lacked information. That is, teams with higher rankings win because they have, on average, better hitting, pitching, fielding, and so on; teams ranked lower lose because of their relative deficiencies in these categories. So if the home team was in first place, playing a visiting team in, say, sixth place, I might safely predict the home team's victory. By comparison, if the home team ranked third and the visitors ranked second, the outcome would be less certain. The point is this: if I can assume that team standings are an appropriate proxy for the particular attributes that affect the outcome of a game, then I can control for them statistically and estimate, much more accurately, the effect of pitching.

To disentangle the influence of Washington representation from the more general set of forces that are believed to be at work, I employ a similar tactic; that is, I rate the parties in each case before the Supreme Court and compare them. This is not difficult to do, since research demonstrates that the actual successes of different litigants usually correspond to the various benefits they are presumed to possess (see, for example, Galanter 1974; Songer and Sheehan 1992; Wheeler et al. 1987). Some parties, such as governments and corporations, win quite often and thus rank high; others, such as businesses, enjoy moderate success and have a more average rating; still others, such as individuals, prevail only infrequently and are placed at the end of the scale. The larger the difference between their ranks, the greater the likelihood that the party with the higher rank will win. So, in a case that pitted the federal government (the litigant of highest status) against an individual (the litigant lowest in the rankings), one would expect the government to win. Similarly, if a case involved two parties of more or less comparable status—say, a state government and a major corporation—their competing resources, litigation strength, and the like might cancel each other out. Accordingly, with the rankings of the parties in hand, I can take their status into account and assess the role of lawyers with greater precision.

My analytic technique, probit analysis, is a statistical procedure that enables one to calculate the effect of some variable or variables on the probability that some event will occur.[11] Probit, therefore, is often used to predict a great many political behaviors, such as whether a person will vote, which candidate will win an election, or, as in this case, whether the petitioner or respondent will win in the Supreme Court. Like all multivariate procedures—those that assess the effects of numerous explanatory variables on some dependent variable—probit analysis also has the virtue of being able to calculate the effect of one variable (for example, pitchers or lawyers) while controlling for the influence of any others. In Table 4-5, I explore a series of explanatory models. In these models, I use party status as well as lawyer-related measures in various combinations to predict the probability of the petitioner's winning the case. For the moment, we need not concern ourselves with the substantive effect of each variable; rather, it is more instructive at this point to track the stability of party status as a predictor across models and to compare the significance of the different types of lawyers.

The most basic proposition—that party status affects the outcome of a case—is tested in model 1. Each party was rated on a ten-point scale of status, with ten being the highest status and one being the lowest. This variable was calculated by subtracting the rating of the petitioner from the rating of the respondent. Larger positive values should increase the likelihood of the petitioner's success; conversely, larger negative values should auger in favor of the respondent.

That is precisely the result. The positive, statistically significant estimate for this variable indicates that the greater the petitioner's status in relation to the opposition, the greater that party's likelihood of success. Alternatively, if the respondent has greater theoretical advantage on balance, that party's chances of winning increase. The "haves" do indeed come out ahead. Still, none of this is news, since it merely confirms what is already known about how party status affects case outcomes.

Consider, though, what happens when Washington lawyers are introduced into the calculus in model 2. Litigant status is reduced slightly and, more important, loses its pow-

Table 4-5 Probit Estimates for Models of Petitioner Success in the Supreme Court

Variable	Model 1	Model 2	Model 3	Model 4	Model 5
Party status	.05*	.03	.03	.02	.03
	(.02)	(.03)	(.02)	(.03)	(.03)
Washington lawyer	—	.34*	—	.23	—
		(.19)		(.20)	
Experienced lawyer	—	—	.38**	.33*	—
			(.15)	(.16)	
Non-Washington, experienced lawyer	—	—	—	—	.21
					(.21)
Washington, experienced lawyer	—	—	—	—	.50**
					(.19)
Intercept	.23	.22	.21	.21	.21
	(.10)	(.10)	(.10)	(.10)	(.10)
Pseudo-R^2	.08	.11	.13	.15	.15

Source: Data on lawyers collected by the author; data on parties drawn from Harold J. Spaeth, *United States Supreme Court Judicial Database* (Ann Arbor, Mich.: ICPSR, 1993). (N=178).

Note: Dash=not applicable. Each lawyer variable is coded as 1 if the lawyer represented the petitioner, -1 if the lawyer represented the respondent, and 0 if the lawyer represented neither party or both parties. Numbers in parentheses are standard errors. An estimate approximately twice the size of its standard error is statistically significant.

* $p < .05$ ** $p < .01$

erful predictive capacity, supplanted by the strength of Washington advocacy. When the lawyer at the podium is a Washingtonian (and the other is not), the party he or she represents has a significantly greater likelihood of winning. Quite apart, then, from wealth or superior litigation strategy or whatever other advantages a party might have, a Washington practitioner makes quite a difference.

As an alternative to the importance of Washington counsel, model 3 measures the role of experienced lawyers, whether in Washington or not. Here again, the various other party strengths pale in the face of legal expertise. As expected, one's chances of winning a case in the Supreme Court are much improved by experienced counsel. In contrast, a lawyer's initiation to the Supreme Court may prove to be a client's downfall.

Of course, a shortcoming of models 2 and 3 is that they treat the two types of counsel in isolation, testing for the effects of Washington's lawyers on the one hand and analyzing the role of experienced lawyers on the other. Necessarily, then, model 4 incorporates both the Washington bar and the lawyers with expertise into the estimation. These results actually have a good bit of intuitive appeal. The effect of the experienced lawyers—virtually unchanged from the previous equation—is moderately greater than the effect of the Washington bar; moreover, the former is statistically significant and the latter is not. How does one interpret this? From the lawyer's perspective, it is who you are, not where you are that appears to matter: having experience before the Court is a great asset in future cases, but working in Washington, while marginally helpful, is not nearly as important. Note also that the significant effect of party status vanishes once again.

The analysis to this point is still less than satisfying. After all, we have seen the centrality of the Washington lawyer for decisions on the merits, but to say that the Washingtonians win just because that is where they practice is not a very convincing argument. This is certainly not to suggest that the Supreme Court's lawyers in Washington are not qualitatively different from other types of lawyers; quite the contrary. In fact, I have devoted a significant portion of this chapter to demonstrating that they are distinctive. The problem is that in one equation, model 2, it is assumed that all of the Supreme Court's practitioners in Washington are the same, when we know that they are not: many have substantial experience in the Court. In model 3 the importance of this experience is recognized, and we find that it counts for a great deal, but geography is ignored. Some of this ambiguity is resolved by the fourth equation, but in this model experienced lawyers and Washington lawyers are put in competition with one another, rather than being permitted to work in tandem. So the solution would be to test simultaneously the effects of experienced lawyers in Washington and experienced lawyers from outside the capital on the outcomes of cases.

Model 5 presents just such results. It provides the clearest picture of the role of legal expertise in the Supreme Court while underscoring the effect of the Washington bar. The effect of experienced lawyers, for example, consistently strong in the earlier models, maintains that strength only in the Washington context. Within the capital, expertise has a considerable influence; outside of Washington, experience carries no statistical clout.

If the lawyers in Washington were really no different from any others, then the size of these two estimates would be more or less the same. That is not the case; the value of the estimate for the Washington lawyers (.50) is more than double that of the non-Washington counsel (.21). Either the system of experienced representation in Washington is qualitatively better, or the veteran litigators in the capital are terribly fussy about the cases they accept and handle only those they think they can win. Although I do not discount completely the possibility of selection bias on the part of lawyers, I think the more realistic hypothesis is that the Washington legal community is just more effective. Few would deny, for example, that the legislative lobbying provided by Washington representatives is influential; it is no less likely that the experienced bar in Washington has credibility in the Court.[12]

Like the earlier models, this fifth equation also suggests that the benefits of parties of higher status are overshadowed by legal expertise. In all fairness, however, I should stress that, because it is so crude, the variable for litigant status probably understates the magnitude of the effects it purports to reflect. Other variables that captured more accurately the kinds of characteristics that I have packaged into a single measure would no doubt provide greater clarity (and perhaps stable statistical significance). As it stands, these variables are being filtered and funneled into one measure, and distortion surely exists. Notwithstanding this limitation, these data carry a sure message: no matter whom they represent in the Supreme Court, the seasoned lawyers in Washington matter, and they matter a great deal.

Just how much is a great deal? The discussion to this point has focused on whether the lawyers in the District of Columbia have a significant effect on the justices' decision making. Having established that they do, an appropriate concern might be the substantive consequences of their participation in a case. One way to handle this issue is to express the consequences of Washington representation in probabilistic terms. If, in an otherwise average case, an experienced lawyer from Washington argued one side of the case, what kind of an effect would he or she have on the outcome?

In the Supreme Court, there is a home-field advantage of sorts; in the majority of cases, the justices reverse, rather than affirm, lower court rulings (Armstrong and Johnson 1982). As a consequence, a model that assumed that the petitioner would prevail over the respondent in every case would account for much of the Court's decision making. In this sample from the 1982 term of the Court, for instance, some 62 percent of the cases were resolved in favor of the petitioning party. Let us assume then that—aside from whatever effect Washington representation may have—in the average case the probability is .62 that the petitioner will win. From this baseline, I present in Table 4-6 the estimated effect of these lawyers.

If the petitioner has the leverage of one of Washington's experienced Supreme Court practitioners, the likelihood of success increases to .81, a substantial boost. Thus, even if the justices come to a case, as they typically do, favorably disposed toward the petitioner, investing in the expertise of one of the capital's leading legal lights still adds abundant strength to the case. Equally impressive are the respondent's chances of prevailing when one of the veteran lawyers in the capital provides the representational advantage. So effective are the Washingtonians, their arguments in favor of affirmance severely undermine— quite critically, it turns out—the petitioners' ordinarily positive odds of winning on the merits. Despite the Court's general proclivity for the petitioners, skilled advocacy in oppo-

Table 4-6 Effect of Experienced Washington Lawyers on
Petitioner Success

Party with experienced Washington lawyer	Probability of petitioner's success
Petitioner	.81
Neither party/both parties	.62
Respondent	.43

Note: Estimates are based on coefficients from model 5 in Table 4-5.

sition can reduce their chances of winning to less than 50 percent. Hence, experienced lawyers who represent petitioners can serve to solidify victory, whereas those who represent respondents can forestall loss, increasing the fortunes of their clients in many instances. Of course, if neither side or both sides enjoy the Washington advantage, the probability of the petitioner's success remains unchanged.

Having said all this, I should add a fairly serious qualification. Because my models measure litigant status by a relatively rough yardstick in conjunction with more precise indicators of legal expertise, the empirical results, at least as far as they apply to the impact of representation, probably present a magnified picture of reality. The probabilities in Table 4-6, therefore, are somewhat misleading; they imply that all that the parties to a lawsuit need do is secure the services of experienced Washington lawyers and they will win. To be sure, other things being equal, the justices are more prone to be persuaded by the effective argument of a Washington specialist than by the unseasoned debut of a lawyer from regions remote from the Potomac, but ultimately the Court is far more concerned with the issues and implications of a case than with the lawyers who articulate them.

Does this mean that corporations, unions, and other big litigants are behaving irrationally by seeking out veteran representation within the capital community? Hardly. The experienced lawyers in Washington offer a far greater payoff than other counsel. Without additional data, however, it is difficult to say how significant that payoff is. Perhaps a profitable line of future inquiry would take more precise account of the other factors that are associated with litigant status. Such research would bring the effect of Washington representation into even greater relief.

Washington Lawyers in Perspective

In Washington, there is a distinct culture of pressure politics, one in which expertise in advocacy makes one a valuable and effective resource. The lawyers who litigate in the U.S.

Supreme Court, it turns out, are no exception to this pattern. Like so many others who represent their clients in the federal government, many of these lawyers locate themselves in the District of Columbia, close to the center of government decision making. Not surprisingly, the same sophisticated clientele that hires the Washington lobbyists to ply their trade in the halls of Congress will likewise hire the Washington lawyers to represent them in the marble palace. Such a concentration of talent has consequences: these lawyers win significantly more often than do other practitioners, even lawyers outside of Washington who have the same amount of experience. Small wonder, then, that institutional players would want them.

What accounts for the pronounced effects of the Supreme Court bar of Washington? One answer would be that these lawyers simply are better at representing interests in the high court than other lawyers; they work in close proximity to the Court, and they have more experience, so naturally they would be closer students of the Supreme Court than most. This is an attractive notion, but it is also a perplexing one, since we know that the decision making of the justices is motivated in large measure by their policy preferences (Segal and Cover 1989). Time and again, this is borne out; for all of his experience and credibility, the solicitor general still loses, and, notwithstanding lackluster lawyers, many other parties succeed.

There are, therefore, obvious limits to the influence of advocacy. No lawyer, no matter how well versed in the finer points of Supreme Court practice, can have much hope of disabusing a justice of his or her long-held policy views. Still, legal skill is important. In the end, it is vital to recognize that the Court consists of justices who—however independent of mind—are open to persuasion. We know that in some areas of the law (abortion and the death penalty, for example) the way arguments have been framed has had a significant effect on the development of the law. Why? "Judges are lawyers. . . . Legal argument is the tool of their trade—the currency with which they conduct their business. It is, thus, not surprising that well-crafted legal arguments appeal to them in their judicial function" (Epstein and Kobylka 1992, 302). If high-quality arguments are the coin of the realm in the Court, then, given Washington's high concentration of wealth, it stands to reason that they would be more successful. What the importance of the experienced Washington bar demonstrates is that, like other government decision makers, justices are willing to listen to those who appear before them. No less than anywhere else in Washington, the quality of one's representation in the Supreme Court can matter a great deal.

Notes

1. The description of this case is adapted from the LEXIS database *Supreme Court Briefs* (Dayton, Ohio: Mead Data Central) and Epstein and Walker 1993b, 10-17.

2. "Brief for Petitioner," Supreme Court Briefs, no. 90-1038, p. 11.

3. For more information on the Judicial Database, see Appendix C of this book.

4. To some, the number of federal government lawyers may seem quite high, since the size of the Office of the Solicitor General is relatively small—roughly two dozen lawyers at any one time. Once one takes account of the various other lawyers within the Justice Department—assistant attorneys general, staff lawyers in specific divisions, and the like—as well as the attorneys from the executive branch departments and administrative agencies, all of whom routinely supplement the work of the solicitor general, the federal bar grows rather quickly.

5. To see why this is important, consider that some 70 percent of all lawyers in the United States—except those in Washington—are in private practice (Curran et al. 1986). All things being equal, then, 70 percent of the Supreme Court lawyers outside of the District of Columbia should be in private practice, and yet they are not; they make up only 48 percent of this group. By comparison, far fewer attorneys in the capital are private lawyers (only 44 percent), but they appear in the Court at a far greater rate, comparatively speaking. So the large number of private practitioners in Washington who appear before the Court is decidedly not a function of there being more lawyers from which parties might choose. Actually, it is just the opposite. There are many Supreme Court lawyers in the private bar in Washington in spite of—not because of—their numbers within the city.

6. Unfortunately, gathering reliable data on the litigation expertise of individual lawyers is a problematic endeavor. To begin with, some lawyers are more conscientious than others when listing their addresses and affiliations on their briefs. So, divining where and in what capacity a lawyer is employed is frequently a daunting task. Matters are further complicated by the fluidity within the bar, because lawyers often move from firm to firm, job to job, and city to city.

7. This does not apply to studies of specific areas of the law, such as search and seizure (Wahlbeck 1994) or capital punishment (George and Epstein 1992), in which we know that experienced lawyers do affect judicial decision making.

8. Furthermore, it is actually a fairly conservative approach, given that many of the most experienced lawyers are engaged, not for oral argument, but rather for consultative roles, such as the preparation of briefs (see McGuire 1993, 108-117). In other words, these data probably understate the use of the experienced Washington bar by parties in the Supreme Court.

9. Twenty-two litigants did not fit readily within any of these categories and are excluded from these figures.

10. The reason the federal government's use of Washington lawyers as shown in Table 4-4 does not equal 100 percent is a statistical artifact of weighting the data. In a handful of cases, multiple parties are consolidated and appear as a single party. When this occurs, as it does in a few cases involving the federal government, more than one lawyer ends up arguing on behalf of the same side of the same case. To count both lawyers who argued would artificially increase the number of cases, and to count only one of the lawyers would discard potentially important information about the other. Where two lawyers argue on behalf of the same side, therefore, the case appears twice—once for each lawyer—but each observation is weighted by 0.5 (that is, counts as half a case). This strategy preserves information about the lawyers while maintaining the proper number of total cases.

11. For more on probit, see Appendix B of this book.

12. The skeptic might argue that the observed relationship between the Washington bar and success in the Court is primarily a function of the solicitor general's participation. This is a reasonable concern, but one to which the data lend little support. The independent effect of the solicitor general's expertise is easily taken into account, and, when it is, the impact of experienced Washingtonians remains strong.

5 The Mysterious Case of Establishment Clause Litigation: How Organized Litigants Foiled Legal Change

Joseph F. Kobylka

According to Arthur Conan Doyle's classic literary figure Sherlock Holmes, in solving a crime, "when you have eliminated the impossible, whatever remains, *however improbable,* must be the truth" (Doyle 1930, 111). In important ways, Holmes also could have been describing the task confronting social scientists. Quite often scholarly research resembles detective work: when we observe patterns of social behavior that deviate from what we would normally expect, we set up a list of suspects (sometimes called hypotheses) that could explain the deviation. With those suspects in hand, we often proceed just as Holmes described: eliminate the impossible and accept whatever is left—however improbable—as the solution.

In this chapter, I seek to solve an intriguing puzzle involving the U.S. Supreme Court: Why has doctrine governing the Religious Establishment Clause of the First Amendment *failed* to experience major legal change? In what follows, I set out this mystery in some detail. For now it is enough to note that, with the onset of Ronald Reagan's presidency in 1981, observers expected the Court either to replace the relatively liberal standard it uses to assess these cases with a far more conservative one, or interpret it in such a way as to produce outcomes more tolerable to some religious interests. This expectation grew when Reagan gained an opportunity to replace some supporters of this liberal standard with justices who presumably would oppose it. The expectation became a near certainty with George Bush's appointments of David H. Souter and Clarence Thomas to replace the liberal stalwarts William J. Brennan, Jr., and Thurgood Marshall. The "sure thing," however, never happened. Although Reagan and Bush—through their appointees—sought and accomplished doctrinal shifts in some areas of the law, they had little effect on religious establishment litigation.

Why did the Court not shift gears in Establishment Clause litigation when virtually all informed observers expected that it would? To solve this mystery, I first map the course of Establishment Clause litigation over the past two decades. Next, I suggest that three possible suspects could explain the lack of legal change in this area: the justices on the Court, the political environment in which the Court rendered its decisions, and the configuration and arguments of organized litigants. By eliminating the "impossible," I come to an "improbable" answer, albeit one that seems to capture the truth. This answer says that even when empirical indicators (such as changes in the membership of the Court and a favorable political environment) suggest a looming change in judicial doctrine, interested litigators can use the *law*—in this case, precedents and the reasoning that supports them—to condition, channel, and, in some instances, frustrate the process of legal change. This group presence is significant, not only in itself, but also because it fosters a *pluralism of argument* that permits justices an opportunity to adjust constitutional doctrine in a fashion that maintains some continuity in "the law" while, at the same time, enabling them to pursue a gentle evolution that leads it toward its future.

The Mystery: A Brief Doctrinal and Political Account of the Establishment Clause

The words of the Establishment Clause of the First Amendment seem simple enough: "Congress shall make no law respecting an establishment of religion." This seeming simplicity, however, is deceptive. Indeed, perhaps no other clause of the Constitution has given the Court so much difficulty, with its resulting rulings marked by confusion, not clarity. Why? The answer lies in the basic difficulty of interpretation posed by the Establishment Clause: the permissible relation between government and religion. Should it resemble Thomas Jefferson's "wall of separation" or a picket fence of accommodation (Jefferson 1905)?

There are two general approaches to this problem (Fowler 1985; Morgan 1968, 1972, 1973; Reichley 1985; Sorauf 1976). *Separationists,* arguing from assumptions grounded in the rationalism of the Enlightenment, posit that the spheres of church and state must be kept distinct and separate so that neither will contaminate the other. The First Amendment, under this argument, requires a high wall of separation between church and state. From an *accommodationist* perspective, government may use its authority to aid religion generally and acknowledge the role it plays in American life, so long as it does not establish an official state church or prefer one religion over others. This is the picket fence view of the Establishment Clause. Both arguments trace their constitutional roots to *Everson v. Board of Education* (1947).

Everson involved a challenge, sponsored by the American Civil Liberties Union (ACLU), to an Illinois statute permitting state reimbursement of transportation costs to the parents of all students, including those who attended sectarian schools. Writing for a bare majority, Justice Hugo L. Black held:

The "establishment of religion" clause . . . means at least this: Neither a state nor the Federal Government can set up a church. Neither can pass laws which aid one religion, aid all religions, or prefer one religion over another. . . . No tax in any amount, large or small, can be levied to support any religious activities or institutions, whatever they may be called, or whatever form they may adopt to teach or practice religion. Neither a state nor the Federal Government can, openly or secretly, participate in the affairs of any religious organizations or groups and vice versa. In the words of Jefferson, the clause was intended to erect a "wall of separation" between church and state. (*Everson*, 1947, 15-16)

Black went on to suggest that the "wall" "requires the state to be a neutral in its relations with groups of religious believers and nonbelievers; it does not require the state to be their adversary" (*Everson*, 1947, 18). In this case, the Court held that the statute provided benefits to all children and their parents, and not to churches per se. This program went to the top of, but not over, the "wall." Four dissenting justices could not square Black's separationist *language* with his accommodationist *decision*. Most memorable were the words of Justice Robert H. Jackson.

[T]he undertones of the opinion, advocating complete and uncompromising separation of Church from State, seem utterly discordant with its conclusion yielding support to their commingling in educational matters. The case which irresistibly comes to mind as the most fitting precedent is that of Julia who, according to Byron's reports, "whispering 'I will ne'er consent,'—consented." (*Everson*, 1947, 19)

The seeming inconsistency of the majority opinion and decision in *Everson* weakened the separationist sentiment at the heart of Black's discussion. It also set the stage for a confused doctrinal legacy. This is seen vividly in the Court's cases immediately after *Everson*: *McCollum v. Board of Education* (1948) and *Zorach v. Clausen* (1952). In *McCollum*, the Court held that "released time" programs—allowing public school students to attend classes of religious instruction taught by volunteers on school premises during school hours—were unconstitutional. In *Zorach*, however, the Court upheld the ruling permitting a released time program that instructed students off-campus. Justice William O. Douglas, writing for the majority, penned what has become the accommodationist creed:[1]

We are a religious people whose institutions presuppose a Supreme Being. . . . When the State encourages religious instruction or cooperates with religious authorities by adjusting the schedule of public events to sectarian needs, it follows the best of our traditions. . . . We cannot read into the Bill of Rights . . . a hostility to religion. (*Zorach*, 313-315)

McCollum and *Zorach* demonstrate that the *Everson* sword cuts both ways. The justices of the Warren Court era (1953-1968 terms), as shown in Table 5-1, continued to wield it to reach both separationist and accommodationist outcomes.

On becoming chief justice, Warren E. Burger sought to end this confusion by framing a comprehensive test to guide resolution of church-state issues (Giannella 1971; Kobylka

Table 5-1 The U.S. Supreme Court and Religious Establishment: Selected Cases and Outcomes, 1948-1980

Case (year)	Issue	Outcome
McCollum v. Board of Education (1948)	Time-release programs	Separationist
Zorach v. Clausen (1952)	Time-release programs	Accommodationist
McGowan v. Maryland (1961)	Sunday closing laws	Accommodationist
Engel v. Vitale (1962)	School prayer	Separationist
Abington School District v. Schempp (1963)	School prayer	Separationist
Epperson v. Arkansas (1968)	Teaching evolutionary principles	Separationist
Board of Education v. Allen (1968)	Textbook loans to parochial schools	Accommodationist
Walz v. Tax Commissioner of the City of New York (1970)	Property tax exemptions for church land	Accommodationist
Lemon v. Kurtzman (1971)	State reimbursement for teachers and instructional materials	Separationist
Tilton v. Richardson (1971)	Construction grants for secular buildings on sectarian college campuses	Accommodationist
	20-year limit on nonsecular use of buildings on college campuses	Separationist
Committee for Public Education and Religious Liberty v. Nyquist (1973)	State grants for maintenance and repair of parochial school buildings and tuition reimbursements-tax credits for parents of children attending parochial school	Separationist
Meek v. Pittinger (1975)	State book loans to parochial schools	Accommodationist
	State-funded material loans, special programs, and counseling for parochial school children	Separationist
Roemer v. Maryland (1976)	Annual state grants used by colleges for secular purposes	Accommodationist
Wolman v. Walter (1977)	State material and equipment loans and field trip assistance to parochial schools	Separationist
	State standardized testing and counseling services to parochial schools	Accommodationist

1989; Morgan 1973). In *Lemon v. Kurtzman* (1971) Burger held that the Court would uphold laws if

- they have a *secular legislative purpose,*
- their principal or *primary effect* neither advances nor inhibits religion, and
- they do not foster "an *excessive entanglement* with religion." (*Lemon,* 1971, 612-613)

This new standard—dubbed the *Lemon* test—combined the "purpose and effect" approach favored by separationists with an accommodationist concept of "excessive entanglement." Soon, however, it became clear that Burger sought to use this three-pronged test to move the Court toward a generally accommodationist rendering of the Establishment Clause. In this he was stymied—at least throughout the 1970s—as the Court simply used *Lemon* as it had *Everson:* to support whatever holdings, separationist or accommodationist, it handed down (Kobylka 1989).

By 1980, however, several factors coalesced to suggest a radical change in the Court's approach to Establishment Clause doctrine, a change that would establish a regime of accommodationism. First, commentators on both sides of the issue called on the Court to clarify this area of law. Second, in the late 1970s, the Court signaled that it too was growing weary of umpiring these controversies. As shown in Table 5-1, one can read decisions such as *Meek v. Pittenger* (1975), *Roemer v. Maryland* (1976), and *Wolman v. Walter* (1977) as gradually pulling *Lemon* doctrine toward a more accommodationist posture. Third, the energy unleashed by the "new right" in the electoral arena began to manifest itself in the courts as groups like the Christian Legal Society turned to litigation to promote a constitutional climate of accommodation.

The final and capping event was Ronald Reagan's election as the fortieth president of the United States. This, more than anything else, seemed to ensure the beginning of the end of a strict, judicially imposed, separation of church and state. The position he took on "the religion issue"—calling for the Court to reverse itself and for passage of a constitutional amendment to permit state-sponsored prayer in public schools—was a significant part of his campaign stump appeal. As president, he (and, later, George Bush) used the solicitors general to push this argument on the Court (Caplan 1987; Fried 1991). Further, as shown in Table 5-2, he was able to reshape the personnel of the Court. Reagan's three appointees—Sandra Day O'Connor, Antonin Scalia, and Anthony M. Kennedy—all *seemed* to fall in line with his philosophical position on the relation between church and state.

At first, the Court gave every indication that the expected legal change would in fact occur; its decisions of the early 1980s gave hope to those who wished to dismantle the stubbornly persisting "wall." In the first four cases in Table 5-3, the Court seemed on the verge of formally adopting an accommodationist reading of the *Lemon* test. In *Committee*

Table 5-2 The Reagan-Bush Effect on the Supreme Court

1980 Court		1991 Court
Warren E. Burger, Chief Justice (1969; Nixon)	⇨	William H. Rehnquist, Chief Justice (1986; Reagan)
William J. Brennan (1956; Eisenhower)	⇨	David H. Souter (1990; Bush)
Potter Stewart (1958; Eisenhower)	⇨	Sandra Day O'Connor (1981; Reagan)
Byron R. White (1962; Kennedy)	⇨	Same
Thurgood Marshall (1967; Johnson)	⇨	Clarence Thomas (1991; Bush)
Harry A. Blackmun (1970; Nixon)	⇨	Same
Lewis F. Powell (1971; Nixon)	⇨	Anthony M. Kennedy (1988; Reagan)
William H. Rehnquist (1971; Nixon)	⇨	Antonin Scalia (1986; Reagan)
John Paul Stevens (1975; Ford)	⇨	Same

Note: Year of appointment and appointing president are given in parentheses.

for Public Education and Religious Liberty (CPERL) v. Regan (1980), a sharply divided Court upheld a New York statute that permitted the reimbursement of all nonpublic schools for costs incurred in performing certain state-mandated procedures (such as data on the state's pupil evaluation program, regents examinations, a state-wide student evaluation plan, and student attendance reports). Justice Byron R. White's majority opinion held that there was "no appreciable risk" that the aid would further the "transmission of religious values" (*CPERL v. Regan*, 1980, 846), and was thus constitutional under *Lemon*. With this, the Court, for the first time, upheld the ruling permitting a direct transfer of government funds to sectarian schools (Giacoma 1980, 406). Three terms later, in *Mueller v. Allen* (1983), the majority let stand a Minnesota law allowing tax deductions for costs associated with sectarian education. It also sustained Nebraska's use of a paid legislative chaplain in *Marsh v. Chambers* (1983). The majority did not even apply the *Lemon* test in *Marsh;* it sufficed that the Congress that wrote the First Amendment retained a paid chaplain.

Table 5-3 U.S. Supreme Court Outcomes and Coalitions in Selected Religious Establishment Cases of the Early and Mid-1980s

Case	Outcome	Majority	Minority
CPERL v. Regan (1980)	Accommodationist	Burger, Powell, Rehnquist, Stewart, White	Blackmun, Brennan, Stevens, Marshall
Mueller v. Allen (1983)	Accommodationist	Burger, O'Connor, Powell, Rehnquist, White	Blackmun, Brennan, Stevens, Marshall
Marsh v. Chambers (1983)	Accommodationist	Blackmun, Burger, O'Connor, Powell, Rehnquist, White	Brennan, Stevens, Marshall
Lynch v. Donnelly (1984)	Accommodationist	Burger, O'Connor, Powell, Rehnquist, White	Blackmun, Brennan, Marshall, Stevens
Wallace v. Jaffree (1985)	Separationist	Blackmun, Brennan, Marshall, O'Connor, Powell, Stevens	Burger, Rehnquist, White
Grand Rapids v. Ball (1985)	Separationist	Blackmun, Brennan, Marshall, Powell, Stevens	Burger, O'Connor, Rehnquist, White
Aguilar v. Felton (1985)	Separationist	Blackmun, Brennan, Marshall, Powell, Stevens, O'Connor (in part)	Burger, Rehnquist, White, O'Connor (in part)

Lynch v. Donnelly (1984) extended the logic of these accommodationist decisions. In upholding the constitutionality of a government-sponsored Christmas display that included a crèche, not only did a five-person majority say that it merely "acknowledged" a national holiday, but it held that the display conformed to *Lemon:* it had a secular purpose (depicting "the historical origins of the holiday"); its effect was only "indirect, remote, and incidental" to the advancement of religion; and it posed no danger of "the 'enduring entanglement' present in *Lemon.*" To rule otherwise, Burger concluded, would "impose a crabbed reading of the [Establishment] clause on the country" (*Lynch,* 1984, 1363-1366). The dissenters in these cases—Harry A. Blackmun, William Brennan, Thurgood Marshall, and John Paul Stevens—clung to the late-1970s version of the *Lemon* test, and came to contrary conclusions.

Just when it seemed that the Court would chart an accommodationist course and dispel the ambiguity that plagued this area of law it abruptly trimmed its sails. (See the last three cases in Table 5-3.) In three cases brought before the Court in 1984, five- and six-person majorities—made up of the dissenting justices in *Regan, Mueller, Marsh,* and *Lynch* plus Justices Lewis F. Powell, Jr., and sometimes O'Connor—applied new mortar to the crumbling wall. In *Wallace v. Jaffree* (1985), they struck down an Alabama law requiring public school teachers to start the day with a "moment of silence for prayer or meditation," and in *Grand Rapids v. Ball* (1985) and *Aguilar v. Felton* (1985) they voided state and federal programs providing public funds for remedial courses in secular subjects taught in sectarian schools. The majority applied the late 1970s separationist version of the *Lemon* test to reach these conclusions.

Following *Wallace, Aguillar,* and *Grand Rapids,* the Court returned to its dual-edged approach in Establishment Clause issues, upholding some accommodations of religion, striking others. Emblematic of this renewed strategy, and the interpretational confusion it generates, was the Court's decision in *County of Allegheny v. American Civil Liberties Union* (1989). The city of Pittsburgh and Allegheny County in Pennsylvania had erected seasonal displays celebrating Christmas and Chanukah. The Christmas display contained a crèche (with figures of the Christ child, Joseph, Mary, shepherds, the wise men, barn animals, and a manger), two evergreen trees, some white poinsettias, a surrounding fence, and an angel bearing a banner declaring "Gloria in Excelsis Deo!" at its apex. Designated as owned by a Catholic group called the Holy Name Society, the display "occupied a substantial amount of space on the Grand Staircase [of the County Courthouse]" (*County of Allegheny,* 1989, 3094). The city's display was outside of the city-county building and included a forty-five-foot decorated Christmas tree, a "Salute to Liberty" sign bearing the mayor's name, and an eighteen-foot menorah owned by Chabad, a Hasidic Jewish organization. Applying a "lemonized" *Lynch* case to these displays, a badly divided Court found the crèche display—but not the display of the menorah—violative of the Establishment Clause.[2]

The Court's interpretational odyssey continues to the present. Even though by 1992 Reagan and Bush appointees held six of the Court's nine seats (see Table 5-2), a five-justice majority found, in *Lee v. Weisman* (1992), that brief prayers offered by a rabbi at a high school graduation ceremony violated the Constitution. In his opinion for the Court, Justice Kennedy pointedly eschewed use of the *Lemon* test and ruled against the practice of such prayers on the basis of "the controlling precedents as they relate to prayer and religious exercise in primary and secondary public schools" (*Lee* 1992, 2655). The following term, however, the Court held unconstitutional the decision of local school authorities to prohibit, based on Establishment Clause concerns, a church from access to school premises to show a movie about family and parenting issues (*Lamb's Chapel v. Center*

Moriches Union Free School District, 1993) and the provision of a sign-language interpreter to a deaf boy attending a parochial high school (*Zobrest v. Catalina Foothills School District*, 1993). The latter decision was 5 to 4, used the *Lemon* test, and saw Kennedy join the *Lee* dissenters to form the majority. Most recently, by a vote of 6 to 3, the Court returned to a more separationist posture in striking down a public school district created by New York to assist a village composed exclusively of Orthodox Jews in *Board of Education of Kiryas Joel Village School District v. Grumet* (1994).[3] In his majority opinion, Justice Souter mentioned *Lemon* only twice and in passing, but he did not repudiate it. Thus, the only consistency in the Court's recent Establishment Clause litigation remains its ambiguity.

When viewed chronologically, as they are in Table 5-4, the Court's decisions since 1980 demonstrate that the justices failed to chart a new and clear course for confronting Establishment Clause issues. Although, on balance, accommodationists may have done somewhat better during this period than their separationist rivals (Ivers 1993), the Court's decisions in cases like *Wallace* (1985), *Grand Rapids* (1985), *Edwards v. Aguillard* (1987), *County of Allegheny* (1989), *Lee* (1992), and *Kiryas Joel* (1994)—as well as its rejection of the overtures of three solicitors general to repudiate formally the battered *Lemon* test—reveal that something stymied a profound legal change; the doctrinal revolution that Reagan, Bush, and Court watchers expected did not occur. Thus, the mystery: why did the law not experience the abrupt change that was so widely anticipated?

The Suspects

To solve our mystery, we must assess the winding path of Establishment Clause litigation against a backdrop of the "usual suspects"—those factors that the literature suggests condition change in constitutional doctrine. A canvass of this literature reveals three "usual" suspects: the justices on the Court, the political environment in which the Court makes its decisions, and the configuration of organized litigators pressing their claims on the Court.

The Court

Scholars have reported on two essentially Court-centered explanations for legal change (or the lack thereof): changes in the thinking of individual justices and personnel turnover. Although the former is unusual, justices occasionally shift their position on the issues that come before them. An example is Justice Blackmun. Appointed by President Richard Nixon to strengthen a constitutional jurisprudence aligned with the "silent majority of law-abiding Americans," Blackmun began his career on the "pro-state" side of the judicial

Table 5-4 U.S. Supreme Court Votes and Outcomes in Establishment Clause Cases, 1979-1992

Case	Subject	Vote	Outcome
CPERL v. Regan (1980)	Money for elementary and secondary schools	5-4	Accommodationist
Stone v. Graham (1980)	Prayer in elementary and secondary schools	5-4	Separationist
Widmar v. Vincent (1981)	Access to colleges	8-1	Accommodationist
Valley Forge Christian College v. Americans United (1982)	Money for colleges	5-4	Accommodationist
Larson v. Valente (1982)	Solicitations	5-4	Separationist
Larkin v. Grendel's Den (1982)	Zoning around schools and churches	8-1	Separationist
Mueller v. Allen (1983)	Money for elementary and secondary schools	5-4	Accommodationist
Marsh v. Chambers (1983)	Legislative chaplain	6-3	Accommodationist
Lynch v. Donnelly (1984)	Christmas	5-4	Accommodationist
Alamo Federation v. Secretary of Labor (1985)	Minimum wage	9-0	Accommodationist
Wallace v. Jaffree (1985)	Prayer in elementary and secondary schools	6-3	Separationist
Thorton v. Caldor (1985)	Sabbath exemptions	8-1	Separationist
Grand Rapids v. Ball (1985)	Money for elementary and secondary schools	5-4	Separationist
Aguilar v. Felton (1985)	Money for elementary and secondary schools	5-4	Separationist
Witters v. Washington (1986)	Money for colleges	9-0	Accommodationist
Edwards v. Aguillard (1987)	Prayer in elementary and secondary schools	7-2	Separationist
Corp. of Presiding Bishop v. Amos (1988)	Employment discrimination	9-0	Accommodationist
Bowen v. Kendrick (1988)	Birth control	5-4	Accommodationist
Texas Monthly v. Bullock (1989)	Taxes	6-3	Separationist
Hernandez v. Commissioner of Internal Revenue (1989)	Taxes	5-2	Accommodationist

Case	Issue	Vote	Classification
County of Allegheny v. ACLU (1989)	Menorah and crèche displays	5-4	Mixed
Swaggart Ministries v. California (1990)	Taxes	9-0	Accommodationist
Board of Education of Westside Community Schools v. Mergens (1990)	Prayer in elementary and secondary schools	8-1	Accommodationist
Lee v. Weisman (1992)	Prayer in elementary and secondary schools	5-4	Separationist
Lamb's Chapel v. Center Moriches Union Free School District (1993)	Access to school building	9-0	Accommodationist
Zobrest v. Catalina Foothills School District (1993)	Money for elementary and secondary schools	5-4	Accommodationist

spectrum but at his retirement was considered to be one of the Court's strongest advocates of individual rights (Kobylka 1992).

The appointment of new justices is more commonly noted as a path to legal change. The literature on judicial decision making tells us that we can understand the actions of justices by viewing them as value-maximizing agents seeking to impose their preferences on public policy (Pritchett 1948; Rohde and Spaeth 1976; Schubert 1965; Segal and Spaeth 1993). Although this "value" or "attitudinal" model hit the discipline of political science like a bolt out of the blue, presidents from the time of John Adams have understood and acted on its implications (Abraham 1985; Goldman 1989; Scigliano 1971; Segal 1987). Thus, when presidents—be they Richard Nixon, Ronald Reagan, or Bill Clinton—turn their attention to filling vacancies in the high court, it is hardly surprising that they seek out candidates whose constitutional values (they think) coincide with their own. The power of nomination gives presidents an opportunity to try to influence the direction of the Court, an opportunity that few have passed by (Schwartz 1988; Tribe 1985).

Obviously, the changes in the justices sitting on the Court must have, in some sense, contributed to the recent Establishment Clause odyssey because they decided the cases in question. Recall, however, that the Court's decisions were not unidirectional *even after* the Reagan and Bush appointments. The mystery thus remains: why did the Court continue to oscillate between the competing doctrinal approaches instead of clarifying and solidifying, once and for all, a single interpretation of the Establishment Clause?

The Court's applications of the *Lemon* test during the 1970s were driven by three blocs of justices (see Morgan 1973). First, there were the "super-separationists"—Brennan, Marshall, and Stevens.[4] *Their* understanding of *Lemon* viewed almost any state aid to religion as violative of its effect and entanglement prongs. As a result, they voted to support separationist outcomes almost exclusively.[5] In direct contrast was the "super-accommodationist" bloc. Its strongest members were White and Rehnquist, but Burger frequently joined them to favor state assistance to or "acknowledgment" of religion. *Their* reading of *Lemon* (although White and Rehnquist's attachment to the three-pronged test was never strong [see Kobylka 1989]), allowed nearly total government accommodation of religion. Between these two extremes were the "moderates"—Potter Stewart, Blackmun, and Powell—who read *Lemon* to prohibit "direct" state aid to religion, especially that aimed at "pervasively sectarian" elementary and secondary parochial schools. With the Court thus constituted, it was institutionally disposed to uphold, by a vote of 6 to 3, some state support of religious concerns and to strike down others by the same margin.[6]

These blocs began to crumble in 1977, when Powell announced that "the risk of significant religious or denominational control over our democratic processes—or even of deep political division along religious lines—is remote, and . . . seems entirely tolerable in light of the continuing oversight of this Court" (*Wolman v. Walter,* 1977, 262-263; see

Table 5-1). In *CPERL v. Regan* (1980), the next significant *parochiaid* case, Powell and Stewart bolted from the moderate bloc to join a White opinion upholding broad state aid to sectarian schools (see Table 5-3).[7] Thus, even before the Reagan onslaught, the Court exhibited some signs of an accommodationist shift—a shift made possible by individual changes of thinking of a few justices.

One would expect the replacement of Stewart, Burger, and Powell with Reagan appointees to cement this shift. Reagan's position on church-state matters was clear. He had long opposed the Court's school prayer decisions—"I don't think that God should ever have been expelled from the classroom" (Reagan 1983, 603)—and made his general position on these issues plain in remarks at the National Prayer Breakfast in 1981: "Our nation's motto—'In God we trust'—was not chosen lightly. It reflects a basic recognition that there is a divine authority in the universe to which this Nation owes homage" (Reagan 1982, 268). Indeed, in replacing Stewart with O'Connor, Reagan switched a lukewarm ccommodationist for a justice seemingly more sympathetic to accommodationist concerns.[8] His subsequent appointments, Scalia and Kennedy (both Roman Catholic), were yet more supportive of government acknowledgment of and support for religion.

The Court's decisions in *Mueller, Marsh,* and *Lynch* confirmed the expected effect of these appointments (see Table 5-3). If *Regan* created a snowball, these decisions provided the hill for that rolling precedent to grow. In all these cases, a five-person majority of Burger, White, Powell, Rehnquist, and O'Connor opposed a four-person dissenting bloc of Brennan, Marshall, Blackmun, and Stevens in upholding government aid to religion and advancing an accommodationist interpretation of *Lemon.*[9] *Lynch* (1984) was the apparent capstone of the shift; if a state-sponsored crèche had a secular purpose and effect and posed no entanglement problems, it was hard to imagine anything running afoul of the "new" *Lemon* test. And yet, without further appointment, the Court ruled against a moment of silence *(Wallace)* and parochiaid legislation (*Grand Rapids* and *Aguilar*) the very next term over the dissents of Burger, White, Rehnquist, and, in part, O'Connor. Seven terms later, with the full complement of Reagan and Bush justices in place, a majority found unconstitutional prayers offered at a high school graduation in *Lee v. Weisman* (1992). Why?

The explanation lies, in a general sense, in the break from the super-accommodationist bloc by Powell and O'Connor in 1985 and by Kennedy in 1992. Powell's defection is difficult to assess, as is Kennedy's. O'Connor foreshadowed her shift, however, with the "endorsement" reading of *Lemon* offered in her *Lynch* concurrence. There she wrote, "The establishment clause prohibits government from making adherence to a religion relevant in any way to a person's standing in the political community" (*Lynch,* 1984, 687). This could happen if there was excessive government entanglement with religion or state "endorsement or disapproval of religion." She went on to explain that "endorsement sends a message to nonadherents that they are outsiders, not full members of the political community, and an accompanying message to adherents that they are insiders, favored members of the political community. Disapproval sends the opposite message" (*Lynch*, 1984, 688). The facts in *Wallace*—the moment-of-silence legislation included explicit mention of using the time to pray—violated O'Connor's endorsement test, and she voted to overrule it.

O'Connor's break from the accommodationist bloc was by no means complete—she still votes with it on occasion—but she is no longer in lock step. Her position in the Court's decisions since its 1984 term marks her as something of an accommodationist-minded "moderate." Indeed, with Rehnquist, Scalia, Thomas, and White firm accommodationists, and with Stevens holding firm to his separationism, O'Connor and Blackmun formed, de facto, the moderate bloc on the Court for the remainder of the Reagan-Bush years. Their moderate position is most apparent in *County of Allegheny*, where they were the only justices to vote against the crèche display but not against that of the menorah. Central for both of them were the contexts of the two displays: the menorah was surrounded by other, secular, objects; the crèche was the centerpiece of its display. Because of these settings, and "applying" the "seasonal context" component of *Lynch*, they found that the crèche "endorsed" religion while the menorah did not.[10] Blackmun's vote is easily explicable: he thinks that the Court's church-state precedents mean something, and that something is essentially captured by the *Meek* (1975) and *Wolman* (1977) framing of the *Lemon* test. O'Connor's vote is a function of the position to which she came (with accommodationist results) in *Lynch* (1984) and sharpened in subsequent cases.

Bush's appointment of Souter and Thomas did little to shake the precarious balance evident in *County of Allegheny*, as they aligned in different camps beginning with *Lee* (1992). Kennedy, whose opinion in *County of Allegheny* made him appear to be a strong accommodationist, has shown in his *Lee* (1992) and *Kiryas Joel* (1994) opinions that, with O'Connor, he lies somewhere in the mushy middle on these issues and is not a sure vote for any bloc. Ginsburg's majority vote in *Kiryas Joel* (1994) suggests that White's retirement will strengthen the separationist position on the Court but not sufficiently to give it ascendancy.[11]

Emerging from this analysis is the conclusion that the Reagan and Bush appointments did not *start* the latest cycle of interpretational confusion, nor did they *cement* the legal change that *Regan, Mueller, Marsh,* and *Lynch* seemed to promise. They *could* have—indeed, at first, they *appeared* to do so—but they did not. Thus, my analysis turns to other suspects.

The Political Environment

At the end of the nineteenth century, a popular fictional character named Mr. Dooley quipped that the Supreme Court "follows th' iliction returns" (Dunne 1938). While perhaps overstating his case, Dooley may have had a point. Jonathan Casper (1972, 293) notes that it is a mistake to depreciate "the importance of the political context in which the Court does its work. . . . [Dooley's] statement recognizes that the choices the Court makes are related to developments in the larger political system." Prominent among such factors are public opinion and the actions of government institutions designed to reflect it. Let us investigate these suspects in turn.

Scholars have demonstrated that there often seems to be a link between court decisions and public opinion (Barnum 1985; Caldeira 1991; Cook 1973; Kuklinski and Stanga 1979; Marshall 1989). There are several reasons why this relation would exist. First, appointed and filtered by a political process, justices may reflect and, in some sense, represent majoritarian preferences. Second, aware of the difficulty of implementing their decisions, they might seek to practice "the art of the possible" by tailoring their decisions with an eye to satisfying the public. Third, the occasional ambiguity of constitutional text leads the justices to seek out the meaning of vague phrases in social sources.

In the Establishment Clause example, if the press of public opinion constrained accommodationist legal change, we would expect to find Americans largely supportive of separationist outcomes. This, as shown in Figure 5-1, is not the case: support for the Supreme Court's decisions forbidding organized prayer or Bible readings in public schools has always been a minority position. The data on parochiaid are more volatile but show a public rather consistently split over the expenditure of tax dollars to assist sectarian education.

These data suggest that the public is highly tolerant of government accommodation of religion (prayer in public schools) or, at the very least, divided over the issue (parochiaid). What is important, however, is that the perception existed on the Court that the former better characterized the viewpoint of Americans. In a 1980 dissent, Justice Blackmun charged that the Court's growing accommodationism was, in part, a reaction to public opinion. Referring to the shift of Stewart and Powell, he wrote: "I am able to attribute this defection only to a concern about the continuing and emotional controversy and to a persuasion that a good-faith attempt on the part of a state legislature is worth a nod of approval" (*Regan*, 1980, 664). Still, despite the perception that its litigation of church-state questions was occurring in a political climate generally supportive of accommodationist claims, the Court continued its decisional and doctrinal oscillations. Indeed, even with its ambivalent gyrations on these issues, it has stood against the press of public opinion urging a greater accommodation of religion. Consider that as recently as 1992 it stuck to its traditional prohibition against formal prayer in school, despite the fact that only about 38 percent of Americans support such a ban.

If public opinion does not help to solve our mystery, perhaps other suspects in the political environment do. Along these lines, political scientists assert that a host of institutionalized actors condition the direction of the decisions of the Court. Of particular

Figure 5-1   Public Opinion on Religious Establishment Issues

Respondents Opposing Supreme Court Decisions Banning School Prayer

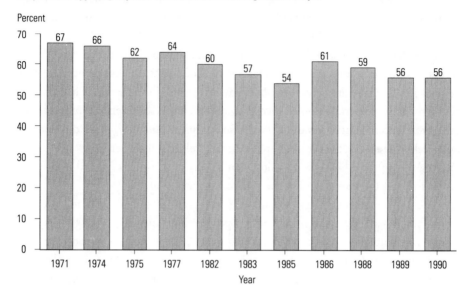

Source: Stanley and Niemi 1992, 21.

Respondents Approving Governmental Aid to Private/Sectarian Schools

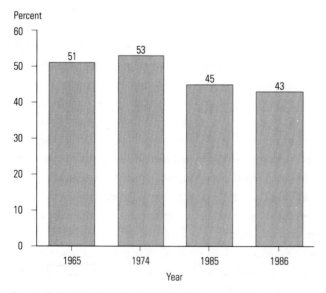

Source: Gallup Poll, 1959–1971, 1974, 1985, 1986 annual editions.

interest here is the role of the president. Studies have shown that the president, through the solicitor general, can affect the Court's agenda (Provine 1980) and enjoy unusual success before it (Puro 1971; Segal 1984 and 1991). Beyond this, the office is increasingly being used to advance the specific political values of the incumbent president (Baker 1992; Caplan 1987; Epstein and Kobylka 1992; Kmiec 1992; Salokar 1992).

As noted previously, court watchers expected Ronald Reagan's ascension to the presidency to prompt profound legal change: it placed a committed accommodationist in the White House. His appeal to the role of religion in American life was a constant theme during his campaigns and a source of great hope to those seeking greater government support of religion and its values. He carried this concern over into his presidency.

We are supposed to have freedom *of* religion. Nothing in the Constitution says freedom *from* religion. (Reagan 1982, 1012)

Our Founding Fathers . . . never intended to construct a wall of hostility between government and the concept of religious belief itself. (Reagan 1983, 361)

[The Founders] found their inspiration, justification, and vision in the Judeo-Christian tradition. (Reagan 1985, 1008)

What's more, Reagan frequently pointed to the Supreme Court as *the* culprit behind the law's skewed separationism. In a press conference in 1981 he argued that "the court ruled wrongly with regard to prayer in schools, for example. . . . Wasn't this a case, maybe, of the court going beyond what the Constitution actually says" (Reagan 1982, 958).

Reagan's attention to church-state issues was substantial, and it extended into legislative and judicial fora.[12] Legislatively, his attack took three routes. First, he proposed to Congress a constitutional amendment to overturn the prayer decisions.[13] Second, he pressed Congress for passage of legislation giving federal tuition tax credits to the parents of children who attended private schools. Finally, he achieved passage of the "Equal Access Act" of 1984—legislation that prohibited secondary public schools from denying "equal access to . . . any students who wish to conduct a meeting within that limited open forum on the basis of the religious, political, philosophical, or other content of the speech at such meetings" (Hertzke 1988; Moen 1989).[14]

Reagan's presidency also brought vigorous advocates of accommodationism to the solicitor general's office (Caplan 1987) and kept an accommodationist perspective on the church-state question before the Court. Part of this office's agenda was to reverse the Court's perceived excessive separationism. Bush, as president, followed these tracks. Rex Lee, Charles Fried, and Kenneth Starr—their solicitors general—appeared before the Court in seventeen Establishment Clause cases (66 percent of the twenty-six decided during this period), arguing ten and filing as amicus curiae in seven.[15] In many of these cases the legal interest of the United States was highly attenuated. In *Lynch* the government cited the fact that it "has in past years sponsored Christmas pageants that included nativity scenes," but it was also more open about its larger and more clearly political interests: "More broadly, the federal government has, from the earliest days of the Republic to the present, felt free to acknowledge and recognize that religion is a part of our heritage and should continue to be an element in our public life and public occasions."

The arguments of the solicitors general were unrelentingly accommodationist. Also significant were the contentions of Edwin Meese who became attorney general in 1985. Meese took an especial interest in church-state cases and used the occasion of the Court's interpretational turn in the 1985 cases as an example of the utility of a jurisprudence of original intent—a belief that the Court should interpret the Constitution to mean *only* what the framers thought it meant. "One finds much merit in Justice Rehnquist's recent dissent in *[Wallace v.] Jaffree*. . . . To have argued . . . that the [First] Amendment demands a strict neutrality between religion and irreligion would have struck the founding generation as bizarre. The purpose was to prohibit religious tyranny, not to undermine religion generally." Meese's suggested replacement for the Court's "jurisprudence of idiosyncrasy" was a doctrine that prohibited the *formal establishment* of a *national* church or preference between religions (Meese 1985, 9). This approach was pressed on the solicitor general's office by, among others, Meese's lieutenant William Bradford Reynolds. The latter's goal was to force the Court to dismantle the "wall of separation" as the operative metaphor defining Establishment Clause doctrine (see Caplan 1987, 98-102). This caused frequent internecine battles at the Department of Justice: Rex Lee, the solicitor general at that time, and his assistant Paul Bator wanted to undermine *Lemon* but had no intention of losing the confidence of the Court or going on a legal "kamikaze mission" by pressing extreme arguments (Caplan 1987, 98-101).

Lee was no great friend of the *Lemon* test (see Lee 1981, 134), but he did have a lawyer's respect for precedent and a solicitor general's respect for the office he held. Not only would he lose an appeal and a case, but he would compromise long-term accommodationist goals if he pushed the Court too far, too fast. Both his briefs and the oral arguments he presented to the Court reflected this cautious, yet determined accommodationism. He pursued his goals by asking the Court not to completely discard the *Lemon* approach but merely to relax its assumptions or use other guideposts for its decisions. Using Black's concept of neutrality in *Everson*, he argued, for example, for a narrow and empirically grounded reading of the effect prong in *Mueller* (1983), *Aguilar* (1985), and *Grand Rapids* (1985); a historically grounded approach to legislative chaplains in *Marsh* (1983); and a showing of some coercion of belief in *Lynch* (1984) and *Wallace* (1985).

The closest Lee came to dismissing the relevance of *Lemon* was in cases like *Marsh*, *Lynch*, and *Wallace*, where he made an argument similar to the one made in *Lynch* that "[w]ooden application [of] legal tests devised for different situations" was inappropriate for issues outside the parochiaid contest.[16] Indeed, one of his major arguments in *Lynch* was that, although government "promotion" of it might be beyond the constitutional pale, government "acknowledgment" of religion—there, in the context of the Christmas display—was perfectly legitimate, *even under Lemon.* O'Connor adopted this language in that case and she still uses it, although in ways that often run counter to Lee's intent. In short, Lee seemed content to undermine separationism by using *Lemon* much as the accommodationist majorities of the early 1980s used it, rather than by asking for its formal reversal. Despite his supposedly greater partisanship, Charles Fried (Lee's successor) continued this very approach in *County of Allegheny* (1989), simply arguing for extended application of the point Lee won in *Lynch.* The obvious difference is that where Lee won *Lynch,* Fried lost *County of Allegheny.*

Kenneth Starr, Bush's solicitor general, generally picked up where his predecessors left off, although he did explicitly call for "reconsideration" of the "so-called *Lemon* 'test' " in *Lee* (1992). He proposed that the Court replace it with "a single, careful inquiry into whether the practice at issue provides direct benefits to a religion in a manner that threatens the establishment of an official church or compels persons to participate in a religion or religious exercise contrary to their consciences."[17] The Court explicitly rejected this invitation and handed Starr his only loss in this area of law.

Scholars have long noted the significance of the participation of the Office of the Solicitor General in Supreme Court litigation. Indeed, Lee Epstein and I found Solicitor General Robert H. Bork's participation in the death penalty cases during the 1975 term of the Court significant in blunting the promise held in 1972 by *Furman v. Georgia* (Epstein and Kobylka 1992, chap. 4). It is conceivable that the office's presence in the church-state realm helped lead the Court's majority to reshape the doctrine governing this realm and bend it to greater accommodationism. This explanation, however, like that relying on public opinion, is not wholly moving. If the presence and argument of the solicitor general was decisive in directing the Court's resolution of *Mueller, Marsh, Lynch, Witters v. Washington* (1986), *Westside Community Schools v. Mergens* (1990), and *Zobrest,* why did it not finish the job in *Wallace, Grand Rapids, Aguilar, County of Allegheny,* and *Lee?* Although the *Lemon* test may be going into eclipse, what Starr called its "constitutional underpinning" in his *Lee* brief stubbornly persists. Participation of Reagan and Bush's solicitors general, even before a Court largely appointed by their administrations, did not carry the day. This clears another suspect.

Group Presence, Argument, and Strategy

Nathan Hakman (1966) once argued that tales of group pressure on the Supreme Court were the stuff of "political science folklore." This argument is no longer—if it ever was — sustainable (O'Connor and Epstein 1983). A growing literature (see Epstein, George, and

Kobylka 1992) demonstrates that groups—by sponsoring cases, filing amicus curiae briefs, coordinating research and publicity—seek to influence judicial decisions. Although groups often have a variety of reasons for taking on the burden of litigation (Epstein and Kobylka 1992, 29-32), paramount among them is a desire to secure favorable judicial rulings that advance their policy goals. Because they bear the attributes of "repeat players" (Galanter 1974), many have succeeded in doing so.

Attention to group litigation created a conventional wisdom that it was an unusually successful path to legal change. Epstein and Rowland (1991) sought to "debunk . . . the myth of interest group invincibility in the courts," but the "myth" persists and the question remains: What is the relation between group litigation and legal change? Groups believe there is a relation, or else it would be hard to explain the magnitude of their litigation activity. Similarly, scholars seem to assume there is a positive relation, or else it would be hard to understand their fascination with this area of study.

In an earlier work, Epstein and I concluded that—at least as concerned the cases of capital punishment and abortion—legal change emanating from the Supreme Court could not be explained simply as a function of group presence in litigation, either alone or in conjunction with other variables (Epstein and Kobylka 1992). Although clearly relevant to doctrinal change, and sometimes sufficient to account for it, it did not fully explain the dynamics associated with interpretive shifts in the law. This finding led us to another suspect.

Our finding, stated simply, is this: *the law and the legal arguments grounded in law* matter, and they matter dearly. The justices that hear these cases and the groups and governments that bring them are relevant factors in their eventual outcomes and the policies they produce, but it is the arguments they hear and make that—at least in the early stages of a doctrinal and decisional shift—seem to influence most clearly the content and direction of the legal change that results. (Epstein and Kobylka 1992, 302, emphasis added)

Pro-choice and abolitionist groups ultimately saw the Court back off from victories they thought they had won. In part, we argued, this was the result of organizational leaders succumbing to "the tyranny of absolutes": the notion that once a case establishes a favorable constitutional precedent, it must be preserved absolutely and exactly on its own terms. This blinded the previously victorious groups to the possible utility of strategic backtracking—a kind of fluidity in doctrinal and argumentational joints—that might have allowed them to preserve the core of their former victories.

If the tyranny of absolutes is necessarily a part of attempts to achieve policy innovations through constitutional litigation, *then* such efforts may be unsteady vessels by which to maintain one-time policy victories: "A tyranny of absolutes—framing what are at core essentially political concerns as basically legal in nature and forcing their maintenance as 'law' to hinge on unbending obeisance to precedent based on unassailable 'rights'—may set the stage for much legal change in controversial areas of public policy" (Epstein and Kobylka 1992, 309). We also, however, noted the following:

In this sense, the tyranny of absolutes may be a logical corollary to what Scheingold (1974) has dubbed "the myth of rights"—the notion that judicially won and crafted rights are self-executing. Scheingold, however, does not say that all judicially claimed rights are open to neglect in regard to implementation but only that they must continue to be pressed on responsible entities to ensure their vitality. Similarly, legal change won through the courts need not *necessarily* fall into this trap. A more flexible approach to the litigation and maintenance of judicial policy judgments—one that makes use of a broad array of legal arguments and does not deify the argument used to win the policy initially—*may* be able to resist the pressures of wholesale legal change. (Epstein and Kobylka 1992, 309, emphases added)

The abortion and capital punishment examples suggested the possibility of such a maintenance strategy, but they did not provide for its test because group attorneys fell prey to the tyranny of absolutes. Because of the vagaries of its development, church-state litigation allows us to examine this suspect in a different context.

The organizational activity in church-state cases is immense. This is not surprising, given previous accounts of this litigation (Ivers 1990 and 1993; Morgan 1968 and 1972; Sorauf 1976). Further, the density of this litigation environment—the number of groups involved in it and the frequency of their participation in any given case (Kobylka 1987)—is staggering. In the twenty-six cases decided by the Court in the fourteen terms from 1979 through 1992, arguments were presented by 128 groups. As noted in Table 5-5, 28 groups appeared in three or more cases, with 11 representing accommodationist interests and 17 articulating a separationist perspective. Did they affect the Court's adjudication of these issues? By structuring the arguments heard by the Court, and by demonstrating the pluralism of perspectives on these difficult questions, I think they did. Understanding the role they played provides a solution to the mysterious lack of legal change in this area of law.

Group involvement in Establishment Clause litigation has a long history. From the separationist perspective, it began with the ACLU consulting with the plaintiffs (Walker 1990, 169) and filing an amicus curiae brief in *Everson* (1947), and snowballed after that. The group again filed as an amicus in the first released time case (*McCollum,* 1948) and was closely involved with the American Jewish Congress (AJC) in the next released time case (*Zorach,* 1952) and in *Engel v. Vitale* (1962), the Court's initial tilt with school prayer (Pfeffer 1975, 199; Sorauf 1976, 43-44). The ACLU and the AJC, joined recently by the Anti-Defamation League of B'nai B'rith (ADBB), are, by volume of cases (see Table 5-5) and expertise, the preeminent separationist litigators.[18]

The ACLU, AJC, and ADBB, while the most active separationist group litigators, are not

Table 5-5 Frequent Group Litigators of Establishment Clause Issues, 1979-1992

Group	Instances of participation (No.)	(%)	No. of sponsored instances of participation
Separationists (17)			
American Civil Liberties Union	21	81	7
AFL-CIO	5	19	0
American Jewish Committee	9	35	0
American Jewish Congress	16	62	0
Americans for Religious Liberty	6	23	0
Americans United for the Separation of Church and State	13	50	1
Anti-Defamation League of B'nai B'rith	16	62	1
Baptist Joint Committee on Public Affairs	9	35	0
Coalition for Public Education and Religious Liberty	12	46	1
Council on Religious Freedom	7	27	0
National Council of Churches of Christ	9	35	0
National Education Association	3	12	0
National Jewish Community Relations Council	5	19	0
National School Boards Association	5	19	0
People for the American Way	6	23	0
Seventh Day Adventists	4	15	0
Synagogue Council	3	12	0
Accommodationists (11)			
American Center for Law and Justice	4	15	3
Association for Public Justice	3	12	0
Catholic League for Religious and Civil Rights	8	31	0
Christian Legal Society	11	42	2
Concerned Women of America	7	27	1
Free Congress Research and Education Foundation	4	15	0
National Association of Evangelicals	10	38	0
National Jewish Commission on Law and Public Affairs	12	46	2
National Legal Foundation	3	12	1
Rutherford Institute and Freedom Council	8	31	1
United States Catholic Conference	10	38	0

the only organized separationist voices appearing before the Supreme Court. Americans United (AU), formerly called Protestants and Other Americans United for the Separation of Church and State, was formed in the immediate aftermath of the Court's decision in *Everson*. Since 1980, it has participated in thirteen (50 percent) of the Court's church-state decisions. Whereas the ACLU approaches these issues from the perspective of secular humanism, and the AJC and ADBB from that of mainstream Jewish thought, traditionally, the AU is more politically conservative and religiously Protestant. Although its greatest percentage of current contributors is Baptist, its "largest per capita contributions come from Christian Scientists, Seventh-day Adventists and Jews" (Hyer 1982). Even with this membership shift, however, it continues to seek to protect churches and believers from state interference, whereas the ACLU, AJC, and ADBB approach these issues from a more secular perspective.

The above-noted groups are the dominant separationist forces, but they are not alone. Other groups also projected themselves into the Court's Reagan era church-state litigation: the late Leo Pfeffer's Committee for Public Education and Religious Liberty (46 percent of the Court's decisions), the American Jewish Committee (35 percent), the Baptist Joint Committee on Public Affairs (BJC; 35 percent), and the National Council of Churches of Christ (NCC; 35 percent) are among the most prominent. Yet, not one of these groups has the litigation record or expertise of the "Big Four," that is, the ACLU, the AJC, the ADBB, and the AU. Only CPERL has sponsored litigation before the Supreme Court; the others have participated only as amicus curiae, and much of their participation has come through cosigning the amicus briefs of one another.

There was no organized accommodationist bar for much of the post-*Everson* period. Through the 1960s, with the exception of occasional amicus participation of the U.S. Catholic Conference, there was little nongovernment opposition to separationist claims. So paltry was the organized support for accommodationist legislation that Sorauf and Morgan, the best chroniclers of the pre-1970 period, could point to little concerted group presence in this area. The most they could locate was the existence of a determined group of attorneys (for example, William Ball, Porter Chandler, Edward Bennett Williams), who were occasionally dispatched by the American Catholic Church to help local attorneys defend accommodationist policies.

This situation changed after 1970, as groups advancing accommodationist arguments turned increasingly to litigation. Foremost here is the National Jewish Committee on Public Affairs (NJCPA) and its counsel Nathan Lewin. In its amicus brief in *Lemon* (1971), Lewin described the group as "a voluntary association organized to combat all forms of religious prejudice and discrimination and to represent the position of the Orthodox Jewish community on matters of public concern." The NJCPA filed its first amicus brief in *Walz v. Tax Commissioner of the City of New York* (1970). Since 1980, it has participated in twelve cases before the Supreme Court. Lewin also presented oral argument to the Court in *Levitt v. CPERL* (1973), *Regan* (1980), *Thorton v. Caldor* (1985), and *County of Allegheny* (1989). These instances represent involvement in 48 percent of the Court's twenty-six cases during this period and act as a counter to the separationist arguments of the AJC and the American Jewish Committee.

This fractionalization of the "Jewish position" presented to the Supreme Court has its parallel on the Protestant side. As noted, the Catholic Church and entities associated with it have pressed accommodationist arguments since *Everson,* but the NCC, the BJC, and the AU presented a relatively solid Protestant separationist front through the 1970s. Starting in 1980, two more Protestant groups entered the establishment fray: the Center for Law and Religion of the Christian Legal Society (CLS; 44 percent) and the National Association of Evangelicals (NAE; 40 percent). The Catholic League for Religious and Civil Rights (29 percent) provided yet another "perspective" on these questions. The legal expertise of the CLS was enhanced when it added Michael W. McConnell, formerly a member of the solicitor general's staff under Rex Lee, to its staff in 1987. It, or its attorneys, argued two cases— *Bowen v. Kendrick* (1988) and *Mergens* (1990). These groups, especially the CLS and NAE, act as accommodationist counterparts to the NCC, BJC, and AU and perform a function akin to that of the NJCPA—they make the justices pointedly aware of the diversity of church-state perspectives in the Christian community.

In addition to these religious groups, other new accommodationist groups have sprung into action. Pat Robertson's National Legal Foundation filed amicus briefs in *County of Allegheny* and *Lee* (1992) and argued *Mergens* (1990)—the decision that upheld the Equal Access Act of 1984. More significantly, it created the American Center for Law and Justice in 1990. Its chief counsel, Jay Alan Sekulow, argued *Mergens* (1990), *Lee* (1992), and *Lamb's Chapel* (1993) and filed an amicus brief in *Zobrest* (1993) for the Deaf Community Center. Concerned Women of America, self-identified as a group "extremely concerned with government programs which deprive individuals and institutions of benefits because of their religious motivations or affiliations," has participated as amicus in seven cases since 1986—58 percent of the Court's cases since the group was founded. The Rutherford Institute, which "undertakes to assist litigants and to participate in significant cases relating to the protection and safeguarding of religious liberties," filed amicus briefs in eight cases, and its attorneys participated in oral arguments in the Louisiana creationism case *Edwards v. Aguillard* (1987). Table 5-5 notes other groups active as friends before the Court.

With the recent creation and activation of these groups, accommodationists are now able to counter the organized separationist perspective that previously enjoyed near-monolithic status before the Court. Added to this newly developed pluralism is the fact that schisms—at least on *some* issues—have formed on the separationist front. In a sense, these fissures find their genesis in different organizational (secular and religious) perspectives. They first became apparent to the Supreme Court in *Walz* (1970) when the AU filed an amicus brief urging the Court to sustain tax exemptions for church property. This put it in opposition to the ACLU. The AJC, unable to come to a position on the question, did not participate at all. This dissension, however, looked anomalous because these groups stayed together on the parochiaid issues that dominated the 1970s.

These separationist schisms grew in the 1980s. As noted in Table 5-6, "separationist" groups joined their usual opponents in many cases to urge an accommodationist interpretation of the Establishment Clause on the Court. A prime example is found in *Thorton* (1986). Here, a man who resigned from his job rather than work on his Sabbath filed a grievance with the Connecticut Board of Mediation and Arbitration against his previous employer for violating a state statute, which said that "[n]o person who states that a particular day of the week is observed as his Sabbath may be required by his employer to work on such day. An employee's refusal to work on his Sabbath shall not constitute grounds for his dismissal." The store from which Thorton resigned rather than accept a demotion or transfer argued that the statute violated the *Lemon* test and the Establishment Clause by providing Sabbath observers an absolute right not to work on their Sabbath—a claimed state advancement of religion.

The Court agreed with the store and struck the statute by a vote of 8 to 1. This decision, no doubt, pleased the groups—unions and business associations—that filed amicus briefs urging separation. It did not please Thorton's attorneys, the NJCPA's Lewin and Marc D. Stern of the AJC. Nor was the AJC the only separationist group urging an accommodationist result in this case. Filing amicus briefs on behalf of Thorton were the Seventh Day Adventists, the ADBB, and the AU. They grounded their accommodationism here on the Free Exercise of Religion Clause of the First Amendment—arguing that the Establishment Clause should not promote hostility to religion—and this put them with groups whose claims they usually oppose and the solicitor general. Similar separationist slippage is also seen in other recent cases.

The cases noted in Table 5-7 pitted traditional allies against one another and presented the Court a confused configuration of organizational arguments. Concerns about free exercise prompted the discordance among the usual separationist voices, but accommodationist groups regularly use that part of the First Amendment's Free Exercise of Religion Clause against the Establishment Clause contentions of separationists. This was a featured argument of several conservative public interest law firms (for example, the Washington Legal Foundation and the Legal Foundation of America) in *Lynch* and of Concerned Women of America and others in *County of Allegheny*. In addition, it was used in the briefs of the United States from *Mueller* (1983) on as a way to get around the coercive edge the Court found problematic in *Engel* (1962) and *Schempp* (1963). By the

Table 5-6 Puralistic Positioning: Cases in which Leading Separationist Groups Took an Accommodationist Position in Supreme Court Litigation, 1979-1992

	Cases argued from an accommodationist position		Total no. of cases argued
Separationist group	No.	%	
AFL-CIO	1	20.0	5
American Civil Liberties Union	2	9.5	21
American Jewish Committee	1	11.1	9
American Jewish Congress	2	12.5	16
Americans for Religious Liberty	0	0.0	6
Americans United for the Separation of Church and State	2	15.4	13
Anti-Defamation League of B'nai B'rith	1	6.3	16
Baptist Joint Committee on Public Affairs	5	55.5	9
Council on Religious Freedom	2	28.6	7
National Coalition for Public Education and Religious Liberty	0	0.0	12
National Council of Churches of Christ	3	33.3	9
National Jewish Community Relations Council	0	0.0	5
National School Boards Association	1	20.0	5
People for the American Way	1	16.7	6

time of *Mergens* (1990), the free exercise argument had gained nearly universal favor among accommodationists as a way of undercutting *Lemon* by requiring coercion to be proven as an element of an Establishment Clause violation.

The more often separationists split on the questions that come before the Court, and they did in ten of the twenty-six cases (38 percent) during this period, the more often they present the justices with mixed cues. This discordance changes the score read by the Court confronting these issues and can do little to advance the *core separationist values* that originally drew them to the courts; at a minimum it creates confusion about the coherence of the separationist understanding of the Establishment Clause. As such, over time it could undermine the ability of these groups to promote precedents favorable to their essentially separationist concerns. This pluralism of argument, coming from groups that previously sang together harmoniously, could give justices inclined to listen greater latitude in re-working, modifying, and recasting the precedents they ponder in deciding their cases.

Whatever confusion the proliferation of accommodationist groups and the occasional discordance of the separationists caused the justices, however, it is clear that neither of these occurrences dramatically affected the overall doctrinal development of the period.

Table 5-7 Discordant Voices in the Separationist Choir: Issue Divisions in Establishment Clause Cases

Case	Organizations taking separationist position	Organizations taking accommodationist position
Widmar v. Vincent (1981)	AJC, ADBB	BJC, NCC
Thornton v. Caldor (1985)	AFL-CIO	AU, ADBB, Seventh Day Adventists
Witters v. Washington (1986)	ACLU, AU, ADBB	American Jewish Committee, AJC
Corp. of Presiding Bishop v. Amos (1988)	AFL-CIO, ADBB	BJC, CRF
Hernandez v. Commissioner of Internal Revenue (1989)	AJC	CRF
Swaggart Ministries v. California (1990)	—	ACLU
Board of Education of Westside Community Schools v. Mergens (1990)	NSBA, ADBB, ACLU, CPERL, ARL, NJCRC, American Jewish Committee, CRF, PAW	BJC, NCC
Lee v. Weisman (1992)	ARL, CPERL, NEA, ACLU, CRF, AU, AJC, BJC, American Jewish Committee, NCC, ADBB, PAW, Seventh Day Adventists, NJCRC	NSBA
Lamb's Chapel v. Center Moriches Union Free School District (1993)	NSBA, ADBB, CPERL	ACLU, AFL-CIO, AJC, AU, BJC, PAW
Zobrest v. Catalina Foothills School District (1993)	CPERL, PAW, ACLU, American Jewish Committee, AU, ADBB, CRF	BJC, NCC

Note: ACLU=American Civil Liberties Union; ADBB=Anti-Defamation League of B'nai B'rith; AFL-CIO=American Federation of Labor-Congress of Industrial Organizations; AJC=American Jewish Congress; ARL=Americans for Religious Liberty; AU=Americans United; BJC=Baptist Joint Committee on Public Affairs; CPERL=Coalition for Public Education and Religious Liberty; CRF=Council on Religious Freedom; NCC=National Council of Churches of Christ; NEA=National Education Association; NJCRC=National Jewish Community Relations Council; NSBA=National School Boards Association; PAW=People for the American Way.

Accommodationist mobilization began with a vengeance in the early 1980s, but it did not deter the Court's separationist decisions in the 1984 term. Similarly, the most prominent discordance in the separationist chorus occurred after the Court's reassertion of separationism in *Wallace, Grand Rapids,* and *Aguilar* and did not keep the Court from deciding *Lee* (or, more recently, *Kiryas Joel*) in a separationist fashion. Although not irrelevant to the resolution of these issues—they clearly set part of the environment in which the Court considers them—changes in pluralistic participation do not account for the shifting tides of Establishment Clause doctrine. A more likely culprit are the arguments presented to the justices.

O'Connor's separate concurrence in *Lynch* made clear that she was the pivotal vote during the mid-1980s. Although she concurred in Burger's majority opinion, she argued that governments could "acknowledge" religion, but not "endorse" it. Since these concepts seemed to be drawn from Lee's accommodationist brief in *Lynch,* it was reasonable to assume that she understood them the way he meant them. Yet, as in the abortion example (Epstein and Kobylka 1992, chap. 6), this assumption was in error. Her votes and opinions in the cases of the 1984 term, especially in *Wallace,* made clear that her accommodationism, although robust, was less so than that of her fellow majority members in *Lynch.* Significantly, separationists picked up on this, as they had not done in the abortion case, and focused their subsequent arguments on getting her vote. Thus, the arguments of Jaffree's attorney and the ACLU's amicus brief specifically pointed to O'Connor's *Lynch* opinion to contend that the moment of prayer and meditation worked "to advance and express endorsement of religion." [19] They did not ask for reversal of *Lynch,* and they won their case and patched a "wall" on the verge of crumbling.[20]

Some accommodationists did not miss the significance of O'Connor's opinion in *Lynch,* either. Although attorneys for Alabama did not mention it in their briefs, Lee's brief explicitly did. O'Connor, however, concurring in the result reached by the majority (but not in its opinion), felt that the peculiar context that generated the moment-of-silence statute constituted an impermissible endorsement of religion.[21] But, even with her defection here, she did not recant her vote in *Lynch,* and she largely went along with the accommodationist bloc in *Grand Rapids* and *Aguilar.* Thus, even after *Wallace,* accommodationist interests remained in a good position: they simply needed to preserve and extend the legal and political gains achieved in *Regan, Mueller, Marsh,* and *Lynch.*

In *County of Allegheny,* accommodationists argued that the crèche-menorah context was no different from the Pawtucket fact setting that the Court previously sustained in *Lynch,* and that *Lynch* was the controlling precedent. The only new argument they advanced concerned the treatment of context in *Lynch.* Burger's opinion there said that the crèche, in the context of the display, raised no establishment problems. What was unclear was whether the relevant context was the physical layout of the display—the surrounding secular symbols—or the general context of a nationally recognized holiday. Accommodationists—an orthodox Jewish group, some conservative organizations, and the solicitor general—maintained that *Lynch* held the latter position: "Our nation is not secular, but pluralistic, and there is nothing wrong with the government attempting to recognize and commemorate the impact of religion in America's historical traditions and cultural heritage." Thus, the displays were merely a *Lynch*-style acknowledgment conveying no "special message of endorsement of religion."[22] If accepted by O'Connor and the Court, this would insulate all sectarian elements of public displays celebrating religious holidays, and another brick would fall from the "wall of separation."

Separationists countered with the revised litigation strategy they unveiled in *Wallace*. With the exception of the AJC, which, joined by the NCC and the AU, filed an amicus brief, none of these groups, including the ACLU, which argued the case, asked the Court to reverse *Lynch*. This strategic decision, grounded in a realization that the former majority remained intact, led them to argue that *Lynch's* contextual elements should be read as closely tied to the *specific fact setting* that case presented. The Pittsburgh displays, adorning the seats of government, clearly constituted the kind of state "endorsement" of religion *Lynch* held beyond the pale. While the separationists argued that both the crèche and the menorah displays fell short of this understanding of *Lynch*—unlike Blackmun and O'Connor, they did not see the "Salute to Liberty" banner and Christmas tree that made up the rest of the menorah display to save its constitutionality—their scaled-down goals and the doctrinal argument that flowed from them clearly influenced the justice (O'Connor) they needed to salvage a partial victory in a case that certainly must have looked like a losing one as it made its way to the Court.

Because it allowed them to avoid the tyranny of absolutes, the separationists' acceptance of *Lynch* in their subsequent litigation was a strategic masterstroke. The argumentational flexibility it afforded enabled them to adapt to an altered Court that was clearly not particularly supportive of their broad claims and to manage, to the degree possible given the context, the process of legal change. This flexibility—and the moderateness of their response to the line of decisions that culminated in *Lynch*—stands in stark contrast to the pressures that *some* accommodationist forces placed on the Court. A good example is *Wallace*. In that case, attorneys for one of the appellants and the Center for Judicial Studies as an amicus endorsed Judge Hand's "wall-breaking" opinion and urged it on the Court. Although the solicitor general successfully dodged political pressures to take a similar stand before the Court (Caplan 1987, 96-103), the justices (particularly O'Connor)—if they were concerned that the Court and constitutional doctrine might appear to be simple pawns in a political game dominated by far-right conservatives—may have recoiled from pressing the accommodationist logic of the early 1980s and gutting long-prevailing doctrine. The separationist strategy provided them ready arguments to stem this tide.

Further, unlike the capital punishment example Lee Epstein and I examined elsewhere (Epstein and Kobylka 1992, chap. 4), none of the major groups involved in this litigation made the strategic error of assuming that *Lynch* absolutely settled the question before the Court. Even the accommodationists, who held a broad view of the contextual dimension of that decision and trivialized the physical context approach as "reindeer counting," [23] said that the display contained sufficient secular objects to save it under the more restrictive approach urged by the separationists. Blackmun and O'Connor accepted this logic, at least as it applied to the menorah.

This analysis supports a confident inference that the law—as explicated in precedents as diverse as *Zorach* and *Engel*, as encapsulated in the *Lemon* approach, and as framed in the legal arguments presented to the Court—mattered and is the culprit that stymied the expected legal change. Perhaps it is more accurate to say that the law mattered to the moderate justices—the separationist and accommodationist blocs were set in their own absolutes—and the major groups arguing before the Court behaved as if it did. Thus, neither side burned argumentational bridges here as the abolitionists had done in *Gregg v. Georgia* (1976) and the pro-choice forces did, to a lesser extent, in *Webster v. Reproductive Health Services* (1989). By accepting and operating in the pluralistic argumentational environment afforded by existing case law, these groups forestalled the kind of legal change characteristic of the abortion and capital punishment examples—a weaker abortion right and the reimposition of the death penalty.

What remains unclear is whether the argumentational pluralism that lurks amid the discordance among usual separationist allies will ultimately so erode the *Lemon* test that the Court will begin anew to fashion a coherent approach to Establishment Clause issues. The success of the accommodationists in the school access cases—*Widmar v. Vincent* (1981), *Mergens* (1990), and *Lamb's Chapel* (1993)—could foreshadow a growing trend among the justices to see establishment issues through the coercion-ground prism of free exercise doctrine. The separationist victory in *Lee* (1992), won largely by the argument that a graduation ceremony is constitutionally equivalent to a classroom, was based more on *Engel* and *Schempp* than on *Lemon*.[24] Further, Kennedy's majority opinion rested, in part, on the "coercive" nature of the event. This language, drawn from the Court's treatment of Free Exercise of Religion Clause cases, prompted Blackmun, Stevens, and O'Connor to issue a concurrence, noting, in part, that "our precedents make clear that proof of government coercion is not necessary to prove an establishment clause violation" (*Lee,* 1992, 2664). Their opinion concludes with a reference to settled law: "I remain convinced that our jurisprudence is not misguided, and that it requires the decision reached by the Court today" (*Lee,* 1992, 2267).

Part 2 of the dissenting opinion in *Lee* by Scalia, joined by Rehnquist, White, and Thomas, ridiculed the notion of any coercion present in the facts of the case. On this point, then, Kennedy and the four *Lee* dissenters agree: coercion is relevant to the resolution of establishment questions. Where they disagree is in what they count as coercive. Their agreement in the next term in *Zobrest* (1993)—over the dissents of Blackmun, Stevens, O'Connor, and Souter—and in *County of Allegheny* (1989) should give separationists pause; so should the retirements of White and Blackmun insofar as they unsettle the Court. The argumentational pluralism that promotes free exercise values over establishment precedents in some instances could end up with the Court's adopting an understanding of establishment with which all separationists would find it difficult to live.

Conclusion

Because the Supreme Court makes its decisions out of public view, the nature of constitutional adjudication seems surrounded by mystery. The process is, to be sure, political and politicized. The judges who decide the issues brought before them are people with partisan beliefs, values, and attitudes. Presidents know this, and this knowledge often guides their judicial nominations (Bronner 1989; Tribe 1985). Those who bring cases into the courts—both the attorneys and the groups (Epstein and Kobylka 1992; Kobylka 1991; McGuire 1993)—are policy entrepreneurs seeking to enshrine their values in the "law of the land." Thus, constitutional interpretation is a part of the political process; it is, in a sense, political decision making under the obscuring cloak of judicial robes. This is the core of our "conventional wisdom," and it is basically true. Yet, elements of the mystery persist.

Noting the political nature of constitutional adjudication does not fully capture the rich and unusual context in which it plays out—a context clearly relevant to constitutional adjudication. Article III of the Constitution provides federal judges considerable independence from the coarse politics of any given day. The "law," although never as clear and pristine as traditional jurisprudes (Fuller 1961) or the advocates of "original intent" (Meese 1985) suggest, is a relevant "out there" for judges; it creates the formal legal context in which they make their decisions and in which they will be critiqued and understood by consumers for whom *the law* is a very real part of their day-to-day lives. At a minimum, judges have to fit their personal predilections into its fabric (Schubert 1965; Segal and Spaeth 1993). At the other end of the spectrum are judges who seek to make their decisions in accordance with the law. The former describes the quintessential "political" judge; the latter, the conventional "legal" judge. Crucial, however, is the fact that both judicial "types" must account for the law in making their decisions.

This reality led C. Herman Pritchett to note that "political scientists who have done so much to put the 'political' in 'political jurisprudence' need to emphasize that it is still 'jurisprudence.' It is judging in a political context, but it is still judging; and, judging is something different from legislating or administering" (1969, 42). It is "something different" because judges must grapple with preexisting rules and precedents. How they do this sets the political field of play for interested litigants and affects the direction of legal development. For example, in *Payne v. Tennessee* (1991), Chief Justice Rehnquist discussed *stare decisis,* the doctrine of precedent, in this way:

Stare decisis is the preferred course because it promotes the evenhanded, predictable, and consistent development of legal principles, fosters reliance on judicial decisions, and contributes to the actual and perceived integrity of the judicial process. . . . Nevertheless, . . . *stare decisis* is not an inexorable command; rather, it "is a principle of policy and not a mechanical formula of adherence to the latest decision." (*Payne,* 1991, 2609-2610)

With this, his majority reversed two precedents that were less than five years old.[25]

Rehnquist's position noted, it was precedent that led Justices O'Connor, Kennedy, and Souter to reaffirm a woman's constitutional right to an abortion in *Planned Parenthood of Southeastern Pennsylvania v. Casey* (1992). Noting at the outset that "Liberty finds no refuge in a jurisprudence of doubt" (*Casey,* 1992, 2803), they rejected the Bush administration's invitation to overrule *Roe v. Wade* (1973):

[W]hatever the premises of opposition [to a controversial precedent] may be, only the most convincing justification under accepted standards of precedent could suffice to demonstrate that a later decision overruling the first was anything but a surrender to political pressure, and an unjustified repudiation of the principle on which the Court staked its authority in the first instance. . . . The promise of constancy, once given, binds its maker for as long as the power to stand by the decision survives and the understanding of the issue has not changed so fundamentally as to render the commitment obsolete. (*Casey,* 1992, 2815-2816)

Stare decisis represents an effort to ease judging from the immediate political plane. In this sense, the law saved the basic holding of *Roe* from predicted reversal.

Obviously the law does not speak in the same voice to all people, lay or litigating. It is, however, an irreducible presence until a majority of the Court decides otherwise. This forces litigators to account for it in making their cases, even if they do not like or accept it. By doing so, litigators can encourage, and indeed facilitate, the growth and development of a pluralistically appropriate array of judicial doctrine. The mysterious case of recent Establishment Clause litigation demonstrates this point.

The accepted empirical indicators of modern political science suggest that the "wall of separation" would not survive the Reagan-Bush assault on it. Yet, even in the face of massive personnel changes, hostile public opinion, and concerted executive branch and group pressure, the Court held the shaky line that characterizes modern Establishment Clause litigation. In the pivotal cases of *Wallace* (1985), *County of Allegheny* (1989), and

Lee (1992), the Court reaffirmed the law—as its predecessors laid it down—to maintain a constitutional regime, eschewing a too close relation between church and state. This is not to say that the balance on the Court is exactly as it was prior to 1980, for it is somewhat more supportive of elements of accommodation than it was previously. The point, rather, is that the legal development in these cases, viewed from the perspective of the 1980, 1984, and 1988 elections, is not what the conventional wisdom about legal change would have led one to expect. Eliminating the usual suspects, one is led to the conclusion that legal argument constrained legal change.

The litigation of Establishment Clause issues nicely demonstrates the capacity of the law to withstand politically directed efforts at change. By accounting for and adapting to the realities of constitutional litigation in the Reagan-Bush era, separationist groups were able to keep the "wall of separation" from being torn down. Avoiding the tyranny of absolutes, they adjusted the arguments they presented the Court to keep part of the *Everson* legacy alive. This meant, for many of them, accepting doctrinal modifications (for example, *Lynch's* version of the *Lemon* test) that, under other circumstances, they would have instantly rejected. Having secured a portion of the past against attack in cases like *Wallace* (1985), *Ball* (1985), *County of Allegheny* (1989), and *Lee* (1992), separationists survived the 1980s with enough doctrinal support to reinvigorate the weakened elements of the law in more favorable circumstances in the future. The decision in *Kiryas Joel* (1994) suggests that this may be occurring now.

One of the lessons of this litigation history is, in a sense, somewhat perverse. It may be a paradox of pluralism as it encompasses the courts, but it seems as if groups facing hostile judicial environments are best served by trimming their argumentational sails and simply keeping afloat in hope of rescue by precedents or future conditions. Put more pointedly, litigating groups in unfriendly contexts may find it to be in their interest to be less formally legal (focused on clear and sequentially building victories) and more self-consciously political (willing to play under the rules of the opposition and lose here and there) in the way they address the Court. In short, groups would approach the courts much as they approach legislatures: use past victories as a piton to secure them from a harsh fall, if not as a way station to a higher perch. Proceeding in this fashion during the Reagan-Bush era, separationist groups protected enough of what they had previously achieved in the law to win the occasional battle and remain alive for the rest of the war. This kind of legal give-and-take does not have the elegance of a well-executed litigation plan, but it does have the virtue of protecting, in the short term, previous accomplishments.

A second lesson of this case study is the precariousness of this kind of strategic, minimize-your-losses approach to constitutional litigation. In a densely populated litigation field, groups generally in agreement may increasingly find themselves at odds on issues related to their consensual core. This promotes a pluralism of argument that could undermine the common values on which they agree. Discordant voices in the separationist choir emerged in the Reagan-Bush years as allied groups took different positions in more than a third of the Court's Establishment Clause cases. Although this pluralism of argument may have helped, in the short term, to preserve some constitutional separationism, it also contributed to the elevation of free exercise values in Establishment Clause interpretation. This, ultimately, could serve to undermine the constitutional values that unite separationist groups.

Having noted dangers of argumentational pluralism in constitutional litigation, I think it is important to return to the success that separationist groups had in staving off, at least in the short term, the end that Ronald Reagan and George Bush wished for them. By making arguments based not on *their* preferred positions but on those with potential appeal to crucial justices, separationist groups maintained a semblance of their values in the decisions of a Court ill-disposed to favor their claims. This is no small feat, especially in light of the fate of organized litigators in other policy areas.

The other side of this organizational success is the receptivity of certain members of the Court to arguments based on precedent. Rehnquist, White, Scalia, and Thomas seemed more than willing to execute the church-state agenda of Reagan and Bush; Brennan, Marshall, and Stevens seemed willing to fight it at nearly every turn; but Blackmun, O'Connor, Kennedy, and Souter seemed to respond to the arguments put before them on matters of law. The willingness of the latter three to do this is especially telling, given that they disappointed the very presidents who appointed them. Each of these justices—O'Connor, beginning in *Lynch* (1984), and Kennedy and Souter in *Lee* (1992)—sought to make sense of the arguments immediately before them in light of cases decided long before them. That they came to somewhat different understandings of what the Establishment Clause requires is less significant than the fact that, at a time when the defection of only one of them would have worked a major doctrinal change, it seems as if they made decisions in accordance with what they thought *the law*—the text and history of the First Amendment, and prior decisions shaping it—required. This drew the ire of their more ideological colleagues and resulted in maintenance of the ambiguous jurisprudential tradition inaugurated in *Everson*. As a result, they helped to sustain rough consistency in constitutional interpretation during a period when few expected it.

Thus ends the mystery of the unsuccessful Reagan-Bush assault on the Establishment Clause. Our investigation has absolved the usual suspects of complicity and revealed the culprit that frustrated the legal change sought by these presidents. It also reminds us that in our investigations of things judicial we must not lose sight of something that was once taken for granted. However improbable it may seem, given our conventional wisdom about the political nature of the judicial process, the language and logic of the law—albeit shaped by an array of political factors—persists as an important element of legal change, conditioning its dynamics. In the hands of skillful attorneys and attentive jurists, this suspect foiled the expected alteration in Establishment Clause doctrine.

Notes

1. Sometime after *Zorach* was decided, Douglas became something of a born-again separationist. By *Abington School District v. Schempp* (1963), his separationism was so extreme that he pondered the constitutional necessity of removing all vestiges of religion from governmental life. This included the motto "In God we trust" on American currency.

2. Blackmun delivered the judgment of the Court in an opinion largely joined by O'Connor. Justices Brennan, Marshall, and Stevens concurred in the judgment against the crèche display but dissented from that sustaining the menorah. Justices Kennedy, William H. Rehnquist, White, and Scalia voted to uphold the ruling permitting both displays, thus concurring in the judgment sustaining the menorah display.

3. Rehnquist, Scalia, and Thomas dissented. *Kiryas Joel* is the first Establishment Clause case on which Justice Ruth Bader Ginsburg, a Clinton appointee, sat. Because it was decided after the twelve-year period of the Reagan and Bush presidencies, it is not included in the formal analysis presented below. Its result, however, is consistent with the conclusions I offer here.

4. Douglas also was a member of the "super-separationist" bloc. His replacement by Stevens thus had no effect on its alignment.

5. They strayed from separationism only on questions of tax exemptions for church property (*Walz v. Tax Commission,* 1970) and secular book loans to sectarian schools (*Wolman v. Walter,* 1977).

6. Examples of the effects of these splits are *Meek* (1975) and *Wolman* (1977), where the super-accommodationists voted with the moderates to uphold some government assistance to sectarian schools, and the super-separationists cast the deciding votes to strike down other elements of the same legislation.

7. I use the term *parochiaid* here and elsewhere to refer to government efforts to aid sectarian schools.

8. Despite his seeming about-face in *Regan,* Stewart supported accommodationist values in only 44 percent of the cases decided between 1970 and his retirement (Kobylka 1985).

9. A minor anomaly is *Marsh,* in which the Court did not apply *Lemon* in upholding the ruling permitting a paid state legislative chaplain and Blackmun silently joined the majority.

10. Brennan, Marshall, and Stevens thought that both displays were constitutionally impermissible, regardless of their physical settings; *Lynch* should be overruled. Rehnquist, White, Scalia, and Kennedy believed that, given *Lynch* and its reliance—from their perspective—on the broader holiday context, the ruling permitting both displays should be upheld. Blackmun and O'Connor, not rejecting *Lynch,* simply read its discussion of the holiday context to refer, not to the general celebratory season, but to the immediate physical setting of the display.

11. Stephen Breyer's replacement of Blackmun will probably be, in regard to bloc formation on *this* issue, a wash.

12. Reagan took his rhetorical trumpeting of accommodationism to the pulpit of the presidency. He frequented National Prayer Day ceremonies, and he regularly addressed groups like the National Religious Broadcasters, the National Association of Evangelicals, and the Women Leaders of Christian Organizations. He also devoted exclusive or substantial attention to this issue in at least five of his weekly Saturday radio addresses to the nation (September 18, 1982; January 22 and November 19, 1983; February 25, 1984; August 24, 1985).

13. "Nothing in this Constitution shall be construed to prohibit individual or group prayer in public schools or other public institutions. No person shall be required by the United States or by any State to participate in prayer." The amendment died after it failed to get the requisite two-thirds Senate approval in March 1984. Reagan, however, continued to submit it to the Senate throughout the rest of his presidency.

14. This act was upheld in *Board of Education v. Mergens* (1990) with only Stevens dissenting.

15. Of the ten cases, the solicitor general argued *Alamo Federation v. Secretary of Labor* (1985), *Corp. of Presiding Bishop v. Amos* (1988), and *Hernandez v. Commissioner of Internal Revenue* (1989), and intervened in *Lynch* (1984), *Wallace* (1985), *Aguilar* (1985), *Grand Rapids* (1985), *Bowen v. Kendrick* (1988), *Mergens* (1990), and *Lee* (1992). The seven cases in which amicus curiae briefs were filed were *Mueller* (1983), *Marsh* (1983), *Thorton v. Caldor* (1985), *Witters v. Washington* (1986), *County of Allegheny* (1989), *Lamb's Chapel* (1993), and *Zobrest* (1993).

16. Brief for the United States in *Lynch,* 1984, 1. Lee never asked the Court to reconsider or reverse *Lemon.* Indeed, his critics on the political right blasted him for exactly this. Note, for example, the comments of James McClellan (1984, 2), head of the Center for Judicial Studies: "Lee has not urged the Supreme Court to overrule a single prior decision, including *Roe v. Wade,* the New York prayer case, and *Mapp v. Ohio.*" Caplan (1987, 99) notes that McClellan was linked to William Bradford Reynolds and was the inspiration for, if not the author of, Judge Learned Hand's district court opinion in *Wallace.* For more on McClellan's links to the Reagan Justice Department, see Schwartz (1988, 4-6).

17. Amicus curiae brief of the United States, requesting a grant of certiorari, *Lee v. Weisman,* (1992, 15; a grant of certiorari formally dockets a case for argument before the Court.)

18. The linkages between the ACLU and the AJC cannot be overstated. Once the church-state issue was taken to the courts, these groups pursued a close and coordinated approach designed to erect and maintain a high "wall of separation." Indeed, scholars have pointed to Leo Pfeffer, a long-time counsel for the AJC, as "one of the most knowledgeable and experienced church-state lawyers in the country" (Morgan 1968, 55); we have no reason to dispute this claim. Pfeffer's reach was amazing. Not only was he active with the AJC, but he also served on the church-state committee of the ACLU, founded and directed the Committee for Public Education and Religious Liberty (CPERL), wrote briefs for other separationist interests (for example, the American Association of School Administrators, the Baptist Joint Committee on Public Affairs, and the Synagogue Council), appeared in untold numbers of cases as a plaintiff attorney, and wrote several books and articles on the constitutional status of religious freedom. He is as close to the historical architect and guide of the legal separationist position as can be imagined.

19. ACLU amicus brief in *Wallace* (1985).

20. In its amicus brief, the AJC, joined by the NJCRC, the ADBB, and the American Jewish Committee, did not focus on either the *Lynch* precedent or O'Connor's "test." It argued that history and precedents demonstrated that the use of public schools to advance religious belief was inherently unconstitutional.

21. The Alabama state senator Donald G. Holmes, a self-described "prime sponsor" of the statute, testified before the district court that the statute was "an effort to return voluntary prayer to our public schools . . . it is a beginning and a step in the right direction," and that he supported it with "no other purpose in mind" than "returning voluntary prayer to our public schools" (*Wallace,* 1985, 2483).

22. Brief for the United States in *County of Allegheny* (1989, 18).

23. Brief for the United States, *County of Allegheny* (1989, 18).

24. The majority opinion in *Kiryas Joel* (1994) treats *Lemon* in much the same fashion.

25. *Booth v. Maryland* (1987) and *South Carolina v. Gathers* (1989).

Part II Trial Courts

"I'll take my case all the way to the U.S. Supreme Court." How many times has that phrase been uttered by actors on television shows or even by average Americans who find themselves involved in some legal dispute. In reality, though, this is a hollow battle cry. During the 1990s, about 100 million criminal and civil cases were filed annually in our nation's federal and state trial courts (Baum 1994, 44-46); in that same period, the U.S. Supreme Court decided about 120 cases per term with an opinion (Epstein et al. 1994, 73). Given those numbers, the probability that the justices would decide any one of the trial court cases bordered on zero.

In marked contrast to the claims made on television shows, then, our experience with the U.S. Supreme Court is likely to be limited to touring the building, hearing oral arguments, or reading its opinions. But the odds are pretty good (as the 100 million figure suggests) that at least once during our lifetimes we will have contact with a trial court. We may be the victim of a crime or even accused of committing one, be it a minor traffic offense or something more serious. We may serve as jurors in civil or criminal trials or become involved as witnesses. Hence, understanding the world of trial courts is not just something we should do as students of the American judiciary. It is knowledge we should possess as citizens who have a vested interest in the courts' work.

The three chapters contained in this part of the book go a long way in helping us to understand the inner workings of trial courts. That they do so is a credit to the authors, for trial courts are not easy to study. They are many in number (ninety-four federal [or U.S. district] tribunals and thousands of state trial courts of limited and general jurisdiction); they possess distinct procedures and operations; and they are filled with numerous and varied actors—from lawyers to judges to jurors. To make general claims about the work of trial courts, thus, is a difficult task indeed. But it is one that the contributors perform well, with each essay providing interesting and important insights.

Thomas W. Church's chapter serves as a reminder that, at least from a quantitative perspective, trials are an insignificant part of our criminal justice system; only about 5 to 15 percent of all prosecutions go to trial. In the remainder, the defendant pleads guilty, usually after arriving at a plea-bargaining arrangement with the prosecutor. In such arrangements the defendant waives the right to a jury trial and agrees to plead guilty in return for certain concessions made by the prosecutor. These concessions normally involve a reduction in the seriousness of the crimes charged, a reduction in the number of counts, or a recommendation for a lenient sentence. Although many citizens look at such arrangements unfavorably, they remain the most common way criminal prosecutions are settled. Why? That is one of the questions Church seeks to address.

To answer it, he develops a most innovative research strategy—one designed to take advantage of the diversity in trial courts and to test theories concerning the influence of local legal culture on court output and practitioner behavior. He wrote a questionnaire that consisted of descriptions of twelve hypothetical cases, each of which included a summary of the victim's story, the facts of the defendant's arrest, a list of witnesses and their expected testimony, a description of the physical evidence, and information on the defendant. He then asked judges and attorneys in four urban trial courts (New York City, Detroit, Miami, and Pittsburgh) how they thought the case should be resolved (for example, a negotiated plea of guilty, jury trial, dismissal). Finally, he compared the survey data with records of cases processed through the particular courts to see how the attitudes and norms of the key players influenced actual system performance.

Among the many findings reported by Church is one that bears directly on the pervasiveness of plea bargaining. Whereas previous research indicated that this arrangement persists because it is an easy and cost-efficient way of handling cases, his study paints a very different picture. In particular, his survey data reveal that attorneys and judges alike view bargaining as an appropriate and fair way to dispose of at least some portion of their cases. As the author points out, this is an especially important finding because it may explain the long history of failed attempts to eliminate plea bargaining.

To be sure, as Church's study reveals, plea bargains, not trials, dominate the criminal justice process. But Kim Lane Schepple's chapter shores up an equally important point: although trials are quantitatively trivial, qualitatively they are significant. Some of the most serious crimes go to trial. In addition, trials educate the public about crime and justice in the community. And they *seem* to embody what Americans treasure so much—truth, objectivity, and open fairness. But do they serve this function? This is one of the issues Schepple explores.

More specifically, at the beginning of her chapter Scheppele asks: "How do judges and juries know when they have found the truth about some event that happened in the past?" This is an important question, for, as she explains, lawsuits are not simply about interpreting the law; they are also about rendering authoritative determinations about "what happened." Yet, for all its significance, most juries and judges don't spend too much time puzzling over their fact-finding mission. Like most of us—they tend to think they "know the truth when they see it."

But "the truth"—for reasons Scheppele describes—is often contested in lawsuits. Thus, the question becomes what happens when different people believe different accounts of the same event? To investigate this, she considers the construction of facts that work to disadvantage women, particularly in cases involving sexualized violence. The end result is a fascinating look into some of the hidden aspects of our legal system. For example, Scheppele finds that women who delay in telling their stories of abuse or harassment (such as Anita Hill) are frequently discredited as liars. But, as she tells us, abused women quite often react in this way—they repress what happened to them. Certainly, this and other findings call into question the conventional notion that judicial actors—or any of us for that matter— know "the truth" when we see it.

The final chapter in this part, by Lynn Mather, brings together and expands on arguments made in the first two. Mather's concerns go to the very heart of the study of trial courts: Do trial courts make policy? If so, how? The answer to the first question, according to Mather, depends on how we define *policy making*. If we rely on narrow and dated definitions (such as the conscious establishment of a new rule or standard for handling problems), then perhaps they do not. But if we turn to more contemporary treatments of policy making, then—as Mather cogently argues—we can observe a wide range of such activities in trial courts. We also learn that judges are not the only legal actors who make policy, nor are their decisions the only vehicles for policy making. As Mather shows, litigants and lawyers contribute by defining problems and formulating policy alternatives; the mass media use cases to dramatize political conflict and set an agenda for action by other actors; and juries create policies through their fact finding and creation of new legal norms.

The answer to the second question—how trial courts make policy—is a bit a more complex but one that Mather handles with clarity and elegance. By taking us through the conventional stages of the trial court process—from filing a legal claim through adjudication, she shows us how actors involved in the trial court process make policy by contributing to problem definition, building agendas, formulating alternatives, and adopting and implementing policy. To build her argument, Mather reexamines studies of trial courts done by other researchers, with the aim of discovering policy-making activity in courts that has often been ignored. She then puts her views to the test, exploring the key events and policy implications of *Yukica v. Leland*, a lawsuit filed by a Dartmouth football coach over a broken employment contract.

In the end, then, the chapters contained in this section focus on different aspects of the trial court process and make use of distinct data sources. Still, all the authors reach an important conclusion: the work of trial courts has meaning far beyond the dispute at hand. Although this lesson may seem an obvious one—especially in an age when those accused of committing violent crimes (the O.J. Simpsons, Lorena Bobbits, and Amy Fishers) regularly make front page news—it is at times not fully appreciated.

6 Plea Bargaining and Local Legal Culture

Thomas W. Church

The popular conception of criminal courts is well illustrated by a television series of the 1960s and 1970s that probably had a key role in forming that understanding: *Perry Mason*. Most of the important action in this program takes place in the courtroom, where momentous questions of guilt and innocence are contested by skillful, dedicated adversaries. Mason is a defense attorney who seems only to defend clients charged with offenses they did not commit. Although these defendants are inevitably exonerated, the audience must worry for much of the hour about whether or not the true perpetrator of the offense will be identified and the innocent party will go free. In the process, the defendants follow a path through the criminal courts characterized by proceedings that are formal, expertly conducted, deliberative, and, at least by the final five minutes of the program, unfailingly accurate and just.

Lawyers, defendants, and criminal justice professionals have always known that this adversarial, courtroom-dominated depiction of the courts has little to do with the reality of criminal justice in the United States. They know that despite television's focus on dramatic trials that frequently result in exoneration of the defendant, the vast majority of criminal defendants have little chance of acquittal at trial and upward of 90 percent plead guilty in abbreviated, if not perfunctory, courtroom ceremonies—usually after out-of-court negotiations with the prosecutor. They know that relations between defense attorneys and prosecutors are seldom as formal and unremittingly hostile as those between Perry Mason and his weekly prosecutorial antagonist, Hamilton Burger. And they know that despite television's implicit depiction of a uniform system of criminal justice in America, there are substantial differences from place to place in how courts function and how similarly situated defendants fare.

The informal process of negotiation through which real-world criminal defendants plead guilty in exchange for some form of sentencing concession is known universally as

This research was supported by grant number 78-MU-AX-0023, awarded to the National Center for State Courts by the National Institute of Justice. A more complete report of the findings of this research can be found in Church 1985.

plea bargaining. Plea bargaining takes a variety of forms, both across courts and even among judges in the same court. In some courts, defendants and their attorneys negotiate with prosecutors about the criminal charge to which the defendant will plead guilty; the typical bargain is for a plea of guilty to a reduced charge—simple robbery rather than armed robbery, for example, or possession of illegal drugs rather than the more serious charge of sale of drugs. These lesser charges carry lower maximum sentences than those originally lodged, so the defendant obtains a reduction in the worst that could happen to him or her, in exchange for forgoing the chance for exoneration at trial. Negotiations can also involve explicit assurances as to sentence, either in the form of a recommendation by the prosecutor that is inevitably followed by the judge, or—less frequently—through negotiations directly with the judge concerning the sentence that will be imposed upon a plea of guilty.[1]

Informal deals between harried prosecutors and criminal defendants in courthouse hallways or back rooms have little in common with the majesty of the criminal courts depicted on *Perry Mason.* Unsurprisingly, as public consciousness of plea bargaining has risen through the visibility provided by the dramatic negotiations conducted by such public figures as Vice President Spiro Agnew and—more recently—Representative Dan Rostenkowski, so has criticism of the process. Some critics argue that plea bargaining results in excessive leniency and lets admitted criminals "get off" with less punishment than they deserve. From the opposite end of the policy spectrum, others contend that plea bargaining is unfair to those charged with criminal offenses; in this understanding, plea bargaining coerces criminal defendants, even innocent defendants, to plead guilty and thereby sacrifice their constitutional right to trial and possible acquittal (see Alschuler 1968, 1975, 1978; Kipnis 1976; Langbein 1978; Schulhofer 1984). As a result of condemnation of the practice, the last decade has seen a number of efforts to reform or abolish plea bargaining. These efforts have seldom proven successful: a peripherally changed but robust system of plea negotiation has typically reemerged from even the most ambitious efforts to change or eliminate the practice (see Church 1975; Clarke 1988; Heumann and Loftin 1979; Nimmer and Krauthaus 1977).

If plea bargaining is both unfair and irrational, why is it so pervasive in American criminal courts? Why have efforts at elimination of plea bargaining frequently been so unsuccessful? These questions are the focus of this chapter.

A Research Strategy: Using Variation across Courts to Examine Plea Bargaining

The existence of fifty-one separate court systems, each with independent organization, funding levels, legal codes, and procedural rules, ensures that the administration of criminal justice in the United States will vary from court to court across the country.[2] Local practitioners—the lawyers and judges who work in the justice system—have long known that American criminal courts are far from uniform, either in operation or in output. Empirical studies have documented the intercourt differences that lawyers observe in their day-to-day work. For example, research has revealed that cases move at quite different speeds, depending on the court in which they are filed: some courts dispose of the typical felony case in a month or two; others consume a year or more from arrest to final disposition (Church et al. 1978; Goerdt 1989; Mahoney 1988). Courts differ in sentencing practices as well, with comparable defendants facing quite dissimilar sentences in different courts (for a summary, see Blumstein et al. 1983). And across courts the proportions differ between cases that are disposed of by trial and those that are disposed of by plea of guilty. Most courts try no more than 20 percent of felony cases, guilty pleas being the predominant mode of disposition for the rest. Other courts have trial rates approaching, and even exceeding, 50 percent (Church et al. 1978).[3]

The existence of variation in the structure and operation of trial courts provides researchers with an opportunity to test their hunches and tentative hypotheses regarding various aspects of criminal court operation, including plea bargaining. In the following sections, I discuss two potential explanations of plea bargaining and examine those explanations using variation across courts to test the hypotheses.

Court Resources

The most common explanation among judges, lawyers, and politicians for the ubiquity and tenacity of plea bargaining is lack of resources in the criminal courts. Although trial by jury is held to be the preferred method to handle all criminal cases, trials are expensive and time-consuming. They require costly courtrooms, highly paid legal professionals and clerical staff, and procedures for procuring jurors and witnesses. A system in which a full-scale trial were held in every criminal case would consume many times the resources—judges, lawyers, court staff, and courtrooms—currently devoted to the criminal courts. Because these resources are not available, it is argued, the system must offer incentives to defendants to plead guilty and thereby eliminate the costs and delays associated with trial; we must make do with a hurried, often harried, semblance of justice because we are unwilling as a society to commit the funds necessary to have trials in all criminal cases. In this view, practitioners engage in plea bargaining not because they regard the practice as appropriate or fair in the cases they are handling but because they must negotiate dispositions in order to get through their heavy caseloads. Inadequate resources are also potentially responsible for the failure of efforts to eliminate plea bargaining, since without adequate resources to provide a trial in every case, some form of plea bargaining is arguably inevitable, regardless of efforts to halt the practice.

If reliance on plea negotiations is caused by, or is at least related to, the amount of resources in the court system, especially the number of judges, available for the disposition of criminal cases, we would expect less plea negotiation and more reliance on trials in court systems that have relatively more resources and the reverse in poorly funded courts. Similarly, if resources in a particular court are increased in relation to caseload, we would expect to see proportionately more trials as the pressure to bargain is reduced; if resources should shrink over time, we would expect the trial rate to drop. Researchers have investigated both of these assertions, without finding support for the hypothesis that the pressure of the caseload causes plea bargaining.

Studies across several courts with dissimilar plea and trial rates reveal virtually no relation between caseload pressure on a court—measured in terms of criminal caseload per judge—and its trial or plea rate. Courts with relatively high judicial caseloads have both high and low trial and plea rates, as do courts with comparatively low caseloads (Church et al. 1978). Furthermore, studies of changes over time in caseload pressure in the same court found no increase in the trial rate as case pressure lessened, nor any decrease as case pressure increased (Feeley 1978; Heumann 1975; Joint Committee on New York Drug Law Evaluation 1978). Although these studies do not definitively disprove the caseload hypothesis, they do cast doubt on its validity as the primary explanation of plea bargaining. If the trial or guilty plea rate is unrelated to differences in court workload—both over time and across different courts—something else must be at work; some other factor must explain courts' reliance on plea bargaining in the face of both changes in workload and efforts to eliminate the practice.

Local Legal Culture and an Organizational Model of Courts

Social scientists have focused considerable attention on criminal courts in the last two decades, and their efforts have done much to increase our understanding of both the observable, quantifiable output of courts and the less formal aspects of their operation. On the basis of interviews with legal practitioners and observational studies in a variety of courts across the United States, researchers have formulated a general model of how criminal courts operate that is both different from and more complex than that depicted either in courtroom dramas on television or by those who see resources and workload as the primary determinants of how courts function. This model views courts as complex *organizations* that have the task of processing large numbers of criminal defendants in a context of relatively scarce resources. These court organizations are dominated by regular participants—judges, defense attorneys, prosecutors, police, court staff—who must cooperate with one another if they are to do their jobs and earn their livelihoods. Although adversarial procedures have a place in this system, trials and other formal proceedings are less significant to a court's everyday work than cooperation and negotiation among regular participants (early examples of this orientation include Blumberg 1964; Eisenstein and Jacob 1977; more recent work includes Eisenstein, Flemming, and Nardulli 1988; Flemming, Nardulli, and Eisenstein 1992; Nardulli, Eisenstein, and Flemming 1988).

Researchers using this organizational framework have examined the pace of litigation in courts, as well as their sentencing and plea-bargaining practices. This research, based in large part on interviews with lawyers and judges, suggests that all of these critical aspects of trial court operation are governed by informal norms that define the proper behavior of judges and lawyers in regard to the disposition of cases. For example, studies of court delay have demonstrated that the pace of litigation differs substantially across courts and that the speed at which cases move in a particular court is related to strong practitioner attitudes regarding the *proper* pace of case disposition. Courts with a comparatively slow pace of litigation tend to have practicing lawyers and judges whose views of the proper pace of litigation support that slow pace, who believe that it is important to let cases "mature" and that a "rush to justice" is unfair; the reverse is true in faster courts, where lawyers and judges express their firm belief that "justice delayed is justice denied" (Church et al. 1978).

Interview-based research also indicates that defendants charged with a criminal act that would be considered relatively minor in one court can be viewed as serious menaces in another. These differences in perception of the seriousness of a case can affect many aspects of how a case is handled in court, including the amount of bail set for defendants (Flemming 1982) and the sentence meted out upon conviction. Sentencing in most criminal cases is based on what are termed *going rates:* implicit normative standards shared by lawyers and judges in a court that define the appropriate sentence for particular types of defendants charged with various crimes (Heumann 1978; Nardulli, Eisenstein, and Flemming 1988). These going rates can differ substantially from court to court.

Research has also suggested that informal norms regarding the seriousness of common types of criminal acts govern plea bargaining and trial decisions in local courts. Lawyers and judges have told researchers that some cases in their courts are viewed as "routine" or "not serious" or "light" or even "garbage." In such cases, lawyers and judges reportedly view a trial as a waste of time and resources, either because they perceive no realistic possibility of acquittal (such cases are termed "dead bang" cases in some courts [Mather 1979]) or because the charges and likely sentence are too trivial to warrant the costs and effort that accompany a trial. These cases are viewed as candidates for a quick plea bargain based on the going rate for sentencing similar defendants charged with analogous crimes (Heumann 1978, 1979).

Informal norms that define the seriousness of cases and unofficial rules and procedures that govern pretrial negotiations, the filing of motions, and the scheduling of cases are seldom written down or even explicitly discussed. Indeed, when lawyers are called on to represent a client in an unfamiliar court, they often report that their biggest problems occur in areas of court operation that cannot be uncovered by reading statutes or local court rules or by looking at case files. Lawyers refer to these variations in norms and ways of doing things as differences in "local practice." Social scientists frequently use the term *local legal culture* to describe this network of unwritten standards and patterns of behavior.[4]

If attorneys and judges evaluate how cases should be disposed of by reference to a set of commonly shared norms regarding the appropriate method for adjudicating particular types of cases, then it is plausible that a major reason for the historically stable pattern of plea and trial rates observed in many courts is the continued existence of these supporting norms. Thus, decisions regarding plea and trial may be influenced more by the shared attitudes practitioners bring into dispositional discussions than by the relationship of resources to workload demands in their court. Further, if existing patterns of decisions regarding plea and trial are grounded in local norms governing how cases *ought* to be handled, these shared attitudes may help explain why efforts to reduce or abolish plea bargaining have so frequently produced entrenched resistance from judges and lawyers and have often proved unsuccessful.

For a social scientist, the concept of legal culture is both promising and problematic. It is promising because it is consistent with the reality observed by both practitioners and researchers in many different contexts and studies. But it is problematic because of the difficulties it poses both for definition and for measurement.

From a definitional perspective, local legal culture is troublesome because of what might be called the chicken-and-egg problem: does local legal culture cause or at least influence a court's output and its practitioners' behavior? Or does cause and effect work the other way around? Are existing patterns of output and behavior simply internalized by new judges and lawyers when they "learn the ropes" in a court, and thereby unconsciously turned into norms of behavior? Unfortunately, even if we establish a demonstrable relationship between actual court output and the norms of practitioners working in that court, it would not be possible to determine which of these two alternative hypotheses is correct. The best that social science can usually provide is evidence of a relationship between two variables—in this case, between practitioner norms and court system behavior. Determining which variable is the causal factor and which is what social scientists call the *dependent variable* is often a speculative exercise.

This definitional quandary may be more apparent than real in this case, however. It is entirely possible for causality to work in both directions: norms can influence behavior, which in turn can influence norms. The hypothesis suggested here is simply that practitioner norms regarding the proper mode of disposition of criminal cases are related to actual dispositional patterns in criminal trial courts. This somewhat muddy notion of causality is not unusual in social science. Research on the operation of Congress, for example, has shown precisely the kind of reciprocal influence of norms on the behavior of members of Congress that the hypothesis concerning local legal culture suggests exists in trial courts in regard to judges and lawyers (see Fenno 1966; Matthews 1960).

The measurement problems that face researchers who wish to investigate the relationship of local legal culture to the output of trial courts are also thorny. How does one empirically demonstrate even the existence of commonly shared attitudes in a court, let alone measure and systematically compare these norms across different courts? I discuss this methodological quandary in the next section.

Measuring Local Legal Culture

The primary elements of legal culture under investigation here are the norms and attitudes of lawyers and judges regarding the proper way to handle criminal cases. Previous research, based on unstructured interviews and observation, suggests that courts are characterized by distinctive sets of practitioner norms regarding which cases should be tried and which should be resolved through a guilty plea or other nonadversarial mode of disposition (Heumann 1978; Mather 1979; Utz 1978). If this prior research is accurate, the variation across courts in patterns of attitudes toward plea bargaining and trial presents an opportunity to assess how local legal culture is related to dispositional practices.

Research based on interviews, although highly instructive for a variety of purposes, is unavoidably subjective and imprecise. It can provide detailed portrayals of how institutions function and of the incentives and perceptions of participants, but it does not produce data that can be used in systematic, quantitative comparisons across courts. When a higher level of precision is wanted regarding the content and strength of individual norms and attitudes, social scientists frequently use questionnaires in which respondents indicate their value preferences in a form that can be quantified. In the research reported here, I examined local norms using attitudinal data obtained from a questionnaire I had given to judges, defense attorneys, and prosecutors in four urban trial courts. The design of the questionnaire was based on the assumption that if local legal culture exists as an influence on the disposition of criminal cases, then its contours might best be ascertained by focusing on attitudes regarding specific factual circumstances.[5]

The questionnaire used in the study consisted of descriptions of twelve hypothetical cases, each of which included a summary of the victim's story, the facts surrounding the defendant's arrest, a list of witnesses and their expected testimony, a description of the physical evidence, and information on the defendant, including past record.[6] The cases were designed to provide variation across the range of seriousness of incident; they thus ran the gamut from relatively minor criminal incidents to quite serious offenses. An attempt was also made to vary the prior records of the hypothetical defendants and the strength of the prosecution's case.[7] The questionnaires were distributed to all judges and attorneys in district attorneys' and public defenders' offices in the general jurisdiction trial courts of the Bronx (a borough of New York City); Detroit, Michigan; Miami, Florida; and Pittsburgh, Pennsylvania.[8]

A note on how these particular courts were chosen is in order here. Because the research methodology used in this project is costly, in both time and money, only a few courts could be analyzed. Unfortunately, reliable, comparable data on plea and trial rates in American trial courts is not readily available, so the choice of courts to be examined was based on unsystematic data on plea and trial rates reported in previous studies and court reports. The four courts chosen were similar in size and urban location but reportedly varied in the proportion of cases disposed of by trial and guilty plea.[9] If legal culture is reflected in actual court practices, then this variation in actual trial and plea rates should be reflected in differing attitudes of practitioners in the courts regarding the kind of cases that ought to be plea-bargained and those that should be tried or disposed of through other means.

The practitioners were asked the same set of questions after each of the case descriptions.[10] The question regarding mode of disposition was phrased in the following way: "Assuming that prosecution, defense, and the court have adequate resources to deal with their caseloads in a fair and expeditious manner, how do you believe this case should be resolved?" The choices included negotiated plea of guilty, guilty plea without charge reduction or sentence assurance, nonjury trial, jury trial, and dismissal or nolle prosequi.[11]

Careful readers will note that the context provided for the answer to this question is a court with adequate resources to dispose of its caseload in a "fair and expeditious manner." The context given for this question was one of the more difficult issues raised in design of the research. Respondents could have been requested to assume existing caseloads and system resources in their court in determining the appropriate mode of disposition of a case. Or, alternatively, they might have been asked to assume an ideal or "perfect" system with no resource constraints. Neither of these two approaches would have been satisfactory. The latter would tie the normative judgments of respondents too closely to existing practices and resources; differences observed between courts on this basis might simply be caused by unequal caseloads of participants, or answers might reflect predictions of *actual* case outcome rather than norms regarding *proper* case outcome. The latter alternative is too ambiguous and speculative to yield consistent results. If legal culture exists as a day-to-day influence on case dispositions in a court, it should be related to cases in a credible system and not to some intangible ideal.

The middle ground chosen represents an attempt to obtain lawyers' and judges' views concerning realistic goals for the criminal courts. Since a major concern of the research was the linkage between practitioners' norms and their resistance to reform, it was hoped that this relationship could best be illuminated by posing the questions in terms of what might reasonably be expected of a criminal court system in the real world.

Trial Rates in Four Criminal Courts

This research is an attempt to relate the actual performance of criminal courts with the attitudes and norms of the lawyers and judges working in those courts. It therefore needs not only a measure of local practitioner attitudes but also measures of actual system performance.

I sampled approximately five hundred closed felony cases in each of the four courts in order to obtain a clear picture of their dispositional practices. Information was collected on the legal charges against the defendant, how the case was disposed of (plea, trial, dismissal, and so forth), and the sentence meted out if the defendant was convicted. The use of information on closed cases for determining how courts compare on plea-bargaining practices poses several methodological problems. Ideally, social scientists would like to know how identical cases would be handled in each court; then any differences observed from court to court in mode of disposition would be based on differences in the courts' case-processing practices rather than on peculiarities of the cases themselves. For obvious reasons, we cannot introduce the same criminal defendants, charged with identical crimes, into different courts and see how they fare. We can only look at closed-case records and try to ascertain how defendants in similar situations are processed through each court. The research problems lie in trying to determine from court records which cases are truly similar and in comparing case procedures and outcomes across courts that often use very different terms and procedures.[12]

An especially perplexing problem lies in defining the seriousness of criminal acts, a factor that has been shown to be critical to almost everything that happens to defendants in the courts. Studies frequently use the formal legal charge in a case—"armed robbery," for example, or "assault"—to measure the seriousness of criminal behavior involved in a case. Unfortunately, the crime charged is often different from the crime on which a defendant is ultimately convicted; and given the bargaining about the charge that takes place between arrest and conviction in many courts, it is seldom clear whether the original or the final charge is the most accurate measure of the seriousness of the criminal behavior. Furthermore, legal crime labels can mean different things in different courts. For example, a charge of "aggravated assault" might be restricted in one court to cases involving serious injuries to the victim and truly malicious behavior by the defendant; in another, it may be charged in the typical barroom brawl. In comparing the trial rates for this offense in these hypothetical courts, one would be comparing apples and oranges.

The *subjective* seriousness with which lawyers and judges view a criminal incident has

Table 6-1 Plea and Trial Rates, Actual Cases

	The Bronx		Detroit		Miami		Pittsburgh	
	N	%	N	%	N	%	N	%
Guilty plea or diversion	424	85	284	82	275	81	312	83
Nonjury trial	11	2	23	7	41	12	49	13
Jury trial	66	13	39	11	23	7	14	4
Total adjudications	501	100	346	100	339	100	375	100

been shown to be the key element in what happens in most criminal cases. In fact, how a defendant's actions are viewed by judges and lawyers is frequently more important in how a case is handled in criminal court than is the legal label under which a defendant is charged or convicted (Mather 1979; Utz 1978).[13] Such factual elements as length of hospital stay for injured victims, amount of property stolen or destroyed, or the use of a lethal weapon have been found in past studies to be indicative of the subjective seriousness with which legal officials view criminal acts. In order to provide a uniform measure of incident seriousness across the four courts and avoid the above-mentioned problems with use of the legal charge, I determined the seriousness of the criminal incident in each of the sampled cases by means of a measuring technique that assigns point values to objective aspects of the criminal incident.[14] Prosecutor and police files were consulted in each case to obtain this information. The sampled cases were then divided into four categories indicative of progressively greater seriousness, from category I, which included relatively minor property crimes such as theft of small amounts of money, to category IV, which encompassed the most serious crimes against the person—armed rape or homicide, for example.[15]

Table 6-1 sets out the way in which these sampled cases were disposed of in the four courts. It indicates the proportion of cases adjudicated in each court through guilty plea, nonjury trial, and jury trial.[16] For example, the Bronx column shows that of the 501 closed cases sampled in that court, 424 (85 percent) were disposed of by plea; 11 cases (2 percent) by nonjury trial; and 66 (13 percent) by jury trial.

The data in Table 6-1 suggest that all four courts dispose of roughly the same proportion of their felony cases by guilty plea—81 to 85 percent. This finding, at least at first blush, seems to indicate that our effort to choose courts with different plea and trial rates was unsuccessful. These figures are, however, aggregates, in which all of a court's cases are lumped together; this practice can be deceptive if courts have different proportions of serious and nonserious cases in their caseload. As indicated earlier, the problem is to ascertain how similar cases are handled in each court. If the four courts have different proportions of serious cases, and different proportions of defendants with prior criminal records,

Figure 6-1 Cases Going to Trial by Seriousness of Charge and Defendant's Prior Record, Actual Cases

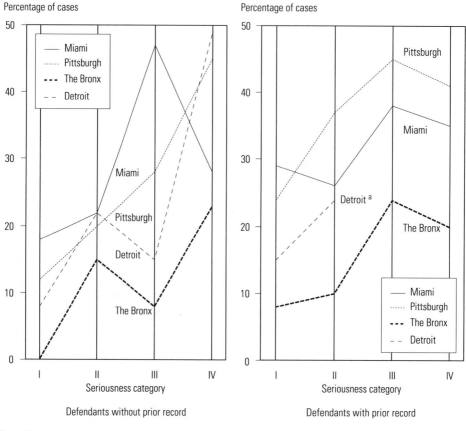

Percentage of cases

Percentage of cases

Defendants without prior record

Defendants with prior record

Note: Seriousness level increases from left to right.

[a] Too few cases to measure in two categories.

then lumping all the cases together may obscure intercourt differences in how similar cases are handled.

In order to address this issue, we need to separate the cases according to seriousness and defendant record and then see how cases in these more precisely drawn categories are handled in each court. The proportion (in percentages) of cases in each seriousness category that goes to trial in each of the four courts is shown in Figure 6-1.

The axes of both parts of the figure are similar: the vertical (y–) axis represents the percentage of cases going to trial. The horizontal (x–) axis represents increasing seriousness levels. For defendants with a prior record appearing in the Bronx court, for example, fewer than 10 percent in seriousness categories I and II were tried; the figure jumps to a bit more than 20 percent for seriousness categories III and IV. This situation contrasts dramatically with the situation in Pittsburgh, where the trial rate was at least twice as high for all categories of seriousness.

The data in Figure 6-1 reveal several important facts concerning mode of disposition in the four courts that were examined. First, it is apparent that case seriousness does affect mode of disposition in the direction suggested in previous research: although there are some exceptions, there is a clear tendency for the proportion of cases tried to increase as seriousness increases. This effect is present both for defendants with prior records and for those without, although the relation is less clear in this latter category.

More important, the data show that the surface similarity in the courts' trial rates in Table 6-1 was indeed a function of differing proportions of more and less serious cases in each court's caseload. The courts clearly diverge in the extent to which similar types of cases are tried. Furthermore, these differences follow a general pattern: in every category of case the lowest proportion of cases are tried in the Bronx. In all but the most serious cases, Detroit's trial rate is consistently 5 to 15 percentage points above that of the Bronx. And Miami and Pittsburgh almost always make more use of trial than Detroit and the Bronx.[17]

It thus appears from the actual case data that for most types of cases, the courts in Pittsburgh and Miami are more "trial oriented" than those in Detroit and, especially, in the Bronx. It should be emphasized, however, that trials are relatively uncommon for all types of cases in all four courts examined. Even in the courts that make the greatest use of trials, consistently fewer than half of the most serious cases—those most likely to be tried—were disposed of by means of a trial. The majority were handled through a guilty plea or its equivalent. In the next section, I examine whether these differences in actual behavior are related to attitudinal differences on the part of the lawyers and judges practicing in those courts.

Plea Bargaining Practices and Local Legal Culture

Earlier I described the hypothetical case questionnaire given to practitioners in the four courts examined in this research. Judges, defense attorneys, and prosecutors were asked to indicate how they believed a court with "adequate resources to deal with [its] caseloads in a fair and expeditious manner" should dispose of each hypothetical case. Figure 6-2 is a summary of how each type of practitioner responded to this question in each of the four courts. The y-axis in this figure measures the percentage of the twelve cases practitioners believed should be disposed of by trial (either jury or nonjury). As an example: Bronx prosecutors, on average, believed that roughly 23 percent of the hypothetical cases should be disposed of by trial; Miami prosecutors believed that nearly 40 percent of the hypotheti-

Figure 6-2 Preferences for Trial, Hypothetical Cases

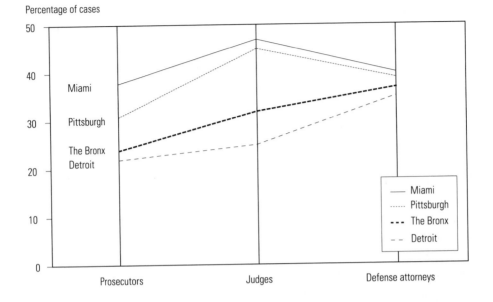

Percentage of cases

cal cases should be disposed of by trial. Interestingly, prosecutors and judges differ in attitudes across courts more than defense attorneys, whose preference for trial is quite similar from court to court.[18]

Figure 6-3 is analogous to Figure 6-2 but describes preferences for plea-bargained dispositions rather than trials. As in Figure 6-2, it sets out the percentage of the hypothetical cases that the average defense attorney, judge, and prosecutor in each city indicated ought to be handled through a negotiated plea of guilty. It should be noted that this graph is not the mirror image of Figure 6-2. Practitioners choosing the plea bargain response on the questionnaire were indicating their view that the case should be disposed of either through "a reduced charge, or sentence assurance, or both."[19] This reply implies that the defendant should receive a sentencing concession or at least an assurance as to what the sentence will be before he pleads guilty. Respondents, therefore, might consider a plea bargain to be inappropriate in a particular case but still not opt for a trial, the obvious alternatives being either a non-negotiated guilty plea or a dismissal.

Figure 6-3, describing normative support for plea bargaining, illustrates stark differences among the four courts in the views of both judges and prosecutors. The Detroit and, especially, the Bronx prosecutors and judges prefer plea bargains in twice as many cases as their counterparts in Miami and Pittsburgh. Defense attorneys, on the other hand, show a

Figure 6-3 Preferences for Plea Bargains, Hypothetical Cases

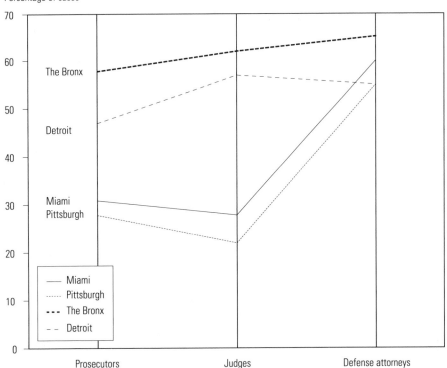

Percentage of cases

The Bronx

Detroit

Miami
Pittsburgh

—— Miami
.... Pittsburgh
- - - The Bronx
– – Detroit

Prosecutors   Judges   Defense attorneys

uniformly high preference for plea bargains in all four courts, even those from the "trial-oriented" courts of Miami and Pittsburgh.[20]

Figures 6-1 and 6-2 are illuminating on many dimensions. Perhaps most significantly, they illustrate that practitioners in all four cities believe that even an adequately funded, "fair and expeditious" criminal court system should dispose of relatively few of the hypothetical cases by trial. Furthermore, they provide little support for the notion that negotiated guilty pleas are considered by practitioners to be a necessary but illegitimate response to inadequate court system resources. The group with the *lowest* proportion of negotiated guilty plea responses—Pittsburgh judges—still believe on average that a quarter of the hypothetical cases should be negotiated and less than half of them tried.

These data support the notion that norms concerning the appropriate mode of disposition for particular types of criminal cases distinguish court systems. Furthermore, when Figures 6-2 and 6-3 are compared with Figure 6-1, there is general congruence. Detroit and the Bronx emerge as cities in which local courthouse norms support a relatively high proportion of guilty pleas and a low use of trial. Practitioners in Miami and Pittsburgh—particularly judges and prosecutors—are much more supportive of trial dispositions and less comfortable with negotiated guilty pleas. The lower proportion of cases actually disposed of by plea in those cities reflects these attitudes.

Although the data in Figures 6-2 and 6-3 suggest the existence of distinctive normative orientations in the four courts regarding proper mode of disposition, they also indicate that these norms are not uniformly held by different groups of practitioners in the same court. Attitudes of judges and prosecutors regarding dispositional mode separate the four courts far more than those of defense attorneys; indeed, the attitudes of defense attorneys in all four courts regarding preferences for both plea bargains and trials are remarkably similar. This similarity in defense attitudes is largely a result of unusually high levels of support for plea-bargained dispositions among defense attorneys in Miami and Pittsburgh.

Several summary observations can be made from these figures. First, the attitudes of practitioners regarding the appropriateness of trials in the hypothetical cases appear to be relatively consistent across practitioner groups within each court: judges, defense attorneys, and prosecutors practicing in a court share similar judgments regarding the kinds of cases that should be tried. And these communal orientations differ from court to court. When the focus is shifted to attitudes toward the appropriateness of plea bargaining in the hypothetical cases, intercourt differences increase, and in two courts (Miami and Pittsburgh), disagreement between defense attorneys on the one hand and judges and prosecutors on the other emerges.

One corollary of the legal culture hypothesis is the expectation of finding general agreement both within and across classes of practitioners in a given court. In other words, the notion of legal culture implies *shared* norms within a jurisdiction, not simply differences across courts. The preceding figures have relied on averages within courts and types of practitioners; but the average cannot tell us how much disagreement exists among the practitioners that make up that figure.

Agreement is in the eye of the beholder: statistics cannot provide an empirically derived breaking point indicative of its presence or absence in a particular group of respondents. Table 6-2 provides one method of looking at agreement within groups of practitioners in the same court. It summarizes data on the twelve individual cases in the questionnaire.

The strongest attitudinal agreement in all four cities relates to preferences regarding trial disposition. Agreement as to the appropriateness, or the inappropriateness, of a trial was achieved at the rather high level of 70 percent in six of the twelve cases in two courts and in five of the cases in the other two courts.[21] Attitudes regarding the appropriateness of plea-bargained dispositions are much less consistent within the courts. In only one city—

Table 6-2 Intracourt Agreement on Proper Mode of Disposition

	The Bronx	Detroit	Miami	Pittsburgh
Negotiated guilty plea [a]				
Most appropriate				
Cases with 3-group agreement[b]	2	1	0	0
Cases with at least 2-group agreement[c]	3	4	2	0
Not most appropriate				
Cases with 3-group agreement	0	0	3	2
Cases with at least 2-group agreement	2	2	7	8
Total cases with 3-group agreement	2	1	3	2
Total cases with at least 2-group agreement	5	6	9	8
Cases with substantial disagreement[d]	1	3	3	2
Trial (jury or nonjury)				
Most appropriate				
Cases with 3-group agreement[e]	0	0	2	0
Cases with at least 2-group agreement[f]	0	2	3	2
Not most appropriate				
Cases with 3-group agreement	5	5	4	6
Cases with at least 2-group agreement	5	7	6	6
Total cases with 3-group agreement	5	5	6	6
Total cases with at least 2-group agreement	5	9	9	8
Cases with substantial disagreement[g]	1	0	2	0

[a] Category includes diversion.

[b] Number of hypothetical cases in which 70 percent or more prosecutors, defense attorneys, and judges agreed that negotiated guilty plea would be most appropriate disposition (out of 12).

[c] Number of hypothetical cases in which 70 percent or more of at least two of the three types of practitioners agreed that a negotiated guilty plea would be most appropriate disposition.

[d] Number of hypothetical cases in which 70 percent or more of at least one group of practitioners indicated that a negotiated plea would be most appropriate and in which 70 percent or more of at least one other group indicated that some other mode would be most appropriate (that is, 30 percent or fewer indicated that a negotiated guilty plea would be most appropriate).

[e] Number of hypothetical cases in which 70 percent or more of prosecutors, defense attorneys, and judges agreed that trial would be most appropriate disposition.

[f] Number of hypothetical cases in which 70 percent or more of at least two of the three types of practitioners agreed that trial would be most appropriate disposition.

[g] Number of hypothetical cases in which 70 percent or more of at least one group of practitioners indicated that a trial would be most appropriate and in which 70 percent or more of at least one other group indicated that some other mode would be most appropriate.

Miami—was there substantial intracourt agreement on plea-bargaining preferences in as many as a quarter of the hypothetical cases.

Practitioners in the Bronx and Detroit tend to agree on cases that are appropriate plea bargains and are not appropriate trials; there is little agreement that any particular case is inappropriate for a plea bargain and virtually no agreement among types of practitioners that any case of the twelve should be tried. The situation in Miami and Pittsburgh is almost the reverse. Practitioners in these courts show little agreement over the appropriateness of plea bargains in any of the hypothetical cases; they agree that two or three of the cases are inappropriate for plea bargaining. As in the Bronx and Detroit, their strongest agreement comes in cases felt to be inappropriate for trial.

These observations support those made from both the actual case data and the summary evaluation of the hypothetical case questionnaires: the felony courts of Miami and Pittsburgh can be characterized as trial oriented, whereas those of Detroit and the Bronx emerge as negotiation oriented. These orientations affect not only the overall frequency with which practitioners choose particular dispositional modes as most appropriate, they also affect the type of agreement that is likely to occur on a particular case. Hence, these data suggest that it is much less likely for a prosecutor, a judge, and a defense attorney in the Bronx to agree that a particular case should be tried than would be the case in Miami and Pittsburgh. The opposite is true regarding agreement that a case should have a negotiated disposition. The differences in actual trial rates in the cities depicted in Figure 6-1 are congruent with these suggestions.

Implications

What are we to make of these findings? Or, in the words of that irreverent but essential question to be asked of all social research, So what? At a minimum, the hypothetical case data, together with the data on actual case dispositions in four courts, provide a useful corrective to the *Perry Mason* view of criminal courts. The actual case data describe courts in which the vast majority of criminal cases are disposed of by means other than trial. Fewer that 15 percent of felony cases were disposed of by trial in the courts examined. Indeed, the most trial-oriented court tried fewer than half of the kind of cases most in appearance on television courtroom dramas: those involving serious criminal incidents such as rapes and homicides. The vast majority of cases in these courts are handled by means of a guilty plea. And although we cannot determine from case records how many of these pleas were actually negotiated, all signs suggest that a great majority involved some form of plea bargaining.

Turning to the hypothetical case data, we see defense attorneys and prosecutors whose attitudes regarding the appropriateness of trial and negotiation differ markedly from those portrayed by Perry Mason and his prosecutorial protagonist, Hamilton Burger. All groups of practitioners in each of the four courts preferred a plea-bargained disposition in several of the hypothetical cases, although the judges and lawyers differed on this dimension both across and within courts. Indeed, the only issue regarding mode of disposition that the lawyers and judges in all four courts uniformly agreed on was the inappropriateness of trial in roughly half of the hypothetical cases. These data also provide at least a step toward an answer to the questions posed at the beginning of this chapter: Why is plea bargaining so pervasive? And why has elimination of plea bargaining proved so difficult?

The hypothetical case data generated in this study provide no support for the commonly held belief that plea bargaining is a result of case pressure, of overworked judges, and lawyers being forced to bargain in order to get through their overloaded calendars. Rather, the data suggest that judges and lawyers believe plea bargaining to be an appropriate and fair way to dispose of at least some portion of their cases, even in an adequately funded court. It would appear that plea bargaining is supported by judges and lawyers, not as a quick-and-dirty means of getting rid of cases, but as a desirable dispositional alternative for particular kinds of cases, independent of workload considerations. These findings are consistent with prior studies that show no relation between court workload and trial and plea rates. All in all, the research suggests that one reason for the pervasiveness of plea bargaining in American courts is a belief among lawyers and judges practicing in those courts that plea bargaining has an important place in even an adequately funded and properly functioning system of criminal justice.

This finding may explain at least a part of the history of failed attempts to eliminate plea bargaining. Local judges and lawyers must implement criminal justice reforms. And if these judges and lawyers believe that plea bargaining is the appropriate way to dispose of a significant proportion of criminal cases, their support and cooperation in attempts to eliminate the practice is unlikely. The result of such efforts is thus likely to be diversionary action to circumvent unwelcome alteration in the status quo. In fact, the criminal justice literature is replete with case studies describing just such successful actions by local practitioners to scuttle policies aimed at reducing or eliminating plea bargaining (Church 1975; Heumann and Loftin 1979; Nimmer and Krauthaus 1977).[22] As one candid judge described his response to a new prosecutorial policy of refusing to plea-bargain in drug sale cases: "When faced with an unpleasant policy, resourceful attorneys, assistant prosecutors, and judges will generally find acceptable ways to get around it" (Church 1975, 400; see, generally, Feeley 1983).

The hypothetical case data do not paint a picture of uniformity in attitudes concerning plea bargaining—either within courts or, especially, across courts. The attitudes of practitioners do follow actual dispositional patterns. Courts in which trials are less frequent tend to be courts in which practitioners tend not to opt for trial as the most desirable mode of disposing of the hypothetical cases. Alternatively, courts with high plea rates are populated by lawyers and judges who are more likely to view plea bargaining as the most appropriate means of disposing of particular criminal cases. But prosecutors and judges have substantial disagreements with defense attorneys regarding the appropriateness of plea bargaining in some of the hypothetical cases, particularly in the trial-oriented cities of Miami and Pittsburgh.

We are left, as in much social science research, with a mixed picture. We see a relation between dispositional patterns and practitioner attitudes regarding the proper mode of disposing of cases. We find substantial agreement in some courts, on some cases, regarding the most desirable mode of disposition. But we also see disagreement within courts that suggests that local attitudes regarding how cases should be disposed of are by no means uniform. At a minimum, the data presented in this chapter show the importance of looking at informal, attitudinal aspects of court systems if we are to understand how they operate. Such data reveal the inadequacy of popular views of criminal justice and suggest that some of the commonly suggested cures for the ailments of the criminal courts may not find support among the very practitioners who must implement them.

Notes

1. Judicial participation in plea-bargaining discussions is illegal in the federal courts and in some state courts. There are less formal norms against such activity in many more. Perhaps the most pervasive form of plea bargaining is what has been termed "implicit plea bargaining" (Heumann 1978), in which defendants plead guilty without explicit negotiations, simply in the belief that they will be treated more leniently if they plead guilty than if they ultimately contest their charges at trial.

2. The fifty-one systems include those of the fifty states plus the federal court system.

3. Courts with such high trial rates inevitably use proceedings before judges alone, without a jury, for most trials. See Schulhofer 1984.

4. Actually, researchers have used a variety of similar terms to describe the same phenomena: "local legal culture" (Church et al. 1978), "local socio-legal culture" (Neubauer et al. 1981), "community legal culture" (Eisenstein, Flemming, and Nardulli 1988). In the context of this research, *local legal culture* will refer to the practitioner norms governing case handling and participant behavior in a criminal court.

5. A more common type of questionnaire includes a series of statements on which respondents are asked to indicate the extent of their agreement or disagreement. For example, to assess support for plea bargaining, respondents could be asked to indicate the level of their agreement with the statement, "Plea bargaining is frequently an appropriate and just means of disposing of criminal cases." These summary statements are necessarily quite broad, and for the purposes of this research, I decided that hypothetical cases could better tease out the specific contours of legal culture.

6. This is the type of information contained in a police report that would be the basis for subsequent decisions by prosecutors and defense attorneys. One of the twelve cases is reprinted in the appendix to this chapter, along with the introductory section of the questionnaire.

7. In fact, the cases were not entirely hypothetical. They were drawn in broad outline from actual criminal cases filed in Detroit Recorder's Court. Particular aspects of the cases, such as the

presence or absence of evidence or the prior criminal record of the defendant were modified in some cases to provide variation on those dimensions.

8. The defense perspective was represented exclusively by state-funded defense agencies in the Bronx, Pittsburgh, and Miami. In each of these courts, between 70 and 90 percent of adult felony defendants were represented by such agencies. In Detroit the defense attorney sample was drawn from attorneys who were most frequently appointed by the court to represent indigent defendants, since the city maintains no public defender office. Sample sizes for each city and category of practitioner varied from 5 (Miami judges) to 42 (Miami prosecuting attorneys). The total number of questionnaires returned was 242. Fully reliable rates of return could not be calculated because questionnaires were usually distributed by office managers and the total number actually distributed was frequently unclear. Rates of return varied from 16 percent to 86 percent. For a discussion of the variation in response rates, see Church 1985, 454-456.

9. Because disposition time and sentencing were also being investigated in the project, the courts were chosen to present variation on these dimensions as well.

10. Once the courts were chosen, systematic samples were taken in each court to determine mode of disposition in a reliable and comparable fashion. In addition to the question on proper mode of disposition, reprinted in the text, there were questions on appropriate sentence if convicted and on proper disposition time. For a full report on findings regarding these other aspects of case disposition, see Church 1985.

11. Nolle prosequi is the decision of the prosecutor to drop criminal charges against the accused. The full text of one hypothetical case, and the responses provided for the mode of disposition question, are set out in the appendix to this chapter.

12. Case records frequently do not contain information that is critical in determining mode of disposition. For example, case records typically contain very sketchy information on the strength of the evidence against the defendant and on the defendant's prior criminal record.

13. Of course, the judge may sentence defendants only within the parameters allowed by the relevant criminal code for the specific conviction charge. Still, the sentencing ranges provided in the statutes usually give the judge substantial discretion as to the actual sentence imposed.

14. The scale was developed by two criminologists, Thorsten Sellin and Marvin Wolfgang (1964). It has been validated in other studies; see Roth 1978.

15. Category I included property crimes involving relatively small amounts of money and person crimes with little or no injury to victims (examples included assault in which medical treatment was unnecessary, burglary of less than $250, theft of a motor vehicle that was recovered undamaged). Category II covered property crimes involving larger amounts of money (burglaries and thefts of more than $250) and person crimes in which injuries required limited medical attention (assaults that required limited medical attention; armed robbery with one victim, no serious injury, and receipt of less than $250). Category III involved serious crimes against the person (assaults in which a victim required hospitalization, rape without the necessity of hospitalization of the victim or use of a weapon). Category IV encompassed the most serious crimes against the person: armed rape, homicide, armed robbery involving serious injury, multiple victims, or larger amounts of money. For a full description of the categories, see Church 1985, Table 3.

16. Included in the guilty plea category are cases resolved in some courts through "pretrial diversion," a practice in which a defendant is diverted from the courts by enrolling in a treatment program, such as one addressing juveniles or substance abuse. Excluded from the table were cases that were dismissed by either the court or the prosecutor.

17. Their respective positions are not consistent, however. Proportionately fewer defendants without criminal records are tried in Pittsburgh than in Miami, a situation that is reversed in most categories of cases involving defendants who have prior records. Category IV, which includes the

most serious crimes, exhibits the least stability in these patterns, particularly for defendants with no prior record. This may be due in part to the fact that this category contains a great deal of variation; homicides can differ substantially in subjective seriousness, for example, depending on such issues as provocation, premeditation, and so forth. This variation may lead to some of the diverse results.

18. The lines connecting participant types in each city do not imply any continuum between the values for prosecutor, judge, and defense attorney. After much experimentation, I determined that this somewhat unorthodox use of figures presented the clearest visual representation of these data.

19. See full text of responses in the appendix at the end of the chapter.

20. These differences are maintained when the hypothetical cases are separated into categories based on overall seriousness (defined in regard to the practitioners' views that a prison term is appropriate upon conviction) and strength of the evidence (defined in regard to the likelihood of conviction at trial). See Church 1985, 477-483.

21. The figure of 70 percent was chosen—more or less arbitrarily—as the point at which substantial agreement existed among a class of practitioners in the same court regarding appropriate mode of disposition.

22. Perhaps the most celebrated effort to eliminate plea bargaining came in Alaska, where the practice was outlawed and allegedly eliminated in the 1970s. Subsequent analysis suggests that some form of exchange system by which defendants are rewarded for their pleas existed throughout the period of elimination and that a more explicit system of plea negotiation grew up in the years following initiation of the reform. Compare Rubenstein and White 1979 with Clarke 1988.

Appendix: National Center for State Courts: Hypothetical Case Questionnaire

(The following are excerpts from the questionnaire used to gather the attitudinal data reported in this chapter.)

Instructions

This questionnaire includes descriptions of 12 hypothetical criminal cases. The information provided summarizes the prosecution's case against each defendant. Also included are antecedent information on the defendant and a brief indication of possible defenses where relevant. No short description can give the full information which a practitioner would require to evaluate an actual case. Please do the best you can with the information provided.

The questions that follow each case are designed to obtain your attitudes and beliefs concerning how the criminal justice system *should* operate, not necessarily how it does operate in this city. We thus are *not* interested in your prediction as to how these cases would be handled in this court. Rather, we want your own belief as to how they might best be resolved given adequate, but not unlimited, resources throughout the court system. . . .

Case #2

A. Complaint. On 8/1/79 at approximately 3:00 p.m. a male, 5 ft. 10 inches, 175 pounds, dark hair, entered Jones' Fried Chicken located at 123 Smith. He was wearing a wide-brimmed hat that partially obscured his face. He approached the service counter operated by complainant and said, "This is a hold up. Give me the money. I'm not playing." The complainant observed that the man had his hand inside a brown paper bag as though he had a gun in it. She took approximately $207 in assorted bills from her cash register and gave it to the man. The man them moved the bag toward the cashier at the next station, Witness A, who then removed approximately $170 from her cash register and gave it to the man. He placed all of the money into the paper bag and ran out the front door. Employees of the restaurant gave chase and the manager, Witness B, observed the subject get into a dark-colored car with license plate ABC 123 and drive away.

Police Officers C and D, patrolling the area in an unmarked car, observed the employees running out of the restaurant and stopped to investigate. They obtained information on the robbery and canvassed the area for suspects. They found the vehicle used for the escape abandoned in an alley nearby (the car was later found to be stolen).

B. Arrest. Approximately two hours later in further scouting the area Officers C and D, still driving in an unmarked police car, observed a Checker cab parked in front of a house four blocks from the scene of the robbery. On the front porch they observed a man answering the description of the man who robbed the restaurant.

The man looked up and down the street, then ran to the cab. Officers C and D followed the cab for several blocks, during which time the man looked furtively out the back window. The officers stopped the cab, showed their identification, and ordered the subject from the cab. He was patted down for offensive weapons and the fruits of the crime. The officers observed a large bulge in the defendant's left front pants pocket. They found it to be a roll of bills totaling $356. The defendant was taken to the police station and advised of his rights. He denied any knowledge of the holdup.

At 8:00 p.m. on the same day a lineup was held in police headquarters at which the complainant made a positive identification of the defendant as the man who robbed the restaurant. Witness A, the other cashier, was uncertain that the defendant was the robber. The defendant's lawyer was present at the lineup.

C. Witnesses.

1. Complainant will testify to being robbed and to identifying the defendant on the lineup.

2. Witness A (the other cashier) will testify to being present at the holdup and to the fact that the defendant looks "similar" to the robber. She can neither confirm nor deny that defendant was the man who robbed the restaurant.

3. Witness B (restaurant manager) will testify to being present during the holdup and obtaining the license number of the getaway car.

4. Officers C and D will testify to observing employees running out of the restaurant, to fact surrounding recovery of the getaway car, and to arrest of defendant.

D. Evidence. $356 in bills obtained from defendant

E. Defendant Information.

1. Age: 19
2. Prior criminal record:
9/17/77 Arrest: breaking and entering occupied dwelling (felony)
Conviction: larceny under $100 (misdemeanor)
Sentence: 10 months county jail; 1 year probation

F. Charge on Indictment. Armed robbery/felony

Questions on Case #2

1. Assuming that prosecution, defense, and the court have adequate resources to deal with their caseloads in a fair and expeditious manner, how do you believe this case should be resolved?

1. negotiated plea of guilty based on either a reduced charge, or sentence assurance, or both
2. guilty plea without charge reduction or sentence assurance
3. non-jury trial
4. jury trial
5. dismissal or nolle prosequi
6. other

[Questions followed on appropriate sentence if the defendant pled guilty, appropriate starting date for a jury trial, and probability of conviction at trial.]

7 Imagined Pasts: Sexualized Violence and the Revision of Truth

Kim Lane Scheppele

How do we know the past? We have tangible remains—photographs, bits of paper, torn clothes, the gun—but just think of all that is left out of those traces. And who gets to say what they mean? We also have records written at the time, but how do we know how accurate they are—or what someone writing the account could not or would not understand? We have our memories, but others' memories of the same event are often different. Mostly, we have our stories that we tell and retell, and the successive retellings reconfirm for us the truth of the story.

So, how do judges and juries know when they have found the truth about some event that happened in the past? Lawsuits are not just about the interpretation of the law; they are also crucially authoritative determinations of "what happened." But despite the difficulty of the task, judges and juries, like the rest of us, manage to operate every day as if the bases of factual judgments were clear and solid. While the idea of truth has been a contested subject among philosophers for as long as philosophy has existed, the idea of truth in daily life seems to generate much less debate. When asked to find "the facts" of a case, judges and juries do not puzzle over the meaning of that instruction. Why? The simple answer is that judges and juries, spectators and litigants, ordinary folks in the dailiness of life, and specialists in the creation of knowledge, "know truth when they see it." Within our own system of truth finding, some cases may be easier and others harder, but the idea of truth itself is rarely in doubt.

But what happens when the truth is contested, when the fault lines in people's understandings of truth run right along major social divisions? What happens when differently

I would like to thank Jane Bennett, Jerome Bruner, Sally Burns, Fernando Coronil, Peggy Davis, John Kitsuse, Richard O. Lempert, Jack Meiland, Francois Rochat, Roger Rouse, Theodore Sarbin, David Scobey, Peter Seidman, Richard Sherwin, Julie Skurski, and Scott Styles as well as seminar participants at the New York Law School, the New York University Law School Clinic, the Michigan Institute for the Humanities, the Stanford Humanities Center, and the Chicago-Kent College of Law for making me believe that earlier versions of this chapter were less adequate than later versions. A longer version of this article appeared under the title "Just the Facts, Ma'am: Sexualized Violence, Evidentiary Habits, and the Revision of Truth" in the *New York Law School Law Review* (1992).

situated social groups believe different accounts of the same event?

In this chapter, I focus on one element among many in the construction of facts that works to the disadvantage of women, particularly women who have suffered from sexualized violence at the hands of men: women who delay in telling their stories of abuse or who appear to change their stories over time about such abuse are particularly likely to be discredited as liars. The very fact of delay or change in the telling of the story is used as evidence that these new stories cannot possibly be true (DuBois 1988; Torrey 1991). But abused women frequently have exactly this response—they repress what happened (Veronen, Best, and Kilpatrick 1979); they cannot speak (Steinberg 1991); they hesitate, waver, procrastinate; they hope the abuse will go away.[1] They cover up for their abusers (Walker 1979, xvi, 74, 213), try harder to be "good girls," and take the blame for the abuse upon themselves (Scheppele and Bart 1983). When they begin to recover from the trauma, women produce delayed or altered stories (Herman 1992, 175-195), stories that are then disbelieved for the very reason that they have been revised.

The disbelief of delayed or changed stories reflects a view that the truth is singular, immediately apparent, and permanent, a view not unique to law. But the construction of facts in law is not based only, or even primarily, on the special expertise of lawyers or on detailed knowledge of the law. Of course, lawyers have a great deal of influence in shaping the facts as they appear at trial. But lawyers, at least successful lawyers, do not just mobilize their legal expertise to work out how to do this. They must also mobilize ordinary storytelling practices that are present outside legal settings, where credibility, coherence, and plausibility are all judged against a background of common knowledge, itself shot through with unexamined assumptions. In American public culture, we have seen this process in action a great deal recently, but nowhere more obviously than in the case of the Supreme Court confirmation hearings of Judge Clarence Thomas.

The Story of Anita Hill

During a riveting weekend of October 1991, large proportions of the American population tuned their television sets to the Supreme Court confirmation hearings of Judge (soon to be Justice) Clarence Thomas, hearings that had turned to the question of sexual harassment allegations against him by his former close aide, Professor Anita Hill. The Republican members of the Senate Judiciary Committee, unfettered by technical rules of evidence that would operate in a court of law, were able to show in stark form just how such a witness could be discredited. They used every strategy they could think of to undermine Anita Hill's testimony—the most effective one, arguably, centering on her delay in reporting the harassment and on the change in her accounts of what the harassment involved as she went through successive retellings of the story.

In the space opened up by Hill's silences and versions, Republican senators attempted to insert various "stock stories" (Lopez 1984; Shank 1991) about the scorned woman, the woman who had lost touch with reality, and the woman motivated by political animus who was making a bid for attention. These stories reveal some popular, common-sense biases in the evaluation of historical accounts, particularly where women are making claims that they have been the target of abuse. To see how popular conceptions of truth can be mobilized to discredit a witness, it helps to look first at the themes that politicians believe will work to undermine a claim and be understandable to the public. Then we can see how these same strategies are used in more formal legal settings in muted form.

Anita Hill's initial delay in reporting the harassment was particularly salient to the senators and to Judge Thomas. Judge Thomas himself emphasized Anita Hill's initial silence in his account of events:

I find it particularly troubling that she never raised any hint that she was uncomfortable with me. She did not raise or mention it when considering moving with me to EEOC [Equal Employment Opportunity Commission] from the Department of Education, and she'd never raised it with me when she left EEOC and was moving on in her life. And, to my fullest knowledge, she did not speak to any other woman working with or around me who would feel comfortable enough to raise it with me.[2]

Trying to put her initial silence in some context, Professor Hill explained how she reacted to Judge Thomas's conduct at the time:

My reaction to these conversations [that were of a sexual nature] was to try to avoid them by eliminating opportunities for us to engage in extended conversations. This was difficult for me because I was his only assistant at the Office for Civil Rights [in the Department of Education]. . . . When Judge Thomas was made chair of the EEOC, I needed to face the question of whether to go with him. I was asked to do so, and I did. The work itself was interesting, and at that time it appeared that the sexual overtures which had so troubled me had ended. I also faced the realistic fact that I had no alternative job.

Professor Hill testified that she talked to close friends about the harassment, but she did not speak to anyone at work. And some of the people to whom she confided the sexual harassment allegations at or close to the time testified on her behalf. But because she had not spoken to anyone official about the alleged harassment at the time, she was distrusted by the senators.

The senators also made a major point of noting how Hill's account of what had happened changed as she reported the story to the Federal Bureau of Investigation (FBI) agents who took her initial account, then repeated the story to the Senate committee staffers, then repeated the story live on television. Because she added new details with each account, they concluded that she could not be trusted to tell the truth. Thomas spoke of these worries:

The facts keep changing, Senator. When the FBI visited me, the statements to this committee and the questions were one thing. The FBI's subsequent questions were another thing, and the statements today as I received summaries of them were another thing. It is not my fault that the facts changed. What I have said to you is categorical; that any allegations that I engaged in any conduct involving sexual activity, pornographic movies, attempted to date her, any allegations, I deny. It is not true. So, the facts can change, but my denial does not.

Thomas clearly was trying to use the idea that statements that remain the same are more reliable than statements that appear to change. He was asserting that his categorical denials were more true than Hill's "changing" facts precisely because his denials had never been subject to revision.

Sen. Arlen Specter's (R-Pa.) questioning of Professor Hill tried to establish crucial inconsistencies and additions, markers of falsehood of the whole account. One statement, surgically cut from its context, was compared with another, similarly surgically cut. Hill, sensing that her story was getting lost in the false concreteness of specificity, told Specter:

I guess one really does have to understand something about the nature of sexual harassment. It is very difficult for people to come forward with these things. . . . And it wasn't as though I rushed forward with this information. I can only tell you what happened and, to the best of my recollection, what occurred and ask you to take that into account. Now, you have to make your own judgment about it from there on, but I do want you to take into account the whole thing.

The *whole* story, Professor Hill argued, was more than the particular details.

Hill's initial silence and then multiple versions of the story left the Senate Judiciary Committee with a lot to pick apart. And much of the strategy of those who won by getting Thomas through the confirmation process and onto the Supreme Court depended on presenting him as the victim of an invented story. They accomplished this in large measure by presenting Hill's story as suspiciously revised after long delay.[3] The Hill-Thomas hearings were not a judicial forum, but the tactics used in an attempt to discredit Hill's testimony borrow both from the courtroom and from daily life.

Silences and Revisions

Anita Hill is not the only woman to have remained silent about sexual harassment. Most women do not report sexual harassment at all. Women who experience rape, domestic abuse, incest, and other forms of sexualized threats and sexualized violence have much the same reaction. When women first talk about the unspeakable to others, they often present initial accounts that try to make things normal again and to smooth out social relations, by minimizing the harm of the abuse, by engaging in self-blame, by telling stories that offer alternative explanations of events so that the full consequences of the abuse do not have to be dealt with at the time, and by disguising the brutality through descriptive distortions.

In psychological terms, women who have been sexually assaulted, whether through rape, incest, domestic brutality, workplace harassment, or extended periods of "domestic captivity" (Herman 1992, 74-76) often show signs of post-traumatic stress disorder. Survivors of extraordinary brutality often literally cannot say what they have seen or put into words the terror that they have felt. Picking through the shards of a former life, survivors can no longer put the pieces into relation with each other to tell a coherent and compelling narrative about the events that occurred. As therapists who have worked with traumatized patients have noted, "the survivor's initial account of the event may be repetitious, stereotyped, and emotionless. . . . It does not develop or progress in time, and it does not reveal the storyteller's feelings or interpretations of events" (Herman 1992, 175). As women's sense of safety in the world has been shattered, so too has their sense of narrative coherence (Scheppele and Bart 1983).

Later, however, brutalized women revise their stories. Women who were silent about the violence, or who said at the time that nothing happened, or who took the blame themselves for anything that did, begin to tell stories of abuse. As these stories are told with more confidence, they "may change as missing pieces are recovered. This is particularly true in situations where [the survivor] has experienced significant gaps in memory" (Herman 1992, 179-180). What the survivor is trying to do at this point is to figure out a story that makes sense of her memories, and that process of making coherence out of previously fragmented knowledge results in adjustments in the details that are recalled or in the way the details are put together. One sign of recovery from the abuse is that women's stories change over time.

Although the influence of extreme trauma on narrative consistency over time is quite pronounced, lesser traumas may produce something of the same effect. Women who have experienced sexual harassment at work also report many of the same symptoms as women who have suffered more extreme forms of physical abuse (Kirstein-Ezzell 1991). Women who have been "merely hassled" also show signs of extreme stress and sometimes leave work or drop out of school without giving explanations. Even Anita Hill, who stayed on the job and tried to ignore the harassment she later publicly described, "was hospitalized on an emergency basis for five days for acute stomach pain which I attributed to stress on the job" (Miller 1994). Eventually, the accounts of what produced the stress may change as the details emerge from a traumatized memory and as the world feels a safer place in which to tell complete stories.

But we should not see this problem of shifting stories as being only a psychological response to individualized events. Larger forces are in play that provide a social and cultural context in which shifting stories appear as a response to sexualized threats and sexualized violence—and in which the threats and the violence are themselves displaced and denied through the fact of delayed accounts. Psychological explanations may be able to tell us how the individually experienced events are cognitively managed, but we need to understand more about the historical and cultural setting to understand why those cognitive strategies seem so compelling in the first place.

Stories that shift in their focus, detail, or attribution of blame through time may be a response to violence that is not "supposed to" happen. Such violence, however, may be common. For example, despite the facts that systematic domestic abuse of women occurs in about one-quarter to one-third of households in the United States (Dobash and Dobash 1979) and that nearly one woman in three will be raped at some point in her lifetime,[4] woman battering and rape are still portrayed as unusual occurrences that need special explanation in the individual case. The normal case is constructed as the nonviolent marriage or the unraped woman, and the battered or raped woman stands out against this picture of normality as an exception. Exceptions are generally explained by models that emphasize deviance from a norm, and the woman subjected to "deviant" practices comes under the spotlight as a participant, perhaps even a willing participant, in deviant conduct. The woman is examined to see if she is to blame. If violence is "not supposed to happen," then it may be hard for a woman to narrate the violence credibly because she must first explain to herself why this particular "I" was singled out for the violence that was not supposed to happen and why this particular "he" did this. To construct such a story, a woman must fight the stereotypes, unless she can cast her experience as a socially comprehensible narrative (Estrich 1987).

The stereotyped stories about sexualized violence that are familiar in American culture are stories of provocation, passion, deranged character, or insanity, told against the backdrop of the assumed rationality of all conduct.[5] People do things for reasons, we learn to believe. If a man is violent, he must have had a reason. Perhaps he was provoked (and it is really the woman's fault). Or perhaps it was evidence of passion (and then perhaps the woman brought it on). Or perhaps it is a "character issue," and the accused is a sexual deviant, a pervert, or a criminal type. Or perhaps he did not have a reason, in which case, he is crazy.

Given the evident social competencies of many men who harass, beat, rape, or assault women, the stories that emphasize insanity or serious character defects are not readily believable.[6] Only "real rapes," those that are committed by strangers, often with weapons, against random women (Estrich 1987), are arguably good candidates for the insanity narrative. That leaves passion or provocation as available, believable narrative strategies for the routine, daily violence that women often experience. But passion narratives contradict the methodical, systematic form that abuse often takes as the man escalates the violence in response to a series of violated threats. Provocation narratives put the blame back on the woman, saying she started it. And women often do tell stories of self-blame and complicity, if they say anything at all, at the time that sexualized violence occurs (Scheppele and Bart 1983). If the victim eventually rejects these options, she may, in a new story, recognize such violence as common, not her personal and individual fault, and this will put the explanatory focus back on men's frequent uses of sexualized and violent methods for getting what they want from women.

These later, revised stories lose their social authority as a statement of truth precisely because they are late in arriving. And they lose their legal power also, for the same reason. Revised stories present problems in law because one of the implicit rules juries and judges use for finding stories to be true is the same rule that the Senate Judiciary Committee invoked in the Hill-Thomas hearings: to be believable, stories must be told immediately and must stay the same in repeated tellings. Truth is supposed to be fixed and stable. Real truth does not shift with time.

Erasing Sexualized Violence in Court

If these presumptions in favor of the immediate stories are deeply part of the way our culture determines facts outside of formal law, then we would expect to see revised stories discredited when women press claims of sexualized violence in court. And this is exactly what happens.

Take *Reed v. Shepard* (1991), for example. JoAnn Reed worked as a "civilian jailer" in the Vandenburgh County (Indiana) Sheriff's Department, beginning in mid-1979. In 1984, Reed was fired, without a hearing, for alleged misconduct in her job, for which there was substantial evidence. She sued on multiple counts, one charging that before she was fired she had been sexually harassed on the job in violation of Title VII of the Civil Rights Act. The story she told about sexual harassment appeared to her co-workers to be revised. According to the trial judge:

Plaintiff contends that she was handcuffed to the drunk tank and sally port doors, that she was subjected to suggestive remarks . . . , that conversations often centered around oral sex, that she was physically hit and punched in the kidneys, that her head was grabbed and forcefully placed in [officers'] laps, and that she was the subject of lewd jokes and remarks. She testified that she had chairs pulled out from under her, a cattle prod with an electrical shock was placed between her legs, and that they frequently tickled her. She was placed in a laundry basket, handcuffed inside an elevator, handcuffed to the toilet and her face pushed into the water, and maced. Perhaps others. (*Reed*, 1991, 486)

"The record confirms these and a number of other bizarre activities in the jail office," the appeals court added. "By any objective standard, the behavior of the male deputies and jailers toward Reed revealed at trial was, to say the least, repulsive" (*Reed,* 1991, 486).

Why, then, did the court go on to conclude that, however offensive the conduct of her male co-workers was, it was *not* sexual harassment? Because, the court found, the conduct was apparently not repulsive to Reed *at the time:* "Reed not only experienced this depravity with amazing resilience, but she also relished reciprocating in kind. . . . Many witnesses testified that Reed revelled in the sexual horseplay, instigated a lot of it, and had 'one of the foulest mouths' in the department" (*Reed,* 1991, 486-487). Moreover, the court noted, Reed never told the men to stop at the time. Why? Reed testified at trial:

Because it was real important to me to be accepted. It was important for me to be a police officer and if that was the only way that I could be accepted, I would just put up with it and [keep] my mouth shut. I had supervisors that would participate in this and you had a chain of command to go through in order to file a complaint. One thing you don't do as a police officer, you don't snitch out [sic] another police officer. You could get hurt. (*Reed,* 1991, 492)

By the time she reached the court, after having been fired, Reed was telling a story that she had been abused. And the Seventh Circuit Court of Appeals did not believe her.

The court indicated that harassment must be so severe or pervasive as "to alter the conditions of [the victim's] employment and create an abusive working environment" (*Reed,* 1991, 491, quoting *Meritor Savings Bank v. Vinson,* 1985, 57) if a claim is to succeed. But to show that this conduct was "in fact" harassing, the victim of such treatment had to indicate *at the time* that she did not welcome the behavior in question—and this Reed had not done. In other words, contemporaneous evidence is required to establish any claim of sexual harassment, and this requirement is part of the legal rule. The judges obviously believed a revenge narrative, one in which a bitter employee recast "horseplay" as "abuse" in order to get back at her co-workers.

But another narrative is possible here. Women who have experienced sexual harassment say, as Anita Hill said, that they want to keep their jobs (Mahoney 1991, 1992). They want the abuse to stop, but they also do not want to make waves (Lewin 1991). They want to fit into the workplace environment as if they really belonged there. And to fit in, they endure the abuse.[7] If women's greatest fears in complaining about sexual harassment are that they will be fired, then the greatest barrier against bringing a complaint is eliminated when they lose their jobs. But victims whose accounts are revised can be blamed for bringing everything on themselves because their narrative instability makes the later story unbelievable.

Exceptions That Reveal the Rule

While the pattern described above is the general rule, there are certain special cases in which revised stories can be presented as credible. Such exceptions include (1) cases in which multiple women establish a pattern of conduct on the part of a particular man, (2) cases in which corroborating physical evidence is available to back up the woman's later account, and (3) cases in which an expert reconstructs the woman's initial story as a delusion because the woman is experiencing stress. It is to these exceptions, the exceptions that demonstrate the solidity of the rule against revised stories, that we now turn.

Safety in Numbers

If women are to be believed when they revise their stories, they have a better chance if they find safety in numbers. Reconstructing as nonconsensual a sexualized relationship that appeared consensual at the time is hard to do in a credible manner. Women typically find that they have to establish that their experience was part of a pattern that other women experienced as well. One example can be found in *Daly v. Derrick* (1991).

In September 1977, when she was fifteen years old, Maura Daly found herself the center of attention of one of her male teachers, who, on a school retreat, initiated a sexual encounter (*Daly* 1991, 709). This initial contact grew into an ongoing relationship that Maura described as a love affair. Her only discomfort at the time in the relationship was that her teacher, Tommy Derrick, also showed a great deal of interest in some of her friends. Nearly a decade later, Daly sought therapy because she was having "sexual difficulties" with her current boyfriend. In the course of therapy, she mentioned that she had been "molested" by a high-school teacher. Later, she filed a lawsuit against Derrick for damages for the harm he had caused her.

This case is one of a growing number now being brought as a result of the "delayed discovery" of childhood molestation. Young girls engage in sexual relationships with older men, sometimes because of force, sometimes because of intimidation, sometimes because of flattery and attention. Sometimes, they may feel that the sexual advances are inappropriate, but they may not know how to articulate this as a conscious matter. Occasionally, a girl claims to enjoy the sexual encounters at the time, valuing the attention they bring. Years later, often in therapy, the now-grown woman "learns" for the first time that this was abuse.

In *Daly* the court was called upon to decide whether the lower court had been correct in throwing out the case on the grounds that more years had passed since the incident than the statute of limitations would allow. Ruling that some of the facts relevant to the case had been only recently discovered and that the statute of limitations did not begin to run until the last relevant fact was discovered, the court let the case proceed. The final outcome of the trial, however, is not recorded.

The *Daly* case presents a stark case of a revised story. Daly clearly thought at the time that her relationship with Derrick was romantic, consensual, and wonderful—usually. Only later did she come to believe that this relationship was abusive and that he had taken advantage of her innocence and immaturity. Although the court allowed her to sue, Daly would probably have had a hard time establishing her initial nonconsent. But she had help.

As it turned out, two other women had experienced the same treatment from Derrick while he was their high-school teacher. In fact, all three of these women were friends in high school and had not realized that Derrick had a sexual relationship with each of them at the same time. Only after Maura Daly came to see Derrick's treatment of her as abusive did Daly's mother then make inquiries and find that two other high-school classmates of Maura's had similar stories to tell. They joined the lawsuit.

Why should three women revising their stories in the same way be more believable than one woman doing this alone? In the case of a lone woman accusing her former lover of abuse, it is easier to tell a stock story about a particular relationship gone sour. But when there are three such relationships that were all being maintained at the same time in an apparently monogamous culture, then each woman appears entitled to adjust her story to take into account the fact that Derrick was misrepresenting to each of them just what the specific relationship was at the time. Derrick's violation of another norm, the norm of monogamy, makes the violation of norms about abuse seem more plausible. He can be constructed as a deviant all around, not the innocent man whose former lover now takes advantage of a convenient feminism to turn him into a monster after the fact. With three women providing evidence of collective misrepresentation, Derrick looks less like a poor guy with bad judgment in relationships and more like a predator. He can be distinguished from ordinary men, who are supposed to engage in one relationship at a time. By finding safety in numbers, women may be able to have their revised stories appear credible.

Corroborating Evidence

Revised stories may also be believed when other evidence, preferably physical evidence, corroborates the changed story. If a revised story is to be credible, it needs something more than itself as proof. For example, in *Simmons v. State* (1987), the Indiana Supreme Court upheld a rape conviction even though the victim told inconsistent stories. First, she said that she had been taken from the Payless Supermarket to the Grandview Golf Course, where she was raped. Later, she said that she started at the Anderson High School parking lot and eventually wound up at some nearby railroad tracks, where the rape took place. The woman later said she was afraid of the rapist, and that was why she had lied. But it helped that the woman had never seen the defendant before the attack, that she had been abducted with the understanding that he had a gun, that he had threatened her with a knife and a heavy pipe during the rape, and that the defendant also stole her car. But most significantly, the police found the pipe with which the defendant had threatened her in the grass by the train tracks. The physical evidence of the pipe and the stolen car backed up her revised story and made it believable.

Expert Testimony

Sometimes a victim's changed story of sexualized abuse can survive scrutiny with the assistance of expert witnesses. These expert witnesses generally testify that the victims of sexualized violence suffer from a form of post-traumatic stress disorder and therefore have first reactions that are not to be trusted, allowing later accounts to be believed.

For example, early one April morning in 1986, L.S. was still sleeping when her former boyfriend, Gregory Frost, appeared in her bedroom (*State v. Frost* 1990). He had broken into her house. As she started to wake up, he hit her. Their baby began to cry, so L.S. picked up the child and ran to the front door to escape. Before she was able to open the door, Frost caught up with her and cut her arm deeply with a razor-edged box cutter.

The relationship between Frost and L.S. had been plagued by Frost's frequent outbursts of violence against L.S., and she estimated that he had hit her at least once per month during the time they had been romantically involved, starting on the second day that they knew each other. Police testified that she had called them to the house at least nine times to stop his violence. After suffering through three and one-half years of battering, L.S. had left Frost and obtained a restraining order to keep Frost away from her and the baby. Eventually Frost was sent to prison for theft from another person. L.S. had been responsible for his arrest in that case and, on the day he broke into her house and cut her with the razor, he had just been let out of prison. His first act as a free man was to seek revenge.

But to everyone who saw her the day of this attack, L.S. had told a different story. At the hospital, where she was given fifteen stitches, L.S. said that she cut her arm on the refrigerator. To others, she said she was fine. She told her mother not to worry. After the stitches, L.S. and Frost were seen spending the day together.

At his trial, on charges of assault, breaking and entering, and violation of the restraining order, Frost claimed that L.S. had agreed to spend time with him that day, which he thought should cast doubt on any claim that he had broken in and attacked her that morning. To respond to this, prosecutors introduced expert testimony to the effect that L.S. was suffering from battered woman's syndrome, an identifiable medical condition that made it impossible for her to leave him.

The effect of the expert testimony was to provide a context within which a jury could believe that all the things L.S. said on the day of the attack were motivated by fear. Such a fear-induced account could be overridden by a revised story later. Without this expert testimony, however, a jury might reasonably conclude, as Frost tried to argue, that she was now trying to get Frost in trouble because they had had a falling out after a pleasant day.

Expert testimony can be very helpful to women in situations like this. But it comes at a price. Such testimony is effective with jurors because it gives them an explanation for a victim's conduct at the time in question by saying she is suffering from a form of mental illness. The victim may have thought things were going to get better, she may have thought he loved her, she may have thought that she wanted to be with him, but she was wrong, deluded, and not a good judge of these things at the time. All this, the expert says, is the result of temporary mental incapacity. The expert allows a woman's revised story to be believed, but at the cost of making her out to be a woman who could not know her own mind.

The Problem of Truth in Law

American courts assume that ordinary citizens know how to find the truth because facts are supposed to be found by juries without specialized training (Scheppele 1988). But truth finding is a culturally complicated and socially situated practice. That means that we all have a set of habits, practices of truth finding, that tell us when a particular story seems more credible or true than another. Never mind that we are often dead wrong in assessing credibility of accounts, regardless of our experience (Ekman and O'Sullivan 1991; Bennett and Feldman 1981). Most of the time, we are successful enough (or blind enough to the consequences of our inaccuracies) not to reevaluate our practices. Whenever we obviously fail at it, we engage in a patch-up effort to work out what went wrong in the particular case, but we rarely reevaluate our entire scheme for evaluating the evidence with which daily life presents us.

So, what do people operating in the legal process see when they are presented with evidence? What interpretive conventions do judges and jurors invoke when called upon to figure out "the facts" of cases? Like the rest of us, judges and jurors bring "evidentiary habits" with them everywhere they go (Bennett and Feldman 1981; Jackson 1988; Papke 1992).

Judges and juries decide whether a particular story is true by evaluating *how the story is constructed* rather than by working out whether the story has a "real" referent out there in the world that gives the story its truth. Of course, this process invokes culturally based expectations about what sorts of stories are credible in the first place, about what seems normal and what seems strange. This is not to say that the reconstruction of the past is completely an exercise in writing fiction. One can have a sense of faithfulness to evidence and still be only assessing the internal properties of stories. And that is what passes for fact, both in life and in law. Stories that stay the same through many retellings are thought to be particularly reliable, and stories that change are not.

Why is this? In courts, judges and juries cannot match testimony against events in the world to see whether the account corresponds to them because events are long over before cases come to trial, and the "reality" in question is not around to provide the match, if such a thing could be done. Most of the time, all that is left over from historical events are accounts by people who were present at or otherwise involved in the event. But the particular "true" story that is selected by judges and juries from among a set of arguably accurate versions of reality may provide a very different impression about what happened than another account that could have been selected just as well. The vexing question is not just whether the descriptions are accurate in some way, although it is crucially important to screen out lies, but rather how it is that some particular description rather than some other comes to be forwarded as the authoritative version of events (Goodman 1978; Sherwin 1988). This raises questions of power and ideology, of the "situatedness" of the descriptions that pass for truth and the social agendas they support (Barrett 1991; Haraway 1991).

All accounts are narratives, and as such they represent strategies for both organizing and making sense of evidence (Bruner 1990, 1991; Carr 1986; Sarbin 1986). No story represents "perception without conception," for there is no such thing. The first versions of stories are *not* merely raw material, processed by the mind without interpretation, that are shaped into revised stories through interpretive processes absent the first time around. We do not first see things "as they are" and then interpret them (Wittgenstein 1976, 194). We "see" with the interpretive frameworks we bring to events as much as we see with our eyes. But when we change interpretive frameworks, especially when the new frameworks create new accounts of blame, others may see us as making things up. But why should we prefer and therefore privilege the first framework that the victim happens to have over another framework that might be brought to bear on the event with more reflection?

Our reluctance to accept revised stories as true is all the more puzzling when we consider that most people believe that reflection aids accuracy in everything but reports of perception. For example, *considered* preferences are usually thought to be more reliable than preferences listed off the top of one's mind. And ethical judgments that have been weighed for a period of time are better than "snap judgments." Even academic papers that have been through revisions are considered better, more polished, than those that have not been through the process of revision. Why is it, then, that reports of "facts" are not similarly thought to be improved with reflection and thought?

We learn to describe as *true* the impressions we have at first because they appear to involve no conscious alteration, even though there may be a physical basis for other reports of those perceptions. Nelson Goodman (1978, 92) suggests that most of us, when we report seeing a round table from an angle, still describe it as round, even though our eyes are perceiving the shape as oval because of the angle of our vision. Clearly, there is a large element of construction, however rapid and implicit, even in the most apparently uncontroversial descriptions. But our first accounts may appear to be "simply" true because they appear to involve no work, whereas revised versions seem to involve a conscious attempt to "make sense" of what has happened. Of course, we are making sense all the time, even before we have had a chance to reflect self-consciously on the sense we are making.

This contrast between a picture of pure and untainted perception (a first account) and an alternative picture of a contaminated and altered (revised) account should now appear naive. If all narratives are constructions and all descriptions make use of concepts and categories that are made available through the cultural location one occupies, why should we privilege the *first* framework that this particular narrator happens to bring to the description of events? In the context of sexualized violence, where a victimized population of women has come to see such abuse as a persistent feature of daily life, saying that initial stories are the only believable accounts amounts to saying that the guilt or liability of a potential defendant rests on the defendant's choice of victim. Women who have accepted continuing victimization with the resignation of self-blame and denial can be abused without anyone's being able to gainsay such women's initial narratives of complicity. When women learn that they do not have to put up with such treatment, however, they see their own pasts differently. But such reconstructions are then discredited as lies. For women who need time to understand what has happened to them because they have learned to accept sexual violence as a feature of daily life and to blame themselves for it as a first-pass explanation (Scheppele and Bart 1983), the exclusion by courts of revised stories works disproportionately against women who are socialized into believing that everyone is reasonable but themselves.

The first stories we tell are not constructed in the absence of frameworks that help us to make sense of what has happened; they are simply constructed with our most unthinking frameworks. My argument does not imply, however, that all revised stories should be believed. It does call into question the believability of first impressions only because they are closer in time to the events in question. Strategies of belief need to be more complicated than we have previously recognized to do justice to the complex conditions that shape our understandings of reality.

Notes

1. Most women do not report sexualized threats and sexualized violence against them. In one survey conducted in San Francisco, only 9.5 percent of the women reported the rapes that had occurred to them (Russell 1984, 31). Estimates of underreporting indicate that only 5 to 50 percent

report rapes (Amir 1971, 27-28; Scheppele 1987, 1097-1098). Of those who do report, many delay before calling the police. One New York source says that most victims wait two to seven days before reporting a rape, and a Massachusetts study reported that half of the rape victims waited before reporting (cited in Torrey 1991, 1013). Apparently, women tend to wait even longer if they know their assailant (Katz and Mazur 1979, 188-190; Torrey 1991). Only about half the domestic violence victims report what has happened to them (Waits 1985). And researchers at Cornell University found that less than 1 percent of female sexual harassment victims filed complaints (cited in Mango 1991). In one government study, researchers found that 52 percent of female sexual harassment victims ignored the harassing conduct and did nothing about it (U.S. Merit System Board 1988, 24).

2. Unless otherwise indicated the quotations in this section come from the Thomas nomination proceedings before the U.S. Senate's Committee on the Judiciary (see Miller 1994).

3. Public perceptions of Hill's story themselves changed over time and varied with different audiences at the same time. Although a majority of the American public at large believed Thomas at the time of the hearings, a survey of judges revealed that two-thirds of them believed Hill at the time (Armstrong 1991). A year later, however, several surveys revealed that more people believed Hill than believed Thomas by 44 to 34 percent, whereas the year before those figures stood at 40 percent for Thomas and only 24 percent for Hill (Smolowe 1992). A *U.S. News and World Report* poll reported a 38-38 percent dead heat in credibility ratings one year after the hearings, whereas polls at the time of the hearings registered 60 to 20 percent in favor of Thomas. Significantly, the percentage that thought Hill had been treated unfairly rose from 8 percent at the time of the hearings to 39 percent a year later (Borger, Gest, and Thornton 1992).

4. This figure is contested. Johnson (1980), using FBI statistics and very conservative assumptions, estimates that 20 to 30 percent of women between twelve and seventy years old will experience a rape attack in her lifetime. Russell and Howell (1983), using somewhat less conservative assumptions, estimate that 46 percent of women will be victims of a rape attack at some point in their lives. A lower estimate can be found in Laycock (1991).

5. Many people believe that most rapes would not happen if only women did not provoke them. Nineteen percent of Anglo men, 25 percent of Anglo women, 73 percent of black men, 23 percent of black women, 32 percent of Mexican-American men, and 70 percent of Mexican-American women believe this to be true (Williams and Holmes 1981, 135, table 17). Check and Malamuth (1985, 416) report that up to 40 percent of both men and women indicate that it is acceptable for a man to force a woman to have sex with him if she has gotten the man sexually excited. When asked whether rapists were "sick, emotionally disturbed men," Williams and Holmes (1981, 136, table 18) report that 91 percent of Anglo men, 92 percent of Anglo women, 83 percent of black men, 98 percent of black women, 87 percent of Mexican-American men, and 63 percent of Mexican-American women believed that this was the case.

6. "Despite . . . numerous efforts to identify ways in which rapists are abnormal, the results have generally indicated very few differences between rapists and nonrapists which would justify any conclusion that rapists are grossly abnormal" (Check and Malamuth 1985, 415).

7. Only 9 percent of women in one survey quit their jobs immediately when harassment started, although more quit later when the harassment escalated (Farley 1978). Another source reports that fewer than 5 percent of sexual harassment victims report the harassment or take other action (Tangri, Burt, and Johnson 1982).

8 The Fired Football Coach
(Or, How Trial Courts Make Policy)

Lynn Mather

Ten years ago, a woman named Rose Cipollone gave a deposition in her suit against three cigarette manufacturers for damage to her health. "I thought it was cool to smoke, and grown-up." Then, she added, "I got hooked." A few months after her deposition Mrs. Cipollone died of lung cancer, so she never knew she had become the first person to be awarded damages—$400,000 to her widower—in a smoking liability case ("A Killing Silence" 1994, A24).

In *Cipollone v. Liggett Group* (1984) Rose Cipollone presented a claim against cigarette manufacturers to obtain compensation for her family for the pain and suffering from her smoking and resulting illness. Although her dispute was an individual one, she was invoking legal norms about harm and product liability to construct and present her case, and her case was publicly argued in a federal trial court in New Jersey. The trial jury's decision to award nearly half a million dollars to her husband was based on the ground that the cigarette companies had misrepresented the risks of smoking. The jury's decision was unprecedented, and indeed, it did not last. The Third Circuit Court of Appeals overturned the ruling, but even after a legal victory at the U.S. Supreme Court, the Cipollone family could not afford the legal fees of a retrial.[1] Since then, the tobacco industry has continued to argue successfully in countless lawsuits that smokers knowingly assume any risks associated with cigarettes and that no conclusive proof exists that smoking caused an individual smoker's illness. The industry has preserved its boast that it has never paid a cent to any smoker who has sued it. That boast may be coming to an end, however.

In spring 1994, members of Congress intensely questioned tobacco company executives about the addictive power of cigarettes. Despite the executives' denial of addictiveness, a "smoking gun" was discovered in the form of internal documents from a major tobacco corporation (said to have been stolen by a former employee of a law firm working for the corporation) that showed that the tobacco executives had known for decades of the addic-

I am grateful to many colleagues for their helpful suggestions and comments on an earlier version of this chapter (Mather 1991). Thanks also to Iris Chiu, Chad Fischer, and Gregory Garre for their research assistance.

170

tive power of nicotine and of the link between cigarette smoking and lung cancer. Then, on August 2, 1994, an advisory panel of the Food and Drug Administration (FDA) rejected the arguments of the tobacco industry to the contrary and voted to declare that nicotine in cigarettes is addictive (Hilts 1994a, A1). This decision allows the FDA, if it so chooses, to regulate cigarettes just as it regulates other drugs. Action by the FDA against cigarettes for their addictive qualities, along with the damaging evidence from within the tobacco industry showing it knew long ago how hazardous and addictive its products were, could lead to more jury rulings like the decision in Rose Cipollone's case. And with more plaintiff victories against cigarette manufacturers, more lawsuits can be expected.

Public health leaders and antismoking lawyers hope that the pressure and cost of litigation will eventually bankrupt the tobacco industry just as the lawsuits by the victims of asbestos-caused diseases succeeded in pushing the $2 billion asbestos manufacturer, the Manville Corporation, into bankruptcy.[2] Indeed, the legal team representing Mrs. Cipollone had extensive experience in litigation against asbestos manufacturers for the illnesses their product caused workers who were exposed to it. And it was the asbestos litigation that sparked the whole wave of smoking lawsuits that began in the 1980s (Rabin 1993). A second wave of smoking lawsuits seems to be building now. "More than 60 suits are now [November 1994] under way in courts around the country, the largest number of anti-tobacco suits ever heading into court at the same time" (Hilts 1994b, 42). Plaintiff lawyers are pooling their resources in class action litigation and are planning to use in court new evidence on nicotine addiction.

While federal legislative and regulatory actions are being debated, and as individuals and lawyers pursue litigation against the tobacco industry, state governments are also taking action to develop new smoking policy. Florida, for example, recently changed its law to allow the state to file a class action lawsuit on behalf of all Medicaid patients in Florida who suffer from smoking-related illnesses.[3] A class-based lawsuit has a greater chance of success than an individual one because of the statistical evidence on demographic health and illness that can be introduced at trial. By facilitating litigation over illnesses that result from smoking, the statute is designed to hold cigarette manufacturers responsible for the health care costs that their products produce. A 1994 state health report found that smoking-related illnesses cost Florida at least $1.2 billion in Medicaid payments since 1989. In signing the bill, Gov. Lawton Chiles declared, "We're going to take the Marlboro Man to court." Florida is anticipating legal challenges to the bill from the tobacco industry, but Governor Chiles predicts eventual victory: "I think this will go through all kinds of legal tests, but at the end, I don't think the tobacco companies are going to be able to brag any longer that they have never paid out a dollar in a lawsuit." Other states are expected to follow Florida's lead, and Mississippi has already filed a similar class action lawsuit against thirteen tobacco companies under existing common law.

As I follow these dramatic events in the political struggle to define and resolve the problem of smoking, I am impressed by the significance of trial courts in the policy process that has been unfolding. The *Cipollone* case contributed to a new way of thinking about the legal responsibility of cigarette manufacturers. The particulars of the case attracted media attention and raised public consciousness about the issues, and the initial victory by the Cipollones and the success of the asbestos lawsuits mobilized other litigants and lawyers to legal action. Robert L. Rabin, a law professor, expresses skepticism, however, about the likelihood of ultimate success of this individual-based litigation strategy against the tobacco industry. He contrasts the dismal record of litigation in the last decade (*Cipollone* remains the only case thus far with a financial judgment against cigarette manufacturers) with the much greater progress made through legislative and regulatory agencies (for example, smoking restrictions in the workplace, restaurants, and public transportation), which have defined the smoking problem as one of collective public health (Rabin 1993). Yet the more successful framing of the issue—as an issue of public health—could still be achieved through judicial proceedings in cases such as Florida's intended class action lawsuit.

The antismoking campaign at present seems to be using a combination of legislative, bureaucratic, and judicial strategies, with state and federal trial courts playing an important role in the policy process. A common textbook view, however, holds that appellate courts make policy and trial courts generally do not (Ball 1987; Carp and Stidham 1993; Jacob 1984). Trial judges, especially at the state level, are seen simply as administrators or bureaucrats who routinely process thousands of individual, private disputes and petty criminal cases. Trial judges are not, except on rare occasions, considered to be policy makers. Despite the frequency with which this view is argued, I think it is fundamentally misguided both for its narrow understanding of the process of policy making and for its incomplete portrayal of trial court activity.

Hence, to me, the key question is not whether trial courts make policy; rather it is how they do so. To address this question, I construct a view of trial courts that emphasizes their political functions and highlights their role in shaping public policies. I draw on the public policy literature and on research about disputing and the mobilization of law to expand our thinking about trial courts as policy makers. In this broader view of trial courts we attend to the behavior of litigants, lawyers, clerks, juries, and audiences to litigation rather than just focusing on the decisions of trial judges. In suggesting the various ways in which trial courts make public policy, I review some of the sociolegal research on litigation strategies, lawyer-client interaction, dispute transformation, pretrial negotiation, the media and trial courts, judicial decision making and the politics of juries. In the last part of the chapter, I illustrate my argument on trial court policy making by analyzing a particular case: a lawsuit brought in New Hampshire by a football coach, Joseph Yukica, to challenge his firing by Dartmouth College.

What Is Policy Making?

The view that trial courts do not make policy rests on a narrow and outdated definition of policy making—namely, the conscious establishment of a new rule or standard for handling problems. Adopting this definition, Herbert Jacob (1965, 1984) was among the first to suggest that only appellate courts engage in policy making, while trial courts function largely as norm enforcers. He explained the distinction this way: "Policy decisions [of appellate courts] are intended to be guideposts for future actions; norm-enforcement decisions [of trial courts] are aimed at the particular case at hand" (Jacob 1984, 37). But, because of the nature of the court process, judicial decisions in trial courts (and usually in appellate courts as well) are nearly always expressed as solutions to "the particular case at hand." Consequently, there will rarely be direct evidence of trial court policy making under a definition that focuses solely on the declaration of a new rule.[4] Where such evidence is found, it is more likely to come from federal trial judges than state judges. Thus, there are some well-known decisions of U.S. district court judges, such as Judge Frank Johnson's order requiring reform of state mental health facilities in Alabama or Judge Stephen Roth's order of cross-district busing to integrate Detroit schools (Cooper 1988). These decisions, however, are depicted as exceptions to the general rule of norm enforcement by trial judges.

A contrasting view of trial courts recognizes how the accumulation of similar individual decisions defines policy just as much as one major decision. Martin Shapiro (1970, 44) argues that any attempt to identify judicial policy making by "the single court decision or the single opinion of the single judge" will miss the aggregation of individual decisions that constitute the "massive, central bodies of judicial activity." Trial judges, just like most appellate judges or administrative decision makers, engage in policy making more often through "the day to day power over small decisions rather than the ability to change dramatically the whole course of government" (Shapiro 1964, 41-42). Thus, a broader definition of policy making, such as "the patterns of impact created by the aggregate of decisions" (Davis and Dolbeare 1968, 242), has led other judicial scholars to give trial courts a much greater policy-making role. Henry R. Glick (1983, 278) discusses the idea of "cumulative policy making" as an "alternative to viewing trial courts mainly as norm enforcers." In this view, trial judges engage in policy making whenever they take a consistent point of view in their decisions, regardless of whether the judges are consciously aware of the policies they create. For example, when judges exercise their discretion to dismiss routinely certain kinds of cases or issue particular court orders, or when they consistently sentence criminal offenders in certain ways, they are creating policies for their communities (see Stumpf 1988).

In the final analysis, the answer to the question, Do trial courts make policy? depends simply on the definition of *policy making* invoked in the discussion because a broad definition tends to give trial courts a significant policy-making role whereas a narrower one does not.[5] Recent literature on public policy provides some guidance here, endorsing a broader definition and suggesting even more inclusive ways in which we should consider the concept of policy making.

First, central to any modern-day treatment of the concept of policy making is an insistence on including the entire policy process, rather than limiting consideration to any one stage of the process. In particular, policy is not made only at the moment a new rule or decision is announced but instead begins from the initial point of problem definition, through the formulation of alternative solutions, to the adoption of a course of action and its final implementation. The process of making new health care policy, for example, has included various definitions of the health care problem; task force, interest group, and expert formulations of alternative plans; and perhaps the adoption of some new health care bill by Congress and the president. Policy analysts typically define the policy-making process as a *series of different stages*. As phrased by Bullock, Anderson, and Brady (1983, 5), these stages include "problem formation, policy agenda, policy formulation, policy adoption, policy implementation, [and] policy evaluation." The process may not be as neat and orderly as conveyed by this sequence of stages, but a real strength of this approach is its broad view of the policy-making process and its rejection of definitions limited solely to the stage of policy adoption.

Second, by recognizing the differentiated nature of policy making, we can avoid the mistake of even imagining that any single political actor or institution could command the entire policy process. That is, public policy is made through the actions and interaction of different political players at different points in the process. Just as Congress may be stronger or weaker than the president on certain issues or at certain stages of policy making (Price 1985), so may the courts be most influential at particular points. Thus, as I wrote earlier, the question is not, Do trial courts make policy? but rather, How (or, in what ways or at what stage in the process) do trial courts make policy? Although trial courts rarely establish new legal rules, they do constitute the actual meaning of legal rules and, in addition, they play an important role in the definition of policy problems, in the formulation of alternatives, and certainly in the implementation and evaluation stages of the policy process.[6]

Third, the policy process is not unidirectional and linear such that one begins with problems and ends with solutions (or the evaluation of those solutions). Feedback loops, interactional effects, and the reverse notion of solutions creating problems, must all be included in any model of policy making. That is, problems that are on policy makers' agendas for action do not arrive full-blown; instead they are socially and politically constructed, and solutions may in fact produce problems. Malcolm Spector and John I. Kitsuse (1977, 84, 128) show how solutions lead to problems "by providing the framework within which those problems can be stated" and how "a prospective solution makes possible the existence of a problem by proposing that some obnoxious aspect of life, heretofore thought to be unalterable ('nothing can be done'), might be alleviated." Trial court outcomes, whether the result of trial or a negotiated settlement, may alert others with a similar "unperceived injurious experience" (Felstiner, Abel, and Sarat 1981, 633) to voice their grievance, with either legal or political action. Rose Cipollone's short-lived trial court victory, for example, signaled others to consider a legal solution for something that previously had been taken for granted as unalterable. Just hearing about someone else's legal claim can change how people view their own problems and, through these changed perceptions, contribute to the collective formation and identification of a problem for public policy. Likewise, awareness of the possible benefits of litigation may lead one to search for an appropriate legal claim to obtain those benefits, a process that parallels occasions of policy making in which one sees "a solution first and then formulates a problem to require the solution" (Stone 1988, 9).[7]

Finally, it is important to remember, as Deborah A. Stone points out, that policy making is fundamentally about ideas:

[T]he essence of policy making in political communities [is] the struggle over ideas. . . . Ideas are at the center of all political conflict. Policy making, in turn, is a constant struggle over the criteria for classification, the boundaries of categories, and the definition of ideals that guide the way people behave. (Stone 1988, 7, emphasis added)

Policy making, in short, is a dynamic process in which political actors do more than just establish standards, solve problems, or allocate resources (although they do all of those as well). That is, they construct, maintain, and change the political order of communities through continual processes of negotiation about the identification and solution of problems. Making policy involves competition over a normative framework for understanding events and relationships and for shaping identities and expectations, as much as it provides the resources and rules for responding to competing claims. Using a definition of policy making that includes the struggle over ideas and the boundaries of categories, we can see more clearly how trial courts make policies and we can better understand the importance for policy making of litigants, lawyers, juries, and trial judges.

Dispute Transformation in Trial Courts

Just as appellate courts make policy by creating categories (such as "fair trial," "clear and present danger," or "fundamental rights") and defining those categories through the classification of various fact situations as within or outside of the category, so do trial courts make policy by defining the categories of "reasonable man," "unfit parent," or "normal burglary" through the repeated disposition of cases. Note that it is in the informal and formal handling of cases by lawyers and judges—not only in the trial judges' decisions—that we should look for this policy activity. Since well over 90 percent of trial court cases are settled without trial, it makes little sense to exclude from consideration the bulk of what occurs in trial courts. Given that lawyers play a central role in case negotiations, we must broaden our investigation of trial court activity beyond the judge to include lawyers and others. Richard S. Wells and Joel B. Grossman (1966) first noted that most notions of judicial policy making were too judge-centered, and since then considerable research (especially on dispute processing and legal mobilization) has demonstrated the importance of nonjudicial participants in trial courts. Current political science work that does acknowledge trial court policy making, however, still limits the discussion to judicial decision making.

Instead of starting with trial court outcomes, we should begin with a disputant's choice to begin legal action. When citizens translate their desires or problems into legal terms, they are mobilizing the law (Zemans 1983). Going to court can be seen as one of several political alternatives for asserting a claim, and indeed, historically, litigation can be understood as an alternative form of political activity (McIntosh 1983). When voicing and responding to claims in trial court, disputants rephrase their concerns to take advantage of the leverage provided by law. Parties in a lawsuit, for example, argue how their claim is similar to (or different from) another legal case, in an effort to obtain the desired outcome. Legal rules are created out of the process of determining similarity and difference among cases, and thus the parties and their lawyers as much as the jury and judge participate in lawmaking (Levi 1949). In presenting their cases to the court, the parties frequently argue about the criteria for classification and the boundaries of categories. For instance, in the case of *Virginia v. Bobbitt*, when Lorena Bobbitt cut off her husband's penis after his repeated acts of marital rape, did her action fall within the category of "temporary insanity" or not? Debate in the specific case shapes the general legal policy, so that the jury's decision to acquit Mrs. Bobbitt by temporary insanity can affect future cases.

A court case is not an objective event or thing but is itself a social and political construct. Disputes that enter court are reformulated or transformed into legal language (for example, a car crash becomes a "tort," a beating becomes an "assault") to facilitate their handling by the legal system (Mather and Yngvesson 1981). *Dispute transformation* refers to change in the form or content of a dispute as a result of the involvement of other participants in the dispute process (Mather and Yngvesson 1981, 777).[8] As disputes—or cases—go into and through the legal system, they change continually as the result of negotiations over interpretation of facts and events. Although a car crash may be a discrete, objective event, the lawsuit that the event gives rise to is a subjective, social construct that may look one way to the victim who files a legal claim, another way as depicted by the defense lawyer before trial, and a third as described by the judge during trial. Even more important, dispute transformation inevitably involves ideas, values, and legal norms, as fact situations are defined in one or more particular normative frameworks. The policy significance of changes that occur in the disputing process lies in the systems of meaning, or categories for classification, used to define and redefine legal claims and disputes.

Courts typically transform cases by imposing conventional categories for classification on events in dispute, that is, by *narrowing*. For instance, lawyers and judges narrow cases by classifying them according to their own particular system of "normal crime," "routine debt," or "ordinary divorce." With the classification comes an expected mode for handling and a typical outcome. Consistent patterns of case outcome in local courts (referred to earlier as cumulative policy making) result from this narrowing of cases. Sometimes, however, courts expand or shift the framework of argument to challenge conventional understandings. Dispute *expansion* changes the normative framework used to interpret events by rephrasing them into a new system of meaning. Thus, an "ordinary" case of parental child abuse is reinterpreted as a case of family discipline based on strong religious faith; or a "routine" firing of an incompetent employee is transformed into an instance of discrimination; or a "typical" hired-gun murder becomes self-defense by a battered wife. Cases may be expanded through the efforts of litigants, their supporters or lawyers, judges or juries, or an audience to the litigation; and legal change is linked to social change in part through the expansion of individual disputes (Mather and Yngvesson 1981).

As others besides the litigants become involved in a case, they bring their own interests, perspectives, and agendas to bear on it. Throughout the court process, the definition (as well as the resolution) of a case is negotiated and renegotiated by various parties. A central problem becomes how to assert and maintain control over the object in dispute. Clearly, the power to transform cases is not equally distributed in court, and tensions frequently arise between lawyer and client, opposing lawyers, lawyer and judge, judge and jury, or even between the court and the wider community. Understanding policy making as it occurs in trial courts involves attention to struggles over the nature and meaning of a case.

The language used to define disputes is of particular importance. The language of law provides the framework in which to present arguments and fix the meaning of disputes. Further, through imaginative use of the linguistic framework, new juxtapositions can be arranged that may change the meaning of old terms. The language in which a case is phrased not only affects its outcome but also connects directly to the political order. For instance, calling an incident a "family fight" suggests the inappropriateness of court action and likely dismissal of charges, but defining the same event as "domestic violence" indicates a serious problem both for the individuals involved and for the polity. "Legal words and practices are cultural constructs which carry powerful meanings not just to those trained in the law" (Merry 1990, 8-9), hence the importance of understanding law as language.[9]

Attempts to create new orderings require linguistic as well as political strategies because those who wish to expand a dispute to change policy must consider public reactions to their formulation. In considering how problems come to be viewed as important and appropriate for political action, Roger W. Cobb and Charles D. Elder (1983, 38) observe that the language of the disputants is "a crucial element in determining the likelihood of an issue attaining access to the political agenda." Another crucial element in agenda building is the scope of the conflict. By enlarging the audience to a particular case, lawyers or interest groups, for example, can change the balance of power in the courtroom (see Schattschneider 1960). Issues that might otherwise be narrowed in conventional ways have greater potential to be redefined through the implicit participation of a wider audience. Defense attorneys are well aware of this strategy, of course, and in high-profile cases we often see attorneys speaking more to the media than to courtroom officials.

By combining these ideas about public policy and dispute transformation, we can see numerous ways in which trial courts contribute to policy making (see also Gambitta 1981). How trial courts make policy is summarized in Table 8-1. Clearly, a judicial decision to adopt a new law is only *one* out of a wide range of policy activities that occur in trial courts. Other important aspects of court policy making include the definition of political problems (including the attention and legitimacy given to the problem by society), the construction of solutions to problems (through the creation of local norms and the implementation of law), and the feedback and evaluation of policy (through the response to litigation and the filing of new legal claims). Note that court cases can contribute to policy making at any stage of the litigation, and at any stage of the policy process. Thus Table 8-1 does *not* depict a developmental sequence of policy making whereby a case begins with "agenda setting" and concludes with the "provision of political or legal resources," although such a sequence could happen.

Policy Making in Trial Courts

To show how trial courts make policy, I review some previous research on courts and present an extended case study of my own. Drawing first on the literature about trial courts, I provide examples of how courts contribute to problem definition, agenda build-

Table 8-1 How Trial Courts Make Public Policy

Aspects of policy making	Examples in trial courts
Agenda setting	Case screening defines what is a "legal" matter and what is not; what is "serious" and what is not.
	Litigation encourages others to file similar claims in same court and elsewhere.
	Interest groups file "test cases" to place issue on agenda of courts.
Forum for political argument	Courts provide public arena for discussion of political issues.
	Cases contribute to definition of policy problem and formulation of alternatives.
	Litigation offers occasion to explain ideas and express beliefs.
Agenda building	Particulars of case publicize issue and attract audience.
	Court hearing gives legitimacy to issue and to litigants.
	Court cases influence agenda of other political actors (appellate courts, legislatures, etc.).
	Media devotes attention to problem through news analyses, talk shows, docudramas, etc.
Mobilization of support or opposition	Litigation arouses sympathy or aversion in mass public.
	Cases spur interest groups to political and legal action.
	New interest groups are formed to lobby issue.
	Political participation increases to address problem.
Definition of local legal norms	Judicial and jury fact-finding leads to construction of local legal categories.
	Norms are set through routine classification of cases (dispute narrowing) in legal negotiation.
	Appellate and statutory law is adapted and implemented for local community.
Creation of new legal norms	Judicial activism leads to new case law.
	Juries substitute their own norms for the formal law (for example, jury nullification).
	Novel legal issue forces judges to create new law.
	Legal framework for interpreting events or relationships changes through dispute expansion.
Political symbolism	Cases act as metaphors for broader problem.
	Individuals and groups associated with litigation attract wider coalitions or cleavages.
	Language of case shapes debate on the policy issues.
Provision of political or legal resources	Groups and individuals benefit by the publicity and legitimacy given their cause.
	Use of legal "rights" provides bargaining leverage in conflicts.
	People change their behavior to avoid potential litigation.

ing, the formulation of alternatives, and the adoption and implementation of policy. This discussion is organized according to conventional steps in the trial court process: filing a legal claim; negotiation; adjudication; and impact of the case. In the last section, I analyze the events and policy implications of *Yukica v. Leland* (1985), a New Hampshire lawsuit about a broken employment contract.

Filing a Legal Claim

The initial decision to file a lawsuit is highly complex, as sociolegal research has clearly shown. Whether someone with a grievance will even seek a lawyer depends on such factors as the person's perceptions of the law, of the court, and of the issues in conflict; the alternatives to law for resolving the dispute; the nature of the relationship between the person and the other party (for example, strangers or not); the goals and resources of the person; and the person's cultural attitudes toward law and conflict.[10] Lawyers then play a critical role in translating issues and events into legal discourse and in adding their own concerns, interests, and beliefs to those of their client (Cain 1979; Mather and Yngvesson 1981). The interaction between lawyer and client is one influence on the final construction of the legal claim (Rosenthal 1974; Sarat and Felstiner 1986); others may be economic concerns (Johnson 1981), cultural norms (Engel 1984), and political interests (Olson 1984).

In a small rural county in Illinois, called Sander County by the researcher, David M. Engel (1984), relatively few personal injury claims were filed in the civil court. A major reason proved to be a reluctance to use tort law for injuries because of deeply ingrained attitudes among most of the residents. These attitudes were reflected—and reinforced—by the local lawyers of the county and by the decisions of trial judges and juries, which tended to give very low awards in such cases. Engel writes that traditional values of individual responsibility, hard work, and self-sufficiency help to explain community pressures against personal injury litigation. That is, most residents felt that to transform a personal injury (even when the fault of another) into a financial and legal claim was an attempt to avoid personal responsibility and an inappropriate effort to cash in on misfortune. In contrast to these negative attitudes and infrequent use of tort law for injuries, however, litigation over broken contracts (even for "routine" debt collection) was quite common (nearly ten times as frequent as personal injury litigation) and met with wide approval. Engel explains that contract litigation "was seen as enforcing a core value of the traditional culture of Sander County: that promises should be kept and people should be held responsible when they broke their word" (Engel 1984, 577).

If we try to evaluate the Sander County civil court using the framework of norm enforcement, we quickly run into the question of which norms are being enforced—the legal norms established by the Illinois Supreme Court and legislature, or the norms of Sander County? By Engel's account it is clearly the latter. In effect, the public policy in Sander

County on personal injuries was adopted and implemented through a complex process—in and around the state trial court—involving an aversion by most victims to define their problems as legal ones because of the social meaning of personal injuries, stigmatization of those few victims who did file legal claims, a reluctance of local lawyers to bring personal injury actions, and hostility toward personal injury plaintiffs by local juries.

The role of civil litigants and private lawyers in shaping civil law is similar to that of victims of crime, police, and prosecutors in shaping criminal law. In particular, police and prosecutors establish criminal law norms for their local communities through their routine policies on arrest and case screening. For example, in the early 1970s the district attorney's office in Los Angeles had an official policy of filing misdemeanor, rather than felony, charges for all offenses with particular fact situations: "possession of dangerous drugs" if ten pills or less; "possession of marijuana" if five cigarettes or less; "assault" if between family members; "bookmaking" if there was no suspicion of organized crime involvement; and so forth (Mather 1979). This policy was written and circulated within the office after the policy had been used for several years as a set of informal guidelines. Other district attorneys' offices in California defined their own—and often very different—policies on the level of charge to be brought and on dismissal of (or refusal to file) charges.[11] Consequently, although the California legislature had adopted general criminal statutes for the entire state, the actual criminal law policies for a given area were determined by prosecutors who set criteria such as these for classifying and assigning meaning to various behaviors. Prosecutors are not entirely free in constructing criteria for case screening, however, since they operate in a close working environment with police, defense attorneys, and judges and are constrained as well by the political and social context of their communities (see Cole 1970; Eisenstein and Jacob 1977; Flemming, Nardulli, and Eisenstein 1992).

In some communities the decision to issue a criminal complaint is made by a lay magistrate, the court clerk, to whom both private citizens and police (if there has been no arrest) must apply. Barbara Yngvesson (1988) describes the politics of this process in neighbor and family conflicts in the "Jefferson County" district court in Massachusetts. When citizens come to the court with their complaints and disputes, the clerk's role is to act as watchdog, distinguishing between "real" criminal conflicts that are worthy of the court's time, and "garbage" cases that require mediation or advice by the clerk but do not merit the issuance of a complaint. The clerk typically dominates the hearings, Yngvesson reports, "by controlling the language in which issues are framed, the range of evidence presented, and the sequence of presentation. He silences some interpretations and privileges others, constructing the official definition of what constitutes order and disorder in the lives of local citizens" (1988, 410). For instance, a complaint by one citizen of assault and threats by another child on her daughter was transformed by the clerk into normal behavior among children (Yngvesson 1988, 434-435). But even while the clerk is helping to define norms and construct the community, community residents are using the clerk and the power of the courthouse to further their own interests in various social and political conflicts, and it is by this interaction that "court and community are mutually shaped" (Yngvesson 1988, 410; see also Yngvesson 1993).

In these examples, the cumulative acts of filing a legal claim, filing criminal charges, or issuing a criminal complaint defined the issues for consideration by the trial courts of Sander County, Los Angeles County, and Jefferson County. This "routine" agenda setting involved important political decisions to define some conflicts as legal matters and other conflicts as essentially private. Even where certain public policies (such as personal injury law or felony statutes) were clearly established by other branches of government, they could not be implemented unless claims on those policies were voiced and then admitted into court by private lawyers, public prosecutors, or court clerks. Moreover, given that "whoever decides what the game is about decides also who can get into the game" (Schattschneider 1960, 105), it is clear that such case screening significantly affects not only the problems to be considered but also the balance of power among different groups and individuals.

Control over the agenda of trial courts is not entirely in the hands of lawyers and legal officials, however; the participation of citizens in voicing their grievances also plays a role. At a very basic level, lawyers need clients to stay in business, and prosecutors need public support to stay in office. But even further, there is an interaction between citizens bringing their demands to legal officials and the decision of those officials to transform private demands into public discourse. For example, when many rape victims had their complaints summarily rejected by prosecutors as not involving "real" crimes, women victims were effectively denied access to the "game" of the criminal courts. The modest improvement that has occurred in the courts' response to rape complaints is only partly due to increased sensitivity and changed consciousness of legal officials. It has also resulted from women's willingness to pursue their grievances in court; the readiness of those at support centers to act as advocates for victims; pressure exerted on officials from political leaders, interest groups, and the courts themselves; and changes in state laws and in ideas about rape and its social meaning.

Sally Merry's (1990) study of court use by working-class plaintiffs shows how they turn to court as an alternative to violence or to the local political authorities, but when they arrive in court they find that their personal problems are not interpreted with the same seriousness by court officials. Instead, the plaintiffs—mostly women—are given advice or referred to mediation. "Court officials," she writes, "endeavoring to provide what they consider justice, convert these problems from legal to moral or therapeutic discourse" (Merry 1990, 179). Questions of where the boundary lies between public and private problems, of how to identify those disputes that are worthy of legal discourse, and of how to classify cases appropriate for court action are questions that are intensely political and fundamentally concern policy. Feminist scholars have been at the forefront in raising these questions, building on the 1960s refrain that the personal is political (see Merry 1990; Minow 1990).

Customary frameworks for classifying certain disputes as "legal" and rejecting others develop their strength through repeated use; but they also change—usually in slow, incremental ways—through their imposition on new and different disputes. Sometimes such change results from an otherwise uneventful case, for example, through publicity that attracts an audience and influences the actions of regular court participants. Media attention, for instance, can disrupt a quietly arranged plea bargain with an alleged child molester and force a prosecutor to proceed harshly and aggressively instead. At other times, litigants or their lawyers consciously seek policy change and plan their litigation strategy accordingly in order to raise new arguments, obtain publicity, gain supporters, and, if not to achieve actual legal change, at least to gain greater legitimacy for their views. Lawyers are critical actors in either situation. They are important politically not just because they seek to advance their clients' interests but because they interpret ideas, struggle with classifications, and at base "work on the law" (Harrington 1994, 56).

Test cases sponsored by social reform organizations are a classic example of policy making in trial courts through the filing of legal claims. Beginning with the litigation campaign started by the National Association for the Advancement of Colored People (NAACP) on behalf of desegregation and continuing through the later use of courts by consumer and environmental organizations, interest groups have used trial courts for the express purpose of defining issues, arguing their cause, formulating solutions, and working generally toward a change in public policy (Handler 1978; Vose 1959).[12] Social reform litigation has increased in frequency in recent years and has also shifted somewhat in style and strategy as a result of greater "rights consciousness," expansion of statutory and regulatory remedies, and easier access to the judicial process for articulating group interests (Olson 1984, 4-5).

In her study of lawsuits brought by disability rights groups to gain access to mass transit, Susan M. Olson shows how litigation merges with political activity outside the courts and how conscious political strategies shape decisions about the form and content of litigation. For example, she describes interest groups "stacking the plaintiffs," a process of choosing the most appealing representative of their claim and also of enlarging the class of plaintiffs to increase their size and their diversity (a kind of "ticket balancing" of plaintiffs) (Olson 1984, 13-16). The disability rights organizations in the lawsuits for accessible transit were especially active clients in the litigation, participating significantly in decisions about case filing and settlement strategy.

In contrast, litigation strategy in class action lawsuits tends to be determined almost exclusively by lawyers. Class actions, an alternative to organizational lawsuits for aggregating large numbers of plaintiffs, are fascinating legal devices that depend on the initiative of a lawyer for their creation. In effect, an entrepreneurial lawyer can create a class—an abstract, formal entity—for the purpose of litigation and, through the class action, can conceivably enforce legal rights against the wishes of class members (Garth 1982). The most successful class actions, however, are likely to be those in which the lawyer not only facilitates access to the courts but also engages in political education and organization of the class members (Paul-Shaheen and Perlstadt 1982). Class actions that both achieve and sustain some kind of policy change tend to combine political and legal strategies; that is, using litigation as a political resource can help mobilize the class, attract supporters to the cause, and change the normative framework of the wider policy debate (Mather 1982; Scheingold 1974).

Lawsuits about pay equity (or comparable worth) during the late 1970s and early 1980s provide an excellent example of litigation acting as a catalyst for a social reform movement: by mobilizing support for the policy; by attracting extensive publicity; by developing legal consciousness about the issue among female workers as they learned to "name" the problem causing their lower pay; and by encouraging other workers to seek pay equity remedies either through collective bargaining or through litigation (McCann 1994). Use of litigation for policy change is not just a strategy of liberal or feminist groups, however (Epstein 1985). Antiabortion legal activists, for example, have pursued various test case strategies to overturn *Roe v. Wade* (1973), in which the U.S. Supreme Court legalized abortion (Horan, Grant, and Cunningham 1987). One of these strategies centers on establishing the legal rights of the unborn in contexts unrelated to abortion. This strategy is being put to the test in state and federal courts around the country in cases involving injury to a pregnant woman (can the fetus recover damages?) or drug consumption by a pregnant woman (is she guilty of delivery of drugs to a minor?).

In sum, the simple act of filing a legal claim in a state trial court can have enormous political—and policy—significance. It may constitute a step in creating new ways of thinking about a problem or it may reaffirm conventional norms. Merely by bringing their demands to the court, litigants participate in the maintenance and development of law; lawyers aid in this enterprise and frequently dominate it.[13] Moreover, the court, as an institution, is defined by the cases filed with it, a definition that in turn shapes how future disputants will view and use the court.

Negotiation

The predominant mode of dispute processing in state trial courts is negotiation, usually just between opposing lawyers, but sometimes with the participation of the judge.[14] Although I distinguish between the negotiation and adjudication phases for purposes of discussion here, it is important to realize that they are not entirely distinct. When negotiation occurs in the context of its alternative—adjudication by adversary trial—then the issues, norms, and principles of trial enter into and influence the course of negotiations. As Robert H. Mnookin and Lewis Kornhauser (1979) entitle their article, there is "Bargaining in the Shadow of the Law." Marc Galanter (1984) notes that negotiation and litigation really comprise a single process—*litigotiation* it might be called—in which parties negotiate through mobilization of the court. Because most case outcomes emerge from negotiations between lawyers and not from trial, more research should be devoted to understanding the normative content and policy implications of the negotiation process.

One reason that political scientists tend to ignore out-of-court bargaining processes could be the belief that such bargaining is shaped solely by individual interests and negotiating skill without reference to norms. Yet this view lacks support in empirical and theoretical studies of dispute negotiation.[15] Melvin A. Eisenberg (1976, 639), for example, reminds us that observations of negotiations reveal that they proceed largely by the "invocation, elaboration, and distinction of principles, rules, and precedents." He suggests that by treating the verbal content of negotiation as meaningful, we find a norm-centered process that is quite similar for both dispute negotiation and adjudication. Bargaining in ordinary litigation, according to one view (Kritzer 1991), falls into three different forms: pro forma or implicit negotiations, in which everyone knows the outcome (or the "going rate" in plea bargaining for certain kinds of cases) and no offers or counteroffers are exchanged; consensus-oriented, appropriate-result negotiations, in which the parties seek jointly to arrive at an appropriate case outcome, rather than seeking a maximal win; and concessions-oriented, maximal-result negotiations, in which parties behave strategically and seek to optimize their gains and minimize their losses. With the first two types of negotiation, norms are clearly involved—in setting the "going rate" and in setting criteria for "appropriate" results. Even in the third type, where bargaining involves concessions, there may be an effort to phrase the compromise in normative terms; significantly, such a transformation reinforces the power of those norms and ideas independently of individual interests that gave rise to the rephrasing.

Most of the empirical research on case negotiation in American courts centers on the plea-bargaining process in criminal court. What emerges from this research is a picture of case dispositions shaped by local understandings and values of the courtroom work group.[16] Attorneys who work regularly with one another develop shared notions of the criteria for distinguishing between cases and informal norms for applying the categories of the criminal statutes to the individual cases. For example, although the penal code does not differentiate between the amount of money or stolen goods involved in a felony theft case, in a local courthouse "everyone knows" that the more stolen, the more serious the case is. This working knowledge is shaped in part by patterns of judge and jury behavior: perceptions of likely trial outcomes thus constitute the law that influences plea bargaining in its shadow. Defense and prosecuting lawyers also create the law themselves through their own criteria for classifying cases and ideas about "what a case is worth." For instance, attorneys in Los Angeles explained plea bargaining in first degree robbery cases as narrowing cases according to whether they involve "real" first degree robberies or not. "We look at the background of the individuals, how much involvement they've had with the law, and the circumstances of the case," one prosecutor explained. A public defender put it more simply: a "real" first degree robbery involves "the meanest guys . . . the least going for them. They're really vicious . . . terrible S.O.B.s . . . backgrounds going 'way back to childhood with crimes of violence. Hostile, very aggressive acts" (Mather 1979, 106, 102). When lawyers engage in plea bargaining, they are negotiating identities and events and transforming them into particular categories of case outcomes. This is an active, political process quite in contrast to passive, administrative enforcement. Or, as Joseph R. Gusfield (1981, 161) describes the disposition of drunk drivers in a local court, it involves a process of negotiating meaning rather than a "consistent, direct implementation of a clearly stated rule and a clearly perceived instance of its violation."

Those few empirical studies we have of out-of-court bargaining in civil cases also show the narrowing of disputes into conventional categories and the use of norms in settlement. In his classic study of personal injury negotiations, H. Laurence Ross (1970) describes the principal issue between attorney and insurance adjuster as whether the case should be considered routine or serious. Although each side used various bargaining tactics, he notes, they also each tried to frame their positions in terms of general, mutually shared principles. Recent research by James D. Atleson (1989) describes the transformation of labor disputes in settlement negotiations between attorneys and judge in Buffalo, New York. In cases of labor union picketing where employers sought injunctions against the picketing, why, asked Atleson, were most actions settled despite strong statutory law against such injunctions? He found that the lawyers, who worked regularly together in a relatively small community representing employers and unions, created their own standards for compromise, standards that were influenced by their perceptions of the role of the police, of the unpredictability of judicial decisions, and of appellate case law. Interestingly, although certain aspects of the formal law were potentially ambiguous, both company and union lawyers acted as if the law were clear; indeed it *was* clear for the lawyers, as Atleson (1989, 61) argues, because they had implicitly created it themselves. Using these shared norms and understandings, lawyers typically transformed a dispute over the union's right to picket into a conflict about interests that could be settled by agreement to limit the number or location of picketers or both.

In the area of divorce negotiations, we see another instance of lawyers creating, in effect, a legal norm. Child support guidelines in Illinois (the formal legal rule) specify the *mini-*

mum amounts that noncustodial parents must pay in support, but according to one recent study (Jacob 1992), divorce lawyers there interpret the rule as a *mandatory* amount to pay. Instead of negotiating to see if child support should be higher than the recommended minimum, lawyers generally accept (and presumably tell their clients) that the amount is already fixed.[17] Within small legal communities, or among lawyers who specialize in certain areas of law (such as divorce or labor-management), we may find more of this kind of pro forma negotiation or negotiation of the "appropriate result" type.[18]

Negotiation to settle cases without formal legal action operates with lawyers in center stage and often reveals lawyers to be the creators as well as the enforcers of legal norms. Consistent patterns of criminal court sentencing, viewed in one sense as cumulative policy making by trial court judges, may actually be more reflective of routine dispute transformation by attorneys. An interesting difference among criminal courts, in fact, is in the extent to which *judges* set sentencing patterns (which then shape plea negotiations between lawyers) or *prosecutors* do (through their plea-bargaining routines, which are then ratified by judges). Central to the negotiation process is the construction of disputes as particular kinds of cases, in which each kind has a well-known path to resolution. Other parties (such as litigants, their supporters, the media, or a trial judge) can actively affect this bargaining process and perhaps urge a different, more unconventional resolution. Although most judges do not participate in plea negotiations in criminal cases, they do play a significant role in the settlement of civil cases. In a nationwide survey, 68.7 percent of state court judges responded that they typically did not attend plea negotiations; in contrast 78.2 percent reported that they normally did intervene in civil settlement discussions, either through the use of cues or suggestions or through the use of direct pressure (Ryan et al. 1980, 175-177). It would be interesting to know more about the nature of such judicial intervention, not just about its style but about its normative content as well.

Although negotiation is the most prevalent way disputes are resolved in the United States, some cases go to adversary trial and some are handled by mediation, arbitration, or other informal alternatives for dispute resolution. Supporters of the alternative methods praise their lower costs and their ability to focus in a nonadversarial way on the interests and needs of the individuals in dispute. In contrast, critics of alternative dispute resolution emphasize how the transformation of cases into individual disputes through mediation tends to depoliticize them, effectively removing legal rights and public policy values from the resolution of the dispute (Harrington 1985; Merry 1990; Silbey and Sarat 1989).

Adjudication

If a settlement is not sought or reached in negotiations, or if alternative methods of dispute resolution do not produce case outcomes acceptable to the parties and their lawyers, then adjudication—an adversary trial before a judge or jury—is the next step in the legal process. Judicial decisions are probably the most common way that we think about policy making in trial courts, either through the cumulative pattern of case outcomes or through an innovative, path-breaking decision. Policy-making judicial decisions do not just come at the end of the trial, or with the pronouncement of sentence, however. The pretrial process provides judges with numerous opportunities to transform cases in distinct ways, to interpret and shape facts into a particular legal framework. When judges rule on questions of jurisdiction, determine the proper parties in the case, define the scope of the issues, or rule on the admissibility of evidence, they are actively constructing the case. This power to define and shape a case has enormous implications politically as well as for the outcome of the individual case. I have heard federal district judges report that they *prefer* their position as trial court judge to that of judge on the higher court of appeals because they feel they have greater decision-making power in the trial court than they would at the appellate level.

The trial judge works on the front lines, facing a raw mass of unsifted and uncategorized facts and interpretations; the judge tries to establish who and what is relevant in the process of narrowing issues and creating a fair and coherent picture. For example, before the first jury trial of the white Los Angeles police officers charged with beating the black motorist Rodney King, the county judge's decision to permit a change of venue (transfer of the case) from the central city court to a suburban one sixty miles away was critical in explaining the final jury verdict of acquittal that resulted in the Los Angeles riots of 1992. This case was an unusual one and had a national audience. Most pretrial judicial decisions, because they fall into predictable aggregate patterns, create cumulative policy for local courts and their communities. The legal rules on admissibility of evidence, for example, are constituted by the routine decisions of trial judges to admit challenged evidence; defense lawyers who know the local routines are not surprised when their motions are denied, despite their occasionally vocal protests in court.

Studies of criminal-sentencing patterns provide most of the empirical evidence for cumulative judicial policy making, with clear differences in the harshness or leniency of sentences given offenders in different urban trial courts (Eisenstein and Jacob 1977; Levin 1977). Trial court researchers have sought to identify and then explain variation in judicial decision making (especially sentencing) by factors such as role orientation and attitudes (Gibson 1978), method of judicial recruitment and social background of judge (Levin 1977), environmental context (Feiock 1989; Gibson 1980), public opinion (Cook 1977; Kuklinski and Stanga 1979), and gender of the judge (Gruhl, Spohn, and Welch 1981).[19]

Trial judges construct local norms through pretrial and trial proceedings, and they also participate in changing policy by defining entirely new legal norms. The creation of new law happens infrequently in both trial and appellate courts, but it is still useful to consider how and when such lawmaking occurs. New norms may result from the leadership (or activism) of an individual trial judge, one who assumes an unusually expansive and creative style that leads to policy innovation. Alternatively, a lawsuit may itself raise issues of unsettled law and force a judge to develop new precedent, regardless of the judge's predisposition toward lawmaking.

Although most research on judicial activism has been done on appellate courts, a few researchers have studied trial judges. Trial judges vary individually and from one locality to another in their willingness to depart from precedent. Austin Sarat (1977) and Gregory A. Caldeira (1977) have used incentive theory to explain why some judges believe the judicial role to be highly creative and discretionary while others favor strict adherence to precedent. That is, the personal incentives or motivations of judges are said to explain their role orientations (which in theory should explain their behavior). In a different approach to identifying variation in trial judges, the anthropologists John M. Conley and William M. O'Barr (1988) applied conversational analysis to the texts of hearings in small claims courts. Their analysis of judicial speech revealed several different judicial types. One of these was the "lawmaker," a judge who uses legal principles primarily as resources rather than constraints and who adapts or invents law in order to pursue justice. Another type of activist judge was the "mediator," a judge who manipulates procedure and exerts his or her own view of a case in order to conciliate the disputants.

Just as judicial activism has many different meanings at the appellate level (Canon 1982a), so it does at the trial level. Marc Galanter, Frank S. Palen, and John M. Thomas (1979) outline several independent activist dimensions along which trial judges may deviate from the prototype of the passive arbiter bound by precedent. For some of these dimensions, it is easy to see how an active judge can contribute significantly to creating new policies. For example, judges who are doctrinally innovative (not bound by precedent), assertive toward other political actors (not deferential), or managerial (not the passive umpire) are more likely to shape cases before them in dynamic and political ways. Two other dimensions also suggest strong potential for proactive policy making by trial judges: a substantive policy orientation (rather than a formal or legalistic approach) and a broad view of cases (rather than seeing them one by one). The last two dimensions are similarly identified in two separate studies (Caldeira 1977; Galanter, Palen, and Thomas 1979). Hence, in the view of these researchers, judicial policy makers are those who use the law to advance policy goals and whose consideration of issues goes beyond the individual case to the community.

New law is created not only through the decisions of an active judge but even more frequently because the issues litigants and lawyers present in their cases compel judicial lawmaking. As legislatures pass new statutes to address society's problems, trial courts must initially give some meaning to those laws. Federal judges have been faulted for imposing their own political preferences on society, but quite often they are simply trying to make sense of a law that Congress has passed. As Robert A. Katzmann (1988, 11) explains, "The view is that courts are usurpers of the electoral process. . . . But this view ignores the irony: judicial action is often a consequence of legislative directives. Congress frequently passes the buck to the courts to avoid controversial choices and then blames judges for issuing decisions that it in fact required."

Stricter constitutional standards developed by the Supreme Court have also forced federal judges to create new law at the trial level. After the landmark case of *Brown v. Board of Education* in 1954, responsibility for defining states' obligation to desegregate public schools fell to the federal district judges. In his book *Fifty-Eight Lonely Men*, J. W. Peltason (1961) describes the conflicting pressures from the Supreme Court and from the local southern communities on federal judges who had to implement the higher court's decision in the southern states. The lawmaking power of these judges should not be underestimated. As Peltason (1961, 21) writes, "The Constitution may be what the Supreme Court says it is, but a Supreme Court opinion means, for the moment at least, what the district judge says it means." This conclusion takes on even greater force when one looks at district court actions involving remedial decrees to enforce constitutional standards on institutions such as mental hospitals, prisons, schools, housing, and the workplace. Phillip J. Cooper's (1988, 328) detailed study of five such lawsuits underscores the inevitability of judicial lawmaking in the cases: "The notion that the controversial remedial decree cases are simply manifestations of a liberal federal judiciary intent upon playing guardian without regard to the consequences of their wide ranging decisions simply does not withstand empirical analysis." Institutional reform cases most frequently appear in federal district courts, but they are also brought in state trial courts. Nearly one-third of large jails throughout the country were under court order in 1991 to correct their unconstitutional conditions; a study of jail litigation in the state of California found that two-thirds of the cases were filed in state courts and one-third in federal courts (Welsh 1992). By the very nature of complex, multiparty litigation, judges are forced to define problems, preside over and mediate between important actors, and construct the appropriate law for dealing with controversial social and political conflicts. The diffuse scope of issues and parties and the continuous interplay of factual and legal issues require that the trial judge actively shape the litigation (Chayes 1976).

Change in legislative and appellate legal rules create occasions for trial court lawmaking. With social, economic, and technological conditions also in flux, people are forever fighting over new problems that were not foreseen by existing law. As lawyers expand legal frameworks to address such conflicts, they force judges to choose between competing interpretations and thus to invent new law. The *Baby M* case illustrates this point well *(In the Matter of Baby M,* 1987). Lawyers representing the biological father and mother of a baby conceived by a surrogate arrangement debated the child custody dispute within conflicting expanded frameworks of contract law and family law. The New Jersey trial judge in the case had to define a new legal norm simply to settle the dispute. Other examples of new issues for trial judges include the determination of custody of frozen embryos in a divorce case, the prosecution for manslaughter of a woman who had used cocaine before delivering a stillborn fetus, or the right of family members and their doctor to disconnect life support for a terminally ill patient. Note that even if the judge's decision at trial is ultimately overturned by an appellate court (as it was in the *Baby M* case), it has still contributed to the creation of new policy. The initial court case on a novel issue tends to symbolize and define the problem as a public issue. Given its symbolic importance and media attention, the case becomes an arena for advancing ideas and interpretations of events not just in the confines of the courtroom but to a broader audience as well. In such a setting the trial judge must fashion a decision for the particular case yet also be aware of how the decision will be used by others to build political support or opposition.

Juries as well as judges preside over adjudication and also play an important role in trial court policy making. Although the trial (petit) jury has a long and rich political history, discussion of juries frequently ignores their political features and concentrates instead on their decision-making processes. Exceptions in this regard are Gary J. Jacobsohn's (1977) and James P. Levine's (1983, 1992) explicit investigations of the ways in which juries participate in the formulation of public policy. Juries make policy through the routine process of fact-finding and through the occasional substitution of their own legal norms for those of the legislature or appellate courts.

Ostensibly, juries only establish the facts in dispute and apply the law as given to them by the trial judge, but it is well known that a clear distinction between facts and law is difficult to maintain. For example, in a negligence case, the jury must evaluate the facts of a defendant's actions to conclude whether or not "reasonable care" was exercised; simply by resolving the facts, the jury is also interpreting the law, that is, the jury is defining what legally constitutes "reasonable care." Jacobsohn quotes the comment of one legal scholar on such cases: "The jury makes policy in the guise of 'finding the facts' " (1977, 80). Interestingly, one can examine trends in jury behavior for the implicit policies they reveal, for example, toward criminal defendants. Early research suggested that juries were more lenient than judges in criminal cases (Kalven and Zeisel 1966). More recent data, however, point to "jury toughness," an increase in the conviction rate by juries over that of judges (Levine 1992). Levine compares conviction rates for state judges and juries over time with public opinion data on criminal justice to conclude that the current severity of juries reflects prevailing conservative ideology.

A second form of jury policy making occurs when juries in effect create their own legal norms for resolving a case. *Jury nullification*, the most commonly cited example of such independent jury action, occurs when juries ignore the formally stated law to reach a verdict based on their particular sense of justice. For instance, juries frequently acquitted obviously guilty offenders of liquor violations during Prohibition to express their hostility to the law, and juries of the late 1960s sometimes did the same for defendants charged with possessing small amounts of marijuana. In another example, from Canada, abortion in Quebec was effectively legalized as a result of jury nullification; believing that abortion should not be a criminal offense, three separate juries between 1973 and 1976 refused to convict a doctor charged with performing illegal abortions. As a result the Quebec government stopped enforcing the federal law.[20] More recently, a jury in Michigan effectively nullified the state law against doctor-assisted suicides by acquitting Dr. Jack Kevorkian for helping a terminally ill man to end his life. Dr. Kevorkian was tried under a 1992 Michigan law that had been specifically enacted to put a halt to his activities (he had assisted some twenty patients commit suicide between 1990 and 1993). Enforcement of the law, however, may not be possible in a political climate of sympathy for the doctor (Margolick 1994).

Rather than invalidating a law through jury nullification, juries may also modify it in particular ways through the informal development of their own substantive rules. Although juries do not officially communicate with each other, they do reflect the norms or attitudes of a local community (as illustrated by jury actions in personal injury cases described by Engel [1984] in Sander County). In a study of jury verdicts in medical malpractice cases in California, James L. Croyle (1979) suggests how the development of substantive jury norms may provide an explanation for the divergence of jury verdicts from appellate court doctrine. As an example, he cites an interesting decision rule of juries that seemed to emerge in his analysis of verdicts:

If the plaintiff goes to a medical practitioner, hospital or clinic with a relatively minor medical problem and comes away from that practitioner or institution with a relatively serious medical problem he will most likely be given a jury verdict regardless of the rules relating to malpractice. Similarly, if he is marginally worse off, or simply bad off in a different way, he is unlikely to win a jury verdict regardless of the question of negligence. (Croyle 1979, 1)

That is to say, juries appear to ignore formal liability doctrine and construct their own policy of compensation.

The Impact of Litigation

The very process of litigation operates to define problems, identities, and relationships; to shape formal law according to local beliefs and conditions; and to create new legal norms. The immediate effect of any particular case is generally restricted to the local community, although occasionally the case may have broader policy ramifications (for example, in test cases brought by interest groups, the introduction of new issues at trial, the broad construction of a case by an activist judge, or instances of jury nullification). Also, some cases that are framed as narrow legal claims and decided accordingly may actually represent far wider interests, and thus the case outcome will also have a broader meaning. For instance, Katherine Bishop (1989) reports from northern California on the use of small claims courts to fight drug dealers. In one of the cases, fifteen neighbors filed individual claims (for the court maximum of $2,000 each) against the owner of a house used for drug use and sale. The plaintiffs argued that the owner was negligent for maintaining a public nuisance. They won a favorable judgment and an award of $30,000 from the court. Subsequently, the owner evicted the drug-dealing tenants, and the city boarded up the house. Thus, although phrased as a narrow legal claim, the case had wider ramifications.

Beyond the local court and community, cases can influence how others in similar situations think about and react to disputes. Regardless of the nature of the final case outcome, the very fact of raising and resolving a claim in court legitimizes the grievance and may encourage others to pursue similar complaints. Informal communications networks among like-minded litigants or lawyers can heighten the impact of litigation. For example, insurance companies, environmentalists, asbestos manufacturers, women's activists, and a host of other groups closely watch the progress of certain lawsuits and attend to the language and strategies used. Specialized groups of lawyers (such as specialists on prisoners' rights, the personal injury bar, employment law experts) devote even more attention to relevant litigation and, when accompanied by political strategies (McCann 1994; Scheingold 1974), can be effective in developing new legal rules. Note that the policy influence of a lawsuit may occur even for parties who lose in court. Gambitta (1981) compared the impact of several lawsuits that challenged school financing laws and found that the "winning" litigants failed to obtain full policy reform, while the "losing" litigants in a separate challenge ultimately succeeded despite their defeat in court.

The most dramatic way in which a trial court case can create widespread policy change is through its role in the process of agenda building. A controversial trial, particularly with extensive media coverage, can lead to the identification of an important public issue and propel its consideration onto the agenda of political decision makers. There are two ways we can think about this process. First, research on agenda building suggests how to conceptualize the process as a sequence of different stages, with pressure for expansion or contraction of conflict depending on the nature of the issues, the groups involved, the type of media coverage, and so forth (Cobb and Elder 1983; Cook 1981; Nelson 1984). A controversial trial initially provides a forum for debate about the definition and solution of a conflict and calls attention to the importance of an issue. The trial may also lead to articulation by the judge or jury of a new legal norm to resolve the dispute and, by extension, the wider problem. Influenced by the trial, supporters and opponents may organize on their own, or in connection with established interest groups. Political leaders may respond to this political mobilization by issuing public statements of concern, initiating legislative change, or urging further judicial action.

For example, immediately after the highly publicized custody trial of the *Baby M* case, the following events occurred to help place surrogate motherhood on the popular agenda: national polls were conducted to gauge public response; newspapers were flooded with letters and editorials; and comments on the dispute were made by President Reagan, Pope John Paul II, and scores of elected officials. Interest groups were formed on both sides of the issue, and leaders of organizations such as the American Civil Liberties Union and the National Organization for Women met to consider their response. Organized moves for policy change occurred in the appellate court of New Jersey (with the filing of numerous amicus curiae briefs), within legislative arenas, and in public hearings through newly created task forces. By December 1987, less than nine months after the trial court's decision in *Baby M*, seventy bills seeking to ban, regulate, or study surrogacy had been introduced in twenty-seven states, three bills had been introduced in Congress, and Louisiana had enacted the country's first law against surrogacy (Peterson 1987).

Second, instead of looking at the trial's effect on policy in a chronological or sequential way, we could focus on its symbolic dimensions. Drawing on ideas about drama, language, and symbolic politics, we could investigate the ways in which trials themselves constitute policy by acting as metaphors for larger social or political concerns. Depending on the elements of a case and the way it is presented by the media, a particular lawsuit may reveal or exacerbate deep social cleavages. When Bernard Goetz shot four black youths in a New York subway in the 1980s, the case threw into sharp relief the city's conflicts over racial tension, crime, and violence. Indeed, the real import of a court or jury trial lies not in the rule that is enforced but in the ritualized acting out of popular beliefs and in the authoritative images that are thus constructed. Trials generally function as a series of object lessons and examples (Arnold 1935), but they also provide an arena for the dramatization of conflicting ideas. To understand more about how trial courts shape public policy, we should explore how they create expectations and influence perceptions of right and wrong.

Filing a legal claim in trial court is one way to influence popular perceptions of right and wrong, to affect the legal construction of a problem, and ultimately to help reshape public policies. When aided by lawyers who are attentive to the broader dimensions of an individual case and by sympathetic media coverage, litigants can succeed in communicating their message to a wider audience whether or not they are successful in their litigation. In the example discussed below, Joseph Yukica's legal claim against Dartmouth College's athletic director played a role in a much wider policy change currently under way in the area of employment law and policy. This New Hampshire lawsuit thus provides an interesting—and unusual—illustration of the ways in which trial courts participate in the policy-making process.

Yukica v. Leland

On November 29, 1985, after a disappointing football season, the head football coach at Dartmouth College, Joseph Yukica, was fired.[21] Three days later, Yukica filed suit in Grafton County, New Hampshire, Superior Court against Edward Leland, Dartmouth's athletic director, charging a breach of contract and seeking a temporary injunction to halt the termination and to prevent Dartmouth from taking steps to hire a new coach. Judge Walter Murphy granted the temporary injunction, but prior to a full hearing on the merits of Yukica's claim, the parties negotiated a settlement out of court. Although the law had clearly favored Dartmouth, Yukica succeeded in continuing as head coach for one more Dartmouth football season.

On the face of it, there is little to commend this case to the student of public policy making. It was a suit involving private law, filed in a New Hampshire county court, that never even went to trial. Although the judge's order to grant a temporary injunction surprised observers, the order had been carefully tailored to the facts of Yukica's contract, and no new law was made. Yet, because of its arguments and the media coverage given it, this case contributed significantly to the politics and law of employment policy, especially in the sports field. *Yukica v. Leland* also illustrates that the "contracts questions that matter, aren't just contracts questions" (Wisconsin Contracts Group 1989, 568).

Yukica became coach at Dartmouth in 1978 with a contract that was renewed every two years. During Yukica's early tenure, the team did extremely well (winning or tying for the Ivy League title three times), but then the team fell into a slump, winning only two games each in the 1984 and 1985 seasons. Just before the 1985 season, Leland sent Yukica a contract renewal letter with warm praise for his coaching, but after the last game of the 1985 season, Leland suggested to Yukica that he resign as head coach. Yukica refused to resign and contacted Michael Slive, a good friend and local lawyer who was also a nationally known expert in sports law and former university athletic director. Four days later Yukica received an official letter of termination from Leland, along with an offer of compensation. Slive and Yukica hired David Nixon, an experienced litigator, to be the trial lawyer; Nixon then initiated the lawsuit on Yukica's behalf. As Yukica described the division of responsibility between his two lawyers in a letter to me on March 14, 1990, "Mike [Slive] was my regular daily contact for advice and media. Dave [Nixon] was our courtroom trial attorney."

In brief, Yukica claimed that he should be allowed to continue for another year as head coach as outlined in his contract. He also charged procedural irregularities in the way Dartmouth had handled the termination. And he sought a temporary injunction, arguing that, were he to be fired, the damage to his professional reputation and career opportunities would cause him, "irreparable harm." These arguments were unusual, seeking to stretch principles of equity in a novel way. In response, Dartmouth College and its athletic director narrowed the case into well-established legal categories with the law weighted on their side. They argued that they had every right to reassign Yukica to other duties within the college as long as they paid his salary and benefits for the remaining eighteen months of the contract. Moreover, Dartmouth argued that the court could not force it to accept Yukica as its football coach; that is, the court could not order the specific performance of Yukica's contract.[22] To do so would contradict the legal precedents on personal services contracts, which have held that compensation ("pay-off"), and not specific performance, is the appropriate legal remedy for a breach of contract.

In firing Yukica while offering monetary compensation, Dartmouth had simply done what colleges around the country had traditionally done when they wanted to change coaches. But Yukica and his lawyers were able to draw support from prominent sports figures who agreed with their view that coaching was in some ways unique, that a broken coaching contract could not be repaired simply through the payment of money. At the preliminary hearing on December 13, Yukica called on numerous witnesses, including Joe Paterno, a coach at Pennsylvania State University; Jack Bicknell, a coach at Boston College; and Bob Blackman, a former Dartmouth football coach. Their testimony furthered the already growing public interest in the case and attracted national media attention. The case was transformed from a fairly routine dismissal into a dispute about the quality of Yukica's twenty-year record of coaching football, the importance of not breaking contracts, and the relative power of institutions and coaches.

A week after the hearing, Judge Murphy granted the temporary restraining order preventing Yukica's dismissal and the college's efforts to replace him. In his order, the judge (himself a former football coach) indicated the likelihood that Yukica would win on the merits of his claim, in part because of procedural irregularities in the dismissal. The procedural question was whether Leland had the sole authority to dismiss Yukica or whether the contract required approval of the dismissal by the sixteen-member athletic council. The judge held that such approval was necessary and offered Dartmouth the chance to obtain it and return to court. That happened in January, as the college brought a motion to dismiss the case on the basis of the minutes of the council meeting in which Yukica's termination was approved. Yukica, however, raised additional procedural issues about the council meeting, and the judge refused to dismiss the case. In addition to the judicial orders, time was clearly on Yukica's side in negotiations, since football recruitment was under way and the college was operating in effect without a head coach. Furthermore, the media coverage of the case put public opinion behind Yukica. As a result, Dartmouth finally settled out of court with an agreement to let Yukica coach for another season.[23]

The temporary injunction by Judge Murphy, although only a pretrial order, played a critical role in the outcome of Yukica's case. The order essentially maintained the status quo and prevented Dartmouth from replacing him. The order also operated to shift power between the two parties, providing Yukica the time and opportunity to argue his case in court and in the press.

Yukica had succeeded in shifting the framework of argument, not just in legal terms but in the wider public debate. National publications reported the case through Yukica's view ("A deal is a deal," "All we're asking is that the college honor a contract") rather than as a dispute about the legal remedy for breach of a personal services contract. For example, the headline above the story in the *New York Times* on December 11, 1985, read, "It's a Matter of 'Principle' for Coach Fighting Ouster"; that in *Sports Illustrated*, January 6, 1986, stated, "Technicalities and Ideals"; and that in *People* magazine for January 20, 1986, said, "Hell No, He Won't Go! Dartmouth's Joe Yukica Fights for His Right to Coach Football." The story in *People* most graphically defined the case in Yukica's terms. The conflict was between a loyal, hard-working coach, fifty-four years old, son of an immigrant steelworker (pictured in one photo with the caption "Alone in the Dartmouth Locker Room") and the athletic director of a powerful Ivy League institution, a thirty-six-year-old "resolute young man and maybe brash as well" (Mano 1986). The images and text of this and other articles tapped deeply held cultural values on the sanctity of contract (see the earlier discussion of Sander County), the ideals of college athletics (rather than an emphasis on winning games), and the struggle of the powerless underdog.

Interestingly, reports on the case seemed to indicate its precedential value despite the limits in the judge's ruling to the particular facts of the contract and despite the fact that it was a negotiated outcome. The president of the American Football Coaches Association, Vince Dooley, was widely quoted as calling *Yukica v. Leland* "a landmark case," and the *Boston Globe* called the judge's initial order a "resounding court victory . . . that could have far-reaching ramifications for the collegiate coaching profession" (Singelais 1985). The *Los Angeles Times*, in a long story about the case that was reprinted in newspapers around the country, described the doctrine of irreparable harm as "a theory that will be mentioned often from now on, no doubt, when coaches challenge the right of employers to pay them off" (Oates 1986, 3). Some might fault the newspapers for oversimplifying and exaggerating the case's import, yet in another sense the accounts were quite accurate.

That is, the lawsuit was highly significant in raising people's consciousness about the issues and symbolizing the problems of a fired coach. Also, through the court hearing and the mass media, Yukica articulated a set of legal ideas—ideas that, in the words of one of his lawyers, challenged "established law and conventional thinking" (Oates 1986, 3). And the fact that the college ultimately did not succeed in dismissing Yukica (albeit through its own agreement to allow him to continue) reinforced the legitimacy of the coach's claim. In addition, the case clearly provided a potential bargaining chip for coaches who might find themselves in conflict with their employers. And employers were forced to pay greater attention to how and when they terminated their employees.

Finally, and perhaps of most importance, it affected how coaching contracts were written, as athletic administrators and coaches began to look more closely at the contract language. Yukica himself published a detailed account of his case ("A Deal Is a Deal") in the 1986 *Summer Manual* of the American Football Coaches Association and provided a fourteen-point listing of his thoughts on contracts (Yukica 1986, 56). And administrators made comments such as, "Contracts obviously are going to be more carefully written by the institution" and "I think it [the case] means when you make contracts with a coach, you better know what you've done" (Asher 1986, E3). It is important to remember that contract law is constituted in part by the way people think about and write their contracts, not just by what happens when a contract is breached. If we think of the contracting process as a sequence of legally significant stages (Tomain 1987), then it seems clear that change has occurred in the early stages involving assumptions, negotiations, and formulation of coaching contracts—even without definitive change at the stage of legal remedy.

Rather than being a completely isolated or aberrant case, *Yukica v. Leland* is one of many recent lawsuits filed by coaches dismissed by their employers. Instead of filing for specific performance, most of the plaintiffs have sought (and some have won) large financial awards not only for compensatory damages but also for the loss of "collateral opportunities" (the perquisites of being a coach beyond salary and benefits). Graves (1986) analyzes these cases (and has a footnote on *Yukica*) in a law review article that begins, "How an Unlikely Group of College and University Figures Is Causing Lawyers and Judges to Reexamine the Traditional Limitations on Recovery in Actions for Breach of Employment Contracts" (545). Indeed, another way to understand the policy importance of *Yukica* is to place it in the larger context of current American employment law. In recent decades the legal rights of employees have been greatly expanded through changes in statutory and case law, but the question of how far to expand those rights is still hotly debated. Cases like this one promote a particular normative interpretation of the problem in ways that distinctly favor employees and encourage legal change.

American legal doctrine on employment has traditionally reflected laissez-faire economics in which employers were free to run their business without government interference. More specifically, by the doctrine of "employment at will," employers have been legally entitled to dismiss their employees for any reason, including a bad reason, or no reason at all. The "at will" doctrine developed at the end of the nineteenth century as a response to particular social and economic conditions and was expressed by the dominant political ideology of the times (Feinman 1976; Moskowitz 1988). With some exceptions, this doctrine still governs the majority of the American work force (Levine 1994; Moskowitz 1988). The exceptions are important, however, because they show the "at will" doctrine eroding through political pressure and legal change. First, certain categories of employees are protected from arbitrary dismissal: unionized employees with collective-bargaining agreements; government and civil service employees; and those with written contracts of fixed terms. Second, employers are prohibited by federal statute from dismissing employees on the basis of race, sex, national origin, handicap, or age. Third, developments in case law have given employees leverage to fight their termination through court rulings on implied contract, the tort of wrongful discharge, and the public policy exception ("Protecting At Will Employees" 1980; Tobias 1988). As a result of these statutory and appellate legal changes, the doctrine of employment at will is undergoing a dramatic transformation, and there are now limits on the ability of private employers freely to terminate employees.

A second way in which employers have been limited in employee dismissals is through the remedies that have been provided to those employees who have been wrongly discharged. Litigation in this area has grown enormously in recent years, and increasing monetary awards have been given to victorious plaintiffs. A study of jury verdicts in California between 1980 and 1984 found that plaintiffs won almost 60 percent of reported wrongful termination suits, with an average award of $173,050 for compensatory damages and $396,650 for punitive damages (Greenan 1984). Juries are thus helping to shape the law in this area through the pattern of their verdicts. The sympathetic response by juries to employee challenges of arbitrary dismissal is not surprising in view of popular attitudes. As one survey revealed, less than 20 percent of those polled knew that employers have the right to fire an employee without giving a reason, and close to 90 percent felt that such employer action was not ethical (quoted in Wisconsin Contracts Group 1989, 564). For employees working with an employment contract (such as Yukica), rather than at the simple discretion of their employer, the legal recourse for an unfair termination is to sue for breach of contract, and the conventional remedy is monetary compensation. In recent years, however, legal scholars have advocated specific performance as a remedy for breach of contract (Schwartz 1979; compare Bishop 1985). Specific performance has also been authorized by civil rights statutes that mandate job reinstatement for employees illegally fired as a result of discrimination. Lawyers for Yukica were thus attempting to accomplish judicially for coaches what had already been done by statute for other groups of employees. Just as Congress made policy when it passed the Civil Rights Act to protect minority employees, so do state trial courts make policy when they extend common law and equitable remedies to protect employees from arbitrary dismissals.

Conclusion

While the concept of policy making includes the adoption of a new rule or remedy, it also involves the definition of problems, agenda setting, the formulation of alternatives, and implementation. Most important, policy making involves conflict over ideas and struggle over a normative framework for interpreting events. Trial courts provide a public arena for the participation of citizens and the influence of lawyers in that struggle, through the transformation of events into legal categories and the construction of law to resolve individual disputes. Whether through informal negotiations or through the adversary proceedings of pretrial and trial, lawyers debate the nature and normative meaning of a case. On occasion, as occurred in the cases of *Cipollone v. Liggett Group*, *In the Matter of Baby M*, and *Yukica v. Leland*, the debate widens to include new meanings as interest groups, the media, or others become involved. Trial courts thus contribute significantly to the formation of public policy through struggles over the meaning of law in the definition and resolution of conflict.

The norm enforcement view of American trial courts has stubbornly persisted in the literature on judicial processes. More than twenty years of research on the political dimensions of trial courts, disputing, and the mobilization of law seem not to have dislodged the paradigm of the trial court as an institution whose sole occupant is a largely passive arbiter of private conflict. By shifting perspectives, political scientists can observe a wide range of policy-making activities in federal and state trial courts: the judge is not the only political actor in court, and formal decisions at the end of a trial are not the only vehicle for making policy. Thus, when litigants and lawyers file legal claims and present arguments, they are defining problems and formulating policy alternatives. Interest groups incorporate litigation as part of their political strategy for changing policy, and the mass media use individual cases to dramatize political conflict and set an agenda for action by others. Lawyers constitute legal rules through patterns of routine negotiation and classification of cases. Juries create policies through their fact finding at trial and through their modification (and occasional nullification) of law. And, finally, judges too make policy—not just by a pathbreaking decision at trial but also by the way in which they frame issues and mold cases, by their consistent patterns of action (in motions, hearings, or sentencing), and by their interactions with lawyers in case negotiation.

Notes

1. The jury's decision in the Cipollone case was only a partial victory for the plaintiff. Rose Cipollone herself was denied damages; her husband was awarded the $400,000. After its defeat at the Third Circuit, the Cipollone family took its case to the U.S. Supreme Court. The Supreme Court, in a splintered and complex 7 to 2 opinion, overturned the Third Circuit decision and sent the case back to the U.S. District Court for a new trial. Several months later the Cipollone family dropped the suit. A colleague of their lawyer commented that "the Cipollones always felt that they got what they wanted out of the case" (Strum 1992, B5). For further discussion of this case and others involving tobacco liability, see Rabin 1993 and Schwartz 1993.

2. As Paul Brodeur (1985) tells the story, asbestos companies knew of the dangers of asbestos dust but failed to protect workers. A products liability lawsuit filed in 1969 in a federal district court in Beaumont, Texas, led to the first court victory against asbestos manufacturers, a decision that was upheld by the Fifth Circuit Court of Appeals. The major asbestos manufacturer, the Manville Corporation, declared bankruptcy in 1982 at a point when it was facing some 17,000 lawsuits brought by victims of asbestos-related cancer and other diseases.

3. All the information in this paragraph comes from Rohter (1994).

4. Trial courts do not make policy, according to Jacob, because even where there is a consistent trend in their decisions, trial judges are often not aware of it, and because few trial court cases challenge an existing norm. "Only when a norm is itself challenged can the courts engage in policy-making" (Jacob 1964, 26). But judicial intent is not necessary for establishment of policy, since the policy consequences of decisions exist whether judges are aware of them or not. In his other writing, Jacob acknowledges the political dimensions of trial courts, but he believes that the essential notion of policy making is rule-announcing behavior.

5. Casper (1976) makes this point about Supreme Court policy making in his influential critique of Dahl (1957). Casper argues that Dahl misrepresents the Supreme Court's contribution to policy because he has adopted an overly narrow definition of policy making.

6. See, for example, Hawkins (1992) on discretionary decision making. As Matheny (1994, 97) writes in a recent book review: "Hawkins and his contributors reconceptualize Dworkin's famous 'doughnut' explanation of discretion. Dworkin argues that discretion is nothing more than the 'hole of the doughnut' which takes shape only because of the surrounding and restrictive legal pastry. The scholars in this volume collectively assert the contrary, i.e., that rules (as law) 'appear' only when viewed through ascending layers of discretionary decision-making."

7. Governor Chiles of Florida seems to be formulating the state's legal claim on behalf of Medicaid patients in order to obtain financial as well as political benefits (he is at this writing running for a second term of office).

8. Barbara Yngvesson and I used the concept of dispute transformation as an analytic framework for comparing dispute processing cross-culturally and for linking the processing of individual disputes to the maintenance and change of political order (Mather and Yngvesson 1981; Yngvesson and Mather 1983; see also Emerson and Messinger 1977; Santos 1977). I draw on that framework here to show how the normative changes as disputes are transformed contribute to policy making in trial courts (see also Yngvesson 1993). In contrast to our emphasis on change in the normative content of cases, Miller and Sarat (1981), for example, examine change in the number of grievances that do or do not become claims, disputes, or court cases (and see Felstiner, Abel, and Sarat 1981).

9. Many sociolegal scholars have analyzed law as language, or as discourse. See, for example, Conley and O'Barr 1990; Kessler 1993; and Merry 1990.

10. For discussion of influences on the decision to file a legal claim, see Boyum 1983; Felstiner, Abel, and Sarat 1981; Miller and Sarat 1981; Silberman 1985; Zemans 1982, 1983.

11. For discussion of prosecutorial filing policies in various California counties, see Mather 1979 on Los Angeles; Utz 1978 on Alameda and San Diego; and Carter 1974 on "Vario County" in northern California.

12. In Chapter 5 of this book, Kobylka examines how interest groups use courts to achieve policy objectives; in Chapter 17, Rosenberg considers the impact of their litigation efforts.

13. As an example of the importance for policy development of the demands litigants bring to court, consider the study done by Canon and Baum (1981) of tort law innovations across the fifty states. They conclude that the pattern of judicial innovativeness is unlike that for legislative initiatives and depends instead on the nature of courts and litigants. Most relevant for my argument is their emphasis on the reactive role of courts in which the ability of state courts to create new legal doc-

trine—at least in the area of torts—was found to depend on the demands of the litigants.

14. For more on negotiation, see Chapter 6 of this volume.

15. In addition to the work cited in the text below, see Cartwright and Schwartz (1973); Comaroff and Roberts (1981); Shapiro (1981); Yngvesson and Mather (1983).

16. The literature on this point is enormous. See, for example, Eisenstein, Flemming, and Nardulli (1988); Eisenstein and Jacob (1977); Feeley (1979); Flemming, Nardulli, and Eisenstein (1992); Heumann (1978); Mather (1979); Neubauer (1974); Utz (1978).

17. In my current research with Richard Maiman and Craig McEwen on negotiations among divorce lawyers in New Hampshire and Maine, we have found the same result with respect to child support guidelines.

18. Most of the research on local legal culture has centered on the shared agreement among lawyers about the pace and procedures of litigation (Church 1982; compare Kritzer and Zemans 1993 for a contrary view). But there is good reason to expect the same kind of shared agreement on substantive legal issues.

19. It is unfortunate that civil court decisions have not received the same scholarly attention as those in criminal court. The imbalance reflects a misguided view that "private law" matters are somehow less appropriate for study by political scientists than are "public law" matters (see Shapiro 1972; Zemans 1983).

20. After Dr. Henry Morgantaler's successful battle to legalize abortion in Quebec, he opened an abortion clinic in Toronto in 1983. Again he was charged by provincial authorities with breaking the federal law, and again he was acquitted by a jury—his fourth acquittal on abortion charges. The crown appealed Dr. Morgantaler's acquittal in Toronto, and the case led to a landmark policy change for the entire country. On January 28, 1988, the Supreme Court of Canada declared the federal abortion law unconstitutional under the new Canadian Charter of Rights and Freedoms (see "Abortion" 1988).

21. Information on this case comes from articles in the local newspaper (the *Valley News*) and other newspapers and magazines; from the pleadings, memoranda, and judicial orders filed in the Grafton County Superior Court; from personal interviews with the litigants and lawyers conducted in fall 1986 by a Dartmouth student, Gregory Garre; and from my own follow-up calls in 1989 and 1994. Gregory Garre also aided in the analysis of the case, and three law professors—Stewart Macaulay, Jack McCrory, and Linda Smiddy—provided useful insights on the case and on contract law.

22. *Specific performance* refers to a remedy for breaking a contract in which parties are ordered to carry out the precise terms of the contract. In this case, *specific performance* would mean that Dartmouth would be ordered to fulfill the terms of its contract with Yukica by allowing him to remain as head coach.

23. During Yukica's final football season, tensions surfaced between the coach and Leland, the athletic director, in regard to many minor issues such as the making of the team's highlights film and removal of Yukica's parking space. These conflicts illustrate why specific performance is rarely ordered in cases involving breach of employment contract: courts do not want to force parties to stay together in an unpleasant personal relationship (Wisconsin Contracts Group 1989).

Part III Lower Appellate Courts

In the introduction to Part I, I noted several distinctions between the way political scientists and journalists think about dimensions of legal processes. Here, I observe a parallel. Just as the media tend to focus their attention on trial court proceedings and U.S. Supreme Court decisions, so do scholars. What both frequently neglect, however, are the lower appellate courts, often called courts of appeals.

In many ways, the omission of these tribunals from newspaper stories and scholarly treatments is surprising.[1] After all, about three-fourths of all states have intermediate courts, and these bodies process a good deal of litigation. In 1990, for example, the Illinois appellate courts disposed of about 8,000 cases—nearly forty times the number handled by the state's supreme court. The figures are equally impressive for lower federal appellate courts. In 1992 the 179 judges of the U.S. courts of appeals disposed of more than 23,000 cases. Furthermore, courts of appeals often render the final decisions in a given case. Research shows that less than 20 percent of the losing parties in lower federal appellate courts ask the U.S. Supreme Court to review their cases (Howard 1981); and, for those who do appeal, there is almost no probability of Supreme Court review. To put it another way, U.S. appellate court rulings are left "undisturbed" in 99.7 percent of the cases (see Songer 1991, 47).

Given the numbers of cases processed by U.S. courts of appeals, not to mention the finality of their decisions, why is it that scholars pay relatively little attention to their work? One reason is that they—like trial courts—vary greatly, making generalizations difficult. State appellate court systems, as Baum (1994, 46) points out, have distinct structures, with some states possessing only a single court of appeals and others providing separate courts for different parts of the state. They also vary in their jurisdiction, with some states requiring their appellate tribunals to hear all cases appealed from trial courts and others permitting them some discretion over their dockets. As we would expect, the U.S. courts of appeals are more uniform, but variations do exist. For example, each court devises its own rules of procedure, which govern everything from oral argument to the responsibilities of the chief judge. Moreover, the individual tribunals develop their own circuit law to help jurists interpret areas of the federal code on which the Supreme Court has not spoken.

Variation, though, is not the only reason scholars have shied away from the study of lower appellate courts; after all, trial courts are far less uniform than courts of appeals, and there is no dearth of research on them. Where the real difference may lie, then, is in the relative visibility of these courts. The O. J. Simpson case, Court TV, and television docudramas have worked to ensure that the business of trial courts remains high on the public's agenda. It is hard to recall, though, the last time a case brought to a court of appeals generated any publicity. Courts of appeals proceedings are not particularly interesting events. They are short (each side typically gets about one-half hour to present its case) and closed to television crews. There are no surprising revelations, no movie stars testifying, no fans cheering on their favored side. It is this lack of glamour and the attendant publicity, I suspect, that keeps the journalists and even the scholars away.

In the end the reason for the absence of treatments of courts of appeals is less important than the simple fact that we do not know much about them. This is troublesome because courts of appeals are, by virtue of the finality of their decisions, important actors in the American judicial system. The chapters in this section, both of which go a long way in filling gaps in our knowledge of U.S. courts of appeals, underscore this point.

In Chapter 9, Christine B. Harrington and Daniel Ward ask a question central to the study of lower appellate courts: Are U.S. courts of appeals similar to one another, or do they manifest characteristics reflecting the regions in which they are located? To address it, Harrington and Ward explore systematically three theories designed to explain patterns of litigation (differences in appeal rates) in the federal courts of appeals. The first two—the social development theory and political culture theory—suggest that conditions external to legal institutions account for the variation. For example, the social development argument holds that litigation rates increase as societies become more complex and modern. In the context of their study, this theory would predict roughly the same litigation activity in circuits that have similar levels of socioeconomic development. A third theory—the institutional theory—takes a rather different tack. As developed by the authors it suggests that courts themselves can affect their own litigation rates. For example, institutional practices that vary from one court to another, such as methods of case processing and reversal rates, may cause diversity in litigation activity.

To test these theories, Harrington and Ward invoke a sophisticated statistical tool called pooled cross-sectional time series (more fully explained in Appendix A). This statistical model allows them to reach some interesting conclusions about variation in litigation activity, not the least of which is that institutional factors seem to have a systematic effect on court caseloads. For example, the more government cases a court of appeals handles summarily (without a full hearing), the fewer of those kinds of cases that come to it the following year. This and other findings lead Harrington and Ward to suggest future research that focuses directly on the circuits themselves.

In Chapter 10, Jeffrey A. Segal, Donald R. Songer, and Charles M. Cameron also explore competitive models, but they concentrate on an area quite distinct from that of Harrington and Ward. They raise the question, How do judges on federal courts of appeals reach their decisions? To address it, they examine three distinct models of judicial behavior: the legal model, which holds that judges make their decisions on the basis of such factors as precedent and the intent of the framers of the Constitution; the attitudinal model, which suggests that judges reach decisions on the basis of their own political preferences; and the hierarchical model, which asserts that judges have political preferences but, as intermediate players in the judicial hierarchy, are limited in their ability to pursue their preferences. In other words, the hierarchical model predicts that both legal and attitudinal factors influence judges.

To determine which of these models best accounts for judges' decisions, Segal and his colleagues drew a sample of cases that arose under the Fourth Amendment to the U.S. Constitution and were decided by U.S. courts of appeals between 1961 and 1990. They then used logistic regression (explained in Appendix B to this book) to see if one of their models better accounted for judicial outcomes than the others. The results indicate that this is the case: the data lend strong support to the hierarchical model. Such is an important finding, as Segal, Songer, and Cameron argue, because it suggests both similarities and differences in the way that court of appeals judges and Supreme Court justices reach decisions. Furthermore, even though they looked at only one area of the law (cases involving searches and seizure), the authors make a good case for the generalizability of their results.

In the final analysis, then, the chapters in Part III have important things to say to scholars and students alike. Perhaps the clearest message is this: Courts of appeals are not only important judicial tribunals but they are distinct from courts above and below them. Accordingly, they deserve far more attention than they have been previously accorded.

Notes

1. I do not mean to imply that there are no scholarly works on courts of appeals. To the contrary, distinguished scholars, including Deborah Barrow and Thomas G. Walker (for example, 1988), Lawrence Baum (for example, 1980), and Donald R. Songer (for example, 1982, 1987), have written extensively on them (see, generally, Songer 1991). The literature, however, is relatively undeveloped compared with what has been written about the U.S. Supreme Court and trial courts.

9 Patterns of Appellate Litigation, 1945-1990

Christine B. Harrington and Daniel S. Ward

In 1891 Congress created the U.S. circuit courts of appeals, resulting in one of the most significant reforms in the history of the federal judiciary. Situating them between the U.S. district courts and the U.S. Supreme Court, Congress hoped that the new appellate courts, by uniformly applying national law, would relieve Supreme Court justices of their burgeoning caseloads and would resolve conflicts among the federal district courts. By the same token, Congress wished to counter the influence of state politics on these newly devised tribunals; after all, it intended that courts of appeals should be free from any undue regional or state pressures in their application of the law. Accordingly, by congressional design, the courts of appeals combine several states within each circuit's jurisdiction.[1]

Still, as shown in Figure 9-1, *regional* formations are present within most circuit boundaries. To be sure, the fit between regional boundaries and circuit court jurisdiction is not perfect. But it is strong enough to raise questions about the extent to which circuit courts are purely national institutions.[2] In particular, is judicial uniformity possible in an institutional setting designed for this purpose, or are the circuits' judicial institutions influenced more by the economic, political, and regional characteristics of their environment? Or, to put it even more simply, how uniform are the courts of appeals? This question is the lens through which we hope to describe and explore circuit court litigation in this chapter.

A Research Strategy

Are courts of appeals performing the function that Congress intended them to perform? Are they resolving conflicts among the federal district courts? And are they doing so by uniformly applying national standards? Based on the low rates of appeal from circuit court decisions (only about 20 percent), scholars assert that they are, in fact, meeting congressional objectives. Yet, because low appeal rates provide only indirect evidence of uniformity, more measures are needed before we can reach any firm conclusions.

We would like to thank Kelley Bevans, Edward Muir, and Alex Reichl for their research assistance on this project.

Figure 9-1 The Thirteen Federal Judicial Circuits

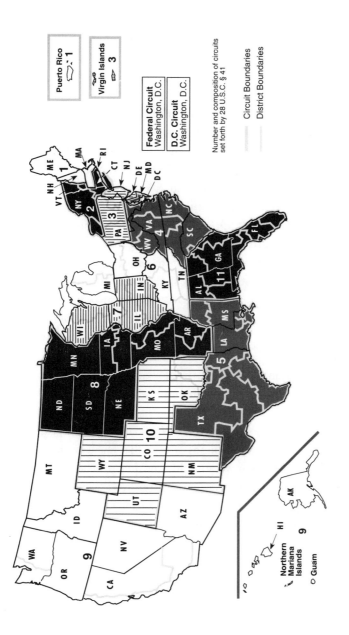

Puerto Rico 1

Virgin Islands 3

Federal Circuit
Washington, D.C.

D.C. Circuit
Washington, D.C.

Number and composition of circuits
set forth by 28 U.S.C. § 41

Circuit Boundaries

District Boundaries

Source: *United States Courts* 1989, 5.

One way of gathering additional measures is to compare doctrinal interpretations among the circuits in a particular area of law, say, the death penalty. Although this kind of strategy would provide a rich analysis of rulings in capital punishment cases, we would learn only about similarities and differences in how circuit courts interpret a particular clause in the U.S. Constitution (in our example, the Eighth Amendment's prohibition against cruel and unusual punishment). If uniformity and stability are central to the *institutional* role of the courts of appeals, we need to know whether these courts are similar to one another or whether they manifest regional characteristics of the environments where they are located.

A more useful approach, then, is to explore the institutional role of circuit courts—that is, the extent to which they are themselves similar to one another and hence more likely to be uniform in their behavior—by providing a historical picture of appellate litigation activity in all the circuits from 1945 to 1990. The U.S. government started keeping systematic records on the number of cases filed by circuit and tracking how the circuits dealt with appeals in the early 1940s (for example, disposed of cases with or without a hearing; reversed or affirmed the lower court or agency decision). The advantage of comparing what cases come to which circuits and how each circuit handles those cases over time is that we can establish a historical context to interpret patterns of appellate litigation. To put it in concrete terms, we know that courts of appeals are hearing more cases than ever before. What we do not know and what these data allow us to do is to identify the types of cases that account for the growth in litigation and to show when, historically, they begin to appear in the circuit courts. Further, we can discover whether growth occurred in all circuits (a general phenomenon) or is limited to circuits in certain parts of the country (an isolated phenomenon). And finally, by examining circuit court litigation over time and across circuits, we can probe issues about the institutional place of the courts of appeals in the federal court system. We can test for patterns of regional diversity that may underlie circuit litigation activity and for stability and uniformity in institutional practices, such as case processing and reversals.

Our research unfolds in the following way. We first consider litigation patterns across the circuit courts by describing the kinds of cases that make up the dockets of the circuit courts from 1945 to 1990. Here we find that *civil litigation* accounts for the most significant growth in appellate litigation, particularly from 1960 to the present. This finding leads us to focus on explanations (theories) for changing rates in civil litigation over time. We then apply those theories to government and private civil litigation in the courts of appeals.

Patterns of Appellate Litigation since 1945

By 1945 the U.S. courts of appeals (then called the circuit courts of appeals) had been in existence for more than fifty years but conducted relatively little business. The ten circuit courts and the U.S. court of appeals in Washington, D.C., averaged fewer than 250 cases apiece that year, and about 30 percent of those cases were disposed of without a hearing.[3] In the cases that were heard, the courts of appeals reversed lower-court decisions 28 percent of the time. So, on average, a circuit court in 1945 reversed the decision in fewer than 50 cases. In contrast, in 1990 the circuit courts heard an average of more than 3,400 cases each. Although nearly 45 percent of these were disposed of without a full hearing, the circuit courts still were left with more than 1,500 cases to hear. Interestingly, the percentage of cases reversed had been cut roughly in half since 1945, producing about 200 reversals per circuit in 1990. Whereas the number of cases increased twelvefold between 1945 and 1990, there were just four times as many reversals in 1990.

The explanations for these patterns are as complex as many of the appellate cases themselves. Some observers suggest that the answer lies in more litigious citizens, interest groups, corporations, and government agencies; others look to broader societal and institutional pressures. In the next section, we discuss several theories that seek to explain litigation rates and we examine the implications of these theories. First, though, we describe the patterns of appellate litigation during a forty-five-year period. We examine the growth in different kinds of cases and diversity in litigation rates across the circuits from 1945 to 1990. Our goal is to identify the kinds of cases most responsible for the dramatic growth in appeals and the circuits that handle a disproportionate number of cases.

The Growth in Appeals and the Changes in Circuit Behavior

The brief portrait of the U.S. courts of appeals in 1945 and 1990 sketched above reveals two very different environments. The most noticeable difference is caseload, the earlier time being characterized by a relatively small and stable workload and the latter by a sharply increased docket size. The growth in the number of appeals between 1945 and 1990 is not a linear trend. In fact, not until the early 1960s do sharp changes occur. Even then, a good deal of the upturn in appellate litigation can be attributed to increases in population. In Figure 9-2 we show the number of cases commenced in the U.S. courts of appeals at five-year intervals, from 1945 to 1990. Data are presented in both raw and per capita figures (that is, the number of cases per 100,000 residents in the circuit).

As we can see, the number of cases increases slowly and steadily from 1945 to 1960 (from 2,730 to 3,899). At the same time, however, the number of cases per capita remains steady, about 2 cases per 100,000 people. In fact, the number *decreases* slightly between 1945 and 1950 and again between 1955 and 1960. Thereafter, the total number of cases

Figure 9-2 Cases Commenced in the U.S. Courts of Appeals: Total and Per Capita Cases, 1945–1990

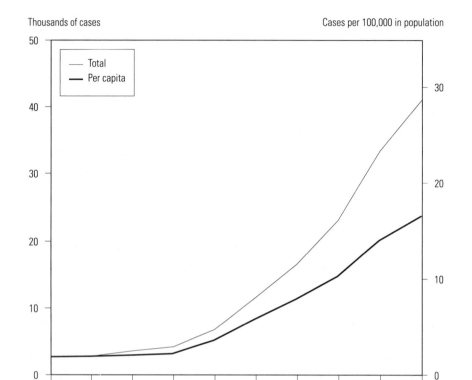

Thousands of cases   Cases per 100,000 in population

Source: Administrative Office of the U.S. Courts, various years.

increases dramatically while the number per capita expands at a more moderate rate. Between 1960 and 1965, for example, there was a 74 percent increase in appeals and a 61 percent rise in per capita appeals. Congress responded to the new caseload pressure on the courts of appeals by authorizing more judgeships. Between 1960 and 1970, Congress created 29 new appellate judgeships, a 43 percent increase in the size of the court of appeals bench. This meant that the number of federal appellate judges went from 68 to 97 in this period. An additional 35 appellate judgeships were authorized by Congress between 1970 and 1979, representing another 36 percent increase in circuit judgeships, or a total of 132 appellate judges by the end of this period (Administrative Office, various years).

One interesting question is whether the increase in caseload is related to other court behaviors. Do judges hear fewer cases on the merits the greater their workload, or are lower-court decisions less likely to be overturned when there is an expanding appellate

Table 9-1 Cases Commenced, Disposed of without Hearing, and Reversed in the U.S. Courts of Appeals (percent)

Year	Change in cases commenced	Disposed of without hearing	Reversed
1945	—	30	20
1950	4	23	17
1955	31	23	21
1960	6	28	18
1965	74	29	13
1970	72	43	12
1975	43	43	10
1980	39	49	9
1985	44	48	9
1990	23	45	7

Source: Administrative Office of the U.S. Courts, various years.

docket? In Table 9-1 we show the percentage change in cases commenced from the previous period, the percentage of cases disposed of without a hearing, and the percentage of decisions reversed for each year.

In the first column are the same data as those displayed in Figure 9-2, but they are shown as the percentage of change from period to period. Once again, the changes are quite dramatic after 1960. The actual percentages for the designated year are shown in the other two columns. As such, of all cases terminated in 1945, 30 percent were disposed of without a hearing and 20 percent were reversed. By 1990, 45 percent of appeals were disposed of without a hearing, and only 7 percent of the lower court or agency decisions were reversed.

The trend we find during the period of rapidly expanding dockets is toward increased procedural terminations (that is, termination without a hearing) and away from reversals of lower-court rulings. For example, prior to 1970, procedural terminations averaged 27 percent of the cases commenced in the courts of appeals. In the period from 1970 through 1990, procedural terminations grew significantly, averaging 46 percent of the cases commenced in this period. In regard to reversal rates, from 1945 to 1960 the courts of appeals reversed lower-court and agency decisions, on the average, in 19 percent of the cases. After 1960, when the number of civil cases began to increase dramatically, the reversal rate drops nearly in half; an average of 10 percent of the cases were reversed in the period from 1965 to 1990. Naturally, this does not indicate a direct causal relation (that is, increased caseload leads to fewer reversals); however, the persistent patterns are worthy of note. We return to these relations in a later section.

The Growth in Appeals and Effects on Case Types

Cases brought to and decided on by the U.S. courts of appeals are broken down into six major categories in official government reports. The most common kind of case appealed to the circuit courts is a civil case. There are two types of civil cases: those involving disputes between private parties and those in which the government is a party, the former being the most prevalent type of appeal. In recent years, these two categories of *civil appeals* have accounted for 65 to 75 percent of the cases before the courts of appeals. A third category is appeals from *criminal* trials. These have constituted 15 to 20 percent of the docket during the past decade. A fourth category encompasses appeals from decisions of *administrative* agencies. Administrative appeals represent only a small portion of the entire circuit dockets and have been in decline in recent years (Harrington 1988). Still fewer cases are *bankruptcy* cases and *original proceedings* in the courts of appeals. We combined bankruptcy and original proceeding cases with a small number of noncategorized cases to create an "other" category for our discussion. Figure 9-3 shows the trend in each of these categories from 1945 to 1990, on a per capita basis.

Private civil cases clearly capture a substantial portion of the overall growth in appellate litigation for this period. In 1990, private civil appeals accounted for 50 percent of the cases in the system, whereas such cases made up just 27 percent of the 1945 docket. In contrast, administrative appeals represented a substantial 16 percent of the 1945 cases, and by 1990 they accounted for only 6 percent of the docket. Criminal cases increased slightly in these forty-five years, from 16 percent to 23 percent of the cases in the courts of appeals.

Another way to explore the components of the increase in appellate litigation and the changing nature of the circuits' dockets is to compare the changes in each category from period to period. The percentage change in the five major categories for each time period is shown in Figure 9-4. By definition, the values for each category are in relation to its raw numbers. Therefore, although private appeals rarely experience the highest level of increase, a 20 percent increase in private civil appeals will bring more cases to court than a 40 percent increase in administrative appeals. By examining percentage change, however, some interesting patterns emerge. For instance, criminal cases appear to be the most volatile category, increasing by more than 100 percent from 1950 to 1955 and from 1965 to 1970, but decreasing in three separate periods. We can also see that whereas private civil appeals always increase in number, their rate of increase tapered off until 1980 but then resurged dramatically. By taking notice of such patterns we can move beyond the simple secular trend of increasing caseloads toward a better understanding of appellate litigation.

It is clear from the data in Figure 9-3 that the most notable change in circuit litigation

Figure 9-3 Per Capita Cases Commenced in the U.S. Courts of Appeals, by Case Type, 1945–1990

Cases per 100,000 in population

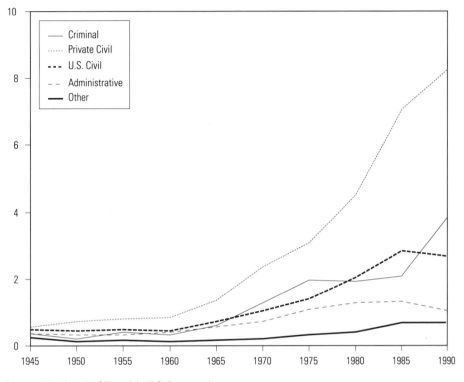

Source: Administrative Office of the U.S. Courts, various years.

during the postwar period is the rise in private civil appeals. Although this trend begins about 1960 and is very visible by 1975, observers of appellate litigation in the early 1980s maintained that the most dramatic shift in the appellate docket was from private economic disputes to disputes involving the government (Baum, Goldman, and Sarat 1981-1982, 306). Our data do not confirm this interpretation; we find the number of *U.S. civil* cases per capita significantly lower than that of private civil cases (see Figure 9-3). That government activity is an important source of litigation in the federal courts has been well documented in studies of federal trial litigation rates and the modern state by Heydebrand and Seron (1986, 1990), yet it appears that at the appellate level the trend is not maintained.

For the purpose of examining the institutional role of circuit courts, we think that by focusing on those cases that account for the most significant growth in appellate litigation (private civil cases), U.S. civil appeals provide an appropriate basis for comparison and

Figure 9-4 Percentage Change in Cases Commenced, by Case Type, 1945–1990

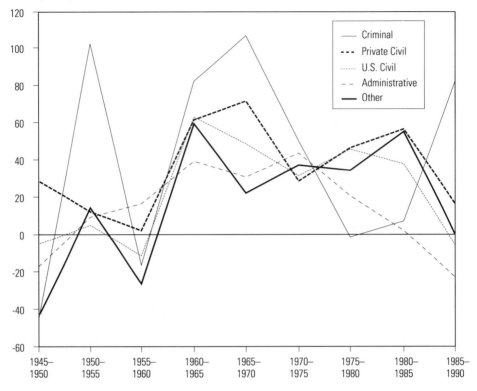

Source: Administrative Office of the U.S. Courts, various years.

analysis. Beyond a description of the changing composition of civil litigation in circuit dockets, we want to know whether those changes are linked to underlying differences in circuit environments, which can be identified by studying the relation between regional political economies and litigation activity within a circuit. We may find, for instance, that these relations function differently for government and private civil appeals. If such relations are found to be strong or weak depending on the kind of civil appeal (government or private), we might better understand the context or circumstances in which economic, political, and regional characteristics of a circuit's environment matter for rates of certain kinds of civil appeals or have little effect.

Diversity among the Circuits

Let us now turn to a final level of differentiation in the appellate system before moving into a more theoretical discussion of factors affecting appellate litigation rates. As we have described, the docket may be broken down by case type. It can also be further broken down by the circuit in which the case was filed. This task becomes more manageable once we limit our discussion to private civil and U.S. civil appeals cases because they make up a substantial portion of the appellate docket. As noted above, the circuits themselves have regional characteristics that may correspond to alternative social, cultural, or economic bases for litigation. Consider, for instance, that the Third Circuit comprises Pennsylvania, New Jersey, and Delaware, one of the most highly industrialized and densely populated regions in the country. It is also a geographically compact circuit. In contrast, the Eighth Circuit encompasses Arkansas, Iowa, Minnesota, Missouri, Nebraska, and the Dakotas. It is largely agricultural, sparsely populated, and geographically sprawling. In 1985, the Third Circuit had 368 residents per square mile, whereas the Eighth Circuit had fewer than one-tenth as many. Per capita income was 18 percent lower in the Eighth than in the Third Circuit in 1985.[4] If such factors affect the rate of litigation, as many of the observers discussed in the next section believe, then we might expect important differences to emerge in litigation rates across the circuits.

The number of U.S. civil and private civil appeals commenced in each circuit for four years during our period of analysis is shown in Figures 9-5 and 9-6. Because population is one of the important features distinguishing the circuits, we have not presented per capita figures, which would tend to "smooth" the pattern. Also, note that the Eleventh Circuit was created out of the Fifth Circuit in 1980, so it appears only in our 1990 data. If the "old" Fifth Circuit were reconstituted, the total number of cases in it in 1990 would be 1,286 U.S. civil appeals and 4,907 private civil appeals, making it the most "litigious" circuit in the system.

One initial observation is that diversity in docket size was quite limited in 1945 and 1960, even absent a control for population size. The difference between the lowest and highest number of *U.S. civil* cases in 1945 (the First and Ninth Circuits, respectively) was just 80 cases. By 1990 the difference between the First and Ninth Circuits (still the lowest and highest in number) was 887 cases. In the *private civil* category (Figure 9-6), the emergence of circuit diversity is even more substantial. In 1945 the Ninth Circuit handled just 131 more private civil cases than the First Circuit. By 1990, the Ninth Circuit took in over 2,400 more cases than the First Circuit. Of course, population is a key factor in a comparison of the First and Ninth Circuits. In 1990 the First Circuit, comprising four small northeastern states, had just 9.4 million residents, whereas the Ninth, including California, Washington, Oregon, and six smaller states, had 45.8 million. Even accounting for this population difference, however, the Ninth Circuit had a higher per capita rate of private civil appeals than the First Circuit.

Population is just one factor that may be used to explain rates of litigation. In the next section of the chapter we introduce theories about influences of other factors on litigation

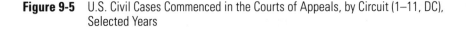

Figure 9-5 U.S. Civil Cases Commenced in the Courts of Appeals, by Circuit (1–11, DC), Selected Years

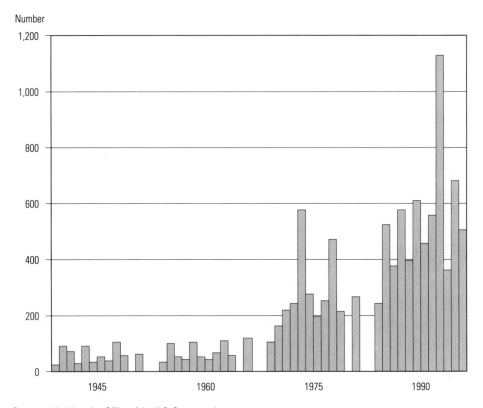

Source: Administrative Office of the U.S. Courts, various years.

rates. In the final section we apply those theories to the data we have presented here on appellate litigation; we focus on civil litigation because it constitutes the largest portion of the appellate docket, having done so for longer than thirty years, and it accounts for the most dramatic growth in appellate litigation.

Factors Affecting Appellate Litigation Rates

What theories of litigation explain differences in appeal rates to the circuit courts? The simple answer to this question is that we know very little about what drives appellate litigation. Thus far, empirically based theories of litigation activity deal with trial court litigation, both state and federal, not appellate litigation. Most studies also deal with total filing in a trial court system rather than filing among courts in a system. Longitudinal

Figure 9-6 Private Civil Cases Commenced in the Courts of Appeals, by Circuit (1–11, DC), Selected Years

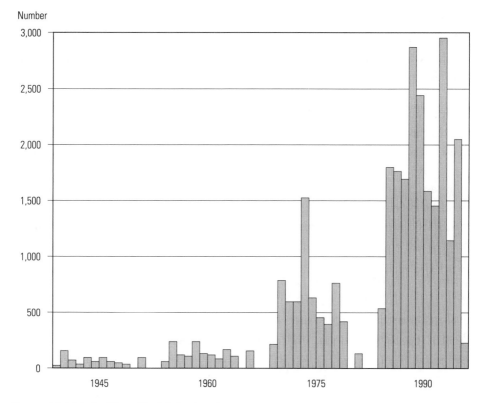

Source: Administrative Office of the U.S. Courts, various years.

studies of federal trial court litigation, for example, report national litigation trends and do not include comparisons of differences among the districts (Clark 1981; Galanter 1983; Grossman and Sarat 1975; Heydebrand 1990; Heydebrand and Seron 1986, 1990). Studies of state courts similarly examine changes in the rates and composition of litigation over time (Atkins and Glick 1976; Kagan et al. 1977; Roper 1986a, 1986b). Cross-sectional studies comparing litigation activity in several states (Grossman et al. 1982), counties (Daniels 1985; Friedman and Percival 1976; Munger 1988), and cities (Wanner 1974, 1975) have also paid little attention to variation among courts. So, although existing research on litigation is limited to trial courts, even that work has not gone far in theorizing about what accounts for differences or similarities among courts within the same system.

Intuitively we might assume that litigants would be deterred because of the added costs, in money and in time, of an appeal and the low odds of winning an appeal—the circuit courts in the last twenty years affirmed at least 90 percent of the appeals they heard (see Table 9-1). This may explain why losing parties at the trial level do not appeal (if data were available to test such a premise), but they do not tell us why appeals are filed. In other words, what factors explain variations or similarities in rates of appeals among the circuit courts?

The two main theories for explaining litigation rates are the social development theory and the political culture theory. The social development theory holds that legal change is dependent on change in society (Friedman 1969; Hurst 1950). Variation in rates of litigation over time is hypothesized to be a "function of the level of complexity, differentiation, and scale of a social structure" (Sarat and Grossman 1975, 1209). The more complex and more hierarchical a society is, the more likely litigation and formal dispute processes will be used. The social development theory, based on a Weberian concept of social relations, posits that litigation will increase as society becomes more "modern." Social development theory assumes that if certain socioeconomic conditions are present, litigation activity will be essentially the same for all courts (Daniels 1984, 754). The theory cannot, however, explain differences among judicial institutions in situations in which, for example, industrialization is positively associated with litigation rates in one court but negatively associated with litigation rates in another. The theory, instead, predicts that if a court is located in a highly industrialized environment, litigation rates will be higher than in those courts located in less industrial settings.

Social scientists have tested the social development theory with measures of industrialization (proportion of work force in manufacturing industries), urbanization (ratio of population per square mile), and legal resources (number of lawyers per population) as surrogates for social complexity. The empirical findings provide mixed support for the theory in some cases, and in others the theory simply does not work. For example, Grossman and Sarat (1975) could not match federal trial court litigation rates to a social development model. In an intensive study of litigation rates over time in one city (St. Louis), however, McIntosh (1983) found some support for a modified version of the social development theory. His data revealed a curvilinear, rather than linear, relation between social and legal development. Subsequent research on county courts in West Virginia also produced weak support for the theory, finding no systematic relation between the pace of industrialization and the rate of litigation (Munger 1988).

The second theory of litigation activity holds that political culture plays an important role in explaining litigation rates. Although judicial research dealing with concepts like political culture has been concerned mainly with plea-bargaining rates in lower criminal courts (Church 1978; Eisenstein and Jacob 1977; Kritzer 1979; Levine 1977), a few political scientists have applied a political culture explanation to litigation use. In a study by

Grossman and others (1982), cultural orientations toward politics were hypothesized as correlating with a propensity to use litigation as a means to resolve a dispute rather than other, less formal, dispute processes, such as arbitration or mediation. The authors defined the concept of political culture as "a cluster of intermediate-level variables which affect or produce a local culture of court usage" (Grossman and others 1982, 91). States and cities within five federal district court jurisdictions were ranked along a political culture spectrum ranging from "moralistic," at which high litigation rates were predicted, to "traditionalistic," at which low rates of litigation were predicted. In between these two points were "individualistic" political cultures. The researchers hypothesized that there would be higher levels of litigation in the political subcultures of moralists (Wisconsin/ Milwaukee and Central California/ Los Angeles) than in those places categorized as traditionalistic political subcultures (New Mexico/ Albuquerque and South Carolina/ Columbia). They expected that litigation levels would be somewhere in the middle for individualistic political subcultures (Eastern Pennsylvania/ Philadelphia). The only place in which litigation rates met their expectations was Philadelphia; in all other places litigation rates were found to be inversely related to the hypothesized political subcultures.

Whether their concept of political culture adequately captured the legal dimension of political culture or not, it is assumed in the political culture theory, as it is in the social development theory, that all litigation is completely dependent on factors that are external to legal institutions. But what about judicial institutions themselves? Do they have an effect on litigation? Perhaps both theories are limited and hence problematic because they do not allow for the possibility that courts themselves may encourage or discourage litigation. Rather than looking outside the courts for an explanation of litigation activity, we might look inside judicial institutions and see if they affect their own litigation rates. This approach offers a third explanation for litigation activity, one we call an *institutional* theory (Harrington and Ward 1993). It draws on research about how courts generate their own agendas by selecting which cases they will hear (Provine 1980) and on work done on the institutional practices of appellate courts (Barrow and Walker 1988; Brigham 1987). Instead of assuming that the use of litigation follows social change or is determined by dominant cultural frames, in an institutional theory it is hypothesized that there is diversity in litigation activity among courts that "results from the effect of differing *local* environmental factors channeled through or mediated by certain key constraints" (Daniels 1984, 754), such as economic and political constraints, but not limited to them. Thus, institutional practices, such as methods of case processing (disposing of cases with or without a hearing) and reversal rates, may operate in particular ways for certain courts and not other courts.

Testing Hypotheses about Litigation

Although the social development and political culture theories of litigation have been applied to trial courts, no one has ever tested their applicability to the courts of appeals. In this section we do so, and we also test the institutional theory. To do this we draw hypotheses from the discussion above and test them in a statistical analysis of civil appeals in the U.S. courts of appeals over time. We distinguish between government and private civil cases to determine whether litigation patterns among these two types of cases respond to different sets of factors. Specifically, we conduct two separate statistical analyses, one with per capita U.S. civil cases in each circuit as the dependent variable (the variable to be explained) and the other with per capita private civil cases as the dependent variable. Here we limit the period of analysis to 1961-1989 because several of the key independent variables (the variables that explain changes in the dependent variable) are not readily available for the 1945-1960 period. In addition, we omit the District of Columbia Circuit because its small population tends to distort the per capita measure and because it is a unique political jurisdiction. It is generally assumed in litigation theories that political and economic conditions affect the decisions of residents in a jurisdiction to make use of its judicial system. A substantial proportion of the cases in the District of Columbia Circuit, however, are generated by the government rather than the citizens of the district (see Harrington 1988; Howard 1981).[5]

Three sets of independent variables—social and economic, political, and institutional—might reasonably be expected to affect the rate of appellate litigation. By seeking to explain litigation rates for a nineteen-year period and across the various circuits, we have the benefit of variation in these factors among the circuits and within individual circuits over time. In the following sections we propose specific hypotheses and detail the variables and measurements used to test them. We then provide a brief, nontechnical, discussion of the statistical model and present the results of the analysis.

Social and Economic Conditions

When we use the per capita litigation rate for the dependent variables we control for population, one of the most important factors used to explain litigation rates. Although individuals are not the primary litigants in many courts of appeals cases, where interest groups and corporations are quite active, larger populations certainly provide greater opportunities for disputes. Included in the analysis as explanatory variables are two factors that have long been held to influence the use of the judicial system: economic pressure and social complexity (McIntosh 1983, 1990). Social development theory suggests that greater wealth and social complexity lead to greater use of the courts. While there are many possible ways to measure wealth and social complexity, we chose the most commonly used measurements. For economic pressure we use per capita personal income, and for social complexity we use population density, or the number of persons per square mile (Durkheim 1960).[6] In both cases we use a lagged measure to account for the pace of the judicial process.

Social development theory suggests two hypotheses:

Hypothesis 1: The higher the per capita income in a circuit, the higher the rate of litigation, everything else being equal.

Hypothesis 2: The higher the population density in a circuit, the higher the rate of litigation, everything else being equal.

Furthermore, we expect private civil appeals to be more responsive to social and economic variables than government cases. Because government litigators are often "repeat players" and thus have a keen knowledge of the judicial process, they may be less affected by social and economic factors than private parties (Galanter 1974; Songer 1991).

Political Conditions

In our consideration of the political conditions of a circuit we are not concerned here with its partisan character. Instead, we are interested in the relation between political opportunity and court use. McIntosh (1983, 1990) and others correlated litigation rates with voter turnout and one-party dominance in certain states to determine whether the use of litigation corresponded with measures of political efficacy. McIntosh found a significant negative relation between voter turnout and litigation rates, and a positive relation between levels of one-party dominance of the state legislature and litigation. Both findings lend support to the thesis that court use increases where the political environment is less responsive. The general expectation is that citizens who are more politically effective will be less likely to turn to litigation. To test this expectation, we include two political variables: competitiveness and participation. Participation is the more easily measured. We simply use the percentage of eligible voters participating in the most recent presidential election. Competition is measured as an index of support for Democratic congressional candidates, ranging from zero for a circuit dominated by one party to fifty for a fully competitive circuit.

Again, two hypotheses are derived from the theory:

Hypothesis 3: The higher the rate of political participation, the lower the litigation rate, everything else being equal.

Hypothesis 4: The higher the level of political competitiveness, the lower the litigation rate, everything else being equal.

As in the case of social and economic conditions, we expect private litigation to be more responsive to political factors in a circuit than government cases. It is generally theorized that the less responsive the political system, the more likely it is that an individual will choose to litigate. But we know from previous research that the judicial system is quite responsive to government litigants (Caldeira and Wright 1988, 1990), so the responsiveness of the political system may be less crucial for these elite actors.

The Institutional Context

We have identified three institutional properties of appellate courts that may affect the flow of appeals to the circuits. Two of these are the handling of cases by the court and the court's treatment of decisions made by a lower court. We have already seen that when the appellate docket began a sharp upward turn in number of cases, there also began a steady trend toward procedural termination of cases (that is, without a hearing) and away from overturning lower-court decisions.

The purpose of this analysis is not to duplicate the findings shown in Table 9-1, but to examine whether, in the midst of these simultaneous trends, differences in institutional properties across the circuits affected the rate of litigation. That is to say, if Circuit X normally gives a case a full hearing and often overturns lower-court decisions, will it draw more cases than a circuit with opposite tendencies? The measurement of these variables is straightforward. Case disposition is simply the percentage of cases dismissed without a hearing in the previous year. Treatment of lower-court decisions is measured as the percentage of cases reversed in the previous year. Naturally, these variables are lagged, so we can logically hypothesize that a court's characteristics affect future decisions of litigators. Thus, we can propose two additional hypotheses:

Hypothesis 5: The higher the rate of procedural terminations, the lower the rate of litigation, everything else being equal.

Hypothesis 6: The higher the rate of reversals, the higher the rate of litigation, everything else being equal.

A third institutional property that we consider is judicial ideology, or partisan identification. This variable is introduced largely as a control to account for the variation in ideology of the circuit benches. Hypothetically, if Republican judges were thought to be especially harsh on prisoner petitions, then we might expect the appeal of such cases to decline in a circuit with a heavily Republican bench. In the aggregate, no particular hypothesis, or a priori expectation, is proposed for this variable. It is measured simply as the percentage of judges claiming Democratic partisan identification (or appointed by a Democrat in the absence of party identification).

One important expectation regarding the institutional context is that U.S. civil cases are more likely to be responsive to institutional factors. As noted above, government litigators play an important role in the judicial process. They are repeat players, indeed, elite actors. As such, government lawyers may be more informed about and responsive to the distinct institutional properties of the various circuits than lawyers for private civil appeals.

Statistical Model and Results

We turn now to a brief elaboration of the model and a presentation of results from our statistical analysis. In cross-sectional statistical analysis, the dependent variable represents observations for different units (individuals, states, nations) at one point in time. Time series analysis entails observations for one unit for many points in time (annual unemployment, for instance). In this study we combine data for multiple circuits over time, which necessitates the use of a pooled time series, cross-sectional statistical model.[7] This model is useful for our study because it controls for the overall national trend of growth in litigation and allows us to focus on the effects of variation in the other independent variables.[8]

In Table 9-2 we present the results of the analysis for both government and private civil litigation from 1961 through 1989. For each variable the hypothesized direction of the regression coefficient is shown as greater or less than zero. For example, because it is hypothesized in the social development theory that litigation would increase with higher per capita personal income, the expectation is that the coefficient for per capital income will be greater than zero.[9] Coefficients and t-statistics (as a test of significance) are shown as well.

Turning first to the social and economic variables, we find that the hypotheses are not confirmed. Per capita income is in the expected direction for U.S. civil cases but is not statistically significant. In contrast, per capital income is statistically significant at the .01 level of significance in the private model, but it is in the opposite direction of that hypothesized. In other words, more private civil appeals appear in circuits with lower levels of per capita income. Population density is statistically significant in the U.S. model, but in the opposite direction of the one hypothesized in the social development theory. The results show that, everything else being equal, more government appeals per capita are found in low-density circuits than in high-density circuits. The fact that population itself has been accounted for in the per capita measure of the dependent variable may explain this discrepancy. That is to say, high-density circuits also tend to be circuits with a high population. Population density is in the expected direction in the model of private appeals but is statistically insignificant.

Moving to the political variables, in accordance with previous research on trial courts, we find that greater political effectiveness tends to be associated with lower levels of court use. Partisan competition is statistically insignificant in both models, but it is stronger and in the hypothesized direction in the model of private appeals. Participation is in the hypothesized direction in both models, although it is statistically significant only for private cases.

Overall, the results for the social, economic, and political variables do not provide strong support for the social development theory. Despite findings that tend to support it at lower levels of the judiciary, it does not perform as well in the federal appellate arena;

Table 9-2 Pooled Analysis of Appellate Litigation Rates, 1961-1989 (cases per 100,000 in population)

	Hypothesis	U.S. civil appeals		Private civil appeals	
		b	t	b	t
Intercept		0.710	2.23*	5.447	7.30**
PINC	>0	0.023	0.23	−0.746	−3.17**
PDEN	>0	−0.001	−4.67**	0.001	1.17
COMP	<0	0.002	0.42	−0.018	−1.49
PART	<0	−0.002	−0.42	−0.036	−2.99**
REV	>0	−0.003	−0.93	−0.026	−2.42**
TERM	<0	−0.005	−2.14*	0.018	3.01**
JID		0.002	1.41	0.010	270**

Note: b=unstandardized coefficient; t=*t* value; PINC=per capita income; PDEN=population density; COMP= political competitiveness; PART=political participation; REV=reversals; TERM=procedural terminations; JID= judicial ideology. For U.S. civil appeals, R^2=.8053; for private civil appeals, R^2=.8870. N=298.

$p \leq .05$ level   ** $p \leq .01$ level.

commonly used measures of the political and social environment do not consistently account in the hypothesized manner for important variation in rates of civil appeals in the U.S. circuit courts of appeals.

Turning to institutional hypotheses, we find that the handling of cases by the circuits *does* appear to have some systematic effect on litigation rates. A circuit's propensity to reverse lower-court decisions, however, *reduces* appellate litigation, although, an acceptable level of statistical significance is achieved only in the model of private civil appeals. This finding may simply capture a long-term relation. Courts with higher workloads tend to reverse fewer cases. The finding on procedural terminations meets with the expectations discussed above for government cases only. That is to say, the more cases a circuit disposes of without a full hearing, the fewer cases come to it in the following term. The opposite is the case for private civil appeals. The results also show that courts that lean toward the Democratic side draw increased litigation, although the coefficient is statistically significant only for private appeals.

Conclusion

Taking the results together, we can build a hypothetical profile of the most and least litigious circuits. For U.S. civil appeals, the highest number of per capita cases would be found in circuits that have low population density and that exhibit a propensity to give cases a full hearing. On the private side, more cases would be found in those circuits in which the per capita income was lower; there was little political participation; and the benches were occupied by Democrats, who tended to dispose of cases without a hearing and rarely overturned lower-court rulings. Overall, there is a slightly better fit for the private than the government model, suggesting that government actors may be less influenced than private actors by environmental factors in their decisions to appeal cases in federal court, as expected. The fact that several of the coefficients emerge in the opposite direction from the one expected, however, does not give us much confidence in this statement, however.

Although some findings of the research in trial litigation have been upheld, the differences for appellate litigation are meaningful. What distinguishes the U.S. courts of appeals from lower courts are the circuits themselves. Future researchers who hope to elaborate on our current knowledge about the appellate process should turn more directly to the circuits, measuring their distinctions in more detail and building those measures into more elaborate explanatory models.

Notes

1. The U.S. Court of Appeals for the District of Columbia and the recently created U.S. Court of Appeals for the Federal Circuit are the only two courts of appeals that do not follow this practice.

2. Political scientists have noted that "regionalism flourished alongside nationalization of judicial values," despite a trend toward greater uniformity in circuit dockets (Howard 1981, 23; also see Baum, Goldman, and Sarat 1981-1982; Carp and Rowland 1983; Goldman 1975; Songer and Davis 1990).

3. All data cited are from the annual reports of the Administrative Office of the United States (various years). "Cases" refer to cases commenced in the year ending June 30.

4. Demographic and political data throughout the analysis are from the *Statistical Abstract of the United States* (U.S. Bureau of the Census, various years).

5. For a more extensive version of this analysis see Harrington and Ward 1993.

6. For purposes of analysis, Alaska is excluded from all measures of the Ninth Circuit because its inclusion tends to distort the population density measure.

7. Although there are several available techniques for carrying out such analysis, we have used the most tractable design, the least-squares with dummy variables (LSDV). See Maddala 1977, 138-139; Sayrs 1989; and Stimson 1985 for further elaboration of the technique. For more details about the statistical tool used in this chapter, see Appendix A of this volume.

8. For readers' information, the equation estimated is:

$$Y_{it} = a + b_1 X1_{it-1} + b_2 X2_{it-1} + b_3 X3_{it} + b_4 X4_{it} + b_5 X5_{it-1}$$
$$+ b_6 X6_{it-1} + b_7 X7_{it-1} + (b_8 T_1 + \ldots + b_{35} T_{28}),$$

where Y = appellate cases per 100,000 in population; a = an intercept term; i = circuit, $i = 1$–10; t = time, $t = 1 - 19$; $X1$ = per capita personal income (in thousands of 1967 dollars), in circuit i, at time $t - 1$; $X2$ = population per square miles, in circuit i, at time $t - 1$; $X3 = 50$ minus the absolute value difference between the mean Democratic percentage of the vote in all congressional districts and 50 percent, in circuit i, in the previous congressional election; $X4$ = percentage of voting age population voting in the last presidential election, in circuit i; $X5$ = percentage of circuit judges self-identified as Democrats, in circuit i, at time $t-1$; $X6$ = percentage of cases reversed in circuit at time $t-1$; $X7$ = percentage of cases disposed of without a hearing in circuit at time $t-1$; $T_1 - T_{28}$ = a series of dummy variables for 1961-1989, the year 1961 being the omitted, or reference, category.

For data normally reported by state (income and voting), the totals for the states within a circuit were aggregated to construct a circuit variable. For instance, total income for a circuit is the sum of income for all states in that circuit, divided by the total population in those states. Participation rates were calculated as the total number of people voting in the appropriate states in the last presidential election divided by the total voting age population in those same states.

9. In order to conserve space we have not reported coefficients for the twenty-eight dummy variables that represent the points of time. We find that the pattern of steady increase in the level of appeals is consistent for both types of cases, indicated by increasing coefficients that show the difference between the given year and the omitted year, 1961. The increase starts more slowly for U.S. cases than for private cases.

10 Decision Making on the U.S. Courts of Appeals

Jeffrey A. Segal, Donald R. Songer, and Charles M. Cameron

The courts of appeals occupy a pivotal position in our political system, the "vital center of the federal judicial system" (Howard 1981, 8). Since their creation in the 1890s, they have been responsible for ensuring the uniformity of national law in a diverse republic in which sectional pressures constantly seek to undermine that uniformity. More recently, they have become the principal means of supervising the myriad federal regulatory agencies. In both these roles, they are important policy makers: the final authoritative interpreters of federal law and the Constitution in the overwhelming majority of all civil and criminal cases filed in the federal courts.[1]

We consider decision making on the U.S. courts of appeals by examining three different models of behavior—the legal model, the attitudinal model, and the hierarchical model. Briefly, the legal model, as its name suggests, holds that judges make decisions based on legal factors such as the intent of the framers of the Constitution and precedent. Alternatively, the attitudinal model holds that judges make decisions based on their own attitudes and values. Finally, the hierarchical model holds that judges on the courts of appeals have attitudes and values but, as intermediate-level players in a complex judicial hierarchy, are limited in their ability to pursue their values. Hence, the hierarchical model combines elements of the other two and encompasses them as extreme cases. We examine these models using a sample of search and seizure cases decided by the U.S. courts of appeals between 1961 and 1990.

Models of Judicial Decision Making

Before we describe these models in greater detail, it may be useful to discuss what a model is and why judicial scholars use them.[2] We start with the premise that the real world is extraordinarily complex. Consider, for instance, the decision of one judge in just one case. What factors influence her decision to rule for one party instead of the other? Those

We thank Robert Ortiz and Kelly Boozer for their research assistance. We gratefully acknowledge the support of National Science Foundation grant SES-9112755.

interested in answering such a question might first consider the facts of the case. They would piece together information from dozens of witnesses to determine what the appellee or defendant may or may not have done and what his intent might have been if and when he did what was alleged. In criminal cases the researchers would have to put together similar information about the police, and in civil cases they would do the same for the appellant. Second, they would consider the beliefs and values of the judge. Is she a Republican or a Democrat, liberal or conservative? Does she have positive or negative feelings toward blacks, whites, Jews, Christians, males, females, senior citizens, handicapped persons, labor, business, or any other type of litigant involved in the suit? Is the judge happy with her job, or is she hoping to get promoted to a higher court or thinking of running for public office? Third, what are the preferences of higher courts, and do they have the ability to impose their preferences on the lower courts? What have higher courts said in cases similar to this? Are the rulings consistent, or is there leeway for the judge? If the rulings are consistent but dated, might new upper courts favor differing interpretations? Will a higher court have the opportunity to review and reverse the lower court? Fourth, what is the political and economic environment like? Is crime a hot issue? Is unemployment up? Do citizens believe local courts are too lenient on crime?

Certainly we could go on. It is, after all, possible to write entire books about particular cases. These typically involve monumental cases such as *Brown v. Board of Education* (1954 [Kruger 1975]) and *Gideon v. Wainright* (1963 [Lewis 1964]), but presumably the same innumerable influences (minus journalistic and scholarly attention) go into decisions in lesser cases as well.[3] One approach to learning, then, is to attempt to learn all you can about as little as possible. Two problems result from this approach. First, human behavior is often so complex that you could spend an entire course studying a particular decision and still in the end not fully understand it. Even a judge might not fully understand all the factors that influenced his or her own decision. Moreover, most of the facts you learn about a single decision are easily forgotten. Second, you are left wondering how generalizable the study of one particular case is to the rest of judicial decision making. You might try to study all the factors that influenced *Roe v. Wade* (1973), but which of those give any clue as to the factors that influenced *Furman v. Georgia* (1972)?[4] Some of the factors that influenced *Roe* probably influenced other decisions as well, but which ones? The detailed study of a single event might provide a useful *description* of events, but it does not and cannot constitute an *explanation* of events that can confidently be carried over to other areas.

An alternative approach is to recognize the complexity of the world around us and to accept the fact that trying to learn everything about one thing may not always be the best way to acquire knowledge. Instead, we can try to examine the most explanatory aspects of a wider set of decisions. Learning the most important factors that influence thousands of decisions might be far more beneficial than learning as much as is humanly possible about a single decision.

This is where models come in. A model is a simplified representation of reality; it does not constitute reality itself. Models purposefully ignore certain aspects of reality and focus instead on a selected set of crucial factors. Such simplifications give us a useful handle for understanding the real world that we could not obtain from more exhaustive and descriptive strategies. For instance, journalistic accounts of presidential elections discuss thousands of factors that might have influenced the final results (for example, White 1961). But if 80 percent of the variance in postwar presidential elections can be explained by changes in real disposable income, then a simplified real-disposable-income model gives us an extraordinarily useful tool for explaining and understanding not just one but a series of presidential elections.

The value of this method of understanding courts has long been appreciated. For example, Oliver Wendell Holmes, in his famous essay "The Path of the Law," advanced a "prediction theory" of the law. Holmes noted that lawyers must be able to predict what judges will do in order to advise their clients appropriately. In fact, Holmes put such stress on prediction that he *defined* the law itself as nothing more than predictions about the behavior of judges. Predictions require models. Hence, models of judicial behavior can be seen as closely connected with the concept of law itself.

From the viewpoint of a social scientist, a successful model achieves two often contradictory goals: it explains the behavior in question, and it does so simply and parsimoniously. A model that does not validly and reliably explain and predict the behavior in question, be it the votes of citizens or the decisions of circuit court judges, is obviously of little value. But an unduly complex model that explains behavior may be almost as worthless, for it fails to give us the grasp on reality that we need from models. Unfortunately, the goals of explanation and parsimony are often contradictory, for the more complex one's model, the more behavior one can "explain." For instance, a judge's vote in a particular criminal procedure case may be based on his or her knowing one of the attorneys well, or knowing a victim of the crime in question. A vote in another case might depend on a different random occurrence. Nevertheless, a good model ignores such idiosyncratic factors and highlights instead variables that explain a high percentage of the behavior in question.

With this explanation in mind, let us now consider the models that may characterize decision making on the U.S. courts of appeals: the legal, attitudinal, and hierarchical models.[5] We do not expect any of the models to be able to tell us everything about judicial decision making; rather, we hope that they will help students of the judiciary better understand how decisions get made.

The Legal Model

We start with the legal model, which postulates that the decisions of courts are based on the facts of the case in light of the plain meaning of statutes and the U.S. Constitution, the intent of the framers, and precedent. Of the three, we focus on precedent, for in our sample of cases (search and seizure decisions), we do not find text or intent to be useful guides to how judges actually resolve disputes.[6] At the level of the U.S. Supreme Court, precedent means deciding cases based on previous high court rulings. This is often not a reliable guide because most attorneys can readily find Supreme Court precedents on either side of the case they are arguing. And even when precedents typically fall on one side only, the Court feels free to ignore them, particularly in constitutional cases.[7] For lower courts, the decision calculus is substantially different: they are supposed to follow the policy preferences set into law by the Supreme Court. The obligation to follow the precedents set by the courts above is a fundamental assumption of our legal system that is constantly reinforced for judges by their law school training, bar associations, and their colleagues on the bench. Without respect for Supreme Court decisions, federal law would mean something completely different in every circuit. And if district courts ignored the circuit courts, federal law would mean something different in every state within a circuit and, in states that had more than one district court, something different in different regions of a state. We are thus not surprised to find evidence that the norm of *stare decisis* has been internalized by most judges. More than 90 percent of the appeals court judges interviewed in one study maintained that when precedent was "clear and relevant" it would have a significant effect on their decision (Howard 1981, 164). Thus, as Supreme Court decisions change, lower courts are obliged to follow suit.

One strand of empirical evidence suggests that this is in fact the case. The decisional trends of both the district and appeals courts shifted to decidedly more liberal patterns in economic policy following the 1937 Supreme Court switch (Songer and Reid 1989; Stidham and Carp 1982). The appointment of Democratic judges to the lower courts before the Supreme Court's policy shift had no substantial effect on policy making in the lower courts. In areas other than criminal procedure (Songer, Rowland, and Carp 1984; Songer and Sheehan 1990), changes in the decisional tendencies of the courts of appeals and district courts likewise followed major changes in policy making in the Supreme Court (Baum 1980; Songer 1987; Songer and Reid 1989; Songer and Sheehan 1990). Still, large-scale noncompliance with Supreme Court decisions has been found by some researchers, thus suggesting that factors other than precedent determine decision making in the lower courts (Beatty 1972; Canon and Kolson 1971; Manwaring 1968; Peltason 1961; Tarr 1977). These studies have typically focused on the school desegregation cases or on other controversial civil liberties decisions of the Warren Court.

Figure 10-1 Justices and Cases in Attitudinal Space

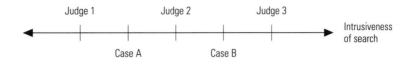

Judge 1   Judge 2   Judge 3

Intrusiveness of search

Case A   Case B

The Attitudinal Model

In contrast to the legal model, the attitudinal model holds that judges decide disputes in light of the facts of the case, given their ideological attitudes and values (Schubert 1965; Segal and Spaeth 1993).[8] To illustrate, imagine a search and seizure whose constitutionality the Court must determine. Assume the police searched a person's house with a valid warrant supported by probable cause. There were no extenuating circumstances. The search uncovered an incriminating diary. Now imagine a second search, similar to the first in that probable cause existed, but in which the police failed to obtain a warrant. Again, there were no extenuating circumstances.

According to the attitudinal model, one can place these searches in ideological space. Since the search without a warrant can be considered less libertarian than the search with the warrant, we place the first search to the left of the second search. This is diagrammed in Figure 10-1, where A represents the first search and B the second. Presumably, any search and seizure will locate on the line; depending on the characteristics of the case, the search will be to the left of A, between A and B (inclusive), or to the right of B. The less prior justification (probable cause or warrant) and the more severe the intrusion (home as opposed to car, or full search as opposed to frisk), the further to the right the search will fall. The more prior justification and the less intrusive the search, the further to the left it will be. The points on the line where the searches lie are referred to as *j*-points.

Next, we place the justices in ideological space. Consider three judges, 1, 2, and 3, who are, respectively, liberal, moderate, and conservative. They could easily be rank-ordered on an ideological scale, with 1 on the left, 2 in the middle, and 3 on the right.

With some additional information we might be able to go a bit further and say that Judge 1 is so liberal that he would not even uphold the search in the first case, perhaps because he believes that police may not search and seize "mere evidence," such as papers and diaries. Thus, we could place Judge 1 to the left of Case A. Judge 2 might not be quite so strict as Judge 1; she would uphold the search of the home with a warrant, but would not uphold the warrantless search. Thus, we could place Judge 2 to the right of Case A but to the left of Case B. Finally, Judge 3 might find the warrant requirement fairly unimportant and would uphold any search he considered reasonable. Since probable cause supported both searches, both are reasonable. Thus, we could place Judge 3 to the right of Case B. The judges are placed in ideological space with the cases in Figure 10-1.

The placement of the judges on the scale constitutes their i-points, or indifference points. A judge will vote to uphold all searches that are dominated by, or are to the left of, the judge's indifference point and will vote to strike all searches that dominate, or are to the right of, the judge's indifference point. Thus, Judge 1 upholds all searches to the left of 1, rejects all searches to the right of 1, and is indifferent whether searches at 1 are upheld or overturned.

Indirect support for the attitudinal model comes from the fact that lower courts have on occasion simply refused to follow Supreme Court precedents (Beatty 1972; Canon and Kolson 1971; Manwaring 1968; Peltason 1961; Tarr 1977). Moreover, the decisions of lower-court judges correlate well with factors such as the judges' partisanship and region (Carp and Rowland 1983; Scigliano 1971; Songer and Davis 1990). The most plausible explanation for such findings is that these variables influence decisions indirectly by working through the judges' ideological predispositions.

The Hierarchical Model

Arguably, the pure attitudinal model has particular relevance for decision making on the Supreme Court. The Supreme Court is a court of last resort whose decisions cannot be overturned by other courts. Supreme Court justices lack electoral or (for the most part) political accountability and have no ambition for higher office. In general, then, they need please no one but themselves.[9] Finally, the Court controls its own jurisdiction and thus can weed out frivolous suits in which text or intent or precedent might be perfectly clear.

These arguments have limited applicability to the judges who sit on the U.S. courts of appeals. First, ambition might be a constraint on the decisions of circuit court judges. Whereas Supreme Court justices have little room to improve their job stature, the same is not true of circuit court judges. We have no accurate count, but it strikes us as reasonable to assume that many of these judges dream of being promoted to the Supreme Court.[10] Thus, the politically acceptable might impinge on the personally preferable. Second, decisions made in circuit courts can be appealed to the Supreme Court. Lower-court judges must then at least consider the preferences of courts above them, although as we shall see, the extent to which they must do so is not always clear. Finally, lack of docket control means that circuit court judges get some cases to decide in which legal discretion is at a minimum, perhaps because of the clarity of a statute or the settling of the issue by the Supreme Court.[11] Although it is impossible to know how often appeals court judges feel that the law or precedents are so clear that any judge would feel constrained to reach the same conclusion, one study estimated that such constraint may exist in as many as 62 percent of their cases (that is, judges may have substantial discretion in only a little over a third of their cases [Songer 1982]).

How might one construct a model of judicial decision making by judges who are constrained by their location in the judicial hierarchy? A detailed answer is far beyond the scope of this chapter; nevertheless, one way to proceed is to use insights from what social scientists refer to as "principal-agent" theory, a theory of strategic decision making within hierarchical settings. Principal-agent theory focuses on situations in which subordinates have different preferences from their hierarchical superiors and the ability to take hidden actions or exploit hidden information relevant to the decisions. According to the theory, monitoring, auditing, and sanctioning become critical in such situations; the theory provides tools for analyzing these and other features of hierarchies.

Application of principal-agent theory to the federal judiciary suggests a "hierarchical model" of circuit courts. At the level considered here, the hierarchical model is mainly conceptual; exact predictions depend on the detailed procedures followed in the hierarchy. For example, tightening or loosening the certiorari process used by the Supreme Court might well alter the decisions coming from the circuit courts. One very general prediction, however, is common across a wide variety of hierarchical models: *superiors rarely find it in their interest to control the behavior of subordinates completely.* The reason may be understood through reference to Figure 10-2.

Figure 10-2 shows the marginal benefits and marginal costs to a higher court of controlling the decisions of a lower court. Costs include greater effort put forth in scrutinizing cases as well as hearing more cases. Benefits include greater conformity between the lower court's doctrine and the upper court's preferences. Marginal costs and benefits are the incremental effect on total costs or benefits of slightly increasing or decreasing the extent of control. As shown, we assume the marginal cost of control increases: at low levels of control an incremental increase in control is likely to require relatively little additional effort because noncompliance is so flagrant that detecting and correcting it is easy. At very high levels of control, however, the few remaining cases of nonconformity probably involve subtle deviations that require considerable effort to detect. We assume that marginal benefits of control are constant across the range of control (arguably, they might fall). The intersection of the cost and benefit curves represents the optimal level of control from the perspective of the higher court: if control were less, an incremental increase in control would bring benefits that exceed costs and would thus enhance the welfare of the higher court. Conversely, if control were greater than the optimal point, a decrease in control would result in a reduction in costs that would more than offset the reduction in benefits. In general, if marginal costs increase while marginal benefits fall or are constant, the two curves will intersect at less than 100 percent control. Accordingly, a general prediction over many hierarchical models is that decision making in the circuit courts depends both on the preferences of the nominal superiors, the Supreme Court, and those of the nominal subordinates, the circuit court judges.

Few studies have directly measured what we call the hierarchical model, but one study

Figure 10-2 The Hierarchical Model: Perfect Control Is Not Optimal

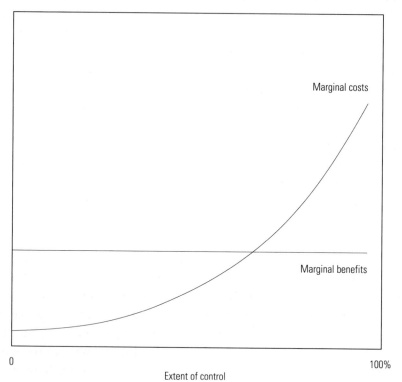

Costs, benefits

Marginal costs

Marginal benefits

0

100%

Extent of control

comes reasonably close. Songer and Reid (1989) examined decision making on the U.S. courts of appeals following doctrinal changes by the Supreme Court in 1936 in substantive due process cases and during the 1950s and 1960s in First Amendment cases (see also Songer, Segal, and Cameron 1994). In so doing they compare two models. The first states that appellate policy making will change as the result of presidential appointments to the appellate courts. If liberals are appointed, the court will become more liberal; if conservatives are appointed, the courts will become more conservative. In our framework, this implies attitudinal decision making. The second model, the legal model, recognizes that circuit court judges are in the middle of a judicial hierarchy and that such judges will more or less faithfully follow the principles of law set down by the Supreme Court.

Songer and Reid found strong support for the legal component of their model. Decision making in the circuit courts did not get more liberal as Roosevelt made appointments between 1933 and 1936. It was not until after the Supreme Court switched its position that the circuit courts started doing the same. Similarly, the circuit courts followed Supreme Court trends on the First Amendment more recently, voting conservatively in the 1950s, liberally in the 1960s, and conservatively again in the 1970s.

Methodological Concerns

Although this analysis and others have added to our understanding of lower-court responsiveness, all the studies previously cited have been hindered by a failure to take into account variation in the factual context in which different courts respond to decisions that announce new precedent. Recall first that fact patterns, or case stimuli, are crucial components of both the legal and attitudinal models. More important, a failure to consider changes in the types of cases courts hear can lead to misleading results. For example, an analysis of agenda change in five state supreme courts shows that the type of issues raised on appeal changed dramatically in response to the decisions in *Mapp v. Ohio* (1961) and *Miranda v. Arizona* (1966). A survey conducted in 1994 by Donald R. Songer revealed that the frequency with which briefs filed for defendants challenged the admissibility of incriminating statements and the frequency with which constitutional errors were alleged in trial court proceedings more than tripled in each state in the ten years following *Mapp.* Since the agendas of appellate courts may change in response to changed Supreme Court policy, analyses of the decisional trends of those courts are difficult to interpret without the addition of controls for changing fact patterns and changing issues. For example, if trial courts, following *Miranda*, severely restricted the ability of prosecutors to introduce confessions while appellate courts encouraged defense attorneys to challenge very subtle forms of coercion, the policy reflected in appeals court decisions might be significantly more liberal than it was prior to *Miranda* although the percentage of appeals court decisions that would be coded as liberal might actually decline. Thus, an analysis of the decisional trends of the courts of appeals that did not take into account the changed facts confronting the appeals court judges would be likely to produce a seriously distorted interpretation of responsiveness. We next examine, then, how we can test our models more carefully.

Hypotheses about Circuit Court Decision Making

The legal, attitudinal, and hierarchical models make different predictions about the factors influencing the decisions of circuit court judges. These differences create the opportunity to test the models. In Table 10-1 we summarize the different predictions.

The first thing to glean from Table 10-1 is that case facts are crucial to all three models. The legal model holds that judges consider the facts of the case in light of text, intent, and precedent. The attitudinal model holds that judges consider the facts of the case in light of their own personal policy preferences. The hierarchical model combines both perspectives: judges consider the facts of the case in light of their own personal policy preferences but

Table 10-1 Factors Affecting Circuit Court Decisions: Predictions from Three Models

		Prediction	
Model	Case facts matter	Supreme Court doctrine matters	Circuit court preferences matter
Legal	yes	yes	no
Attitudinal	yes	no	yes
Hierarchical	yes	yes	yes

are likely to be somewhat constrained by text, intent, and precedent, depending on the tools available to higher courts to control lower ones. Because all three models agree about the importance of case facts, fact variables cannot be used to test the models. Instead, fact variables must serve as control variables. That is, the inclusion of facts in our model will allow us to make sure that any results we achieve with regard to legal and attitudinal variables are the result of those factors and not changes in the types of cases heard by the courts of appeals.[12]

The situation differs concerning the influence of Supreme Court doctrine. The legal model and the hierarchical model suggest that the decisions of circuit court judges are affected by Supreme Court doctrine. In contrast, the attitudinal model suggests that Supreme Court doctrine plays little role in the decision making of the circuit court judges. So the importance of Supreme Court doctrine can be used to test the legal and hierarchical model versus the attitudinal model, but not against each other. In other words, if Supreme Court doctrine proves to be important in circuit court decision making, the data reject the attitudinal model as a complete explanation of circuit court decision making.

The attitudinal model and the hierarchical model suggest that circuit court decision making will be affected by the attitudes of the judges on the case, independent of the policy or doctrinal trends on the Supreme Court. The legal model, however, suggests that attitudinal variables play little role in judicial decision making. Therefore, attitudinal variables can distinguish the attitudinal and hierarchical model from the legal model. In other words, if attitudinal variables prove important, the data reject the legal model as a complete explanation of circuit court decision making.

Combining these tests implies the following: if either the attitudinal or the doctrinal variables prove unimportant, the data reject the hierarchical model. If both prove important, both the attitudinal and legal models are dominated by the hierarchical model as an explanation of circuit court decision making.

Research Design

We test the three models on a stratified random sample of votes by circuit court judges in search and seizure cases between 1961 and 1990.[13] Critical variables are the facts of the case, contemporary Supreme Court doctrine, and the attitudinal predisposition of the particular judge.

As discussed earlier, all three models consider the facts of the case to be important. Consistent with the models, we employ the fact-pattern model developed by Segal (1984). Segal's model examined the place of the intrusion (for example, home, business, car), the extent of the intrusion (full search or lesser intrusion), the prior justification (warrant and probable cause), and various exceptions to the warrant requirement (for example, searches incident to arrest).

The legal and hierarchical models suggest that the decisions of circuit court judges are affected by *contemporary* Supreme Court doctrine (Howard 1981; Richardson and Vines 1971), which may or may not be the same as previous doctrine. Therefore, we need to assess how Court doctrine has changed during our sampling period. We accomplished this by the following procedure. First, we estimated the search and seizure fact-pattern model discussed above on the decisions of the Supreme Court between 1961 and 1990 (see Segal and Spaeth 1993, chap. 6, for details). We then added a variable to capture how the Supreme Court's decision-making balance might have changed during this period. We hypothesized that each replacement of a Warren Court justice with a Republican appointee made the Court more conservative. Thus, the variable for Supreme Court change takes the value "zero" during the Warren Court and increases by one each time a Warren Court justice is replaced by a Republican appointee. This variable, which we call "Change," will measure circuit court responsiveness to changing Supreme Court preferences.

The attitudinal and hierarchical models suggest that decision making in the circuit courts is affected by the attitudes of the judges on the case, independent of the policy or doctrinal trends on the Supreme Court. Although much evidence suggests that lower-court judges are responsive to Supreme Court precedent, such studies have their limits, as noted above. Moreover, these studies contradict the overwhelming finding that federal judges' decisions correlate reasonably well with the judges' party identification (Goldman 1966, 1975; Howard 1981). If circuit court judges were merely proxies for the Supreme Court, their own attitudes and backgrounds simply would not matter.

One test of the attitudinal approach to circuit court decision making would add to our model a variable representing the ideology of each judge voting on the particular case. After we controlled for the facts of the case and the policy trends of the Supreme Court, this would tell us how much the judges' own preferences mattered. Unfortunately, we do not have direct, independent measures of the ideology of hundreds of circuit court judges, nor is it feasible to obtain them. We can, however, use two separate indicators that should correlate with their ideology. Those indicators are the party identification of the judge's appointing president (Carp and Rowland 1983; Scigliano 1971; Tate 1981; Tate and Handberg 1991) and whether the judge is from the South (Songer and Davis 1990; Tate, 1981; Tate and Handberg 1991).

Results

We first present the results from the basic fact-pattern model, which is a shared component of all three models. Our dependent variable, the variable we are trying to explain, is whether each judge voted to allow or disallow the search in question. The independent variables (those that are supposed to explain the dependent variable) are the facts of the case as originally modeled by Segal (1984). These include the extent of the intrusion and the prior justification for the search. The extent of the intrusion includes, first, where the search took place—such as one's home, one's business, one's car, or one's person—and second, the actual extent of the intrusion, which distinguishes between full searches on the one hand and stop-and-frisks and other limited intrusions on the other. The prior justification variables include the arrest, probable cause, and warrant variables. We measure whether searches are incident to a lawful arrest, after a lawful arrest, or after an unlawful arrest. Searches incident to arrest are those that take place at the time and place of an arrest. Searches after a lawful arrest are those that take place following an arrest, but not at the immediate time and place. *Unlawful arrests* are those that are deemed unlawful by the court from which the appeals court case was appealed. The variable *warrant* represents the existence of a warrant, and *probable cause* represents the determination by the court below the appeals court as to the existence of probable cause. Finally, the *except* variable measures certain exceptions to the warrant requirement, such as border searches or consent searches (see Segal 1984 for details).

We use these independent variables in our statistical model to try to predict our dependent variable, whether the judge voted to uphold the search or not.[14] We report our results in Table 10-2. The column labeled MLEs, or maximum likelihood estimates, represent changes in the likelihood that the search will be upheld when the variable in question is present.[15] The most important thing to know about the MLEs is that a positive MLE indicates that the variable in question increases the probability of a search being found reasonable, whereas a negative coefficient decreases the probability of a search being found reasonable.

The column labeled "Sig $(p < x)$" presents the significance levels of the different variables. Significance levels tell us how likely it is that the MLEs we observe could have oc-

Table 10-2 Logistic Regression of Search and Seizure Fact Pattern Model, 1962-1990

Variable	MLE	S.E.	Sig (p<x)	Impact
Home	−0.60	0.31	0.03	−0.15
Business	−0.91	0.42	0.02	−0.22
Car	−0.31	0.32	n.s.	−0.08
Person	−0.47	0.37	0.10	−0.12
Incident	0.48	0.22	0.02	0.12
After	0.33	0.27	0.02	0.08
Unlawful	−1.42	1.08	0.10	−0.31
Warrant	0.67	0.23	0.01	0.16
Probable cause	1.03	0.22	0.01	0.22
Extent	−0.22	0.37	n.s.	−0.05
Except	0.70	0.19	0.01	0.17
Constant	−0.59	0.45	—	—

Note: Percentage predicted correctly: 66.0; $N = 573$. MLE = maximum likelihood estimate; S.E. = standard error; Sig = significance level; n.s. = not significant; dash = not applicable.

curred by chance. Consider, for example, asking a sample of people their party identification. If we observed fifty Democrats and fifty Republicans it would be reasonable to assume that the sample came from a population in which half the people were Democrats and half the people were Republicans. If we observed sixty Democrats and forty Republicans, it is still possible that the sample could have come from a population in which there was an even split between Democrats and Republicans. But if we observed eighty Democrats and twenty Republicans it would be highly unlikely that our sample came from a population with an even partisan split. In our example, significance levels tell us the probability (p) that the MLE we observe could have come from a population in which the true MLE is zero, that is, in which the variable in question has no effect on the judges' decisions. Typically, we like significance levels to be below .05, or at the very least, below .10. A significance level of .05 (that is, $p < .05$) tells us that there is less than a 5 percent chance that the MLE from our sample could have come from a population with a true value of zero (that is, a population in which the variable has no influence on the dependent variable).

The final column in the table, "Impact," represents the change in the probability that a search will be found reasonable when the variable in question is present and the search otherwise has a 50 percent chance of being upheld. Thus when a search has a 50 percent chance of being upheld, a search of one's home lowers the probability that a search will be found reasonable by .15.

Table 10-2 presents us with the following information. First we examine the place of the search. Here, the variables are all compared to a baseline category of a place where one does not have a property interest. Thus, searches of one's home and one's place of business significantly decrease the probability that a search will be found reasonable compared with a search of a place where one does not have a property interest, such as the home of a friend. One's person receives slightly more protection than the baseline category, whereas one's car does not receive significantly more protection than a place in which one does not have a property interest. We will see shortly, though, that in our more complete models the variable crosses the threshold into statistical significance.

We next consider the arrest variables, which are all compared to a baseline where no arrest took place. Searches incident to a lawful arrest are much more likely to be upheld than exactly similar searches that were not preceded by an arrest. In contrast, searches that are after but not incident to a lawful arrest just miss the .10 significance level. Searches after unlawful arrests slightly decrease the probability that the search will be found reasonable.

The existence of warrants and probable cause strongly and significantly increases the probability of a finding that a search was reasonable. Both variables are significant at $p <$ .005.[16] That is, the probability that these results are due to chance is less than 1 in 200. Full intrusions, compared with lesser intrusions, do not appear to receive more stringent treatment from courts of appeals judges. Finally, various exceptions to the warrant requirement significantly increase the probability that a search will be found reasonable.

Overall, the model is significant at $p < .001$. We predict the outcome of 66 percent of the judges' votes correctly.[17] This suggests that case stimuli, important to both the legal and the attitudinal models, do influence circuit court decisions. Moreover, our model suggests that we have done a fairly good job of controlling for the facts of the case and thus can examine additional factors with a reasonable degree of confidence.

We next consider whether circuit court judges are responsive to changes in decision making by the U.S. Supreme Court, as suggested by the legal model. We accomplish this by adding to our fact-pattern model a variable that represents changing Supreme Court preferences from the end of the Warren Court through 1990. The results are presented in Table 10-3.

The results of the fact pattern are essentially the same as in the first model. One important difference, though, is that the "Car" variable is now significant at the .10 level and remains significant through subsequent models. More important, the variable "Change" demonstrates that circuit court judges did get more conservative in search and seizure cases as the Supreme Court got more conservative. The estimate for change is significant at $p < .001$, and the MLE suggests that a search that had a 50 percent chance of being upheld in 1969 would have a 75 percent chance of being upheld in 1990 after controlling for the facts of the case.[18] Nevertheless, the percentage of the judges' decisions predicted correctly barely improves, rising from 66.0 percent to 67.2 percent.

Table 10-3 Logistic Regression of Search and Seizure Fact Pattern Model Plus Supreme Court Change, 1962-1990

Variable	MLE	S.E.	Sig (p<x)	Impact
Home	−0.69	0.31	0.02	−0.16
Business	−1.10	0.43	0.01	−0.25
Car	−0.41	0.32	0.10	−0.10
Person	−0.56	0.37	0.07	−0.14
Incident	0.88	0.25	0.01	0.21
After	0.52	0.28	0.04	0.13
Unlawful	−0.98	1.08	n.s.	−0.23
Warrant	0.73	0.24	0.01	0.17
Probable cause	1.00	0.22	0.01	0.23
Extent	−0.12	0.38	n.s.	0.03
Except	0.63	0.20	0.01	0.15
Change	0.16	0.04	0.01	0.25
Constant	−1.33	0.49	—	—

Note: Percentage predicted correctly: 67.2; $N = 573$. MLE = maximum likelihood estimate; S.E. = standard error; Sig = significance level; n.s. = not significant; dash = not applicable.

Our next test concerns attitudinal variables. Although we do not have direct measures of the judges' ideology, we know at least two factors related to their ideology. First, we know the partisanship of their appointing president. Innumerable studies have demonstrated that Republican presidents on average choose more conservative judges than do Democratic presidents (Carp and Rowland 1983; Scigliano 1971; Tate 1981, 1991). We also know the region of the judge. Again, we know that southern judges tend on average to be more conservative than nonsouthern judges (Songer and Davis 1990; Tate 1981, 1991). We added these attitudinal surrogates to our fact-pattern model from Table 10-2 and present the results in Table 10-4.

Both variables are in the proper direction, are highly significant, and substantively meaningful. A search that has a 50 percent chance of being upheld by a Republican appointee has only a 28 percent probability of being upheld by a Democrat. Alternatively, a search that has a 50 percent chance of being upheld by a northern judge would have a 70 percent chance of being upheld by a southern judge. Knowing these factors increases our ability to predict the judges's decisions from a 66 percent baseline (fact patterns only) to 71.2 percent. Thus, knowing factors related to the judges' ideology not only significantly increases our ability to predict their decisions, it offers a substantially greater improvement than did the legal variable, Supreme Court change. That is, it is much more important in understanding these decisions to know the circuit court judges' preferences than it is to

Table 10-4 Logistic Regression of Search and Seizure Fact Pattern Model Plus Attitudinal Measures, 1962-1990

Variable	MLE	S.E.	Sig (p<x)	Impact
Home	−0.64	0.32	0.03	−0.15
Business	−1.08	0.44	0.01	−0.25
Car	−0.43	0.33	0.10	−0.11
Person	−0.41	0.39	n.s.	−0.10
Incident	0.68	0.24	0.01	0.16
After	0.50	0.29	0.05	0.12
Unlawful	−1.63	1.09	0.07	−0.30
Warrant	0.79	0.24	0.01	0.19
Probable cause	0.97	0.23	0.01	0.23
Extent	−0.28	0.39	n.s.	−0.07
Except	0.68	0.20	0.01	0.16
Democratic president	−0.94	0.20	0.01	−0.22
Southern	0.84	0.22	0.01	0.20
Constant	−0.25	0.49	—	—

Note: Percentage predicted correctly: 71.2; $N = 559$. MLE = maximum likelihood estimate; S.E. = standard error; Sig = significance level; n.s. = not significant; dash = not applicable.

know the Supreme Court's preferences.

Finally, we combine our legal and attitudinal variables into a single model to create the hierarchical model. Thus, we can statistically determine whether attitudinal and legal factors exert independent influence on circuit court decisions after each is controlled for the other. Note the following: Between 1969 and 1990, the Supreme Court became increasingly conservative because of the appointments by Richard Nixon, Gerald Ford, Ronald Reagan, and George Bush. So too did the circuit courts become more conservative, for essentially the same reasons.[19] The hierarchical model allows us to determine whether the conservatism of the circuit court judges was due to their own conservatism, the Supreme Court's conservatism, or both. We present the results in Table 10-5.

The results indicate that our legal variable, Supreme Court Change, and our attitudinal variables, measuring region and party, continue to exert a strong influence on the decisions of circuit court judges. All are significant below the .01 level, and all have the ability to shift dramatically the likelihood that a search will be upheld.

Returning to Figure 10-2, we can now draw some conclusions about the three models. The data reject the legal model as a complete explanation of circuit court decisions because the attitudes of circuit court judges clearly have an effect on their decisions, even when there is a control for the facts in the cases. The data also reject the pure attitudinal model as

Table 10-5 Logistic Regression of Search and Seizure Fact Pattern Model Plus Supreme Court Change and Attitudinal Measures, 1962-1990

Variable	MLE	S.E.	Sig (p<x)	Impact
Home	−0.72	0.32	0.02	−0.17
Business	−1.23	0.45	0.01	−0.27
Car	−0.50	0.33	0.07	−0.12
Person	−0.48	0.39	n.s.	−0.12
Incident	1.02	0.27	0.01	0.24
After	0.66	0.30	0.02	0.16
Unlawful	−1.22	1.09	n.s.	−0.27
Warrant	0.83	0.25	0.01	0.20
Probable cause	0.94	0.23	0.01	0.22
Extent	−0.21	0.39	n.s.	−0.05
Except	0.63	0.21	0.01	0.15
Change	0.13	0.04	0.01	0.21
Democratic president	−0.93	0.20	0.01	−0.22
Southern	0.78	0.22	0.01	0.19
Constant	−0.86	0.53	—	—

Note: Percentage predicted correctly: 72.3; $N = 559$. MLE = maximum likelihood estimate; S.E. = standard error; Sig = significance level; n.s. = not significant; dash = not applicable.

a complete explanation of their decisions because changes in Supreme Court doctrine affect the decisions of circuit court judges, even when there are controls for facts and attitudes. Instead, the data demonstrate that the hierarchical model, as applied to circuit court decisions, dominates both alternatives: as predicted by that model, both attitudes and Supreme Court doctrine matter. Of course, this does not mean the hierarchical model is "true" in some transcendental sense. But the hierarchical model does provide a simple and useful starting place for understanding the decision making of lower-court judges. Clearly this class of models deserves more attention.

Conclusion

From an empirical standpoint, several elements are prominent. First, our data show that circuit court judges consistently respond to case stimuli or fact patterns in deciding cases, at least in search and seizure law. Plus, the similarity in the way judges on the courts of appeals and the Supreme Court respond to these fact patterns is remarkable. This finding raises two possibilities: (1) either the long-term precedents established by the Court (for example, that a search pursuant to a warrant should carry a greater initial presumption of validity than a similar search without a warrant) have a substantial effect on the decisions of the appeals court, or (2) the attitudinal filters that appeals court judges use to evaluate cases are similar to those employed by the justices on the Supreme Court. That is, the extreme similarity in appeals court and Supreme Court decision making may reflect either institutional constraints imposed on lower courts or attitudes shared by higher and lower courts. Because of the inherent ambiguity of the fact-pattern analysis, efforts to distinguish between the two possibilities must move beyond case stimuli. We do so here by examining changing Supreme Court preferences and the attitudinal predispositions of the judges. Both sets of factors add to our understanding of circuit court decisions. But substantially more explanatory power comes from the attitudinal factors than the legal factor.

Obviously, care must be taken in interpreting these findings. First, we have useful but imperfect measures of legal and attitudinal variables. Stronger measures might lead to stronger results. Second, we have examined only one set of issues, search and seizure cases. We cannot be sure our discovered mix of legal and attitudinal influences would hold in other areas of the law, nor even whether these factors would continue to explain circuit court decisions at all.

Nonetheless, the findings have interesting implications for theories of judicial decision making. Judicial scholars have long debated the relative merits of the legal and the attitudinal models for understanding Supreme Court decision making. At the level of the Supreme Court, the evidence supporting the attitudinal model is strong (Segal and Spaeth 1993). Nonetheless, many scholars believe that legal factors must be important, if only in subtle ways (Epstein and Kobylka 1992; George and Epstein 1992; Rogers Smith 1988). Our evidence for the hierarchical model can be seen as bolstering this view, at least for judges below the apex of the judicial hierarchy. In addition, we believe our brief discussion of the hierarchical model—viewing lower-court judges as value driven, as in the attitudinal model, but constrained by institutional rules and procedures from the free exercise of those values—hints at a productive way to move the theoretical debate.

Finally, despite the inherent limits of studying only one branch of the law, the results may be more generalizable than they first appear. Previous research has suggested that controversial civil liberties decisions of the Warren Court are among those that lower courts are *least* likely to comply (Baum 1978). Thus, our finding of responsiveness to the Supreme Court in civil liberties law may suggest even greater responsiveness in other areas.

Notes

1. Fewer than one-half of 1 percent of the decisions of the courts of appeals are reviewed by the Supreme Court (Songer 1991).

2. For more on models, see Chapter 1 of this book.

3. The *Brown* decision outlawed the "separate-but-equal" system of racially segregated schools. The *Gideon* decision guaranteed all defendants accused of a felony in state courts the right to court-appointed counsel if they could not afford it.

4. *Roe v. Wade* created a constitutional right to abortion that could not be abridged through the first two trimesters of pregnancy. *Furman v. Georgia* struck down capital punishment laws as then imposed in the United States. The Supreme Court allowed states to reinstitute the death penalty in a series of decisions in 1976.

5. In Chapter 13, Harold J. Spaeth considers the applicability of legal and attitudinal models to decision making on the U.S. Supreme Court.

6. The Fourth Amendment details the requirements for a warrant but does not state when a warrant is required. The amendment's prohibition is on *unreasonable* searches and seizures, a term that it does not define. Nor do we find the intent of the framers useful in explaining how the circuit courts actually answer questions regarding telephone wiretaps, border searches, drug testing, or other modern problems.

7. See *South Carolina v. Gathers* (1989) at 892 [Scalia dissenting] and *Payne v. Tennessee* (1991) at 737.

8. This section relies on Segal and Spaeth 1993, 67–68.

9. Congress can overturn the Court's statutory decisions, but the extent to which the Court actually considers such future actions in its decisions is not clear.

10. These dreams may be fed by the knowledge that fourteen of the last twenty people nominated for the Supreme Court were appeals court judges at the time of their nomination.

11. For example, when David Windsor filed suit claiming that he sought to foil Saint Peter who was actually the Black Devil and the father of Judas Iscariot and that therefore the authorities should arrest the widow of Martin Luther King (alias Matilda Winfield) before she could destroy the Roman Catholic Church by installing herself as a "Black Popess," the court of appeals presumably felt it was compelled by precedent to affirm the ruling of the district court that Windsor lacked standing to bring his suit *(Windsor v. Pan American Airways*, 1984).

12. For example, it could be that cases in the 1980s, when the Supreme Court was more conservative, were more likely to contain warrants. Conservative lower-court decisions could be the result of a more conservative Supreme Court or more reasonable searches by the police. By controlling for whether warrants existed, we can determine whether it was a more conservative Supreme Court that led to changes in lower-court decisions.

13. We used Westlaw, a computerized legal information service, to identify all published decisions of the courts of appeals that considered the admissibility of evidence secured through a search and seizure of evidence. A random sample of forty cases per year was selected from these decisions. But since our dependent variable (whether the search was upheld) would be seriously skewed in such a sample, we selected a subset of cases for analysis that consisted of all cases in which the court declared the evidence from the search inadmissible and an 11 percent random sample of those in which the validity of the search was upheld.

14. For more on the statistical tool used in this chapter, see Appendix B of this book.

15. MLEs represent the change in the log of the odds ratio of finding a search reasonable. See Segal and Spaeth (1993, appendix) for a discussion.

16. We report only through the .01 level in the tables.

17. The mean of our stratified sample is .503, for a 32 percent reduction in error.

18. We report the effect of this variable in the tables as it changes over its full range of 0 to 7.

19. Although the Democrat Jimmy Carter made no Supreme Court appointments, he did make fifty-six circuit court appointments. Thus the conservative tide on the courts of appeals was temporarily reversed from 1977 to 1980.

Part IV The U.S. Supreme Court

On the surface, the Supreme Court of the United States is a trivial body. It is composed of only nine jurists; its total budget of $26 million is a mere drop in the bucket compared with, say, the Justice Department's budget of $6 billion; it employs fewer than 400 persons (the Justice Department pays more than 65,000 civilian employees); it meets in session just nine months of the year; and it hears arguments in only about 120 cases per term.

Yet, figures can be deceiving, for the U.S. Supreme Court is probably the most well-studied legal tribunal in the world. In the past century, thousands of articles and books have dissected its business, its decisions, and its members; there are even bibliographies devoted exclusively to cataloguing scholarly work on the Court (for example, Martin and Goehlert 1990). Its decisions make front page news here and abroad; and popular novelists occasionally weave the Court into their plot lines (for example, John Grisham's *The Pelican Brief*).

Why is the Supreme Court the object of so much attention? One answer is that it is, perhaps, the most important court on the planet. How the Court accumulated so much power is a question scholars have long debated. But it seems reasonably clear that its decisions can change the way Americans think and behave, not to mention that it structures the rules constraining the choices citizens make (for more on the Court's impact, see Part V of this volume).

Another answer centers on the dominating role the Court plays in various fields of study. Specialists in constitutional interpretation, for example, quite naturally pay close attention to the Court because it is the authoritative interpreter of our nation's charter. Analysts of judicial decision making who are more behaviorally and choice oriented also focus heavily on the Court. Indeed, for these scholars the Court has been a traditional source of concern because the pioneers of the study of judicial decision making, C. Herman Pritchett, Glendon A. Schubert, and Harold J. Spaeth, all explored explanations for its output. Quite naturally, their studies set the tone for generations of scholars to come.

A final reason, I suspect, is that the Supreme Court is relatively easy to study compared with other tribunals. As I pointed out in the introductions to Parts II and III, conducting research on trial and lower appellate courts is a difficult task because of their numbers and the variation among them. This, of course, is not the case for the Supreme Court. There is only one Court, and its procedures and practices have varied little, at least since the 1930s. Moreover, obtaining information about the Court is not difficult.[1] Almost all law and even public libraries contain copies of Supreme Court opinions; and there are numerous reference books that contain data and other information useful for studying the institution. This is in marked contrast to the dearth of information readily available on trial and lower appellate courts, especially at the state level (sources of data are discussed in Appendix C).

Given the extensive attention the Supreme Court has received, is there anything left to learn about it? As the essays contained in this part indicate, the answer is yes: not only are there many gaps in our knowledge about the Court, but scholars disagree about what is and is not known. Chapter 11, by Richard L. Pacelle, Jr., shores up these points about an important dimension of Supreme Court activity: its agenda. After all, Pacelle notes, the Supreme Court receives more than 5,000 petitions for review each year but decides only about 5 percent of them. Hence, numerous questions emerge; for example, Why does the Court decide some cases and reject others? Does the Court's agenda—consisting of those cases it accepts—periodically undergo transformations?

Answers to the first question abound. Scholars have produced dozens of studies explicating the factors that make a case worthy of Supreme Court review (for recent treatments, see Caldeira and Wright 1988; Perry 1991). But the second question went largely unaddressed until Pacelle turned to it here and elsewhere (see Pacelle 1991). In particular, his chapter explores dimensions of change in agenda building by the Rehnquist Court and considers the implications of such alterations for the Court as an institution.

That Pacelle takes the Rehnquist Court as his primary empirical reference point is by no means a coincidence. In the past few years, some analysts have commented that the Court's agenda is in flux—that it is deciding fewer civil liberties cases (and more economic ones) than it has in decades. Pacelle confirms this decline, noting that particular kinds of civil liberties take up far less space on the Rehnquist Court's agenda than they did during the tenure of Earl Warren and even Warren E. Burger. The question, though, is whether that decline is part of a broader trend that might continue and gain momentum. The answer Pacelle reaches, through a discussion of the agenda-building process that is rich in theory, is that the systematic disfranchisement of civil liberties from the Court's agenda may be a logical extension of a philosophy that emphasizes judicial restraint and deference to the elected branches of government—a philosophy apparently held by some of the more recent appointees to the Court. Still, Pacelle suggests that because it would represent an extreme change in institutional rules and goals, a dramatic transformation in the Court's agenda would take time before it could be realized.

Chapters 12 and 13, by Leslie Friedman Goldstein and Harold J. Spaeth, respectively, pick up where Pacelle's chapter leaves off: they consider what happens to cases once the Court has placed them on its agenda. At first blush, the concerns of Goldstein and Spaeth are quite similar. Both explore the world of Supreme Court decision making. But from there their interests depart dramatically. Goldstein examines how justices *should* decide cases, and Spaeth asks how they *do* decide cases.

This subtle but crucial difference gives rise to highly divergent research strategies. Consider, first, Goldstein's approach. After reviewing traditional types of constitutional theory—frameworks of principles for guiding judges in their task of constitutional interpretation—she argues that the most contemporary theories focus on the structure, or essential features, of the American regime, or polity. She then provides examples of that trend, asserting that they demonstrate an important convergence among these regime-focused scholars on the principled baseline of government by consent of the governed. Finally, she explores, from the perspective of recent scholarship, the relation between that baseline and constitutional jurisprudence. Because Goldstein developed one of these perspectives, she herself engages in constitutional theory, invoking history and Court cases to provide an answer to the question of what should guide judges in their decision making.

Harold Spaeth's chapter could not be more different in analytic style. Even though he, like Goldstein, describes various theories of judicial decision making and advances one over the others, he takes a data-intense approach. In other words he translates Supreme Court outcomes (for example, liberal and conservative) and (some) theories into numbers and asks which one best characterizes the outcomes. His answer is unequivocal: the attitudinal model provides the most parsimonious and accurate explanation of Court decisions. Under this model, justices base their decisions solely on the facts of cases vis-à-vis their ideological attitudes and values. Or, as Spaeth put it elsewhere (Segal and Spaeth 1993, 65), "Rehnquist votes the way he does because he is extremely conservative; Marshall voted the way he did because he is extremely liberal." As readers will see, these are not statements Spaeth makes lightly; to the contrary, he devotes many pages of his chapter to considering alternative explanations for Court decisions. None of them, however, according to Spaeth, provides as holistic and as elegant an answer to his research question.

Spaeth's conclusion about the value of the attitudinal model is one echoed by many scholars of the judicial process, and not just those working in the area of decision making. Indeed, analysts have invoked it to study this important question: What role does the Supreme Court play in American society? As Thomas G. Walker and I explain in Chapter 14, this question has divided scholars into two primary camps: those who argue that the Supreme Court should and usually does act to protect minority interests and those who assert that the Court usually chooses to protect the interests of the ruling regime—the elected institutions. Despite these differences, as we demonstrate, the two schools rest on a common assumption about the nature of judicial decision making: Justices do not decide a priori to protect minority rights or to legitimate the ruling regime. Rather, they base their votes on their political ideologies, with a consequence being that liberal justices *tend* to protect minority interests, while conservative ones *tend* to legitimate the ruling regime. In other words, scholarly work on the role of the Court in American society has adopted Spaeth's attitudinal model.

Walker and I argue that this model is inadequate or, at the very least, incomplete. We believe that the role the Court plays in a democratic society is not merely the product of the individual political preferences of the justices; it is also a function of the preferences of other political actors, particularly Congress and the president, and of the political context in which the actors operate. To put it in different terms, we argue that to understand the role the Court plays in American society it is important to consider events taking place outside of the marble palace. To develop this argument, we explore a sequence of events occurring in the wake of the Civil War: Congress's attempt to reconstruct the defeated Southern states and the Court's response.

Thus, I end where I started: the U.S. Supreme Court may be the most studied Court in the world but we still have much to learn about important dimensions of its work, its decisions, its relations with the other branches of government, and, as the next part of the book indicates, its impact and influence. What is more, scholars are rather divided about how we should be studying these dimensions. Fortunately, readers will have a chance to consider some of these divisions because the chapters that follow are as varied in design and strategy as they are in substance.

Note

1. It is, of course, true that the Court deliberates cases in private. That is, only the justices attend conferences at which cases are discussed and important decisions made. Still, using the private papers of the justices, scholars have been able to piece together the deliberative process in regard to particular cases. See, for example, Howard 1968; Murphy 1964; Schwartz 1983, 1990.

11 The Dynamics and Determinants of Agenda Change in the Rehnquist Court

Richard L. Pacelle, Jr.

Agenda building, the process by which the Supreme Court culls the cases and issues it wants to address from the mass of the petitions on its docket, arguably involves the most important decisions the Court makes. The Court faces a flood of petitions every year, in recent years more than 5,000 per term (O'Brien 1993, 233). The Court, however, has the institutional capacity to hear only a fraction of these cases. Traditionally, however, the Court has decided only about 200 to 250 cases each term, representing about 5 percent of the petitions. Most of the petitions that reach the Supreme Court's docket seek a writ of certiorari. The Court has complete discretion in granting writs of certiorari and operates under the so-called rule of four: if four justices (less than a majority) want to accept the case, the petition is granted. Like any government agency, the Court must winnow out frivolous demands, requests that cannot be met for some reason, and issues whose time has not yet arrived. Issues and cases that fail to be accepted are effectively denied any further consideration. For half of the cases that are accepted the Court hears oral arguments and issues a written opinion. I define these cases as the Court's agenda. For the remainder, the justices give cursory, brief decisions.

My objective in this chapter is to examine the properties and structure of agenda change in the Supreme Court. In particular, I am concerned with the changes in agenda building in the Court under Chief Justice William H. Rehnquist and the implications of such changes for the Court as an institution. I consider these changes in the context of previous trends in the composition of the agenda and theories about agenda change and decision making.

Properties of Agenda Building

The factors that govern the selection of cases and the construction of an annual agenda are closely tied to the factors that explain the justices' decisions on the merits of cases. The values and attitudes of individual justices are traditionally viewed as the most important determinant of judicial decision making (Rohde and Spaeth 1976; Segal and Spaeth 1993).[1] Those attitudes are sometimes tempered by justices' conceptions of the judicial role, which

251

might induce them to vote against their values in order to support a past precedent, establish consistency in the law, or achieve unanimity or a stronger majority in a decision (James 1968; Pacelle 1991). Given the close connection between case selection and agenda building on the one hand and the Court's decisions on the merits of cases on the other (Perry 1991; Ulmer 1972, 1978), it is useful to consider these as integrated steps in the same basic process of decision making (Pacelle 1991).

Researchers have examined both very sophisticated (Schubert 1962) and more basic strategies (Brenner 1979; Perry 1991) of voting on certiorari petitions. Perry (1991) and Ulmer (1984) have shown that justices' votes on petitions for certiorari are consistent with their votes on the merits of the case. Justices typically grant certiorari in order to reverse a lower-court decision they do not support, evidence that the values and attitudes of the justices hold great importance. They also vote to accept cases when there is confusion or a conflict between lower courts (Perry 1991; Ulmer 1984). Frequently, cases involving similar issues arise in different circuit courts at approximately the same time. The different courts may use different standards and reach different conclusions. The Supreme Court often grants certiorari for the express purpose of resolving the differences. Occasionally, justices cast "defensive denials"; that is, even though they disagree with the lower-court decision, they vote to deny a case because they do not think they can muster five votes on the merits of the case. Better, the strategic justice would reason, to allow a bad lower-court decision to prevail in one jurisdiction than to call the case up, lose on the merits, and have a harmful precedent for the country (Perry 1991).

Because agenda building is an important component of the broader process of decision making, a theory of decision making developed by Rohde and Spaeth (1976) can be extended to agenda building to explain and evaluate the form of agenda change. Rohde and Spaeth maintain that Court decisions result from the interaction of three factors: goals, rules, and situations. *Goals* refer to the individual and collective values and attitudes of the members of the Court, the most significant determinants of decision making (Segal and Spaeth 1993). *Rules* comprise formal procedures, norms, and rule structures of the institution. Institutional rules structure the aggregation of individual preferences (values) within a decision-making body. For example, the rule of four, the order of discussion of cases, and the assignment of the writing of opinions affect individual decision making.[2] The most important rule for the justices is the judicial role. Thus, decisions are not merely the collective expression of the individual preferences of its members (the sum of the nine justices' values) but are a function of the interaction of individual preferences and institutional structures and rules (Epstein, Walker, and Dixon 1989). Finally, the existence of certain *situations* or conditions can enhance or retard processes of decision making. Any number of situations could affect decision making. For instance, changes in the priorities of the solicitor general (the attorney who litigates U.S. Supreme Court cases for the United States government), the rise of various groups in an issue area or their exit from it, the opinions of lower courts, and the opinions of specialized publics can have an effect on the Court's decisions.[3]

The Importance of Agenda Building

The dynamics involved in building an institutional agenda have many procedural and substantive implications for the Court and for political litigation. First, the justices are, to a significant degree, constrained by past decisions (an effect of rules) in their selection of cases. Second, the time spent in gatekeeping, the process of selecting the small number of cases to accept from the mass of petitions, impinges on the time spent dealing with other responsibilities of the Court (another constraint imposed by rules). Third, agenda priorities affect substantive access (which groups get access) to the Court (goals). Finally, the decision to grant a writ of certiorari is often a first vote on the merits of the case (goals). Let me consider each of these in some detail.

The Effects of Past Agenda Priorities and Decisions

There are significant institutional constraints (rules) on the construction of an agenda. The construction of judicial policy and legal doctrine is a dynamic process. No single decision, no matter how important, ever settles an area of law. The Court's work has been compared to building a mosaic (Greenhouse 1985). Court decisions create new questions and new interstices to be filled. As a positive process, the Court may seek to build or expand policy (furthering individual or institutional goals). As a result, the justices screen petitions for cases that will help them build doctrine and fill gaps. The tone of the Court's decisions may encourage litigants to bring additional cases in that policy area or in related areas. Some of the Court's influence is negative. Confusion in doctrine creates uncertainty for lower courts (leading to conflicting decisions) and for litigants and generates subsequent rounds of cases aimed at resolving the uncertainties (fulfilling institutional rules).

The Demands of Case Screening

The investment in time required to screen the flood of petitions limits the Court's ability to fulfill its other responsibilities, most notably those of constructing doctrine and monitoring lower courts. In considering changes that would allow the Court to shift its resources to other duties, attention has focused on case screening. Members of the Court have advocated and occasionally Congress has provided changes in the case-screening process to facilitate the ability of individual justices and the Court as an institution to review the petitions. The creation of the discretionary writ of certiorari coupled with periodic reductions and finally the virtual elimination of mandatory writs of appeals have given the

Court increased control over its docket.[4] The numbers of petitions and the press of other Court business, however, still leads justices to complain about the process and seek further remedies.

Access to the Agenda

Some analysts claim that the Court's problems are of its own making (the influence of goals on rules). The vast expansion of rights and remedies that occurred during the tenure of Chief Justice Earl Warren (1953-1969) offered groups an alternative to the other branches of government and encouraged further use of the courts (Casper and Posner 1976). Organized interests, lacking political muscle, could turn to the judiciary. Later, groups turned to the Supreme Court to protect the gains they had accrued in the other branches of government. In particular, conservative groups responded to the changes in the Court's membership and the tenor of the decisions coming from the Court when Warren E. Burger was chief justice (1969-1986; Epstein 1985). As a consequence, the demands on the Court increased. To some analysts, the initial step in solving the problems that attend an overloaded docket must be taken by the judiciary. The Court, to some degree, possesses the tools to limit or reverse the flow of petitions.

If the Court were to limit access to its agenda, the perceived results would not be substantively neutral. Liberalizing access to the Supreme Court through the creation and expansion of constitutional and statutory rights, lowering jurisdictional hurdles, and moderating the rules of access (like standing) served to help those who were relatively powerless in the "political" branches of government. Measures that would limit standing and raise jurisdictional barriers (modifying institutional rules) would serve to deny access to groups that would presumably need it the most.

The First Vote on the Merits

The Court accepts a number of cases in order to reach desired policy outcomes. The Warren Court accepted Civil Liberties cases in order to advance individual rights.[5] The more restrictive Rehnquist Court might accept similar types of cases in order to limit those same rights and liberties. Indeed, there is a widespread perception that the Rehnquist Court is interested in reversing or limiting the decisions of the Warren Court. Less obvious, perhaps, is that this is part of a change in the philosophical and jurisprudential outlook of the majority that has emerged on the Rehnquist Court and that this new outlook may serve as an impetus for a recasting of the role of the Supreme Court. The evidence I have gathered shows that the processes of agenda building are being revised, which suggests broader implications for the role of the Supreme Court.

Data and Measurement

The data for this study come from several sources, most notably the United States Supreme Court Judicial Database.[6] The database covers the period from 1953 through 1990 and codes the Court's decisions across a large number of variables. Of particular interest for this analysis are the variables that measure the reason the Court granted certiorari, the bases of decisions, the direction of the decisions, and the votes of individual justices. Because the time frame for the analysis predates and antedates some of the database, I collected additional data for cases that were heard during 1937-1952. I have also coded cases for the 1991 and 1992 terms, adhering as closely as possible to the coding rules set out in the Supreme Court Judicial Database code book and documentation.

Included in my study are all the cases on which the Supreme Court issued an opinion longer than one page in the 1933 through 1992 terms.[7] These requirements yielded 8,183 cases, all but 6 of which were placed into one of fourteen general policy areas described in Table 11-1. Theoretically and empirically, some of these fourteen issues cluster together into broader dimensions. For instance, Due Process, Substantive Rights, and Equality constitute a broader, Civil Liberties, dimension. The unit of analysis is the policy area and the allocation of agenda space by the Court. The variation in the agenda across time is measured as a function of the variation in the relative shares of agenda space allocated to the different policy areas.

The Trends in Supreme Court Agenda Building, 1933-1992

In order to understand the current trends in agenda change that may be unfolding and assess their potential implications, it is necessary to place the nature of agenda change in its historical context. The Court's allocation of agenda space to the four major issue clusters (Economic issues, Federalism, Regulation, and Civil Liberties) during the 1933-1992 terms is presented in Figure 11-1. This period spans some of the most significant changes in American government and politics in the United States.

As shown in the figure, economic concerns (such as Internal Revenue, State Regulation, and Ordinary Economic cases), which dominated the agenda prior to 1937, were gradually and effectively eliminated from the Court's agenda. The decline in the importance of these issues in the Court provides evidence that changes in the Court's agenda did not occur in a vacuum. The Great Depression created the conditions (situation in the theory of judicial decision making) that made this transformation possible. First, the Court was directly involved in interpreting the constitutionality of various state and federal programs that sought to cope with the economic ravages of the Depression. Initially, a slim majority of the Court resisted these programs, overturning some of the New Deal legislation. But in

Table 11-1 Description of the Different Issue Areas

Issue	Description
Due Process[a]	Criminal procedure (for example, search and seizure, *Miranda* rights, right to counsel), civil due process cases (administrative searches, hearings prior to job dismissal) ($n = 1,674$ cases; 20.5% of the total agenda space)
Substantive Rights[a]	First Amendment (for example, freedom of speech, freedom of the press, freedom of religion), privacy, and abortion rights ($n = 743$; 9.1%)
Equality[a]	Fourteenth Amendment—equal protection (for example, race, gender, age, disability), voting rights ($n = 702$; 8.6%)
Criminal Law	Interpretation of criminal statutes (for example, definition of kidnapping or postal regulations) ($n = 210$; 2.6%)
Government as Provider	Social Security and public welfare ($n = 62$; 0.8%)
Separation of Powers	Interpretations of the powers of the three branches of government ($n = 77$; 0.9%)
Foreign Affairs	Cases involving relations between the United States and foreign governments ($n = 123$; 1.5%)
Federalism	Cases involving the division of power between the central government and the subnational (state and local) governments (for example, commerce clause, federal laws and local control) ($n = 837$; 10.2%)
U.S. Regulation	Cases involving regulation of business by the central government (for example, securities regulation, labor relations, environmental regulation) ($n = 2,140$; 26.2%)
State Regulation	Cases involving regulation of business by the state government (for example, state taxation of business) ($n = 284$; 3.5%)
Internal Revenue	Cases involving the Internal Revenue Service and federal taxation ($n = 603$; 7.4%)
United States as Litigant	Cases involving the liability of the U.S. government (for example, tort claims against the government) ($n = 163$; 2.0%)
State as Litigant	Cases involving the state government as a litigant (for example, state disputes over boundaries or water rights) ($n = 99$; 1.2%)
Ordinary Economic	Cases involving individual litigants (for example, tort claims against business or insurance companies) often turning on jurisdictional questions (whether the federal court is the appropriate forum or whether state or federal law is controlling) ($n = 460$; 5.6%)

Notes: n = total number of cases decided in an opinion longer than one page, 1933-1992 terms; percentages are of the total number of cases accepted (8,183), 1933-1992 terms. Some of the fourteen issue areas form common dimensions, based on the common or similar principles that govern decisions, the input of the same groups, and similar patterns of voting by the justices (Rohde and Spaeth 1976). Due Process, Substantive Rights, and Equality issues make up the cluster Civil Liberties; Internal Revenue, State Regulation, State as Litigant, United States as Litigant, and Ordinary Economic issues form the Economic cluster.

[a] Groups like the American Civil Liberties Union and the National Association for the Advancement of Colored People litigate in the three areas of Due Process, Substantive Rights, and Equality and use the same types of arguments in each; the preferred-position doctrine also dominated the decisions in each of these areas for many cases; many of the justices tend to be consistently liberal or conservative in each of these areas.

Figure 11-1 Supreme Court Allocation of Agenda Space to Major Issue Areas, 1933–1992 Terms

Percentage

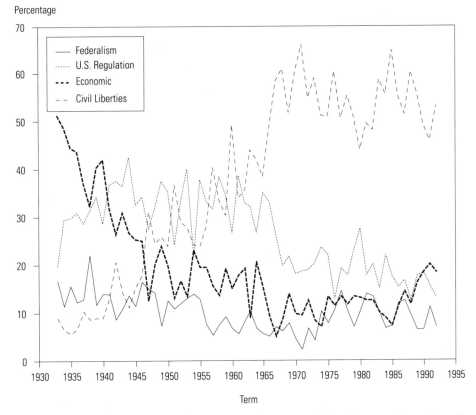

Term

1937, after President Franklin Delano Roosevelt proposed his Court-packing plan, the justices began upholding the building blocks of the New Deal—sometimes called "the switch in time that saved nine."[8] As a result, the Court finally moved into step with the reigning political order in economic matters.

Hence, it is hardly surprising to find economic cases dominating the Court's agenda during this period; they represented the major concerns of the nation. By the same token, Federalism cases surged during the New Deal period. That was because many of the New Deal programs increased the reach of the central government into areas that had traditionally been the province of state governments. Still, the ultimate decision to leave the foundation of the New Deal intact left the Court in a curious position, which brings me to the second way that the Depression contributed to the transformation of the Court's agenda.

Having capitulated to Roosevelt, the Court might have relegated itself to a subordinate role, rubber-stamping presidential and legislative prerogatives. But instead, the Supreme Court used its affirmation of executive and legislative initiatives as a point of departure for its own transformation. The Supreme Court had to reestablish its legitimacy and find its proper niche in the government structure. Thus, in a direct, if delayed, sense the Depression and the programs designed to combat it affected both the authority and the role of the Supreme Court.

This transformation occurred soon after "the switch in time," when Justice Harlan Fiske Stone advocated a new role for the Supreme Court. In an otherwise insignificant case, *United States v. Carolene Products* (1938), Stone included a footnote—now heralded as "Footnote Four"—which created a so-called double standard: in economic matters, the Court would generally defer to Congress unless litigants challenging such regulations could demonstrate clear, inherent flaws. Concurrently, the Court would give more exacting scrutiny to possible violations of individual liberties and the rights of insular minorities, who would merit additional judicial protection (Mason 1956). In cases involving civil liberties, the burden would be placed on the government to justify why it needed such restrictions. During the next half-century, this preferred-position doctrine dominated the decisions in civil liberties and civil rights cases and served as the philosophical impetus for a transformation of the Court's agenda (Pacelle 1991).

To be sure, proponents of the preferred-position doctrine have not always had a majority on the Court. But through the years they have woven the threads of the preferred-position doctrine into the fabric of constitutional law. The Warren Court, in particular, advanced a virtual constitutional revolution with its expansion of individual liberties and civil rights. For the first time since Justice Stone proposed the double standard, however, no member of the Supreme Court subscribes to its principles. Justice John Paul Stevens may vote in a liberal direction in civil liberties cases, but he is not a long-time proponent of the preferred-position doctrine. Justice Ruth Bader Ginsburg has demonstrated support for this philosophical tenet in her work as a litigant and a lower-court judge, but it is too early to assess her work as a justice. Justice Stephen Breyer had a moderate-to-liberal voting record as a lower-court judge, which does not suggest an overwhelming commitment to the tenets of the preferred-position doctrine. As a consequence of membership changes, the Rehnquist Court stands on the brink of a potentially new era in American constitutional law. The retreat from the preferred-position doctrine will likely change the shape of the Court's agenda, the substantive nature of constitutional law, and ultimately the very role of the Supreme Court.

The data displayed in Figure 11-1 provide some initial support for these possibilities. As indicated, the increase in the number of Civil Liberties cases accepted began haltingly, but by the early 1960s these cases had supplanted Regulation cases as the most significant consumers of agenda space. During the time of the Burger Court, however, the allocation of agenda space for Civil Liberties cases began a pattern of decline that has continued in the Rehnquist Court. In Figure 11-2, I trace the expansion and decline of the agenda space

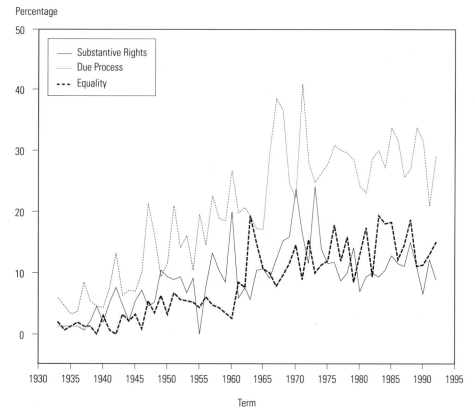

allocated to the components of Civil Liberties: Due Process, Substantive Rights, and Equality. Once again, the trends suggest a reversal of past priorities. During the Rehnquist Court terms, Due Process cases have reached a two-decade low, and cases dealing with Equality and Substantive Rights have also ebbed to levels that match their pre-growth spurts. Given the high percentage of agenda space allocated to such areas, some decline would seem natural. The question remains whether that decline is systematic and part of a broader trend that might continue and gain momentum. Addressing it requires some consideration of the explanations of the structure of the agenda change depicted above.

Explaining the Structure of Agenda Change

As I described earlier, the interaction of goals, rules, and situations helps to explain the structure of agenda change. Since the 1940s, the preferred-position doctrine has dominated decisions in civil liberties and civil rights cases and served as the philosophical impetus for a transformation of the Court's agenda (Pacelle 1991). Indeed, the Supreme Court became known as the protector of individual rights and liberties. To accomplish this, the Court had to create agenda space for Civil Liberties cases. Given the finite amount of agenda space available, the Court had to reduce the space granted other issues.

The goals of the Court appeared to shift in the wake of Footnote Four, but significant membership turnover temporarily elevated justices who preferred balancing approaches to the preferred-position doctrine. Moreover, the second generation of individual rights cases began when the Court was just coming to grips with its new role, and they raised significantly more complex questions. For instance, the early cases concerning freedom of religious exercise posed relatively easy questions for the Court. These cases, however, gave way to the first cases concerning the establishment of religion which involved small amounts of government aid to religion and raised more difficult questions (see Pritchett 1954, 3-4). The external situation in the country was also not conducive to the expansion of individual rights and liberties, given World War II and the advent of the cold war. Congress and many states passed antisubversive acts, and the Court was inclined at that time to defer to the elected officials. Even some civil libertarians (including leaders of the American Civil Liberties Union) were caught up in the anti-Communist hysteria, afraid of being tied to Communism (Walker 1990, 186). As a consequence, the growth of Civil Liberties cases on the agenda was far from linear and frequently interrupted.

Rules, defined as institutional norms, limited the extent of change toward an agenda dominated by individual liberties and civil rights, the core of the preferred-position doctrine, during its initial process of evolution. The Court had an existing agenda that was dominated by Economic cases, which consumed significant agenda space and needed to be addressed before the justices could turn their attention to emerging civil liberties concerns. The case selection literature maintains that policy values and attitudes (goals) govern the selection of some cases (Perry 1991; Ulmer 1978), and the strictures imposed by the judicial role (rules) are responsible for the selection of other cases (Perry 1991; Ulmer 1984).

The Court's role (the most significant of the "rules") induces it to expend precious, finite agenda space that might otherwise be reserved for issues viewed as more significant by the justices. Thus, the role of the Court appears to be an omnipresent limitation the Court imposes on its agenda building, which affects long-term patterns of change. Interviews conducted by Perry (1991) with Supreme Court justices and their clerks confirm the influence of judicial role. Each of the justices interviewed professed that they often used their values and attitudes to determine which cases to accept. Each justice also cited the need to accept other cases in order to correct mistakes made by lower courts, clarify doctrine, or resolve lower-court disputes.

These constraints suggest that we cannot necessarily think about the Supreme Court's agenda as a single entity. In theory, the Court has almost complete discretion over the cases it wants to accept. In practice, the Court exercises its own restraint. To label portions of the agenda mandatory would be misleading, but to claim complete discretion would minimize the influence of the judicial role. It may be that the Supreme Court's agenda is actually bifurcated and thus comprised of two components. One portion, labeled the *exigent agenda*, consists of those issues that require judicial attention to settle questions and resolve lower-court disputes. Thus, institutional rules and norms structure the processes of agenda building. The remaining cases make up the *volitional agenda*, which holds those cases that fulfill the policy designs (goals) of its members. Because of the finite nature of agenda space, the need to attend to exigent agenda issues places limits on the size of the volitional agenda (Pacelle 1991).

The nominations of Earl Warren and William J. Brennan, Jr., were significant in changing the leadership of the Court; they profoundly altered the goals of the institution and mitigated the effects of the rules on change. With William O. Douglas and Hugo L. Black, proponents of the preferred position, already on the Court, a majority was built to advance the protections for individual liberties and civil rights on the volitional portion of the agenda. Subsequent nominations provided a critical mass that allowed the later Warren Court to overcome many of the constraints imposed by institutional rules (Baum 1992a). Indeed, the most pronounced growth of Civil Liberties cases occurred during this time. Given the dynamics of the process, this growth would ensure significant Court attention to such issues for the foreseeable future, even with changes in the goals of the institution.

The Warren Court modified its agenda priorities and conditioned future agendas through many of its decisions. Certainly, *Brown v. Board of Education* (1954), which sought to end segregation in the schools, was a major landmark that changed the nature of the Equality agenda. But it also had ripple effects that spilled over into other areas. Other decisions and changes in institutional rules opened the agenda to civil liberties cases. The momentum toward the application of the Bill of Rights to the states encouraged litigation (Cortner 1981). Decisions in the areas of libel and obscenity expanded the First Amendment and opened new areas of law. For example, *New York Times v. Sullivan* (1964) protected newspapers from libel suits by public officials, and *Roth v. United States* (1957) narrowed the definition of what constitutes obscene material, so more expression was protected under the First Amendment. Thus the Court was forced to reallocate agenda resources. The Court also eased restrictions on in forma pauperis and habeas corpus petitions, facilitating use of the Court by prisoners and the poor. In addition, in many decisions the Court eased its rules of access, lowering the barriers to standing.[9] Such rulings led to significant growth spurts in cases filed (Casper and Posner 1976). It is shown in Figure 11-2 that the growth in the percentage of agenda space allocated to Due Process, Substantive Rights, and Equality cases occurred in the wake of liberalizing Warren Court cases.

Due Process cases began to increase soon after the adoption of the preferred-position doctrine but had sustained bursts of growth during the later Warren Court years. Substantive Rights and Equality cases gained agenda space later. The growth of the three areas continued through the early tenure of the less sympathetic Burger Court.

Decisions that expanded civil rights and civil liberties, resulting from the goals of the Court, had another effect: they created a conducive situation for group litigation. Decisions that expanded rights and liberties and provided broadly based equity remedies (McDowell 1982) encouraged the National Association for the Advancement of Colored People to continue to use the courts, which served as a model for other groups. Loosening restraints on standing encouraged groups to expand their activities and enter new areas of law. This made the sequencing of litigation by groups an easier task. In some areas, lowering the hurdles to standing was critical to doctrinal development. Establishment-of-religion doctrine, for example, could not evolve until the Court permitted taxpayers to undertake suits to challenge government aid to religious institutions (Morgan 1972; Sorauf 1976). The rise of interest group litigation has been well-documented (Epstein 1985). As repeat players in the Court, these groups sought to achieve favorable precedents and rule structures that would facilitate the achievement of their policy goals (Galanter 1974).

Constraints on Agenda Change

While the post-1937 Court set a dynamic in motion, the Warren Court provided the momentum to spur its development. To change the agenda in any meaningful way, the Court would have to alter the dynamics that underlay its construction. That would require changing the nature of its substantive decisions and perhaps its philosophies. In regard to the theory of decision making, the goals of the membership should change (most likely through replacement), institutional rules would need to be modified, and a propitious situation or conditions would be needed to induce and abet such changes. These were the prospects as the Burger Court began.

The goals of the institution changed as Republicans took control of the White House after 1969 and made the selection of Supreme Court justices a central component of issues like law and order, family values, and judicial restraint. The replacement of members of the Warren Court, particularly those who were proponents of the preferred-position doctrine, ushered in a new majority that was less sympathetic to civil liberties and civil rights (Baum 1988, 1992a). The Burger Court was not completely antithetical to civil liberties, however. The widespread busing to achieve desegregation, remedies to counter gender discrimination, the creation of the right to an abortion, and the remedy of affirmative action to correct past discrimination had their first Supreme Court recognition during Chief Justice Burger's tenure.

In other areas, such as criminal procedure, the Burger Court was significantly more conservative than its predecessor. Such a reversal in ideological direction does not alter the dynamics of the agenda, for if the Court wants to create exceptions to existing protections or refine precedents, it must continue to allocate agenda space to guide lower courts and flesh out doctrine. Indeed, as the Burger Court's decisions became increasingly more conservative in the area of criminal procedure, the levels of agenda space allocated to Due Process cases did not decline significantly. One change, however, was evident: during the Warren Court the preponderance of Due Process cases were brought by the defendants; increasingly during Burger's tenure, the state appealed adverse decisions (Hellman 1985). In general, conservative groups took advantage of the more propitious environment (situation) to initiate and expand their litigation and to influence the Court through an increase in their amici curiae efforts (Epstein 1985).

The Court needed to expand agenda space in order to attend to Civil Liberties cases and modify doctrine. To create this space, the Burger Court began to clear some items off the volitional agenda. The Court made two significant changes to achieve this. First, it contracted its exigent agenda by changing its informal screening rules. Instead of settling circuit conflicts as they arose, the Court let the conflicts percolate to multiple circuits (Hellman 1983; Tiberi 1993). More significantly, the Burger Court transplanted some venerable volitional agenda issues to the exigent agenda. The Court began to treat most issues concerned with Regulation differently. Except for antitrust regulation and labor relations cases, the percentage of Regulation cases that were accepted to settle a circuit conflict (the essence of the exigent agenda) and that were decided unanimously grew significantly (Pacelle 1991). As these issues moved from the center of the institution's concerns, attention could be directed toward civil liberties issues. The additional agenda space allowed the Burger Court to continue to flesh out the issues it initiated and, in some areas, to continue to refine, limit, or dismantle the doctrine left by the Warren Court.

Some changes in precedent did modify the dynamics of the agenda. In a series of decisions beginning in 1957 in *Roth v. United States*, the Warren Court used a liberal test that made convictions for obscenity very difficult to obtain. Because the standard was vague, it also forced the Court to accept many cases in this area. *Miller v. California* (1973) changed the Court's standard for judging the alleged obscenity. In that case, the Burger Court significantly changed obscenity standards by allowing local communities to determine their own obscenity standards. Once the Court had let the *Miller* decision percolate through to other districts for a few terms and had clarified its direction, the agenda space allocated to such areas declined markedly. The Court decided fifty-four obscenity cases in the decade preceding *Miller* and only four in the decade after the decision.

The effect of membership changes on the institutional goals varies over time (Segal 1986). As such changes accrue, they become more visible and provide the votes to change doctrine, the overall ideological direction of the decisions, and the agenda. There is a brake on the system, however, in the form of institutional rules. The Court's formal and informal rules were predisposed to ensure that groups interested in protecting civil liberties would have access to the agenda. The underlying philosophy that guided the Court's decisions, the preferred-position doctrine, was still in place, buttressed by a large number of precedents. The judicial role, manifested empirically in attention to the exigent agenda, prohibited wholesale changes without the construction of an extensive foundation.

Overcoming the Constraints: Strategies for Changing Agenda Priorities

The resignations of Justices Brennan and Marshall, proponents of the preferred-position doctrine (further changing the goals), placed the Court in a position that appears to be ripe for a possible change in the dominant philosophies underlying doctrinal development and perhaps the Court's very institutional role. Goals and situations suggest that agenda, decisional, and doctrinal changes were in the offing as the Rehnquist Court increasingly took shape. Rules, however, dampen the immediate prospects for agenda and doctrinal change. If the Rehnquist Court is in the process of transforming the institutional agenda, it would be the result of dynamics set in motion by the Burger Court when it altered the exigent agenda and modified its substantive decisions.

The decisions of the Rehnquist Court have begun to demonstrate some evidence of change. On the whole, the decisions appear to be only marginally more conservative than those of the later Burger Court, but there is a perception that doctrinally the Rehnquist Court has taken a sharper turn to the right.[10] Perhaps more important, significant changes in the underlying philosophy of the Court have begun to emerge in some areas of law. Such philosophies have not captured majority support on the Court, but they have altered the tenor of debate. The influence of policy advocates can be felt in direct and indirect ways. If a cadre of justices has the votes to control decisions, they can dominate the specification of alternatives. Lacking a majority, justices (and litigants) may still have the ability to introduce different perspectives to the debate and force opponents to deal with the substantive and philosophical nature of their positions.[11] The appointments made by President Bill Clinton do not appear to be pushing the Court far to the left, but they may arrest any further migration to the right.

On the current Court, William Rehnquist (Davis 1989) and Antonin Scalia (Brisbin 1990; Wyszynski 1989) propound relatively coherent judicial philosophies that structure their decisions. The effect of membership changes provides Rehnquist and Scalia with the votes to pursue aggressive philosophical precepts and may ultimately change the nature of the theory that has underpinned judicial decisions since the "switch in time" and the mandate of Footnote Four. The "new" philosophy, which represents a return to past doctrines, advocates attention to the original intent of the framers of the Constitution and a stricter construction of the document. In practical terms, these justices (and others on the

Court) desire to place individual rights and competing social interests on a more equal footing than the preferred-position doctrine would advocate. This theory is complemented by an increased willingness to defer to Congress and the executive branch in civil liberties and civil rights issues, thus rejecting the twentieth-century liberalism that has guided Court decisions and policy making in individual rights cases (Smith 1985). Even as the Burger Court undermined many precedents that came from the Warren Court, the nature of debate occurred within the context of the theoretical framework that had been in place since the ascension of the preferred-position doctrine. The changes that might accompany the rejection of this theory would have the effect of altering the nature of debate, the standards of decision making, and maybe the institutional role of the Supreme Court.

Concurrently, the Court begins to show signs of reopening parts of the Federalism agenda. Membership changes have elevated a majority that would recast the doctrine of intergovernment relations. The changes in doctrine, which had exposure in the *National League of Cities v. Usery* (1976) decision, reflect a retreat from national supremacy and a renewal of a form of dual federalism. Such a change would strengthen the powers reserved to the states. O'Brien (1989, 411) claims that "at no time in the last half-century have there been stronger defenders of states' sovereignty on the U.S. Supreme Court" than Rehnquist and Sandra Day O'Connor. In a dissent in a later case that overturned *National League of Cities* (*Garcia v. San Antonio Metropolitan Transit Authority*, 1985), Rehnquist prophesied further changes in doctrine that would alter the dynamics of the agenda in this area.

With the extensive scope of federal activity in all aspects of life, a change in Federalism doctrine would trigger a spate of cases and stake a renewed claim to significant agenda space. Such a process appears to be under way. The dynamics of the agenda reveal that growth patterns normally gain momentum and lead to further expansion of agenda space. The costs must be borne by contracting the agenda space granted to other issues. The most likely candidate would be the component areas that make up Civil Liberties.

Changes in Federalism doctrine may have wide-ranging spillover effects as well. If the Court advances a coherent, broadly based constitutional philosophy that supports the exercise of state prerogatives across a variety of domains, the effects may be felt outside the economic realm. The Warren Court extended nationalization of the law from economic to civil liberties. A reversal of Federalism doctrine might encourage a similar process, changing the nature of individual rights as well. Most notably, the Court could reverse some of the incorporation decisions and permit broader latitude for state police power in individual rights cases. Justices O'Connor (Cook 1991; Gelfand and Werhan 1990) and Anthony Kennedy (Melone 1990; Williams 1988) have advocated loosening restraints on states in such matters, particularly criminal procedure. The Court's recent abortion decisions certainly reflect a desire to give states some control over the trappings of the right to an abortion and in determining the course of school desegregation. For different reasons,

Table 11-2 Percentage of Cases in Selected Issue Areas Accepted to Resolve Circuit Court Conflict, 1938-1992 Terms

Policy areas	1938-1952	Warren Court (1953-1969)	Burger Court (1969-1985)	Rehnquist Court (1986-1992)
Internal Revenue	84	65	77	87
Ordinary Economic	66	35	45	53
U.S. as Litigant	67	36	63	72
U.S. Regulation	19	19	22	52
Due Process	10	8	23	32
Substantive Rights	5	5	13	14
Equality	15	9	21	49
N	1,793	1,754	2,237	766

because they are seen as a potentially more favorable forum, some proponents of individual rights support use of the state courts and state constitutions to protect civil liberties (Brennan 1977; Latzer 1991).

There is some compelling empirical evidence to suggest that the Rehnquist Court is altering the dynamics of agenda building. First, the decline in the percentage of agenda space allocated to Civil Liberties that began during the Burger Court has continued, and the rate of that decline has accelerated. The raw numbers mask the substantive nature of that decline, particularly in the Due Process area, in which cases concerned with the rights of prisoners have increased during the past two decades to offset partially the large-scale declines in criminal procedure cases. The Court appears to be interested in reinvigorating some dormant areas of law (such as federalism and property rights). If that is the case, then Civil Liberties is a logical candidate to sacrifice agenda space.

The most direct evidence comes from changes in the Court's case-screening processes and perhaps its priorities. The percentage of Internal Revenue and Ordinary Economic cases accepted to resolve a circuit conflict (a central tenet of the exigent agenda) has risen during the Rehnquist Court, even though the levels were quite high during the Burger Court (Table 11-2). Changes in the volitional agenda cases have been even more dramatic. Whereas less than a quarter of the cases concerned with Regulation were accepted to resolve a circuit conflict during the Burger Court, fully one-half of the accepted Regulation cases during the Rehnquist Court cite this as the reason for granting certiorari. The percentage of Due Process cases accepted to resolve circuit conflict has risen significantly, from 22 percent to almost a third of the cases. The most striking change is in cases about Equality, where the rate rose from 21 percent to just under half the cases accepted to resolve a lower-court conflict. The Court appears to be less tolerant of percolation, accepting many of these conflict cases before the conflict has spread to multiple circuits.

The numbers suggest two possibilities: one relatively narrow and the other more sweeping. The narrow interpretation of the trends is that the Court is in the process of transforming some of these issues. In the areas of Equality and Regulation, the Rehnquist Court may be in the process of transplanting some of the subareas in these broader policy domains from the volitional to the exigent portion of the agenda. In Regulation, for instance, the Court continues to treat labor relations and antitrust cases in the manner of volitional cases (that is, they are accepted for the importance of the question, the decisions are nonunanimous, and there is ideological division between justices). Most of the other areas within the Regulation domain are treated in a manner similar to Internal Revenue cases: they are accepted solely to address the circuit conflict, one question is culled from a number raised by the litigants and even that question is typically narrowed by the Court, and the decision is likely to be unanimous. The treatment of Equality cases and, to a lesser degree, some Due Process cases may be the harbinger of a transformation of those issues from the volitional agenda to the exigent agenda.

In a sense, the Court has appeared to be reducing the volitional portion of its agenda and expanding exigent agenda space. There seems to be less percolation in that the Rehnquist Court is settling more circuit conflicts as they arise. This would shrink the space available to volitional agenda cases. This is in marked contrast to many of the Court's agenda-building policies that had been in force since 1937. Proponents have often argued that the Court should concentrate on settling problems in the lower courts and paying attention to the judicial role rather than pushing the individual policy dispositions of the dominant majority. Even though the members of the Court could certainly pursue ideological designs through the exigent agenda, the discretion provided by the volitional agenda makes it less difficult and more efficient to do so.

Other trends suggest that a broader interpretation is possible. The number of full opinions issued by the Court has declined markedly in the past few terms. In the 1986-1988 terms, the slight decrease in full decisions did not appear to represent more than a temporary aberration. In the 1989-1992 terms, the decline has been more pronounced and, when coupled with the data on case selection, appears to have systematic elements. The number of full decisions in 1990 (112 cases), 1991 (115), and 1992 (113) decreased from a "normal" agenda load by more than 20 percent. This has occurred despite increasing record numbers of case filings.

The decline in the number of accepted cases is coincident with the change made by Congress in 1988 in the institutional rules, whereby the mandatory writs of appeal were virtually eliminated and the justices were left with almost complete discretion over their docket. Still, it is difficult to attribute the entire decline to a change in the mechanism of case screening. The rules may have become more favorable for changing agenda priorities, but the will to change those priorities (institutional goals) must also be present.

The goals of the Court have led the justices to adopt significant, at least symbolic, internal rule changes. Three changes in the Due Process area suggest that the reduction in the number of such cases on the agenda is merely a part of a broader plan to pare the Court's attention to these cases. In the past, although the Supreme Court has not traditionally accepted every individual challenge to capital punishment, most of the justices claimed that such petitions earned very close scrutiny due to the ultimate nature of the punishment (Epstein and Kobylka 1992; Perry 1991). But in the last decade the Court has been considerably more likely to respect the judgment of the jury if proper procedures have been followed, and it has adopted a tougher stance regarding the acceptance of petitions from death row inmates. This may not, however, reduce the number of death penalty cases reaching the Court because the defendant has nothing to lose by filing such a petition.

The other changes may affect levels of demand for hearings by the Court. The Warren Court made it relatively easy for a state criminal defendant to use the writ of habeas corpus to get into the federal courts. The Court has placed tighter restrictions on the use of habeas corpus as a collateral attack in state criminal procedure cases. In addition, over three dissents, Supreme Court Rule 39, which provided for access for the poor, was amended to permit the Court to deny "frivolous or malicious" *in forma pauperis* filings. The former justice Thurgood Marshall penned the most pointed dissent, claiming that the Court's traditional guarantee will now read: "All men and women are entitled to their day in Court only if they have the *means* and the *money.*" [12] Although the practical effects of the amended Rule 39 may be unclear, the symbolic message is testimony to the ideological changes in the Court's membership.

One decision in the 1990 term may be influential in altering the dynamics of the agenda as well. In *Arizona v. Fulminante* (1991), a majority of the Court extended the "harmless error" standard to the admission of involuntary confessions. Under this standard, a procedural irregularity in gaining a confession that is not essential to the conviction can be considered a harmless error and disregarded. The effect is to grant greater latitude to state enforcement officials, giving them the opportunity in court to defend their procedures. The increasingly broad sweep and application of the harmless error standard continues to resemble the vague fair trial standard of *Twining v. New Jersey* (1908) that was abandoned by the Warren Court. The immediate effect of the *Fulminante* decision on the agenda may not be evident. The Court will continue to accept such cases because the harmless error standard is unclear and states will encourage the Supreme Court to expand the discretion granted officials.

In the Equality area, the Court has tightened the restrictions on civil rights suits, limited affirmative action remedies, made it easier to challenge affirmative action and set aside programs for women and blacks, reversed earlier desegregation decisions, and avoided expanding the net of equal protection to groups seeking the heightened levels of scrutiny traditionally granted racial and gender discrimination cases.

The area of Substantive Rights has been less directly touched by the Court's decisions, at least since the decision in *Miller v. California* virtually ended agenda access for cases involving allegedly obscene materials. The predicted demise or reconstruction of establishment-of-religion, abortion, and libel doctrine has not purged these cases from the docket. The confusion in doctrine or the incremental dismantling of existing precedents keeps these issues viable and on the agenda. Groups continue to press such issues to get the Court to clarify and flesh out its intentions.

These concurrent trends suggest that the Court may be undergoing an institutional transformation similar (if philosophically opposed) to the changes wrought in the wake of Footnote Four. The changes in the goals of the institution and the situation facing the Court may represent the beginning of a transformation of the Court's agenda. If the goals and rules are effectively changed, then those changes will induce a reformulation of the volitional and exigent portions of the agenda. In one sense, some transition is virtually guaranteed. The levels of allocation of Civil Liberties cases to the agenda have reached an effective ceiling. Such a change might not appear to be profound in any broad sense. After all, not every subarea of Due Process, Substantive Rights, and Equality would be moved to the exigent agenda. More likely, the transition would take a form that resembles the transformation that occurred in U.S. Regulation cases during the Burger Court. Some subareas, like labor relations and antitrust, continued to hold space on the volitional agenda, whereas most subareas of Regulation exhibited the tendencies seen in exigent agenda cases (growing numbers of limited, unanimous decisions and cases accepted solely to settle a circuit conflict).

Significant changes that are not yet visible at the aggregate level may be under way. In other words, the Court may systematically move some subareas off the volitional agenda while it continues to address other subareas within the broader domain. As a result, the agenda space granted to Civil Liberties overall may not decline significantly even though important underlying changes may be occurring. In fact, if the Court is interested in removing certain issues from its agenda, in the short term justices may need to address additional cases from that area to establish some consistency and provide guidance for lower courts. If such a process is unfolding, it will take a while to manifest its full dimensions.

An agenda change of the magnitude suggested would have important consequences for the role of the Supreme Court, the nature of public policy, and the rights of individuals. The surest manifestation of agenda change would be sharp, long-term reductions in the percentage of agenda space allocated to Civil Liberties. To abdicate its responsibilities in the various areas of individual rights would be akin to the Court's retreat from economic matters in 1937. At the time of that transformation, the Court had an outlet: civil liberties and civil rights. What would fill the vacuum that would be left if Civil Liberties issues were delegated to other political actors is uncertain. The Court could delve back into the economic areas, but it would be on turf claimed by other actors. This would place the Court in an interstitial, secondary role. The Court could rewrite Federalism doctrine. Redrawing the lines between the levels of government could take a number of years to implement and could require the expenditure of significant space on the agenda.

In a study in which they oppose proposals like the National Court of Appeals and the Inter-Circuit Tribunal, Estreicher and Sexton (1986) advocate a managerial role for the Supreme Court. The authors suggest that the Court divide its cases into the priority and discretionary dockets. They maintain that the Court should concentrate its energies and resources on the priority docket, which is made up of those cases that should be addressed immediately. The discretionary docket, in contrast, consists of cases with tolerable lower-court conflict that could be allowed to percolate in the circuits for a while longer. Once the priority docket cases have been considered, then the Court can turn to the discretionary docket.

Although they are not yet well-developed, there are hints and harbingers that the Rehnquist Court is redefining its agenda and possibly its role. It is impossible to assess the relative significance of the cases accepted, but the selection policies of the early Rehnquist Court appear to reflect some of the recommendations of Estreicher and Sexton (1986). Taking cases that both fulfill policy goals and resolve lower-court disputes suggests something akin to the priority docket.

While it may be premature to speculate on this trend, the changes in the last few terms are not without policy-related consequences for the role of the institution. Estreicher and Sexton do not explicitly consider these implications. The decision to expand the exigent agenda and concentrate on cases with lower-court conflicts would appear to have one significant short-term cost: coherence in doctrinal construction. To the extent that the Court confines its case selection to those petitions demonstrating clear lower-court conflict that has spread to multiple circuits, its ability to construct coherent doctrine is affected (Tiberi 1993). Cases on the exigent agenda arise much less systematically than volitional agenda cases. Estreicher and Sexton (1986) implicitly recognize this in advocating that the Court address individual cases rather than focusing on issues. Because the cue for the Court is the existence of conflict, such cases are not sequenced as well as cases that have more significant policy implications. Groups using the courts have developed litigation strategies that often attempt to build on previous decisions, which introduces some structure to the dynamic processes of policy making. Experienced groups would undoubtedly adapt to the managerial role and might fabricate or exaggerate the existence of lower-court conflict (Perry 1991). This would force the Court to invest more resources in case screening, leaving less time for other responsibilities.

In volitional agenda cases, justices and litigants are often able to gauge the broad direction of doctrinal construction. This affords litigants the opportunity to be relatively systematic in bringing the types of cases that will be logical extensions of the recent decisions. The Court can be somewhat proactive in selecting those cases that fit the next stage of development. The justices also have the opportunity to manipulate the petitions. Exigent agenda cases, however, force the Court into a more reactive stance. The cases are selected not because they are the next logical questions to be addressed but because lower courts have disagreed about the interpretation of similar fact situations. Although coherent policy making would not be impossible, it would be more difficult.

Such a transformation of the agenda and the Court's role would affect the Court's agenda-building and policy-making capacity. The reactive stance that would result from these changes would undermine the nature of agenda building. In effect, the agenda would be reduced to the mere selection of cases. The interrelationships between current and subsequent agendas and between policy areas competing for agenda space would be reduced significantly. The Court has developed a few devices to enhance its ability to construct its agenda, such as pairing cases and developing on-off cycles.[13] The ability to use these mechanisms would be impaired by case selection policies directed primarily at resolving lower-court disputes. The reduction in the number of cases accepted by the Rehnquist Court may suggest that agenda capacity is strained by the increased attention to circuit conflicts and the costs hypothesized in shrinking the volitional agenda.

Changing the role of the Court would have significant implications for notions of pluralism. Since 1937, insular minorities and unpopular groups have had a forum in the Supreme Court. If this avenue were foreclosed, it might mean the systematic disfranchisement of many groups. One remaining point of access would be the state courts, which might create a patchwork of protections that would vary from state to state or region to region. The vast expansion of the Civil Liberties agenda was a result of the Warren Court's attempts to standardize the law through the incorporation or application of the Bill of Rights to the states and an expansive interpretation of the Fourteenth Amendment. These processes expanded the agenda space allocated to Substantive Rights, Due Process, and Equality.

The systematic removal of Civil Liberties cases from the Court's agenda seems unlikely, but such an action is a logical implication of a philosophy that emphasizes judicial restraint and deference to the elected branches of government. Despite the fact that justices who espouse such views have increasingly been nominated to the Court, such removal would take a long while to implement and would represent an extreme change in institutional rules and goals.

Conclusion

The historical trends strongly suggest that the road to a transformation in the role of the Court is fraught with potential obstacles. The apparent change in the philosophies of the Court has not extended across all policy domains and may not do so. The center of the Court (marked by Justices O'Connor and David H. Souter) appears to hold a balance of power, as it traditionally does. Analysts have speculated that the Court's right wing has become too strident and too polemic, thus chasing O'Connor, Souter, and sometimes Kennedy toward the middle, where they can use their influence to build majorities with either wing. To get their votes, Scalia and Rehnquist may have to moderate their views. While in some areas, like Due Process and Federalism, evidence of change in philosophical direction is clear, in other areas the battle for governing standards continues.

In the long term, such policies might well signal a new role for the Supreme Court, consistent with the judicial philosophies of many of the current justices. Such a role would appear to incorporate judicial restraint and deference to other agencies of government, the core of traditional normative values. Most fundamentally, these changes have implications for the treatment of individual rights and liberties, the staple of the volitional agenda. Civil liberties issues may receive the same type of balancing tests the Court has used in economic issues. The Court would, therefore, be less directly involved in the fundamental construction of policy than its predecessors in the Warren Court.

The potential change in the paradigm that guides decision making has historical antecedents, and so does the incremental process of putting it into effect. Ultimately, it took proponents of the preferred position a long time to become ascendant and begin to control the tenor of debate. Similarly, any sweeping revision in the Court's philosophy and role could be vulnerable. The emergence of a new paradigm could be threatened or even undermined by changes in the political environment. A few additional opportunities to "pack" the Court could defuse the construction of the nascent paradigm and reinvigorate a battle for the philosophical core of the Court, a battle that seemed lost just a year earlier. In fact, in recent terms, some of the justices appear to have reexamined the consequences of the wholesale changes that were being urged on the Court and retreated from the precipice.

A Court with two strong ideological and philosophical wings would represent a change in the goals of the institution. Those changes would undoubtedly create the impetus for some changes in institutional rules. Taken together, the goals and rules would create new conditions (situations) for group litigation. Ironically, all this foment might create some elements of stability in the Court's agenda. As the pendulum swings and the Court finds its new center, history suggests that the newly constituted Court will continue to grapple with the issues that comprise its current agenda and to modify the doctrine, expanding it in some areas and contracting it in others. Those are the conditions that keep issues on the Court's volitional agenda.

Notes

1. For more on judicial attitudes, see Chapter 13.

2. The order of discussion of cases begins with the chief justice and continues through to the most junior justice. This gives the chief justice some opportunity to structure the discussion and force the next justices to address the chief's remarks. Similarly, the chief justice gets to assign the writing of the majority opinion when he or she votes in the majority. Thus a chief justice might vote with the majority even if he or she is not in agreement with those views in order to assign the opinion (Danelski 1989). For example, if Chief Justice Rehnquist was in the minority, senior justices William J. Brennan, Jr. (when he was on the Court) or John Paul Stevens would get to assign the opinion. In most instances, Brennan or Stevens would assign the opinion to someone who would write a more liberal ruling that would expand rights. If Rehnquist voted with the majority, he could assign the majority opinion to a more moderate or conservative justice. Thus, the majority opinion, which creates a precedent and is, in effect, the law of the land, would be closer to his views than if he allowed a more liberal justice to assign it.

3. The solicitor general repeatedly argues cases in the Court and is a respected player; his or her arguments therefore carry a great deal of weight with the justices (Caplan 1987; Scigliano 1971). Thus, personnel changes or revisions in the priorities of the solicitor general's office would be reflected in the cases brought to the Court or in the legal arguments presented. When a group enters an area of law it can bring a new perspective and new arguments. Similarly, when a group leaves an area of law, it can alter the dynamics of that area (Kobylka 1987). The Supreme Court may give more attention to decisions made in lower courts that have an ideological focus different from its own than to decisions made in a compatible lower court. Specialized publics include respected legal theorists and law review articles that sometimes affect judicial decisions (Epstein and Kobylka 1992, 26-27).

4. Prior to 1925, the Court lacked discretion over the cases on its docket. As a result, the Court had to accept every case properly brought before it. In 1925, Congress divided the Court's jurisdiction into mandatory writs of appeal and discretionary writs of certiorari. The Court also found ways to deal with frivolous or trivial writs of appeal, which by law it was obligated to accept. The Court could "deny the writ as improvidently granted" (d.i.g.). In 1988, Congress again expanded the Court's discretionary jurisdiction, reducing sharply the numbers of cases the Court was obligated to accept under its mandatory jurisdiction.

5. When I refer to the issue areas as I have coded them, I capitalize the terms (for example, Due Process, Equality, Civil Liberties, Economic, Regulation) to distinguish them from the common usage of the words. When I refer to the common usage of the terms, I lowercase them.

6. For more on the database, see Appendix C of this book.

7. The minimum of one page is designed to eliminate cases that the Court could decide with one sentence because of an existing precedent. The theoretical rationale is borne out by the empirical reality; very few decisions are contained on one page. Most of the Court's decisions are full opinions, brief memoranda decisions published in the back of the *United States Reports*, or terse per curiam decisions (unsigned decisions, usually brief opinions for the Court). Longer per curiam and memoranda decisions are included because their length indicates their importance and substance (Pacelle 1991, 17-18).

8. After his resounding 1936 electoral victory, President Roosevelt sought by way of his famous "Court-packing plan" to pressure the Court to fall into line with his New Deal policies. Ostensibly

designed to help the overworked "nine old men," the plan sought to add one justice to the Court for every current member over the age of seventy. In reality, Roosevelt hoped to stack the Court with new justices sympathetic to his New Deal.

9. In a variety of cases the Court loosened jurisdictional restraints in order to get to the substantive issue in important areas of law. In *Baker v. Carr* (1962), the Court made what Chief Justice Warren called the most important decision of his tenure, deciding that reapportionment was a justiciable issue, not a political question. In *Flast v. Cohen* (1968), the Court granted standing and allowed a taxpayer suit against public spending for textbooks for religious schools (Morgan 1972, 129-131).

10. The aggregate levels of support are not much different, but the perception is that the Rehnquist Court has gone considerably further in restricting individual rights and liberties. Indeed, in civil liberties, criminal procedure, and due process, the decline in levels of support for the liberal side has been almost imperceptible. In civil rights, support for the liberal side actually grew from 52 percent to 55 percent (Epstein et al., 1994, 166). Certainly, the abortion decisions have allowed greater restrictions, although opponents of *Roe v. Wade* could not muster the fifth vote to overturn that precedent in *Casey v. Planned Parenthood of Southeastern Pennsylvania* (1992). In *Employment Division, Department of Human Resources of Oregon v. Smith* (1990), the Court rewrote free exercise-of-religion doctrine, making it more restrictive and breaking from precedents established thirty years earlier.

11. Litigants occasionally get involved in an attempt to change the nature of the debate, even if the prospects for winning are not great. Groups may attempt to get a line of reasoning into law review articles to influence special publics (Epstein and Kobylka 1992). Solicitor General Charles Fried (1985-1989) admitted raising issues or rationales to provide allies on the Court with ammunition or to insert the reasoning in the debate in the hope that support would be forthcoming later (Caplan 1987; Fried 1991; Salokar 1992). In death penalty cases, Solicitor General Robert H. Bork's brief in *Gregg v. Georgia* (1976) helped transform the nature of the debate and was the core of a new standard (Epstein and Kobylka 1992). Similarly, in *Akron v. Akron Center for Reproductive Health Services* (1983), the solicitor general offered the "undue burden" standard, upon which Justice Sandra Day O'Connor built what has become the core of the Court's standard in such cases (Epstein and Kobylka 1992).

12. In re Amendment to Rule 39, 111 S. Ct. at 1574 (1990 term).

13. The Court can use such tools, in effect, to expand the capacity of its annual agenda. To "expand" its agenda, the Court will often take a number of similar cases concurrently, allowing the justices to address a number of questions simultaneously and thus more fully. Relatedly, the Court will then put that area aside and let its decisions percolate at the lower-court level for a term or two and turn to other areas of law and pair those cases. These devices increase the Court's decisional capacity because it takes less time to screen, decide, and write opinions on related cases than to do so on the same number of unrelated cases.

12 By Consent of the Governed: Directions in Constitutional Theory

Leslie Friedman Goldstein

How should judges reach decisions? To address this question, scholars often invoke *constitutional theory* or *constitutional philosophy*—phrases that refer to a framework of principles for guiding judges in their task of constitutional interpretation. Although analysts have long expounded such theories, scholarly interest in constitutional philosophy often increases in eras when the output of the U.S. Supreme Court is exceptionally controversial. For example, the felt need for such a framework intensified in a number of stages immediately prior to the 1970s. And, after the Court's decision in *Roe v. Wade* (1973), the felt need was so overwhelming that it led to a veritable flowering of constitutional theory in the scholarly world.[1]

In this chapter, I review the judicial events that prompted the scholarly reaction and examine the types of constitutional theory that have resulted. I argue that the most recent trend in constitutional theory has been an outcropping of theories that focus on the structure, or essential features, of the American regime or polity—in other words, on the nature of the American "state" in the sense of the essential features of its governmental form. I then provide examples of that trend, arguing that they demonstrate an important convergence among these regime-focused scholars on the principled baseline of government by consent of the governed. The relation between that baseline and constitutional jurisprudence is then explicated from the perspective of this recent scholarship. Since one of these perspectives is my own, I proceed to defend a particular version of popular-consent-oriented constitutional theory and to compare that one with other recent versions of the general approach. To the extent that this chapter contains a defense of certain aspects of this consent-focused approach, it, too, engages in constitutional theory, attempting to answer the question, "What should guide the judges?"

The Rise of Constitutional Theory: *Brown v. Board of Education of Topeka* and Its Aftermath

In the 1950s and 1960s, the Supreme Court, under the chief justiceship of Earl Warren produced an extraordinary number of innovative constitutional interpretations. These expanded the rights of individual Americans to vote *(Harper v. Virginia State Board of Elections,* 1966), to be free of state-established religion *(School District of Abington Township v. Schempp,* 1963), to be free of state policies that result in penalties on the exercise of religion *(Sherbert v. Verner,* 1963), to advocate radical politics *(Brandenburg v. Ohio,* 1969), to read purportedly obscene literature *(Memoirs of a Woman of Pleasure v. Massachusetts* [the *Fanny Hill* case], 1966), to have legislative districts of the same population size as other districts in the same state *(Reynolds v. Sims,* 1964), to attend desegregated schools *(Brown v. Board of Education I,* 1954; *Brown v. Board of Education II,* 1955; *Cooper v. Aaron,* 1958), and to be protected in several ways if accused of crime. For example, indigents acquired assurance of the assistance of defense counsel *(Gideon v. Wainwright,* 1963), and persons searched unlawfully or pressured by the police in unlawful ways into confessions of crime acquired security against being convicted by the fruits of those illegal procedures *(Mapp v. Ohio,* 1961; *Escobedo v. Illinois,* 1964; *Miranda v. Arizona,* 1966).

These and other Warren Court decisions triggered debates about "judicial activism" as opposed to "judicial restraint," debates that focused on how often or under what circumstances courts should exercise judicial review (Bickel 1962; Black 1960; Choper 1980; Gunther 1964; Halpern and Lamb 1982; Perry 1982). More relevant here is the interest these cases generated in constitutional theory, which considers what courts ought to be doing when they are exercising judicial review. The first decision from the Warren Court to trigger an invigoration of constitutional theory was the one that is to this day its most famous, *Brown v. Board of Education* (1954), the decision announcing an end to the doctrine of "separate but equal" in public schools.

In immediate response to the *Brown* decision, Alexander Bickel (of Yale Law School) wrote a much-cited article published in the *Harvard Law Review* in 1955 that increased the salience of the old political question doctrine. According to this doctrine, matters of political discretion (that is, policy choices), are left to the (legislative and executive) branches elected by the people, or to the people themselves in their constitution-writing mode. What judges do, by contrast, is settle not these "political questions" but, rather, *legal* questions in which policies adopted by the political branches are interpreted and applied to particular cases. Legal questions include the interpretation of America's highest law, the Constitution, which "we the people" adopted in clear anticipation that it would override legislative or executive enactments that conflict with it *(Marbury v. Madison* 1803, 166-177).[2]

Bickel's article demonstrated, by thorough historical research, that "section 1 of the Fourteenth Amendment [which contains the equal protection clause at issue in *Brown*] . . . carried out . . . relatively narrow objectives and hence, as *originally understood,* was meant to apply neither to jury service [cf. *Strauder v. West Virginia,* 1880], nor suffrage, nor anti-miscegenation statutes, nor segregation" (1955, 58). Bickel went on to argue, however, that the Warren Court was quite justified in refusing to follow the "original understanding" of the sovereign people who had written and adopted the Fourteenth Amendment, because those people knew the Constitution to be a "broadly worded organic law not [to be] frequently or lightly amended." And, operating with this knowledge, the framers of the Fourteenth Amendment had deliberately rejected proposed language of a narrow and concrete focus in favor of wording "more receptive to 'latitudinarian' construction," in order to put into the supreme law of the United States a language "sufficiently elastic to permit reasonable future advances"—"a line of growth" in the direction of a higher societal morality than that for which the citizens of 1868 were ready (1955, 59-64).

Bickel was suggesting that in many of its parts—the "open-textured" ones—the Constitution as an organic law is a constitution of aspiration, containing moral principles meant to endure but also meant to evolve along with the moral level of the people themselves. He urged justices to take this hope for growth into account when they interpreted the document, even to the degree of contravening the known purposes of the congressional authors of a constitutional amendment.[3]

Admitting that the known intentions of the Constitution's authors should sometimes be violated, however, opened up a veritable Pandora's box of judicial-power possibilities. If the conscious and announced intent of the law's author could be transgressed by a court purporting to interpret *that law*, what, if anything, remained of the political question doctrine? In other words, what remained of the idea that courts interpret and apply the will of the sovereign rather than ruling as sovereign themselves?

Bickel's next three books attempted to answer this question (1962, 1970, 1975), as did two influential articles published in 1959 in the *Harvard Law Review*—one by Henry M. Hart and one by Herbert Wechsler.[4] As guides for "constitutional interpretation," Herbert Wechsler suggested following "the text of the Constitution when its words may be decisive," and giving weight to "history" and "precedent" as well. He argued at length that the assessing of the relative role of these three elements in the interpretive task is to be done by means of reasoned principles. To deny, he insisted, that there are proper criteria to guide the Court in its interpretive task would be to render the Court "a naked power organ" rather than a "court of law" (1959, 6, 10, 12, 15-17).

Hart cited Wechsler approvingly (1959, 99 n. 34). And when he described the Supreme Court as "destined to be the voice of reason, charged with the creative function of discerning afresh and of articulating and developing impersonal and durable principles," Hart made clear that he was talking about principles for interpreting the law. The rest of his sentence reads thus: "principles of constitutional law, and impersonal and durable principles for the interpretation of statutes and the resolution of difficult issues of decisional law" (1959, 99).

And Bickel wrote of the Court that, in acting on "its power *to construe and apply the*

Constitution," it must ever be mindful of constitutional text, history, and precedent as "sources of inspiration"—if not the "wellspring" of judgment—but that the Court must also find its reasoned principles in "the evolving morality of our tradition" and must prudently refrain from taking cases when the application of firm, reasoned principles to them would be politically unwise (Bickel 1962, 235ff. and also chap. 4).[5]

Another leading work of this period, by Charles L. Black—while not denying any of the guidelines of text, precedent, history, societal moral tradition, or reasoned principle—added an argument for the wisdom and propriety of finding guidance in the plan embedded in the overall structure of government. But, again, he proffered this suggestion in order to guide the courts in interpreting "the great vague words of the Constitution" (Black 1960, 48).

Thus the battle among critics of the Court in the post-*Brown* decade concerned whether the Court was following the proper guidelines in doing its job of interpreting the more malleable phrases of the Constitution—those phrases like "due process" and "equal protection" that had been, as it were, *intended* by the framers to take on *unintended* meaning as society evolved. Those parts of the constitutional text were intended by the framers to evolve and grow in meaning as society developed, and to grow in ways that simply could not be foreseen, or in any literal sense planned on, in advance. Text, history, precedent, societal moral tradition, reasoned principle, and government structure were all recommended as guides for judges deciding how to apply the more plastic portions of the constitutional text. Still, the judicial task was conceptualized as preeminently that of interpreting a legal text. This changed with the right-to-privacy decisions, *Griswold v. Connecticut* (1965) and *Roe v. Wade* (1973).

The Second Plateau of Constitutional Theory: *Griswold* and Its Aftermath

In *Griswold v. Connecticut* (1965) the Supreme Court reasserted the long-discredited doctrine of "substantive due process" in order to protect a right nowhere mentioned in the Constitution—one the justices called "marital privacy," which meant, in *Griswold*, a right for married people to be free of government interference into their decision whether to use birth control devices.[6] Although the official "Court" opinion for *Griswold*, authored by Justice William O. Douglas, specifically denied reliance on substantive due process, several other justices so identified the reasoning.[7]

The doctrine of substantive due process had been discredited on a variety of grounds, but the criticism of interest here would go as follows: Substantive due process reads the due process clauses of the Fourteenth and Fifth Amendments as licensing U.S. judges to decide (for and by themselves) what rights are fundamental in the United States. If *they* believe certain rights to be of fundamental importance in American society (that is, in the good society), then—even if the Constitution neither mentions them nor alludes to them—the courts may so announce.[8] Once they have pronounced a particular right "fundamental"—such as the right to use contraception (*Griswold*), or the right to be free from government interference in "decisions so fundamentally affecting the person as the decision whether to bear or beget a child" (*Eisenstadt v. Baird* 1972, 453-454)—the electorally responsive branches of government may not, absent very compelling exigency, abridge it.[9] So-called substantive due process turns the justices from interpreters of a legal text (albeit an opaque, amorphous, malleable one) into grand prohibitors of legislation who may prohibit any law that strikes them as a bad one on the grounds that the particular freedom invaded by this law is fundamental in American society. Once so prohibited, the law will continue to stay prohibited (short of a judicial overruling) as long as at least one-third plus one of the membership of either house of Congress also dislikes the law, or at least one legislative house in each of thirteen of the fifty states does. In other words, it is highly impracticable for the people of the United States, if they disagree with the Court on the fundamentalness of any particular aspect of freedom, to override the Court through constitutional amendment. *Through substantive due process the court can directly legislate rights. The justices do not have to derive them from any expression of the sovereign will.* So the distinction put forth in the original political question doctrine disappears; and Americans wind up, on various topics, ruled by nine persons appointed for life who are more or less immune to the influence of majority sentiment.

These implications were apparent in 1965, but not very many Americans cared to oppose the idea that married couples who wanted to use contraceptive devices should be allowed to; so *Griswold v. Connecticut* went more or less unnoticed. After 1973, however, when *Roe v. Wade* extended the Court's logic about a right to contraception and struck down the criminal abortion statutes of all but a handful of the states, a kind of pandemonium broke loose in judicial scholarship. No longer was the Court legislating at the margins against curious, outdated, and nationally unpopular state laws; now it was legislating in bold and broad strokes, dramatically shaping the life of the nation. And it was doing so in its grand prohibitor mode, with no apparent embarrassment at the idea that it needed no referent in the constitutional text for its assertion that there is a fundamental right to choose to have an abortion.[10] The justices were obviously doing something other than merely *interpreting* law, and they were doing it in ways that had tremendous impact on society. This new approach, because many scholars wanted to defend it on grounds other than "substantive due process," was given a variety of labels: fundamental-rights jurisprudence, extratextualism, noninterpretivism, to name the frequently appearing ones. The basic theme of this approach was the idea that federal judges should protect fundamental rights against legislation abridging them, whether or not the particular rights are mentioned or even specifically implied in the written Constitution. Scholars lined up on either side of this new development; a searching reexamination of the role of judicial review in American society began.

The Terrain of Contemporary Constitutional Theory

Some scholars, as might have been expected, reacted against this new development. Raoul Berger took up the outpost at the furthest extreme opposing the new trend—insisting that the only legitimate role for judges was to follow the exact and specific intent of the framers where such intent was discoverable (unless the Constitution were formally amended to the contrary). For him, even *Brown* was an illegitimate use of judicial power (1977). Berger is the most consistent and most prominent defender of intentionalism, and very few of his followers maintain the approach as rigidly and thoroughly as he. Others who claim to espouse intentionalism—for instance, the former judge Robert Bork—tend to waiver when their favorite clauses are at stake (1971). A narrow intentionalism of the Berger variety can be criticized on several grounds—impracticality; the impossibility of deciding which framers' intentions get priority, since they disagreed among themselves; the multiplicity of approaches in the past, even within the "founding" generation (1776-1820); and the fact that the framers themselves evidently disagreed with Raoul Berger (see Goldstein 1991, chaps. 1 and 3). Thus, as either a scholarly or a practical matter, the impact of Berger and of his approach has been quite limited.

John Ely produced the most impressive of the criticisms along the traditional (the political question doctrine) axis—that is, when they engaged in extratextualist jurisprudence, the judges were stepping outside the role of judges and this was illegitimate (1973). Then, in a book-length work, he modified his opposition to unwritten rights in the following respect: calling his new approach "the ultimate interpretivism," Ely argued that unless judges inferred their constitutional rules either from the text of the Constitution itself or from the type of regime (representative government) established by the text, they were exercising inappropriate power (1980). Ely's critique appears to have been of enduring influence, and the reasons for that will be explored in the next section.

Nonetheless, the vast majority of constitutional theorists have staked out a position not in opposition to extratextualism but in favor of it. Support for the idea that American judges have legitimate authority to single out for protection whatever liberties strike them as fundamental in our society is overwhelming among the law school professoriate. The doctrine has been endorsed on several grounds. Some scholars have supported it on historical grounds, arguing that a long tradition of neglected precedent supports such extratextual decision making by Supreme Court justices (for example, Grey 1974, 1978, 1988a, 1988b; Murphy 1978) or that the "original" intent of many of the framers was that this would go on (Grey 1974, 1978, 1988a, 1988b; Sherry 1987). Others have defended it on the grounds that the spirit and structure of our Constitution establish limited government and that if the legislators fail to honor appropriate limits, it then becomes appropriate for judges to force them to do so (for example, Bobbitt 1982, chaps. 7-12; Tribe 1978, chap. 15, especially at 893). Still others have argued that a nonelected branch is more capable of engaging in reasoned reflection as to what ought to be the core values of our society, and this moral leadership power therefore should be accorded to judges simply to make America a better country (for example, Perry 1982, chap. 4). Another group of scholars has defended judicial declarations of extratextual rights on the basis of the text itself, citing the Ninth Amendment (for example, Bobbitt 1982; Murphy 1978, 1980) or the Privileges or Immunities Clause (for example, Bobbitt 1982).[11] Finally, some scholars, influenced variously by legal realists, by contemporary philosophic trends, or by developments in recent literary theory, have argued that texts are indeterminate in their meaning, so legal texts cannot constrain judges anyway; the old political question doctrine has never been more than a comforting myth, and judges have always imposed their own values on the citizenry, purporting to be interpreting the law but in fact making it up as they go along (for example, Carter 1985; Miller 1982; Unger 1986).

Something like a middle ground between textualism and extratextualism was also staked out. Some scholars, of whom Ronald Dworkin is the most prominent, selected parts of the Constitution, such as the word *justice* in the Preamble or the word *equal* in the Equal Protection Clause, and then used these textual anchors to symbolize "vague" ideas—called "concepts" by Dworkin.[12] These "concepts" amount to empty vessels into which justices of different generations would be expected to pour content derived from the moral philosophy of their day (Dworkin 1977, 134-137).[13] These scholars go through the ritual of attaching their constitutional theory to a bit of the text, but the level of abstraction involved, for all practical purposes, amounts to an authorization of extratextual jurisprudence.

New Directions: Consent of the Governed and the American Regime

A survey of the terrain of American constitutional theory as of 1990 makes evident that neither text nor precedent nor history alone can settle the question of whether justices should feel free to constitutionalize as rights whatever values strike them as fundamental. Although proponents of such jurisprudence can cite pieces of history in its favor, so can opponents. For instance, there is the awkward fact that the Constitutional Convention specifically debated whether to include Supreme Court justices with the president in a Council of Revision, in which they would share a general, political veto power (analogous to extratextual jurisprudence, except that it would have been overridable by a two-thirds vote in both houses of Congress). At the convention James Wilson defended this power as one that would let justices strike down laws that were "unwise" or "unjust" but not "so unconstitutional as to justify the judges in refusing to give them effect" (Farrand 1966, 2:73). The convention specifically voted against this idea twice, the successful side arguing that the Supreme Court would be reviewing laws for constitutionality, anyway, and the justices should not participate in passing laws that they would later have to judge (Farrand 1966, 2:73-80, 298). Similarly, while proponents of extratextualism can spin out theories strengthening the Ninth Amendment or plausibly insist on the wrongfulness of neglecting the Fourteenth Amendment privileges or immunities clause, opponents can point to those words in the text that reserve "legislative" (law-making) power to Congress and that give only "judicial" (law-interpreting) power to the Supreme Court. They can also point to the phrasing of those parts of the Constitution that describe the judicial power: the Supremacy Clause in authorizing the judicial voiding of state laws mentions only the grounds of a conflict with national treaties, national laws, or "this Constitution"; and the clause of Article III that confers federal court jurisdiction refers only to cases "arising under" national laws, national treaties, or the national Constitution.[14] Likewise, while obscure precedents can be cited that relied on natural rights, or the spirit of our free institutions (as discerned by the justices, of course), on behalf of the judicial defense of unwritten rights, it is also true that precedents like *Marbury v. Madison* (1803) and *West Coast Hotel v. Parrish* (1937) can be cited to condemn non-text-based constitutional jurisprudence.[15]

The idea here is not that the U.S. Constitution and judicial precedents interpreting it are incoherent; many of the scholars involved in the extratextualism debate have developed reasonably coherent analyses in which they answer to their own satisfaction the points cited by the other side. Rather it is that the choice for or against extratextualism for the U.S. Supreme Court cannot be made on purely legal grounds. It is a political choice, a choice of regime—in other words, a choice of basic government structure. In my view, history, text, and precedent on the whole counsel in favor of a textualist jurisprudence, but I concede that plausible arguments can also be made to the contrary. If the constitutional text is susceptible to opposed interpretations, how is one to choose? One has to look at the text as a whole and in light of its historic context and historic development in order to get a sense of the regime type that is being established. The regime will be an expression of certain normative political principles, of a political theory. Ultimately, one's political theory is the foundation of one's constitutional theory (see also Dworkin 1981, 1982).

Thus the question of regime is central. Charles Black (1960, 1969) emphasized regime structure during the growth spurt of constitutional theory in the 1960s, but at that time regime structure was brought into the picture merely as one among many guidelines for interpreting the text. It was Ely (1980) who gave center stage to the matter of regime structure in his book *Democracy and Distrust*. In the book Ely defends the enhancing of an egalitarian, representative political process as the guideline-setting goal for judicial review, not on the grounds that this process is favored by Ely's own political theory but rather that it is the political theory implicitly endorsed by the whole Constitution. The extratextualists can challenge Ely with the reminder that the text nonetheless includes clauses like the Privileges or Immunities Clause that seem to license judges to roam all over the map of social policy, striking down any law that evokes in them a powerful feeling that it is wrong. And Ely appears to have no answer for the extratextualists because he does not give an account of his own desire to find constraints on judicial power in the text. Yes, one can find them if one wants to constrain judicial discretion, but one can also find discretion-enhancing clauses if one sets out to look for them.

In other words, Ely's argument is essentially as follows: the Constitution sets up a representative form of government; the Supreme Court is not very tightly bound to the representative process; so let's look for ways to constrain its discretion in order to limit the Court's power to enhancing the representative process. One could as easily argue a contrary view: the Constitution provides a series of checks on majoritarian, legislative power; the Supreme Court can provide such a check; so let's look for ways to enhance its discretion in order to let it do more checking.

Because Ely did not defend the grounds of his choice, more or less taking for granted that all who looked would agree with him that the essential nature of the American regime was that it was a representative democracy, his book received a great deal of criticism. But its wisdom in focusing on the regime question did bear fruit. In the early 1990s four different constitutional theory books that argue the centrality of the regime question were published (Ackerman 1991; Burt 1992; Goldstein 1991; and Sunstein 1993). In all four the arguments coalesce in emphasizing one or more aspects of "government by consent of the governed" as the central theme of American constitutionalism. This important development may eventually modify the fundamental-rights jurisprudence of the U.S. Supreme Court.

Consent-Oriented Constitutional Theory I: Goldstein Version

Below I summarize my core argument for an American constitutional theory (presented in greater detail in Goldstein 1991) and then explain ways in which its focus on "government by consent of the governed" is echoed in arguments made in the recent books of Bruce Ackerman (1991), Robert Burt (1992), and Cass Sunstein (1993). I will then offer some concluding reflections on the relation between this trend in constitutional theory and the Supreme Court's fundamental-rights jurisprudence.

I have argued (Goldstein 1991, chaps. 1 and 3), and indeed still would argue, that the meaning of the slogan "government by consent of the governed," like judicial review itself in the United States, evolved dramatically in the first few decades after independence. Political development itself became less elitist, moving from a system of state constitutions adopted by state legislatures to one where constitutions faced ratification by the people themselves and came to be viewed as, for that reason, higher than legislative authority. Contemporaneously, judicial review evolved from a power to check legislatures on the basis of the (elite) judges' pronouncement of "natural law" or the "law of nations" (which review was so unpopular as to provoke mass protest meetings, threats to impeach judges, votes of legislative censure, and the like) to one based on a theory that the people are the true sovereign, and they express their will in a written constitution that is to be treated as higher law and upheld (if need be) by judges. This new version of judicial review, unlike what preceded it, was immediately accepted across American jurisdictions.

The new version followed on the adoption of the new national Constitution of 1787-1791, and its theory was most prominently explicated in *Federalist* No. 78, and in *Marbury v. Madison*. It is a theory that responds to a problem explored in *Federalist* Nos. 10 and 51. Americans were establishing a government responsive through the election system to the will of the majority. In this sense, popular majorities would rule. But majorities sometimes want bad things; they may threaten the rights of individuals or of minorities (*Federalist* No. 10). One solution to this problem is to have the people as a whole write down in founding documents the basic rules of the game, indicating those rights that may not be violated. Judges then can protect these rights, responding to the long-term wishes of the people against temporary bad majorities (*Federalist* No. 78, and *Marbury*). Also, persons elected by the people to rule may be tempted to abuse their power. "If men were angels we wouldn't need government" (*Federalist* No. 51). Judges (with their own ambitions) could be used to "counteract ambition" (*Federalist* No. 51), employing judicial review to secure the basic rules chosen by the people from abuses of power by other government officials (*Federalist* No. 78, and *Marbury*).

In the regime of this type of judicial review the people consent to government at two levels. The higher level is that of constitution formation through the original ratification and the amending process put forth in Article V. The "governed" in their lower level as elective majorities give consent to legislative policies. In both of these, granted, "the people" still express their will through elected representatives, but the assumption is that if support for a rule is so widespread that it can garner the combination needed for formal constitutional amendment—namely, two-thirds majorities in each house of Congress, and majorities in three-quarters of the state legislatures, so many folks must want it that this should count as the voice of the people themselves. Therefore, a given policy of lower-level consent is not allowed to contravene the will of the people as a whole. In this sense the people as constitution-adopters are the ultimate sovereign, and their will is to be enforced by courts exercising text-based judicial review.

So goes the old-fashioned narrative. But no American alive today was there when most of the Constitution was adopted; how is "consent of the governed" a living reality for the late twentieth century? My answer is that there is a system of ongoing informal, constitutional politics. For the most part, Americans acquiesce in current constitutional doctrine, just as they do toward other laws, many of which were adopted before they came of voting age. And from time to time voters go to the polls, vaguely aware that they are voting to put people in office who will have to swear to uphold the Constitution.

Buttressing these modes of passive consent to the basic rules is the system of active constitutional politics, through which the voting public produces informal constitutional amendments by political mobilization contrary to existing Supreme Court interpretations, which mobilization causes the Court to alter constitutional doctrine. Such a doctrinal reversal has sometimes come in response to an all-but-successful movement for a formal constitutional amendment,[16] and it can also be brought about through politics, when the president and members of Congress pledge to use the appointment process and control over the size of the Court to reverse (or enforce) a controversial Supreme Court decision. Such a campaign is precisely what Lincoln pledged in response to the *Dred Scott* decision (1857);[17] Richard Nixon, in response to decisions in the 1960s that were alleged to "coddle criminals"; and Ronald Reagan, in response to *Roe v. Wade*. Indeed, the fact that such responses do sometimes occur renders credible the claim that when they do not, the passive acquiescence deserves to be taken seriously as a kind of consent. Still, such "consent" does not represent the public's firmest, most authoritative voice. Rather, it is the public speaking tentatively, provisionally, and until circumstances change. And the nonconsent of active constitutional politics represents the public asking the Court to reconsider. If the Court fails to do so, the voting public may become so dissatisfied that it will formally amend the Constitution.

In a sense, then, there are three levels of authority in the American regime. The formally adopted Constitution is the voice of the people at its firmest and most authoritative. It is to be honored even at the cost of frustrating—the bottom level—particular legislative majorities at particular moments. Between the will of elected legislative majorities and the will of the Constitution-ratifying people, there is the amorphous, fluid world of constitutional politics—the ongoing dialogue between the people and the Supreme Court about the meaning of their constitutional law. The Court is to be attentive to this dialogue, but it is not subordinate to it in the sense that it is subordinate to the formal Constitution.

In this three-level constitutional regime that I have described, the will of the Constitution-forming people is the only authority higher than legislative majorities. (In the middle level there is no clear authority but a dialogic, interpretive process of mutual, shifting influence, with all interpreting parties looking to the formal Constitution as their authority.) If I am correct in pinpointing "government by consent of the governed" as the domi-

nant theme of the American regime, then it makes sense to adopt judicial-power-con-
straining readings of those infinitely expandable clauses the Ninth Amendment and the
Privileges or Immunities Clause. It makes sense to interpret them in such a way that they
channel rather than unleash judicial power, limiting the judiciary to implementing some
expression of the will of the sovereign people. The latter clause forbids state governments
to abridge the "privileges or immunities of citizens of the United States." What are these?
A good answer might be, those privileges or immunities perceived as important enough to
have been specifically mentioned in the Bill of Rights. (The Supreme Court has never
agreed to this rather common-sensical interpretation but has instead protected most of
those rights at the state level via a sometimes strained reading of the Fourteenth Amendment's Due Process Clause. The Court basically ignores the Privileges or Immunities
Clause—a posture hardly respectful of the idea that it is duty-bound to implement the
Constitution.) As to the Ninth Amendment, in my view, according to the best historical
evidence, it was meant to protect rights secured in state bills of rights against the idea that
the listing of rights in the federal Constitution (including rights against state governments
in Article I, Sec. 10) was an exclusive listing and was meant to be interpreted because of the
Supremacy Clause as eliminating all other rights against state government (Goldstein 1991,
112-14).

Three important arguments exist for viewing this system, grounded in popular sovereignty, as pointing to a textually constrained constitutional theory. First, as noted above,
both the constitutional wording describing judicial power and the convention history of
decision making about a Council of Revision point to a regime structured around a tripartite system of governing branches, two of which—the legislative and the executive—were
to be accountable to electoral majorities, and one of which was not. That "consent of the
governed" to which appointed-for-life judges were to be responsible was the will expressed
in the constitutional document, for judges, like other officials, are required to take an oath
to uphold that document. The tripartite structure of government is built on the premise of
the political question doctrine (explained in the discussion of *Brown v. Board of Education*,
above). If the Court were to be free to announce new rights as it went along, there would be
no reason for not treating it as a third house of the legislature.

Second, the political history of the American people's own reaction to fundamental-
rights jurisprudence indicates, in my view, a deep and enduring negative response to it. As
already noted above, the earliest instances of judicial review in America predated the theory and practice of constitutionalism based on popular sovereignty. Those early exercises
of judicial review based on unwritten rights met with open and widespread hostility.
Moreover, an examination of the fate of the unwritten rights decisions of the past two
hundred years has led me to the conclusion that they tended to get overruled, unless there
was readily available a well-reasoned, textually oriented alternative basis for the decision

(Goldstein 1991, 130-31, 146 nn. 46-50). I shall return to this important fact below. For now, I wish to point out that the nation's response to the unwritten rights jurisprudence that periodically crops up has been repeatedly negative. I would argue that the inference to be drawn from this history is that the enhancement of judicial power produced by such jurisprudence does not resonate comfortably with the elements of the American regime that are based on popular sovereignty.

Third, a moral premise underlies the regime based on popular sovereignty that I have described. Strangely enough (or perhaps not so strangely, since American constitutional theorists all inhabit the same actual American regime), the same moral premise underlies the jurisprudence of fundamental rights. At the core of the extratextualist position is the belief that the Supreme Court should strike down any law that conflicts with justice, and this group of scholars defines justice in such terms as every person's right to equal concern and respect (for example, Ronald Dworkin; Kenneth Karst 1977), or, similarly, respect for human dignity or for the inherent worthiness of every human being (Murphy 1980). The commitment to government by consent of the governed stems from the same moral theory—from the view that in a moral sense all people are created equal. But a careful look at the regime structures favored, respectively, by the extratextualist scholars and by advocates of textually constrained judicial power yields the conclusion that the regime preferred by the latter honors the moral premise shared by both groups more thoroughly than does the regime of the extratextualists.

The political theory that defends a regime in which judges exercise extratextual power gives great weight to the importance of moral reasoning in any society and to the justices' institutional position, which facilitates tranquil, reasoned reflection. In this account of the American regime, the justices speak as the voice of moral reason and are given authority to check majority impulses because the electoral majority may behave tyrannically. The people (that is, ordinary citizens) acquiesce in this system because they know that they may, on any given day, find themselves among the victimized minority. If the Court ever gets too wild, there remains the remedy of impeachment via activation of the elected representatives of the people. For less egregious cases there remain the more gradual remedies of electoral influence over Court appointments, legislative regulation of jurisdiction, and constitutional amendment. Short of these extremes, the electoral majorities must submit to judicial will and hope for the best. In this political theory of a "good" representative democracy, distrust of electoral majorities weighs heavily. A frequently added ingredient of the theory is the claim that supposedly representative (that is, electoral) institutions are elitist and unrepresentative anyway. Although the Court is not depicted as any more representative, it is viewed as a useful check on those branches that are driven by forces more vulgar than moral reasoning, such as the crass striving for reelection.

By contrast, in the political theory of textually constrained jurisprudence, priority is given to the written Constitution and, to some degree, to what the founding generation understood the text to mean. The people in their role as ratifiers of the Constitution are the ultimate sovereign. They adopt the fundamental rules of the game by consenting to a written version of those rules so that all people will know what they have agreed to. Governing authorities are the people's deputies, assigned to carry out the rules. If government agents violate the rules, judges enforce them by judicial review: they declare void the rule-breaking statutes.

It is true that all members of the government are duty bound to enforce the rules, but members of the judiciary have a special responsibility in that regard; it is "emphatically" their "province and duty" (as Marshall noted in *Marbury*). In this political theory the particular responsibility of the judiciary to enforce the rules is justified by the judges' specialized training as construers of law and also by the institutional structure that removes them from electoral pressures. The absence of those pressures reduces the incentives for judges to distort the rules in their own self-interest.

In this political system the values of individual autonomy and equality of respect for each human being are built into the base of the system by means of popular consent to the fundamental rules in the process of amending the Constitution, rather than guarded as policy outcomes by a tiny elite removed from popular control; in that sense, this system honors the ultimate moral authority of the will of the people. The basic difference between the role of the judge in this political system and in the system of the fundamental-rights jurists is that here the judges are duty bound to interpret the written Constitution, not morality or up-to-date public opinion. The judges look to the written text because it is the expressed will of the people—expressed through the tacit consent system of constitutional politics—that this text be the highest law of the nation. Justices' selection among plausible interpretations of the text—and there always is a range of choice or we would not need judges—will of course be colored by their sense of morality or justice. And it is also appropriate for them to consider the constitutional politics going on around them.

It seems to me that this contrasting picture of alternative regimes and their respective political theories makes evident that the extratextualists' regime raises judges above the rest of the people for their role as moral guardian. To that degree it dishonors the supposed commitment of the extratextualists to "equal respect and concern" for all people. In other words, the regime defended by the extratextualists does not do as good a job of honoring their own central moral premise as does the regime defended by their textualist opponents.

Consent-Oriented Constitutional Theory II: Ackerman, Sunstein, Burt

The proliferation of unresolved debate about fundamental-rights jurisprudence in the 1970s and 1980s has led other scholars besides myself to focus their attention on regime for guidance in the 1990s. In the same year that my book presenting these arguments appeared (1991), Ackerman's *We the People: Foundations* was published.

His arguments parallel mine in several respects. He too looks to the theory of the American regime as set forth in *The Federalist Papers* for guidance as to the basic commitments and theoretical assumptions of the American constitutional system (Ackerman 1991, chap. 7). Whereas I concluded that we have three levels of constitutional authority based on popular sovereignty, Ackerman concludes that the United States is in its essence a *dualistic democracy*. The duality comes from the same two levels I focus on: that of electoral legislative majority of the moment, and "we the people" acting in sovereign capacity as adopters of the Constitution. He too takes note of the importance of what I describe as a third, middle level of constitutional politics. In fact he elevates constitutional politics some of the time so that what I have called informal constitutional amendments become for him the equivalent of formal constitutional alterations, as binding on the judges as those that follow the method of amending found in Article V. (It is not entirely clear why he counts some but not other successes of constitutional politics as having produced a real we-the-people level constitutional change; for instance, he counts the New Deal period as having produced a new constitutional regime but does not count the civil rights era of 1954-1968 as having done so.)[18] Still, even though he calls his system dualistic, he does acknowledge the importance of the same three levels I discussed. And he also aligns himself against those who advocate the "moral prophet" role for judges, insisting that the judicial role within the American regime of dualistic democracy is to preserve through interpretation the will of the sovereign people against onslaughts from temporary legislative majorities. Such majorities can rule most of the time, as long as they remain within the bounds set forth in the higher law mandated by the sovereign people.

Ackerman's analysis improves on my own in explaining why "we the people" are to be understood as more authoritative than temporary legislative majorities. My analysis focused on the widespreadness of "the people"—if two-thirds of Congress and three-fourths of the states favor something, that breadth of support represents opinion that is about as close to unanimous consent as it is practical to demand in real-world politics. Such broad consensus on the need for a rule would seem to warrant treating the rule as fundamental. Ackerman adds the important insight that at certain times of social crisis the mass public is roused from its usually all-absorbing private concerns to think seriously about critical issues facing the government. In these crisis situations people are provoked to think in the mode of public-spirited citizens, deliberating seriously about what is good for the nation. Such public-spirited deliberation comes at rare moments from the general population, but when it does, it deserves to be honored as the voice of "the people." If a mobilized citizenry can succeed over a course of years in one of these hyper-alert eras to gain repeated support, in response to opponents' counterattacks, for the regime change that they favor, the American constitutional regime indicates that such change should count as new higher law. (Ackerman treats Article V as establishing one mode for such change and urges readers to recognize parallel modes as equally binding on judges. I agree with him on the importance of parallel modes of constitutional politics; I simply argue that these should be viewed as less powerfully binding than formal amendments. This difference is why his system is "dualistic" and mine has three authority levels.)[19]

Implicit in both our treatments of "consent of the governed" is a notion of better and worse selves. The assumption in my (and the Constitution's) emphasis on widespreadness is that if the public has come to a genuine consensus on a given principle, that principle is not likely to be one that detracts from the public interest rightly understood. Such principles are meant to endure in the face of mere temporary (and less widespread) majorities who may well be acting on the basis of group selfishness (as the factions of *Federalist* No. 10). Judicial review is to be employed to guard the fruits of our better selves (constitutional rules) against the wishes of our lesser selves (preferences of mere legislative majorities). Similarly, Ackerman's mobilized citizenry, aroused by the constitutional crisis, provoked into serious deliberation about the public interest for a long enough time that political forces produce a constitutional amendment, is viewed as the better self of a public that tolerates more self-interested, nonreflective group influence in the ordinary day-to-day legislative process. Again, for Ackerman, judicial review preserves the fruits of our better selves against the occasional inclinations to the contrary of our lesser selves.

Ackerman's focus on public-spirited deliberation and its importance for the American regime is also a theme in Sunstein's book *The Partial Constitution*. Sunstein, too, focuses on aspects of consent of the governed and takes that concept as the key to judicial review: he wrote of judicial review, "Its basic purpose was to protect the considered judgments of the people, as represented in the extraordinary law of the Constitution, against the ill-considered or short-term considerations introduced by the people's mere agents in the course of enacting ordinary law" (Sunstein 1993, 23). Whereas Ackerman calls the American system "dualist democracy," in order to emphasize the role of the Supreme Court in policing the relation between the two levels, Sunstein calls it "deliberative democracy," in order to emphasize *why* the formal rules of the Constitution are to check later (less deliberative) temporary majorities. Sunstein aims, in general, to flesh out the details of the *kind* of representative democracy set forth in 1787-1791—in a sense completing the project that John Ely barely began, that of describing the nature of the regime goals, as discernible from the constitutional document understood in historic context and as a whole, so that these principled goals might guide constitutional development. As both Ackerman and I reject a "moral prophet" role for the Court, so Sunstein concludes,

If interpretive principles are generally to grow out of democratic commitments, it follows that a judicial role in social reform will frequently be unjustified. We might even be able to generate a set of criticisms of an aggressive role for the judiciary in the name of the Constitution. . . .

Reliance on the courts may impair democratic channels for seeking change, and in two ways. It might divert energy and resources from politics, and the eventual judicial decision may foreclose a political outcome.

On both counts the impairment of democracy can be very serious. . . .

[A]n aggressive Court is the furthest thing from an unambiguous good; and this is so even if the Court's goals are sound (1993, 144-146).

Similarly, Sunstein shares the view that the principles of the constitutionally established regime, rather than the personal moral philosophies of the justices, are what should guide judicial review. Rights inferable as necessary preconditions for the liberal democracy aimed at by the Constitution, such as the right to vote or the right to debate political issues, need to be protected by the courts (because their absence could pervert the process of discerning the consent of the governed). In sum, "[I]nsistence on the democratic character of American constitutionalism provides the right source of interpretive principles. In most cases that view would lead to judicial caution. In others it would lead to a more aggressive role. In all cases it would provide a helpful orientation" (Sunstein 1993, 144).

Finally, Burt's contribution to regime-focused constitutional theory, *The Constitution in Conflict* (1992), goes in a rather different direction, but it, too, stresses "consent of the governed" as the guiding principle for American judicial review. Burt claims to be taking his bearings from a remark by Abraham Lincoln about wanting to be neither slave nor master, but in fact Burt's theory owes more to the spirit of John C. Calhoun. Burt, like Calhoun, feels that it is important for a viable democracy that the winners as well as the losers feel that they have consented to government policies.[20] The way that this can happen, he believes, is if institutional pressures push both sides toward a mutually palatable compromise. Toward this end, he zeros in on the dialogic process I have described above as constitutional politics, and he argues that the Supreme Court should structure its decisions in such a way as to maximize recourse to this process. The paradigm model for Burt is the "all deliberate speed" decision of *Brown v. Board of Education II* (1955), in which the Supreme Court reaffirmed its refusal to tolerate white coercion against individual black school children but itself refrained from imposing coercion on the southern white majority, "leaving the consequences of [the] decree for renewed argument, though at indeterminate and multiply repeated intervals" (Burt 1992, 280). While political prudence may necessitate such an approach from time to time, and may even make it advisable as a general matter, I believe that Burt errs in reading the guidance of the Constitution this way. Still, he touches on an important truth in the course of his argument: that principles enforced as higher law by the Court must be ones on which the people have come to a widespread consensus. For me, expression by formal amendment to the Constitution is enough to count as evidence of such consensus. For Burt, such consensus as to particular rules is better left to the political branches to work out through the give and take of compromise before the Court actually enforces them.[21] For each of us, however, "government by consent of the governed" is the key to the American regime and to appropriate judicial review therein.

Conclusion

In conclusion, I return to the matter of judicial declaration of unwritten fundamental rights. As the reader by now is aware, the textualist constitutional theory that I have defended would not produce a constitutional right of sexual privacy as such, since this right is not plausibly implied by any part of the constitutional text. Current, official constitutional doctrine, nonetheless, does embrace *Roe v. Wade* and the right of sexual privacy (except for homosexuals, as five justices declared in *Bowers v. Hardwick*, 1986).[22] As I noted above, however, all previous unwritten rights decisions have eventually been overturned, except in instances where an alternative textual foundation for the right is readily available. There is afoot (perhaps consequently?) a minor flurry of activity to develop an equal protection argument for abortion freedom, one that would not rely on the more shaky unwritten rights foundation of current doctrine.

One version of such an argument runs as follows: As long as the state does not impose a good-samaritan obligation of intrusive bodily donation (for example, kidney donation for a needed transplant) on parents of *both* genders when their offspring's life is endangered, it violates the equal protection clause to impose such an obligation (of a kind of body-lending) only on pregnant women, as criminal abortion statutes have done (for example, Sherry 1989; Sunstein 1993, 272-277). The fact that the second newest Supreme Court justice, Ruth Bader Ginsburg, has frequently endorsed an equal protection argument to defend abortion freedom was a much publicized element of her confirmation hearings. In the current political climate, it does not appear probable that the Supreme Court will abandon its commitment to the right to sexual/familial privacy,[23] but it is safe to predict that the more the American public becomes convinced that abortion rights for women really are implied in a sensible interpretation of "equal protection of the laws" (or some other clause actually in the Constitution), the more secure those rights will be.

Notes

1. In *Roe v. Wade* (1973, 153), the Supreme Court ruled that the "right to privacy, whether it be founded in the Fourteenth Amendment's concept of personal liberty and restrictions upon state

action, as we feel it is, or . . . in the Ninth Amendment's reservation of rights to the people, is broad enough to encompass a woman's decision whether or not to terminate her pregnancy." For more on *Roe v. Wade*, see Chapter 17 of this volume.

2. Chief Justice John Marshall's opinion in *Marbury v. Madison* is best known for establishing the doctrine of judicial review—the authority to review and strike down government actions that are incompatible with the U.S. Constitution.

3. "If the fourteenth amendment were a statute, a court might well [be] . . . foreclosed from applying it to segregation in public schools. The evidence of congressional purpose is as clear as such evidence is likely to be" (Bickel 1955, 59).

4. This was the year following *Cooper v. Aaron* (1958), signed by all nine justices, in which the Court reaffirmed the *Brown* holding and declared itself "supreme in the exposition of the law of the Constitution" *(Cooper v. Aaron*, 1958, 18).

5. See also Bickel 1975, 25, to the effect that the Court's obligation "to give us principle," bounded by the need that it be rigorously reasoned and that the justices consider both "history and changing circumstances," originates in "the Constitution as the Framers wrote it." Also, Bickel 1970, 86-87, clarifies that Bickel's references to the Court's use of the method of "moral philosophy" was an effort to describe an approach to constitutional interpretation: "The justification must be that the *constitutional judgment* turns on issues of moral philosophy"—that is, "the method of reason familiar to the discourse of moral philosophy, and in *constitutional adjudication*, the place only for that" (as specifically contrasted to policy preferences either of the justices or of the public). Emphasis added in both text and note.

6. "Substantive due process" refers to the use of the Fourteenth (or Fifth) Amendment due process clause to protect from government abridgment *all* liberties viewed by the Court as "fundamental," whether or not those liberties have any connection to the "process" by which government deprives people of life (executes them), of liberty (imprisons them), or of property (fines them). The wording of the Fourteenth Amendment due process clause is, "No state shall deprive any person of life, liberty, or property without due process of law." Thus, on the surface it appears to be about the process that is owed ("due") within the arena of criminal procedure (for example, privilege against self-incrimination, against double jeopardy, and so forth). From 1905 to 1937 the Supreme Court interpreted the clause as also saying, "Government may not deprive persons of fundamental liberties unless it has exceptionally strong reasons for doing so." The Court then used this "substantive due process" doctrine to declare that the freedom to make an employer-employee contract at substandard wages or for inhumanely long working hours was "fundamental" and could not be violated. So the Court declared unconstitutional such things as minimum wage laws. In 1937, during the Great Depression, under intense political pressure, the Supreme Court abandoned this doctrine.

In 1965, however, several justices once again turned to it to protect what they called the "right to marital privacy." Later, in *Roe v. Wade* (1973), Justice Potter Stewart—who had dissented in *Griswold* but then concurred in follow-up right-to-privacy cases—as well as most of the original *Griswold* majority, acknowledged that the doctrine of substantive due process to support unmentioned constitutional rights had been readmitted to U.S. constitutional law (*Roe v. Wade*, 1973, 152-153 and 167-168). See also *Eisenstadt v. Baird* (1972), where Stewart switched to the side he had opposed in *Griswold*.

7. Justice John Marshall Harlan openly admitted that the doctrine of substantive due process was being resurrected; but also concurrences by Justices Byron R. White and Arthur J. Goldberg (whose opinion was joined by Earl Warren and William J. Brennan, Jr.) can be read as implicitly saying as much, and the dissents so characterized the decision.

8. I reserve the phrase "substantive due process" for the creation by the Court of unwritten fundamental rights, even though one could argue that the Court had long been using that doctrine

for the "written" rights (both express and implied) of the First Amendment. I would argue that the application of First Amendment rights against state governments is legitimate, not as a matter of substantive due process, but either because these are "privileges and immunities of citizens of the United States" (see discussion of this clause in the next text section) or because these are rights essential to a democratic lawmaking process and thus are "due" to Americans as procedural "due process." The merger of these two arguments is a central theme in John Ely's book *Democracy and Distrust* (1980).

9. The formal argument went as follows: The Constitution forbids the state or the federal government to take "life, liberty or property without due process of law." Some liberties are so fundamental that the "process" that is "due" if the government wishes to abridge them is that the government must have a compelling justification and may abridge the freedom no further than is necessary for attaining that compelling interest. This is the same test that the Supreme Court uses for such explicit constitutional rights as freedom of speech and press.

10. See, for example, the quote from *Roe* cited in note 1. It is worth noting in this context that not even one of the justices who currently oppose the idea that there is a constitutional right to seek an abortion wishes to abandon the doctrine that the due process clause licenses judges to decide which rights are fundamental for Americans. And the resistance to this doctrine by the Supreme Court nominee Robert Bork is widely viewed as what caused the Senate to refuse to confirm him to the Court.

11. The Ninth Amendment states that "[t]he enumeration in the Constitution, of certain rights, shall not be construed to deny or disparage others retained by the people." Even though Ely (1980) aimed to constrain fundamental rights jurisprudence, he nonetheless wrote a lengthy argument defending the plausibility of this use of the Ninth Amendment.

The Privileges or Immunities Clause of the Fourteenth Amendment states that "[n]o State shall make or enforce any law which shall abridge the privileges or immunities of citizens of the United States." I have argued that the Privileges or Immunities Clause provides a much firmer textual grounding for extratextualism than does the Ninth Amendment (Goldstein 1991, 101-103, 112-114) even though I too (like Ely) did so within the context of a book trying to constrain extratextualism. (In other words, both of us concede that there is some textual grounding for extratextualism but see extratextualism as a danger to the overall constitutional project of establishing a representative democracy and therefore try to constrain it.)

12. The Preamble to the U.S. Constitution reads as follows: "We the People of the United States, in Order to form a more perfect Union, establish Justice, insure domestic Tranquility, provide for the common defence, promote the general Welfare, and secure the Blessings of Liberty to ourselves and our Prosperity, do ordain and establish this Constitution for the United States of America." The Equal Protection Clause of the Fourteenth Amendment states, "nor shall any State . . . deny to any person within its jurisdiction the equal protection of the laws."

13. Similarly, Michael Perry (1988, chapter 6) calls on the justices to implement the "highly indeterminate" (149) "values or ideals" of the Constitution (163); and Walter Murphy (1978; 1980) focuses on terms like *justice* in the Preamble as authorizations of fundamental values jurisprudence.

14. The Supremacy Clause of Article VI states: "This Constitution, and the Laws of the United States which shall be made in Pursuance thereof; and all Treaties made, or which shall be made, under the Authority of the United States, shall be the supreme Law of the Land; and the Judges in every State shall be bound thereby, any Thing in the Constitution or Laws of any State to the Contrary notwithstanding." Section 2 of Article III states: "The judicial Power shall extend to all Cases, in Law and Equity, arising under this Constitution, the Laws of the United States, and Treaties made, or which shall be made, under their Authority."

15. In *West Coast Hotel v. Parrish*, the Court upheld a state law setting minimum wages for

women and children employees. In so doing, it overruled several earlier decisions that had made use of the substantive due process doctrine to declare that the freedom to make an employer-employee contract (even at substandard wages) was "fundamental" and could not be violated. See note 6.

16. This has happened at least twice. One time was in response to support in 70 percent of state legislatures and 90 percent in each house of Congress for, but official failure of, the Equal Rights Amendment (the doctrinal change took place in *Craig v. Boren*, 1976; see Goldstein 1987). Another time was in response to growing support for the Child Labor Amendment (*West Coast Hotel v. Parrish*, 1937, and *United States v. Darby Lumber*, 1941; see Vose 1972).

17. In *Dred Scott v. Sandford* (1857) the Court struck down the Missouri Compromise (which had been repealed by Congress prior to the Court's decision), ruling that Congress did not have the constitutional power to regulate slavery in the territories. In so doing, the justices claimed that blacks could not be considered in a legal sense to be citizens of the United States. The Fourteenth Amendment overturned this part of the Court's ruling.

18. He grants that *Brown v. Board of Education* (1954) ended up inspiring "the most successful constitutional movement of our time," in which a widely mobilized American people was to "renew and expand its constitutional commitment to racial equality" (136-140). Yet he is unwilling to put this movement on the same footing as the New Deal. Apparently his view is that the New Deal really changed the Constitution, whereas the civil rights movement merely reinvigorated what was already in the post-Reconstruction Constitution. (My aim here is not to endorse all the particulars of his analysis nor to critique the ones with which I disagree. It is to note the parallel points in our analyses.)

19. I should add that despite our agreement on broad regime principle and on proper judicial role, Ackerman disagrees with me on the specific matter of substantive due process and its use to protect liberty of contract and sexual-marital privacy. He believes those principles were constitutionalized by the people. I remain unconvinced.

20. Toward this end, Calhoun's famous *Disquisition on Government* (1853) advocated requiring consent from every affected interest group before allowing any government policy. Burt does not go so far, but his goal of widespread consensus for any contested governmental action is similar to Calhoun's.

21. Burt (1992, 21-22) attributes the origin of this view to Bickel (1962, 239).

22. In *Bowers v. Hardwick* the Court upheld a Georgia law that prohibited oral and anal sex. The majority opinion dealt exclusively with "consensual homosexual sodomy," expressing "no opinion . . . on other acts of sodomy."

23. I base this conclusion on the failed confirmation hearings of Robert Bork. It was dramatically evident that his principled opposition to the "right to privacy" was a major reason for his defeat.

13 The Attitudinal Model

Harold J. Spaeth

What explains why judges, at least those on the U.S. Supreme Court, decide cases the way they do? To answer this question we need to focus on judges' decisions rather than on the reasons they give in their opinions for deciding the way they have. For the explanations that persons—including judges—give for what they have done do not necessarily correspond to their actions. If human beings have any unlimited capability, it is their capacity to rationalize their behavior. We all desire to put the best face on our deeds, public officials no less than anyone else. Indeed, the authoritative character of government action and the need that public officials have for public acceptance, if not approval, commonly causes them to take special pains to justify their decisions and make them palatable to those who are governed by them.

Since the onset of our constitutional system, and even well before then, judges at all levels of the judicial system have unfailingly justified their decisions exclusively in terms of the legal model of decision making. This model holds that judges make decisions on the basis of the facts in the cases before them, as these facts pertain to one or more of the following considerations: (1) the language of the applicable law, (2) the intentions or motivations of those who made the law, (3) the precedents established in previously decided cases, and (4) a balancing of societal interests. As discussed below, the legal model fails to explain judicial behavior, at least insofar as the U.S. Supreme Court is concerned. As a result, scholars have formulated an alternative model—the attitudinal model—that does explain the Court's behavior. In contrast to the legal model, the attitudinal model states that the Court's decisions are based on the facts of a case in light of the ideological attitudes and values of the participating justices; in other words, on the basis of the individual justice's personal policy preferences.

In this chapter, I examine both the legal and the attitudinal models of judicial decision making. My conclusion is straightforward and unequivocal: evidence overwhelmingly supports the attitudinal model and, equally overwhelmingly, fails to support the legal model as an explanation of why the justices decide their cases as they do. The remainder of this chapter documents the accuracy of this nonobvious assertion.

Some Preliminaries: Models and Judicial Decision Making

What is a model and why is it useful?[1] A model does not reflect reality; it only represents it. A model focuses only on the most explanatory aspects of the activity in question, while ignoring less revealing ones. Models have two objectives: to explain the behavior in question and to do so parsimoniously. These objectives commonly conflict with one another. A relatively full account of some phenomenon—such as judicial voting—may contain a large number of variables. It is axiomatic, of course, that one may explicate any phenomenon if the number of variables used in the explanation equals the number of times the phenomenon has occurred. Thus, if the reasons given for the Court's decisions in the 1992 term differ for each of the cases the justices decided, we have learned nothing systematic about the justices' voting. All we know is unique—idiosyncratic—to each case.

A good model does not function in this fashion. It focuses, rather, on a small number of factors—variables—common to all or most of the observed phenomena that explain a high proportion of the behavior in question. The test of whether a model provides a valid and reliable explanation is its ability accurately to predict future outcomes.

The Legal Model

With this in mind, I turn first to the legal model. As mentioned, this model contains four major variants: plain meaning, legislative and framers' intent, precedent, and the balancing of societal interests. Each has its own adherents, some being more popular than others. Apart from precedent, no one of them is more empirically testable than the others. As a result, it is not possible to present their deficiencies in any systematic fashion. I can only illustrate their subjectivity anecdotally and in no particular order of importance. Because the focus of this chapter is the U. S. Supreme Court, I exemplify the shortcomings of the legal model by reference to the Court's own decisions. I also employ this focus in my treatment of the attitudinal model.[2]

Plain Meaning

This version of the legal model applies not only to the language of statutes and constitutional provisions but also to that of judicially created rules. It simply holds that judges rest their decisions on the plain meaning of the pertinent language. So if Article I, Section 10, of the Constitution declares that no state shall pass any law impairing the obligation of contract, then the Court will strike down any law that does so. Alternatively, courts should not judicially create rights that the Constitution does not explicitly contain.

In one regard, plain meaning may be said to be the preferred aspect of the legal model. Excerpts from decisions of a recent term indicate that the justices all agree that resolution of their cases "begin with the text" (*Gollust v. Mendel*, 1991, 118). "In deciding a question of statutory construction, we begin of course with the language of the statute" (*Demarest v. Manspeaker*, 1991, 614). "When we find the terms of a statute unambiguous, judicial inquiry should be complete except in rare and exceptional circumstances" (*Freytag v. Commissioner of Internal Revenue*, 1991, 776). And if "the plain language . . . disposes of the question before us," intent will not be assessed (*Toibb v. Radloff*, 1991, 151).

The primacy accorded plain meaning does not detract from the legal model. The problem lies in the model's failure to specify the point at which plain meaning terminates and one of the other variants begins. As an example, consider a case that required the Court to determine the meaning of the phrase "noncurriculum related student group," which appears in a congressional statute requiring public schools to give student religious groups the same access to school facilities that nonreligious extracurricular student groups have. The majority and dissenting opinions both noted that the law failed to define "noncurriculum related student group," and that even the law's sponsors did not know what the phrase meant. In dissent, Justice Stevens observed that

the word "noncurriculum" is not in the dictionary. Neither Webster nor Congress has authorized us to assume that "noncurriculum" is a precise antonym of the word "curriculum." "Nonplus," for example, does not mean "minus" and it would be incorrect to assume that a "nonentity" is not an "entity" at all. (*Westside Community Schools v. Mergens*, 1990, 207, 211, 236, 242)

The majority, instead, focused on the word *curriculum*, which the act does not use. Finding that word also inadequate, the majority turned to the act's purpose. This they also found "less than helpful" (208). To decide the case, the majority used a third variant of the legal model, precedent, resting its decision on the "logic" of a 1981 decision.

Even more distressing than the legal model's failure to provide empirically grounded rules governing the propriety of one variant rather than another is the matter of ambiguity. Almost every word in the English language has an abundance of different meanings, some of which contradict one another. *Sanction*, for example, may mean to reward as well as to punish. When words are strung together, the probability of ambiguity increases exponentially. Consider, for example, the operative language of the Mann Act, which prohibits the transportation of females across a state line for any "immoral purpose." The Court sequentially held that this language applied to the transportation of one's mistress across a state line, that it did not apply to a madam who took two of her employees with her on a vacation to Yellowstone National Park, and that it did apply to polygamous Mormons who traveled from one state to another with their several wives (*Caminetti v. United States*, 1917; *Mortensen v. United States*, 1944; *Cleveland v. United States*, 1946). Of the twenty-six justices who participated, only the bare minimum that was needed to produce an opinion of the Court concurred in each of these cases.

The use of plain meaning does not preclude the Court from writing its own definitions. Consider the word *citizens* in Article III of the Constitution. Chief Justice John Marshall ruled that the word encompassed corporations even though no dictionary defined it so broadly (*Bank of the United States v. Deveaux*, 1809). And though the justices may resort to the dictionary to determine statutory or constitutional meaning, they do not necessarily agree on which dictionary is appropriate. In *Sullivan v. Stroop* (1990), for example, the majority used the *Random House Dictionary of English Usage*, second edition, while the dissenters resorted to *Black's Law Dictionary*.

Neither does plain meaning prevent the Court from denying what the law clearly states. In *Maryland v. Craig* (1990), the majority ruled that the Confrontation Clause of the Sixth Amendment does not mean what it says—"In all criminal prosecutions, the accused shall enjoy the right . . . to be confronted with the witnesses against him"—if the witness is a child in a child abuse case. Clearly, explicit constitutional language may be subordinated to currently favored public policy if a majority so rules, as Justice Antonin Scalia in dissent pointed out.

Finally, the Court's own words can sometimes be found to render false "plain meaning" as a reliable guide to why the justices decide the way they do. In an important freedom-of-communication case, the majority initially cited seven of its precedents, which arose in seven different contexts, that "above all else, the First Amendment means that government has no power to restrict expression because of its message, its ideas, its subject matter, or its contents." The operative constitutional language after all is "make no law." The Court, however, immediately qualified the quoted language:

This statement . . . read literally . . . would absolutely preclude any regulation of expressive activity. . . . But we learned long ago that broad statements of principle, no matter how correct in the context in which they are made, are sometimes qualified by contrary decisions. (*Young v. American Mini Theatres*, 1976, 65)

The Court has a second string to its bow whereby it may qualify plain meaning. This tactic allows plain meaning to be discounted by offsetting it against the intent of those who proposed or enacted the law in question. The justification for so doing is "a familiar rule," several centuries old, "that a thing may be within the letter of the statute and yet not within the statute, because not within its spirit, nor within the intention of its makers" (*Church of the Holy Trinity v. United States*, 1892, 459). A classic illustration of its use occurred in *Steelworkers v. Weber* (1979), which upheld a collectively bargained affirmative action plan notwithstanding the plain language of Title VII of the 1964 Civil Rights Act, which prohibits an employer or a labor union to "discriminate against any individual because of his race." A union and employer had agreed to establish a training program to eliminate the racial imbalance that resulted because jobs had traditionally been reserved for whites.

Clearly then, plain meaning does not explain why the justices vote as they do because the justices simply do not mean what they say in the opinions that are supposed to explain their decisions. Furthermore, the justices provide us with no meaningful criteria that indicate which of their statements are true and which are false.

Legislative and Framers' Intent

"Legislative and framers' intent" refers to construing statutes and the Constitution according to the preferences of those who originally drafted and supported them. The sole substantive difference between these two types of intent is that the former pertains to the interpretation of statutes, whereas the latter applies to constitutional provisions.

Hence, like plain meaning, intent governs statutory construction as well as constitutional interpretation. But unlike plain meaning, where the legal language is empirically delimited by a finite set of words, almost any aspect of the historical record leading up to the enactment of the provision in question may be considered grist for the mill of intent. Three problems inhere in this approach. First, the historical record is often sketchy and sometimes nonexistent. We know little about the Constitutional Convention except for the contents of a carelessly kept journal; James Madison's notes, which he edited for publication thirty-two years after the event; and a few written comments from eight other delegates to the Convention (Farrand 1966, xi-xxv). Virtually no records exist from the state ratifying conventions, on whose approval the adoption of the Constitution depended. Similar situations also obtain for much current legislation, state as well as congressional. Furthermore, existing records are not necessarily accurate. Until 1978, for example, members of Congress were free to add, delete, insert, and edit the remarks they made—or ostensibly made—on the floor of the House and Senate. Members, for example, filled 112 pages of the *Congressional Record* on a day when the Senate met for only eight seconds and the House not at all (Hunter 1985).

Second, who are the "framers"? Very few of the delegates to the Constitutional Convention stayed the course. Many came and went. Only thirty-nine signed the final document. What about those elected to the state ratifying conventions? How about the intentions of those who elected these delegates? At the legislative level, should only the motives of those who voted for the bill be assessed? What about the desires of those who voted them into office in the first place?

Third, and most perplexing, how is intent determined? One legislator's motive may be antithetical to the purpose of another. Even assuming complete and accurate records, fathoming intent is an exceedingly risky enterprise even at the individual level. As the abundance of psychiatrists and therapists evidences, people often do not know why they do what they do. To assume, at the group level, that all who vote or respond similarly possess a common motivation is simply absurd. Two current members of the Court have so stated,

Justices Scalia and John Paul Stevens. Scalia has been an especially harsh critic of this aspect of the legal model. Although he was most tellingly so in the highly charged context of teaching "creation science" in the public schools, his acerbic comments apply across the board.

The number of possible motivations, to begin with, is not binary, or indeed even finite. In the present case, for example, a particular legislator need not have voted for the Act either because he wanted to foster religion or because he wanted to improve education. He may have thought the bill would provide jobs for his district, or may have wanted to make amends with a faction of his party he had alienated on another vote, or he may have been a close friend of the bill's sponsor, or he may have been repaying a favor he owed the Majority Leader, or he may have hoped the Governor would appreciate his vote and make a fundraising appearance for him, or he may have been pressured to vote for a bill he disliked by a wealthy contributor or a flood of constituent mail, or he may have been seeking favorable publicity, or he may have been reluctant to hurt the feelings of a loyal staff member who worked on the bill, or he may have been mad at his wife who opposed the bill, or he may have been intoxicated and entirely *un*motivated when the vote was called, or he may have accidentally voted "yes" instead of "no," or, of course, he may have had (and very likely did have) a combination of some of the above and many other motivations. To look for *the sole purpose* of even a single legislator is probably to look for something that does not exist.

    Putting that problem aside, however, where ought we to look for the individual legislator's purpose? We cannot . . . assume that every member present . . . agreed with the motivation expressed in a particular legislator's pre-enactment floor or committee statement. . . . Can we assume . . . that they all agree with the motivation expressed in the staff-prepared committee reports . . . [or] post-enactment floor statements? Or post-enactment testimony from legislators, obtained expressly for the lawsuit? . . . media reports on . . . legislative bargaining? All these sources, of course, are eminently manipulable.

    . . . If a state senate approves a bill by a vote of 26 to 25, and only one intended solely to advance religion, is the law unconstitutional? What if 13 of 26 had that intent? What if 3 of the 26 had the impermissible intent, but 3 of the 25 voting against the bill were motivated by religious hostility or were simply attempting to "balance" the votes of their impermissibly motivated colleagues? Or is it possible that the intent of the bill's sponsor is alone enough to invalidate it—on a theory, perhaps, that even though everyone else's intent was pure, what they produced was the fruit of a forbidden tree. (*Edwards v. Aguillard*, 1987, 636-638)

Scalia's colleagues essentially disagree with his anti-intent position because "common sense suggests that inquiry benefits from reviewing additional information rather than ignoring it" (*Wisconsin Public Intervenor v. Mortier*, 1991, 547 n. 4).

    At least one commentator suggests that Scalia's opposition to intent governs only his construction of statutory language:

When interpreting statutes, Scalia claims to be a "textualist," refusing to look beyond the "plain meaning" of the words for evidence of the original intention of the Congress. When interpreting the Constitution, however, Scalia claims to be an "originalist," insisting that each provision should be interpreted in light of the original understanding of its framers and ratifiers. (Rosen 1993, 20)

Rosen, however, adds that in some cases Scalia's "passions lead him to betray his principles" (1993, 21).

Precedent

Also known as *stare decisis*, the word *precedent* in law means adherence to what has been decided. Like plain meaning and intent, precedent applies to the interpretation of constitutional provisions as well as to the language of statutes. Unlike plain meaning and intent, however, all courts cite previously decided cases to justify their decisions. As a result, this aspect of the legal model appears far more often than the others. But the mere fact that a court cites precedent provides no evidence that precedent actually determines the outcome of the case. Certainly not at the appellate level. Precedents support the contentions of both parties to the lawsuit. As federal judge Frank M. Coffin points out: "Precedent is certainly real and we learn to live with it. But if precedent clearly governed, a case would never get as far as the Court of Appeals: the parties would settle." Similarly, Judge Frank H. Easterbrook: "Given that litigation is so expensive, why are parties willing to take their cases up? . . . It's because precedent doesn't govern. Precedent governs the major premise. But the mind-set of the judge governs the minor premise" (Greenhouse 1988).

Because precedents lie on both sides of appellate court controversies, *stare decisis* provides no sure guide to decision. A court will choose those precedents that support the majority's contention, while disregarding or disparaging those to the contrary. The most irrefutable evidence that this is the case may readily be had by simply consulting a decision that contains a dissenting as well as a majority opinion. Both will likely contain a roughly equivalent number of citations to previously decided cases. Reference to these will show that they do indeed respectively support the contrary contentions of the disputants.

One way to test the extent to which the justices adhere to precedent is by determining whether those who dissent from landmark decisions subsequently adhere to them. Analysis of a random sample of such decisions decided between the beginning of the Warren Court and the end of the 1992 term shows that the justices who dissented in these highly important cases overwhelmingly refused, in subsequent decisions, to adhere to the precedents they established. Of 148 votes cast by those initially opposed to the precedent, only 15 (or 10.1 percent) acceded to the precedent in question in subsequent cases. Of the fourteen justices involved, only Potter Stewart and Lewis F. Powell, Jr., were even moderately influenced by precedent, while seven others unfailingly voted against precedent at every opportunity (Segal and Spaeth 1994).

Accordingly, precedent really appears to be only a matter of style rather than a substantive limit on a judge's discretion. Good legal form merely requires that judges lard their opinions with citations to previously decided cases. And on those rare occasions when a court finds itself confronted by a restrictive line of precedents, devices exist that allow judges to avoid adherence to what has been decided, all of which comport with good legal form:

1. Obiter dicta, commonly known as dicta, allow a judge to declare portions of a previous opinion to be surplus verbiage and thereby not part of the precedent that this opinion established. Thus, for example, the Supreme Court had initially held that an act of Congress that denied the president power unilaterally to remove officials in the executive branch of the federal government was unconstitutional. The Court subsequently qualified this language by ruling that the president could remove only those officials whose duties were exclusively executive and who were not protected by civil service (*Myers v. United States*, 1926; *Humphrey's Executor v. United States*, 1935).

2. A court may distinguish a precedent; that is, it simply asserts that the facts of the case to be decided are sufficiently dissimilar from those of a precedent the court does not wish to follow. This tactic is less drastic than declaring part of an earlier opinion to be dicta. In no way does the court alter the scope of the precedent; it merely says that because of factual dissimilarities the early decision does not control the outcome of the case at hand. Inasmuch as facts always differ from one case to another, precedents may be distinguished at will. All the court need do is specify the factual differences. Thus, for example, in a pair of Louisiana cases involving the inheritance rights of illegitimate children, the Supreme Court initially ruled that wrongful death actions could not be prohibited if they involved intimate familial relationships. But a state may nonetheless treat illegitimate offspring differently when it seeks to establish, protect, or strengthen family life (*Levy v. Louisiana*, 1968; *Labine v. Vincent*, 1971). I will not dispute a judgment that these purposes merely amount to variant ways of saying the same thing. But the fact remains that the one formulation sustains the law's constitutionality, the other does not.

3. A court may limit a precedent in principle. More drastic than distinguishing a precedent, its effect closely approximates declaring language to be obiter dicta. The difference is that when a precedent is limited in principle, it permanently loses its original scope. When a court distinguishes a precedent, it only says that it is not applicable to the case at hand. Its original scope remains intact. The constitutional right of a woman to an abortion nicely illustrates this device. The Supreme Court originally ruled that during the first six months of pregnancy a woman could secure an abortion so long as it was performed by a competent person in a sanitary environment. Subsequently, the Court qualified this decision, ruling that a woman only had a right to an abortion without undue government

interference (*Roe v. Wade*, 1973; *Maher v. Roe*, 1977; *Webster v. Reproductive Health Services*, 1989).

4. Finally, a court may formally overrule a case it or an inferior court has decided. Courts tend to avoid overrulings because they jar the notion that the law is fixed and stable. A recent study identifies only 115 decisions in which the Supreme Court formally altered precedent during the forty-six-year period between 1946 and 1992, an average of two and one-half times per term (Brenner and Spaeth 1995). Unlike the other three limitations on precedent, overruling is amenable to empirical analysis. Brenner and I have shown that liberal Courts, such as that presided over by Earl Warren, overrule conservative precedents, and conservative Courts—those of Warren E. Burger and William H. Rehnquist—alter liberal precedents. Within the analyzed Courts, liberal and conservative justices behaved similarly. Liberal justices voted to overrule conservative precedents; conservative justices the opposite. Justices aligned with neither wing fall on both sides of the divide. These patterns of behavior, of course, conform to the attitudinal model of decision making rather than the legal model.

Balancing

The final aspect of the legal model manifests itself in an opinion that sets off the interests of society—that is, the common good, the national interest, the general welfare—against the life, liberty, or property interests of individual persons. Sometimes a conflict occurs between private interests, as when one person's freedom of communication conflicts with another's right to a fair trial. The Supreme Court uses either an ad hoc or a definitional approach to balancing. The latter resorts to specific rules, tests, or principles to justify a decision, while ad hoc balancing features the facts of the case without reference to any previously formulated rule or test.

When the Supreme Court resorts to balancing, it does not hesitate to label it as such. Balancing may be viewed as a surrogate for reasonableness—the concept that dominates decision making in trial courts. Both types of balancing provide courts and judges with a degree of decisional flexibility that enables them to decide cases on the basis of their individual merits. As such, balancing appears preferable to its variants, the rigid rule and the subjective utility tests. The former straitjackets the facts into a decision-making framework in which the rules are applied literally—no matter how foolish the resulting decision. For example, a law that prohibits noise above a certain decibel level after 10:00 p.m. is clearly silly in a community with a population density of one person per square mile, or in most college dormitories. Subjective utility, in contrast, bases decision on the intensity of likes and dislikes. Hence, the person who passionately dislikes rock music should be compensated more for a disturbance of the peace than those who object only to the noise.

Of course, what one person deems reasonable, another finds unreasonable. Nonetheless, it is hard to fault a decision that a court justifies as reasonable. Furthermore, notwithstanding the inherent subjectivity of the concept, judges and legal analysts commonly label it as an objective criterion.

Conclusion

Neither the Supreme Court nor any lower court has provided empirically identifiable criteria to indicate when it will use one of the aspects of the legal model rather than another. Precedent, of course, appears in virtually every opinion the justices write. Not uncommonly, precedent will be conjoined with plain meaning, intent, or balancing. Nor has the Court formulated any criteria for using any of the limitations on precedent. Although analysts may validly and reliably identify their use after the fact, the Supreme Court, at least, has provided no systematic guide to their application in advance of decision. Any objective observer, therefore, necessarily must conclude that at the very least the legal model cannot be tested because its key concepts, except for precedent, cannot be specified or defined in any evenhanded fashion. As an explanation of Supreme Court behavior, it does not even marginally pass muster. Not uncommonly, the majority and dissenting opinions will both use the same aspect of the legal model—say, plain meaning or intent—to support their antithetical conclusions. This, of course, does not gainsay the utility of the legal model as a cloak to conceal the real bases for the justices' decisions and to provide them with means to rationalize their votes. Commentators and legal scholars endlessly squabble about the respective value of these normative factors, but their bickering does nothing to further our understanding of why the justices decide as they do.

The Attitudinal Model

The attitudinal model differs from the legal in several respects. First, it rests on a common set of assumptions; namely, that the justices decide their cases on the basis of the interaction of their ideological attitudes and values with the facts of a case. Justice William J. Brennan, Jr., decided cases as he did because he was liberal; Justice William Rehnquist or Warren Burger, because they were conservative. In other words, the justices vote as they do because they want their decisions to reflect their individual personal policy preferences. Attitudinal modelers differ among themselves in the level of generality with which they conduct their analyses. Some proceed microanalytically, examining behavior in narrowly defined issue areas: the death penalty, commercial speech, affirmative action. Others proceed more globally, investigating, for example, the justices' voting in such broad areas as civil rights or business regulation. Analysts also disagree about the source of attitudes—whether an individual acquires them genetically or as a result of environmental experi-

Figure 13-1 Hypothetical Cases and Justices in Ideological Space

ences—and whether the justices' personal policy preferences extend to normative considerations, such as judicial restraint and strict construction, or to procedural matters, such as venue and mootness, or operate only substantively. Such differences do not affect the attitudinal model's underlying assumptions, however. They only concern the analyst's focus, microscopic or macroscopic, and whether or not the attitudes motivating behavior pertain only to the merits of the litigation—for example, the justices' attitudes toward sex discrimination, hate speech, and wiretapping—or extend more broadly to include instrumental and procedural values.

Second, the justices do not admit the validity of the attitudinal model as an explanation of their votes. They will occasionally accuse their colleagues, who disagree with their position, of deciding on the basis of their policy preferences. But they assert that they themselves strictly adhere to one or more of the variants of the legal model.

Third, because the various aspects of the legal model cannot be operationalized, the legal model cannot be empirically tested. Precedents exist on both sides of appellate controversies; the majority and the dissenters assert equally plausible objectives as the motivation of those who enacted the legal provision at issue; and the legal language itself supports the contentions of both sides. In contrast, the attitudinal model operationalizes its constructs in a concrete fashion and subjects them to empirical testing.

The Formulation of the Attitudinal Model

In reaction to the formalistic jurisprudence that characterized legal scholarship, which asserted that judging is a nondiscretionary exercise in which judges merely find or discover law in the same way that children hunt for Easter eggs or an astronomer discovers a new star, a small group of scholars, so-called legal realists, asserted that judging necessarily involved the exercise of discretion; that, willy-nilly, judges made law. The legal realists did not explain how judges exercised discretion, but they did call for an empirical, scientific study of the law. Scholars responded slowly. Not until 1965 did a detailed attitudinal model emerge (Schubert 1965). It assumed that the stimuli presented by the facts of a case and the justices' policy preferences could be ordered along ideological dimensions as illustrated in Figure 13-1.

Imagine that cases 1 and 2 involved the searches of homes, in which the police had probable cause to suspect criminal activity. The searches uncovered incriminating evidence. A search warrant had been issued for the search in case 1, but not for that of case 2.

Because of the warrant, the search in case 1 was more protective of individual liberty than that in case 2. As such, it is placed to the left of the second search. According to Schubert, all search and seizure cases can be similarly positioned in ideological space. If, for example, a third search of a home had occurred, this one without either a warrant or even probable cause, it would fall to the right of case 2 because it invades privacy more.

The justices who decide these cases are also positioned in the space portrayed in Figure 13-1. Their location indicates that Justice A is liberal, B moderate, and C conservative. According to Schubert, justices will uphold any search to the left of their point in the space and void those to the right. Accordingly, Justice A will vote in support of the defendant in both cases, B in case 1 only, and C will consider both searches to be constitutional.

David W. Rohde and I (1976) formulated an alternative model. We contended that the justices seek policy goals, and that in deciding their cases each justice desires the Court's decision to approximate as closely as possible his or her personal policy preferences. Because the justices do not stand for reelection, serve for life, and are subject to no higher court, they are able to vote their individual policy preferences in deciding their cases. Central to the Rohde-Spaeth formulation is the construct of attitudes, which we define as a set of interrelated beliefs about at least one attitude object and the situation in which it is encountered. Attitude objects are the classes of litigants the justices encounter—the direct and indirect parties to the litigation; for example, criminal defendants, broadcasters, women, blacks, indigents, businesses. The attitude situation is the dominant legal issue that the case presents; for example, double jeopardy, freedom of communication, sexual harassment, employment discrimination, welfare benefits, the antitrust laws.

In our focus on attitudes, Rohde and I begin at a microanalytic level by gathering the Court's decisions into discrete sets based on an attitude object and the situation in which it is encountered. Thus, cases involving the right to vote are divided among those pertaining to access to the ballot, residency requirements, the amended Voting Rights Act of 1965, reapportionment, and a residual set of constitutional questions regarding the right to vote. We assume that sets of cases forming around similar attitude objects and situations will correlate with one another to form issue areas (for example, criminal procedure, civil rights, judicial procedure, federalism) in which an interrelated set of attitudes—which we call a "value" (for example, freedom, equality, libertarianism)—will explain and predict the individual justice's votes.

Testing the Attitudinal Model

It is one thing to formulate a model or a theory and another matter to test it. As noted, except for precedent, the legal model cannot be tested because its concepts do not lend themselves to meaningful, empirical definition. Attitude, the key construct of the attitudinal model is, however, amenable to testing. Valid and reliable analytical techniques exist that enable scholars to explain and predict why the justices vote as they do. The method most often used is cumulative, or Guttman, scaling. Created during World War II for the purpose of ordering social psychological data from one extreme to another (Stouffer et al. 1950), it simply assumes that persons who respond favorably to a given question will also respond favorably to all less extreme questions. "Extremeness" is not defined on the basis of the questions themselves but rather on the basis of the proportion of the respondents who agree or disagree with them. Consider, for example, a set of three questions on a given subject. Seventy-five percent agree with the first statement, 50 percent with the second, and 30 percent with the third. Ideally, the 30 percent who agree with the third statement should also agree with the other two inasmuch as more than 30 percent support them. Conversely, those who do not agree with the first statement should also reject the second and third ones. In other words, each respondent should reply in one of the following ways: yes-yes-yes, yes-yes-no, yes-no-no, or no-no-no.

Beginning in the late 1950s and early 1960s, political scientists began to use cumulative scaling to identify the justices' attitudes (for example, Schubert 1959, chap. 5; Spaeth 1963; Ulmer 1960). If a justice begins to oppose an hypothesized attitude, say, toward capital punishment, in a given case, he should continue to oppose it in all more extremely decided cases; that is, those decided by a larger anti-capital punishment vote. Thus, if the justice voted with the majority in a case that voided the punishment by a vote of 6 to 3, he should also be among the majority in cases that invalidate the penalty by votes of 7 to 2, 8 to 1, and of course 9 to 0. Similarly, if the justice dissented in a 5-to-4 decision in which the death penalty was prohibited, he should vote with the majority in all cases sustaining capital punishment regardless of the vote. If all the justices behave in a similarly consistent fashion, one may safely assume that the hypothesized variable—attitude toward capital punishment—explains the justices' voting behavior. Table 13-1 illustrates such a pattern of responses.

In case 1 the defendant's allegation that he was unconstitutionally subject to the death penalty was unanimously upheld, whereas in case 11 the defendant unanimously lost. Note that the cases are ordered solely on the basis of the proportion of "+" and "-" votes. Case 7 is less extreme from the government's standpoint than case 4 because fewer justices supported the claimant in the latter than in the former. Or, to view these cases from the opposite (that is, liberal) perspective, case 4 is less extreme from the defendant's standpoint because fewer justices supported the government's contentions than they did in case 7.

Note that each justice votes in a perfectly consistent fashion. Justice A is the most liberal, supporting the person subject to capital punishment in every case except 11. Justice I is most conservative, voting to uphold the death sentence in all except case 1. The likelihood that such a pattern occurred by chance is most improbable. Nine justices participat-

Table 13-1 Hypothetical Cumulative Scale

Case	Justices									Vote
	A	B	C	D	E	F	G	H	I	
1	+	+	+	+	+	+	+	+	+	9-0
2	+	+	+	+	+	+	+	+	−	8-1
3	+	+	+	+	+	+	−	−	−	6-3
4	+	+	+	+	+	−	−	−	−	5-4
5	+	+	+	+	−	−	−	−	−	4-5
6	+	+	+	+	−	−	−	−	−	4-5
7	+	+	+	−	−	−	−	−	−	3-6
8	+	+	−	−	−	−	−	−	−	2-7
9	+	+	−	−	−	−	−	−	−	2-7
10	+	−	−	−	−	−	−	−	−	1-8
11	−	−	−	−	−	−	−	−	−	0-9

ing in a case may be arrayed in 256 different combinations: $(N!/R!) / (N - R)!$, where N = the number of participating justices and R = the number of justices voting either + or −. Thus, in the case of a 5-to-4 vote, $(9!/4!) / (9 - 4)! = (362{,}880/24) / 120 = 126$. Similarly, a 6-to-3 vote produces eighty-four combinations, 7-to-2 thirty-six, 8-to-1 nine, and 9-to-0 one. Because each combination may produce an outcome favorable to one party or the other—may, in other words, support or oppose the hypothesized attitude—its total number must be doubled to 512.

A cumulative scale need not display perfect voting consistency to be valid. Louis Guttman, the creator of cumulative scaling, formulated a measure, the coefficient of reproducibility (R), to describe the goodness of a scale. Cases decided unanimously or with only a single dissenting vote are excluded from its calculation. In a unanimous decision all the justices necessarily vote consistently, and in a case containing a solo dissent, eight of the nine justices perforce vote consistently. To include such cases in the calculation of the coefficient artificially inflates the appearance of consistent voting. The number of inconsistent or nonscale votes (*nsr*, or nonscale responses) is therefore subtracted from unity (1) and divided by the total participations: $R = 1 - (nsr/N)$. R should reach 0.950 if one is to infer that the hypothesized attitude explains the justices' behavior, and in addition the pattern of nonscale votes should be randomly dispersed rather than concentrated in a couple of cases or disproportionately located among the votes of one or two justices (Spaeth and Peterson 1971). The presence of either of these conditions suggests that the cases in question tap an attitude other than the hypothesized one, or that the justice(s) in question are motivated by a different attitude.

Although the robustness of the scales constructed by various scholars supports a "confident inference" (Kobylka 1989, 550) that attitudes explain, and thus motivate, the justices' behavior, from a strictly scientific standpoint cumulative scaling is inherently defective: one cannot demonstrate that attitudes explain votes when the attitudes are operationalized from those same votes. Circularity results. An independent measure is needed. Because scholars have been constructing scales covering most of the Court's decision making in the twentieth century, in addition to a limited period of the nineteenth century, it is now possible to use the rank order of the justices on a narrowly focused scale from an earlier period to predict the votes of the justices in more recently decided cases. Such a procedure was not feasible earlier because of the lack of narrowly focused scales that extended over a considerable period of time.

A valid application and test of the attitudinal model may therefore be had by comparing the justices' votes at an earlier time with those votes cast later. Consider affirmative action, an issue that both the Burger and Rehnquist Courts addressed. Table 13-2 displays the cumulative scale of the justices' votes in the cases that the Burger Court formally decided, excluding those with only a single or no dissents. Three Burger Court justices—Black, Douglas, and Harlan—do not appear because they participated in none of these cases. This scale was formed on the assumption that the justices' attitudes toward affirmative action motivated their behavior. The array of votes scales acceptably, producing a coefficient of reproducibility $(R) = 0.957$. The rank order of the justices is not as refined as one might wish because of ties. Harry A. Blackmun, William Brennan, and Thurgood Marshall invariably supported affirmative action. Powell is ranked ahead of Stevens because a greater proportion of his votes supported affirmative action and because Stevens cast two inconsistent antiaffirmative action votes. Although Justices Byron R. White and Sandra Day O'Connor are technically tied, White is placed ahead of O'Connor because six of his eleven votes supported affirmative action, as compared with only one of O'Connor's five. Stewart, who retired before the end of the Burger Court, comes next, followed by Burger and Rehnquist.

On the basis of the well-documented presumption that the justices' attitudes—like those of adults generally—are relatively stable, we anticipate that the holdover Burger Court justices will rank themselves in the Rehnquist Court's affirmative action cases similarly to the ranking that is displayed in Table 13-2. Because Justices Anthony M. Kennedy and Antonin Scalia did not serve on the Burger Court, other indicators must be found to determine their attitudes toward affirmative action. One that has proved to be reliable and replicable is newspaper editorials that characterize nominees prior to confirmation as liberal or conservative toward civil rights and liberties (Segal and Cover 1989; Segal and Spaeth 1993, 226-231; Segal et al., forthcoming). This measure shows that both Kennedy and Scalia are conservative, Scalia the more so. Indeed, Scalia matches Rehnquist as most

Table 13-2 Votes of the Burger Court Justices toward Affirmative Action

Justice	Cases										
	1	2	3	4	5	6	7	8	9	10	11
Blackmun	+	+	+	+	+	+	+	+	+	+	+
Brennan	+	+	+	+	+	+	+	+	+	+	+
Marshall	+	+	+	+	+	+	+	+	+	+	+
Powell				+	+	+	+	−	−	−	−
Stevens				[−]	[−]	+	+	+	−	−	−
White	+	+	+	+	+	−	−	−	[+]	−	−
O' Connor						+	−	−		−	−
Stewart	+	+	+	−	−				−		
Burger	−	−	−	[+]	−	−	−	−	−	−	−
Rehnquist	−	−	−	−	−	−	−	−	−	−	−
Vote	5-2	5-2	5-2	6-3	5-4	6-3	5-4	4-5	4-5	3-6	3-6

Note: 1 = *Steelworkers v. Weber* (1979); 2 = *Kaiser v. Weber* (1979); 3 = *United States v. Weber* (1979); 4 = *Fullilove v. Klutznick* (1980); 5 = *Regents v. Bakke* (1978); 6 = *Firefighters v. Cleveland* (1986); 7 = *Metal Workers v. EEOC* (1986); 8 = *Wygant v. Jackson Board of Education* (1986); 9 = *Regents v. Bakke* (1978); 10 = *Firefighters v. Stotts* (1984); 11 = *Memphis Fire Dept. v. Stotts* (1984); + = supporting vote; − = opposing vote; empty cells = not participating.

conservative. Kennedy's conservatism, although less than Scalia's, exceeds that of O'Connor. I arrive, then, at the ordinal ranking from liberal to conservative, depicted in Figure 13-2.[3]

Table 13-3 displays the votes of the Rehnquist Court justices. The predicted pattern obtains for all cases except the first, where O'Connor rather than White should have been the third dissenter. In the other seven cases, the justices rank themselves in the order specified above. Note that our ability to predict on the basis of the justices' past votes requires knowledge of the direction of the decision (whether liberal or conservative) and the number of justices who dissented, along with the names of any justice(s) who did not participate. This degree of precision is a far cry from a full and complete prediction that would tell us the issue the justices will decide in any given case and how each of the justices will vote. Nonetheless, the accuracy of the limited prediction shown above validates the explanatory power of the attitudinal model, at least to the extent that the hypothesized variable alleged to explain the justices' votes did not likely occur by chance.

Calculation of the probability that the predicted votes did not occur by chance is rather problematic. One could assume randomness and simply contend that because each justice is a free agent, together they may produce 126 different 5-to-4 vote combinations, with a resultant probability of predicting the correct one equaling .0079. But all six of the 5-to-4

Figure 13-2 Ordinal Ranking of Justices on the Rehnquist Court

decisions in the Rehnquist Court's affirmative action cases conform to our predictions, so arguably .0079 should be multiplied six times for a result of .0000000000002. Such astronomical probabilities distort reality, however. As pointed out above, the attitudinal model decrees that if a given justice is the sole liberal dissenter in a case conservatively decided on a specific issue, he or she must also vote liberally in all cases in which one or more of the other justices also vote liberally—that is, those conservatively decided by a 7-to-2, 6-to-3, or 5-to-4 vote—in addition to being among the majority in all liberally decided cases that bear on the issue in question. Consequently, although it is theoretically possible, it is most unlikely that a Justice Scalia, Rehnquist, or Thomas will be the sole liberal dissenter in a conservatively decided civil liberties case, or that a Brennan or Marshall would have dissented alone or with one another in a liberally decided such case.

Accordingly, I take a much more conservative approach to estimating probability. Albeit arbitrarily, I simply assume that no more than three justices are likely to be the marginal dissenter in any given case. Thus, if the vote is 8 to 1, the candidates are Justices G, H, and I. If the vote is 7 to 2, I becomes a given, with F joining G and H as the other probable one. Similarly for cases with three and four dissenters. Hence, the probability of predicting how all the justices vote in a given case becomes .33. Applying this estimate to the Rehnquist Court's affirmative action decisions gives us $.33^7$ (the number of cases correctly predicted) x .67 x 8 (the number of ways one can get any seven of eight predictions correct—that is, 8![7! x 1!])—which equals .002. Compatibly with convention, any probability less than .05 is statistically significant and supports the truth of the hypothesized explanation.

Although the foregoing approach validates the attitudinal model, the pattern of past votes may also enable one to make predictions other than those that require knowledge of the direction of the predicted decision and the number of dissenters. For example, if past decisions show the Court overwhelmingly supportive of certain litigants when caught up in a certain situation, one could predict that the Court's behavior will not change absent marked change in the policy preferences of the Court's majority. Similarly, one could predict with virtually absolute certainty that no death penalty case would be unanimously decided against the convicted person as long as Brennan or Marshall sat on the Court. Not only had they never voted to uphold the death penalty, in each and every case in which they participated they formulaically reiterated their unequivocal opposition to the death penalty.

Table 13-3 Votes of the Rehnquist Court Justices toward Affirmative Action

Justice	Cases							
	1	2	3	4	5	6	7	8
Blackmun	+	+	+	+	+	+	+	+
Brennan	+	+	+	+	+	+	+	+
Marshall	+	+	+	+	+	+	+	+
Powell	+			+				
Stevens	+	+	+	+	+	+	+	−
White	[−]	+	+	−	−	−	−	−
O'Connor	+	−	−	−	−	−	−	−
Kennedy		−	−	−	−	−	−	−
Scalia	−	−	−	−	−	−	−	−
Rehnquist	−	−	−	−	−	−	−	−
Vote	6-3	5-4	5-4	5-4	4-5	4-5	4-5	3-6

Note: 1 = *Johnson v. Transportation Agency* (1987); 2 = *Metro Broadcasting v. FCC* (1990); 3 = *Astroline v. Shurberg* (1990); 4 = *United States v. Paradise* (1987); 5 = *Martin v. Wilks* (1989); 6 = *Personnel Board v. Wilks* (1990); 7 = *Arrington v. Wilks* (1990); 8 = *Richmond v. Croson Co.* (1989); + = supporting vote; − = opposing vote; empty cells = not participating.

Discussion: The Limits of the Attitudinal Model

Notwithstanding the overwhelming evidence supporting the attitudinal model, it does have limitations. Only recently has it been applied systematically to any lower court (see Chapter 10 of this book), largely because of limited scholarly resources and personnel. Lower courts do operate in an environment distinctly different from that of the Supreme Court. These differences may cause lower-court judges to decide on bases other than their personal policy preferences. They may be electorally accountable and as a result render decisions that enhance their reelection. Others may seek higher positions—either inside or outside the judiciary—and color their decisions accordingly. Most courts are subject to appellate review. Judges thereon may decide according to their superiors' dictates rather than their own preferences. And with the exception of some state supreme courts, judges do not have control of their dockets as the justices do. Hence, their decision making may involve run-of-the-mill litigation in which policy matters are either absent or not amenable to discretion because a jury decides or because matters are open and shut.

The application of the attitudinal model to the Supreme Court is timebound for two reasons. First, most analysts have, for reasons of currency and the availability of data, preferred to focus on the present rather than the past. Political scientists are not historians. Second, during many periods in the Court's history—the Marshall Court, and those between the Civil War and the 1930s—dissents were few and far between. The attitudinal model cannot be rigorously applied and tested when all but a handful of cases are unanimously decided. If everyone agrees about the outcome, the possibility of disconfirming a hypothesized basis for decision cannot readily be tested.

Finally, with a few very limited exceptions the attitudinal model has only been applied to the justice's voting behavior, and then only to the final vote—the one specified in the reports of the Court's decisions. Scholars have not appreciably addressed such matters as coalition formation and opinion writing. Nor have they analytically addressed decisional stages antedating the final vote. I do not know enough to say whether voting coalitions form for reasons other than attitudinal affinity. In those issues in which the attitudinal model explains behavior, presumably not. But opinion coalitions and opinion writing may be a matter where nonattitudinal variables operate. To date, no one has conducted an empirically systematic investigation. Although data about decisions that antedate the final vote are gradually becoming available (for example, Palmer 1990), analyses of the justices' voting in their secret conference are only beginning to be a focus of scholarly attention.

Notes

1. For more on models, see Chapter 1 of this book.
2. In Chapter 10, the authors consider the applicability of legal and attitudinal models to decision making on the U.S. courts of appeals.
3. This ranking excludes David H. Souter, Clarence Thomas, and Ruth Bader Ginsburg, none of whom had participated in any affirmative action case as of this writing. Editorial data pertaining to Ginsburg show that she will be among the Court's most liberal members (Segal et al., forthcoming); Souter should position himself between Stevens and White; and Thomas will join conservatives Scalia and Rehnquist (Epstein et al. 1994, 291).

14 The Role of the Supreme Court in American Society: Playing the Reconstruction Game

Lee Epstein and Thomas G. Walker

The historian of the Court should keep his watch in the halls of Congress, not linger within the chamber of the Court.

—Charles Fairman, *History of the Supreme Court of the United States: Reconstruction and Reunion*

During the American Civil War, Abraham Lincoln had his hands full. Not only did he have to stave off the Confederate army, but he also had to concern himself with the presence of Confederate supporters in the northern and border states.[1] Particularly worrisome to Lincoln were the large numbers of Southern sympathizers, known as Copperheads, active in Indiana, Illinois, Ohio, and Missouri. Because they were located so close to enemy lines, Lincoln knew that the Copperheads could provide substantial support to Southern forces without actually joining the Confederate army. But combating these civilian enemies posed a difficult problem for Lincoln. Military action provided the most efficient method of dealing with them, yet the army had no legal authority to arrest and try civilians where no hostilities were occurring. The regular state and federal courts were in full operation and capable of trying civilians charged with treason or other crimes.

To resolve this problem, Lincoln issued orders expanding military control over civilian areas, permitting military arrests and trials of civilians, and suspending habeas corpus.[2] As a result, arrests of suspected traitors and conspirators became common and often were based on little evidence. But were Lincoln's actions constitutional? In *Ex parte Milligan* (1866) the U.S. Supreme Court said they were not. The justices held that Lambdin P. Milligan, a Confederate sympathizer living in Indiana, could not be arrested and tried by

We gratefully acknowledge research support provided by the National Science Foundation (grants SES-9024640 and SES-9024851). We also thank Jack Knight, Charles M. Cameron, and other participants at the 1993 Conference on the Political Economy of Public Law, W. Allen Institute of Political Economy, University of Rochester, who brought this line of research to our attention. Jeffrey A. Segal provided a biting (but welcome) critique of the general argument we offer. Finally, we appreciate the efforts of Carla Molette Ogden, Edward Stephens, Madhavi McCall, and Christina Wolbrecht, who helped gather the data reported in this chapter.

the military when civilian courts were in full operation and the area was not a combat zone. As a general principle, according to the Court's majority, neither the president nor the Congress, acting separately or in agreement, could suspend the writ of habeas corpus under such circumstances.

Just three years later, though, the Court *seemed* to have a change of heart. In the case of *Ex parte McCardle* (1869), the Court turned down the claims of William McCardle, a Southern journalist who was charged with writing "incendiary and libelous articles" about the Republican-led Congress. When he was arrested and held for a trial before a military tribunal, McCardle—like Milligan—asserted that he was being illegally detained, and— again like Milligan—petitioned for a writ of habeas corpus. But the Court dismissed McCardle's case, refusing to provide the requested relief.

The disparity between the Court's treatment of Lambdin Milligan and William McCardle raises many questions, some of which we shall consider later in this chapter. For now, it is enough to note that these decisions support two versions of the role the judiciary plays in our society. On the one side are those analysts who argue that the Supreme Court should and usually does act to protect minority interests, as it did in *Milligan*. Under this school of thought, the Court is the only institution that can act on behalf of disaffected interests because it lacks an electoral connection. Members of Congress and the president must respond to majority interests to retain their jobs; the Court is not so hindered. On the other side are those scholars who assert that the Court could play the role of minority-protector but that it usually chooses to legitimate the interests of the ruling regime—the elected institutions—as it did in *McCardle*. The predominant explanation for the Court's presumed behavior, as we shall soon see, centers on the appointment process, which—it is argued—ensures that Court decisions will never be far removed from majority preferences.

Despite these differences, the two schools rest on a common assumption about the nature of judicial decision making: Justices do not decide a priori to protect minority rights or to legitimate the ruling regime. Rather, they base their votes on their political ideologies, with a consequence being that liberal justices *tend* to protect minority interests, whereas conservative ones *tend* to legitimate the ruling regime. Under this thinking, *Milligan* came out the way it did because the Court was composed of civil liberties-minded jurists—and not because the justices were purposefully playing the role of minority protectors. Likewise, theorists of both schools would argue that *McCardle* did not reflect a belief on the part of the justices that they should go along with the interests of elected institutions; rather it represented the Court's political attitudes toward the issues raised in the case. In other words, these two approaches assume that the role the Court carves out for itself—be it minority protector or regime supporter—rests with the justices and that it is merely a byproduct of their political ideologies. A liberal court, for example, will usually protect the oppressed; a court of the law-and-order-minded, conversely, will generally sustain government assertions (although exceptions to this rule have occurred).

Our argument is that this assumption is inadequate or, at the very least, incomplete. We believe that the role the Court plays in a democratic society is not merely the product of the individual political preferences of the justices; it is also a function of the preferences of other political actors, particularly Congress and the president, and of the political context. To put it in different terms, we agree with the sentiment of Charles Fairman (1971): to understand the role the Court plays in American society it is important to consider events occurring outside of the Marble Palace. As we shall see, *Milligan* came out the way it did not only because the justices sincerely preferred the derived outcome but because they thought that the president and Congress would not overturn their decision. In contrast, *McCardle* did not reflect the sincere preferences of the Court; instead it represented the best course of action the justices thought they could take in the face of a threatening political environment.

We develop our argument in the following steps. First, we review some of the traditional literature on the Court's role in a democratic society. Second, we present a theory in response to this literature, which takes into account the strategic context of judicial decision making. Third, we explore the model's predictions by examining a crucial series of post-Civil War Supreme Court decisions, from *Milligan* to *McCardle* and beyond. Finally, we consider ways that future researchers could put our argument to more general tests. Along the way, we hope to quell a traditional concern about the Court: that when it acts to protect minority interests, it necessarily does so in ways that subvert majority will, that it is a counter-majoritarian institution. We argue that the Court would rarely take this path for fear that its decisions would be overturned or its institutional integrity impeded by the elected institutions.

The Role of the Supreme Court in a Democratic Society

In resolving the *Milligan* and *McCardle* cases the Supreme Court took two very different actions. In the first, the justices opposed Lincoln's congressionally supported military policies and upheld the rights of an individual who espoused a particularly unpopular cause. In the second, the justices turned down William McCardle's petition, thereby reaffirming the pro-military policies of the Reconstruction Congress. As we noted earlier, these decisions illustrate two differing views of the Supreme Court's role in our society. One claims that the Court is part of *the ruling regime* and generally reinforces the policies of the legislative and executive branches. The other holds that the Court is an independent actor capable of playing a unique role as *a protector of individual and minority rights*.

The Ruling Regime Thesis

In his classic study of the Supreme Court's role, Robert Dahl (1957) advanced the ruling regime thesis. At the core of Dahl's argument is the assertion that the policy decisions of the Supreme Court will never be substantially out of line with those of the existing law-making majorities. Accordingly, the justices will usually reach decisions consistent with the preferences of the elected branches. The primary reason for this, Dahl argues, is quite simple. On average, presidents have the opportunity to appoint two new justices during the course of a four-year term. Presidents usually nominate justices with philosophies similar to their own, and the Senate generally confirms only nominees who have views consistent with the contemporary political mainstream. As a result of this regular turn-over, the Court's majority rarely represents a political ideology in conflict with the president and Congress. That is why, Dahl explains, the Supreme Court does not often strike down federal legislation. Such laws reflect the positions of Congress, the president, and—by virtue of the regularity and nature of the appointment process—the Court as well. Under this logic, the Court almost never assumes an antimajoritarian role. Rather, it will typically represent and, therefore, legitimate the interests of the ruling regime.

The data Dahl invokes seem to support his argument. They show that between the 1780s and the 1950s the Court struck down relatively few federal laws and, when it did exert judicial review in this way, the action tended to come more than four years after the particular laws were passed. To Dahl this indicates that the Court is much more likely to strike down legislation passed by congressional majorities that are no longer in power than it is to void the acts of current legislative majorities. By striking down legislation more than four years after enactment, the Court may be reflecting the will of the new political majority that no longer desires the legislation enacted in earlier years (see Epstein and Walker 1993b, chap. 7).

Dahl renders moot any normative debate about what the role of the Court should be in a democratic society. Analysts no longer need worry about whether the Court should or should not act as a counter-majoritarian body because, at least according to Dahl, it will almost never take on this role. Rather, it will typically represent and, therefore, legitimate the interests of the ruling regime.

The Court's decision in *Ex parte McCardle* appears consistent with Dahl's thesis. The justices allowed the military policies of the incumbent Congress to stand against pleas made by an individual that the policy was violative of his constitutional rights. The Court supported the ruling regime.

The Minority-Protector Thesis

However persuasive Dahl's argument might be, it was not the last word on the subject. Some political observers view the Court in much different terms. Rather than subscribe to

Dahl's thesis that the Court inevitably falls into line with the elected branches of government, they argue that the Court is essentially an independent actor capable of challenging the political majorities and defending the rights of individuals and minorities. The Court's ability to play such a role flows from those constitutional provisions designed to ensure judicial independence, especially the life tenure without electoral accountability that federal judges enjoy.

Jonathan Casper, a political scientist, is one of the most prominent advocates of the independent actor thesis. Casper argues that Dahl's conclusions reflect an earlier era and cannot be generalized to the modern period. In an influential article published in 1976, Casper contends that the years immediately following the period Dahl studied gave witness to an entirely different court role. The Warren Court (1953-1969) hardly acted to protect the interests of the ruling regime; rather, in numerous decisions it served as a protector of minority interests. As Casper explains,

Dahl's article was published in 1957, appearing at the end of a decade that had seen one of our periodic episodes of national political repression. . . . The rulings of the Supreme Court in this period did not mark it as a bastion of individual rights standing against a fearful and repressive national majority. . . .

Since then, we have witnessed the work of the Warren Court. . . . The Warren Court, by general reputation at least, was quite different than most of its predecessors. Indeed, one associates with it precisely the characteristics that Dahl found lacking in the Supreme Court—activism and influence in national policy making and protection of fundamental rights of minorities. (Casper 1976, 52)

Surely, Warren Court decisions on such matters as school desegregation, obscenity, the rights of the criminally accused, school prayer, and reapportionment were often inconsistent with the preferences of the legislative and executive branches as well as the majority of the public. By the same token, the Burger (1969-1986) and Rehnquist (1986-) Courts that followed the Warren era handed down decisions on busing, abortion, flag burning, and affirmative action that *may* have generated social change but were often not supported by political majorities. Finally, members of the Burger and Rehnquist Courts were much more prone to strike down laws recently passed than were justices of earlier periods. It is just this kind of evidence that leads Casper and others to conclude that, contrary to Dahl's thesis, the Court does not inevitably act as a legitimator of the ruling regime. Rather, it is quite capable of protecting individuals and minorities against the actions of those in power.

Turning back to the Civil War era, we find that the justices' decision in *Ex parte Milligan* appears consistent with Casper's view of the Court. Here the justices behaved as independent actors, ruling against the preferences of Congress while protecting the rights of an individual representing a political minority.

Common Assumptions about the Role of Ideology

Dahl and Casper make diametrically opposed claims about the Court's role in American society. To Dahl, the nomination and confirmation process guarantees that the Court will operate as a majoritarian institution—one that reflects prevailing political preferences. To Casper, the selection process guarantees no such thing; rather, the Court is an important and independent actor, one that can protect minority interests against majority tyranny.

Despite these differences, Dahl and Casper operate under a common assumption about the nature of Court decision making: judicial decisions are a function of the political attitudes of the justices. That is, the justices do not make an a priori decision to legitimate the policies of the other branches or to assume the role of protector of minorities; rather, the role played by the Court is merely a byproduct of the ideologies of its members. For Dahl, the Court tends to reinforce prevailing political majorities because the selection process is biased in favor of choosing justices who have political attitudes consistent with those of incumbent presidents and legislators. For Casper, the justices are capable of defending the rights of minorities because they are free to act in accordance with their own political ideologies and need not respond to the views of other officeholders or of public opinion.

That Dahl and Casper agree about the nature of judicial decision making and its effect on the Court's role is not too surprising. Their views are based on a movement of the 1950s—behavioralism—that has had an enormous influence in political science and that has been transported to the study of courts in the form of the attitudinal model.[3] In this model, cases raise issues on which the justices have established political attitudes. Those attitudes, in turn, trigger a behavior—a judicial vote. In other words, justices base their decisions solely on the facts of cases in light of their ideological attitudes and values. They are "single-minded seekers of legal policy" whose ideologies dictate their votes (George and Epstein 1992, 325). Or, as two leading proponents of the attitudinal model put it, "Rehnquist votes the way he does because he is extremely conservative; Marshall voted the way he did because he is extremely liberal" (Segal and Spaeth 1993, 65). Thus, this "attitudinal" approach focuses exclusively on the ideologies of the justices. It leaves no room for the role of other institutions, such as Congress or the president; Rehnquist will take the conservative position and Marshall will take the liberal one, regardless of where Congress or the president stand on a particular issue.

Taken along with the perspectives of Dahl and Casper, then, the traditional argument about the Court's role in society comes together in the following way: whether the Supreme Court acts to protect minorities or supports the ruling regime depends exclusively on the political attitudes of the Court's majority. In short, ideological attitudes drive the role the Court will play, and not vice versa. Or, as Segal and Spaeth (1993, 332) assert, "not only judicial restraint, but also judicial activism, serve only to cloak the individual justices' policy preferences."

Figure 14-1 Hypothetical Distribution of Preferences

Source: Adapted from Eskridge 1991a, 1991b.

Note: J=majority of Supreme Court; C(M)=committees' indifference point; C=relevant congressional committees; M=median member of Congress; P=president.

To see the implications of the attitudinal approach to the Court's role, consider Figure 14-1.[4] On the horizontal line—which represents possible interpretations the Court could give to, say, a civil rights statute ordered from most liberal to most conservative—we place the preferences of several key political actors. We denote the Court's and the president's most preferred positions as "J" and "P," respectively. "M" signifies the preferred position of the median member of Congress and "C" of the congressional committees with jurisdiction over civil rights bills.[5] "C(M)" represents the committee's indifference point "where the Court can set policy which the committee likes no more and no less than the opposite policy that could be chosen by the full chamber" (Eskridge 1991a, 378; see also Eskridge 1991b). To put it another way, because C(M) and M are equidistant from C, the committee likes C(M) as much as it likes M; it is indifferent between the two.

As we can see, the Supreme Court is to the left of Congress, the key committees, and the president. This means, in this illustration, that the Court favors more liberal policy than do the other institutions. Now suppose that the Court has a civil rights case before it, one involving the claim of a woman who says that she has been sexually harassed at her place of employment in violation of federal law. How would the Court decide this case? In Dahl's and Casper's "attitudinal" approach the justices would vote exactly the position shown on the line; they would set the policy at J. They would vote their "attitudes," even though they would know that the threat of congressional reaction loomed large. That is because the policy articulated by the attitudinally driven Court would be to the left of the indifference point of the relevant committees, giving them every incentive to introduce legislation lying at their preferred point of C. Congress would support such legislation because it would prefer C to J, and the president would sign it because he too likes C better than J.

If the Court risked congressional reversal and merely voted its attitudes, as Casper, Dahl, and Segal and Spaeth predict, it would be (at least in this example) supporting Casper's version of the Court's role in our society: the Court would be protecting the woman—a minority interest—in a civil rights case. In response, scholars like Dahl would simply argue that the Court is temporarily out of step with the majoritarian institutions because of some fluke—such as an unusually long period of time without a presidential appointment to the Court, a realigning election, and so forth. In such a situation, Dahl might argue, the justices will continue to vote their attitudes, fully aware that Congress could and probably would reverse the Court's position. In time, however, the periodic replacement of justices would bring the Court back into line with the elected branches.

A Rational Choice View of the Court's Role in American Society

A natural question emerges from our portrait of the attitudinal approach to the judicial role: Why would the Court take a position that Congress would overturn? The answer that attitudinalists provide is a simple one: justices are "single-minded seekers of legal policy" whose ideology dictates their votes. They will always vote their sincere preferences regardless of the positions of their colleagues or pressure from outside forces.

Our argument is that this perspective often fails to capture the realities of Supreme Court decision making and, accordingly, of the Court's role in American society. If justices are "single-minded seekers of legal policy," would those justices not care about the ultimate state of that policy? To rephrase the question, why would justices who are policy-maximizers take a position they know Congress would overturn? To argue that justices would do this—merely vote their attitudes—is to argue that the Court is full of myopic thinkers, who consider only the shape of policy in the short term. It is also to argue that justices do not consider the preferences of other political actors and the actions they expect others to take when they make their decisions and simply respond to stimuli before them. Such a picture does not square with much important writing about the Court (Eskridge 1991a, 1991b; Howard 1968; Murphy 1964; Pritchett 1961; Rodriguez 1994) or with the way many social scientists now believe that political actors make decisions (see, for example, Ordeshook 1992).

We thus reject this attitudinal vision and propose a rational choice one in its stead. Many rational choice theories of judicial decision making begin with the same assumption as that of the attitudinal model—that justices are goal-directed, single-minded seekers of legal policy (Eskridge 1991a and 1991b).[6] But, from there, the two approaches veer away from each other dramatically (see Knight and Epstein 1994). Unlike the attitudinal approach, choice theories of judicial decisions emphasize that these goal-directed actors operate in a *strategic* or interdependent decision-making context. The justices know that their "fates" depend on the preferences of other actors—such as Congress, the president, and their colleagues on the Court—and the choices they expect these other actors to make, not just on their own preferences (see Ordeshook 1992, chap. 1).[7]

This notion of interdependent choice is important for the following reason. If justices really are single-minded seekers of legal policy, then they necessarily care about the "law" broadly defined. And if they care about the ultimate state of the law—about generating legal policy that other institutions will not overturn—then they must act strategically, taking into account the preferences of others and the actions they expect others to take. Occasionally, such calculations will lead them to act in a sophisticated fashion (that is, in a way that does not reflect the justices' sincere or true preferences) so as to avoid the possibility of seeing their most preferred policy being rejected by their colleagues in favor of their least preferred one, of Congress replacing the justices' preference with its own, of political noncompliance, and so forth (Murphy 1964; Rodriguez 1994).[8] In short, goal-oriented justices must—as Fairman (1971) put it—keep their watch in the halls of Congress and sometimes in the Oval Office of the White House.

In the final analysis, then, the rational choice theories of judicial decisions suggest that the Court will decide cases "with reference to the likelihood that its decisions will be reversed by another political institution."[9] They highlight the fact that under a government system of checks and balances, goal-directed public officials, including Supreme Court justices, act strategically; they make their choices with some attention to the policy preferences of the other key political actors and the actions they expect those other actors to take. If they truly care about policy, in other words, they cannot—as the attitudinal school would argue—operate as if they were in a vacuum.

To see the implications of the rational choice theory of judicial decisions, return to Figure 14-1. Given the distribution of the most preferred positions of the actors in this figure, strategic justices—unlike attitudinal justices—would not be willing to take the risk and vote their sincere preferences: they would see that Congress could easily override the Court's position and that the president would support Congress. In fact, in this instance the rational course of action—the best choice for justices interested in policy—is to place the policy near $C(M)$.[10] The reason is simple: since the committees are indifferent between $C(M)$ and M, they would have no incentive to introduce legislation to overturn a policy set at $C(M)$. Thus, the Court would end up with a policy close to, but not exactly on, their ideal point without risking adverse congressional reaction.

Accordingly, rational choice arguments have an important implication for empirical and normative debates about the role of the Court in American society. They suggest that the Court will not often be significantly out of step with the other branches, but for reasons different from those offered by Dahl. Recall that Dahl argues that the Court will rarely strike down congressional legislation because the majority of the Court, the median member of Congress, and the president generally share the same values. Choice perspectives, in contrast, argue that because justices take into account the preferences of the ruling regime (even if they do not necessarily share those preferences) and of the actions they expect the regime to take, the Court's decisions typically will never be far removed from what contemporary institutions desire. (For circumstances under which this would not hold, see Eskridge 1991a, 1991b.)

Figure 14-2 Hypothetical Distribution of Preferences

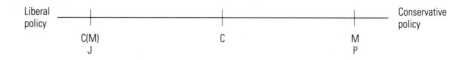

Note: C(M)=committees' indifference point; J=majority of Supreme Court; C=relevant congressional committees; M=median member of Congress; P=president.

This does not mean, however, that the Court will never play the role of minority protector or that it will never strike down federal laws. Indeed, if the preferences of the contemporary regime and of the Court support those weapons, the Court will feel free to deploy them. Nor does it suggest that the Court can never vote its sincere preferences. An example of how both these possibilities could occur is shown in Figure 14-2. Given the displayed distribution of preferences, the Court would be free to set policy in a way that protects minority interests and that reflects its raw preferences. For if it voted its preferences (which are comparatively liberal) and set the policy at J, the relevant congressional committees would have no incentive to waste precious legislative resources to override the Court. Since C(M) = J, they would be indifferent between the policy preferred by the Court and that preferred by the median member of Congress.

To summarize, rational choice accounts of judicial decisions suggest that the role of the Court in American society is not simply a function of the preferences of the Court but also of the other relevant institutions and of the actions the Court expects them to take. The Court—comprised of strategic "single-minded seekers of legal policy"—prefers to avoid reaching decisions considerably outside the range acceptable to the legislature and the president. As strategic actors the justices realize that by doing so the ultimate state of the law could end up farther away from their ideal points than is necessary.

The Reconstruction Game

To illustrate the explanatory power of the rational choice approach, we consider two U.S. Supreme Court decisions—*Ex parte Milligan* (1866) and *Ex parte McCardle* (1869)—reached in the wake of the Civil War. This was a critical period in American history, one marked by a dramatic series of events involving all three branches of government. It began in April of 1865, with the South—represented by General Robert E. Lee—surrendering to General Ulysses Grant at the Appomattox court house. And it ended just a few years later in 1870, when all the Southern states were readmitted into the Union. In between, a president was impeached, the Southern states were put under military authority, and the Constitution was amended three times.

These events were dramatic indeed. But for our purposes, the most important of all the Reconstruction activities centered on and occurred within the Supreme Court of the United States. A political struggle was waged there over a policy issue of enormous importance: the extent to which the Constitution allows military jurisdiction over civilians in noncombat areas. With their 1866 decision in *Milligan*, the justices provided a sign of hope to the defeated Southern states; they indicated that they would be willing to protect individuals against congressionally approved military control. But in the 1869 *McCardle* case, the justices switched course and failed to block tough congressional Reconstruction measures; in other words, they served as legitimizers of the ruling regime.

How can we explain this turnabout? In what follows, we invoke the logic of rational choice theory to show that in *Milligan*, the justices were—given the configuration of the key political actors—able to vote their sincere or raw preferences (the J point in the figures). By the time of *McCardle*, however, those configurations had changed markedly, enough so that the justices could not vote sincerely without facing severe consequences. Hence, they acted in a sophisticated fashion in *McCardle*, reaching a decision that reflected political realities, rather than their raw preferences.

The Milligan *Decision*

The Court's decision in *Ex parte Milligan* came at the onset of the Reconstruction period, although the case itself started even before the Civil War had ended (see Table 14-1). In October 1864, military authorities in Indiana, acting under the presidential proclamation of 1863 (which, pursuant to the Habeas Corpus Act of 1863, permitted the president to suspend the writ of habeas corpus in certain areas), arrested Milligan for inciting insurrection and assisting the enemy. A military commission found him guilty and sentenced him to be hanged on May 19, 1865 (for more details see Nevins 1987). In the meantime, events of great moment were occurring. The Civil War ended and, with Lincoln's assassination, the nation saw the ascension of a new president, Andrew Johnson.

At first, it seemed that Johnson would take a hard line on the sort of treasonous activity Milligan committed (Fairman 1971, 197-199). Indeed, he had been in office less than a month when he sustained Milligan's execution order. But that did not stop Milligan's lawyers from seeking further recourse. Eight days after Johnson's action, they sought a writ of habeas corpus in a federal court in Indianapolis, grounding their request in the 1863 Habeas Corpus Act. This law, as we noted above, permitted the president to suspend the writ of habeas corpus during times of rebellion, but, at the same time, it had a provision that allowed for the release of prisoners (like Milligan) if a grand jury did not issue an indictment (see Hughes 1965, 585). Since no indictment was returned against Milligan, his lawyers argued that he should be tried in a civilian court. The lawyers also suggested that the federal government could not try Milligan before a military tribunal when the civil

Table 14-1 Key Events Leading Up to *Ex parte Milligan*

Date	Event
Mar. 3, 1863	Congress passes the Habeas Corpus Act of 1863, which serves as the basis for *Milligan*.
Sept. 15, 1863	Pursuant to the 1863 Habeas Corpus Act, Lincoln suspends the writ and declares martial law in effect throughout the United States.
Oct. 5, 1864	Milligan arrested.
Oct. 21, 1864	Milligan is tried before a military commission and sentenced to be hanged on May 19, 1865.
Apr. 9, 1865	Lee surrenders to Grant at Appomattox Court House.
Apr. 15, 1865	Lincoln dies; Andrew Johnson becomes president.
May 2, 1865	Johnson sustains order that Milligan be executed.
May 10, 1865	Milligan's attorneys seek a writ of habeas corpus in a federal circuit court.
May 16, 1865	Circuit court judges certify questions in *Milligan* to the U.S. Supreme Court.
May 29, 1865	Johnson begins his "restoration" policy.
May 30, 1865	Justice John Catron dies.
Dec. 4, 1865	Start of the Thirty-ninth Congress. With the exception of Mississippi, all Southern states have met Johnson's requirements for readmission into the Union; they send delegations to Congress, but Congress refuses to seat them.
Dec. 14, 1865	Congress establishes the Joint Committee on Reconstruction, with Radical Republican Thaddeus Stevens named as head.
Jan. 15, 1866	Lyman Trumbull, chair of the Senate Judiciary Committee, introduces the Freedmen's Bill and the Civil Rights Bill.
Feb. 4, 1866	Freedmen's Bill passes in Senate and House on straight party votes.
Feb. 19, 1866	Johnson vetoes Freedmen's Bill.
Feb. 20, 1866	Senate cannot override Johnson's veto of Freedmen's Bill, Johnson's last major legislative victory.
Mar. 5–13, 1866	Court hears arguments in *Milligan*.
Mar. 13, 1866	Congress passes Civil Rights Bill.
Mar. 27, 1866	Johnson vetoes Civil Rights Bill.
Apr. 3, 1866	Court announces, without reasons, its decision in *Milligan*.
Apr. 9, 1866	Congress overrides Johnson's veto of the Civil Rights Bill.
June 20, 1866	Report of the Joint Committee on Reconstruction issued.
June 26, 1866	Congress passes revised Freedmen's Bill.
July 16, 1866	Johnson vetoes new Freedmen's Bill, and Congress overrides Johnson's veto.
July 23, 1866	Congress reduces size of Supreme Court; Johnson will be unable to replace Catron or James Wayne, when he dies on July 5, 1867.
Aug. 14, 1866	Johnson organizes National Union party to offset Radical Republicans in Congress.
Fall 1866	Radical Republicans are big winners in 1866 elections; they now have sufficient votes to ensure successful veto overrides.
Dec. 3, 1866	Start of second session of the Thirty-ninth Congress, which debates numerous Reconstruction proposals.
Dec. 17, 1866	First motion to attempt to impeach Johnson is made; it fails. Court issues formal opinions in *Milligan*.

courts were open and functioning, as they were in Indiana.

The particular circuit court that heard Milligan's dispute was composed of District Judge David McDonald and U.S. Supreme Court Justice David Davis.[11] Both were obviously upset by the case; they went so far as to send a letter to President Johnson, begging him to intercede and stop the execution (Fairman 1971, 197-199). Whether or not they received a response is unclear;[12] what we do know is that Davis, in particular, had such "hatred" of the "arbitrary arrests" at issue in *Milligan* that he was "determine[d] to rid the land of them forever." To this end, he sought to ensure that the case would reach the Supreme Court (Hughes 1965, 585-586) by asking it to resolve the three key questions *Milligan* raised:

1. On the facts stated in the petition and exhibits, ought the writ of habeas corpus to be issued?
2. Ought Milligan to be discharged?
3. Did the military commission have jurisdiction legally to try and sentence Milligan?

While Milligan awaited Supreme Court action, the political environment was undergoing substantial change: President Johnson began to lose political support. His downfall began when, at the time the circuit court was considering the charges against Milligan, he proposed a plan for the defeated states (see Table 14-1). Called "restoration," the proposal involved a series of measures designed to bring the South back into the Union swiftly and graciously. "[I]n broad outline," Johnson's call for "restoration" was similar to the plan Lincoln was contemplating at the time of his assassination (Kelly, Harbison, and Belz 1991, 324).

Perhaps that is why, at least initially, restoration received a warm reception in Congress (see Fairman, 1971, 105), despite the fact that Johnson was a Democrat and Congress Republican. As historians now tell it, "[p]olitical circumstances favored Andrew Johnson on his accession to the executive office in April 1865." At the time,

[m]ost Republicans were moderates who wanted to secure the results of the war by guaranteeing genuine freedom to emancipated slaves and by excluding leading Confederates from reconstruction politics. Convinced of the soundness and virtue of their party's free-labor, free-speech, and equality-before-the-law principles, they wanted to extend these principles to the South. Their purposes were to republicanize the region, unite the nation, and secure political control of federal and state governments for their party. But the main body of Republicans was averse to political, social, and economic revolution in the South, and was prepared to accept the leadership of the new president in the initial stages of reconstruction (Kelly, Harbison, and Belz, 1991, 324).

By the end of 1865, however, relations between the president and Congress began to sour. Apparently believing that they had met Johnson's criteria for readmission into the

Union, the Southern bloc sent delegations to the Thirty-ninth Congress. But the existing Congress refused to seat them. It was enraged by the audacity of the Southern states, many of whose delegates included prominent members of the Confederacy (for example, Georgia sent Alexander Stevens, who was vice president of the Confederate states). Besides, Congress believed that the old Confederacy was seeking to undermine the spirit of "restoration" by enacting black codes—precursors to Jim Crow laws.

Congressional refusal to seat the Southern delegates revealed major flaws in Johnson's plan: it did not deal explicitly with the terms under which states would be readmitted to the Union and it was weak on racial issues. The flaws, in turn, highlighted the differences between the desires of the Democratic president and those of Radical Republican members of Congress. Whereas Johnson believed that the Southern states remained a part of the Union after the war and only had to be restored, Radical Republicans began to argue that they had committed "state suicide" and had to be wholly reconstructed. Since Johnson's plan had no mechanism for such "reconstruction," these members of Congress believed they needed to take matters out of Johnson's hands and into their own.

As shown in Table 14-1, the first step taken by the Radicals was the establishment of the Joint Committee on Reconstruction. The purpose of this committee was to "inquire into the condition of the States which formed the confederacy" (Fairman 1971, 118). But it would eventually do far more than "inquire"; under the leadership of the Radical Republican Thaddeus Stevens, it became the guiding force behind the Fourteenth Amendment, as well as the military reconstruction plan at issue in *McCardle* (discussed below). Next, the Radicals—led by Lyman Trumbull, chair of the Senate Judiciary Committee—proposed two measures designed to further their interests in reconstructing the South and in protecting black rights: the Freedmen and Civil Rights bills. Among other provisions, the first proclaimed that any person charged with depriving freedmen (former slaves) of their rights would be tried by a military, not civilian, tribunal. The Civil Rights Bill was aimed at ensuring the rights of blacks by, among other things, granting full citizenship to anyone born in the United States.

On February 4, 1866, Congress passed the Freedmen's Bill, with all the Republicans supporting it and all the Democrats opposing it. About two weeks later, however, Johnson vetoed the bill, asserting that the provision for military tribunals violated the Constitution. The Radicals attempted to override Johnson's veto but could not muster the necessary two-thirds vote.

It was within this political environment—just two weeks after the Radicals failed to override Johnson's veto—that the Supreme Court heard arguments in *Ex parte Milligan*. The case itself seemed to turn on a simple question: Could the federal government invoke a military tribunal to try Milligan when civilian courts were functioning in his state? And that is the way the attorneys representing Milligan (including David Dudley Field, the brother of Justice Stephen J. Field, and Jeremiah Black, a close friend of Justice Davis) chose to present it in what Chief Justice Rehnquist (1987, 159) later called a "very good argument." U.S. attorneys, though, turned it into a broader question. As Rehnquist (1987, 159-160) characterized their argument,

The government's response . . . was made by James P. Speed of Kentucky, surely one of the nation's least-gifted attorneys general. . . . [He] argued that in time of war the president was "the sole judge of exigencies, necessities, and duties of the occasion. . . . During the war his power must be without limit. . . ." Insofar as the guarantees of the Bill of Rights, such as the right to jury trial, "these, in truth, are all peace provisions of the Constitution, and . . . are silence amidst arms."

By making this claim, according to historians, the government opened the door for the justices "to rule on the broader substantive questions of congressional power in Reconstruction" (Urofsky 1988, 464). In other words, in *Milligan* the justices simply were asked to determine if military tribunals could be used to try civilians living in states where the civilian courts were operating. But the case also presented them the opportunity—should they choose to take it—to comment on the kind of Reconstruction by military imposition desired by the Radicals. It is no wonder that all eyes in Washington, D.C., were carefully watching the Court.

What would the justices do? Under a rational choice approach to judicial decision making, we first must consider the preferences of the justices in regard to military involvement in Reconstruction. In Table 14-2 we present the information we collected to locate those preferences. At first blush, it would be easy to conclude that the Court would go along with the use of military tribunals. After all, most of the justices had been appointed by Lincoln, who clearly desired the invocation of military authority, at least during the war. But that conclusion would not be accurate. First, recall that Johnson's restoration plan was quite similar to the one Lincoln planned to propose. Both presidents, unlike the Radical Republicans, had "no thought of erecting regimes manned by ever-loyal Unionists" in the South or elsewhere once the war had ended (Fairman 1971, 103). Apparently, two of Lincoln's appointees, particularly Davis and Field, shared these views (see Table 14-2). They were Lincoln supporters, and they wanted to see the nation repaired—but not at the expense of military rule over civilians. Second, there remained on the Court four holdovers from Democratic regimes. These justices were avowed opponents of the Radical Republicans (see Table 14-2). Accordingly, even though we cannot fix with certainty the attitudes of all the justices (especially Chief Justice Salmon P. Chase), it seems clear that a majority of six (Nathan Clifford, Davis, Field, Robert C. Grier, Samuel Nelson, and James M. Wayne) or seven (depending on how one counts Chase) opposed military involvement in states where the civilian courts were functioning—even in those that had been part of the Confederacy.

Given the assumptions of the choice model, we cannot stop with identifying the prefer-

Table 14-2 Background Information of the Justices: Preferences before *Ex parte Milligan*

Justice (party)	Appointing president	Position before Milligan
Chase (Rep.)	Lincoln	Even members of the Lincoln administration were "apprehensive [that] Chase will fail . . . on the question of habeas corpus and State arrests" (Warren 1926, 420). Also, in a December 11, 1865, diary entry, Chase writes that he had dinner with Thaddeus Stevens and could "not adopt Stevens view about holding States as Territories . . ." (Fairman 1971, 118-119). Still, because there was "no man with more fierce aspirations than Chase," who was perceived to use the Court "to promote his personal ends," his vote was unpredictable (Warren 1926, 420).
Clifford (Dem.)	Buchanan	A "holdover appointee of pro-Southern Democratic President" (Hughes 1965, 582); his "adherence to Democratic fundamentalism was beyond question" (Fairman 1971, 509).
Davis (Rep.)	Lincoln	His "hatred of such 'arbitrary' arrests [as the one at issue in *Milligan*] led him to determine to rid the land of them forever. As Circuit Judge [in *Milligan*] he made certain that the case would come to the Supreme Court" (Hughes 1965, 585-586; see also Fairman 1971, 61, for a letter Davis wrote in which he "comments disapprovingly" on restoration plans for the South).
Field (Dem.)	Lincoln	He "made no attempt to conceal his narrow view of the powers which he felt the Constitution allowed the national government in peacetime" (Hughes 1965, 582-583). In his view, "recriminatory acts against the South—such as . . . governing them by arbitrary military tribunals . . . were to be deplored and to be checked wherever possible" (Swisher 1963, 165).
Grier (Dem.)	Polk	A "holdover appointee of pro-Southern Democratic President"; he "was closely attached to the pro-Southern wing of the Democratic Party and its pre-war leader . . . former President James Buchanan" (Hughes 1965, 582).
Miller (Rep.)	Lincoln	Although Miller's correspondence shows disdain of some Radical Republican plans (see Fairman 1971, 124-125), he was considered a "safe" vote for congressional authorization of military reconstruction.
Nelson (Dem.)	Tyler	A "holdover appointee of pro-Southern Democratic President"; "Even during the war [he] actively opposed the Republican's conception of the extent of the national government's legitimate area of power" (Hughes, 1965, 582).
Swayne (Rep.)	Lincoln	A "safe" vote for the Radical Republicans; his son was an agent of the Freedmen's Bureau; and he "maintained political connections . . . with the radicals" (Hughes 1965, 583).
Wayne (Dem.)	Jackson	Although he was "somewhat of a nationalist," he was also a strong States Rights Democrat. He "could scarcely be expected to view with pleasure any stern measures imposed upon his native South in peacetime" (Hughes 1965, 582).

ences of the Court; we must also consider those of the other involved political actors. For what good would it do the Court to rule in favor of Milligan if Congress had the desire and the ability to override (or alter) it and the president would sustain congressional action? This was a particularly important consideration given the context of the times—a period during which the Court was trying to regain its credibility. As Hughes (1965, 581) put it, "Not only was the Court's influence probably at an all time low during the period from its ill-fated 1857 decision in the *Dred Scott* case through the Civil War, but the Court was widely distrusted even by moderate Republicans."[13]

To locate the preferences of the other key relevant actors, we begin with the policy space depicted in Figure 14-3, one centering on military jurisdiction over civilians.[14] Based on the above discussion, we place the president quite close to the Court (he vetoed the Freedmen's Bill on the ground that military tribunals violate the Constitution), the median member of Congress to the right of the president (Congress passed the Freedmen's Bill),[15] and the relevant committee chairs (for example, Trumbull and Stevens) farthest to the right (they were the ones who pushed for Reconstruction legislation). Finally, "when the president is aligned with the Court [as he is in our Figure 14-3], a new point becomes relevant—"the pivotal veto member," namely, that point in each chamber for which one-third of the legislators are on one side, and two-thirds on the other" (Eskridge 1991a, 381). Given the political environment under which the Court heard *Milligan*, we place the pivotal veto member close to the president and the Court (recall that the Senate could not override Johnson's veto of the Freedmen's Bill).

In this version of the Reconstruction game, the Court is free to vote its sincere preferences. The committee chairs obviously will not like the decision, but they will not propose legislation to override it (or otherwise to impinge on the institutional integrity of the Court), for Johnson would veto it. And, given the point of the pivotal veto member, the key congressional players would be unable to obtain a successful override.

Hence, the model predicts that the Court will vote its unconstrained preference and the key committee chairs will not attempt to override its decision. This, at least initially, is what happened. On the last day of its term (April 3, 1866), the Court announced its holding in *Milligan*: "the writ of habeas corpus should be issued; petitioners ought to be discharged according to the Act of March 3, 1863; the military commissions had been without jurisdiction." In other words, it handed Milligan a rather complete victory. But, at the time, the Court provided no justification for its decision. Chief Justice Chase announced that the opinions would be issued next term "when such of the dissenting judges as see fit to do so will state their grounds of dissent" (Fairman 1971, 143-144).

The full opinions did follow in December 1866, but no dissents were issued. Instead, four of the justices filed a concurring (or, at most, a partial dissenting) opinion, disagreeing only with the breadth of the decision and not the result.[16] As Urofsky (1988, 464) put it,

Figure 14-3 Distribution of Preferences at the Time the Court Heard *Ex parte Milligan*

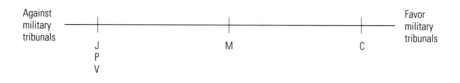

Note: J=majority of Supreme Court; P=president; V=pivotal veto member; M=median member of Congress; C=relevant congressional committees.

All the justices agreed that the military court had failed to live up to the terms of the 1863 act. While the President certainly had a right and a duty to suspend habeas corpus where the civil courts were closed, he could not do so where they remained opened. . . . The justices divided, however, over who had the power to decide when a crisis justified the expediency of imposing martial law. [For the majority] Justice Davis . . . noted that a military commission did not meet the constitutional description of a court created by Congress, and he doubted that Congress had the power to create such tribunals.

The separate opinion, written by Chief Justice Chase "claimed Congress did have the power to determine when military justice should be established in areas remote from the actual theater of war" (Urofsky 1988, 464).

Of course, the content of these opinions was unknown in April 1866; only the Court's short order had been made public. Did Congress or other relevant actors respond to this order? Our model predicts that they would not—or, more pointedly, that Congress would not attempt to override it. And that, at least in the spring of 1866, was the case. As Fairman (1971, 144) writes, the Court's order in *Milligan* "occasioned little notice at the moment." He posited two explanations for the lack of attention. First, "[t]here was no knowing what ground the opinion would take, or what might be said in dissent." Second, the Radicals had managed to pass the Civil Rights Bill (described above), but Johnson had vetoed it. The attention of Congress was focused on efforts to override the veto.

By issuing the orders it did, the Court took the rational course of action in the spring of 1866. It voted its preferences believing that Congress would not enact legislation to override *Milligan*. Key to this reasoning was the fact that President Johnson generally supported the Court's position and the Radicals had yet to demonstrate that they had sufficient strength to override any presidential veto. Consequently the president's ever-growing opposition to Radical initiatives provided a measure of protection for the justices.

From Milligan *to* McCardle

Between the spring and summer of 1866, before the Court issued its full opinions in *Milligan*, the political situation worsened considerably for President Johnson and, ulti-

Figure 14-4 Distribution of Preferences after the Fall Elections of 1866

Note: J=majority of Supreme Court; P=president; M=median member of Congress; V=pivotal veto member; C=relevant congressional committees.

mately, for the Court. As shown in Table 14-1, the Radical Republicans were beginning to show some muscle: they overrode Johnson's veto of the Civil Rights Bill and passed a revised version of the Freedmen's Bill, again over Johnson's veto. So, too, they managed to enact a bill reducing the size of the Court so that Johnson would be unable to replace Justice John Catron (who had died before *Milligan*) and would be unlikely to make any future appointments.[17] Finally, and most important, in the fall elections of 1866 Johnson's supporters lost a substantial number of seats, despite the president's attempts to garner votes for members of the newly formed National Union Party (a vehicle designed to counter the Radical Republicans). Indeed, the results for the Republicans in the autumn elections represented to that time "the most decisive and complete victory ever won in American politics" (Fairman 1971, 133). In each house of the Fortieth Congress the ability to override presidential vetoes would no longer be hit or miss: the two-thirds majority required to override a veto was clear and convincing.

The importance of this election cannot be sufficiently stressed. As we note in Figure 14-4, it changed the preference configuration. No longer would Johnson have any chance of successfully vetoing congressional legislation. Reconstruction would now lie in the hands of the Congress, not the president. This became apparent immediately. Although the Fortieth Congress would not meet until March 1867, the Radicals—buoyed by their electoral success—in December devised numerous measures to "reconstruct" the South in accordance with the state suicide theory. In other words, most of the contemplated proposals centered on imposing military authority over the defeated region.

It was in the midst of these congressional debates that the Court handed down its formal opinions in *Milligan*. Of course, given the distribution of preferences revealed in Figure 14-4, it is tempting to say that the Court never would have reached the decision it did had it not issued the order in April 1866. The political environment had changed that much. What looked to be a rational course of action in April 1866 was, by December of that year, one that begged for congressional response. For, "[i]n the context of the moment, the opinion came as a shock, a breach of the comity between the Court and Congress. It gave warning that as Congress was about to deal with intransigent Southern States supported by the president, it must reckon with an unfriendly Court" (Fairman 1971, 236). Radicals asserted that the Court had now "joined hands with President Johnson in an effort to destroy the Congressional plans for Reconstruction" (Warren 1926, 447).

President Johnson continued to oppose the Congress with unprecedented vigor, but also with a spectacular lack of success. During his four years in office, Johnson vetoed twenty-one bills; fifteen of those vetoes were overridden by the Radicals. The overrides included all of Johnson's vetoes of important legislation: the Civil Rights Act, the revised Freedmen's Bill, the Tenure of Office Act, the Reconstruction Act and all the Supplemental Reconstruction Acts, and various state admission laws. By comparison, the sixteen presidents serving before Johnson had cast only thirty-six regular vetoes and had experienced only six congressional overrides (and five of those were suffered by a single president, John Tyler). The consequences for the Court were disastrous. No longer could the president be considered a protector, or even a viable ally. His veto power was not a realistic buffer against congressional reaction.

Worse yet, with the issuance of the *Milligan* decision, the Radicals saw the Court as being in league with Johnson. The opinions unleashed a furor of Republican emotions, with the Radical Republican press predicting the worst for the justices. As one editor noted, "Every Republican member of Congress with whom I have conferred on the subject is out and out for abolishing the Supreme Court at once, upon the ground that if Congress does not abolish it, it will abolish Congress, for the president stands ready to execute its nefarious decision with an iron hand" (Fairman 1971, 221-222).[18] "These accounts," according to Warren (1926, 445-446) "were not exaggerated; for the reports of statements made by the president that the Supreme Court was prepared to follow its *Milligan* decision to its logical consequences and to hold unconstitutional any legislation which contemplated the government of the Southern States by military force, aroused the Republican leaders to a consideration of means of curbing the Court." This was so even though *Milligan* dealt only with the use of military tribunals in states where the civilian courts were functioning, not in the defeated region—and only with executive power at that. But members of Congress thought it denied their institution the power to authorize military commissions in the South (see Fairman 1971). Given this interpretation, Congress was more than a bit concerned that the Court would strike down the Reconstruction proposals it was in the process of considering—many of which called for military authority in the Southern states.[19]

Accordingly, as Warren (1926) indicates, legislators considered numerous proposals to curb the Court.[20] For example, on January 21, 1867, one member of Congress introduced a bill to require a unanimous vote by the Court to invalidate a federal law; the next day a proposal was offered that would have excluded from the federal bar those guilty of a felony or who helped in the rebellion.

Although Congress did not immediately take any of these steps, it may have been attempting to signal the justices of its displeasure with the *Milligan* ruling and to show them the necessity of voting strategically (not sincerely) should the issue arise again. If this was the case, the signal was picked up clearly by members of the Court. For during the spring of 1867 the Court "transformed its stance from one of belligerent assertiveness to one of retiring prudence" (Hughes 1965, 588).[21] For example, in April the Court handed down *Mississippi v. Johnson* (1867), followed in May by *Georgia v. Stanton* and *Mississippi v. Stanton* (1868).[22] In these decisions the Court held that it had no jurisdiction to rule on the constitutionality of Reconstruction Act enforcement.

With these signals apparently sent and received, Congress turned to the real business at hand: dealing with the Southern states. To this end the first months of 1867 saw a wave of legislation passed—all of which Johnson vetoed and Congress overrode. The most important piece was the Military Reconstruction Act of 1867. This act divided the Southern states into five military districts, each governed by a military general. These military governments were given the authority to hold trials and punish offenders.

At the time this act was passed, many observers and members of Congress thought that it overrode *Milligan*. In the wake of its passage, one editor wrote that "[t]he Supreme Court is literally dead. So dead—and so proved to be by numerous events of late—that it is utterly impotent against Congress. . . . Congress does not intend that the Supreme Court shall obstruct its policy. The impotency of that tribunal alone protects it from an act for its reorganization" (Fairman 1971, 314). That Congress took this step, again, is hardly surprising, given the configuration of preferences displayed in Figure 14-4; in fact, it is exactly what rational choice accounts would predict. Congress had the desire and the wherewithal to overcome the Court, and it did.

Ex parte McCardle

As indicated in Table 14-3, about the time Congress passed the Military Reconstruction Act, it also enacted the Habeas Corpus Act of 1867. Seemingly trivial in comparison to the Military Reconstruction Act, this piece of legislation actually served as the catalyst to *Ex parte McCardle*, one of history's most important showdowns between Congress and the Court.

As its name suggests, the Habeas Corpus Act of 1867 centered on writs of habeas corpus, a subject of some familiarity to Congress. In fact, in one of its first major acts—the 1789 Judiciary Act—Congress sought to codify the writ, as guaranteed in the U.S. Constitution (Article I, Section 9).[23] Under the 1789 act and subsequent legislation, however, access to the federal courts on habeas corpus grounds was very limited, especially for those persons incarcerated by state officials (see Van Alstyne 1973). No explicit appellate jurisdiction had been granted to the Supreme Court to hear habeas corpus cases, but the Court

Table 14-3 Key Events Leading Up to *Ex parte McCardle*

Feb. 5, 1867	Congress passes the Habeas Corpus Act of 1867.
Feb. 20, 1867	Both Houses pass the Military Reconstruction Act of 1867.
Mar. 2, 1867	Johnson vetoes the Military Reconstruction Act; Congress overrides Johnson's veto. Thirty-ninth Congress adjourns.
Mar. 4, 1867	The Fortieth Congress convenes nine months ahead of schedule to continue to control Reconstruction and weaken Johnson's control; passes several laws designed to curb presidential power.
Mar. 11, 1867	Johnson acquiesces to Congress and appoints commanders for the five military districts specified in the Military Reconstruction Act.
Apr. 15, 1867	In *Mississippi v. Johnson,* Court dismisses a challenge to presidential enforcement of the Reconstruction Act.
May 13, 1867	In *Georgia v. Stanton,* Court dismisses a second challenge to enforcement of the Reconstruction Act.
Spring 1867	House begins to investigate Johnson to see if grounds for impeachment exist.
July 5, 1867	Justice Wayne dies; under the terms of a judicial act of July 23, 1866, the Court remains at eight members.
Nov. 8, 1867	McCardle arrested; a military commission is directed to convene and try him on November 20, 1867.
Nov. 11, 1867	McCardle's counsel seek writ of habeas corpus in circuit court under Habeas Corpus Act of 1867.
Nov. 25, 1867	Circuit court rules against McCardle; he is released on bail pending his direct appeal to the U.S. Supreme Court.
Dec. 23, 1867	McCardle's attorneys file case in U.S. Supreme Court.
Jan. 1868	Various Court-curbing bills proposed in Congress by Trumbull and others.
Jan. 13, 1868	House passes bill that would have required a two-thirds majority on the Court to strike congressional legislation.
Jan. 21, 1868	Trumbull files motion in Court that justices should dismiss *McCardle* for lack of jurisdiction.
Jan. 31, 1868	Court hears arguments on whether *McCardle* should be dismissed for lack of jurisdiction.
Feb. 17, 1868	Court rejects Trumbull's motion; *McCardle* will advance. Trumbull proposes bill in Congress to remove Court's jurisdiction over Reconstruction cases.
Feb. 24, 1868	House votes to impeach Johnson.
Mar. 1868	Senate prepares for Johnson impeachment trial with Chief Justice Chase presiding. The case is heard from March 30, 1868 to May 16, 1868.
Mar. 2–9, 1868	Court hears arguments in *McCardle.*
Mar. 12, 1868	Congress passes bill to repeal the section of the Habeas Corpus Act of 1867 that permits appeals to the Supreme Court (the repealer bill).

Mar. 21, 1868	Court meets in conference to discuss *McCardle*; over the dissents of Grier and Field it votes to postpone deciding the case until Johnson acts on the repealer bill.
Mar. 25, 1868	Johnson vetoes the repealer bill.
Mar. 27, 1868	Congress overrides Johnson's veto of the repealer bill.
Apr. 6, 1867	Supreme Court adjourns, announcing its decision to hold *McCardle* over until next term.
May 16-26, 1868	Senate fails to convict Johnson.
Summer 1868	Seven states readmitted to the Union.
Nov. 3, 1868	Republicans are big winners in 1868 elections; Ulysses S. Grant elected president by a landslide.
December 1868	Court sets rearguments in *McCardle* for March 19, 1869.
February 1869	Trumbull proposes and Senate passes bill to increase the Court's size and to relieve the justices of circuit court duty; passed by House on March 3, 1869.
Mar. 4, 1869	Grant sworn in as president.
Mar. 19, 1869	Court hears rearguments in *McCardle*.
Apr. 10, 1869	Bill to increase size of court and relieve justices of circuit duty is augmented with pension provision for the justices. Becomes law on this date.
Apr. 12, 1869	Court issues opinions in *McCardle*.

had occasionally decided such appeals using certiorari jurisdiction. The 1867 act expanded the habeas corpus role of the federal judiciary by stipulating that the federal courts had the power to grant writs of habeas corpus in *all cases* where *any person* may be restrained of his or her liberty in violation of the Constitution, laws, or treaties of the United States. Furthermore, the act conferred appellate jurisdiction in such cases on the U.S. Supreme Court.

Why would the Congress expand the Court's authority at a time when it was considering many pieces of legislation to curb it? The answer is simple:

The immediate concern was to enforce the grant Congress had made by a resolution to encourage enlistments, in 1865: where a slave volunteered, his wife and children should be forever free. But it was discovered that if the master still held them to service, the federal judiciary had no authority to issue habeas corpus. [In other words, this legislation was meant to help North, not South.] Accordingly, the House instructed its Judiciary Committee to report a bill, which it did . . . whose broad effect was "to enlarge the privilege of the writ of habeas corpus, and to make the jurisdiction of the courts and judges of the United States co-extensive with all the powers that can be conferred upon them." If the detention was in violation of some federal right, the writ was now available. Moreover, there was a direct line of "appeal" to the Supreme Court. (Fairman 1971, 448)

But, as Fairman notes (1971, 448): "Like the rain, the law impartially blesses the just and unjust. Congress had set out to protect the wife and children of the Negro soldier— and within the year 1867 counsel for ex-Confederate McCardle would grasp the statute in an effort to prostrate Congressional Reconstruction, and preserve white supremacy." In other words, the act was passed to protect blacks, but one of the first to take advantage of it was William McCardle, who was arrested in November 1867 by military authorities in Mississippi for publishing "incendiary and libelous" articles about Congress and Reconstruction. Under the Reconstruction legislation, a military commission was supposed to hear his case. But, using the 1867 Habeas Corpus Act, McCardle sought a writ of habeas corpus in circuit court, arguing that the Reconstruction Acts were unconstitutional. That court ruled against McCardle, so, under the terms of the 1867 act, his attorney sought relief in the U.S. Supreme Court. Congressional lawyers—including Trumbull, the chair of the Judiciary Committee and a Radical Republican—immediately countered that the Court should not hear the case for want of jurisdiction (see Table 14-3). Their particular argument was that the 1867 act did not "apply to this case, because that statute was intended to apply to prisoners of *state* officials; McCardle had committed a 'military offence,' and therefore fell" within an exceptional category. They further suggested that if the 1867 act "did not apply . . . the Court had no jurisdiction otherwise to review the case, since no such appellate authority was conferred by the Judiciary Act of 1789" (Schubert 1960, 279).

Unconvinced by Trumbull's argument, the Court agreed to hear the oral arguments in the case, setting the date for March 2, 1868. As Chief Justice Chase wrote, "Prior to the passage of [the Habeas Corpus Act of 1867] this court exercised appellate jurisdiction over the action of inferior court by *habeas corpus*... aided by a writ of certiorari." He went on to provide examples of cases in which the Court had taken that very step.

The decision on the part of the justices just to hear arguments in *McCardle* once again unleashed a furor in Congress (see Table 14-3). On the very day the Court refused to dismiss *McCardle* for lack of jurisdiction, Trumbull proposed a bill that would, in essence, remove the Court's jurisdiction to hear cases growing out of reconstruction measures. This move was akin to the "cocking of a gun, audible in the nearby Supreme Court chamber" (Fairman 1971, 464). Moreover, talk of impeachment abounded (see Swisher 1963, 162, for an interesting story concerning Justice Field), and not just of Supreme Court justices. Shortly after the Court agreed to hear arguments in *McCardle*, the House voted to impeach President Johnson (see Table 14-3).

It was amidst this incredibly charged political environment that the Court heard arguments in *McCardle*. All in Washington recognized the importance of the case. To the Radicals, it provided the justices with a vehicle to eradicate their entire Reconstruction program; to President Johnson, whose impeachment proceedings were getting under way in the Senate at the very time the Court was hearing arguments (in fact, Chase had to leave in the middle of arguments to help the Senate prepare for the trial), it represented a potential source of vindication of his policies. The Court obviously understood these hopes and fears: it allowed six hours for each side to present its case (twice the normal amount).

Not surprisingly, then, the oral arguments were an extraordinary event. The several attorneys representing McCardle (including, once again, Justice Field's brother David Dudley Field) "professed to be 'extremely embarrassed' ... because the case was so very simple, and the law [for example, *Milligan*] was all on his [McCardle's] side!" (Fairman, 1971, 452). But their strategy "was nothing less than to free the Old South from the grasp of Congress: they did not aim merely to free McCardle from the general" (Fairman 1971, 456). More specifically, they presented the following arguments on behalf of McCardle:

1. Trial by court-martial infringed on his Fifth and Sixth Amendment rights.
2. Exigent circumstances did not warrant the use of martial rule and the suspension of the right to trial by jury.
3. Application of the Reconstruction Act to McCardle's editorials would violate the First Amendment.
4. Much of the act of Congress of March 2, 1867, which placed the ten states under military jurisdiction, was itself unconstitutional (see Van Alstyne 1973, 238).

The government, represented again by Trumbull and others, found that the "Bench was not friendly." Trumbull's "main effort was to induce the Court to acknowledge that Congress in reconstructing the rebel States was exercising a power not subject to judicial control" (Fairman 1971, 454). Along these lines, the government reiterated its jurisdictional concerns.

In all of this, one might have expected a lively exchange between the attorneys and the justices. But this was not the case: "counsel arguing McCardle were not interrupted by questions from the bench. The issues were clear and familiar. One supposes that no Justice was still making up his mind" (Fairman 1971, 456). To push the observation one step farther, it is clear that the Court's preferences lay with McCardle (see Figure 14-4).[24]

Congress, as well as the informed public, sensed that the Court was leaning toward a ruling for McCardle. One contemporary writer (a good friend of Chief Justice Chase) laid out the situation after oral argument this way:

The apprehension has been almost universal, among Republicans, that the decision [in *McCardle*] would pronounce the Reconstruction laws unconstitutional, and that, on the strength of this, Mr. Johnson would at once withdraw the troops from the Southern States. The current belief has been that five out of the eight Judges would so decide—Nelson . . . Grier . . . Clifford . . . Field, and Davis. Mr. Davis is known to have expressed disapproval of some of the reconstruction legislation; but it is not certain that he will go to the length of pronouncing it all unconstitutional. . . .

On the other hand, Justices [Noah H.] Swayne . . . and [Samuel F.] Miller . . . are believed to regard the reconstruction legislation as constitutional, and to be certain so to decide. Mr. Chief Justice Chase's position has been much questioned. . . . [I]t may be considered certain that he will take counsel . . . solely of his judgment and his conscience. But he is known to have said that the most ardent desire of his life was to see the Southern States restored to their normal relations to the Union, under the reconstruction policy of Congress. And in the decision in [*Milligan*], he has put on record his opposition to the trial of citizens before military courts, in time of peace. From these two facts it might perhaps be inferred that his decision would be adverse to the right of military trials, but not to the general reconstruction policy (Fairman 1971, 465)

Given this assessment, coupled with the preference distribution displayed in Figure 14-4 (which remained the same throughout this period), we should not be surprised that Congress reached the conclusion that the "Court must be curbed" (Fairman 1971, 461). To this end, it returned to Trumbull's proposal to take away the Court's jurisdiction in all Reconstruction cases. But instead of enacting it, in a "bit of craftiness" the Republicans proposed just to repeal the 1867 Habeas Corpus Act. Because they put the repealer in an otherwise "harmless and unimportant Senate bill to extend to the Court's appellate jurisdiction in cases involving customs and revenue officers" (Warren 1926, 474), the move flew through the Senate and House on March 12 virtually unnoticed.

But that invisibility did not last long. The Radical Republican press was giddy with delight: "The passage of that little bill which put a knife to the throat of the *McCardle Case* was a splendid performance. . . . Congress will not abandon its Reconstruction policy to please any Court, because it sincerely believes that the welfare of the Nation depends upon the success of that policy" (Warren 1926, 476). Supporters of President Johnson were nervous. They suspected that he would veto the legislation, and that the timing would hardly be auspicious: the bill had passed the day before his Senate impeachment trial would commence. Moreover, they felt that it undermined the Court's authority. As one supporter had written in his diary: "By trick, imposition and breach of courtesy, an Act was slipped through both houses, repealing the [1867 Habeas Corpus Act], the effect of which is to take from the Supreme Court certain powers and which is designed to prevent a decision in the *McCardle* Case. Should the Court in that case, as it is supposed they will, pronounce the Reconstruction Laws unconstitutional, the military government will fall and the whole Radical fabric will tumble with it" (Warren 1926, 476).

Most important, for our purposes, was that the Court knew precisely what was happening; by March 21, 1868, when it was to decide *McCardle*, the justices were well aware of Trumbull's proposals to curb the Court, of the repealer bill, and of the fact that Johnson had not yet acted on it. What would the Court do? The answer to that question depends on one's perspective of judicial decision making. The attitudinal model would predict that the Court would merely decide the case in accord with the raw preferences displayed in Figure 14-4 and rule in McCardle's favor. Approaches grounded in assumptions of rationality, however, suggest that the Court would act in a way to avoid congressional override (or, as in this case, to avoid the severe institutional consequences of the sort Trumbull proposed).

In this particular instance, the choice approach yields the more accurate prediction. Despite the fact that Justices Field and Chase told intimates that all of the justices (except Swayne) wanted to decide the case in McCardle's favor at the March 21 conference (see Fairman 1971, 467-474),[25] the Court voted to postpone its final decision until the next term. The justices must have known, as did virtually all of Washington, that Johnson would veto the repealer bill (which he did, on March 25) and that Congress would override his veto (which it did on March 27). Had the Court decided the case *before* Johnson acted, they knew they would face a congressional override or, worse yet, legislation to curb the Court, proposals to impeach members, and so forth.

Thus, despite the existence of other options, the Court took the rational, not attitudinal, course of action (see, especially, Hughes 1965; Murphy 1964; Van Alstyne 1973, 244-247).[26] Of course, the move helped to avoid a collision with Congress (see Figure 14-4), but it also had an additional virtue: the Court knew that it would eventually obtain another case in which it could invoke its appellate jurisdiction, under the 1789 act and previous precedent, over habeas corpus cases. It made this quite clear when it eventually (in April 1869) issued a formal opinion in *McCardle*. Although the justices dismissed the case for lack of jurisdiction (and therefore conceded the constitutionality of the repealer act), the last paragraph of the opinion is instructive on this point:

Counsel seem to have supposed, if effect be given to the repealing act in question, that the whole appellate power of the court, in cases of *habeas corpus*, is denied. But his is an error. The act of 1868 [the repealer act] does not except from that jurisdiction any cases but appeals from Circuit Courts under the act of 1867 [the Habeas Corpus Act]. It does not affect jurisdiction which was previously exercised.

In other words, the Court was attempting to have its cake and eat it too. It knew that it would lose to Congress in a battle over Reconstruction by military imposition. What's more, by the time the Court decided the case, the Reconstruction era was coming to an end; virtually all the Southern states had been readmitted to the Union and, thus, were no longer under military authority. So, in *McCardle*, it voted in a sophisticated fashion—with Congress. Still, the above paragraph shows that it had hope of reading its sincere preferences over habeas corpus into law in future cases. All it would take was a case grounded in the 1789 Judiciary Act, rather than the repealed 1867 law.

If that was the case, the Court did not have to wait very long. Just two months after the Court dismissed McCardle's suit for lack of jurisdiction, Edward M. Yerger stabbed and killed Major Joseph Crane, an army officer assigned to act as mayor of Jackson, Mississippi. Since Mississippi was still under military rule, Yerger was tried by a military commission. His lawyers objected to this and sought a writ of habeas corpus in a federal circuit court. When that court denied their request, they appealed to the U.S. Supreme Court. There, "Yerger's lawyers picked up on Chase's suggestion in [the last paragraph of] *McCardle* and argued that the Supreme Court's appellate jurisdiction over habeas corpus derived not from the 1867 act, but from the Judiciary Act of 1789. The 1867 law merely amended and augmented the Court's power, and consequently, the 1868 repeal did no more than reduce the Court's authority to the 1789 limits" (Urofsky 1988, 468). In October 1869 the justices agreed. They made it clear that the "repealing statute took away only the jurisdiction conferred in 1867, not that which had been confirmed in 1789" (see Currie 1988, 306). In the final analysis, then, *Ex parte Yerger* (1869) provided the Court with the vehicle to etch its preferences in regard to habeas corpus into law while avoiding a battle with Congress about Reconstruction.

A reasonable question is why the Court would act this way, given the preferences of Congress. Did it not fear a congressional backlash? While it is true that members of Congress proposed several Court-curbing bills in the wake of *Yerger*, it was clear that their chances of passage were minimal, and the justices probably knew this. Why? What had changed between 1868 and 1869? For one thing, *McCardle* had shown the legislature that the Court would hardly make a contest with Congress. Even the Radicals no longer viewed the Court as a threat. Second, the Court's decision in *Yerger* had virtually no adverse effect on Reconstruction, since by then almost all the Confederate states had been readmitted (see Warren 1926, 496). This significantly reduced the probability of an adverse congressional response. After all, Congress had engaged in battle with President Johnson and the Supreme Court in order to preserve Reconstruction policy—not because of any particular concern over appellate jurisdiction in habeas corpus cases (see Currie, 1985, 307; Kutler 1968, chap. 5).

Discussion

At the time the Court agreed to postpone a decision in *Ex parte McCardle*, anti-Radicals lambasted it. One member of Johnson's administration wrote: "The judges of the Supreme Court have caved in, fallen through, failed, in the *McCardle* case" (Schwartz 1994, 141). The former Supreme Court justice Benjamin R. Curtis agreed: "Congress, with the acquiesce of the country, has subdued the Supreme Court" (Schwartz 1994, 141). Even scholars have tended to concur with this view. As Schwartz notes (1994, 154): "The traditional view of the Supreme Court during the Civil War and Reconstruction has been that it played a more subdued role than at any time in its history—that it had been weakened, if not impotent, ever since the *Dred Scott* decision." As a result, "[b]iting criticism has been reaped on the Justices over the years for [their] refusal to meet the Radicals head-on in constitutional combat" (Murphy 1964, 194).[27]

Here, we present a different view, one more in line with contemporary thinking about *McCardle* (for example, Currie 1985; Kutler 1968). By acting strategically, not attitudinally, the Court "performed like an expert, if aged, escape artist" (Hughes 1965, 595). It was able to stave off a major attack on its legitimacy while giving up—in light of *Yerger*—little. Or, as Murphy (1964, 194) put it:

Whatever doubts one might have about the courage or the ethics of *McCardle*, its prudence is not open to question. The Court emerged from this conflict somewhat battered but with its power basically intact. Although the justices submitted to temporary legislative domination, by maintaining their power potential they had helped insure that this domination would be short-lived. The Justices turned what threatened to be a battle of annihilation into a stinging and humiliating but still not disastrous defeat.

The Court's decisions in *Milligan* and *McCardle* illustrate that there are occasions when, in order to accomplish long-term policy goals and preserve the integrity of their institution, the justices must abandon the practice of deciding cases consistent with their political ideologies. This may be especially true in times of political crisis, when the legislative and executive branches are sufficiently aroused to use their constitutional powers to check the Court. Under such conditions the justices may act strategically, taking a step backward in order to preserve the ability of attaining long-term objectives. To be sure, as Murphy

(1964, 193-195) concluded, "[a]doption of this 'passive' alternative is hardly the sort of choice a Justice would make if he were free to act as he would prefer, but it may be the best choice available under particular circumstances."

Notes

1. We derive this account from Epstein and Walker 1992, 199-200.

2. Habeas corpus is a legal procedure with roots extending back into English legal history. It permits an arrested person to have a judge determine whether the detention is legal. If the court concludes that there are no legal grounds for the arrest, it may order the release of the detained individual. Habeas corpus is essential to the doctrine of checks and balances because it gives the judiciary the right to intervene if the executive branch abuses the law enforcement power.

3. For more on the Supreme Court and the attitudinal model, see Chapter 13.

4. See also Ferejohn and Shipan 1989.

5. In denoting these preferred points of J, M, P, and C, we assume that the actors prefer an outcome that is nearer to that point than one that is further away. Or, to put it more technically, "beginning at [an actor's] ideal point, utility always declines monotonically in any direction. This . . . is known as single-peakedness of preferences" (Krehbiel 1988, 263).

6. Accordingly, these rational choice accounts would concur with the assumption made by Dahl and Casper, namely, political preferences lead justices to act as restraintists or activists, and not vice versa.

7. In rational choice models of judicial decisions, thus, it is not enough to say, as the attitudinal mode does, that Justice X chose action 1 over action 2 because X preferred 1 to 2. Rather, the strategic assumption suggests the following proposition: Justice X chose 1 because X believed that the other relevant actors—perhaps Justice Y or Senator Z—would choose 2, 3, and so forth, and given these choices, action 1 led to a better outcome for Justice X than did alternative actions (see Ordeshook 1992, 8).

8. Not only can political actors pass legislation or propose constitutional amendments to negate Court decisions, but they also can take out their frustrations in other ways: alter the jurisdiction of the Court, reduce its budget, change its size, and even threaten to impeach (Murphy 1964). Justices who are concerned with policy obviously are in no position to make it if they are impeached or if their decisions are being overturned.

9. To be more precise and technical about it, rational choice approaches to judicial decision making assume that decision making is interdependent (see note 7), that institutions (or rules) influence individual actions, that actors are goal directed, and that actors make decisions that reflect their beliefs about the political context in which they operate—whether it favors, in their estimation, achievement of their goals or not (Eskridge 1991a and 1991b; Knight and Epstein 1994; see generally, Ordeshook 1992, 8-11).

10. Alternatively, the Court could try to persuade the committee to shift its preferences to the left. See Eskridge 1991a, 380.

11. The circuit courts did not have judges of their own. Instead, cases were decided by combinations of district court judges and Supreme Court justices. Consequently, it was a normal occurrence for a Supreme Court justice to hear a case in the lower courts. This practice ended in 1891 with the creation of the courts of appeals.

12. Weeks later, however, the president reduced the sentence to life at hard labor.

13. In *Scott v. Sandford* (1857), the Court struck down the Missouri Compromise (which had

been repealed by Congress prior to the Court's decision), ruling that Congress did not have the constitutional power to regulate slavery in the territories. In so doing, the justices claimed that blacks could not be considered in a legal sense to be citizens of the United States. Not only do some scholars suggest that *Scott* was a cause of the Civil War but that it also severely strained the credibility of the Supreme Court for decades to come.

14. We assume that the key actors viewed this issue as separate from the one concerning the treatment of blacks. Evidence to support this comes from various sources, including this passage from a letter Chase wrote on September 1, 1868: "I hold my old faith in universal suffrage, in Reconstruction upon that basis, in universal amnesty, and in inviolate public faith; but I do not believe in military government for American States, nor in military commission for the trial of American citizens, nor in the subversion of the Executive and Judicial Departments of the General Government by Congress."

15. To simplify matters, we treat the houses of Congress as one.

16. Justice Davis's opinion for the majority was signed by four of the Court's five Democrats (Clifford, Field, Grier, Nelson). Only Wayne broke party lines to sign Chase's concurrence. For more on this point, see Currie 1985, 288-292.

17. In 1863 Congress increased the size of the Court to ten justices. The 1866 legislation reduced the size to seven, to be implemented by the future deaths or resignations of justices. The law was specifically enacted by the Republicans to deprive President Johnson of any influence over the Court's membership. The Court never reached seven justices because in 1869, shortly after Ulysses S. Grant was elected to replace Johnson in the White House, Congress raised the size of the Court to nine, where it has remained.

18. Johnson, as indicated in Figures 14-3 and 14-4, was in full accord with the Court's opinion. Right after the formal opinions came down, he issued an order dismissing all trials against civilians by the military "in Virginia and in other States in which the Republicans were claiming that a condition of war still existed" (Warren 1926, 442).

19. Indeed, just two days after the opinion came down, the Radical Thaddeus Stevens said that *Milligan* "showed that prompt legislation on the government of the rebel States was 'absolutely indispensable.' " He also noted that *Milligan* "might appear 'not as infamous as the *Dred Scott* decision,' but in truth it was 'far more dangerous' by reason of 'its operation upon the lives and liberties of the loyal men,' black and white, in the South." He then declared Congress to be " 'the sole guardian' of the sovereignty of the people; no officer, from the President and the Chief Justice down, could do any act save as directed by the legislative power" (Fairman 1971, 267-68).

20. They also sought to curb the president. In January 1867 a resolution was put forth to investigate Johnson, with the eventual goal of impeaching him. Although this resolution failed, later efforts to accomplish the same end succeeded.

21. By the same token, several members of the Court were extremely distraught by congressional reaction to *Milligan*. See, in particular, Davis's letter of February 24, 1867 (Fairman 1971, 231-234), and Field's comments recorded in Swisher (1963, 152).

22. Although the Court announced its decisions in *Georgia v. Stanton* and *Mississippi v. Stanton* in May 1867, formal opinions were not issued until February 1868.

23. "The Privilege of the Writ of Habeas Corpus shall not be suspended, unless when in Cases of Rebellion or Invasion the public Safety may require it."

24. Furthermore, Fairman (1971, 467-474) reports that both Field and Chase told friends that the Court wanted to vote in favor of McCardle. See also Warren 1926, 480.

25. Again, these preferences seemed widely known in and outside of Washington. About the time of the Court's conference, the *Boston Post*, for example, wrote that "[i]t is well ascertained that Justices Chase, Nelson, Grier, Clifford and Field believe the Reconstruction Acts to be unconstitu-

tional. . . . The decision is made up, and they have the power and the right to deliver it. Whether they have the nerve to be an independent Judiciary remains to be seen" (Warren 1926, 480 n. 2).

26. As Van Alstyne (1973, 244-247) and Fairman (1971, 449) point out, the Court could have (1) held that the provision for military trials was inconsistent with specific constitutional guarantees, without condemning the entire [congressional Reconstruction] scheme; (2) held that the repealer act was irrelevant, since it already had established its jurisdiction over the case; (3) held that the repealer act did not apply to McCardle, since it became effective only after the case had been heard on the merits. All these options, as Fairman and Van Alstyne acknowledge, would have provoked a congressional reaction.

27. *McCardle* has also generated an extensive scholarly literature on whether Congress can remove the Court's appellate jurisdiction (see Berger 1969; Hart 1953; Ratner 1960; Sager 1981), and even debate among the justices (compare Harlan's and Douglas's opinions in *Glidden Co. v. Zdanok* [1962], where Harlan says that "Congress has consistently [with Article III] withdrawn the jurisdiction of the Court to proceed with a case then sub judice, *Ex parte McCardle,*" and Douglas asserts that "there is serious question whether *McCardle* could command a majority view today.").

Part V The Impact of Courts

After the Supreme Court announced its decision in *Brown v. Board of Education* (1954), many observers predicted that grand social and political change would follow. Representatives of the National Association for the Advancement of Colored People, for example, asserted that segregation in the nation's public schools would be completely eliminated within five years (see Rosenberg 1991, 43); others argued that Americans—even those opposed to desegregation—would express outrage over racially discriminatory practices because *Brown* would serve to enlighten them.

But did these and other predictions hold? The analysis by Rosenberg (1991) of the impact of the *Brown* decision suggests that they did not: neither desegregation nor vast changes in public opinion occurred in the wake of *Brown*. Even more broadly, Rosenberg argues that *Brown* "contributed little" to furthering the cause of civil rights. Richard Kluger (1975, 944), though, reaches quite a different conclusion. In his view, "*Brown* signaled the beginning of the nation's efforts to rid itself of the consuming demons of racism."

To be sure, this particular debate pertains only to the case of *Brown v. Board of Education*. But it serves to highlight two more general points about the Court's impact and influence. The first is that scholars are divided with regard to the degree to which courts can generate major societal and political changes. Rosenberg represents a particular school of thought, which suggests that jurists cannot evoke significant societal alterations without the support of the public and other key actors in the system. There are several reasons for this, an important one being that courts lack the institutional authority to implement their own decisions. When the Supreme Court handed down its decision on *Brown*, for example, the justices could not go into every school district in the United States to monitor progress toward desegregation. Rather, they had to depend on others to ensure compliance with their ruling. Often, these "others" were unwilling to implement Court rulings. This was surely also true of the prayer-in-school rulings of the 1960s. As I pointed out in Chapter 1, noncompliance with these decisions was rampant: years after the justices banned prayer, more than half of the public schools in the South continued to endorse some form of Bible reading in their classes. The problems were that (1) the key actors charged with implementing the Court's decision—teachers and principals—were, at least in some school districts, unwilling to do so, and (2) the public did not support the Court's rulings. In light of the limited capacity to execute their own decisions, these were obstacles that the justices could not overcome.

Kluger's comment about *Brown* is typical of another school of thought, which underscores the agenda-setting role of courts. In this line of thinking, courts alone may not be able to execute their decisions, but they can change public opinion, which in turn can reset the priorities of the political institutions. The logic here is as follows: given the high regard with which the public holds the Supreme Court, it can play the role of republican schoolmaster, providing Americans with an "example of the way good republicans should behave." In other words, when "the Court rules, it confers legitimacy on the position it favors ... [which] leads to increased public support for the position taken by the argument" (Franklin and Kosaki 1989, 752). Once the public turns to support the Court's position, it places pressure on elected officials to codify and execute Court policies. To some scholars, *Brown* nicely illustrates this logic: after the decision, Congress passed several major pieces of legislation designed to eradicate race discrimination in voting, employment, public facilities, and so forth. To those analysts who view courts as facilitators of social and political change, these laws were a direct result of the agenda-setting opinion in *Brown*; without the decision, Congress would not have acted so quickly or forcefully.

The disagreement between Kluger and Rosenberg with regard to *Brown*'s efficacy shores up a second point: in looking at precisely the same case, these scholars reached wholly different conclusions. To put it more generally, the study of the Court's impact and influence is bedeviled by methodological problems: whether one agrees with Rosenberg or Kluger depends on the data one invokes and how one interprets and analyzes them. Take *Roe v. Wade*, another salient Court case, as an example. Researchers (for example, Blake 1977a, 1977b; Combs and Welch 1982) looking at aggregated data (here, the percentage of the public supporting abortion at a given point in time) typically conclude that the Court's decision had no effect on public opinion. But analysts who turn to data supplied at the individual level find evidence that it did. As Franklin and Kosaki (1989) assert, if citizens were pro-choice before the decision, they became even more so after; the same held true for those opposed to abortion.

Because these and many other problems confound the interpretation of a given case, it takes very little imagination to understand the difficulty of reaching generalizations about the impact and influence of the Court. If we cannot agree on whether a specific decision (such as *Brown* or *Roe*) generated real social or political change or had any other kind of effect, then how can we begin to characterize all or even some Court decisions? Even if we could draw comparisons between, say, *Brown* and *Roe*, is it fair to generalize from them? Because they were highly salient, controversial decisions—with all the attendant media coverage—they are hardly representative of the vast majority of disputes the Court resolves.

These are just some of the many questions and issues with which the authors of the chapters in this section grapple. In so doing, they are all mindful of the difficulties—both theoretical and methodological—that plague this line of inquiry. Still, they manage to contribute significantly to our understanding of the impact and influence of the Supreme Court, in particular, in American society. Charles H. Franklin and Liane C. Kosaki (Chapter 15) investigate a link missing in many studies of the effect of the Court on public opinion—the media. After all, the Court could hardly be expected to affect—much less change—societal views if the media did not provide information about its decisions.

In examining the role media coverage plays in informing citizens about Supreme Court decisions and the consequences that information has for citizen evaluation of the Court, Franklin and Kosaki rely on public opinion surveys as well as other information about media attention to particular Court opinions. As we might expect, these data show that coverage of the Court is highly episodic. Although it receives much less attention than the president or Congress, there are periods when the Court receives intense coverage. Hence, rather than learning about the Court from a long and continuous stream of news, as occurs with the other two branches, citizens are much more likely to encounter the Court only occasionally and in the context of controversial decisions. Equally as episodic, according to Franklin and Kosaki, is the media's coverage of particular Court cases, the result being that citizens vary considerably in their knowledge of specific decisions. Still, when the media do cover a case, they have a strong and dramatic effect on the public's awareness of the decision. High levels of coverage make a very large proportion of the public aware of decisions; low levels of coverage result in much less awareness. This finding, as the researchers show, has an important implication for studies of the impact of judicial decisions: because the media tends to focus on controversial cases, the public receives information about only a small portion of the Court's work.

Finally, Franklin and Kosaki explore the consequences of knowledge for the evaluations citizens form of the Court. They demonstrate that information about the Court tends to accumulate over time. People with low levels of information must base their evaluations on outdated facts, whereas those with high levels of information are able to use recent events in their evaluations. More specifically, the authors show that among the less informed, liberals are more approving of the Court than are conservatives. As information rises, Franklin and Kosaki report a dramatic reversal of this pattern, and conservatives become far more approving of the Court.

Lauren Bowen (Chapter 16) is also concerned with public response to judicial rulings, but she focuses on one case, *Bates v. State Bar of Arizona* (1977; in which the Court struck down regulations explicitly banning all advertising activity by lawyers), and on the response of a specific subset of the population, attorneys. Her research question is simple enough: Why did members of some law firms take advantage of *Bates* and begin to advertise their services while others did not? Or, to put it more generally, why do some members of the target population of a Court decision alter their attitudes and behaviors in light of a shift in the legal status quo and others do not? To address this question, Bowen mailed a survey to the senior partner (someone equipped to speak on behalf of the firm) of small law firms located in the states of Illinois, Kentucky, Louisiana, and Massachusetts. The survey asked whether the firm was currently advertising its services and included other questions designed to ascertain why some firms advertise their services and others do not.

Her primary finding was that response to *Bates* was largely a function of attitudes—that is, attorneys with unfavorable attitudes toward advertising were less apt to advertise their services than were those with tolerant attitudes. Although this may be a less-than-startling proposition, it is one with which other scholars have taken issue. For example, in studying parental choices with regard to busing (in response to *Brown* and the lower-court rulings it generated), Giles and Gatlin (1980) found that attitudes were not sufficient to determine behavior. Instead, the relative costs and benefits of different courses of action provided the best explanation.

Why her findings differ markedly from those of Gatlin and Giles is an intriguing question, and one that Bowen considers in some detail. In the main she argues that *Bates* set up a voluntary consumption situation (that is, attorneys had the option of doing nothing in response to *Bates*), while the *Brown* lineage of cases established a mandatory choice situation (that is, parents of school-age children had to decide whether to have their children bused to public schools or to place their children in schools not subject to the busing order; doing nothing was not an option). The lesson she draws, then, is that in a voluntary consumption situation the impetus for change appears to be a function of a favorable or tolerant disposition toward the new policy. This is significant, as Bowen explains, because it suggests that if consumers (in her case, attorneys) are hostile to a decision (as they were in *Bates*), then they will not change their behavior in appreciable numbers. As a result, even salient rulings—such as the one in *Bates*—may turn out to be something less than the "landmarks" the media and others anticipate.

Finally, in Chapter 17, Gerald N. Rosenberg, too, seeks to address issues centering on the impact and implementation of Court decisions, but his concerns and, accordingly, his theoretical perspective and methods vary from those of Bowen. Rosenberg focuses on the effect of the Court's abortion decisions, both *Roe* and *Doe* and other key rulings based on them. How did the public, politicians, medical professionals, and interest groups react to them? Were the decisions implemented? Did they bring safe and legal abortions to all American women? To some American women? Or, to put these specific questions more generally: Are there conditions under which Court decisions on behalf of relatively power-less groups are more or less likely to be implemented?

Through a detailed examination of the public opinion data, historical materials, and government documents, Rosenberg demonstrates that the impact and implementation of the Court's abortion decisions have been neither straightforward nor simple. Political response has varied and access to legal and safe abortion has increased, but in an uneven and nonuniform way. These findings, according to Rosenberg, are best explained by two, related factors. First, at the time of the 1973 abortion decisions, there was widespread support for legal abortion from several sets of actors, including relevant political and professional elites on both the national and local level, from the public at large, and from activists. Second, the Court's decisions, by allowing clinics to perform abortions, made it possible for women in some places to obtain abortions if hospitals refused to provide them. As Rosenberg shows, however, implementation by private clinics has led to uneven availability of abortion services and has encouraged local political opposition.

In the final portion of his chapter, Rosenberg seeks to extract more general lessons about the implementation of constitutional rights. His general argument is that constitutional rights have a greater likelihood of being implemented when they reflect the preexisting beliefs of politicians, relevant professionals, and the public. When at least some of them are opposed, locally or nationally, implementation is less likely. To put it another way, Supreme Court decisions are not implemented automatically. They are merely one part of the broader political picture. At best, they can contribute to the process of change. In and of themselves, according to Rosenberg, they accomplish little.

Whether readers find Rosenberg's claims—or, for that matter, those of the other contributors—persuasive depends a great deal on the interpretation of evidence. As I implied earlier, data invoked in this area of inquiry are never quite as clear or clean as we would like. Nor are the analyses particularly simple. But that is precisely why these essays, taken as a whole, are so intriguing. By taking different tacks to address questions relating to the impact of courts, they highlight the key debates in this field and provide much for us, the readers, to contemplate.

15 Media, Knowledge, and Public Evaluations of the Supreme Court

Charles H. Franklin and Liane C. Kosaki

Knowledge is not a prerequisite for opinion. Uninformed opinion runs especially rampant in politics. Our political ideologies, partisanship, and perhaps even personalities predispose us to evaluate policy proposals, candidates, and events in ways consistent with our prior beliefs, even when we know very little about the substance of these phenomena. Sometimes our prior beliefs serve us well, as when a Republican voter assumes that the Democratic candidate is more liberal than the Republican candidate. Most of the time this is true. The assumption by the same Republican voter that the Republican candidate is more honest than the Democrat, more intelligent, or more competent, however, enlarges the room for error substantially. Neither party has a monopoly on honesty, intelligence, or competence, so reliance on predispositions without knowledge can lead to wildly erroneous evaluations. Uninformed opinion may lead us astray.

Public evaluation of the Supreme Court may be particularly open to uninformed opinion. Although the Court is the ultimate arbiter of the law in the United States, it is not the most visible institution. Studies of public opinion often find low public knowledge of the Court. An oft-cited example is a poll that was conducted by the *Washington Post* that found more people could identify Judge Wapner of television's *People's Court* than could identify Chief Justice William H. Rehnquist of the United States Supreme Court (Caldeira 1991a). Beyond the names of the justices, the substance of Court decisions is also frequently beyond the ken of average citizens. Many cases are complex and hence difficult to understand. More important, many of the cases that the Court decides are virtually invisible in the mass media. In 1989 the Court handed down full decisions in 144 cases. Of these, less than a quarter (35 cases, 24 percent) received any network television news coverage, and only 16 (11 percent) were covered on all three networks (Larson and Tramont 1993). With this low level of coverage in a society in which most people get their news from television, it is not surprising that the public lacks intimate familiarity with the decisions of the Court.

This image of massive public ignorance of the Court, however, is misleading. Most cases do remain invisible. But for some cases, the Court and its decisions are as visible, as controversial, and as widely known as any political debate in the nation. *Brown v. Board of*

Education (1954) and *Roe v. Wade* (1973) are only the most extreme examples of decisions that draw the Court into the spotlight of public attention. Other cases, such as those dealing with redistricting, defendant's rights, school prayer, the death penalty, affirmative action, and free speech, often are headline news and become widely known and debated.

What accounts for the differences in levels of awareness among Court decisions? And what are the consequences of these levels of awareness for the public's evaluation of the Supreme Court? The importance of these questions lies in the legitimacy that the Court is able to command from the public. Because the Court has little power to enforce compliance with its decisions, it is left with the power of persuasion, a power that is strongest when its legitimacy is high.[1] If legitimacy is weakened by unpopular decisions, however, greater public knowledge could be damaging to the Court. In contrast, if the public has little awareness of the Court's decisions, then legitimacy should not be much affected.

It should come as no surprise, then, that researchers have given considerable thought to questions concerning public awareness of Court decisions. Some efforts have focused on the role of newspapers and television in determining levels of awareness. These works suggest that although the media may not be able to tell the public what to think, they are important in shaping the public perception of what to think about (see, generally, Iyengar and Kinder 1987). To put it another way, previous work has shown that the media (especially television news) are important players in determining how much the public knows about Court decisions. Other researchers have considered the dynamics of public awareness (Franklin and Kosaki 1991; Franklin, Kosaki, and Kritzer 1993). They have found that those who are most aware of Court decisions are more highly educated and more interested in politics and that public awareness of Court decisions varies greatly. While some cases are the talk of the town, others barely register in the public consciousness. Still, it is not clear what these different levels of awareness signify for evaluations of the Court. On the one hand, the momentousness and consequences of highly visible decisions may be enough to make a lasting impression on the public and influence its evaluations of the Court. On the other, the addition of one more piece of knowledge to already low levels of knowledge about the Court may have little effect on the public's evaluation of the institution.

In this chapter, we examine the factors that influence the public's awareness of Supreme Court decisions, paying special attention to media coverage. We find that although media coverage is a crucial variable, it is not the only one. Media coverage interacts with personal characteristics. We develop and test a model that predicts levels of awareness for different kinds of cases and for individuals. Then we turn our attention to the relation between levels of awareness and evaluations of the Supreme Court.

Factors That Influence the Public's Awareness of Supreme Court Decisions

The media are an obvious influence on the visibility of the decisions of political institutions. The quantity of media coverage serves as an important cue, affecting the public's judgment about which issues are important (Iyengar and Kinder 1987).

Although much of the Court's business is conducted behind the scenes—even oral argument is closed to television cameras—claims about the media's importance apply to our highest judicial body too. The Supreme Court's importance as a national policy maker compels media coverage, and the amount of coverage given to its decisions sends a powerful message to the public about the significance of a case and of the Court's decision.[2] Accordingly, we expect those people who are more active in monitoring the media to be more likely to see news about the Court's decisions. Because television is widely regarded as more influential in this process than the print media, we also expect that exposure to television news plays a more important role than that of print media.

The media, however, do not operate in a vacuum. Although coverage of decisions in the media is important, so is the social environment. Some researchers (Neuman 1990; Sniderman et al. 1975) argue that the type of issue plays a role in determining the extent of public response to media coverage. While some issues receive large amounts of public attention after being covered by the media, others receive very little attention from the public no matter how much coverage the media give them. Thus, although levels of awareness are correlated with levels of media attention, the relation is far from perfect and varies, depending on the type of issue. For example, Neuman (1990) shows that whereas public attention and levels of media coverage are highly correlated for crisis issues like the Vietnam War, issues involving chronic problems like crime show little correlation between media coverage and public attention. We need to consider, then, what other factors besides media coverage might influence levels of awareness.

One such factor is the public reaction to decisions, especially reactions from elites. Some cases bring little reaction from political elites, yet others spawn outcries for constitutional amendments. Although it is true that elites will respond to public reactions to events, in the short run it is their actions that are most likely to promote awareness of a decision in the days following a Court ruling. If elites rally in support of or in opposition to a decision, then the news media will produce stories reporting this reaction. If elite response is muted, continuing coverage of the decision is unlikely. By highlighting the controversy over the Court's decision and thus extending media coverage of the case, elite response increases public awareness.

News reports often evoke different reactions among different demographic groups; thus, a personal characteristic like race or gender may be associated with a predisposition toward an issue. Price and Zaller (1993) find that the extent of recollection of news items differed among a set of "issue publics." Issues had a higher level of salience for those groups that had some personal experience or interest in them. An example of this is a news item on the Stealth bomber, about which, it was found, men remembered more than women (Price and Zaller 1993, 153-155). Thus, higher levels of awareness of a Court decision may be the result of a greater sensitivity to the issue involved, either because of interest, prior media coverage, or social interaction. In sum, different levels of public attention to Supreme Court decisions may be due to many factors: media coverage of the decision, elite response, preexisting personal interest, prior media coverage of the issue involved, and social interaction.

Study Design and Data Sources

In order to study public awareness of the Court and its decisions, we need data on both individuals and on the news coverage of the Court to which they are exposed. The awareness of individuals can be easily measured through surveys, but their exposure to the media is more difficult to capture. Rather than use a national survey, we designed a study of a single metropolitan area, St. Louis, Missouri. The advantage of using a single location is that the media coverage is uniform over the entire population. We can easily determine the coverage of the Court presented by newspaper and television. In a national study, by contrast, we would need data on the media coverage of dozens, if not hundreds, of newspapers. The price we pay is that St. Louis is no more representative of the country as a whole than any other single location. Our interest, however, is not in the level of awareness nationally but rather in the effects of media coverage and of individual characteristics on awareness of Court decisions. For these purposes, national representation is not as important as is the ability to measure media content.

The data for this research were collected in a telephone survey of the St. Louis metropolitan area.[3] A total of 545 interviews were completed. Interviews were conducted from July 10 to July 27, 1989. This period was chosen because it was soon after the Court announced several highly controversial decisions. These decisions, all announced in the last weeks of the Court term, included an important abortion case, *Webster v. Reproductive Health Services* and the highly controversial flag-burning case, *Texas v. Johnson*.[4] Also decided were a significant affirmative action case, *Martin v. Wilks*; a case dealing with the death penalty for minors, *Stanford v. Kentucky*; and *Sable Communications v. FCC*, involving the regulation of so-called "dial-a-porn" services.[5] Despite their importance, however, these cases varied substantially in prominence, in subject matter, and in the news coverage devoted to each.

For the media coverage, we collected all stories carried by the local daily newspaper, the *St. Louis Post-Dispatch*, and the national television network news. We did not collect data on local television news. This is somewhat unfortunate because one of our cases (*Webster v. Reproductive Health Services*) involved a local abortion clinic and the state's attorney general. Local coverage of this decision was substantial. One advantage of our design, however, is that all our respondents were exposed to the same, unmeasured, local coverage. This means that differences we find across individuals cannot be due to differences in the local coverage. Although we may underestimate the total number of stories to which they were exposed, we should not be in danger of confusing these effects with those that most concern us.

News Coverage of the Court

Very few people have direct contact with the Supreme Court and its decisions. Journalists may cover the Court, and lawyers may read some of its decisions, but the vast majority of Americans encounter the Supreme Court only indirectly, through the media or perhaps conversation. How the media cover the Court and how much attention they devote to decisions therefore determine to a significant extent what the citizenry knows about the Court.

One of the peculiarities of the Supreme Court as an institution is that its activity is highly episodic and mostly private. Except on the days when it hears oral argument and the days when it hands down a decision, there is literally nothing to watch. The justices meet in private, they circulate draft opinions in private, and they talk among themselves in private. Political scientists tell us that this is a crucial time of negotiation and decision making (Baum 1992b; Murphy 1964), but because it is private, it is invisible to the media. In contrast, even before it takes a vote, Congress holds hearings, committee and subcommittee meetings, and floor debates; and party leaders and other members make statements, visit the White House, and appear on television interview shows. In comparison with the Supreme Court, Congress is a veritable hotbed of activity. The president is even more visible.

Given these differences in institutional structure and practice, it is not surprising to find that the Supreme Court is much less frequently covered in the media. The consequence of this is nonetheless important. As one of the three branches of the federal government, the Court is co-equal with the president and Congress. Yet it is far from co-equal in visibility and hence in the knowledge that citizens have about it and its decisions.

To compare coverage of the Court with that of the president and Congress, we used the Vanderbilt University Television News Index and Abstract. From January 1989 through July 1990 we coded every news story that involved the president, Congress, or the Court. The number of news stories involving each of these institutions is shown in Figure 15-1.[6]

For each of the nineteen months included in our data, the president received more news coverage than did Congress, which received more than did the Supreme Court. The

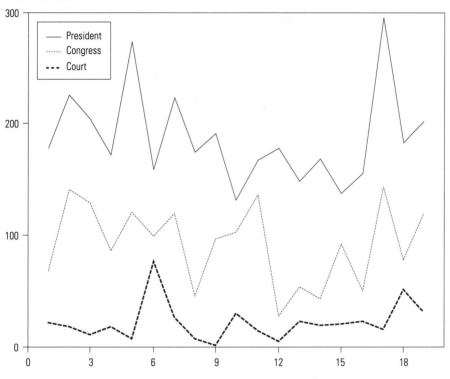

Number of stories

Months from January 1989

Court's coverage peaks in June, when major decisions tend to be handed down. There is also a modest upturn in coverage when the Court begins its term in October. In the nineteen months we studied, there were 3,566 stories about the president, 1,754 about Congress, and only 429 about the Supreme Court.[7] In short, the president receives 8.3 times as much coverage as the Court, and Congress gets 4.1 times as much.

Another way of looking at these data is to consider the average number of stories per day per network. This more closely approximates the typical exposure of citizens, who seldom watch more than one network newscast per day. We find that the president is featured in an average of 2.1 stories per day for each network. Congress appears in an average of 1.0 stories. For the Court the average is 0.25 stories per day. This means that whereas, on average, citizens can expect to see two presidential stories and one congressional story per day, they will wait for four days between Court stories.

Still another way to think about the prominence of stories is to consider the probability that an average citizen goes for a week without seeing any stories about each of the branches of government. For the president and Congress, the probability of not seeing a story in a week is about 1 percent. For the Court, the probability of not seeing a story is 39 percent.[8] Put simply, citizens are virtually guaranteed to see stories about the president and Congress. It is far more likely that a citizen will miss the few stories that appear about the Court.

Coverage of the Court is generally low, but it is substantial during its peak in June. In June 1989 the Court was featured in seventy-seven network news stories. This was higher than for Congress in six of the nineteen months in our data. While this compares the peak of Court coverage with the nadir of congressional visibility, it demonstrates that the Court does, occasionally, reach a visibility level similar to that of Congress, although never close to that of the president. This is in keeping with our argument that the Court is visible only episodically, in contrast to the continuous coverage given the president and the near-continuous coverage afforded Congress. When there is an episode of Court coverage, however, it can become a much more visible institution than it normally is. In the most intensely covered months, media stories about the Court's decisions are very unlikely to be missed. For example, we estimate the probability that the average respondent went for a week in June 1989 without seeing a Court story at only 1.9 percent.

What stands out most clearly from these data is that the Court is not only less likely to be covered than the other branches of the federal government but that the average citizen is far more likely to miss what Court coverage there is. This is not the entire story, however. In keeping with our argument for the episodic coverage of the Court, we find that when the Court is particularly visible, it begins to rival the other branches in prominence and the likelihood that citizens will be exposed to news about it. This seeming paradox is now clear: the Court is often ignored and invisible, but at times it becomes quite visible indeed. Thus, citizens may know little about the Court in general, yet be exposed to quite a lot of news about it in a short period of time.

The cases in June and July 1989 dealt with abortion, flag burning, affirmative action, the death penalty, and regulation of pornography. We chose these cases to study in particular because we expected them to vary in the coverage they received and in the knowledge citizens had about them.

In Table 15-1 we show the number of stories and prominence of coverage for the five cases from June 1 through July 31. There are modest differences in coverage between newspaper and television. These differences, however, are not of major concern here. Rather, we are most concerned with the level of coverage. Of these cases, the abortion and flag-burning cases received the highest coverage, from three to seven times as much as the other three cases. The three less visible cases, received little coverage, making it much more likely that citizens would fail to hear of these decisions.

Table 15-1 Coverage of Five Supreme Court Decisions, June-July 1989

Case content	Newspaper		Television	
	Number of stories	Prominence of stories [a]	Number of stories	Prominence of stories (minutes)
Abortion	36	62	31	82.8
Flag burning	20	29	37	76.0
Affirmative action	6	10	5	8.8
Death penalty	3	5	5	11.7
Dial-a-porn	2	4	3	6.3

[a] Front page story = 3; story on first page of inner section = 2; story on inner page = 1.

Not only is the total amount of coverage given to a decision important, but the frequency with which stories appear matters as well. A story that is carried by the news on five successive nights is likely to reach a wider audience than if all five stories were run on a single night. If news is concentrated into a single day, the probability that an average citizen misses it is 49 percent. If the news is spread over five days, the probability that it is missed entirely is just 3 percent.[9]

The number of days that at least one network news show carried a story about these decisions is presented in Table 15-2, as is the estimated probability that an average citizen would fail to see a story on the case. It is virtually certain that a citizen with average television news viewing habits would be exposed to at least one story on each of the two more visible cases. It is considerably more likely that stories on affirmative action and the death penalty would be missed, and it is very likely that the dial-a-porn decision would be missed.

The amount of coverage of each case by network news and by the *St. Louis Post-Dispatch* is shown in Figure 15-2. Both the abortion and flag-burning cases received very prominent coverage and this coverage continued through the month following the decision. This is in striking contrast to the other three decisions. Each of these received coverage on the day of the decision (or in the newspaper on the following day) but very little thereafter. Even what little followed was spread over a considerable period of time rather than the day or two following the decision.

The abortion and flag-burning cases differ slightly in their pattern of coverage. The abortion decision received immediate and extraordinarily high coverage. Even at its height, the flag case received barely half of the maximum of the abortion coverage on television and even less in the newspaper. Another difference is the pattern of flag coverage compared with that for abortion. The abortion coverage peaks immediately after the deci-

Table 15-2 Days of Coverage and Probability of Missing All Coverage of Five Supreme Court Decisions

Case content	Number of days stories aired	Probability of missing all coverage (percent)
Abortion	12	0.02
Flag burning	16	0.001
Affirmative action	3	11.5
Death penalty	3	11.5
Dial-a-porn	1	48.6

sion and then declines steadily thereafter. The peak in the flag case, in contrast, doesn't come until about a week after the decision, when there is a new upturn in coverage. This surge occurred when President Bush called for a constitutional amendment banning the desecration of the flag and was followed by presidential and congressional newsmaking about this issue. Judging from the pattern of coverage in the first week following the decision, it seems likely that the flag issue would have vanished from the news almost as quickly as did the affirmative action decision. What reenergized the issue was the reaction of political elites, in this case the president and Congress. The lesson to be learned from this is that even controversial and unpopular decisions, such as the flag-burning case, are likely to vanish quickly from the media unless they provoke sustained elite reaction. By the same token, elites can keep some Court decisions on the media's agenda if they sustain a reaction.

To summarize, the Court is generally covered much less than the president and Congress. When it renders major decisions, however, it is possible for the Court to receive substantial coverage, although for most cases the coverage is over a fairly short span of time. Coverage varies considerably across cases, both in the amount of coverage and in the frequency with which stories appear. Both the total number of stories and their repetition over a period of days are likely to be important elements in the public's awareness of the Court and its actions.

Individual Awareness of Decisions

We have seen that media coverage differs across cases, but we have not yet considered individuals' awareness of decisions. It is entirely possible, for example, that an individual is exposed to media coverage of a decision yet fails to remember the decision later. In the previous section, we estimated the likelihood that individuals were exposed to stories but did not consider how probable it was that they remembered this exposure. Thus, while exposure to news coverage is a necessary condition for awareness, it is not sufficient. Here we turn to our survey data on individual citizens to examine their knowledge of Supreme Court decisions.

Whether a citizen knows about a decision depends both on characteristics of the individual and on characteristics of the case. Citizens who are interested in politics and who pay close attention to the media, for example, are more likely to know of Court decisions than are those who are uninterested and who do not watch the news or read the papers. By the same token, cases that become highly visible in the media and may become the topic of conversation are much more likely to be known to citizens, even inattentive ones, than are cases that receive little coverage. Finally, there may be complex interactions between individual characteristics and the nature of the cases. For example, members of groups who are directly affected by a decision may be more likely to hear of that case than are those not so affected.

In this section we estimate a model of awareness of Court decisions. This model allows for both differences across cases and across individuals.[10] From this we can see how much each affects citizen awareness. The statistical model includes the individual-level effects of age, religion, race, sex, education, political conversations, television news viewing, and newspaper readership. The model also incorporates the effects of case coverage in the news, both television and newspaper, plus any other factors unique to each case.[11] We use the models to estimate the probability that each individual in our sample is aware of the Court's decision on each of the five cases. For the technically minded reader, the estimated coefficients are presented in the Table 15-3. But, in general, our focus is on the predicted probabilities. These probabilities show us the distribution of awareness of the cases, some citizens being unlikely to have heard of a case whereas others are nearly certain to know of the decision.

In Figure 15-3 we show the distribution of probability of awareness for each case. The average awareness of each case is indicated by the vertical line in each figure. The spread of the distribution around this average shows how much variation in awareness there is. If the characteristics of the case were the most important determinant of awareness, and individual characteristics played little role, the distribution would be tightly packed around the average awareness. Alternatively, if case characteristics mattered very little, the distributions would all appear similar and the average awareness would be the same for all cases.

What we see in this figure is that both case and individual characteristics matter quite a lot. Each distribution has a substantial spread, showing that individual characteristics matter. But the medians of the distributions (indicated by the vertical line) also move from left

Figure 15-2 Comparison of News Coverage for Selected Public Issues

St. Louis Post-Dispatch Coverage

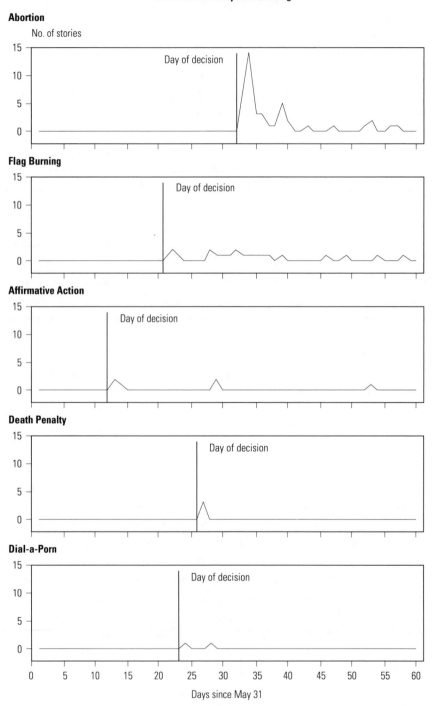

Days since May 31

Figure 15-2 Comparison of News Coverage for Selected Public Issues *(continued)*

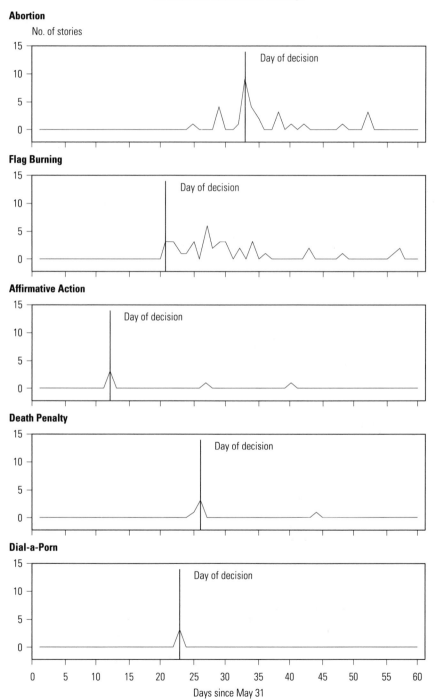

Network Television News Coverage

Figure 15-3 Distribution of Awareness: Comparisons of Selected Public Issues

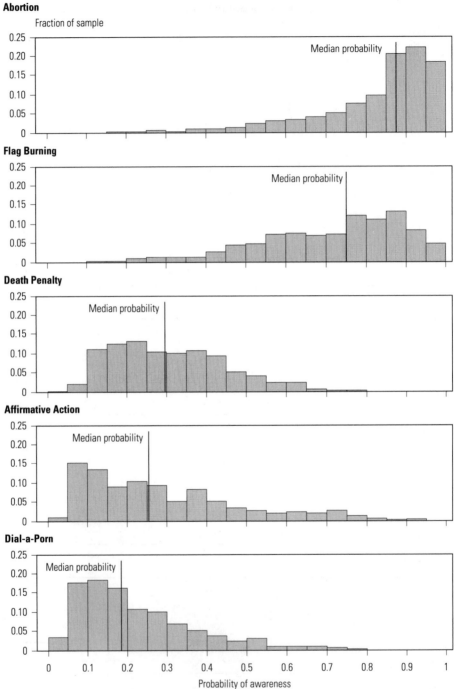

Table 15-3 Estimated Models of Awareness (Logit Estimates)

Individual characteristics	Abortion	Flag burning	Affirmative action	Death penalty	Dial-a-porn
Constant	0.276	−1.191	−3.782*	−3.002*	−4.716*
	(0.860)	(0.730)	(0.755)	(0.698)	(0.822)
Age	−0.029*	−0.009	0.010	−0.001	0.005
	(0.009)	(0.007)	(0.008)	(0.007)	(0.008)
Catholic	0.428	−0.200	−0.291	0.358	−0.543*
	(0.294)	(0.230)	(0.238)	(0.214)	(0.258)
Nonwhite	−0.931*	−1.059*	0.450	0.338	−0.086
	(0.319)	(0.277)	(0.290)	(0.271)	(0.310)
Female	−0.075	−0.349	−0.899*	−0.506*	−0.112
	(0.267)	(0.221)	(0.219)	(0.203)	(0.231)
Years of school	0.177*	0.159*	0.134*	0.097*	0.162*
	(0.052)	(0.044)	(0.043)	(0.041)	(0.047)
Political talk	0.348*	0.278*	0.297*	0.104*	0.186*
	(0.093)	(0.072)	(0.054)	(0.050)	(0.053)
TV news watching	0.012	0.066	0.037	0.109*	0.157*
	(0.051)	(0.043)	(0.044)	(0.041)	(0.047)
Newspaper readership	−0.010	0.072	0.116*	0.102*	0.053
	(0.048)	(0.040)	(0.040)	(0.038)	(0.043)

Note: Standard errors are in parentheses.

* $p < .05$.

to right as we go from abortion to dial-a-porn. This shift shows that the average awareness differs substantially across cases, demonstrating that the effect of case characteristics is also quite substantial.

This set of cases illustrates the range of different public responses to Court decisions. The least visible case, dial-a-porn, has the low average probability of awareness of 0.18, and the great majority of people in our sample have a low (less than 0.30) probability of recalling the decision. The distribution is concentrated at the low awareness end of the graph, with a skew to the right. This indicates that although most people are quite unlikely to hear of this case, there are some who are considerably more likely to know of it. Some people pay close enough attention to the Court to be aware of even its less visible cases.

The affirmative action case shows the average awareness shifting a little to the right, to 0.24, while also evincing a much more spread-out distribution. While the average awareness is only a little more than for the pornography case, there are quite a few more people with a predicted probability over 0.50. The greater spread is also due to some shifts in who responds to news about this decision. Both minorities and men are more sensitive to news about affirmative action, and this contributes to greater variation in the effect of individual characteristics.

The death penalty distribution is shifted more to the right and also begins to approach symmetry. While still skewed a bit to the right, it is not nearly so skewed as the previous two cases. For decisions with an average probability of awareness of about 0.50, we might expect a roughly symmetric distribution, with about as many less likely than average to be aware as more likely. None of our actual cases is very close to this evenly balanced awareness, so we must extrapolate from the pattern of the cases we do observe.

The flag-burning and abortion cases show that it is possible for large portions of the public to be very likely to be aware of some Court decisions. The median probability for the flag case is 0.75, whereas for the abortion case it is 0.88. These are very high rates of awareness. What is more, the skew of the distributions is now reversed from that of the other three cases. Here, the bulk of cases is concentrated on the aware end of the scale. In the first three cases, it was unusual to find people who were very likely to be aware of the decisions. In the cases of flag burning and abortion this is reversed: it is unusual to be unaware of the cases.

The most important conclusion from these results is that there is substantial variation in awareness of Supreme Court decisions, both from case to case and across individuals. This demonstrates that when a case becomes highly visible, as the abortion and flag cases were, public awareness can become very high. This contrasts with the image of the Court as a nearly invisible institution. Sometimes it is, as the dial-a-porn case demonstrates. But it can also be highly visible, as the abortion and flag cases show. Citizens, therefore, do not receive a complete picture of the Court. They are much more likely to become aware of controversial issues that produce substantial and continued media coverage, while remaining ignorant of most other decisions. Only those most consistently interested in politics and the Court are likely to know of the full range of its work and decisions. As we shall see, this has some important consequences for what they think of the Court.

The Effect of Media Coverage on Awareness

While we found substantial differences among cases in the previous section, we did not estimate the effect of media coverage per se. In this section we turn to this task. For each of our five cases, most media coverage, both television and newspaper, had ended by the time we conducted our interviews in mid-July. For the abortion and flag cases, a handful of stories appeared during interviewing, but not enough to estimate their effect reliably. Despite this, we can estimate the effect of coverage on awareness by pooling the five cases. To do this, we count the number of stories carried on network newscasts and in the newspaper up to the day we interviewed each respondent. By including these counts of news stories in our model of individual awareness and pooling all cases, we can estimate the effect of each story on knowledge of decisions.[12]

As shown in Table 15-1, actual media coverage ranges from a low of two stories in the newspaper to a high of thirty-seven stories on network television. The coverage is also quite highly correlated: both television and newspapers gave high coverage to abortion and flag burning and low coverage to the other three cases (although television gave noticeably more coverage to the flag case than did the newspaper). In our estimates below, we consider a range of coverage from none to forty stories. We assume that for each newspaper story there is a television story and vice versa. By this assumption, we ignore the differences between cases and simplify coverage patterns in order to clarify the effects. Because the effect of newspaper and television stories is similar, and because coverage is highly correlated between media, this is not a drastic simplification.

The statistical estimates of the model are presented in Table 15-4. Both newspaper and television stories exert a statistically significant influence on awareness. As coverage rises, so does awareness. The effect of newspaper stories appears slightly higher than that for television news. This comparison should be treated cautiously, however, because of the differences in exposure to the newspaper and to television. A story broadcast by one network is not seen by viewers of other networks, whereas a newspaper story has a broader potential audience in a one-newspaper town such as St. Louis.

To understand the magnitude of these effects, consider a person who has a 0.50 chance of knowing of a decision, based on his or her individual characteristics. The effect of one additional newspaper story leads to a change in the probability of awareness from 0.50 to 0.516.[13] For a television news story, the effect is somewhat less, a change of about 0.01, from 0.50 to 0.51. These shifts may seem very small, but it is important to remember that this is the marginal effect of a single story. A string of ten such stories would produce a cumulative effect about ten times as large.

A better way to visualize the effect of news stories is to consider the probability that an average person will become aware of a decision across the range of possible news coverage. In Figure 15-4 we plot the predicted probability of awareness of a Court decision against the possible number of news stories. We use the range of zero to forty stories, since this is roughly the range observed in our data. Arguably, the flag and abortion cases represent near highwater marks for coverage of Court decisions, so we would not expect many decisions to receive more coverage than forty stories. The figure also assumes that both newspaper and television carry the same number of stories, so forty stories means forty in each medium.

It can be seen in Figure 15-4 that the effect of combined newspaper and television news coverage can be very great indeed. For the least-covered cases, the average citizen has a less

Table 15-4 Estimated Media Effects on Awareness
(Logit Estimates)

Independent variables	Estimated effect
Constant	−3.800
	(0.346)
Newspaper coverage	0.066*
	(0.009)
Television coverage	0.041*
	(0.007)
Age	−0.005
	(0.003)
Catholic	−0.042
	(0.104)
Nonwhite	−0.240
	(0.132)
Female	−0.378*
	(0.098)
Years of school	0.138*
	(0.020)
Political talk	0.218*
	(0.026)
TV news watching	0.079*
	(0.020)
Newspaper readership	0.073*
	(0.018)

Note: Standard errors are in parentheses.   * $p < .05$.

than 0.20 chance of having heard of the decision. As coverage rises, so does awareness. The grid in the figure shows the number of stories required to reach 0.25, 0.50, 0.75, and 0.90 probability of awareness. Four stories are sufficient to produce a 0.25 probability of awareness. Fourteen stories boosts this to 0.50. And twenty-four stories will reach about 0.75 of average citizens. After this point, it becomes increasingly difficult to raise awareness. Between 0.25 and 0.75 awareness, it takes about ten stories to raise awareness by 0.25. This accords with our estimates of the marginal effect above, where we estimated an effect of $0.016 + 0.01 = 0.26$ per newspaper and television story combined, as we find here. Above 0.75, increases in coverage affect awareness levels less and less. An increase from twenty-four to thirty-five stories raises awareness from 0.75 to 0.90, a 0.15 change. This is to be expected. News coverage has a declining marginal effect that is especially noticeable at high levels of awareness.

Figure 15-4   Effect of News Coverage on Awareness of Court Decisions

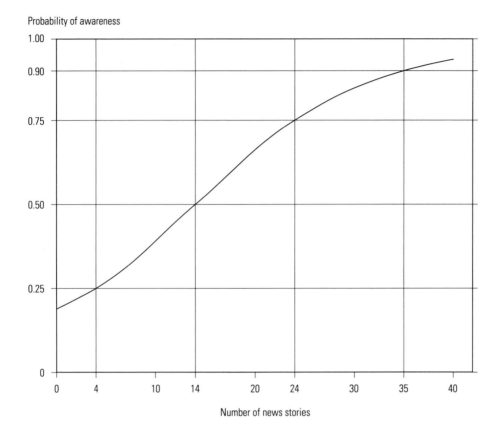

Probability of awareness

Number of news stories

Our estimates show that media coverage of the Supreme Court is a key determinant of what people know of its decisions. For the very low levels of coverage that are typical of most decisions, less than a quarter of the population should be expected to know that the Court has done anything at all. Knowledge of cases receiving low coverage is based on the individual's interest in public affairs and close attention to what little news is reported. For those less interested or less attentive to news, the likelihood of awareness of decisions is small. Thus, for run-of-the-mill cases, which receive little coverage, awareness is concentrated in a very unrepresentative fraction of the public. As media coverage rises, however, awareness spreads rather quickly. If there are slightly more than a dozen stories, awareness is predicted to reach half of the population.

It is important to put "a dozen stories" in perspective. That amounts to just four stories on each of the three networks, and a dozen stories in the newspaper (which might carry a couple per day). Viewed in this light, a modest amount of coverage can enlighten a substantial fraction of the public. Still, this is more than twice the coverage devoted to the affirmative action and death penalty decisions. When a major decision, such as the abortion case, is handed down, the media devotes far more coverage to the case. In this circumstance, quite substantial proportions of the public are likely to become aware of the decision.

Knowledge and Evaluation of the Supreme Court

Democratic government rests on the support of the public. In the case of the Supreme Court, which is unelected and unaccountable to the public, trust and approval are especially important. If the Court is seen as acting against the wishes of the public, its stability as an institution is threatened. In extreme cases, such lack of support can lead to attempts to force the Court to respond, as in President Franklin Roosevelt's Court-packing plan of the 1930s. Yet the Court is also a political body. Its members are appointed by presidents and approved by the Senate in a process that has become increasingly politicized in recent years. And the actions of the Court are inherently entangled with political ideology. Issues such as affirmative action and abortion carry strong ideological meanings. When the Court deals with such cases, it necessarily chooses among ideologically charged alternatives. It is therefore to be expected that a citizen's judgments of the Court should depend on the ideological leanings of the citizen and the perceived direction of the Court. In other words, those who find that the Court's decisions are compatible with their own ideological preferences are more likely to view the Court favorably.

Our results on media coverage and individual awareness, however, imply that not all citizens are equally knowledgeable about the Court's actions and the tenor of its decisions. The episodic nature of Court decisions and the irregular coverage it receives means that substantial portions of the public will fail to hear of many decisions. The high coverage given a few cases means that those that are most visible will constitute a biased sample of the Court's decisions. And differences in awareness across citizens means that some will judge the Court on the basis of far greater information than will others.

Those who are most interested in the Court are likely to have up-to-date information about its actions and decisions. We would expect their evaluations of the Court to be based on reasonably accurate perceptions of the ideological cast of recent Court decisions. As we move toward those who have less interest in the Court, however, we expect two things to occur. First, there should be less information. Second, what information exists is likely to be a combination of relatively old knowledge and some newly acquired perceptions. Whereas the knowledgeable are able to discard old information because they know how the Court has changed, the less informed are less able to distinguish relevant from irrelevant information. Having once thought the Court to be liberal, they have less ability to know when it has turned in a conservative direction, for example.

The Reagan years had a substantial effect on the composition of the Court and on its ideological balance. The liberal activist majority of the Warren Court of the 1960s was eroded under Nixon, yet Nixon's Burger Court retained a generally liberal majority. Reagan's appointments finished what Nixon had started, producing a solid conservative majority and a substantial shift in the Court's decisions. We would expect that conservative citizens who were familiar with the Court would recognize this shift and evaluate the Court more favorably than would equally knowledgeable liberals. For those who are less knowledgeable about the Court, we would expect this relationship to be much less sharp. And among those least well informed, we would expect considerable confusion, with images and evaluations resting on long-outdated notions of the Court and its behavior.

To examine these possible effects, we stratify our sample from least knowledgeable to most knowledgeable, based on the average probability of awareness of the five decisions we have examined. We then compare the least knowledgeable 25 percent of the sample with the middle 50 percent and the most knowledgeable 25 percent. If our expectations are met, we would expect the top 25 percent to have the most accurate perceptions, and the lowest 25 percent to exhibit reactions to the Court that are substantially out of touch with the current behavior of the Court.

We also constructed a conservatism scale, based on the probability that a respondent calls him- or herself a "conservative" as opposed to a moderate or a liberal. The predicted probability is constructed from an ordered logit model of the three-point ideology scale. The regressors were the same demographic variables used in the awareness model. Predicted values range from near zero to 0.80. To measure evaluation of the Supreme Court, we use a 100-point "feeling thermometer." This question asks the respondent to rate the Court on a scale of 0 to 100, where 100 means the respondent feels very warm or favorable to the Court, 0 means the respondent feels very cool or unfavorable, and 50 indicates neither warm nor cool feelings. We regress the feeling thermometer score on conservatism for the low-, medium-, and high-knowledge groups in the sample. The results are shown in Figure 15-5. The coefficients for conservatism are -9.1, 18.5, and 51.2 for the low-, medium-, and high-information groups, respectively. Similar results also hold for an alternative measure of evaluation based on whether the respondent has a great deal of confidence in the Court to do what is right. We use the feeling thermometer because of its more intuitive scale.

Among the quarter of the population least likely to know about Court decisions, liberals are more approving of the Court, whereas conservatives are more disapproving. The difference amounts to about 9 points on the 100-point feeling thermometer. As we move up the level of awareness of the Court, this pattern reverses. The middle group shows a posi-

Figure 15-5 Predicted Evaluation of the Supreme Court Among Low-, Medium-, and High-Information Respondents

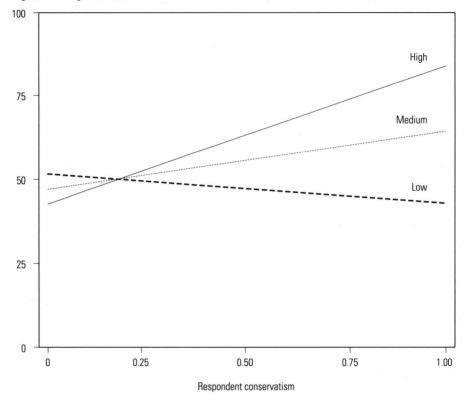

Degrees on feeling thermometer

tive relationship between conservatism and approval. For the middle 50 percent of our sample, conservatives were 18.5 points more approving of the Court than were liberals. Also, liberals rated the court slightly below 50 on the thermometer. This shows a closer connection between ideology and evaluation, and one that is more reflective of the Court as it stood in 1989. But it is the most knowledgeable 25 percent of the sample who show the most powerful effects of information. Among these people, conservatives are an amazing 51 points more favorable to the Court than are liberals. The most liberal citizen is expected to rate the Court at just 38 degrees on the feeling thermometer, whereas the most conservative person is expected to place the Court at 89 degrees. This disparity shows how great the differences in perception of the Court can be when citizens are well informed of its actions.

Citizens are free to hold any evaluation of the Court that suits them. But we have seen that when these judgments are based on a combination of little information and outdated information, it can lead to incorrect assessments. In contrast, informed citizens are far more accurate in their assessments and recognize the changes that have taken place on the Court. We have also seen that evaluations of the Court are closely tied to the respondents' ideological preferences and to the shifting nature of the Court. Those who judge the Court based on substantial information are far more accurate in their assessments, while those relying on meager stores of information actually work against their own preferences.

Conclusion

The story of public awareness of the decisions of the Supreme Court is complex. It is full of qualifications. Although citizens are generally unaware of the Court's decisions, given the right circumstances public knowledge of a decision can be quite high. Clearly, media coverage of decisions plays a crucial part in influencing levels of awareness, but it must filter through a mesh of the personal characteristics of the individual. Finally, levels of public awareness of the Court's decisions affect public evaluation of the Court.

Although knowledge is not a prerequisite to opinion, it is a prerequisite to accurate opinion. The significance of this observation can be seen if we consider that evaluations of the Court rely on an understanding of the current patterns of the Court's decisions. Those who follow the Court can accurately gauge its direction, and that assessment is reflected in their evaluations of how warmly they feel toward the Court. This finding raises the question of how the Court's ability to persuade the public of the legitimacy of its decisions is affected by the accurate perception of its decisions. Does the knowledgeable citizen become cynical and conclude that the Court follows the election returns?

More important, we have found some evidence here that the public's evaluation of the Court responds to their awareness of the substance of Court decisions. This suggests that the dynamics of the public's evaluations of the Supreme Court may be much like those for Congress and the presidency. Thus, the stability of the Court's evaluations over time may be a function of insufficient knowledge rather than an enduring level of trust in what seems to be a Jovian institution (Redlawsk and Lau 1994). If this is so, then we might well wonder if greater awareness of the Court would result in more volatile evaluations and more problems of enforcement and compliance for an institution whose major currency is legitimacy.

Notes

1. For more on compliance with Court decisions, see Chapters 16 and 17.
2. The media may be important channels of information, but their reporting of Court action

has generally been criticized rather than praised. Early on, Newland (1967) expressed concern about the quality and accuracy of coverage of the Court. And these problems persist despite efforts to increase reporters' qualifications (Shaw 1981; Slotnick and Segal 1992). Katsh's (1983) analysis of network newscasts indicated that coverage was highly selective, with only about 20 percent of the Court's decisions receiving network news coverage, even though the amount of coverage differed little among the networks. In his examination of television coverage of the decision in *Regents v. Bakke* (1978)—which held that absent a history of racial discrimination, affirmative action programs that set quotas for particular racial or ethnic groups violate the Constitution but that minority status may play a role in the admissions process—Slotnick (1991) notes that the coverage failed to put the case in historical context, tended to take a "win-lose" approach that was not appropriate to the complexity of the case outcome, and presented the facts of the case selectively.

3. The sample used random digit dialing with clustering within residential central office codes. Objective respondent selection was used throughout, allowing no substitutions. Up to ten callbacks were made in an attempt to complete an interview. No refusal conversion was attempted, however. The response rate, based on the total number of working numbers drawn, was 48 percent.

4. In *Webster*, the Court upheld a Missouri law, which, among other restrictions, required viability testing and barred public employees from performing abortions. The Court did not, however, overturn *Roe v. Wade*, as it was widely expected to do. In *Johnson*, the Court struck down, on First Amendment grounds, a Texas law that prohibited the desecration of the American flag.

5. In *Martin*, the Court held that white firefighters, who argued that they were denied promotions in favor of less qualified blacks, could challenge the employment practices, even though they had not participated in earlier proceedings. In *Stanford*, the Court held that the Constitution does not prohibit imposition of the death penalty for those who committed crimes when they were sixteen or seventeen years old. In *Sable Communications*, the Court ruled that Congress could prohibit obscene telephone messages but not adult access to messages that were indecent but not obscene.

6. The January 1989 count of presidential stories is actually a count of the number of stories concerning George Bush, who was not sworn in as president until January 21. The coverage of outgoing President Reagan was somewhat lower. We also noticed that a large number of congressional stories in February and March of 1989 concerned the confirmation of President Bush's cabinet nominees. Except for these instances, the coverage does not seem to be affected by unusual events or special circumstances. We concluded our coding at the end of July 1990 because the Iraqi invasion of Kuwait in August produced a huge upturn in presidential coverage.

7. Our count includes stories that mention more than one institution. For example, if the president comments on a Court decision, this story is counted in the total for both president and Court.

8. This calculation is based on the average viewership of television news and the number of stories carried. The respondents in our St. Louis survey watched an average of 3.6 television newscasts per week. This implies a probability of 0.514 of watching the news each evening. The probability that the president and Congress will be covered on the evening news is near 1.0, while for the Court the probability is about 0.247. If we assume that the probability of watching is independent of the content of the news (an assumption that is not entirely correct but good enough for purposes of illustration), then the probability of seeing a story on any single day is the product of the probability of watching the news times the probability that a story is carried. For the Court, this gives 0.514 x 0.247 = 0.127. The probability of going a week without seeing any story on the court is $(1—0.127)7 = 0.39$ (assuming that each night's news content is independent of each other night's content). We've cheated a little in these calculations by ignoring the fact that sometimes the Court may be featured in more than one story in a single night. The effect of this is to overestimate the probability that the Court appears and to underestimate the probability that a viewer goes a week without seeing a Court story. Our estimate of 39 percent is therefore a conservative estimate.

9. We estimate that the chance an average citizen watches the evening news is 0.514. The chance that such a person misses news that is on for k nights is $(1 - 0.514)k$, again assuming independence between viewing and news content.

10. The model we estimate is a logit model in which the dependent variable is a dichotomous indicator of awareness of a decision (for more on logit models, see Appendix B of this volume). We estimate five such models, one for each case. This allows for variation in coefficients across cases; for example, minorities may be more sensitive to affirmative action or death penalty cases than to dial-a-porn. It also incorporates differences in media coverage through the intercept term, which estimates the level of awareness when all independent variables are equal to zero. Since coverage is a constant within each case, these effects are absorbed by the intercept and are not otherwise identifiable. Later we pool cases to allow estimation of the effect of media on knowledge. The results presented in the text are predicted probabilities from each of these models. The full models are presented in Table 15-3.

11. All of these case-specific effects are captured in the intercept for each model. They are not directly measured and included in the estimation.

12. In pooling the cases, we also restrict the individual characteristics to have constant effects across all cases. This constraint simplifies estimation and should have very little consequence for our estimates of media effects, our central concern in this section.

13. In this calculation we use the marginal effect evaluated at a probability of awareness of 0.50. The formula is $dP / dx = \beta_x P(1 - P)$. For $P = 0.50$ this is simply $\beta_x / 4$. For newspaper stories, $\beta_x = 0.066$. For TV news stories, $\beta_x = 0.041$.

16 Do Court Decisions Matter?

Lauren Bowen

In the case of *Bates v. State Bar of Arizona* (1977), the U.S. Supreme Court held that the First Amendment precluded an absolute ban on the advertising of legal services. In so doing, it struck down regulations explicitly banning all advertising activity by lawyers. This decision followed *Bigelow v. Virginia* (1975) and *Virginia State Board of Pharmacy v. Virginia Citizens Consumer Council* (1976), in which the Supreme Court held that economic or commercial speech was worthy of constitutional protection.

These cases and others pertaining to professional advertising, in particular, highlight a significant question about the impact of government decisions.[1] In *Bates* there was no mandate by the government; no particular behavior was being demanded of lawyers. Rather, the Court gave attorneys the choice of whether or not to advertise their services, which was an option that had not previously existed. Of course, the Court's majority (*Bates*, 1977, 378) thought that lawyers would take advantage of the policy change because it could increase their visibility and, presumably, increase their client base and profits. But was the Court right?

My aim in this chapter is to explore and explain the impact of *Bates* on lawyers, the group most directly affected by the decision. My fundamental question is why did members of some law firms take advantage of *Bates* and begin to advertise their services whereas others did not? Or, to put it more generally, can we explain why some members of the target population of a Court decision alter their attitudes and behaviors in light of a shift in the legal status quo and others do not?

By addressing these questions, I hope to shed light on the relevance of judicial action for those most directly affected by the rendering of judicial decisions. To this end, I invoke attitudinal theory to generate expectations about the impact of *Bates* on the advertising practices of attorneys. I then examine the size and nature of the impact of *Bates* on lawyers, with the goal of explaining why some took advantage of the decision and others did not.

This research was supported by National Science Foundation Grant 8907008. The author would like to thank Kevin Snape for his comments on earlier drafts of this chapter and Bradley Canon and James Garand for their assistance over the course of this project.

Figure 16-1 Populations Affected by Judicial Decisions

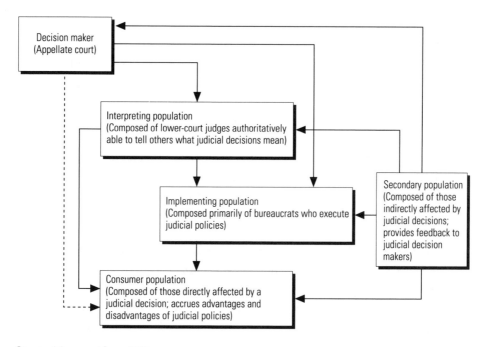

Source: Johnson and Canon 1984.

Attitude Theory

Johnson and Canon (1984) provide a useful framework by which to organize information about judicial impact. They delineate four populations that are potentially affected by them: interpreters, implementers, consumers, and secondary populations.

Consumers make up the population that is perhaps most neglected by researchers of the impact of judicial decisions. Defined as those most directly affected by a judicial decision, consumers are an ever-shifting population, given the variety of judicial policies. The responses of this population, then, need to be gauged to assess the extent to which policies made by the judiciary influence the behavior of those targeted by judicial decisions. As Canon (1982b, 21) has noted, "consumption is the ultimate measure of impact."

There is evidence to suggest that those most directly affected by a judicial decision do not always change their behavior in the wake of the policy change (see Bond and Johnson 1982; Levine 1973). Why do some potential consumers become actual consumers and others do not?

Answering this question requires an acknowledgment of the differences in the nature of judicial policies. Some policies provide members of the target population with choices but require a behavioral adjustment. I call this "mandatory choice." For example, consumers of busing decisions (parents of school-age children) had to decide whether to have their children bused to public schools or place their children in schools not subject to the busing order. Maintaining the status quo was not an option. Mandatory choice can be contrasted with "voluntary consumption." This occurs when judicial rulings (such as that in *Bates*) give the target population (such as attorneys, who fall under the ruling in *Bates*) the choice of doing nothing or of altering their behavior.

When judicial decisions fall into the category of voluntary consumption, it makes sense to gauge the attitudes of consumers and then assess the influence of those attitudes on behavior.[2] Attitudes may play *the* determinant role in explaining whether a behavioral change occurs because if there is no behavioral mandate and if the option of doing nothing exists, there are no structural forces (for example, a legal requirement to act) to undermine one's beliefs.

The proposition underlying the attitudinal framework is that reactions to the substance of the policy decision in question should have a substantial effect on one's reaction to a judicial decision. In the context of my study, attorneys favoring a ban on advertising are deemed to have negative attitudes toward advertising, whereas those opposing a ban are said to be more tolerant of advertising. Thus, the attitudinal approach generates the expectation that those favoring a ban will be less likely to advertise than will those in opposition to a ban on the advertising of legal services.

Although the idea that attitudes predict behavior seems obvious and intuitive, the evidence about the effect of attitudes on consumption of judicial decisions is mixed. Among those finding their influence consequential are Levine (1973), who argued that the attitudes of booksellers influenced their decision to stock sexually explicit materials, and Bond and Johnson (1982), who found that whether or not a hospital provided nontherapeutic abortions was primarily a function of the preferences of hospital administrators. Yet Milner (1971) found that although a vast majority of police officers disagreed with the holding in *Miranda v. Arizona* (1966), they complied with it.[3] Along the same lines, Giles and Gatlin (1980) suggest that costs and benefits shaped responses to school-busing decisions, even though attitudes may have shaped the willingness of consumers to accept busing as a policy.

Perhaps the conflicting results are attributable to the difference in settings. Milner (1971) and Giles and Gatlin (1980) were looking at a mandatory choice situation, whereas Levine (1973) and Bond and Johnson (1982) were concerned with voluntary consumption. Given that *Bates* falls into the voluntary consumption category, it seems appropriate to expect that the attitudes of lawyers about the propriety of advertising their services will influence their response to the choices provided in *Bates*.

Data

To explore this expectation, I needed to gauge the response of lawyers, the consumers, to the decision in *Bates*. To this end, I mailed a survey questionnaire to the senior partner (someone equipped to speak on behalf of the firm) of small law firms located in the states of Illinois, Kentucky, Louisiana, and Massachusetts between November 1988 and March 1989.[4] One of the questions asked was whether the firm was currently advertising its services; others were designed to ascertain why some firms advertise their services and others do not. Of the 1,780 lawyers to whom I mailed the survey, 797 lawyers (or 44 percent) responded.

Measuring Attitudes

At the outset, I should note one potential problem with exploring the impact of attitudes on behavior. It is impossible to prove definitively any theory of human behavior. The best we can hope to do is present evidence that links theory and behavior in a way that suggests that the theory (here, attitudinal theory) explains behavior (here, lawyer advertising). Linking attitudes and behaviors, then, is dependent on some key assumptions. For example, I assume that lawyers' attitudes (the independent variables—or factors that I think explain the variation in attorney response to *Bates*) influence whether or not they advertise legal services (the dependent variable) and not vice versa. That means that I am predicting that attorneys' attitudes about advertising shape their behavior—and not that advertising behavior, which is caused by some other reason, leads to certain attitudes about advertising. But because I gathered all my data at one point in time rather than tracking attorneys' attitudes for several years and then tracking attorneys' advertising behavior, I am looking at attitudes and behaviors simultaneously. So I must assume—with some evidence to support me—that attitudes exist independently of the behavior in question.

But I do more than assume. To demonstrate that attitudes about advertising are not a function of whether one advertises, I use my survey responses and consider (1) whether the issue is still salient and attitudes do, in fact, continue to vary across the legal profession and (2) whether attitudes appear to be strongly held. The results of this analysis indicate that the attitudes exist independently of whether or not attorneys chose to advertise.

Salience of Advertising and Variation in Attitudes

Perhaps the most useful question I asked of respondents to gauge their attitude toward the concept of legal services advertising was, "Do you favor or oppose a ban on advertising?" Sixty-three percent of those asked favored a ban on lawyer advertising, whereas 34 percent opposed a ban; 3 percent did not respond. Some respondents suggested that al-

Table 16-1 Attitudes about the Propriety of Advertising in the Legal Profession, from Survey

Survey statement	Agree		Disagree	
	N	%	N	%
The law is a profession, not a trade, and advertising should be banned.	454	57	328	41
The public is ill-equipped to evaluate lawyer advertising.	530	67	252	32
Lawyer advertising provides useful information to the public.	162	21	620	78
Advertising by lawyers is inherently misleading.	266	34	515	65
Advertising by lawyers must be allowed because of the First Amendment.	27	34	515	65
Advertising is necessary for new lawyers entering the profession.	61	8	721	91
Only factual advertising (change of address, etc.) is appropriate.	318	40	464	59

though advertising is not inherently misleading or in poor taste, much of the advertising currently done falls into those categories. Given this response, it would seem that the issue is still salient to attorneys and that there continues to be variation in attitude.

Respondents were also asked if they agreed with a series of statements about the propriety of advertising. These statements were designed to measure attitudes toward the concept of advertising and its practice in the aggregate. The distribution of responses suggests again that attitudes do vary among small firms (see Table 16-1). For example, 57 percent of the respondents agreed that the law is a profession, not a trade, and therefore the advertising of legal services should be banned. Only about a third of the respondents concurred with the *Bates* holding, agreeing with the statement that the First Amendment guarantees lawyers the right to advertise their services. Roughly a third maintained that lawyer advertisements are inherently misleading as well, again suggesting that although a majority would ban advertising, that view may have more to do with the nature of advertising as it currently exists rather than with the concept of advertising by attorneys. Two-thirds of those surveyed, however, agreed that the public is ill-equipped to evaluate advertisements for legal services. And only 20 percent agreed that advertisements provide useful information to the public.

These observations suggest that attitudes vary about the advertising of legal services. There appears to be significant opposition to the concept of advertising in the abstract, as reflected in Table 16-1, and in the proportion of respondents willing to ban it. Some respondents seem to view advertising as improper and a violation of professional etiquette, which was one justification for banning it in the first place. Others seem more concerned that advertising is ultimately a disservice to those seeking to retain an attorney. Yet, support for the concept exists as well. Some of that support appears to emerge from the belief that such speech deserves constitutional protection, and some seems to arise from a conviction that advertisements are not intrinsically harmful and may actually be informative. In any event, it is clear that there is a sufficient range in attitudes to assess the relationship between attitudes and behavior and determine whether attitudes toward the concept of lawyer advertising shape individual decisions of whether or not to advertise.

An additional indication of the salience of the topic of lawyer advertising is the infrequency with which lawyers have no opinion as to the propriety of advertising. The survey included a series of questions asking lawyers if advertising across a variety of media (the context or location of the advertisement) as well as the inclusion of different pieces of information (the content of the advertisement) lessened the dignity of the profession. Those answering the questionnaire could indicate for each of these questions that they had no opinion on the issue, if that was the case. The number who had no opinion fluctuated, depending on the question, but no more than 16 percent of the respondents fell into this category for any question. On some questions, as many as 95 percent of the respondents were willing to indicate a view. The distribution of "no opinion" responses as compared with those indicating whether or not the dignity of the profession was lessened are shown in Table 16-2. Given the responses, I conclude that questions about the propriety of the advertising of legal services continues to be salient to members of the legal profession.

Strength of Attitudes

Gauging the strength of attitudes is also useful because it gives us some sense of whether responses are random and subject to fluctuation. Respondents had the opportunity to share their particular attitudes about advertising by writing comments on the survey questionnaire. Ninety-five of 792 respondents took advantage of this option and wrote comments about advertising generally. These responses indicate that advertising is still a salient issue for many members of the legal profession. Some were quite adamant in their views. For example, one lawyer who clearly believes that mass media advertisements should be permitted wrote: "Big firms advertise—or rather market—their services and testimonials constantly—at the country club, at parties, by soliciting the government for business. The 'dignity of the profession' is a joke. We are not dignified but out for a buck so why be hypocritical about it?" Others were equally negative in their views. For example, one respondent noted that "advertising is turning a once dignified profession into a fraternity of charlatans." Others seemed concerned that lawyers who advertise would never pay the necessary dues in the profession. This idea is perhaps best summarized by the following

Table 16-2 Attitudes toward Specific Components of Lawyer Advertising, from Survey

Location and content of advertisement	Lessens dignity		Does not lessen		No opinion	
	N	%	N	%	N	%
Location						
Yellow pages	290	36.6	389	49.1	93	11.7
Newspaper	544	68.7	143	18.1	87	11.0
Direct mail	593	74.9	104	13.1	77	9.7
Radio	637	80.4	86	10.9	48	6.1
Television	655	82.7	78	9.8	40	5.1
Content						
Included information about office hours	199	25.1	450	56.8	126	15.9
Included information about areas of practice	238	30.1	417	52.7	118	14.9
Included "no charge for initial consultation" statement	340	42.9	320	40.4	119	15.0
Included information about the personal qualifications	384	48.5	268	33.8	122	15.4
Included prices	457	57.7	215	27.1	106	13.4
Included testimonials of past clients	676	85.4	37	4.7	63	8.0

observation from one of the respondents: "Advertising usually helps those the most who have little experience, have less business or who desire to increase business faster than their skill would ordinarily increase their business."

Negative comments were more numerous (57 percent) than positive comments (31 percent); 13 percent were ambivalent, which parallels the results reported in Table 16-2. Although the relatively small numbers preclude generalizations of any kind, I conclude that advertising does still prompt a reaction from many lawyers and that those attitudes vary widely.

Measuring Effects of Attitudes on Advertising Behavior

Now that I have demonstrated that attitudes about advertising are not dependent on whether attorneys advertise, I turn to addressing my primary research question: Do attitudes, as I expect, explain behavior? As noted above, those favoring a ban on the advertising of legal services are deemed to have negative attitudes toward advertising, whereas those opposing a ban are said to be more tolerant of advertising. Thus, the expectation is that those favoring a ban will be less likely to advertise than will those in opposition to a ban.

To explore this expectation, I needed, first, to develop measures of attitudes that could be used to assess their influence on the decision to advertise.[5] The three indicators used to measure attitudes and their range of measurement are delineated in Table 16-3. The first of these, "Banning of advertising" is straightforward; I simply asked respondents whether or not they favored a ban on advertising. I expect to find that attorneys who favor the ban do not advertise, whereas those who oppose it do. For the second attitudinal measure, "Context of advertising," I asked respondents whether advertising in certain forums (for example, the yellow pages, newspapers, radio) "lessens the dignity of the legal profession." I assume a positive relationship between context and attorney advertising. That is to say, I expect those who think that a particular advertising forum does *not* lessen the dignity of the profession to be more likely to advertise. The third measure, "Content of advertisement," covers whether respondents think that the inclusion of particular information in advertisements (for example, such phrases as "no charge for initial consultation," prices for services, office hours) "lessens the dignity of the profession." Again, I assume a positive relationship between content and the decision to advertise. In other words, the more information the respondent was willing to allow the advertisement to include, the more likely his or her firm would be to advertise.

With these attitudinal measures in hand, I sought to determine the extent to which they explained the decision of the respondent firm to advertise. To do so, I employed logistic regression, or logit.[6] This is an appropriate statistical tool to use for my study, since the dependent variable (the decision to advertise) is dichotomous: the respondent's firm advertises or does not advertise.

Findings

The results of my analysis are reported in Table 16-4. As we can see, all the signs of the coefficients are in the expected direction (positive), and two of the three independent variables are statistically significant. Attitudes about both the content and the context of advertising appear to be significantly related to the decision to advertise. Only the "Oppose/favor ban" question does not have a statistically significant relationship to the decision to advertise. It seems that asking respondents their views on an advertising ban is probably not a valid measure of their attitude about advertising.

Another possibility is that attitudes about *banning* advertising do not predict the deci-

Table 16-3 Attitudinal Theory Measures Used in Survey

Question/indicators	Value
Banning of advertising	
Does respondent favor or oppose ban on advertising?	0 = favor ban 1 = oppose ban
Context of advertising: mass media	
Questions designed to determine whether advertising in various kinds of media lessens the dignity of the legal profession.[a]	0 = advertising in *all* media lessens dignity 1 = advertising in yellow pages does not lessen dignity but all other advertising does 2 = advertising in at least one of the non-yellow pages or "intrusive" media does not lessen dignity
Content of advertisement: information included	
Questions designed to determine whether the inclusion of different pieces of information in the advertisement lessens the dignity of the profession.[b]	0-5 additive scale

[a] These questions concerned advertising (1) in the yellow pages, (2) in newspapers, (3) on radio, (4) on television, and (5) via direct mailings.

[b] The different pieces of information included (1) a "no charge for initial consultation" statement, (2) prices, (3) areas of practice, (4) office hours, (5) personal qualifications, and (6) testimonials by clients.

sion to advertise. Why might this be? Perhaps opposing a ban on advertising is a function of an attitude toward free speech or a tolerance for advertising rather than support for the actual practice of advertising. Some respondents might be opposed to policy being dictated by the government but would be comfortable with the internal regulation of advertising practices in the profession. Others might not approve of advertising but view its legality to be a necessary evil.[7] We could determine whether this explanation has any merit by estimating an additional logit model that controlled for attitudes about the First Amendment's guarantee of free speech. The results of such an analysis indicate that attitudes about the First Amendment were not the reason that the "Oppose/favor ban" question lacked a statistically significant relationship to the decision to advertise. Thus, we are left with the conclusion that attitudes about banning advertising (regardless of the source of those attitudes) have no bearing on the decision to advertise. Instead, attitudes about the nature of advertising—its context and content—are extremely influential.

Turning to the ability of the attitudinal variables taken as a whole to predict the decision

Table 16-4 Logit Analysis for Attitudinal Model

Independent variables	Beta	Standard error	t-value
Intercept	−1.35	0.65	2.07
Oppose/favor ban	−0.23	0.31	0.75
Context of ad	0.50*	0.19	2.62
Content of ad	0.25*	0.08	3.20
Chi-square	74.46*		

Note: The frequency of the dependent variable is 0.66 for nonadvertisers and 0.34 for advertisers. The proportion correct for the entire sample is 0.71; for advertisers, 0.84; for nonadvertisers, 0.46.

* $p \leq .01$ level.

to advertise, we see that the model correctly predicts behavior approximately 71 percent of the time, which is an improvement of roughly 5 percent over the modal category. This means that if we simply guessed that all firms would be nonadvertisers, we would be right approximately 66 percent of the time. Although the independent variables taken together correctly predict about 83 percent of the nonadvertisers, only 46 percent of the advertising respondents are appropriately classified, suggesting that the problem lies in identifying those respondents that are going to advertise. All in all, this initial analysis lends limited support to the attitudinal model, because the model does provide some improvement over random predictions.

Further analysis also suggests modest support for the attitudinal model. The average predicted probability for actual nonadvertising cases was 0.28. As this is below 0.50, most nonadvertising cases were correctly predicted. The average predicted probability for firms that actually do advertise was 0.46. As this probability also falls below the prediction threshold of 50 percent, most advertising firms were also predicted to be nonadvertisers. Nonetheless, the average predicted probability of cases that represent those advertisers is significantly higher than the average predicted probability of nonadvertisers. I can conclude from this that the model does have the power to distinguish advertisers from nonadvertisers based on the statistically significant differences in the averages. So, to a certain extent, the initial examination of the results is misleading. Although the model is only a 5 percent improvement over the modal category, it is truly a significant improvement over random predictions because of the distinction between advertisers and nonadvertisers.

Based on these analyses, I am satisfied that attitudes can influence behavior in the voluntary consumption situation and have done so with regard to advertising by law firms. This is worth noting because, as previously indicated, the link between attitudes and behavior has not been fully explored in the judicial impact literature. These findings are confined to the voluntary consumption situation, but there is evidence to suggest that when potential consumers have a choice about whether to change their behavior, their attitudes toward the behavior in question are relevant, although perhaps not the sole determinants of behavior.

Discussion

It may seem to be intuitive that attitudes predict behavior and that those with unfavorable attitudes are less apt to engage in advertising activity than are those with tolerant attitudes. As my discussion of previous studies revealed, however, scholars disagree about this proposition. Most pointedly, Giles and Gatlin's study (1980) of parental choices in the busing of children for the purpose of desegregation found that although attitudes predict attitudes, an assessment of costs and benefits predicts behavior. Indeed, Giles and Gatlin argue that attitudes shape the willingness to accept a policy change. Yet these attitudes were not sufficient to determine behavior. Instead, the relative costs and benefits of different courses of action determined behavior. The findings of the research reported in this chapter are in sharp contrast to theirs.

The reason, as I suspected from the outset, is that I explored a situation of voluntary consumption, whereas they considered one that was mandatory. Indeed, for the most part, the findings presented here are consistent with other research on voluntary consumption. For example, in his study of bookseller practices in the wake of expansive obscenity rulings, Levine (1973) found that personal preferences or attitudes tended to dictate response. Market variables were not particularly powerful in his analysis, as they were not in the present study. Personal distaste for "obscene" materials was the most powerful determinant of whether or not a potential consumer would become an actual consumer; in much the same way, negative attitudes toward advertising usually precluded it as a behavioral option, whereas tolerant attitudes were able to predict with some success who would advertise. Similarly, my results conform to the findings of Bond and Johnson (1982) in their analysis of why some hospitals provided abortions after the decision of *Roe v. Wade* (1973) and other hospitals did not. Bond and Johnson found that whether or not a hospital provided abortions was primarily a function of the preferences of hospital administrators; similarly, whether or not a law firm advertised its services was found to be primarily a function of the preferences or attitudes of the senior partner of the firm.

In this context, the findings of Giles and Gatlin make sense. The parents of schoolchildren in their study did not have the option of doing nothing. Their children were going to be bused unless they paid private school tuition or moved. The decision of parents to pay tuition or move is not likely to be solely a function of attitudes because these choices entail incurring monetary costs and may mean changing many other aspects of their lives. Thus, parents who acquiesced in having their children bused may have done so because they could not afford the alternatives rather than because they had positive or supportive attitudes toward the new policy. Costs and benefits, then, predict behavior in the mandatory choice setting,[8] whereas attitudes have more power in the voluntary consumption setting.

To put it simply, I am arguing that attitudes influence behavior in the voluntary consumption situation, and that is what separates my study from most others (except for Levine 1973 and Bond and Johnson 1982) in the literature on the impact of judicial decisions. Because members of the consumer population can maintain their old behavior or the status quo without penalty in a voluntary consumption situation, it seems convincing that attitudes provide the impetus for changes. This is in direct contrast to the mandatory choice setting, where some behavioral adjustment is required (as in the Giles and Gatlin study [1980]). In those situations, attitudes alone are insufficient to shape behavior.

Therefore, on the basis of my research, I argue that in a voluntary consumption situation, the impetus for change or for taking advantage of a seemingly beneficial policy change appears to be a function of a favorable or, at least, tolerant disposition toward the new policy. At the same time, it seems likely that a major impetus for resisting change or maintaining the status quo is the lack of a favorable disposition or some hostility to the new behavior allowed by the policy change. Inertia is no doubt a factor as well, but attitudes, I maintain, have some bearing on whether or not inertia will be overcome such that behavior changes.

Conclusion

The primary finding of this study—that responses to judicial decisions in voluntary consumption situations are primarily a function of attitudes—is significant in understanding the scope and meaning of judicial decisions. If the attitudes and beliefs of members of the consumer population, those most directly affected by the decisions, influence their behavioral responses, then it stands to reason that these attitudes will ultimately define the meaning of the judicial policy. We know that a majority of lawyers are opposed to advertising by attorneys, in spite of *Bates*, and that many lawyers feel that the dignity of the profession is diminished by the various forms that advertising takes. Not surprisingly, only one-third or so of the lawyers I surveyed have availed themselves of the new policy option.

So while *Bates* expanded the meaning of the First Amendment to the U.S. Constitution by broadening the protection afforded economic speech, the aftermath of the decision suggests that the change in policy may not have been as profound or meaningful as originally anticipated. This discussion demonstrates how an emphasis on impact—one that focuses on consumer response—can complement and expand our knowledge of the judicial process. Analyses of the factors that affect why judges vote the way they do are quite important, but they provide only a partial glimpse into the judicial process. Studying the responses to judicial decisions, or their impact, enriches our understanding of that process.

Notes

1. See, for example, *Ohralik v. Ohio State Bar Association* (1978), in which the Supreme Court held that solicitation for pecuniary gain was not protected speech; *In re Primus* (1978), in which mail solicitation was protected as speech if the business was not being solicited for profit; *In re R.M.J.* (1982), in which the Court held that state regulations of advertising could be no broader than reasonably necessary to prevent deception; *Zauderer v. Office of Disciplinary Counsel of the Supreme Court of Ohio* (1985), in which it held that states cannot ban the use of illustrations in newspaper advertising but that regulations regarding misleading information are acceptable; *Shapero v. Kentucky State Bar Association* (1988), in which targeted mailings to prospective clients with legal problems were protected.

2. The distinction between these mandatory and voluntary choice situations is subtle, for in both, the consumer population is given choices. In the mandatory choice situation, where some behavioral change is required, the basic question of why some potential consumers become actual consumers is not particularly meaningful. Thus, in examining this question, we must use a policy of "voluntary consumption," in which no policy-imposed constraints face the consumer population. Once again, the decisions of lawyers about advertising constitute such a policy area.

3. In *Miranda v. Arizona* (1966), the Supreme Court held that suspects taken into police custody must be informed that they have a right to remain silent, that anything they say can be used against them, that they have the right to an attorney, and that, if they cannot afford an attorney, one will be obtained for them.

4. Following *Bates*, the American Bar Association (ABA) put forth two model codes to be considered by the state authority responsible for revising lawyer advertising rules. The first, labeled Model Code A by the ABA and the "regulatory" model by Lori Andrews, the first chair of the ABA Commission on Advertising established post-*Bates* (1981), in her discussion of *Bates* and its implications for the legal profession, specified what kinds of information could be included. The second, labeled Model Code B by the ABA and the "directive" model by Andrews, stated what lawyers *could not* do with regard to advertising. To control for the effects of region, law firms in two northern states (one which had adopted an approximation of model code A, or the regulatory model, detailed above, and one with a directive code) as well as two southern states (one with a restrictive code and one with a directive code) were sampled. Louisiana and Massachusetts had directive codes, whereas Illinois and Kentucky had restrictive codes. The results of the multivariate analyses did not reveal any significant differences in likelihood to advertise across region or state bar code. Accordingly, for the remainder of the analysis, respondents in the sample will not be distinguished on the basis of the state in which they practice.

Other sampling considerations were relevant as well. There is evidence that advertising has increased most dramatically in small law firms, suggesting that the distinction between potential and actual consumers is most meaningful in this group (Reskin, 1986). Large firms, containing five or more members, were therefore excluded from the sample. All small firms listed in the *Martindale-Hubbell Legal Directory* are included in the sample.

5. For more on measurement, see Chapter 1 of this book.

6. For more on logit, see Appendix B of this book.

7. A corollary to this would be the contemporary debate about pornography. Many people are opposed to pornography in principle, but they may also be troubled by the possibility of the government's banning it because they perceive that to be censorship under the First Amendment to the Constitution.

8. I can say this with even greater confidence because, in a separate inquiry, I examined whether or not costs and benefits predicted advertising behavior. I found that costs and benefits do not predict the behavior of attorneys—most likely because they had the option of doing nothing and did not have to change their behavior in some way.

17 The Real World of Constitutional Rights: The Supreme Court and the Implementation of the Abortion Decisions

Gerald N. Rosenberg

In *Roe v. Wade* and *Doe v. Bolton* (1973) the Supreme Court held unconstitutional Texas and Georgia laws prohibiting abortions except for "the purpose of saving the life of the mother" (Texas) and where "pregnancy would endanger the life of the pregnant mother or would seriously and permanently injure her health" (Georgia). The Court asserted that women had a fundamental right of privacy to decide whether or not to bear a child. Dividing pregnancy roughly into three trimesters, the Court held that in the first trimester the choice of abortion was a woman's alone, in consultation with a physician. During the second trimester, states could regulate abortion for the preservation and protection of women's health, and in approximately the third trimester, after fetal viability, could ban abortions outright, except where necessary to preserve a woman's life or health. Although responding specifically to the laws of Texas and Georgia, the broad scope of the Court's constitutional interpretation invalidated the abortion laws of almost every state and the District of Columbia.[1] According to one critic, *Roe* and *Doe* "may stand as the most radical decisions ever issued by the Supreme Court" (Noonan 1973, 261).

Roe and *Doe* are generally considered leading examples of judicial action in support of relatively powerless groups unable to win legislative victories. In these cases, women were that politically disadvantaged group; indeed, it has been claimed, "No victory for women's rights since enactment of the 19th Amendment has been greater than the one achieved" in *Roe* and *Doe* ("A Woman's Right" 1973, A4). But women are not the only disadvantaged interests who have attempted to use litigation to achieve policy ends. Starting with the famous cases brought by civil rights groups, and spreading to issues raised by environmental groups, consumer groups, and others, reformers have over the past decades looked to the courts as important producers of political and social change.[2] Yet, during the same period, students of judicial politics have learned that court opinions are not always implemented with the speed and directness that rule by law assumes (Becker and Feeley 1973; Johnson and Canon 1984; Wasby 1970). This is particularly the case with decisions that touch on controversial, emotional issues or deeply held beliefs, such as abortion.

This chapter contains an exploration of the effect of the Court's abortion decisions, both *Roe* and *Doe*, and the key decisions based on them. How did the public, politicians, medical professionals, and interest groups react to them? Were the decisions implemented? Did they bring safe and legal abortions to all American women? To some American women? If the answer turns out to be only some, then I want to know why. What are the factors that have led a constitutional right to be unevenly available? More generally, are there conditions under which Court decisions on behalf of relatively powerless groups are more or less likely to be implemented.[3]

The analysis presented here shows that the effect and implementation of the Court's abortion decisions have been neither straightforward nor simple. Political response has varied and access to legal and safe abortion has increased, but in an uneven and nonuniform way. These findings are best explained by two related factors. First, at the time of the initial decisions there was widespread support for legal abortion from several sets of actors, including relevant political and professional elites on both the national and local level, the public at large, and activists. Second, the Court's decisions, by allowing clinics to perform abortions, made it possible for women to obtain abortions in some places where hospitals refused to provide them. Implementation by private clinics, however, has led to uneven availability of abortion services and has encouraged local political opposition.

The Abortion Cases

Roe and *Doe* were the Court's first major abortion decisions, but they were not its last.[4] In response to these decisions, many states rewrote their abortion laws, ostensibly to conform with the Court's constitutional mandate but actually with the goal of restricting the newly created right. Cases quickly arose, and continue to arise, challenging state laws as inconsistent with the Court's ruling, if not openly and clearly hostile to it. In general, the Court's response has been to preserve the core holding of *Roe* and *Doe* that a woman has a virtually unfettered constitutional right to an abortion before fetal viability, but to defer to legislation in areas not explicitly dealt with in those decisions. These cases require brief mention.

Areas of Litigation

Since *Roe* and *Doe*, the Court has heard three kinds of cases on abortion. One type involves state and federal funding for abortion. Here, the Court has consistently upheld the right of government not to fund abortion services and to prohibit the provision of abortions in public hospitals, unless the abortion is medically necessary. In perhaps the most important case, *Harris v. McRae* (1980), the Court upheld the most restrictive version of the so-called Hyde Amendment, which barred the use of federal funds for even medically necessary abortions, including those involving pregnancies due to rape or incest.

A second area that has provoked a great deal of litigation is the degree of participation in the abortion decision constitutionally allowed to the spouse of a pregnant married woman or the parents of a pregnant single minor. The Court has consistently struck down laws requiring spousal involvement but has upheld laws requiring parental notification or consent, as long as there is a "judicial bypass" option allowing minors to bypass their parents and obtain permission from a court.

A third area generating litigation involves the procedural requirements that states can impose for abortions. Most of these cases have arisen from state attempts to make abortion as difficult as possible to obtain. Regulations include requiring all post-first trimester abortions to be performed in hospitals; the informed, written consent of a woman before an abortion can be performed; a twenty-four-hour waiting period before an abortion can be performed; a pathology report for each abortion and the presence of a second physician at abortions occurring after potential viability; the preservation by physicians of the life of viable fetuses; and restrictions on the disposal of fetal remains. The Court's most recent pronouncement on these issues, *Planned Parenthood of Southeastern Pennsylvania v. Casey* (1992), found informed consent, a twenty-four-hour waiting period, and certain reporting requirements constitutional.

Trends in Court Treatment of Abortion Cases

Since the late 1980s, as *Casey* suggests, the Court has upheld more restrictions on the abortion right. In *Webster v. Reproductive Health Services* (1989), the Court upheld a 1986 restrictive Missouri law, and in 1991, in *Rust v. Sullivan*, it upheld government regulations prohibiting family-planning organizations that receive federal funds from counseling patients about abortion or providing abortion referrals. Most important, in *Casey* the Court abandoned the trimester framework of *Roe*. Although the justices did not agree on the proper constitutional standard for assessing state restrictions on abortion, Justices Sandra Day O'Connor, Anthony M. Kennedy, and David H. Souter adopted an "undue burden" standard. Under this standard, states may regulate abortion but may not place an undue burden on women seeking an abortion of a nonviable fetus.

Many commentators expected *Casey* to generate an avalanche of litigation centering directly on the abortion rights. Given the ambiguity of the undue burden standard, they expected expanded state activity to limit abortion. These expectations may yet be fulfilled, but, interestingly, Court cases since *Casey* have not specifically focused on the abortion right per se. Rather, in recent litigation the Court has been asked to resolve questions concerning access to abortion; namely, what steps can courts take to prevent antiabortion advocates from interfering with public access to family-planning and abortion clinics? The reason these kinds of questions arose is not difficult to discern; the 1990s has seen the rise of militant tactics—ranging from boisterous protests to harassment of clinic workers and even to the murder of physicians performing abortions—by certain segments of the anti-abortion movement.

These "access" cases have generated mixed Court rulings. In *Bray v. Alexandria Women's Health Clinic* (1993), the Court rejected an attempt by pro-choice groups to use the 1871 Ku Klux Klan Act as a way to bring federal courts into this area. But, in *Madsen v. Women's Health Center* (1994), the Court upheld parts of a Florida trial court injunction permanently enjoining antiabortion protesters from blocking access to an abortion clinic and from physically harassing persons leaving or entering it. With the enactment by Congress of the Freedom of Access to Clinic Entrances Act in 1994, and the immediate filing of a legal challenge, it is likely that the Court will have another opportunity to address this issue (Marcus 1994).

Implementing Constitutional Rights

How have the public, politicians, medical professionals, and interest groups reacted to the Court decisions since *Roe* and *Doe?* How has access to legal and safe abortion changed in the wake of these decisions? In other words, when the Supreme Court announces a new constitutional right, what happens?

Legal Abortions: The Numbers

An obvious way to consider this question, at least in the abortion realm, is to look at the number of legal abortions performed before and after the 1973 decisions. For, if the Court has had an important effect on society in this area, we might expect to find dramatic increases in the number of legal abortions obtained after 1973. Collecting statistics on legal abortion, however, is not an easy task. Record keeping is not as precise and complete as one would hope. Two organizations, the public Centers for Disease Control and Prevention in Atlanta and the private Alan Guttmacher Institute in New York, are the most thorough and reliable collectors of the information. The data they have collected on the number of legal abortions performed between 1966 and 1992 and the yearly percentage change are shown in Figure 17-1.

Interestingly, these data present a mixed picture of the effect of the abortion decisions. On the one hand, they suggest that after *Roe* the number of legal abortions increased at a strong pace throughout the 1970s (the solid line in Figure 17-1). On the other hand, they reveal that the changes after 1973 were part of a trend that started in 1970, three years before the Court acted. Strikingly, the largest increase in the number of legal abortions occurs between 1970 and 1971, two years before *Roe!* In raw numerical terms, the increase between 1972 and 1973 is 157,800, a full 134,500 fewer than the pre-*Roe* increase in 1970-1971. It is possible, of course, that the effect of *Roe* was not felt in 1973. Even though the

Figure 17-1 Legal Abortions, 1966–1992

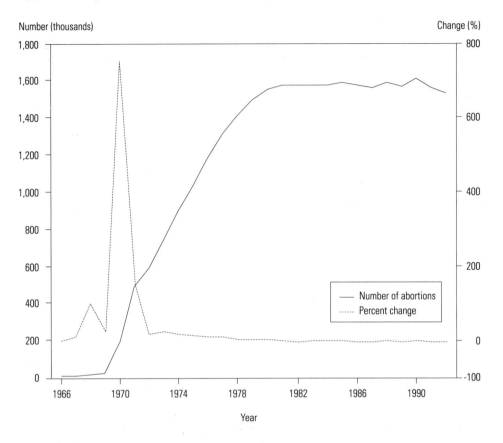

Sources: Estimates by the Alan Guttmacher Institute and the Centers for Disease Control and Prevention in Henshaw and Van Vort 1994, 100–106, 112; Lader 1973, 209; U.S. Congress 1974, 1976; Weinstock et al. 1975, 23.

Note: When sources differed, I have relied on data from the Alan Guttmacher Institute since its estimates are based on surveys of all known abortion providers and are generally more complete. Data points for 1983, 1986, and 1990 are estimates based on interpolations made by the Alan Guttmacher Institute.

decision was handed down in January, perhaps the 1973-1974 comparison gives a more accurate picture. If this is the case, the increase, 154,000, is still substantially smaller than the change during 1970-1971. And while the number of legal abortions continued to increase in the years immediately after 1974, that rate eventually stabilized and by the 1990s had actually declined. The dotted line in Figure 17-1 (representing the percentage change in the number of legal abortions performed from one year to the next) shows, too, that the largest increases in the number of legal abortions occurred in the years prior to *Roe*.

Yet another way of analyzing the data is presented in Table 17-1, where two- and three-

Table 17-1 Increase in the Number of Legal Abortions

Period	Increase
1969-1971	463,100
1970-1972	393,300
1971-1973	258,800
1972-1974	311,800
1973-1975	289,600
1969-1972	564,100
1972-1975	447,400
1973-1976	434,700

year comparisons are given. The largest increase during a two-year period is in 1969-1971, when there was an increase of 463,100 legal abortions. The 1970-1972 period is next, show-ing an increase of 393,300, about 26 percent higher than the 1972-1974 increase of 311,800. The increase during 1971-1973 is only 258,800. Even the 1973-1975 increase is only 289,600. The largest increase over three years comes in the pre-*Roe* period of 1969-1972, during which there were an additional 564,100 legal abortions. The 1972-1975 period saw an increase of 447,400 legal abortions, and between 1973 and 1976 the increase was 434,700.

The data presented above show that the largest numerical increases in legal abortions occurred in the years prior to initial Supreme Court action. This holds both for single and multiyear comparisons: There was no steep or unusual increase in the number of legal abortions following *Roe*. To be sure, it is possible that without constitutional protection for abortion no more states would have liberalized or repealed their laws and those that had done so might have overturned their previous efforts. And the fact that the number of legal abortions continued to increase after 1973 suggests that the Court was effective in easing access to safe and legal abortion. But those increases, while large, were smaller than those of previous years. Hence, the growth in the number of legal abortions can be only partially attributed to the Court; it might even be the case that the increases would have continued without the Court's 1973 decisions.

What Happened?

Particularly interesting about the data presented above is that they suggest that *Roe* itself failed to generate major changes in the number of legal abortions. This finding is compat-ible with political science literature, in which it is argued that Supreme Court decisions, particularly ones dealing with emotional and controversial issues, are not automatically and completely implemented. It also appears to fit nicely with an argument I have made elsewhere (Rosenberg 1991), which suggests that several factors must be present for new constitutional rights to be implemented. These include widespread support from political and professional elites on both the national and local level, from the public at large, and from activists and a willingness on the part of those called on to implement the decision to act accordingly. This is true, as Alexander Hamilton pointed out two centuries ago, because courts lack the power of "either the sword or the purse." To a greater extent than other government institutions, courts are dependent on both elite and popular support for their decisions to be implemented.

To fill out my argument in greater detail, I examine both pre- and post-1973 actions as they relate to the implementation of the abortion right. In so doing, I reach two important conclusions. First, by the time the Court reached its decisions in 1973, little political opposition to abortion existed on the federal level, relevant professional elites and social activists gave it widespread support, it was practiced on a large scale (see Figure 17-1), and public support for it was growing. These positions placed abortion reform in the American mainstream. Second, in the years after 1973, opposition to abortion strengthened and grew.

Pre-*Roe* Support

In the decade or so prior to *Roe*, there was a sea change in the public position of abortion in American life. At the start of the 1960s, abortion was not a political issue. Abortions, illegal as they were, were performed clandestinely, and women who underwent the procedure did not talk about it.[5] By 1972, however, abortion had become a public and political issue. While little legislative or administrative action was taken on the federal level, a social movement, organized in the mid- and late 1960s, to reform and repeal prohibitions on abortion met with some success at the state level, and public opinion swung dramatically from opposition to abortion in most cases to substantial support.

Elites and Social Activists

Although abortions have always been performed, public discussion did not surface until the 1950s. In 1962 the American Law Institute (ALI) published its Model Penal Code on abortion, permitting abortion if continuing the pregnancy would adversely affect the physical or mental health of the woman, if there was risk of birth defects, or if the pregnancy resulted from rape or incest. Publicity about birth defects caused by Thalidomide, a drug prescribed in the 1960s to cure infertility, and a German measles epidemic in the years 1962-1965 kept the issue prominent. By November 1965 the American Medical Association Board of Trustees approved a report urging adoption of the ALI law.

In 1966, reform activists began making numerous radio and television appearances.[6] By then there were several pro-choice groups, including the Society for Humane Abortion in California; the Association for the Study of Abortion in New York, a prestigious board of doctors and lawyers; and the Illinois Committee for Medical Control of Abortion, which advocated repeal of all abortion laws. Abortion referral services were also started. Previously, pro-choice activists had made private referrals to competent doctors in the United States and Mexico, who performed illegal but safe abortions. But by the late 1960s, abortion referral groups operated publicly. In New York City, in 1967, twenty-two clergy announced the formation of their group, gaining front-page coverage in the *New York Times* (Fiske 1967). The Chicago referral service took out a full page add in the *Sun-Times* announcing its services. In Los Angeles, the referral service was serving more than a thousand women per month. By the late 1960s pro-choice organizations, including abortion-referral services, were operating in many major U.S. cities. And by 1971, the clergy referral service operated publicly in eighteen states with a staff of about 700 clergy and lay people (Hole and Levine 1971, 299).

In order to tap this emerging support, the National Association for the Repeal of Abortion Laws (NARAL) was founded.[7] Protesting in the streets, lecturing, and organizing "days of anger" began to have an effect. Women who had undergone illegal abortions wrote and spoke openly about them (see Schulder and Kennedy 1971). Seventy-five leading national groups endorsed the repeal of all abortion laws between 1967 and the end of 1972, including twenty-eight religious and twenty-one medical groups. Among the religious groups, support ranged from the American Jewish Congress to the American Baptist Convention. Medical groups included the American Public Health Association, the American Psychiatric Association, the American Medical Association, the National Council of Obstetrics-Gynecology, and the American College of Obstetricians and Gynecologists. Among other groups, support included the American Bar Association and a host of liberal organizations. Even the YWCA supported repeal (U.S. Congress 1976, 4:53-91).

The Federal Government

In the late 1960s, while the abortion law reform battle was being fought in the states, the federal arena was quiet. For example, although states with less restrictive laws received Medicaid funds that paid for some abortions, for "six years after 1967, not a single bill was introduced, much less considered, in Congress to curtail the use of federal funds for abortion" (Rosoff 1975, 13). The pace momentarily quickened in 1968 when the Presidential Advisory Council on the Status of Women, appointed by President Lyndon Johnson, recommended the repeal of all abortion laws (Lader 1973, 81-82).

Still, abortion was not a major issue in the 1968 presidential campaign. Despite his personal beliefs, the newly elected president, Richard M. Nixon, did not take active steps to limit abortion, and the U.S. government did not enter *Roe* nor, after the decision, did it give support to congressional efforts to limit abortion.[8] Although it is true that in 1973 and 1974 President Nixon was occupied with other matters, his administration essentially avoided the abortion issue.

In Congress there was virtually no abortion activity prior to 1973. In April 1970, Sen. Bob Packwood (R-Ore.) introduced a National Abortion Act designed to "guarantee and protect" the "fundamental constitutional right" of a woman "to control her own fertility" (U.S. Congress 1970b). He also introduced a bill to liberalize the District of Columbia's abortion law (U.S. Congress 1970c). Otherwise, Congress remained essentially inactive on the abortion issue.

The States

It is not at all surprising that the president and Congress did not involve themselves in the abortion reform movement of the 1960s. Laws banning abortion were state laws (see Mohr 1978), so most of the early abortion law reform activity was directed at state governments. In the early and middle parts of the decade there was some legislative discussion in California, New Hampshire, and New York. By 1967, reform bills were introduced in twenty-eight states, including California, Colorado, Delaware, Florida, Georgia, Maryland, Oklahoma, New Jersey, New York, North Carolina, and Pennsylvania (Rubin 1982). The first successful liberalization drive was in Colorado, which adopted a reform bill, modeled on the ALI's Model Penal Code. Interestingly, another early reform state was California, where Gov. Ronald Reagan, despite intense opposition, signed a reform bill.

These victories further propelled the reform movement, and in 1968, abortion legislation was pending in some thirty states (Monroe 1968). During 1968-1969 seven states—Arkansas, Delaware, Georgia, Kansas, Maryland, New Mexico, and Oregon—enacted reform laws based on or similar to the ALI model (Lader 1973, 84). In 1970, four states went even further. In chronological order, Hawaii, New York, Alaska, and Washington essentially repealed prohibitions on abortions in the first two trimesters.

To sum up, in the five or so years prior to the Supreme Court's decisions, reform and repeal bills had been debated in most states, and seventeen plus the District of Columbia acted to liberalize their laws (Craig and O'Brien 1993, 75). State action had removed some obstacles to abortion, and safe and legal abortions were thus available in scattered states. And, as indicated in Figure 17-1, in 1972, nearly 600,000 legal abortions were performed. Activity was widespread, vocal, and effective.

Public Opinion

Another important element in the effectiveness of the Court is the amount of support from the population at large. By the eve of the Court's decision in 1973, public opinion had dramatically shifted from opposition to abortion in most cases to substantial, if not majority, support. Indeed, in the decades that have followed, opinion on abortion has remained remarkably stable.[9]

Looking at the 1960s as a whole, Blake (1971, 543, 544) found that opinions on discretionary abortion were "changing rapidly over time" and polls were recording "rapidly growing support." For example, relying on data from Gallup polls, Blake (1977b, 49) found that support for elective abortion increased approximately two and one-half times from 1968 to 1972. One set of Gallup polls recorded a fifteen-point drop in the percentage of respondents disapproving of abortions for financial reasons in the eight months between October 1969 and June 1970 (Blake 1977a, 58). Relying on data from the National Opinion Research Center (NORC), and averaging responses to six abortion questions, Granberg and Granberg (1980, 252) found an increase of over 50 percent between 1965 and 1972 in supportive responses, with an average of 41 percent approving of abortion in 1965 and 63 percent approving in 1972. And in 1971, a national poll taken for the Commission on Population Growth and the American Future found 50 percent of its respondents agreeing with the statement that the abortion "decision should be left up to persons involved and their doctor" (Rosenthal 1971, 22). Thus, in the words of one study, "[b]y the time the Supreme Court made its ruling, there was strong public support behind the legalization of abortion" (Ebaugh and Haney 1980, 493).

Much of the reason for the growth in support for the repeal of the laws on abortion, both from the public and from organizations, may have come from changes in opinion by the professional elite. Polls throughout the late 1960s reported that important subgroups of the American population were increasingly supportive of abortion law reform and repeal. Several nonscientific polls of doctors, for example, suggested a great deal of support for abortion reform. A scientific poll of nearly thirteen thousand respondents in nursing, medical, and social work schools in the autumn and winter of 1971 showed strong support for repeal. The poll found split opinions among nursing students and faculty but found that 69 percent of medical students, 71 percent of medical faculty, 76 percent of social work students, and 75 percent of social work faculty supported "freely accessible abortion" (Rosen et al. 1974, 165). And a poll by the American Council of Education of 180,000 college freshmen in 1970 found that 83 percent favored the legalization of abortion (Currivan 1970). It is clear that in the late 1960s and early 1970s, the public was becoming increasingly supportive of legal abortion.

Post-*Roe* Activity

The relative quiet of the early 1960s has yet to return to the abortion arena. Rather than settling the issue, the Court's decisions added even more controversy. On the federal level, legislative and administrative action dealing with abortion has swung back and forth, from more or less benign neglect prior to 1973 to open antipathy to modest support. State action has followed a different course. Legislative efforts in the 1960s and early 1970s to reform and repeal abortion laws gave way to efforts to limit access to abortions. Public opinion remained stable until the *Webster* decision, after which there was a noticeable shift toward the pro-choice position. Finally, the antiabortion movement grew both more vocal and more violent.

The Federal Government: The President

On the presidential level, little changed in the years immediately after *Roe*. Nixon, as noted, took no action, and Gerald R. Ford, during his short term, said little about abortion until the presidential campaign in 1976, when he took a middle-of-the-road, antiabortion position, supporting local option, the law before *Roe*, and opposing federal funding of abortion (Craig and O'Brien 1993, 160-161). His Justice Department, however, did not enter the case of *Planned Parenthood of Central Missouri v. Danforth*, in which numerous state restrictions on the provision of abortion were challenged, and the Ford administration took no major steps to help the antiabortion forces.[10]

The Carter administration, unlike its Republican predecessors, did act to limit access to abortion. As a presidential candidate Carter opposed federal spending for abortion, and as president, during a press conference in June 1977, he stated his support for the Supreme Court's decisions allowing states to refuse Medicaid funding for abortions (Rubin 1982, 107). The Carter administration also sent its solicitor general into the Supreme Court to defend the Hyde Amendment.

Ronald Reagan was publicly committed to ending legal abortion. Opposition to *Roe* was said to be a litmus test for federal judicial appointments, and Reagan repeatedly used his formidable rhetorical skills in support of antiabortion activists. Under his presidency, antiabortion laws enacted included prohibiting fetal tissue research by federal scientists, banning most abortions at military hospitals, and denying funding to organizations that counseled or provided abortion services abroad. His administration submitted amicus curiae cases in all the Court's abortion cases, and in two (*Thornburgh v. American College of Obstetricians and Gynecologists*, 1986, and *Webster*) urged that *Roe* be overturned (see Epstein and Kobylka 1992). Yet, despite the rhetoric and the symbolism, these actions had little effect on the abortion rate (see Figure 17-1). As Craig and O'Brien (1993, 190) put it, "in spite of almost eight years of antiabortion rhetoric, Reagan had accomplished little in curbing abortion."

The administration of George Bush was as, if not more, hostile to the constitutional right to abortion as its predecessor. It filed antiabortion briefs in several abortion cases and urged that *Roe* be overturned. During Bush's presidency, the Food and Drug Administration placed RU-486, a French abortion drug, on the list of unapproved drugs, making it ineligible to be imported for personal use. And, in the administration's most celebrated antiabortion action, the secretary of the Health and Human Services Department, Louis W. Sullivan, issued regulations prohibiting family-planning organizations that received federal funds from counseling patients about abortion or providing referrals (the "gag rule" upheld in *Rust*).

President Bill Clinton brought a sea change to the abortion issue. As the first pro-choice president since *Roe*, he acted quickly to reverse decisions of his predecessors. In particular, on the third day of his administration, and the twentieth anniversary of *Roe*, Clinton issued five abortion-related memos.

1. He rescinded the ban on abortion counseling at federally financed clinics (negating *Rust*).
2. He rescinded restrictions on federal financing of fetal tissue research.
3. He eased U.S. policy on abortions in military hospitals.
4. He reversed Reagan policy on aid to international family planning programs involved in abortion-related activities.
5. He called for review of the ban on RU-486, the French abortion pill (Toner 1993).

In addition, in late May 1994, he signed the Freedom of Access to Clinic Entrances Act, giving federal protection to facilities and personnel providing abortion services. And, in early August 1994, the U.S. Justice Department sent U.S. marshals to help guard abortion clinics in at least twelve communities around the country (Thomas 1994). Furthermore, his two Supreme Court appointees as of 1994, Ruth Bader Ginsburg and Stephen Breyer, are apparently both pro-choice.

The Federal Government: Congress

In contrast to the executive branch, Congress engaged in a great deal of antiabortion activity after 1973, although almost none of it was successful, and some supportive activity actually occurred in the late 1980s and early 1990s. By means of legislation designed to overturn *Roe*, riders to various spending bills, and constitutional amendments, many members of Congress made their opposition to abortion clear. Perhaps the most important congressional action was the passage of the Hyde Amendment, which restricted federal funding of abortion: First passed in 1976, and then in subsequent years, the amendment prohibited the use of federal funds for abortion except in extremely limited circumstances. Although the wording varied in some years, the least limited version allowed funding only to save the life of the woman, when rape or incest had occurred, or when some long-lasting health damage, certified by two physicians, would result from the pregnancy. The amendment has been effective and the number of federally funded abortions fell from 294,600 in 1977 to 267 in 1992 (Daley and Gold 1994, 250).

Despite the amount of congressional activity, the Hyde Amendment was the only serious piece of antiabortion legislation enacted.[11] And, in 1994, Congress actually enacted legislation granting federal protection to abortion clinics. Thus, Congress was hostile in words but cautious in action with abortion. While not supporting the Court and the right to abortion, congressional action did not bar legal abortion.[12]

The States

Prior to 1973 the states had been the main arena for the abortion battle, and Court action did not do much to change that. In the wake of the Court decisions, all but a few states had to rewrite their abortion laws to conform to the Court's constitutional mandate. Their reactions, like those on the federal level, varied enormously. Some states acted to bring their laws into conformity with the Court's ruling, while others reenacted their former restrictive laws or enacted regulations designed to impede access to abortion. Since abortion is a state matter, the potential for state action affecting the availability of legal abortion was high.

At the outset, a national survey reported that state governments "moved with extreme caution in implementing the Supreme Court's ruling" (Brody 1973, A1). By the end of 1973, Blake (1977b, 46) reports, 260 abortion-related bills had been introduced in state legislatures and 39 enacted. In 1974, 189 bills were introduced and 19 enacted. In total, in the two years immediately following the Court decisions, 62 laws relating to abortion were enacted by 32 states. And state activity continued, with more abortion laws enacted in 1977 than in any year since 1973 (Rubin 1982, 126, 136).

Many of these laws were hostile to abortion. "Perhaps the major share," Blake (1977b, 61 n. 2) believes, was "obstructive and unconstitutional." They included spousal and parental consent requirements, tedious written-consent forms describing the "horrors" of abortion, funding limitations, waiting periods, hospitalization requirements, elaborate statistical reporting requirements, and burdensome medical procedures. Other action undertaken by states was simple and directly to the point. North Dakota and Rhode Island, for example, responded to the Court's decisions by enacting laws allowing abortion only to preserve the life of the woman (Weinstock et al. 1975, 28; "Rhode Island" 1973). Virginia rejected a bill bringing its statutes into conformity with the Court's order (Brody 1973, 46). Arkansas enforced a state law allowing abortion only if the pregnancy threatened the life or health of the woman ("Abortions Legal for Year" 1973, A14). In Louisiana, the attorney general threatened to take away the license of any physician performing an abortion, and the state medical society declared that any physician who performed an abortion, except to save the woman's life, violated the ethical principles of medicine (Weinstock et al. 1975, 28). The Louisiana State Board of Medical Examiners also pledged to prevent physicians from performing abortions (Brody 1973). In Pennsylvania, the state medical society announced that it did "not condone abortion on demand" and retained its strict standards (King 1973, 35). And in Saint Louis, the city attorney threatened to arrest any physician who performed an abortion (King 1973). Given this kind of activity, it can be concluded that in many states the Court's intent was "widely and purposively frustrated" (Blake 1977b, 60-61).

Variation in state response to the constitutional right to an abortion continues to this day. Although legal abortions are performed in all states, the availability of abortion services varies enormously. As noted, a variety of restrictions on abortion have been enacted across the country. In the wake of the Court's decision in *Webster* (1989), which upheld a restrictive Missouri law, a new round of state restrictions on abortion was generally expected. Indeed, within two years of the decision nine states and Guam enacted restrictions. Nevertheless, four states enacted legislation protecting a woman's right to abortion (Craig and O'Brien 1993, 280). The Pennsylvania enactments were challenged in *Casey* (1992), in which the "undue burden" standard was announced. The lack of clarity in this standard virtually ensures that restrictions will continue to be enacted.

Public Opinion

As shown in Figure 17-2, public opinion changed little from the early 1970s (pre-*Roe*) until the *Webster* decision in 1989, after which a small but important growth in pro-choice support occurred. Although differently worded questions produce different results, it is clear that the American public remains strongly supportive of abortion when the woman's health is endangered by continuing the pregnancy, when there is a strong chance of a serious fetal defect, and when the pregnancy is the result of rape or incest. The public is more divided when abortion is sought for economic reasons, by single unmarried women unwilling to marry, and by married women who do not want more children.[13] "The overall picture that emerges is that a majority supports leaving abortion legal and available to women unfortunate enough to need it, though many in the majority remain concerned about the moral implications" (Craig and O'Brien 1993, 269).

It is important to note, however, that many Americans are unaware that the Supreme Court has issued an opinion on the constitutionality of abortion. In 1975, two years after *Roe* and *Doe*, a Gallup Poll found that "less than half of American adult respondents were informed about the 1973 decisions" (Blake 1977b, 57-59). In 1982, nearly a decade after the decisions and two years into the Reagan administration and its loudly proclaimed commitment to ending legal abortion, 59 percent of a national survey sample answered either "Don't Know" or "No" to a question about whether the Supreme Court had issued an opinion permitting abortion in the first three months of pregnancy ("Americans Evaluate" 1982, 25). These results were highlighted in 1990 by eleven focus groups held around

Figure 17-2 Public Opinion and Abortion, Selected Years, 1975–1992

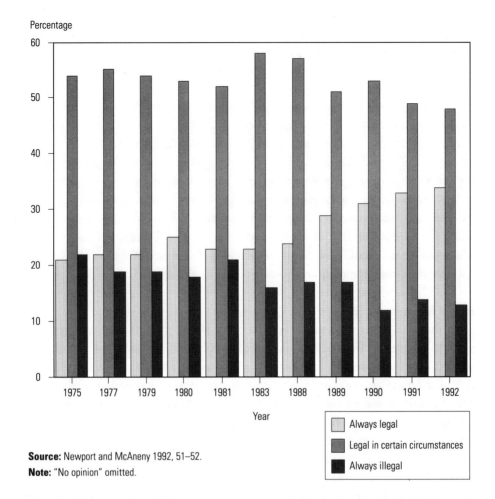

Percentage

Source: Newport and McAneny 1992, 51–52.
Note: "No opinion" omitted.

Legend:
- Always legal
- Legal in certain circumstances
- Always illegal

Year

the country for teenagers by the Center for Population Options in Washington, D.C. Summing up their findings, Stone and Waszak (1992, 55) reported: "Many of the participants thought it [abortion] was illegal in most states, although participants seemed to know that abortion was legal in their own state. No participants said that abortion was legal in all 50 states (many were surprised to learn the truth), and only a few of the teenagers could identify *Roe v. Wade* or explain its significance." Public support for abortion choice may be growing, but knowledge of the Court's decisions appears low.

Anti-Abortion Activity

Organized opposition to abortion increased dramatically in the years following the

Table 17-2 Abortion Clinics Reporting Harassment, 1985 and 1988
(in percent)

Activity	1985	1988
Picketing	80	81
Picketing with physical contact or blocking	47	46
Demonstrations resulting in arrests	—	38
Bomb threats	48	36
Vandalism	28	34
Picketing homes of staff members	16	17

Source: Surveys of all abortion providers taken by the Alan Guttmacher Institute in Henshaw (1991, 246-252, 263).

Note: Dash = question not asked.

Court's initial decisions. National groups such as the American Life Lobby, Americans United for Life, the National Right to Life Committee, the Pro-Life Action League, and Operation Rescue and numerous local groups have adopted some of the tactics of the reformers. They have marched, lobbied, and protested, urging that abortion be made illegal in most or all circumstances. In addition, in the 1980s, groups like Operation Rescue began to adopt more violent tactics. And, since 1982, the U.S. Bureau of Alcohol, Tobacco and Firearms has reported 146 incidents of bombing, arson, or attempts against clinics and related sites in thirty states, causing more than $12 million in damages (Thomas 1994). The high level of harassment of abortion clinics is shown in Table 17-2.

The level of harassment appears to have increased over time. In just 1992 and 1993 the U.S. Bureau of Alcohol, Tobacco and Firearms recorded thirty-six incidents, which resulted in an estimated $3.8 million in damages (Thomas 1994). The National Abortion Federation, representing roughly half of the nation's clinics, noted that incidents of reported vandalism at its clinics more than doubled from 1991 to 1992 (Barringer 1993). From May 1992 to August 1993 the U.S. Bureau of Alcohol, Tobacco and Firearms reported that 123 family-planning clinics were bombed or burned (Baum 1993). In 1992 more than forty clinics were attacked with butyric acid (a chemical injected through key holes, under doors, or into ventilation shafts), forcing clinic closures and requiring costly repairs (Anderson and Binstein 1993, C27). One of the aims of this violence appears to be to raise the cost of operating abortion clinics to such an extent as to force their closure. In 1992 and 1993, for example, arson destroyed clinics in Missoula and Helena, Montana, and in Boise, Idaho. The clinics have either been unable to reopen or have had great difficulty in doing so because of the difficulty of finding owners willing to rent to them and obtaining insurance coverage. In 1990, in the wake of such violence, one major insurer,

Traveler's Insurance Company, decided not to insure any abortion-related concerns (Baum 1993).

Another tactic aimed at shutting down abortion clinics is to conduct large, sustained protests. During the summer of 1991, for example, Operation Rescue staged forty-six days of protest in Wichita, Kansas, resulting in the arrest of approximately 2,700 people. During the summer of 1993, Operation Rescue launched a seven-city campaign with similar aims. In addition, there have been individual acts of violence against abortion providers. Dr. David Gunn was murdered in March 1993 outside an abortion clinic in Pensacola, Florida; Dr. George Tiller was shot in August 1993 in Wichita, Kansas; and Dr. John Britton and his escort, James Barrett, a retired air force lieutenant colonel, were murdered in late July 1994, also in Pensacola. Commenting on the murders of Dr. Britton and James Barrett, Don Treshman, director of the antiabortion group Rescue America, issued an ominous warning: "Up to now, the killings have been on one side, with 30 million dead babies and hundreds of dead and maimed mothers. On the other side, there are two dead doctors. Maybe the balance is going to start to shift" (quoted in Lewin 1994, A7).[14] In sum, as Forrest and Henshaw (1987, 13) concluded, "antiabortion harassment in the United States is widespread and frequent."

Two important facts can be gleaned from the foregoing discussion. First, at the time of the 1973 abortion decisions, large segments of the political and professional elite were either indifferent to or supported abortion reform. Second, after the decisions, many political leaders vociferously opposed abortion. Congress enacted antiabortion legislation as did some of the states. In addition, activist opposition was growing. How this opposition affected the implementation of the decisions is the focus of the next section.

The Effect of Opposition on the Implementation of Abortion Rights

On the eve of the abortion decisions, there was widespread support from critical professional elites, growing public support, successful reform in many states, and indifference from most national politicians. Is this sufficient for the implementation of constitutional rights?

Constitutional rights are not self-implementing. That is, to make a right a reality, the behavior of individuals and the policies of the institutions in which they work must change. Because abortion is a medical procedure, and because safe abortion requires trained personnel, the implementation of abortion rights depends on the medical profession to provide abortion services. When done properly, first-term and most second-term abortions can be performed on an outpatient basis, and there is less risk of death in the procedure than there is in childbirth or in such routine operations as tonsillectomies.

Thus, no medical or technical reasons stand in the way of the provision of abortion services. Following Supreme Court action, however, the medical profession moved with "extreme caution" in making abortion available (Brody 1973, 1). Coupled with the hostility of some state legislatures, barriers to legal abortion remained.

These barriers have proved to be strong. Perhaps the strongest barrier has been opposition from hospitals. In Table 17-3, I track the response of hospitals to the Court's decisions. The results are staggering. Despite the relative ease and safety of the abortion procedure, and the unambiguous holding of the Court, both public and private hospitals throughout America have refused to perform abortions. *The vast majority of public and private hospitals have never performed an abortion!* In 1973 and the first quarter of 1974, for example, slightly more than three-quarters of public and private non-Catholic general care short-term hospitals did not perform a single abortion (Weinstock et al. 1975, 31). As illustrated in the table, the passage of time has not improved the situation. By 1976, three years after the decision, at least 70 percent of hospitals provided no abortion services. By 1992 the situation had further deteriorated: only 18 percent of private non-Catholic general care short-term hospitals and only 13 percent of public hospitals provided abortions. As Stanley Henshaw (1986, 253, emphasis added) concluded, reviewing the data in 1986, "most hospitals have *never* performed abortions."

These figures mask the fact that even the limited availability of hospital abortions detailed here varies widely across states. In 1973, for example, only 4 percent of all abortions were performed in the eight states that make up the East South Central and West South Central census divisions (Weinstock et al. 1975, 25).[15] Two states, on the other hand, New York and California (which are home to about 20 percent of all U.S. women), accounted for 37 percent of all abortions in 1974 (Alan Guttmacher Institute 1976). In eleven states, "not a single public hospital reported performance of a single abortion for any purpose whatsoever in all of 1973" (Weinstock et al. 1975, 31). By 1976, three years after Court action, no hospitals, public or private, in Louisiana, North Dakota, and South Dakota performed abortions (Hansen 1980). The Dakotas alone, had thirty public and sixty-two private hospitals. In five other states, which had a total of eighty-two public hospitals, not one performed an abortion. In thirteen additional states, less than 10 percent of each state's public hospitals reported performing any abortions (Forrest, Sullivan, and Tietze 1979a, 46). Only in the states of California, Hawaii, New York, and North Carolina and in the District of Columbia did more than half the public hospitals perform any abortions during 1974-1975 (Alan Guttmacher Institute 1976, 30). By 1992, the situation was little better, with five states (California, New York, Texas, Florida, and Illinois) accounting for 49 percent of all legal abortions (Henshaw and Van Vort 1994, 102).

This refusal of hospitals to perform abortions means that women seeking them, particularly from rural areas, have to travel, often a great distance, to exercise their constitu-

Table 17-3 Hospitals Providing Abortions, Selected Years, 1973-1992 (percent)

Year	Private, short-term, non-Catholic, general	Public
1973	24	—
1974	27	17
1975	30	—
1976	31	20
1977	31	21
1978	29	—
1979	28	—
1980	27	17
1982	26	16
1985	23	17
1988	21	15
1992	18	13

Sources: Forrest, Sullivan, and Tietze 1978, table 5; Henshaw 1986, 253; Henshaw et al. 1982, table 7; Henshaw, Forrest, and Van Vort 1987, 68; Henshaw and Van Vort 1990, 102-108, 142; Henshaw and Van Vort 1994, 100-106, 122; Rubin 1982, 154; Sullivan, Tietze, and Dryfoos, 1977, figure 10; Weinstock et al. 1975, 32.

Note: Dash = unavailable.

tional rights. In 1973, for example, 150,000 women traveled out of their state of residence to obtain abortions. By 1982 the numbers had dropped, but more than 100,000 women were still forced to travel to another state for abortion services. In Table 17-4, I list the states from which 10 percent or more of female residents seeking abortions have had to travel to other states to obtain them. As late as 1987, nearly fifteen years after the initial Court decisions, more than 20 percent of women residing in ten states went to other states to obtain abortions, as did an additional 10 to 19 percent of women residing in nine states.

Even when women can obtain abortions within their states of residence, they may still have to travel a great distance to do so. In 1974, the year after *Roe*, the Guttmacher Institute found that between 300,000 and 400,000 women left their home communities to obtain abortions (Alan Guttmacher Institute 1976). In 1980, across the United States, more than one-quarter (27 percent) of all women who had abortions had them outside of their home counties (Henshaw and O'Reilly 1983, 5). And in 1988, fifteen years after *Roe*, an estimated 430,000 (27 percent) women who had abortions in nonhospital settings traveled more than fifty miles from their home to reach their abortion provider. This includes over

Table 17-4 Women Going Out of State of Residence to Obtain Abortions, Selected Years (percent)

State of residence	20% or more				10%-19%			
	1979	1980	1985	1987	1979	1980	1985	1987
Alabama	22							14
Arizona		25	24					
Arkansas		20	26		10			19
Connecticut						11		
Delaware	23	23					11	
Idaho	33	26	20	28				
Indiana	28	25	26	29				
Iowa					18	18	16	17
Kansas						10	12	
Kentucky	27	26	30	23				
Louisiana					15	15	10	11
Maine						11	18	
Maryland	29	26	27	26				
Mississippi	45	38	27	32				
Missouri	31	25	21	23				
New Hampshire	24	24		29			15	
New Jersey					14	12		
New Mexico							17	16
North Dakota	28	24						13
Oklahoma						14	13	
Oregon					12			
Rhode Island					17	14		
South Carolina					15	14	17	18
South Dakota	52	52	23	47				
Vermont	21					19	13	10
Virginia					15	15	14	16
West Virginia	51	52	28	35				
Wyoming	52	54	52	56				
Total	15	14	10	10	10	10	10	9

Sources: 1979 and 1980: Henshaw and O'Reilly 1983, table 9; 1981: Henshaw et al. 1985, table 7; 1982: Henshaw, Forrest, and Van Vort 1987, table 4; 1985: Henshaw and Van Vort 1990, table 34; 1987: Henshaw and Smith 1991, table 6.

140,000 women who traveled more than 100 miles to obtain a legal abortion (Henshaw 1991, 248).[16]

The general problem that faces women who seek to exercise their constitutional right to abortion is the paucity of abortion providers. From the legalization of abortion in 1973 to the present, at least 77 percent of all U.S. counties have been without abortion providers. And the problem is not merely rural. In 1980, seven years after Court action, there were still fifty-nine metropolitan areas in which no facilities could be identified that provided abortions (Henshaw et al. 1982, 5). The most recent data suggest that the problem is worsening. In 1992, 84 percent of all U.S. counties, home to 30 percent of all women of reproductive age, had no abortion providers. Ninety-one of the country's 320 metropolitan (28 percent) areas have no identified abortion provider, and an additional 14 (4 percent) have providers who perform fewer than fifty abortions per year. The 91 metropolitan areas with no abortion providers are located in thirty-seven states and include areas such as Bradenton, Florida; Springfield and four other Illinois cities; seven Indiana cities; Sioux City, Iowa; Battle Creek, Michigan; Bismarck, North Dakota; six Ohio cities; Erie and six other Pennsylvania cities; Rapid City, South Dakota; Abilene, Amarillo, Galveston, Waco, and nine other Texas cities; Provo, Utah; Kenosha, Racine, and five other Wisconsin cities; and Cheyenne, Wyoming (Henshaw and Van Vort 1994, 101). Overall, in 1992 in "22 states, no more than five counties have a facility that reports providing at least one abortion . . . and in only 11 states do as many as half the counties have any abortion services" (Henshaw and Van Vort 1994, 103).

Even when abortion service is available, providers have tended to ignore the time periods set out in the Court's opinions. In 1988, fifteen years after the decisions, only 43 percent of all providers perform abortions after the first trimester. More than half (55 percent) of the hospitals that perform abortions have refused to perform second-trimester procedures, a time in pregnancy at which hospital services may be medically necessary. Only at abortion clinics have a majority of providers been willing to perform abortions after the first trimester (Henshaw 1991, 252). Indeed, in 1988 a startling 22 percent of all providers refused to perform abortions past the tenth week of pregnancy, several weeks within the first trimester, during which, according to the Court, a woman's constitutional right is virtually all-encompassing (Henshaw 1991, 251).

Finally, although abortion is "the most common surgical procedure that women undergo" (Darney et al. 1987, 161) and is reportedly the most common surgical procedure performed in the United States (Baum 1993), an *increasing* percentage of residency programs in obstetrics and gynecology do not provide training for it. A survey taken in 1985 of all such residency programs found that 28 percent of them offered no training at all, a nearly fourfold increase since 1976. According to the results of the survey, approximately one-half of the programs made training available as an option, while only 23 percent included it routinely (Darney et al. 1987, 160). By 1992 the percentage of programs requiring abortion training had dropped nearly to half, to 12 percent (Baum 1993). In a study done in 1992 of 216 of 271 residency programs, it was found that almost half (47 percent) of graduating residents had never performed a first-trimester abortion, and only 7 percent had ever performed one in the second trimester (Cooper 1993). At least part of the reason for the increasing lack of training is harassment by antiabortion activists. "Anti-abortion groups say these numbers prove that harassment of doctors, and in turn, medical schools which train residents in abortion procedures, is an effective tactic," Cooper reported. " 'You humiliate the school. . . . We hope that in 10 years, there'll be none' that train residents how to perform abortions" (Randall Terry, founder of Operation Rescue, quoted in Cooper 1993, B3).

These findings are well illustrated by a few examples. In Illinois, the sixth largest state in the Union, abortion services are available in only 12 of 102 counties, and only 21.6 percent of hospitals with obstetric services perform abortions. Five metropolitan areas lack abortion services, including the capital, Springfield, a city of 100,000. The result is that "many women have to drive for several hours to find a willing physician" (Lipinski 1989, 12). In 1992 in twelve states there were fewer than ten abortion providers per state. In the country as a whole, there is an average of 4.0 providers per 100,00 women aged fifteen to forty-four, and states like California and New York have 7.7 and 6.8 providers, respectively, per 100,000 women, yet seventeen states have fewer than 2.0 providers per 100,000 women. At the furthest extreme, there is only one provider in each of North Dakota and South Dakota (Henshaw and Van Vort 1994, 105). As the lead sentence in a *New York Times* story in July 1989 put it, "outside of the nation's biggest cities, women who seek abortions must drive four hours and often cross state lines to reach a doctor willing to perform one" (Belkin 1989, 1).

It is clear that hospital administrators, both public and private, refused to change their abortion policies in reaction to the Court decisions. In the years since the Court's decisions, abortion services have remained centered in metropolitan areas and in those states that reformed their abortion laws and regulations prior to the Court's decisions. In 1976 the Alan Guttmacher Institute (1976, 13) concluded that "[t]he response of hospitals to the legalization of abortion continues to be so limited . . . as to be tantamount to no response." Jaffe, Lindheim, and Lee (1981, 15) concluded that "the delivery pattern for abortion services that has emerged since 1973 is distorted beyond precedent." Reviewing the data in the mid-1980s, Henshaw, Forrest, and Blaine (1984, 122) summed up the situation this way: "There is abundant evidence that many women still find it difficult or impossible to obtain abortion services because of the distance of their home to the nearest provider, the cost, a lack of information on where to go, and limitations on the circumstances under which a provider will make abortions available." Most recently, Henshaw (1991, 253) con-

cluded that "an American woman seeking abortion services will find it increasingly difficult to find a provider who will serve her in an accessible location and at an affordable
cost."

Implementing Constitutional Rights: The Market

The foregoing discussion presents a seeming dilemma. There has been hostility to abortion from some politicians, most hospital administrators, many doctors, and parts of the
public. On the whole, in response to the Court, hospitals did not change their policies to
permit abortions. Yet, as demonstrated in Figure 17-1, the number of legal abortions performed in the United States continued to grow. How is it, for example, that congressional
and state hostility seemed effectively to prevent progress in civil rights in the 1950s and
early 1960s but did not prevent abortion in the 1970s? The answer to this question not only
removes the dilemma but also illustrates why the Court's abortion decisions were effective
in making legal abortion more easily available. The answer, in a word, is *clinics.*

The Court's decisions prohibited the states from interfering with a woman's right to
choose an abortion, at least in the first trimester. They did not uphold hospitalization
requirements, and later cases explicitly rejected hospitalization requirements for second-
trimester abortions.[17] Room was left for abortion reformers, population control groups,
women's groups, and individual physicians to set up clinics to perform abortions. The
refusal of many hospitals, then, to perform abortions could be countered by the creation of
clinics willing to do the job. And that's exactly what happened.

In the wake of the Court's decisions the number of abortion providers sharply increased
(see Table 17-5). In the first year after the decisions, the number of providers grew by
nearly 25 percent. Over the first three years the percentage increase was almost 58 percent.
The number of providers reached a peak in 1982 and has declined more than 18 percent
since then. These raw data, however, do not indicate who these providers were.

It can be clearly seen in Table 17-6 that the number of abortion providers increased
because of the increase in the number of clinics. To fill the void that hospitals had left,
clinics opened in large numbers (Schultz 1977). Between 1973 and 1974, for example, the
number of nonhospital abortion providers grew 61 percent. Overall, between 1973 and
1976 the number of nonhospital providers grew 152 percent, nearly five times the rate of
growth of hospital providers. In metropolitan areas (not shown in the table), the growth
rate was 140 percent between 1973 and 1976, five times the rate for hospital providers; in
nonmetropolitan areas it was a staggering 304 percent, also about five times the growth
rate for nonmetropolitan hospitals.

The growth in the number of abortion clinics was matched by the increase in the number of abortions performed by them. By 1974, nonhospital clinics were performing ap-

Table 17-5 Number of Abortion Providers, Selected Years, 1973-1992

Year	Number	Change from previous year	Percent change from previous year
1973	1,627	NA	NA
1974	2,028	401	24.7
1975	2,398	370	18.3
1976	2,567	169	7.1
1977	2,688	121	4.7
1978	2,753	65	2.4
1979	2,734	−19	−0.7
1980	2,758	24	0.9
1981	2,896	138	5.0
1982	2,908	12	0.4
1984	2,710	—	—
1985	2,680	−30	−1.1
1987	2,618	62[a]	−2.3[a]
1988	2,582	−36	−1.4
1992	2,380	−202[b]	−7.8

Sources: 1973-1985: Henshaw, Forrest, and Van Vort 1987, table 1; 1987: Henshaw and Van Vort 1990, 102-108, 142; 1988 and 1992: Henshaw and Van Vort 1994, 100-106, 112.

Note: NA = not applicable. Dash = unavailable.

[a] Change between 1985 and 1987.   [b] Change between 1988 and 1992.

proximately 51 percent of all abortions, and nearly an additional 3 percent were being performed in physician's offices. Between 1973 and 1974, the number of abortions performed in hospitals rose 5 percent, while the number performed in clinics rose 39 percent. By 1976, clinics accounted for 62 percent of all reported abortions, despite the fact that they were only 17 percent of all providers (Forrest, Sullivan, and Tietze 1979a). From 1973 to 1976, the years immediately following Court action, the number of abortions performed in hospitals increased by only 8 percent, whereas the number performed in clinics and physicians' offices increased by a whopping 113 percent (Forrest et al. 1979a).[18] The percentages continued to rise, and by 1992, 93 percent of all abortions were performed in nonhospital settings. Clinics satisfied the need that hospitals, despite the Court's actions, refused to meet.

In permitting abortions to be performed in clinics as well as hospitals, the Court's decisions granted a way around the intransigence of hospitals. The decisions allowed individuals committed to safe and legal abortion to make use of the market and create their own

Table 17-6 Facilities That Provided Abortions, Selected Years, 1973-1992

Year	Hospitals		Nonhospitals [a]	
	Number	Abortions performed (%)	Number	Abortions performed (%)
1973	1,281	52	346	48
1974	1,471	47	557	54
1975	1,629	40	769	60
1976	1,695	35	872	65
1977	1,654	30	1,055	70
1978	1,626	25	1,127	75
1979	1,526	23	1,208	77
1980	1,504	22	1,254	78
1982	1,405	18	1,503	83
1985	1,191	13	1,489	87
1988	1,040	10	1,542	90
1992	855	7	1,525	93

Sources: Forrest, Sullivan, and Tietze 1978, table 5, 1979a, 1979b, 329, 338; Henshaw, Forrest, and Blaine 1984, tables 5 and 6; Henshaw, Forrest, Sullivan, and Tietze 1982, tables 7, 8, 13; Henshaw, Forrest, and Van Vort 1987, table 5; Henshaw and O'Reilly 1983, 11; Henshaw and Van Vort 1994, tables 5 and 6; Sullivan, Tietze, and Dryfoos 1977, figure 10; Weinstock et al. 1975, 23.

[a] Abortion clinics, clinics that provide services in addition to abortion, and physicians' offices.

structures to meet the demand. They also provided a financial incentive for services to be provided. At least some clinics were formed solely as money-making ventures. As the legal activist Janice Goodman put it, "Some doctors are going to see a very substantial amount of money to be made on this" (quoted in Goodman, Schoenbrod, and Stearns 1973, 31). Nancy Stearns, who filed a pro-choice amicus brief in *Roe*, agreed: "[In the abortion cases] the people that are necessary to effect the decision are doctors, most of whom are not opposed, probably don't give a damn, and in fact have a whole lot to gain . . . because of the amount of money they can make" (quoted in Goodman et al. 1973, 29). Even the glacial growth of hospital abortion providers in the early and mid-1970s may be due, in part, to financial considerations. In a study of thirty-six general hospitals in Harris County (Houston), Texas, the need for increased income was found to be an important determinant of whether hospitals performed abortions. Hospitals with low occupancy rates, and therefore low income, the study reported, "saw changing abortion policy as a way to fill beds and raise income" (Kemp, Carp, and Brady 1978, 27).

Although the law of the land was that the choice of an abortion was not to be denied a woman in the first trimester, and regulated only to the extent necessary to preserve a woman's health in the second trimester, American hospitals, on the whole, do not honor the law. By allowing the market to meet the need, however, the Court's decisions resulted in at least a continuation of some availability of safe and legal abortion. Although no one can be sure what might have happened if clinics had not been allowed, if the sole burden for implementing the decisions had been on hospitals, hospital practice suggests that resistance would have been strong. After all, the Court did find abortion constitutionally protected, and most hospitals simply refused to accept that decision.

The implementation of constitutional rights, then, may depend a great deal on the beliefs of those necessary to implement them. The data suggest that without clinics the Court's decisions, constitutional rights notwithstanding, would have been frustrated.

Court Decisions and Political Action

It is generally believed that winning a major Supreme Court case is an invaluable political resource. The victorious side can use the decision to dramatize the issue, encourage political mobilization, and ignite a political movement (see McCann 1994; Scheingold 1974, 131, 148). In an older view, however, this connection is dubious. Writing at the beginning of the twentieth century, Thayer (1901) suggested that reliance on litigation weakens political organizing. Because there have been more than twenty years of litigation in regard to abortion, the issue provides a good test of these competing views.

The evidence suggests that *Roe* and *Doe* may have seriously weakened the political effectiveness of the winners— pro-choice forces—and inspired the losers. After the 1973 decisions, many pro-choice activists simply assumed they had won and stopped their activity. According to J. Hugh Anwyl, then the executive director of Planned Parenthood of Los Angeles, pro-choice activists went "on a long siesta" after the abortion decisions (quoted in Johnston 1977, 1). Alfred F. Moran, an executive vice president at Planned Parenthood of New York, put it this way: "Most of us really believed that was the end of the controversy. The Supreme Court had spoken, and while some disagreement would remain, the issue had been tried, tested and laid to rest" (Brozan 1983, A17). These views were joined by a NARAL activist, Janet Beals: "Everyone assumed that when the Supreme Court made its decision in 1973 that we'd got what we wanted and the battle was over. The movement afterwards lost steam" (quoted in Phillips 1980, 3). By 1977 a survey of pro-choice and antiabortion activity in thirteen states nationwide revealed that abortion rights advocates had failed to match the activity of their opponents (Johnston 1977).[19] The political organization and momentum that had changed laws nationwide dissipated in reaction to Court victory. This may help explain why abortion services remain so unevenly available.

Reliance on Court action seems to have harmed the pro-choice movement in a second way. The most restrictive version of the Hyde Amendment, banning federal funding of abortions even where abortion is necessary to save the life of the woman, was passed with the help of a parliamentary maneuver by pro-choice legislators. Their strategy, as reported the following day on the front pages of the *New York Times* and the *Washington Post*, was to pass such a conservative bill that the Court would have no choice but to overturn it (Russell 1977; Tolchin 1977; this tactic is also noted in Gelb and Palley 1979 and Jaffe et al. 1981). This reliance on the Court was totally unfounded. With hindsight, Karen Mulhauser, a former director of NARAL, suggested that "had we made more gains through the legislative and referendum processes, and taken a little longer at it, the public would have moved with us" (quoted in Williams 1979, 12). By winning a Court case "without the organization needed to cope with a powerful opposition" (Rubin 1982, 169), pro-choice forces vastly overestimated the power and influence of the Court.

By the time of *Webster* (1989), however, pro-choice forces seemed to have learned from their mistakes, while right-to-life activists miscalculated. In early August 1989, just after *Webster*, a spokesperson for the National Right to Life Committee proclaimed: "[F]or the first time since 1973, we are clearly in a position of strength" (Shribman 1989, A8). Pro-choice forces, however, went on the offensive by generating a massive political response. Commenting on *Webster*, Nancy Broff, NARAL's legislative and political director, noted, "It finally gave us the smoking gun we needed to mobilize people" (quoted in Kornhauser 1989, 11). Membership and financial support grew rapidly. "In the year after *Webster*, membership in the National Abortion Rights Action League jumped from 150,000 to 400,000; in the National Organization for Women [NOW], from 170,000 to 250,000" (Craig and O'Brien 1993, 296). Furthermore, NARAL "nearly tripled" its income in 1989, and NOW "nearly doubled" its income, as did the Planned Parenthood Federation of America (Shribman 1989, A8). In May 1989 alone, NARAL raised $1 million (Kornhauser 1989).

This newfound energy was turned toward political action. In gubernatorial elections in Virginia and New Jersey in the fall of 1989, pro-choice forces played an important role in electing the pro-choice candidates L. Douglas Wilder and James J. Florio over antiabortion opponents. Antiabortion legislation was defeated in Florida, where Gov. Bob Martinez, an opponent of abortion, called a special session of the legislature to enact it. Congress passed legislation that allowed the District of Columbia to use its own tax revenues to pay for abortions and that essentially repealed the so-called gag rule, but President Bush vetoed both bills, and the House of Representatives failed to override the vetoes. As Paige Cunningham, of the antiabortion group Americans United for Life, put it: "The pro-life movement has been organized and active for twenty years, and some of us are tired. The pro-choice movement is fresh so they're operating with a much greater energy reserve. They've really rallied in light of *Webster*" (quoted in Berke 1989, 1).

This new understanding was also seen in *Casey*. Although pro-choice forces had seen antiabortion restrictions upheld in *Webster* and *Rust,* and the sure antiabortion vote of Justice Clarence Thomas had replaced the pro-choice vote of Justice Thurgood Marshall on the Supreme Court in the interim, pro-choice forces appealed the lower-court decision to the Supreme Court. As the *New York Times* reported, this was "a calculated move to intensify the political debate on abortion before the 1992 election" (Berke 1989, 1). Further increasing the stakes, they asked the Court either to reaffirm women's fundamental right to abortion or to overturn *Roe.* Berke (1991, B8) declared that "[t]he action marked an adjustment in strategy by the abortion rights groups, who seem now to be looking to the Court as a political foil rather than a source of redress."

All this suggests that Thayer may have the stronger case. That is, Court decisions do seem to have a mobilizing potential, but for the losers![20] Both winners and losers appear to assume that Court decisions announcing or upholding constitutional rights will be implemented, but they behave in different ways. Winners celebrate and relax, whereas losers redouble their efforts. Note, too, that in the wake of *Webster,* public opinion moved in a pro-choice direction, counter to the tenor of the opinion. Court decisions do matter, but in complicated ways.

Conclusion

"It does no good to have the [abortion] procedure be legal if women can't get it," stated Gwenyth Mapes, the executive director of the Missoula (Montana) Blue Mountain Clinic destroyed by arson in March 1993 (quoted in Baum 1993, A1).

Courts do not exist in a vacuum. Supreme Court decisions, even those finding constitutional rights, are not implemented automatically or in any straightforward or simple way. They are merely one part of the broader political picture. At best, they can contribute to the process of change. In and of themselves, they accomplish little.

The implementation of the Court's abortion decisions, partial though it has been, owes its success to the fact that the decisions have been made in a time when the role of women in American life is changing dramatically. Out of the social turmoil of the 1960s grew a women's movement that continues to press politically, socially, and culturally for ending restrictions on women's opportunities. Access to safe and legal abortion is part of this movement. In 1973 the Supreme Court lent its support by finding a constitutional right to abortion. And in the years since, it has maintained its support for that core constitutional right. Yet, I have argued that far more important in making safe and legal abortion available are the beliefs of politicians, relevant professionals, and the public. When these groups are supportive of abortion choice, that choice is available. Where they have opposed abortion, they have fought against the Court's decisions, successfully minimizing access to abortion. Lack of support from hospital administrators and some politicians and intense opposition from a small group of politicians and activists have limited the availability of abortion services. On the whole, in states that were supportive of abortion choice before Court action, access remains good. In the states that had the most restrictive abortion laws before *Roe*, abortion services are available but remain difficult to obtain. As Gwenyth Mapes put it, "[I]t does no good to have the [abortion] procedure be legal if women can't get it."

This analysis suggests that in general, constitutional rights have a greater likelihood of being implemented when they reflect the preexisting beliefs of politicians, relevant professionals, and the public. When at least some of these groups are opposed, locally or nationally, implementation is less likely. The assumption that the implementation of Court decisions and constitutional rights is unproblematic both reifies and removes courts from the political, social, cultural, and economic systems in which they operate. Courts are political institutions, and their role must be understood accordingly. Examining their decisions without making the political world central to that examination may make for fine reading in constitutional-law textbooks, but it tells the reader very little about the lives people lead.

Notes

1. Alaska, Hawaii, New York, and Washington had previously liberalized their laws. The constitutional requirements set forth in *Roe* and *Doe* were basically, although not completely, met by these state laws.

2. For an in-depth look at the involvement of interest groups in the judicial process, see Chapter 5 of this book.

3. For a fuller examination, see Rosenberg 1991.

4. In 1971, before *Roe* and *Doe*, the Court heard an abortion case (*United States v. Vuitch*) from Washington, D.C. The decision, however, did not settle the constitutional issues involved in the abortion controversy.

5. Estimates of the number of legal abortions performed each year prior to *Roe* vary enormously, ranging from 50,000 to nearly 2 million. See Rosenberg 1991, 353-355.

6. The following discussion, except where noted, is based on Lader 1973.

7. After the 1973 decisions, NARAL kept its acronym but changed its name to the National Abortion Rights Action League.

8. Nixon's "own personal views" were that "unrestricted abortion policies, or abortion on demand" could not be squared with his "personal belief in the sanctity of human life" (quoted in Lader 1973, 176-177).

9. Franklin and Kosaki (1989, 762) argue that in the wake of *Roe* opinions hardened. That is, those who were pro-choice before the decision became even more so after; the same held true for those opposed to abortion. Court action did not change opinions; abortion opponents did not become abortion supporters (and vice versa). See Epstein and Kobylka 1992, 203.

10. Ford did veto the 1977 appropriations bill containing the Hyde Amendment. He stated that he did so for budgetary reasons (the bill was $4 billion over his budget request) and reasserted his support for "restrictions on the use of federal funds for abortion" (quoted in Craig and O'Brien 1993, 161).

11. The Congressional Research Service reports that Congress enacted thirty restrictive abortion statutes during 1973-1982 (Davidson 1983).

12. The growth in violent attacks on abortion clinics, and illegal, harassing demonstrations in front of them, may demonstrate a growing awareness of this point by the foes of abortion.

13. For recent poll data, see "Abortion" 1989; *American Enterprise* 1993; Dionne 1989; Hugick 1992; Lewin 1989; Newport and McAneny 1992.

14. Treshman is not the only antiabortion activist to express such views. Goodstein (1994, A1) writes that "there is a sizable faction among the antiabortion movement's activists ... who have applauded Hill [the convicted killer of Dr. Britton and Mr. Barrett] as a righteous defender of babies."

15. The East South Central states are Kentucky, Tennessee, Alabama, and Mississippi. The West South Central states are Arkansas, Louisiana, Oklahoma, and Texas. Together, these eight states contained 16 percent of the U.S. population in 1973.

16. It is possible, of course, that some women had personal reasons for not obtaining an abortion in their home town. Still, that seems an unlikely explanation as to why 100,000 women each year would leave their home states to obtain abortions. For data on this phenomenon, see Forrest and Henshaw 1987, 66; Forrest, Sullivan, and Tietze 1979b, 332; Henshaw, Forrest, and Van Vort 1987; Henshaw and O'Reilly 1983, 9; Sullivan, Tietze, and Dryfoos 1977, 124.

17. *Akron v. Akron Center for Reproductive Health* (1983); *Planned Parenthood v. Ashcroft* (1983). The vast majority of abortions in the United States are performed in the first trimester. As early as 1976, the figure was 90 percent. See Forrest et al. 1979a, 32.

18. The percentage for clinics is not artificially high because there were only a small number of clinic abortions in the years preceding Court action. In 1973, clinics performed more than 330,000 abortions, or about 45 percent of all abortions (see Alan Guttmacher Institute 1976, 27).

19. Others in agreement with this analysis include Tatalovich and Daynes (1981, 101, 164), participants in a symposium at the Brookings Institute (in Steiner 1983), and Jackson and Vinovskis (1983, 73), who found that after the decisions "state-level pro-choice grounds disbanded, victory seemingly achieved."

20. This also appears to have been the case in 1954 with the Court's school desegregation decision, *Brown v. Board of Education*. After that decision, the Ku Klux Klan was reinvigorated and the White Citizen's Councils were formed, with the aim of preserving racial segregation through violence and intimidation.

Reference Material

Appendix A: Regression and Pooled Cross-Sectional Time Series

David C. Nixon

Many of the chapters in this book examine the relationships among some plausibly interconnected variables. Often, the authors seek to explain one particular variable. This is called the *dependent* variable. *Independent* variables are those that are thought to cause variation in the dependent variable. Consider the relationship, depicted in Figure A-1, between a dependent variable *(Y)*—the number of cases filed in U.S. Courts of Appeals—and an explanatory variable *(X)*—time (fiscal year). Note that for each observation in this set of data, the values of X and Y define a unique point. So, for example, the number of cases filed in 1915 is 1,452; in 1916, 1,518; and so forth. Also observe that a positive relationship exists between X and Y. That is, higher values of Y are associated with higher values of X, while lower values of Y are associated with lower values of X. Here, this means that the number of cases filed has increased over time.

It is one thing to say that two variables are associated, as is true of the variables *cases filed* and *time*. But it is quite another matter to talk about the strength of the relationship between a dependent and an independent variable, a desirable undertaking in social scientific research. That is why scholars invoke regression analysis: it provides a robust technique for estimating the strength of the relationship between variables.

The mechanics of linear regression are relatively straightforward.[1] In its simplest form, it begins with the assumption that the relationship between an independent and dependent variable is a straight line that can be expressed in this way:

$$(A-1) \qquad\qquad Y = a + bX,$$

where Y is the dependent variable (in our example, the number of cases filed), coefficient a is the height of the line (called an intercept, or constant), coefficient b is the steepness of the line (called the slope), and X is the independent variable (here, time). Various computer-driven statistical software packages can be used to obtain estimates of the coefficients for a and b.[2] For the example shown in Figure A-1, a regression indicates that Y is linearly related to X in the following way,[3]

Figure A-1 Caseload of the U.S. Court of Appeals, 1915–1936

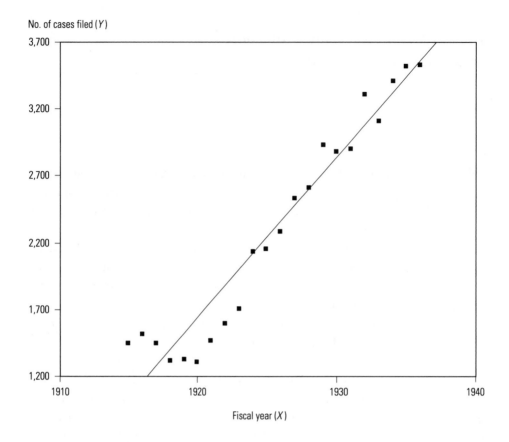

No. of cases filed (*Y*)

Fiscal year (*X*)

Source: Epstein et al. 1994, 642.

(A-2)   Number of cases filed = 911.35 + 119.92(time).[4]

This tells us that the number of case filings increased by about 120 each year. In addition, these estimates can be used to generate a prediction about the number of cases filed in any given year. The predicted value of the dependent variable for a given observation is the value of the independent variable multiplied by its coefficient, plus the intercept. Thus, in Figure A-1, an observation with a value of 3 (in our case that would be the third year, 1917) is predicted to have a value of 1,271. Or,

(A-3)   Predicted number of cases filed in 1917 = 911.35 + (119.92 x 3) ≈ 1,271.

Interestingly, as this number makes clear, we cannot perfectly predict the number of cases filed based solely on knowledge of what year it is; the actual number of cases filed in 1917 was 1,446, not 1,271. The line fitted to the data in Figure A-1 reinforces this conclusion because not all the observations fall on it. What this means is that the relationship between time and cases filed is not exact.

What would an exact fit look like? Consider Figure A-2, a display of a hypothetical set of caseload data. The regression estimates for these data are:

(A-4)   Number of cases filed = 900 + 100(time).

This means that case filings increase by 100 with each passing year and that the predicted value for year 1 (1915) would be 1,000; for year 2, 1,100; and so forth. But note the difference between these data and those displayed in Figure A-1: Y is an exact linear function of X. If X increases one unit in value then Y increases exactly 100 units; no observations sit off the regression line. In other words, if the year is known, the number of case filings can be perfectly predicted.

Unfortunately, as Lewis-Beck (1980, 10) makes clear, very few relationships in the social sciences are this exact. More tend to look like Figure A-1 than Figure A-2. Accordingly, it would be better to rewrite equation A-1 in this way:

(A-5) $Y = a + bX + e,$

where e represents the existence of error. It captures the fact that, in most of our work, X will not perfectly predict Y, just as time does not perfectly predict case filings. The smaller the errors, the more accurate the predictions, or the more fully one can claim to have "explained" the dependent variable.

Multiple Regression

What causes error? Why doesn't every value of Y fall exactly on the line depicted in Figure A-1? Answers to these questions abound. But one that readily comes to mind in our illustration is this: as Christine B. Harrington and Daniel Ward suggest in Chapter 9, we would not expect "time" to be the sole cause of variation in the dependent variable. Other factors, such as increases in population and in the number of judges, probably affect case filings, as well. The same holds for almost all political phenomena: they are best explained by more than one independent variable. To understand why, consider all, or at least some, of the factors affecting a voter's choice in an election. A *bivariate* model (that is, one that includes only one independent variable, as in our use of time to predict caseload) would

Figure A-2 Hypothetical Caseload Data Showing Exact Linear Relationship between *X* and *Y*

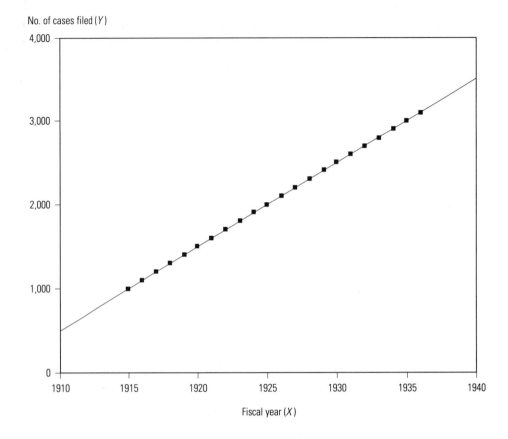

No. of cases filed (*Y*)

Fiscal year (*X*)

take into account only one explanatory variable, say, party identification. In a *multivariate* model (one that includes more than one independent variable) many other explanatory factors are considered, such as a person's gender, education, race, or preference on specific policy items (for example, abortion). In this instance, as in most in the social sciences, it is clear that a multivariate model would provide a more realistic picture of the voting decision.

Happily, regression with one independent variable (bivariate), as in the previous example, is easily generalized to multiple independent variables (multivariate). Each coefficient in a multivariate regression indicates the expected change in the dependent variable for a hypothetical one-unit change in the independent variable, holding all other variables constant. For example, Harrington and Ward estimate that the effect of per capita income on private civil appeals is –0.746 (see Table 9-2). Each additional dollar of per capita income in a circuit reduces the predicted number of appeals per 100,000 population by –0.746.

Taking the average circuit population of 21,000,000 as our baseline, a circuit with a per capita income of $20,000 is predicted to have 157 fewer appeals than a circuit with a per capita income of $21,000, all else being equal (–0.746 x 1 x 210 = 156.6).

Cross-Sectional versus Longitudinal Data

As Harrington and Ward note, data may be either *cross-sectional* or *longitudinal.* For longitudinal data, an identical unit (say, a *single* appellate court) is observed at multiple time points. (Figure A-1 provides an example of longitudinal data.) The effect of an explanatory variable, as indicated by the regression coefficient for that variable, is the predicted change in the dependent variable resulting from a hypothetical increase of one unit of the explanatory variable, holding all other explanatory variables constant. This is the more traditional understanding of what is normally considered an *effect.*

For cross-sectional data, multiple units (say *all* U.S. Courts of Appeals) are observed at a single moment. Rather than explaining changes in the dependent variable over time, regression with cross-sectional data explains differences in the dependent variable between observational units. The effect of a variable, as indicated by the regression coefficient, is the change in the prediction of the dependent variable for a hypothetical change of one unit in the explanatory variable *at that time.*

The distinction between longitudinal and cross-sectional effects may seem subtle, but it is crucial when both cross-sectional and longitudinal data are combined, as they are in Chapter 9. This is called a *pooled cross-sectional* design.

Consider a hypothetical data set consisting of three observational units observed at three time points each, as in Figure A-3. Each unit is indicated by a unique symbol. There are three observations for each unit, representing three different time points.

What effect should we infer in this example? The cross-sectional effect is a positive one. Units with higher values for the explanatory variable are associated with units with higher values for the dependent variable. The longitudinal effect is a negative one, however. For each observational unit, increases in the explanatory variable are associated with decreases in the dependent variable over time. This hypothetical example illustrates that two logically separate effects are present when longitudinal and cross-sectional observations are pooled together. Of course, more subtle confounding scenarios are possible. The cross-sectional and longitudinal effects may be in the same direction but may differ in magnitude. Separating the effects is crucial to establish a valid description of the relationship between the independent and dependent variables.

The most common approach to this problem is regression with dummy variables. Dummy, or *dichotomous,* variables are typically coded as 1 (the characteristic is observed, the event occurs) or 0 (the characteristic is not observed, the event does not occur). In

Figure A-3 Hypothetical Pooled Cross-Sectional Data Set

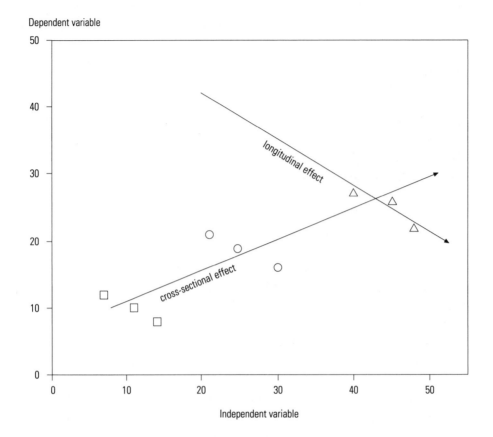

addition to the explanatory variables of interest, dummy variables for all but one of the time points or all but one of the observational units are included in the regression. Har-·rington and Ward adopt this tactic by including forty-five dummy variables (one each for the years 1945-1990) in the regression. This controls for variation over time and guarantees that the regression-estimated effects of the explanatory variables are strictly cross-sectional in nature. The alternative method is to include ten dummy variables (one each for ten of the circuits) in the regression. This technique would eliminate all cross-sectional effects, guaranteeing that the regression-estimated effects are strictly longitudinal in nature. Obviously, Harrington and Ward are more interested in the former approach because they are interested in variation between circuits and not variation over time.

Regression with dummy variables controls for variation over time or variation across units. As implemented in Harrington and Ward, the technique removes all time-specific variation by, roughly speaking, averaging over time for each circuit. The analysis of interest, explaining differences between circuits, may then proceed. Of course, this technique may obscure what the data can tell us, for it eliminates all longitudinal information. But the technique's virtue is that the inferences about effects are no longer plagued by the possibility of confounding factors. We can have confidence that we are properly estimating the cross-sectional effect of the independent variables.

Notes

1. I adapt this discussion from Lewis-Beck 1980, which provides an excellent and straightforward introduction to regression analysis.

2. I used SYSTAT to estimate the coefficients depicted in equation A-2. Many other statistical packages are available to estimate a linear regression.

3. A regression chooses the slope for a line by minimizing the sum of the squared vertical differences between the data points and the line implied by the regression estimate. Hence, linear regression is also referred to as *ordinary least-squares* regression.

4. To simplify presentation I used a counter to represent time, rather than year, so that 1915 = 1; 1916 = 2; and so forth.

Appendix B: Probit and Logit

David C. Nixon

A great many political variables are *discrete:* an event either happens or it doesn't; we either observe a characteristic or we don't. *Probit* and *logit* models are common statistical tools for analyzing such discrete (or dichotomous) dependent variables—outcomes that can take on only one of two possible values.[1] In Chapter 4, for example, Kevin T. McGuire uses the probit model to predict whether a petitioner will be successful in the Supreme Court or not. In Chapter 10, Jeffrey A. Segal, Donald R. Songer, and Charles M. Cameron invoke the logit model to determine the circumstances under which the Supreme Court will uphold or strike down a search and seizure. Charles H. Franklin and Liane C. Kosaki apply the logit model in Chapter 15 to explain individuals' awareness of particular Court decisions. Finally, Lauren Bowen, in Chapter 16, uses logit to discover whether or not attorneys advertise their services. To put it another way, all four of these chapters are seeking to predict dichotomous dependent variables: petitioner success (they win or they don't); court outcomes (liberal or conservative); public awareness of Court decisions (they are aware or not); and attorney behavior (they advertise or they don't).

It is easiest to understand and interpret the probit and logit models by focusing on the *probabilities* of observing these discrete dependent variables. That is, what are the chances of observing one outcome rather than the other? Suppose that the probability, which may be represented as π_i, of observing the characteristic in question is somewhere between zero and one for case *i*. In McGuire's context, this is the equivalent of saying that the probability of a petitioner's success is π_i. Instead of presuming that each individual or, in McGuire's case, petitioner has the same probability of success, we have some notions about the kinds of petitioners that are likely to succeed and the kinds that are likely to fail in a given case. A good social scientist specifies plausible and interesting conditions that affect the probability of observing a particular value of the dependent variable. McGuire uses the status of the lawyers on a case to predict success, with the perfectly straightforward hypothesis that more experienced lawyers are more successful. Segal, Songer, and Cameron use the facts of a case to predict whether or not a search will be upheld. And Bowen suggests that attorneys who favor advertising are more likely to advertise than those who do not. These *explanatory variables* (also called *independent variables*) are used to test whether the conditions

430

they indicate increase or decrease the probability of observing the dependent variable to a statistically significant degree.[2] For McGuire, then, the expectation is that as the independent variable (attorney status) increases (that is, as attorneys achieve higher status), the dependent variable (the chances of Court success) increases too.

Independent variables are significant to varying degrees in predicting the dependent variable. Logit and probit models employ a numerical technique, *maximum likelihood,* to derive estimates of *coefficients* for each of the explanatory variables. These coefficients, which may be represented as β, indicate the direction and strength of the relationship between the independent and dependent variables. If a coefficient is positive, then larger values of that independent variable are associated with a higher probability of observing a 1 for the dependent variable. Bowen, for example, finds that as attorney's attitudes toward advertising become more positive, their probability of advertising increases. The positive coefficients for attitudes in her table support that assertion. McGuire and Segal, Songer, and Cameron find support for their main hypotheses as well.

Regardless of the sign of β, smaller values of β result in flatter curves and less responsiveness between the independent variable and the dependent variable. If β is zero, then there is virtually no difference (in predicted probability of observing a 1 for the dependent variable) between observations with high values for the independent variable and those with low values. If a coefficient is large enough, we may legitimately conclude that the independent variable is a significant aid in predicting the dependent variable.

The relationship between an explanatory variable and the probability of observing the characteristic indicated by the dependent variable is illustrated in Figure B-1, for three possible values of β. To see how this works, consider the analysis in the chapter by Segal, Songer, and Cameron, in which the odds that a search will be upheld by the Supreme Court are examined. The estimated coefficient for probable cause is 0.94 (see Table 10-5). This corresponds to the positive curve in Figure B-1. At maximum effect, if X increases from 0 to 1 (which is to say, if the authorities meet the requirements to show probable cause in their search), the probability that the search will be upheld increases from approximately 38 percent to 62 percent. As a second example, McGuire's estimated coefficient for party status in model 1 is 0.05. The curve for that coefficient is not illustrated in Figure B-1. We know, however, that the curve will be flatter than those in the figure because the coefficient is nearer to zero. It turns out that at its maximum effect, as attorney status increases from 1 to 10 (which is to say, as status increases from the lowest to the highest), the probability of success before the Supreme Court increases from approximately 44 percent to 56 percent.

The McGuire example illustrates a problem: when do we declare that a relatively minor influence (such as party status) is insignificant? The effect of that variable at its maximum, increases the odds of winning by a mere 10 percent. The data in McGuire's Table 4-5

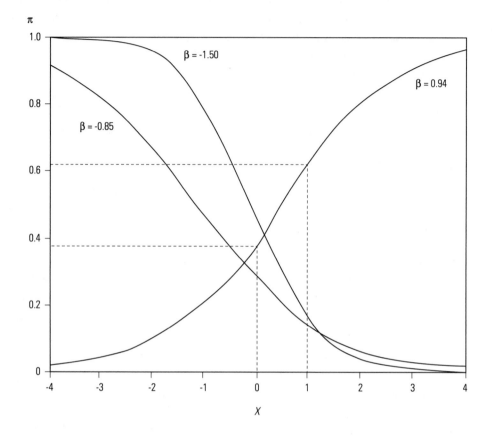

indicate that this variable is not significant at the .05 level for four of the five models estimated. One way to think about significance of effects is to realize that estimates for β are always imperfect. Indeed, one should view an estimate for β as a "best guess," which could be expected to vary within some range just by chance. A simple misprint of the data in a primary source, or the accidental omission of an observation in the records could conceivably alter the statistical results. If the expected range of the coefficient is very large, then we have less confidence that the estimate we obtained is a good one. And if that range includes zero, then we have some reason to question whether β is different from zero. Perhaps β really is zero (the independent variable is completely unrelated to the dependent variable), but mere chance has produced the estimate we observe. That is the logic behind the statistical tests on practically every multivariate model in social science.

Statistical analysis allows us to state that we have 95 percent confidence that the real value for β lies within 1.96 standard errors of our estimate. So if β is more than two standard deviations larger (or smaller) than zero, we are 95 percent confident that the independent variable is related to the dependent variable (β is nonzero). To revisit one of our running examples, McGuire's model 1 estimates β for party status as 0.05 with a standard error of 0.02. We can declare with 95 percent confidence that the true value for β lies between 0.01 and 0.09. This range may seem fairly large. The important point is that it does not include zero. We are 95 percent confident that party status does help to predict success in the Court. Yet the coefficient for that variable does not lie more than 1.96 standard errors from zero for McGuire's models 2 through 5. Overall, we should conclude that party status has a minor role at most and probably does not have any effect at all on success before the Supreme Court.

Notes

1. Dichotomous variables, also called dummy variables, are typically coded as 1 (the characteristic is observed, the event occurs) or 0 (the characteristic is not observed, the event does not occur). To analyze such variables, as I note above, scholars often invoke logit (the logistic specification) and probit (the normal curve specification) models. For more information on the difference between the two, see Aldrich and Nelson 1984.

2. When more than one explanatory, or independent, variable is included in a model, it is called a *multivariate* model. Most political phenomena are best modeled through multivariate techniques. To understand why, consider the factors affecting a voter's choice in the ballot box. A *bivariate* model would take into account only one explanatory variable, say, party identification. In a multivariate model, many other explanatory factors are considered, such as a person's gender, education, race, or preference on specific policy items (such as abortion).

Appendix C: Conducting Research on Law and Courts: Sources of Data

In what follows, we provide information on data sources that students might find useful in their research. Two words of clarification are in order. The first is that we aimed at something short of comprehensiveness, choosing instead to describe sources that are unique or are readily available and accessible. Second, we occasionally mention the archive of the Inter-university Consortium for Political and Social Research (ICPSR) at Ann Arbor, Michigan. The ICPSR's archive is a major repository for databases collected by social scientists. ICPSR disseminates these databases (along with accompanying documentation) free of charge to faculty, staff, and students of colleges and universities that are members of the consortium; individuals at nonmember schools can gain access to the data for a fee. For more details, contact your school's ICPSR representative or write to: ICPSR, The University of Michigan, Institute for Social Research, P.O. Box 1248, Ann Arbor, MI 48106.

Actors in the Legal System

Information about *state court judges* is available from a number of sources. The *Book of the States* (1992) lists the plans invoked by states to select their judges; Hoffman's *The American Bench* (various years) identifies current state court judges, as does Want's *Federal-State Court Directory* (various years). *State Court Caseload Statistics* (Court Statistics Project, various years) contains data on court caseloads, the number of authorized judgeships per state, and the structure of state court systems. Some of this information is also available in Epstein et al. 1994, Tables 10-18 through 10-25, along with data on the U.S. Supreme Court's treatment of state court decisions (Table 10-26).

Many volumes contain information on *federal court judges*. The U.S. Senate Committee on the Judiciary keeps records of federal judicial nomination proceedings; Mersky and Jacobstein (various years) have compiled official congressional hearings and reports of U.S. Supreme Court nominations since 1916. Tables 4-10 through 4-14 in Epstein et al. 1994 also include information on Supreme Court nominees, such as Senate votes and interest group participation. In 1958, the Senate Judiciary Committee produced a useful report containing the names of judges who served on the U.S. circuit courts from 1801 through 1958. More recent information can be gleaned from Brownson's *1993 Judicial Staff Directory* (1993), Want's *Federal-State Court Directory* (various years), Hoffman's *The American Bench* (various years), and *Judges of the United States* (1983). These volumes identify all current members of the federal judiciary and provide some biographical information. Data on the number of authorized judgeships and on caseloads can be found in the annual reports of the director, Administrative Office of the U.S. Courts (various years). *The Statistical Abstract of the United States* (prepared by the U.S. Bureau of the Census) and Epstein et al. 1994 (Tables 10-4 through 10-6, 10-12) also contain caseload data. Reams and Haworth (1978) and Reams (1994) have compiled virtually all congressional hearings and reports on matters pertaining to the federal courts. Finally, the ICPSR-archived database *Survey of Judges on the Role of Courts in American Society* (no. 7824) contains the results of a questionnaire put to federal and state court judges in five districts. The data include information about the amount of time judges spend on certain kinds of cases, their suggestions for dispute resolution, and their demographic characteristics.

Martindale-Hubbell Law Directory (various years) and *The American Bar* (various years) list the names of attorneys practicing in the United States. *Who's Who in American Law* contains brief profiles of prominent lawyers, judges, and professors. The American Bar Foundation has produced a series of statistical profiles of the U.S. legal profession (see especially Curran et al. 1986). It also has published a report on legal education in the United States (American Bar Association 1991). Several ICPSR-archived studies are worthy of note. John P. Heinz and Edward O. Laumann's "Chicago Lawyers Survey, 1975" (no. 8218) contains information on the social organization of the Chicago Bar; Ronald L. Hirsch's "National Survey of Lawyers' Career Satisfaction, 1984" (no. 8975) holds data designed to assess career satisfaction among young lawyers, such as their job descriptions, educational background, and psychological characteristics. The U.S. Department of Justice, Bureau of Justice Statistics (BJS), "National Prosecutors Survey, 1990," also archived at the ICPSR (no. 9579), contains the results of a survey of chief state prosecuting attorneys about the handling of felony cases within their districts.

Information on *interest groups* that litigate is available from several sources. Phase II of the *United States Supreme Court Judicial Database* contains the following information on amicus curiae participation in the U.S. Supreme Court case: total number of amicus curiae participants in a given case, the solicitor general's role, citation to amici in the Court's opinions, and the names and positions taken by amici.[1] Tables 7-20 through 7-22 in Epstein et al. 1994 provide summary information on the participation of groups during certain periods of the Court's history, as does Lawrence 1990 (Appendix C), which also gives the win-loss records of key organizations. O'Connor and Epstein 1989, the Council for Public Interest Law 1976, and the Foundation for Public Affairs 1988 house descriptions of many public interest law groups. Finally, Kurland and Casper (various years) have compiled the briefs of the parties and amici curiae filed in landmark constitutional cases.

Trial Courts

State court caseload data are available in *State Court Caseload Statistics;* federal court data can be found in the annual reports of the director, Administrative Office of the United States Courts. The *Statistical Abstract of the United States* contains a good deal of longitudinal data on the caseloads of federal district courts, including the disposition of certain kinds of criminal disputes. Hoffman's *The American Bench* (various years) lists the names of current judges, as does Want's *Federal-State Court Directory* (various years). And Goldman (1965, 1991, 1993) provides a wealth of data on the background characteristics of U.S. district court judges.

Sources of data on crime and criminal justice in the United States include the many reports of the BJS: *Sourcebook of Criminal Justice Statistics, Criminal Victimization in the United States, Prisoners in State and Federal Institutions,* and *National Survey of Courts,* to name just a few.[2] *Crime in the United States,* an annual publication of the Federal Bureau of Investigation (FBI), includes data on crimes reported by state and local authorities.[3] The *Statistical Abstract of the United States* contains key tables included in these reports, such as crime rates by state, homicide victims by race and sex, and federal and state prisoner populations. Several ICPSR-archived studies are also worthy of note. They include Thomas W. Church's "Assessing Local Legal Culture" (no. 7808), which looks at local legal culture in four criminal courts (see Chapter 6 of this volume) and Nardulli, Eisenstein, and Flemming's "Comparing Court Case Processing in Nine Courts, 1979-1980" (no. 8621), which contains information on the characteristics of officials involved in the processing of court cases.[4]

Civil litigation is explored by Herbert M. Kritzer, David M. Trubek, William L. F. Felstiner, Joel B. Grossman, and Austin Sarat in *Civil Litigation in the United States, 1977-1979* (ICPSR no. 7994). The database consists of information (such as negotiation proceedings and relations between clients and lawyers) on a sample of disputes processed in the United States between 1977 and 1979. In a related project (*Survey of Households in Five Judicial Districts in the United States: A Civil Litigation Project, 1977-1979;* ICPSR no. 9743), David M. Trubek et al. surveyed households involved in lawsuits. The database includes demographic characteristics and information about the disputes. Allan G. Lind et al. (ICPSR no. 9699) gathered data on tort litigants in three state courts in 1989 and 1990. And C. K. Rowland's *Federal District Court Civil Decisions, 1981-1987: Detroit, Houston, and Kansas City* (ICPSR no. 9367) contains information on unpublished civil cases filed in three district courts, including the date of termination, the nature of the decision, and whether a monetary award was granted.

Lower Appellate Courts

For information on judges and caseloads, see *State Court Caseload Statistics;* the annual reports of the director, Administrative Office of the U.S. Courts (various years); and Epstein et al. 1994, Tables 10-2 through 10-6. Donald R. Songer is in the process of amassing an important database on decisions made in U.S. courts of appeals, which includes information on case issues, the votes of judges, and amicus curiae participants, among many other things. The database will be archived with the ICPSR in 1996. Wheeler and Harrison (1989) have produced a useful volume detailing the history of the federal circuit courts; some of their data are summarized in Epstein et al. 1994, Table 10-1. A 1958 report of the Senate Judiciary Committee contains the names of judges who served on the U.S. circuit courts from 1801 through 1958. The *1993 Judicial Staff Directory* (Brownson 1993), Want's *Federal-State Court Directory* (various years), *The American Bench* (Hoffman, various years), and *Judges of the United States* (1983) identify all current members of the federal judiciary. And Goldman (1965, 1991, 1993) provides information on the background characteristics of U.S. courts of appeals judges.[5]

The U.S. Supreme Court

Epstein et al. 1994 contains data and other information on the following dimensions of Court activity: institutional development, review process, opinions and decisions, judicial backgrounds, voting patterns, and impact. Witt (1990) summarizes the holdings of landmark Court cases and provides brief biographies of the justices. And John R. Schmidhauser's ICPSR database (no. 4720) houses data on justices who served between 1789 and 1958. More comprehensive biographical information is available in Cushman (1993) and Friedman and Israel (1969-1978). Martin and Goehlert 1990 is an annotated biography of scholarly writings on the Court. *The Constitution of the United States of America* (prepared by the Congressional Research Service, Library of Congress) lists state and federal acts overturned by the Supreme Court, as well as Court decisions overruled by subsequent decisions. Harold J. Spaeth's *United States Supreme Court Judicial Database, 1953-Current Terms* (ICPSR no. 9422), provides a wealth of data beginning with the Warren Court through to the present.[6] Among the many attributes of Court decisions coded by Spaeth are the names of the courts making the original decision, the identities of the parties to the cases, the policy context of a case, and the votes of each justice. Spaeth and Jan Palmer are now expanding the database to include the conference votes cast by justices of the Supreme Court under Fred M. Vinson (1946-1952 terms) and Earl Warren (1953-1968 terms) (see also Palmer 1990, which lists the conference votes in cases decided between the 1946 and 1953 terms).

The Influence of Courts

The Gallup Poll, the Harris Survey, and the National Opinion Research Center are sources for data on *public opinion* and the judiciary, especially the U.S. Supreme Court. Chapter 8 of Epstein et al. 1994 contains many tables summarizing public views of the Supreme Court and issues related to the legal system. Questions reviewed include "How knowledgeable is the public about the Court?" and "To what extent does the public support the Court's resolution of specific controversial issues?" The results of a survey, done under the auspices of the BJS, on national attitudes toward courts and justice are reported in "Public Image of Courts, 1977" (ICPSR nos. 7703, 7704). No. 7703 is a survey of the general public; no. 7704 is a survey of judges, lawyers, and community leaders.

Data on the impact of court decisions on certain public policy questions are available in Chapter 9 of Epstein et al. 1994. Abortion, capital punishment, school desegregation, voter registration, and reapportionment are examples of the issues covered. Becker 1969, Becker and Feeley 1973, and Johnson and Canon 1984 contain information on the impact and implementation of many landmark decisions. Rosenberg 1991 also has a good deal of data on salient Court cases, especially *Brown v. Board of Education* (1954) and *Roe v. Wade* (1973).

Notes

1. These data will soon be deposited at the ICPSR.
2. Many of the studies from the BJS are archived with the ICPSR, including "Capital Punishment in the United States" (nos. 9210, 9337, 9507), "Census of State Felony Courts" (no. 8667), "Commercial Victimization Surveys" (no. 8002), and "Historic Statistics on Prisoners in State and Federal Institutions" (no. 8912).
3. Again, many of the FBI's studies are archived with the ICPSR, including its uniform crime reports (nos. 9252, 9226, 9163).
4. The ICPSR archive contains many other databases pertaining to matters of criminal justice. Interested readers should consult the *ICPSR Guide to Resources and Services.*
5. Along the same lines, Gerard Gryski, Gary Zuk, and Deborah Barrow have amassed an important database of the background characteristics and retirement patterns of lower federal court judges, *Multi-User Database on the Attributes of U.S. Courts of Appeals Judges, 1891-1992,* which will soon be archived with the ICPSR.
6. Spaeth is in the process of backdating the database to include the Vinson Court era.

References

Aberbach, Joel D. 1990. *Keeping a Watchful Eye.* Washington, D.C.: Brookings Institution.

"Abortion." 1988. *MacLean's* 101:8-16.

"Abortion: Rights and Wrongs." 1989. *Public Opinion* 11:35-39.

"Abortions Legal for Year, Performed for Thousands." 1973. *New York Times,* December 31, sec. A.

Abraham, Henry. 1985. *Justices and Presidents.* 2d ed. New York: Oxford University Press.

Abramowicz, Michael. 1992. "Page Puts on Big Rush in Minnesota Court Bid." *Washington Post,* October 24, sec. G.

Abramowitz, Alan I., and Jeffrey A. Segal. 1992. *Senate Elections.* Ann Arbor: University of Michigan Press.

Ackerman, Bruce. 1991. *We the People: Foundations.* Cambridge, Mass.: Belknap Press.

Adamany, David, and Philip Dubois. 1975. "The 'Forgetful' Voter and an Underreported Vote." *Public Opinion Quarterly* 39 (Summer): 227-231.

Adamany, David, and Mack C. Shelley II. 1980. "Encore! The Forgetful Voter." *Public Opinion Quarterly* 44:234-240.

Administrative Office of the U.S. Courts. Various years. *Annual Reports.* Washington, D.C.: Administrative Office of the U.S.

Ainsworth, Scott, and John A. Maltese. 1992. "Early Policy Influence of the National Grange at the Federal Level: 1878-1881." Paper presented at the annual meeting of the Southern Political Science Association.

Alan Guttmacher Institute. 1976. *Abortion 1974-1975: Need and Services in the United States, Each State and Metropolitan Area.* New York: Planned Parenthood Federation of America.

Aldrich, John, and Charles Cnudde. 1975. "Probing the Bounds of Conventional Wisdom." *American Journal of Political Science* 19:571-608.

Aldrich, John H., and Forrest D. Nelson. 1984. *Linear Probability, Logit, and Probit Models.* Sage University Paper series, Quantitative Applications in the Social Sciences, 07-045. Beverly Hills, Calif.: Sage Publications.

Alschuler, Albert W. 1968. "The Prosecutor's Role in Plea Bargaining." *University of Chicago Law Review* 36:50-112.

___. 1975. "The Defense Attorney's Role in Plea Bargaining." *Yale Law Journal* 84:1179-1314.

___. 1978. "Sentencing Reform and Prosecutorial Power: A Critique of Recent Proposals for 'Fixed' or 'Presumptive' Sentencing." *University of Pennsylvania Law Review* 126:550-577.

The American Bar. Various years. Sacramento, Calif.: Forster-Long.

American Bar Association. 1989. *Model Rules of Professional Conduct and Code of Judicial Conduct.* Chicago: American Bar Association.

___. 1991. *A Review of Legal Education in the United States, Fall 1990.* Chicago: American Bar Association.

American Enterprise. 1993. Vol. 4 (January/February), 103.

"Americans Evaluate the Court System." 1982. *Public Opinion* 5:24-27.

Amir, Menachim. 1971. *Patterns in Forcible Rape.* Chicago: University of Chicago Press.

Anderson, Jack, and Michael Binstein. 1993. "Violent Shift in Abortion Battle." *Washington Post,* March 18, sec. C.

Andrews, Lori B. 1980. *Birth of a Salesman: Lawyer Advertising and Solicitation.* Chicago: American Bar Association Press.

___. 1981. "Lawyer Advertising and the First Amendment." *American Bar Foundation Journal* 1981:967-1021.

Armstrong, Scott. 1991. "Women Seeking Office Quickened by Thomas Flap." *Christian Science Monitor,* October 22, U.S. sec.

Armstrong, Virginia C., and Charles A. Johnson. 1982. "Certiorari Decisions by the Warren and Burger Courts: Is Cue Theory Time Bound?" *Polity* 15:141-150.

Arnold, Thurman W. 1935. *The Symbols of Government.* New York: Harcourt, Brace and World.

Asher, Herbert B., Randall B. Ripley, and Karen C. Snyder. 1991. "Political Attitudes and Behavior of Union Members: The 1990 Ohio Elections." Paper presented at the annual meeting of the American Political Science Association, Washington, D.C.

Asher, Mark. 1986. "Yukica-Dartmouth Case Raises Contract Questions." *Washington Post,* February 16, sec. E.

Ashman, Allan, and James J. Alfini. 1974. *The Key to Judicial Merit Selection: The Nominating Process.* Chicago: American Judicature Society.

Aspin, Larry T., and William K. Hall. 1989. "Friends and Neighbors Voting in Judicial Retention Elections: A Research Note Comparing Trial and Appellate Court Elections." *Western Political Quarterly* 42:587-596.

Atkins, Burton M., and Henry R. Glick. 1976. "Environmental and Structural Variables as Determinants of Issues in State Courts of Last Resort." *American Journal of Political Science* 20:97-115.

Atleson, James B. 1989. "The Legal Community and the Transformation of Disputes: The Settlement of Injunction Actions." *Law and Society Review* 23:41-73.

Aumann, Francis R. 1931. "The Selection, Tenure, Retirement, and Compensation of Judges in Ohio." *University of Cincinnati Law Review* 5:408-428.

Babbie, Earl. 1992. *The Practice of Social Research.* Belmont, Calif.: Wadsworth.

Baker, Nancy V. 1992. *Conflicting Loyalties: Law and Politics In The Attorney General's Office, 1789-1990.* Lawrence: University Press of Kansas.

Ball, Howard. 1987. *Courts and Politics: The Federal Judicial System.* Englewood Cliffs, N.J.: Prentice-Hall.

Barber, Kathleen. 1971. "Ohio Judicial Elections—Nonpartisan Premises with Partisan Results." *Ohio State Law Journal* 32:762-789.

___. 1972. "Selection of Ohio Appellate Judges: A Case Study in Invisible Politics." In *Political Behavior and Public Issues in Ohio,* edited by John J. Gargan and James G. Coke. Kent, Ohio: Kent State University Press.

Barnum, David. 1985. "The Supreme Court and Public Opinion: Judicial Decision Making in the Post-New Deal Period." *Journal of Politics* 47:652-666.

Barrett, Michele. 1991. *The Politics of Truth: From Marx to Foucault.* Stanford, Calif.: Stanford University Press.

Barringer, Felicity. 1993. "Abortion Clinics Said to Be in Peril." *New York Times,* March 6, sec. A.

Barrow, Deborah J., and Thomas G. Walker. 1988. *A Court Divided: The Fifth Circuit Courts of Appeals and the Politics of Judicial Reform.* New Haven, Conn.: Yale University Press.

Baum, Dan. 1993. "Violence Is Driving Away Rural Abortion Clinics." *Chicago Tribune,* August 21, sec. A.

Baum, Lawrence. 1978. "Lower Court Response to Supreme Court Decisions: Reconsidering a Negative Picture." *Justice System Journal* 3:208-219.

___. 1980. "Responses of Federal District Judges to Courts of Appeals Policies: An Exploration." *Western Political Quarterly* 33:217-224.

___. 1983. "The Electoral Fates of Incumbent Judges in the Ohio Court of Common Pleas." *Judicature* 66:420-430.

___. 1987. "Explaining the Vote in Judicial Elections: The 1984 Ohio Supreme Court Elections." *Western Political Quarterly* 40:361-371.

___. 1988. "Measuring Policy Change in the U.S. Supreme Court." *American Political Science Review* 82:905-912.

___. 1988-1989. "Voters' Information in Judicial Elections: The 1986 Contests for the Ohio Supreme Court." *Kentucky Law Journal* 77:645-670.

___. 1992a. "Membership Change and Collective Voting Change in the United States Supreme Court." *Journal of Politics* 54:3-24.

___. 1992b. *The Supreme Court.* 4th ed. Washington, D.C.: CQ Press.

___. 1994. *American Courts.* Boston: Houghton-Mifflin.

Baum, Lawrence, Sheldon Goldman, and Austin Sarat. 1981-1982. "Research Note: The Evolution of Litigation in the Federal Courts of Appeals, 1895-1975." *Law and Society Review* 16:291-309.

Beatty, Jerry K. 1972. "State Court Evasion of United States Supreme Court Mandates during the Last Decade of the Warren Court." *Valparaiso Law Review* 6:260-285.

Beck, Paul Allen, Lawrence Baum, Aage Clausen, and Charles Smith. 1992. "Patterns and Sources of Ticket-Splitting in Subpresidential Voting." *American Political Science Review* 86:916-928.

Becker, Theodore L. 1969. *The Impact of Supreme Court Decisions.* New York: Oxford University Press.

Becker, Theodore L., and Malcolm M. Feeley, eds. 1973. *The Impact of Supreme Court Decisions.* 2d ed. New York: Oxford University Press.

Belkin, Lisa. 1989. "Women in Rural Areas Face Many Barriers to Abortions." *New York Times,* July 11, sec A.

Bennett, Lance, and Martha Feldman. 1981. *Reconstructing Reality in the Courtroom.* New York: Sage Books.

Berger, Raoul. 1969. *Congress v. the Supreme Court.* Cambridge, Mass.: Harvard University Press.

___. 1977. *Government by Judiciary.* Cambridge, Mass.: Harvard University Press.

Berk, Richard A. 1983. "An Introduction to Sample Selection Bias in Sociological Data." *American Sociological Review* 48:386-398.

Berke, Richard L. 1989. "The Abortion Rights Movement Has Its Day." *New York Times,* October 15, sec. 4.

___. 1991. "Groups Backing Abortion Rights Ask Court to Act." *New York Times,* November 8, sec. A.

Berkson, Larry. 1979. "The U.S. Circuit Judge Nominating Commission: The Candidates' Perspective." *Judicature* 62:466-482.

Bernstein, Robert A., and James A. Dyer. 1984. *An Introduction to Political Science Methods.* Englewood Cliffs, N.J.: Prentice-Hall.

Berry, Jeffrey M. 1989a. *The Interest Group Society.* Boston: Little, Brown.

___. 1989b. "Subgovernments, Issue Networks, and Political Conflict." In *Remaking American Politics,* edited by Richard Harris and Sidney Milkis. Boulder, Colo.: Westview Press.

Berry, William, and Stanley Feldman. 1985. *Multiple Regression in Practice.* Beverly Hills, Calif.: Sage Publications.

Bickel, Alexander. 1955. "The Original Understanding and the Segregation Decision." *Harvard Law Review* 69:1-65.

___. 1962. *The Least Dangerous Branch.* Indianapolis, Ind.: Bobbs-Merrill.

___. 1970. *The Supreme Court and the Idea of Progress.* New York: Harper and Row.

___. 1975. *The Morality of Consent.* New Haven, Conn.: Yale University Press.

Bickel, Alexander M., and Benno Schmidt, Jr. 1984. *The Judiciary and Responsible Government, 1910-1921.* New York: Macmillan.

Bishop, Katherine. 1989. "Neighbors in West Use Small Claims Court to Combat Drugs." *New York Times,* October 17, sec. A.

Bishop, William. 1985. "The Choice of Remedy for Breach of Contract." *Journal of Legal Studies* 14:299-319.

Black, Charles. 1960. *The People and the Court.* New York: Macmillan.

___. 1969. *Structure and Relationship in Constitutional Law.* Baton Rouge: Louisiana State University Press.

Blake, Judith. 1971. "Abortion and Public Opinion: The 1960-1970 Decade." *Science,* February 12.

___. 1977a. "The Abortion Decisions: Judicial Review and Public Opinion." *In Abortion: New Directions for Policy Studies,* edited by Edward Manier, William Liu, and David Solomon. Notre Dame, Ind.: University of Notre Dame Press.

___. 1977b. "The Supreme Court's Abortion Decisions and Public Opinion in the United States." *Population and Development Review* 3:45-62.

Blumberg, A. 1964. *Criminal Justice.* New York: Triangle Books.

Blumstein, Alfred, Jacqueline Cohen, Susan E. Martin, and Michael H. Tonry, eds. 1983. *Research on Sentencing: The Search for Reform.* Washington, D.C.: National Academy Press.

Bobbitt, Philip. 1982. *Constitutional Fate: Theory of the Constitution.* New York: Oxford University Press.

Bond, Jon, and Charles A. Johnson. 1982. "Implementing a Permissive Policy: Hospital Abortion Services after Roe v. Wade." *American Journal of Political Science* 26:1-24.

Bone, Hugh. 1990. "Washington Primary: Judicial Politics." *Comparative State Politics* 11:45-48.

Book of the States, 1992-93 Edition. 1992. Lexington, Ky.: Council of State Governments.

Borger, Gloria, Ted Gest, and Jeannye Thornton. 1992. "The Untold Story." *U.S. News and World Report,* October 12.

Bork, Robert. 1971. "Neutral Principle and Some First Amendment Problems." *Indiana Law Journal* 47:1-35.

___. 1990. *The Temperature of America.* New York: Basic Books.

Boyd, Jo Ann. 1983. "Despite Setbacks, Reagan's Assault on Legal Services Corp. Bears Fruit." *National Journal,* March 12.

Boyum, Keith O. 1983. "The Etiology of Claims: Sketches for a Theoretical Mapping of the Claim-Definition Process." In *Empirical Theories about Courts,* edited by Keith O. Boyum and Lynn Mather. New York: Longman.

Brehm, John. 1993. *The Phantom Respondents: Opinion Surveys and Political Representation.* Ann Arbor: University of Michigan Press.

Brennan, William. 1977. "State Constitutions and the Protection of Individual Rights." *Harvard Law Review* 90:489-504.

Brenner, Saul. 1979. "The New Certiorari Game." *Journal of Politics* 41:649-655.

Brenner, Saul, and Harold J. Spaeth. 1995. *Stare Indecisis: The Alteration of Precedent on the Supreme Court, 1946-1992.* New York: Cambridge University Press.

Brigham, John. 1987. *The Cult of the Court.* Philadelphia: Temple University Press.

Brisbin, Richard. 1990. "The Conservatism of Antonin Scalia." *Political Science Quarterly* 105:1-29.

Brock, David. 1993. *The Real Anita Hill.* New York: Free Press.

Brodeur, Paul. 1985. *Outrageous Misconduct: The Asbestos Industry on Trial.* New York: Pantheon Books.

Brody, Jane E. 1973. "States and Doctors Wary on Eased Abortion Ruling." *New York Times,* February 16, sec. A.

Bronner, Ethan. 1989. *The Battle for Justice: How the Bork Nomination Shook America.* New York: W. W. Norton.

Brownson, Ann, ed. 1993. *1993 Judicial Staff Directory.* Mt. Vernon, Va.: Staff Directories.

Brownstein, Ronald. 1984. "With or Without Supreme Court Changes, Reagan Will Reshape the Federal Bench." *National Journal,* December 8.

Brozan, Nadine. 1983. "Abortion Ruling: 10 Years of Bitter Conflict." *New York Times,* January 15, sec. A.

Bruner, Jerome. 1990. *Acts of Meaning.* Cambridge, Mass.: Harvard University Press.

____. 1991. "The Narrative Construction of Reality." *Critical Inquiry* 18:1-21.

Bullock, Charles S., III, James E. Anderson, and David W. Brady. 1983. *Public Policy in the Eighties.* Monterey, Calif.: Brooks/Cole.

Burris, William. 1987. *Duty and the Law: Judge John J. Parker and the Constitution.* Chapel Hill: University of North Carolina Press.

Burt, Robert A. 1992. *The Constitution in Conflict.* Cambridge, Mass.: Belknap Press.

Byrne, Gary C., and J. Kristian Pueschel. 1974. "But Who Should I Vote for for County Coroner?" *Journal of Politics* 36:778-784.

Cain, Maureen. 1979. "The General Practice Lawyer and the Client: Towards a Radical Conception." *International Journal of the Sociology of Law* 7:331-354.

Caldeira, Gregory A. 1977. "Judicial Incentives: Some Evidence from Urban Trial Courts." *Justitia* 4:1-28.

____. 1991a. "Courts and Public Opinion." *In The American Courts,* edited by John B. Gates and Charles A. Johnson. Washington, D.C.: CQ Press.

____. 1991b. "The Supreme Court and Democratic Accountability." *American Political Science Review* 85:984-988.

Caldeira, Gregory A., and Charles E. Smith. 1993. "Campaigning for the Supreme Court: The Dynamics of Public Opinion on the Thomas Nomination." Paper presented at the annual meeting of the American Political Science Association, Washington, D.C.

Caldeira, Gregory A., and John R. Wright. 1988. "Organized Interests and Agenda Setting in the U.S. Supreme Court." *American Political Science Review* 82:1109-1127.

___. 1990. "The Discuss List: Organized Interests and Agenda-Setting." *Law and Society Review* 24:807-836.

___. 1994. "Lobbying for Justice: Organized Interests and the Bork Nomination in the United States Senate." Ohio State University.

Calhoun, John C. 1853. *Disquisition on Government.* New York: D. Appleton.

Cameron, Charles M., Albert D. Cover, and Jeffrey A. Segal. 1990. "Senate Voting on Supreme Court Nominees: A Neoinstitutional Model." *American Political Science Review* 84:525-534.

Canon, Bradley C. 1982a. "A Framework for the Analysis of Judicial Activism." In *Supreme Court Activism and Restraint,* edited by Stephen C. Halpern and Charles M. Lamb. Lexington, Mass.: Lexington Books.

___. 1982b. "Studying the Impact of Judicial Decisions: A Period of Stagnation and Prospects for the Future." Paper presented at the annual meeting of the American Political Science Association, Denver, Colo.

___. 1991. "Courts and Policy: Compliance, Implementation, and Impact." In *The American Courts: A Critical Assessment,* edited by John B. Gates and Charles A. Johnson. Washington, D.C.: CQ Press.

Canon, Bradley C., and Lawrence Baum. 1981. "Patterns of Adoption of Tort Law Innovations: An Application of Diffusion Theory to Judicial Doctrines." *American Political Science Review* 75:975-987.

Canon, Bradley C., and Kenneth Kolson. 1971. "Compliance with Gault in Rural America: The Case of Kentucky." *Journal of Family Law* 10:300-326.

Caplan, Lincoln. 1987. *The Tenth Justice.* New York: Vintage Books.

Cardozo, Benjamin. 1921. *The Nature of the Judicial Process.* New Haven, Conn.: Yale University Press.

Carmines, Edward, and Richard Zeller. 1979. *Reliability and Validity Assessment.* Beverly Hills, Calif.: Sage Publications.

Carp, Robert A., and C. K. Rowland. 1983. *Policymaking and Politics in the Federal District Courts.* Knoxville: University of Tennessee Press.

Carp, Robert A., and Ronald Stidham. 1993. *Judicial Process in America.* 2d ed. Washington, D.C.: CQ Press.

Carr, David. 1986. *Time, Narrative, and History.* Bloomington: Indiana University Press.

Carter, Lief H. 1974. *The Limits of Order.* Lexington, Mass.: Lexington Books.

___. 1985. *Contemporary Constitutional Lawmaking: The Supreme Court and the Art of Politics.* New York: Pergamon.

Cartwright, Bliss C., and Richard D. Schwartz. 1973. "The Invocation of Legal Norms: An Empirical Investigation of Durkheim and Weber." *American Sociological Review* 38:340-354.

Casper, Gerhard, and Richard Posner. 1976. *The Workload of the Supreme Court.* Chicago: American Bar Federation.

Casper, Jonathan D. 1972. *The Politics of Civil Liberties.* New York: Harper and Row.

———. 1976. "The Supreme Court and National Policy-Making." *American Political Science Review* 70:50-63.

Chafee, Zechariah, Jr. 1941. *Free Speech in the United States.* Cambridge, Mass.: Harvard University Press.

Champagne, Anthony, and Judith Haydel, eds. 1993. *Judicial Reform in the States.* Lanham, Md.: University Press of America.

Chayes, Abram. 1976. "The Role of the Judge in Public Law Litigation." *Harvard Law Review* 89:1281-1316.

Check, James, and Neil Malamuth. 1985. "An Empirical Assessment of Some Feminist Hypotheses about Rape." *International Journal of Women's Studies* 8:414-423.

Choper, Jesse. 1980. *Judicial Review and the National Political Process.* Chicago: University of Chicago Press.

Church, Thomas W. 1975. "Plea Bargains, Concessions, and the Courts: Analysis of a Quasi-Experiment." *Law and Society Review* 10:377-401.

———. 1982. *Examining Local Legal Culture—Practitioner Attitudes in Four Criminal Courts.* Williamsburg, Va.: National Center for State Courts.

———. 1985. "Examining Local Legal Culture." *American Bar Foundation Research Journal* 1985: 449-518.

Church, Thomas W., A. Carlson, J. L. Lee, and T. Tan. 1978. *Justice Delayed: The Pace of Litigation in Urban Trial Courts.* Williamsburg, Va.: National Center for State Courts.

Clark, David. 1981. "Adjudication to Administration: A Statistical Analysis of Federal District Courts in the Twentieth Century." *Southern California Law Review* 55:55-152.

Clark, Peter B., and James Q. Wilson. 1961. "Incentive Systems: A Theory of Organizations." *Administrative Science Quarterly* 6:129-166.

Clark, Timothy B. 1981. "Affirmative Action May Fall Victim to Reagan's Regulatory Reform Drive." *National Journal,* July 11.

Clarke, S. H. 1988. *The Effect of the Prohibition of Plea Bargaining on the Disposition of Felony Cases in Alaska Criminal Courts.* Chapel Hill: Institute of Government, University of North Carolina.

Clausen, Aage R., Lawrence Baum, Paul Allen Beck, and Charles E. Smith, Jr. 1992. "The Dynamics of Information Acquisition in Subpresidential Contests." Paper presented at the annual meeting of the Midwest Political Science Association, Chicago.

Close, Arthur C., J. Valerie Steele, and Michael E. Buckner. 1993. *Washington Representative 1993.* 17th ed. Washington, D.C.: Columbia Books.

Cobb, Roger W., and Charles D. Elder. 1983. *Participation in American Politics: The Dynamics of Agenda-Building.* 2d ed. Baltimore: Johns Hopkins University Press.

Cohen, Richard E. 1981. "Knowing One When They See One." *National Journal,* June 6.

———. 1988. "Labor Comes Alive." *National Journal,* July 16.

Cole, George F. 1970. "The Decision to Prosecute." *Law and Society Review* 4:331-343.

Comaroff, John L., and Simon Roberts. 1981. *Rules and Processes.* Chicago: University of Chicago Press.

Combs, Michael W., and Susan Welch. 1982. "Blacks, Whites, and Attitudes toward Abortion." *Public Opinion Quarterly* 46:510-520.

"Committee for Public Education and Religious Liberty v. Regan: New Possibilities for State Aid to Nonpublic Schools." *St. Louis University Law Journal* 24:406-424.

Congressional Research Service, Library of Congress. Various years. *The Constitution of the United States of America.* Washington, D.C.: Government Printing Office.

Conley, John M., and William M. O'Barr. 1988. "Fundamentals of Jurisprudence: An Ethnography of Judicial Decision Making in Informal Courts." *North Carolina Law Review* 66:467-507.

___. 1990. *Rules versus Relationships: The Ethnography of Legal Discourse.* Chicago: University of Chicago Press.

Converse, Philip E. 1962. "Information Flow and the Stability of Partisan Attitudes." *Public Opinion Quarterly* 26:578-599.

Cook, Beverly Blair. 1973. "Sentencing Behavior of Federal Judges: Draft Cases 1972." *University of Cincinnati Law Review* 42:597-633.

___. 1977. "Public Opinion and Federal Judicial Policy." *American Journal of Political Science* 21:567-600.

___. 1991. "Justice Sandra Day O'Connor: Transition to a Republican Agenda and Values." In *The Burger Court: Political and Judicial Profiles,* edited by Charles Lamb and Stephen Halpern. Champaign: University of Illinois Press.

Cook, Fay Lomax. 1981. "Crime and the Elderly: The Emergence of a Policy Issue." In *Reactions to Crime,* edited by Dan A. Lewis. Beverly Hills, Calif.: Sage Publications.

Cooper, Helene. 1993. "Medical Schools, Students Shun Abortion Study." *Wall Street Journal,* Midwest edition, March 12, sec. B.

Cooper, Phillip J. 1988. *Hard Judicial Choices: Federal District Court Judges and State and Local Officials.* New York: Oxford University Press.

Cortner, Richard. 1981. *The Supreme Court and the Second Bill of Rights.* Madison: University of Wisconsin Press.

Council for Public Interest Law. 1976. *Balancing the Scales of Justice: Financing Public Interest Law in America.* Washington, D.C.: Council for Public Interest Law.

Court Statistics Project. 1992. *State Court Caseload Statistics: Annual Report 1990.* Williamsburg, Va.: National Center for State Courts in Cooperation with the Conference of State Court Administrators.

___. Various years. *State Court Caseload Statistics.* Williamsburg, Va.: National Center for State Courts in Cooperation with the Conference of State Court Administrators.

Craig, Barbara Hinkson, and David M. O'Brien. 1993. *Abortion and American Politics.* Chatham, N.J.: Chatham House.

Croyle, James L. 1979. "The Impact of Trial Courts on the Public Policy of Private Law: Medical Malpractice Jury Verdicts in California." Paper presented at the annual meeting of the Western Political Science Association, Portland, Ore.

Curran, Barbara A., Katherine J. Rosich, Clara N. Carson, and Mark C. Puccetti. 1986. *Supplement to the Lawyer Statistical Report: The U.S. Legal Profession in 1985.* Chicago: American Bar Foundation.

Currie, David P. 1985. *The Constitution in the Supreme Court: The First Hundred Years.* Chicago: University of Chicago Press.

Currivan, Gene. 1970. "Poll Finds Shift to Left among College Freshmen." *New York Times,* December 20, sec. 1. .

Cushman, Clare. 1993. *The Supreme Court Justices: Illustrated Biographies, 1789-1993.* Washington, D.C.: Congressional Quarterly Inc.

Dahl, Robert A. 1957. "Decision-Making in a Democracy: The Supreme Court as a National Policy-Maker." *Journal of Public Law* 6:279-295.

Daley, Daniel, and Rachel Benson Gold. 1994. "Public Funding for Contraceptive, Sterilization, and Abortion Services, Fiscal Year 1992." *Family Planning Perspectives* 25:244-251.

Danelski, David J. 1964. *A Supreme Court Justice Is Appointed.* New York: Random House.

___. 1989. "The Influence of the Chief Justice in the Decisional Process of the Supreme Court." In *American Court Systems,* 2d ed., edited by Sheldon Goldman and Austin Sarat. New York: Longman.

Daniels, Stephen. 1984. "Ladders and Bushes: The Problem of Caseloads and Studying Court Activities over Time." *American Bar Foundation Research Journal* 1984:751-798.

___. 1985. "Continuity and Change in Patterns of Case Handling: A Case Study of Two Rural Counties." *Law and Society Review* 19:381-420.

Darney, Philip D., Uta Landy, Sara MacPherson, and Richard L. Sweet. 1987. "Abortion Training in U.S. Obstetrics and Gynecology Residency Programs." *Family Planning Perspectives* 19:158-162.

Davidson, Roger H. 1983. "Procedures and Politics in Congress." In *The Abortion Dispute and the American System,* edited by Gilbert Y. Steiner. Washington, D.C.: Brookings Institution.

Davis, James R., and Kenneth M. Dolbeare. 1968. *Little Groups of Neighbors: The Selective Service System.* Chicago: Markham Publishing.

Davis, Richard. 1993. "The Supreme Court in the News: Covering a Political Institution." Paper presented at the annual meeting of the Midwest Political Science Association, Chicago.

Davis, Sue. 1989. *Justice Rehnquist and the Constitution.* Princeton, N.J.: Princeton University Press.

Dionne, E. J., Jr. 1989. "Poll on Abortion Finds the Nation Is Sharply Divided." *New York Times,* April 26, sec. A.

Dobash, R. Emerson, and Russell Dobash. 1979. *Violence against Wives: A Case against the Patriarchy.* New York: Free Press.

Doyle, Arthur Conan. 1930. *The Complete Sherlock Holmes.* Garden City, N.Y.: Doubleday.

DuBois, Dawn. 1988. "A Matter of Time: Evidence of a Victim's Prompt Complaint in New York." *Brooklyn Law Review* 53:1087-1115.

Dubois, Philip L. 1980. *From Ballot to Bench: Judicial Elections and the Quest for Accountability.* Austin: University of Texas Press.

___. 1984. "Voting Cues in Nonpartisan Trial Court Elections: A Multivariate Assessment." *Law and Society Review* 18:395-436.

Dunne, F. P. 1938. *Mr. Dooley at His Best.* New York: Charles Scribner's Sons.

Dunne, Gerald T. 1977. *Hugo Black and the Judicial Revolution.* New York: Simon and Schuster.

Durkheim, Emile. 1960. *The Division of Labor in Society.* Glencoe, Ill.: Free Press.

Dworkin, Ronald. 1977. *Taking Rights Seriously.* Cambridge, Mass.: Harvard University Press.

___. 1981. "The Forum of Principle." *New York University Law Review* 56:469-518.

___. 1982. "Law as Interpretation." *Texas Law Review* 60:527-550.

Ebaugh, Helen Rose Fuchs, and C. Allen Haney. 1980. "Shifts in Abortion Attitudes: 1972-1978." *Journal of Marriage and the Family* 42:491-499.

Eisenberg, Melvin A. 1976. "Private Ordering through Negotiation: Dispute Settlement and Rulemaking." *Harvard Law Review* 89:637-681.

Eisenstein, James, and Herbert Jacob. 1977. *Felony Justice: An Organizational Analysis of Criminal Courts.* Boston: Little, Brown.

Eisenstein, James, Roy B. Flemming, and Peter F. Nardulli. 1988. *The Contours of Justice: Communities and Their Courts.* Boston: Little, Brown.

Ekman, Paul, and Maureen O'Sullivan. 1991. "Who Can Catch a Liar?" *American Psychologist* 46:913-920.

Ely, John. 1973. "The Wages of Crying Wolf: A Comment on Roe v. Wade." *Yale Law Journal* 82:920-949.

___. 1980. *Democracy and Distrust.* Cambridge, Mass.: Harvard University Press.

Emerson, Robert M., and Sheldon L. Messinger. 1977. "The Micro-Politics of Trouble." *Social Problems* 25:121-134.

Emerson, Thomas I. 1970. *The System of Freedom of Expression.* New York: Vintage.

Engel, David M. 1984. "The Oven Bird's Song: Insiders, Outsiders, and Personal Injuries in an American Community." *Law and Society Review* 18:551-582.

Epstein, Lee. 1985. *Conservatives in Court.* Knoxville: University of Tennessee Press.

___. 1990. "Interest Groups and the Courts." *In The American Courts: A Critical Assessment,* edited by John B. Gates and Charles A. Johnson. Washington, D.C.: CQ Press.

Epstein, Lee, and Joseph F. Kobylka. 1992. *The Supreme Court and Legal Change.* Chapel Hill: University of North Carolina Press.

Epstein, Lee, and C. K. Rowland. 1991. "Debunking the Myth of Interest Group Invincibility in the Courts." *American Political Science Review* 33:825-841.

Epstein, Lee, and Thomas G. Walker. 1992. *Constitutional Law for a Changing America: Institutional Powers and Constraints.* Washington, D.C.: CQ Press.

___. 1993a. *Constitutional Law for a Changing America: Institutional Powers and Constraints.* Supplement. Washington, D.C.: CQ Press.

___. 1993b. *The Supreme Court of the United States: An Introduction.* New York: St. Martin's Press.

Epstein, Lee, Tracey E. George, and Joseph F. Kobylka. 1992. *Public Interest Law: An Annotated Bibliography and Research Guide.* New York: Garland Publishing.

Epstein, Lee, Jeffrey A. Segal, Harold J. Spaeth, and Thomas G. Walker. 1994. *The Supreme Court Compendium: Data, Decisions, Development.* Washington, D.C.: Congressional Quarterly Inc.

Epstein, Lee, Thomas G. Walker, and William Dixon. 1989. "The Supreme Court and Criminal Justice Disputes: A Neo-Institutional Perspective." *American Journal of Political Science* 33: 825-841.

Ericsson, K. Anders, and Herbert A. Simon. 1984. *Protocol Analysis: Verbal Reports as Data.* Cambridge, Mass.: MIT Press.

Eskridge, William N., Jr. 1991a. "Overriding Supreme Court Statutory Interpretation Decisions." *Yale Law Journal* 101:331-417.

___. 1991b. "Reneging on History? Playing the Court/Congress/President Civil Rights Game." *California Law Review* 79:613-684.

Estreicher, Samuel, and John Sexton. 1986. *Redefining the Supreme Court's Role.* New Haven, Conn.: Yale University Press.

Estrich, Susan. 1987. *Real Rape.* Cambridge, Mass.: Harvard University Press.

Fagin, Dan. 1983. "In Winning His Battle for Rights Commission, Did Reagan Lose the War?" *National Journal,* December 17.

Fairman, Charles. 1971. *The History of the Supreme Court of the United States: Reconstruction and Reunion 1864-1868.* Part 1. New York: Macmillan.

Farley, Lin. 1978. *Sexual Shakedown: The Sexual Harassment of Women on the Job.* New York: McGraw-Hill.

Farrand, Max, ed. 1966. *The Records of the Federal Convention of 1787.* Rev. ed. 4 vols. New Haven, Conn.: Yale University Press.

Feeley, Malcolm M. 1978. "The Effects of Heavy Caseloads." In *American Court Systems: Readings in Judicial Process and Behavior,* edited by Sheldon Goldman and Austin Sarat. San Francisco: W. H. Freeman.

___. 1979. *The Process Is the Punishment.* New York: Russell Sage Foundation.

___. 1983. *Court Reform on Trial: Why Simple Solutions Fail.* New York: Basic Books.

Feinman, Jay M. 1976. "The Development of the Employment at Will Rule." *American Journal of Legal History* 20:118-135.

Feiock, Richard C. 1989. "Support for Business in the Federal District Courts: The Impact of State Political Environment." *American Politics Quarterly* 17:96-104.

Felice, John D., and John C. Kilwein. 1992. "Strike One, Strike Two . . .: The History of and Prospect for Judicial Reform in Ohio." *Judicature* 75:193-200.

Felstiner, William L. F., Richard L. Abel, and Austin Sarat. 1981. "The Emergence and Transformation of Disputes: Naming, Blaming, Claiming. . . ." *Law and Society Review* 15:631-654.

Fenno, Richard. 1966. *The Power of the Purse.* Boston: Little, Brown.

Ferejohn, John A., and Charles R. Shipan. 1989. "Congressional Influence on Administrative Agencies: A Case Study of Telecommunications Policy." In *Congress Reconsidered,* 4th ed., edited by Lawrence C. Dodd and Bruce I. Oppenheimer. Washington, D.C.: CQ Press.

Fiorina, Morris P. 1992. *Divided Government.* New York: Macmillan.

Fish, Peter G. 1988-1989. "Spite Nominations to the United States Supreme Court: Herbert C. Hoover, Owen J. Roberts, and the Politics of Presidential Vengeance in Retrospect." *Kentucky Law Journal* 77:545-576.

Fiske, Edward B. 1967. "Clergymen Offer Abortion Advice." *New York Times,* May 22, sec. A.

Flemming, Roy B. 1982. *Allocating Freedom and Punishment: Pretrial Release Decisions in Detroit and Baltimore.* New York: Longman.

Flemming, Roy B., Peter F. Nardulli, and James Eisenstein. 1992. *The Craft of Justice: Politics and Work in Criminal Court Communities.* Philadelphia: University of Pennsylvania Press.

Forrest, Jacqueline Darroch, and Stanley K. Henshaw. 1987. "The Harassment of U.S. Abortion Providers." *Family Planning Perspectives* 19:9-13.

Forrest, Jacqueline Darroch, Ellen Sullivan, and Christopher Tietze. 1978. "Abortion in the United States, 1976-1977." *Family Planning Perspectives* 10:271-279.

___. 1979a. *Abortion 1976-1977: Need and Services in the United States, Each State and Metropolitan Area.* New York: Alan Guttmacher Institute.

___. 1979b. "Abortions in the United States, 1977-1978." *Family Planning Perspectives* 11:329-341.

Foundation for Public Affairs. 1988. *Public Interest Profiles.* Washington, D.C.: Congressional Quarterly Inc.

Fowler, Robert Booth. 1985. *Religion and Politics in America.* Metuchen, N.J.: Scarecrow Press for American Theological Library Association.

Frank, John P. 1991. *Clement Haynsworth, the Senate, and the Supreme Court.* Charlottesville: University of Virginia Press.

Franklin, Charles H., and Liane C. Kosaki. 1989. "Republican Schoolmaster: The U.S. Supreme Court, Public Opinion, and Abortion." *American Political Science Review* 83:751-771.

____. 1991. "Public Awareness of Supreme Court Decisions." Paper presented at the annual meeting of the Midwest Political Science Association, Chicago.

Franklin, Charles H., Liane C. Kosaki, and Herbert M. Kritzer. 1993. "The Salience of U.S. Supreme Court Decisions." Paper presented at the annual meeting of the Southern Political Science Association, Atlanta.

Freedom of Access to Clinic Entrances Act. 1994. U.S. Public Law 103-259, 108 Stat. 694.

Fried, Charles. 1991. *Order and Law: Arguing the Reagan Revolution—A First Hand Account.* New York: Simon and Schuster.

Friedman, Lawrence M. 1969. "Legal Culture and Social Development." *Law and Society Review* 4:29-44.

Friedman, Lawrence M., and Robert V. Percival. 1976. "A Tale of Two Courts: Litigation in Alameda and San Benito Counties." *Law and Society Review* 10:267-301.

Friedman, Leon, and Fred L. Israel, eds. 1969-1978. *The Justices of the United States Supreme Court.* New York: R. R. Bowker.

Friedman, Richard D. 1983. "The Transformation in Senate Response to Supreme Court Nominations: From Reconstruction to the Taft Administration and Beyond." *Cardozo Law Review* 5:1-95.

____. 1986. "Tribal Myths: Ideology and Confirmation of Supreme Court Nominations." *Yale Law Review* 95:1283-1320.

Fuller, Lon. 1978. "The Forms and Limits of Adjudication." In *American Court Systems,* 1st ed., edited by Sheldon Goldman and Austin Sarat. San Francisco: W. H. Freeman.

Galanter, Marc. 1974. "Why the 'Haves' Come Out Ahead: Speculations on the Limits of Legal Change." *Law and Society Review* 9:95-160.

____. 1983. "Reading the Landscape of Disputes: What We Know and Don't Know (and Think We Know) about Our Allegedly Contentious and Litigious Society." *UCLA Law Review* 31:4-71.

____. 1984. "Words of Deals: Using Negotiation to Teach about Legal Process." *Journal of Legal Education* 34:268-276.

Galanter, Marc, Frank S. Palen, and John M. Thomas. 1979. "The Crusading Judge: Judicial Activism in Trial Courts." *Southern California Law Review* 52:699-741.

Gallup Poll. Various years. *The Gallup Poll.* Wilmington, Del.: Scholarly Resources.

Gambitta, Richard A. L. 1981. "Litigation, Judicial Deference, and Policy Change." In *Governing through Courts,* edited by Richard A. L. Gambitta, Marlynn L. May, and James C. Foster. Beverly Hills, Calif.: Sage Publications.

Garth, Bryant G. 1982. "Introduction: Toward a Sociology of the Class Action." *Indiana Law Journal* 57:371-383.

Gelb, Joyce, and Marian Lief Palley. 1979. "Women and Interest Group Politics: A Comparative Analysis of Federal Decision-Making." *Journal of Politics* 41:362-392.

Gelfand, David, and Keith Werhan. 1990. "Federalism and Separation of Powers on a 'Conservative' Court: Current and Cross-currents from Justices O'Connor and Scalia." *Tulane Law Review* 64:1443-1476.

George, Tracey, and Lee Epstein. 1992. "On the Nature of Supreme Court Decision Making." *American Political Science Review* 86:323-337.

Giacoma, James M. 1980. "Committee for Public Education and Religious Liberty v. Regan: New Possibilities for State Aid to Nonpublic Schools." *Saint Louis University Law Journal.* 24:406-424.

Giannella, Donald A. 1971. "Lemon and Tilton: The Bitter and the Sweet of Church-State Entanglement." *Supreme Court Review* 1971:147-200.

Gibson, James L. 1978. "Judges' Role Orientations, Attitudes, and Decisions: An Interactive Model." *American Political Science Review* 72:911-924.

___. 1980. "Environmental Constraints on the Behavior of Judges: A Representational Model of Judicial Decision Making." *Law and Society Review* 14:343-370.

Giles, Micheal, and Douglas Gatlin. 1980. "Mass Level Compliance with Public Policy: The Case of School Desegregation." *Journal of Politics* 42:722-746.

Glick, Henry R. 1983. *Courts, Politics, and Justice.* New York: McGraw-Hill.

Glick, Henry R., and Craig F. Emmert. 1987. "The Recruitment of State Supreme Court Judges." *Judicature* 70:228-235.

Goerdt, J. 1989. *Examining Court Delay: The Pace of Litigation in 26 Urban Trial Courts, 1987.* Williamsburg, Va.: National Center for State Courts.

Goings, Kenneth W. 1990. *The NAACP Comes of Age: The Defeat of Judge John J. Parker.* Bloomington: Indiana University Press.

Goldman, Sheldon. 1965. "Characteristics of Eisenhower and Kennedy Appointees to the Lower Federal Courts." *Western Political Quarterly* 18:755-762.

___. 1966. "Voting Behavior on the United States Courts of Appeals, 1961-1964." *American Political Science Review* 60:374-383.

___. 1975. "Voting Behavior on the United States Courts of Appeals Revisited." *American Political Science Review* 69:491-506.

___. 1983. "Reagan's Judicial Appointments at Mid-Term: Shaping the Bench in His Own Image." *Judicature* 66:335-347.

___. 1985. "Reaganizing the Judiciary: The First-Term Appointments." *Judicature* 68:315-337.

___. 1989. "Judicial Appointments and the Presidential Agenda." In *The Presidency in American Politics,* edited by Paul Brace, Christine B. Harrington, and Gary King. New York: New York University Press.

___. 1990. "Reagan's Judicial Legacy: Completing the Puzzle and Summing Up." *Judicature* 72:318-330.

___. 1991. "The Bush Imprint on the Judiciary: Carrying on a Tradition." *Judicature* 74:294-306.

___. 1993. "Bush's Judicial Legacy: The Final Imprint." *Judicature* 76:282-297.

Goldstein, Leslie Friedman. 1987. "The ERA and the U.S. Supreme Court." *Research in Law and Policy Studies* 1:145-61.

___. 1991. *In Defense of the Text.* Savage, Md.: Rowman and Littlefield.

Goodman, Janice, Rhonda Copelon Schoenbrod, and Nancy Stearns. 1973. "Doe and Roe." *Women's Rights Law Reporter* 1:20-38.

Goodman, Nelson. 1978. *Ways of Worldmaking.* Indianapolis, Ind.: Hackett Publishing.

Goodstein, Laurie. 1994. "Life and Death Choices: Antiabortion Faction Tries to Justify Homicide." *Washington Post,* August 13, sec. A.

Granberg, Donald, and Beth Wellman Granberg. 1980. "Abortion Attitudes, 1965-1980: Trends and Determinants." *Family Planning Perspectives* 12:250-261.

Graves, Judson. 1986. "Coaches in the Courtroom: Recovery in Actions for Breach of Employment Contracts." *Journal of College and University Law* 12:545-558.

Greenan, James S. 1984. "The Problems of Wrongful Termination." *California Lawyer* 4:29-31.

Greenhouse, Linda. 1985. "Of Tents with Wheels and Houses with Oars." *New York Times,* May 16, sec. A.

___. 1988. "Precedent for Lower Courts: Tyrant or Teacher." *New York Times,* January 29, sec. A.

Grey, Thomas S. 1974. "Do We Have an Unwritten Constitution?" *Stanford Law Review* 27:703-718.

___. 1978. "Origins of the Unwritten Constitution: Fundamental Law in American Revolutionary Thought." *Stanford Law Review* 30:843-893.

___. 1988a. "The Original Understanding and the Unwritten Constitution." In *Toward a More Perfect Union: Six Essays on the Constitution,* edited by Neil L. York. Provo, Utah: Brigham Young University Press.

___. 1988b. "The Uses of an Unwritten Constitution." *Chicago-Kent Law Review* 64:211-238.

Griffin, Kenyon N., and Michael J. Horan. 1979. "Merit Retention Elections: What Influences the Voters?" *Judicature* 63:78-88.

___. 1983. "Patterns of Voting Behavior in Judicial Retention Elections for Supreme Court Justices in Wyoming." *Judicature* 67:68-77.

Grossman, Joel B. 1965. *Lawyers and Judges: The ABA and the Politics of Judicial Selection.* New York: John Wiley and Sons.

Grossman, Joel B., and Austin Sarat. 1975. "Litigation in the Federal Courts: A Comparative Perspective." *Law and Society Review* 9:321-346.

Grossman, Joel B., and Stephen Wasby. 1972. "Haynsworth and Parker: History Does Live Again." *South Carolina Law Review* 23:345-375.

Grossman, Joel B., Herbert M. Kritzer, Kristin Bumiller, Austin Sarat, Stephen McDougal, and Richard Miller. 1982. "Dimensions of Institutional Participation: Who Uses the Courts and How?" *Journal of Politics* 44:87-111.

Gruhl, John, Cassia Spohn, and Susan Welch. 1981. "Women as Policymakers: The Case of Trial Judges." *American Journal of Political Science* 25:308-322.

Gunther, Gerald. 1964. "The Subtle Vices of the 'Passive Virtues'—A Comment on Principle and Expediency in Constitutional Law." *Columbia Law Review* 64:1-25.

Gusfield, Joseph R. 1981. *The Culture of Public Problems.* Chicago: University of Chicago Press.

Hakman, Nathan. 1966. "Lobbying the Supreme Court: An Appraisal of Political Science Folklore." *Fordham Law Review* 35:15-50.

Hall, Kermit L. 1979. *The Politics of Local Justice.* Lincoln: University of Nebraska Press.

___. 1980. "The Children of the Cabins: The Lower Federal Judiciary, Modernization, and the Political Culture." *Northwestern University Law Review* 75:423-471.

Hall, William K., and Larry T. Aspin. 1987. "What Twenty Years of Judicial Retention Elections Have Told Us." *Judicature* 70:340-347.

Halpern, Stephen C., and Charles M. Lamb, eds. 1982. *Supreme Court Activism and Restraint.* Lexington, Mass.: Lexington Books.

Handler, Joel F. 1978. *Social Movements and the Legal System: A Theory of Law Reform and Social Change.* New York: Academic Press.

Hannah, Susan B. 1978. "Competition in Michigan's Judicial Elections: Democratic Ideals vs. Judicial Realities." *Wayne Law Review* 24:1267-1306.

Hansen, John Mark. 1991. *Gaining Access: Congress and the Farm Lobby, 1919-1981.* Chicago: University of Chicago Press.

Hansen, Susan B. 1980. "State Implementation of Supreme Court Decisions: Abortion Rates Since Roe v. Wade." *Journal of Politics* 42:372-395.

Haraway, Donna. 1991. "Situated Knowledges: The Science Question in Feminism and the Privilege of Partial Perspective." In *Simians, Cyborgs and Women: The Reinvention of Nature,* edited by Donna Haraway. New York: Routledge.

Harrington, Christine B. 1985. *Shadow Justice: The Ideology and Institutionalization of Alternatives to Court.* Westport, Conn.: Greenwood Press.

___. 1988. "Regulatory Reform: Creating Gaps and Making Markets." *Law and Policy* 10:293-316.

___. 1994. "Outlining a Theory of Legal Practice." In *Lawyers in a Postmodern World: Translation and Transgression,* edited by Maureen Cain and Christine B. Harrington. Buckingham, U.K.: Open University Press.

Harrington, Christine B., and Daniel Ward. 1993. "Rethinking Litigation Activity." Paper presented at the annual meeting of the American Political Science Association, Washington, D.C.

Harris, Joseph P. 1951. *The Advice and Consent of the Senate.* Washington, D.C.: Brookings Institution.

Harris, Richard. 1970. *Decision.* New York: E. P. Dutton.

Hart, Henry M., Jr. 1953. "The Power of Congress to Limit the Jurisdiction of Federal Courts: An Exercise in Dialectic." *Harvard Law Review* 66:1362-1402.

___. 1959. "The Supreme Court—Foreword: Time Chart of the Justices." *Harvard Law Review* 73:84-125.

Hawkins, Keith. 1992. *The Uses of Discretion.* Oxford: Clarendon Press.

Haynes, Evan. 1944. *The Selection and Tenure of Judges.* Newark, N.J.: National Conference of Judicial Councils.

Heclo, Hugh. 1977. *A Government of Strangers: Executive Politics in Washington.* Washington, D.C.: Brookings Institution.

Heinz, John P., and Edward O. Laumann. 1982. *Chicago Lawyers: The Social Structure of the Bar.* New York: Russell Sage Foundation.

Hellman, Arthur. 1983. "The Supreme Court, the National Law, and the Selection of Cases for the Plenary Docket." *University of Pittsburgh Law Review* 44:521-634.

___. 1985. "Case Selection in the Burger Court: A Preliminary Inquiry." *Notre Dame Law Review* 60:947-1055.

Henderson, Lynne N. 1987. "Review Essay: What Makes Rape a Crime?" *Berkeley Women's Law Journal* 3:193-229.

Henshaw, Stanley K. 1986. "Induced Abortion: A Worldwide Perspective." *Family Planning Perspective* 18:250-254.

___. 1991. "The Accessibility of Abortion Services in the United States." *Family Planning Perspectives* 23:246-252, 263.

Henshaw, Stanley K., and Kevin O'Reilly. 1983. "Characteristics of Abortion Patients in the United States, 1979 and 1980." *Family Planning Perspectives* 15:5.

Henshaw, Stanley K., and Jennifer Van Vort. 1990. "Abortion Services in the United States, 1987 and 1988." *Family Planning Perspectives* 22:102-108, 142.

___. 1994. "Abortion Services in the United States, 1991 and 1992." *Family Planning Perspectives* 26:100-106, 122.

Henshaw, Stanley K., Nancy J. Blinkin, Ellen Blaine, and Jack C. Smith. 1985. "A Portrait of American Women Who Obtain Abortions." *Family Planning Perspectives* 17:90-96.

Henshaw, Stanley K., Jacqueline Darroch Forest, and Ellen Blaine. 1984. "Abortion Services in the United States, 1981 and 1982." *Family Planning Perspectives* 16:119-127.

Henshaw, Stanley K., Jacqueline Darroch Forrest, and Jennifer Van Vort. 1987. "Abortion Services in the United States, 1984 and 1985." *Family Planning Perspectives* 19:63-70.

Henshaw, Stanley K., Jacqueline Darroch Forrest, Ellen Sullivan, and Christopher Tietze. 1982. "Abortion Services in the United States, 1979 and 1980." *Family Planning Perspectives* 14:5-15.

Henshaw, Stanley K., Lisa M. Koonin, and Jack C. Smith. 1991. "Characteristics of U.S. Women Having Abortions, 1987." *Family Planning Perspectives* 23:75-81.

Herman, Judith Lewis. 1992. *Trauma and Recovery.* Cambridge, Mass.: Harvard University Press.

Hertzke, Allen D. 1988. *Representing God in Washington: The Role of Religious Lobbies in the American Polity.* Knoxville: University of Tennessee Press.

Heumann, Milton. 1975. "A Note on Plea Bargaining and Case Pressure." *Law and Society Review* 9:515-528.

___. 1978. *Plea Bargaining: The Experiences of Prosecutors, Judges, and Defense Attorneys.* Chicago: University of Chicago Press.

___. 1979. "Thinking about Plea Bargaining." In *The Study of Criminal Courts: Political Perspectives,* edited by Peter Nardulli. Cambridge, Mass.: Ballinger.

Heumann, Milton, and C. Loftin. 1979. "Mandatory Sentencing and the Abolition of Plea Bargaining: The Michigan Felony Firearm Statute." *Law and Society Review* 13:393-430.

Heydebrand, Wolf. 1990. "Government Litigation and National Policymaking: From Roosevelt to Reagan." *Law and Society Review* 24:477-495.

Heydebrand, Wolf, and Carroll Seron. 1986. "The Rising Demand for Court Services: A Structural Explanation of the Caseload of U.S. District Courts." *Justice System Journal* 11:303-320.

___. 1990. *The Rationalization of Justice: Historical Change and Structural Contradictions of the Federal Justice System.* Albany: State University of New York Press.

Hilts, Philip J. 1994a. "F.D.A. Panel Takes Step toward Setting Control on Nicotine." *New York Times,* August 3, sec. A.

___. 1994b."Lawsuits against Tobacco Companies May Be Consolidated." *New York Times,* November 6, sec. 1.

Himmelstein, Jerome. 1990. *To the Right: The Transformation of American Conservatism.* Berkeley: University of California Press.

Hinckley, Barbara. 1980. "House Re-Elections and Senate Defeats: The Role of the Challenger." *British Journal of Political Science* 10:441-460.

Hinckley, Barbara, Richard Hofstetter, and John Kessel. 1974. "Information and the Vote: A Comparative Election Study." *American Politics Quarterly* 2:131-158.

Hine, Darlene Clark. 1977. "The NAACP and the Supreme Court: Walter F. White and the Defeat of John J. Parker, 1930." *Negro History Bulletin* 5:753-757.

Hoffman, James R., ed. Various years. *The American Bench: Judges of the Nation.* Sacramento, Calif.: Forster-Long.

Hojnacki, Marie, and Lawrence Baum. 1992. " 'New-Style' Judicial Campaigns and the Voters: Economic Issues and Union Members in Ohio." *Western Political Quarterly* 45:921-948.

Hole, Judith, and Ellen Levine. 1971. *Rebirth of Feminism.* New York: Quadrangle.

Holmes, Oliver Wendell, Jr. 1897. "The Path of the Law." *Harvard Law Review* 10:457-478.

Hoover, Kenneth R. 1988. *The Elements of Social Scientific Thinking*. New York: St. Martin's Press.

Horan, Dennis J., Edward R. Grant, and Paige C. Cunningham, eds. 1987. *Abortion and the Constitution: Reversing Roe v. Wade Through the Courts*. Washington, D.C.: Georgetown University Press.

Howard, J. Woodford. 1968. "On the Fluidity of Judicial Choice." *American Political Science Review* 62:43-56.

____. 1981. *Courts of Appeals in the Federal Judicial System: A Study of the Second, Fifth, and District of Columbia Circuits*. Princeton, N.J.: Princeton University Press.

Hughes, David F. 1965. "Salmon P. Chase: Chief Justice." *Vanderbilt Law Review* 18:589-614.

Hugick, Larry. 1992. "Abortion: Public Support Grows for Roe v. Wade. . . ." *Gallup Poll Monthly* 316 (January): 5-9.

Hunter, Marjorie. 1985. "Case of the Missing Bullets." *New York Times*, May 15, sec. A.

Hurst, James Willard. 1950. *The Growth of American Law: The Law Makers*. Boston: Little, Brown.

Hyer, Marjorie. 1982. "Americans United's Role in Church-State Separation." *Washington Post*, January 16.

Ivers, Gregg. 1990. "Organized Religion and the Supreme Court." *Journal of Church and State* 32:775-94.

____. 1993. *Redefining the First Freedom: The Supreme Court and the Consolidation of State Power*. New Brunswick: Transaction Press.

Iyengar, Shanto, and Donald R. Kinder. 1987. *News That Matters*. Chicago: University of Chicago Press.

Jackson, Bernard. 1988. *Law, Fact, and Narrative Coherence*. Merseyside, U.K.: Deborah Charles Publications.

Jackson, John E., and Maris A. Vinovskis. 1983. "Public Opinion, Elections, and the 'Single-Issue' Issue." In *The Abortion Dispute and the American System*, edited by Gilbert Y. Steiner. Washington, D.C.: Brookings Institution.

Jacob, Herbert. 1965. *Justice in America*. 1st ed. Boston: Little, Brown.

____. 1984. *Justice in America*. 4th ed. Boston: Little, Brown.

____. 1992. "The Elusive Shadow of the Law." *Law and Society Review* 26:565-590.

Jacobsohn, Gary J. 1977. "Citizen Participation in Policy-Making: The Role of the Jury." *Journal of Politics* 39:73-96.

Jaffe, Frederick S., Barbara L. Lindheim, and Phillip R. Lee. 1981. *Abortion Politics*. New York: McGraw-Hill.

James, Dorothy. 1968. "Role Theory and the Supreme Court." *Journal of Politics* 30:160-186.

Jamieson, Kathleen Hall. 1992. *Dirty Politics: Deception, Distraction, and Democracy.* New York: Oxford University Press.

Jefferson, Thomas. 1905. *Writings.* Vol. 16. Washington, D.C.: Thomas Jefferson Memorial Association of the United States.

Johnson, Alan. 1990. "Governor Campaigns Used up $16 Million." *Columbus Dispatch,* December 15, sec. B.

Johnson, Allan Griswold. 1980. "On the Prevalence of Rape in the United States." *Signs* 6:136-146.

Johnson, Charles A., and Bradley C. Canon. 1984. *Judicial Policies: Implementation and Impact.* Washington D.C.: CQ Press.

Johnson, Earl, Jr. 1981. "Lawyers' Choice: A Theoretical Appraisal of Litigation Investment Decisions." *Law and Society Review* 15:567-610.

Johnston, Laurie. 1977. "Abortion Foes Gain Support as They Intensify Campaign." *New York Times,* October 23, sec. 1.

Joint Committee on New York Drug Law Evaluation. 1978. *The Nation's Toughest Drug Law: Evaluating the New York Experience.* Washington, D.C.: U.S. Department of Justice.

Judges of the United States. 1983. Washington, D.C.: Judicial Conference of the United States.

Kagan, Robert A., Bliss Cartwright, Lawrence M. Friedman, and Stanton Wheeler. 1977. "The Business of State Supreme Courts, 1870-1970." *Stanford Law Review* 30:121-156.

Kalman, Laura. 1990. *Abe Fortas.* New Haven, Conn.: Yale University Press.

Kalven, Harry, Jr., and Hans Zeisel. 1966. *The American Jury.* Chicago: University of Chicago Press.

Karst, Kenneth. 1977. "Foreword: Equal Citizenships." *Harvard Law Review* 91:1-68.

Katsh, Ethan. 1983. "The Supreme Court Beat: How Television Covers the Supreme Court." *Judicature* 67:6-12.

Katz, Sedelle, and Mary Ann Mazur. 1979. *Understanding the Rape Victim: A Synthesis of Research Findings.* New York: John Wiley and Sons.

Katzmann, Robert A. 1988. "The Underlying Concerns." In *Judges and Legislators: Toward Institutional Comity,* edited by Robert A Katzmann. Washington, D.C.: Brookings Institution.

Kelly, Alfred H., Winfred A. Harbison, and Herman Belz. 1991. *The American Constitution: Its Origins and Development,* 7th ed. New York: W. W. Norton.

Kemp, Kathleen A., Robert A. Carp, and David W. Brady. 1978. "The Supreme Court and Social Change: The Case of Abortion." *Western Political Quarterly* 31:19-31.

Kessler, Mark. 1993. "Legal Discourse and Political Intolerance: The Ideology of Clear and Present Danger." *Law and Society Review* 27:559-597.

"A Killing Silence." 1994. *New York Times.* May 12, sec. A.

King, Wayne. 1973. "Despite Court Ruling, Problems Persist in Gaining Abortions." *New York Times,* May 20, sec. 1.

Kipnis, Kenneth. 1976. "Criminal Justice and the Negotiated Plea." *Ethics* 86:93-106.

Kirstein-Ezzell, Tina. 1991 "Eradicating Title VII Sexual Harassment by Recognizing an Employer's Duty to Prohibit Sexual Harassment." *Arizona Law Review* 33:383-399.

Kluger, Richard. 1975. *Simple Justice.* New York: Knopf.

Kmiec, Douglas W. 1992. *The Attorney General's Lawyer: Inside the Meese Justice Department.* New York: Praeger.

Knight, Jack, and Lee Epstein. 1994. "On the Struggle for Judicial Supremacy." Washington University, St. Louis, Mo.

Kobylka, Joseph F. 1985. "Justice Harry A. Blackmun and Church-State Questions: A 'Born-Again Separationist'?" Paper presented at the annual meeting of the Law and Society Association, San Diego.

___. 1987. "A Court Related Context for Group Litigation: Libertarian Groups and Obscenity." *Journal of Politics* 49:1061-1078.

___. 1989. "Leadership on the Supreme Court of the United States: Chief Justice Burger and the Establishment Clause." *Western Political Quarterly* 42:545-568.

___. 1991. *The Politics of Obscenity: Group Litigation in a Time of Legal Change.* Westport, Conn.: Greenwood Press.

___. 1992. "The Judicial Odyssey of Harry Blackmun: The Dynamics of Individual-Level Change on the U.S. Supreme Court." Paper presented at the annual meeting of the Midwest Political Science Association, Chicago.

Kornhauser, Anne. 1989. "Abortion Case Has Been Boon to Both Sides." *Legal Times,* July 3.

Krehbiel, Keith. 1988. "Spatial Models of Legislative Choice." *Legislative Studies Quarterly* 13:259-319.

Kritzer, Herbert M. 1979. "Political Culture, Trial Courts, and Criminal Cases." In *The Study of Criminal Courts,* edited by Peter Nardulli. Cambridge, Mass.: Ballinger.

___. 1991. *Let's Make a Deal: Understanding the Negotiation Process in Ordinary Litigation.* Madison: University of Wisconsin Press.

Kritzer, Herbert M., and Frances Kahn Zemans. 1993. "Local Legal Culture and the Control of Litigation." *Law and Society Review* 27:535-557.

Kuklinski, James H., and John E. Stanga. 1979. "Political Participation and Government Responsiveness: The Behavior of California Superior Courts." *American Political Science Review* 73:1090-1099.

Kurland, Philip B., and Gerhard Casper. Various years. *Landmark Briefs and Arguments of the Supreme Court of the United States.* Frederick, Md.: University Publications of America.

Kutler, Stanley I. 1968. *Judicial Power and Reconstruction Politics.* Chicago: University of Chicago Press.

Lader, Lawrence. 1966. *Abortion.* New York: Bobbs-Merrill.

_____. 1973. *Abortion II: Making the Revolution.* Boston: Beacon Press.

Lamm, Jocelyn B. 1991. "Easing Access to the Courts for Incest Victims: Toward an Equitable Application of the Delayed Discovery Rule." *Yale Law Journal* 100:2189-2208.

Langbein, J. H. 1978. "Torture and Plea Bargaining." *University of Chicago Law Review* 46:3-22.

Larson, Stephanie Greco, and Bryan Tramont. 1993. "The Supreme Court and Television: Predicting Case Coverage." Paper presented at the annual meeting of the Midwest Political Science Association, Chicago.

Latzer, Barry. 1991. *State Constitutions and Criminal Justice.* Westport, Conn.: Greenwood Press.

Lawrence, Susan E. 1990. *The Poor in Court.* Princeton, N.J.: Princeton University Press.

Laycock, Douglas. 1991. "Vicious Stereotypes in Polite Society." *Constitutional Commentary* 8:395-407.

Lee, Rex. 1981. *A Lawyer Looks at the Supreme Court.* Provo, Utah: Brigham Young University Press.

Levi, Edward H. 1949. *An Introduction to Legal Reasoning.* Chicago: University of Chicago Press.

Levin, Martin A. 1977. *Urban Politics and the Criminal Courts.* Chicago: University of Chicago Press.

Levine, James P. 1973. "Constitutional Law and Obscene Literature: An Investigation of Bookseller Practices." In *The Impact of Supreme Court Decisions,* 2d ed., edited by Theodore Becker and Malcolm Feeley. New York: Oxford University Press.

_____. 1983. "Using Jury Verdict Forecasts in Criminal Defense Strategy." *Judicature* 66:448-461.

_____. 1992. *Juries and Politics.* Pacific Grove, Calif.: Brooks/Cole.

Levine, Martin A. 1977. *Urban Politics and Criminal Courts.* Chicago: University of Chicago Press.

Levine, Marvin J. 1994. "The Erosion of the Employment-at-Will Doctrine: Recent Developments." *Labor Law Journal* 45:79-89.

Lewin, Tamar. 1989. "Views on Abortion Remain Divided." *New York Times,* January 22, sec. 1.

_____. 1991. "A Case Study of Sexual Harassment." *New York Times,* October 11, sec. A.

_____. 1994. "A Cause Worth Killing For? Debate Splits Abortion Foes." *New York Times,* July 30, sec. A.

Lewis, Anthony. 1964. *Gideon's Trumpet.* New York: Vintage.

Lewis-Beck, Michael S. 1980. *Applied Regression—An Introduction.* Sage University Paper Series on Quantitative Applications in the Social Sciences, 07-022. Beverly Hills, Calif.: Sage Publications.

Lhotka, William C., and Tim Brant. 1992. "Missouri Judge Voted Out for 1st Time in 50 Years." *St. Louis Post-Dispatch,* November 5, sec. C.

Lipinski, Ann Marie. 1989. "Abortion Clinics Face Must-Win Case." *Chicago Tribune,* August 6.

Lisio, Donald J. 1985. *Hoover, Blacks, and Lily-Whites: A Study of Southern Strategies.* Chapel Hill: University of North Carolina Press.

London, Robb. 1990. "For Want of Recognition, Chief Justice Is Ousted." *New York Times,* September 28, sec. B.

Lopez, Gerald. 1984. "Lay Lawyering." *University of California Los Angeles Law Review* 32:1-60.

McCann, Michael W. 1994. *Rights at Work: Pay Equity Reform and the Politics of Legal Mobilization.* Chicago: University of Chicago Press.

McClellan, James. 1984. "A Lawyer Looks at Rex Lee." *Benchmark* 1:1-16.

McDowell, Gary. 1982. *Equity and the Constitution.* Chicago: University of Chicago Press.

McGuigan, Patrick B., and Jeffrey O'Connell, eds. 1987. *The Judges War.* Washington, D.C.: Institute for Government and Politics.

McGuigan, Patrick B., and Dawn Weyrich. 1990. *Ninth Justice: The Fight for Bork.* Washington, D.C.: University Press of America.

McGuire, Kevin T. 1993. *The Supreme Court Bar: Legal Elites in the Washington Community.* Charlottesville: University Press of Virginia.

McIntosh, Wayne V. 1983. "Private Use of a Public Forum: A Long Range View of the Dispute Processing Role of Courts." *American Political Science Review* 77:991-1010.

____. 1990. *The Appeal of the Civil Law.* Champaign: University of Illinois Press.

Mackenzie, G. Calvin. 1981. *The Politics of Presidential Appointments.* New York: Free Press.

MacKerron, Conrad. 1981. "Legal Services Corp. Supporters Fear It May Be 'Block Granted' to Death." *National Journal,* February 28.

McKnight, R. Neal, Roger Schaefer, and Charles A. Johnson. 1978. "Choosing Judges: Do the Voters Know What They're Doing?" *Judicature* 62:94-99.

Maddala, G. S. 1977. *Econometrics.* New York: McGraw-Hill.

Mahoney, B. 1988. *Changing Times in Trial Courts.* Williamsburg, Va.: National Center for State Courts.

Mahoney, Martha. 1991. "Legal Images of Battered Women: Redefining the Issue of Separation." *Michigan Law Review* 90:1-94.

____. 1992. "Exit: Power and the Idea of Leaving in Love, Work, and the Confirmation Hearings." *Southern California Law Review* 65:1283-1319.

Maltese, John Anthony. 1990. "The Selling of Clement Haynsworth: Politics and the Confirmation of Supreme Court Justices." *Judicature* 72:338-347.

Mango, Kimberly A. 1991. "Students versus Professors: Combatting Sexual Harassment under Title IX of the Education Amendments of 1972." *Connecticut Law Review* 23:355.

Manheim, Jarol B., and Richard C. Rich. 1991. *Empirical Political Analysis.* White Plains, N.Y.: Longman.

Mano, D. Keith. 1986. "Hell No, He Won't Go! Dartmouth's Joe Yukica Fights for His Right to Coach Football." *People,* January 20.

Manwaring, David R. 1968. "The Impact of Mapp v. Ohio." In *The Supreme Court as Policy-Maker: Three Studies on the Impact of Judicial Decisions,* edited by D. H. Everson. Carbondale: Southern Illinois Press.

Marcus, Ruth. 1994. "President Signs Clinic Access Law; Foes File Lawsuit." *Washington Post,* May 27, sec. A.

Margolick, David. 1994. "Jurors Acquit Dr. Kevorkian in Suicide Case." *New York Times,* May 3, secs. A, B.

Marsh, Jeanne C., Alison Geist, and Nathan Caplan. 1982. *Rape and the Limits of Law Reform.* Boston: Auburn House.

Marshall, Tom. 1989. *Public Opinion and the Supreme Court.* Boston: Unwin Hyman.

Martin, Fenton S., and Robert U. Goehlert. 1990. *The U.S. Supreme Court—A Bibliography.* Washington, D.C.: Congressional Quarterly Inc.

Martindale-Hubbell Law Directory. Various years. Summit, N.J.: Martindale-Hubbell.

Mason, Alpheus Thomas. 1946. *Brandeis: A Free Man's Life.* New York: Viking Press.

___. 1956. *Harlan Fiske Stone: Pillar of the Law.* New York: Viking Press.

Massaro, John. 1990. *Supremely Political: The Role of Ideology and Presidential Management in Unsuccessful Supreme Court Nominations.* Albany: State University of New York Press.

Matheny, Albert R. 1994. *Review of The Uses of Discretion,* by Keith Hawkins. *Law and Politics Book Review* 4:96-98.

Mather, Lynn. 1979. *Plea Bargaining or Trial? The Process of Criminal Case Disposition.* Lexington, Mass.: Lexington Books.

___. 1982. "Conclusion: The Mobilizing Potential of Class Actions." *Indiana Law Journal* 57:451-458.

___. 1991. "Policy Making in State Trial Courts." In *American Courts,* edited by John B. Gates and Charles A. Johnson. Washington, D.C.: CQ Press.

Mather, Lynn, and Barbara Yngvesson. 1981. "Language, Audience, and the Transformation of Disputes." *Law and Society Review* 15:775-821.

Matthews, Donald. 1960. *U.S. Senators and Their World.* Chapel Hill: University of North Carolina Press.

Mayhew, David. 1990. *Divided We Govern.* New Haven, Conn.: Yale University Press.

Medalie, Richard, Leonard Zeitz, and Paul Alexander. 1968. "Custodial Police Interrogation in Our Nation's Capital: The Attempt to Implement Miranda." *University of Michigan Law Review* 66:1347-1422.

Meese, Edwin. 1985. "Remarks before the American Bar Association." In *The Great Debate: Interpreting Our Constitution*. Occasional Paper 2). Washington, D.C.: Federalist Society.

Melone, Albert. 1990. "Revisiting the Freshman Effect Hypothesis: The First Two Terms of Justice Anthony Kennedy." *Judicature* 74:6-14.

Merry, Sally Engle. 1990. *Getting Justice and Getting Even: Legal Consciousness among Working-Class Americans.* Chicago: University of Chicago Press.

Mersky, Roy M., and J. Myron Jacobstein. Various years. *The Supreme Court of the United States Nominations.* Buffalo: William S. Hein.

Miller, Anita, ed. 1994. *The Complete Transcripts of the Clarence Thomas-Anita Hill Hearings: October 11, 12, 13, 1991.* Chicago: Academy Chicago Publishers.

Miller, Arthur S. 1982. *Toward Increased Judicial Activism: The Political Role of the Supreme Court.* Chicago: Greenwood.

Miller, Richard E., and Austin Sarat. 1981. "Grievances, Claims, and Disputes: Assessing the Adversary Culture." *Law and Society Review* 15:525-566.

Milner, Neal. 1971. *The Court and Local Law Enforcement.* Beverly Hills, Calif.: Sage Publications.

Minow, Martha. 1990. *Making All the Difference: Inclusion, Exclusion, and American Law.* Ithaca, N.Y.: Cornell University Press.

Mnookin, Robert H., and Lewis Kornhauser. 1979. "Bargaining in the Shadow of the Law: The Case of Divorce." *Yale Law Journal* 88:950-997.

Moen, Matthew C. 1989. *The Christian Right and Congress.* Tuscaloosa: University of Alabama Press.

Mohr, James C. 1978. *Abortion in America: The Origins and Evolution of National Policy, 1800-1900.* New York: Oxford University Press.

Monroe, Keith. 1968. "How California's Abortion Law Isn't Working." *New York Times Magazine,* December 29.

Moon, David. 1990. "What You Use Depends on What You Have." *American Politics Quarterly* 18:3-24.

Morgan, Richard E. 1968. *The Politics of Religious Conflict.* New York: Pegasus.

___. 1972. *The Supreme Court and Religion.* New York: Free Press.

___. 1973. "The Establishment Clause and Sectarian Schools: A Final Installment?" *Supreme Court Review* 1973:57-97.

Moritz, Amy. 1988. "The New Right, It's Time We Led: Conservatism's Parched Grass Roots." *Policy Review* 1988: 22-25.

Moskowitz, Seymour. 1988. "Employment-at-Will and Codes of Ethics: The Professional's Dilemma." *Valparaiso Law Review* 23:33-73.

Mueller, John E. 1970. "Choosing among 133 Candidates." *Public Opinion Quarterly* 34:395-402.

Munger, Frank. 1988. "Law, Change, and Litigation: A Critical Examination of an Empirical Research Tradition." *Law and Society Review* 22:57-101.

Murphy, Bruce Allen. 1988. *Fortas: The Rise and Ruin of a Supreme Court Justice.* New York: William Morrow.

Murphy, Walter F. 1964. *Elements of Judicial Strategy.* Chicago: University of Chicago Press.

___. 1978. "The Art of Constitutional Interpretation." In *Essays on the Constitution of the United States,* edited by M. Judd Harmon. Port Washington, N.Y.: Kennikat Press.

___. 1980. "An Ordering of Constitutional Values." *Southern California Law Review* 53:703-760.

___. 1990. "Reagan's Judicial Strategy." In *Looking Back on the Reagan Presidency,* edited by Larry Berman. Baltimore: Johns Hopkins University Press.

Nakanishi, Masao, Lee G. Cooper, and Harold H. Kassarjian. 1974. "Voting for a Political Candidate under Conditions of Minimal Information." *Journal of Consumer Research* 1:36-43.

Nardulli, Peter F., James Eisenstein, and Roy B. Flemming. 1988. *The Tenor of Justice: Felony Courts and the Guilty Plea Process.* Champaign: University of Illinois Press.

Nelson, Barbara J. 1984. *Making an Issue of Child Abuse: Political Agenda Setting for Social Problems.* Chicago: University of Chicago Press.

Nelson, Robert L., John P. Heinz, Edward O. Laumann, and Robert H. Salisbury. 1988. "Lawyers and the Structure of Influence in Washington." *Law and Society Review* 22:235-300.

Neubauer, David W. 1974. *Criminal Justice in Middle America.* Morristown, N.J.: General Learning Press.

Neubauer, David W., Marcia J. Lipetz, Mary Lee Luskin, and John Paul Ryan. 1981. *Managing the Pace of Justice: An Evaluation of LEAA's Delay Reduction Program.* Washington, D.C.: Government Printing Office.

Neuman, W. Russell. 1990. "The Threshold of Public Attention." *Public Opinion Quarterly* 54:159-176.

Nevins, Allan. 1987. "The Case of the Copperhead Conspirator." In *Quarrels That Have Shaped the Constitution,* edited by John A. Garraty. New York: Harper and Row.

Newland, Chester A. 1967. "Press Coverage of the U.S. Supreme Court." *Western Political Quarterly* 17:15-36.

Newport, Frank, and Leslie McAneny. 1992. "Whose Court Is It Anyhow? O'Connor, Kennedy, Souter Position Reflects Abortion Views of Most Americans." *Gallup Poll Monthly* 322 (July): 51-53.

Nimmer, Raymond T., and Patricia Ann Krauthaus. 1977. *Plea Bargaining Reform in Two Cities.* Justice System Journal 3:6-21.

Noonan, John T., Jr. 1973. "Raw Judicial Power." *National Review,* March 2.

Oates, Bob. 1986. "He Fought the System . . . and Won." *Los Angeles Times,* March 30, sec. III.

O'Brien, David M. 1988. "The Reagan Judges: His Most Enduring Legacy?" In *The Reagan Legacy: Promise and Performance,* edited by Charles O. Jones. Chatham, N.J.: Chatham House.

___. 1989. "Federalism As a Metaphor in the Constitutional Politics of Public Administration." *Public Administration Review* 49:411-419.

___. 1993. *Storm Center.* 3d ed. New York: W. W. Norton.

O'Connor, Karen, and Lee Epstein. 1983. "The Role of Interest Groups in Supreme Court Policy Formation." In *Public Policy Formation,* edited by Robert Eyestone. Greenwich, Conn.: JAI Press.

___. 1985. "Bridging the Gap between Congress and the Supreme Court: Interest Groups and the Erosion of the American Rules Governing Awards of Attorneys Fees." *Western Political Quarterly* 38:238-249.

___. 1989. *Public Interest Law Groups.* New York: Greenwood Press.

Olson, Susan M. 1984. *Clients and Lawyers: Securing the Rights of Disabled Persons.* Westport, Conn.: Greenwood Press.

Ordeshook, Peter C. 1986. *Game Theory and Political Theory.* Cambridge: Cambridge University Press.

___. 1992. *A Political Theory Primer.* New York: Routledge.

Orren, Karen. 1976. "Standing to Sue: Interest Group Conflict in the Federal Courts." *American Political Science Review* 70:723-741.

Overby, L. Marvin, Beth M. Henschen, Michael H. Walsh, and Julie Strauss. 1992. "Courting Constituents? An Analysis of the Senate Confirmation Vote on Justice Clarence Thomas." *American Political Science Review* 86:997-1006.

Pacelle, Richard. 1991. *The Transformation of the Supreme Court's Agenda: From the New Deal to the Reagan Administration.* Boulder, Colo.: Westview Press.

Palmer, Jan. 1990. *The Vinson Court Era: The Supreme Court's Conference Votes.* New York: AMS Press.

Papke, David, ed. 1992. *Narrative and Legal Discourse: A Reader in Storytelling and the Law.* Liverpool, U.K.: Deborah Charles Publications.

Paul-Shaheen, P. A., and Harry Perlstadt. 1982. "Class Action Suits and Social Change: The Organization and Impact of the Hill-Burton Cases." *Indiana Law Journal* 57:385-423.

Peltason, J. W. 1961. *Fifty-Eight Lonely Men: Southern Federal Judges and School Desegregation.* New York: Harcourt, Brace and World.

Perry, H. W. 1991. *Deciding to Decide: Agenda Setting in the United States Supreme Court.* Cambridge, Mass.: Harvard University Press.

Perry, Michael. 1982. *The Constitution, the Courts, and Human Rights.* New Haven, Conn.: Yale University Press.

___. 1988. *Morality, Politics, and Law: A Bicentennial Essay.* New York: Oxford University Press.

Pertschuk, Michael, and Wendy Schaetzel. 1989. *The People Rising: The Campaign against the Bork Nomination.* New York: Thunder's Mouth Press.

Peterson, Iver. 1987. "States Assess Surrogate Motherhood." *New York Times,* December 13, sec. 1.

Pfeffer, Leo. 1975. *God, Caesar, and the Constitution.* Boston: Beacon Press.

___. 1984. *Religion, State, and the Burger Court.* Buffalo, N.Y.: Prometheus Books.

Phelps, Timothy, and Helen Winternitz. 1992. *Capitol Games.* New York: Hyperion.

Phillips, Richard. 1980. "The Shooting War over 'Choice' or 'Life' Is Beginning Again." *Chicago Tribune,* April 20, sec. 12.

Pierce, Neal R. 1981. "Some Friends in High Places May Save Legal Aid Funding Program from Extinction." *National Journal,* June 6.

Pomper, Gerald. 1966. "Ethnic and Group Voting in Nonpartisan Municipal Elections." *Public Opinion Quarterly* 30:79-97.

Price, David E. 1985. "Congressional Committees in the Policy Process." In *Congress Reconsidered,* 3d ed., edited by Lawrence C. Dodd and Bruce I. Oppenheimer. Washington, D.C.: CQ Press.

Price, Vincent, and John Zaller. 1993. "Who Gets the News? Alternative Measures of News Reception and Their Implications for Research." *Public Opinion Quarterly* 57:133-164.

Pritchett, C. Herman. 1948. *The Roosevelt Court.* New York: Macmillan.

___. 1954. *Civil Liberties and the Vinson Court.* Chicago: University of Chicago Press.

___. 1961. *Congress versus the Supreme Court.* Minneapolis: University of Minnesota Press.

___. 1969. "The Development of Judicial Research." In *Frontiers of Judicial Research,* edited by Joel B. Grossman and Joseph Tanenhaus. New York: John Wiley and Sons.

"Protecting At Will Employees against Wrongful Discharge: The Duty to Terminate Only in Good Faith." 1980. *Harvard Law Review* 93:1816-1844.

Provine, Doris Marie. 1980. *Case Selection in the United States Supreme Court.* Chicago: University of Chicago Press.

Puro, Steven. 1971. "The Role of *Amicus Curiae* in the United States Supreme Court." Ph.D. diss., State University of New York at Buffalo.

Pusey, Merlo J. 1951. *Charles Evans Hughes.* New York: Columbia University Press.

Rabin, Robert L. 1993. "Institutional and Historical Perspectives on Tobacco Tort Liability." In *Smoking Policy: Law, Politics, and Culture,* edited by Robert L. Rabin and Stephen D. Sugarman. New York: Oxford University Press.

Rabkin, Jeremy. 1988. "Micromanaging the Administrative Agencies." *Public Interest* 100:116-130.

Rahn, Wendy M., John H. Aldrich, Eugene Borgida, and John L. Sullivan. 1990. "A Social-Cognitive Model of Candidate Appraisal." In *Reasoning and Choice: Explorations in Political Psychology,* principal authors Paul M. Sniderman, Richard A. Brody, and Philip E. Tetlock. Cambridge: Cambridge University Press.

Ratner, Leonard. 1960. "Congressional Power over the Appellate Jurisdiction of the Supreme Court." *University of Pennsylvania Law Review* 109:157-202.

Rauh, Joseph L., Jr. 1990. "A Personalized History of the Supreme Court from Roosevelt to Bush." Regents' Lecture, University of California, San Diego, Calif., February 13 and 15.

Raymond, Paul. 1992. "The American Voter in a Nonpartisan, Urban Election." *American Politics Quarterly* 20:247-260.

Raymond, Paul, and Peter Paluch. 1994. "The American Voter in a Local, Judicial Election." Paper presented at the annual meeting of the Midwest Political Science Association, Chicago.

Reagan, Ronald. 1982. *Public Papers of the President.* Washington, D.C.: U.S. Government Printing Office.

___. 1983. *Public Papers of the President.* Washington, D.C.: U.S. Government Printing Office.

___. 1984. *Public Papers of the President.* Washington, D.C.: U.S. Government Printing Office.

___. 1985. *Public Papers of the President.* Washington, D.C.: U.S. Government Printing Office.

Reams, Bernard D., Jr. 1994. *Congress and the Courts: A Legislative History.* Buffalo: William S. Hein.

Reams, Bernard D., Jr., and Charles Haworth. 1978. *Congress and the Courts: A Legislative History.* Buffalo: William. S. Hein.

Redlawsk, David P., and Richard R. Lau. 1994. "The Effect of Political Expertise on Support for the United States Supreme Court, 1980-1992." Paper presented at the annual meeting of the American Political Science Association, New York.

Rehnquist, William H. 1987. *The Supreme Court—How It Was, How It Is.* New York: William Morrow.

Reichley, A. James. 1985. *Religion in American Public Life.* Washington, D.C.: Brookings Institution.

Reskin, Lauren Rubinstein. 1986. "LawPoll: How Lawyers Vote on Tough Ethical Dilemmas." *American Bar Association Journal* 72:42.

"Rhode Island Abortion Law Is Declared Unconstitutional." 1973. *New York Times,* May 17, sec. A.

Richardson, Richard J., and Kenneth N. Vines. 1970. *The Politics of Federal Courts: Lower Courts in the United States.* Boston: Little, Brown.

Rodgers, Harrell, and Charles S. Bullock. 1972. *Law and Social Change: Civil Rights Laws and Their Consequences.* New York: McGraw-Hill.

Rodriguez, Daniel B. 1994. "The Positive Political Dimensions of Regulatory Reform." *Washington University Law Quarterly* 72:1-150.

Rohde, David W., and Harold J. Spaeth. 1976. *Supreme Court Decision Making.* San Francisco: W. H. Freeman.

Rohter, Larry. 1994. "Florida Prepares New Basis to Sue Tobacco Industry for People on Medicaid." *New York Times,* May 27, secs. A, B.

Roper, Robert T. 1986a. *A Preliminary Examination of Available Civil and Criminal Trend Data in State Trial Courts for 1978, 1981, and 1984.* Williamsburg, Va.: National Center for State Courts.

___. 1986b. "The Propensity to Litigate in State Trial Courts, 1981-1984, 1984-1985." *Justice System Journal* 11:262-281.

Rosen, Jeffrey. 1993. "The Leader of the Opposition." *New Republic,* January 18.

Rosen, R. A. Hudson, H. W. Werley, Jr., J. W. Ager, and F. P. Shea. 1974. "Health Professionals' Attitudes toward Abortion." *Public Opinion Quarterly* 38:159-173.

Rosenberg, Gerald N. 1991. *The Hollow Hope: Can Courts Bring About Social Change?* Chicago: University of Chicago Press.

Rosenthal, Douglas E. 1974. *Lawyer and Client: Who's in Charge?* New York: Russell Sage Foundation.

Rosenthal, Jack. 1971. "Survey Finds 50% Back Liberalization of Abortion Policy." *New York Times,* October 28, sec. A.

Rosoff, Jeannie I. 1975. "Is Support for Abortion Political Suicide?" *Family Planning Perspectives* 7:13-22.

Ross, H. Lawrence. 1970. *Settled Out of Court: The Social Process of Insurance Claims Adjustments.* Chicago: Aldine.

Ross, William G. 1990. "Participation by the Public in the Federal Judicial Selection Process." *Vanderbilt Law Review* 43:1-84.

___. 1994. *A Muted Fury: Populists, Progressives, and Labor Unions Confront the Courts, 1890-1937.* Princeton: Princeton University Press.

Roth, J. 1978. "Prosecutor Perceptions of Crime Seriousness." *Journal of Criminal Law and Criminology* 69:232-242.

Rubenstein, M., and T. White. 1979. "Alaska's Ban on Plea Bargaining." *Law and Society Review* 13:367-383.

Rubin, Eva R. 1982. *Abortion, Politics, and the Courts.* Westport, Conn.: Greenwood Press.

Russell, Diana E. H. 1984. *Sexual Exploitation: Rape, Child Sexual Abuse, and Workplace Harassment.* Beverly Hills, Calif.: Sage Publications.

Russell, Diana E. H., and Nancy Howell. 1983. "The Prevalence of Rape in the United States Revisited." *Signs* 8:688-695.

Russell, Mary. 1977. "House Bars Use of U.S. Funds in Abortion Cases." *Washington Post,* June 18, sec. A.

Ryan, John Paul, Allan Ashman, Bruce D. Sales, and Sandra Shane-DuBow. 1980. *American Trial Judges: Their Work Styles and Performance.* New York: Free Press.

Sager, Lawrence Gene. 1981. "Foreword: Constitutional Limitations on Congress' Authority to Regulate the Jurisdiction of the Federal Courts." *Harvard Law Review* 95:17-89.

Salisbury, Robert H. 1990. "The Paradox of Interest Groups in Washington—More Groups, Less Clout." In *The New American Political System,* edited by Anthony King. Washington, D.C.: AEI Press.

Salokar, Rebecca Mae. 1992. *The Solicitor General: The Politics of Law.* Philadelphia: Temple University Press.

Santos, Boaventura de Sousa. 1977. "The Law of the Oppressed: The Construction and Reproduction of Legality in Pasargada." *Law and Society Review* 12:5-105.

Sarat, Austin. 1977. "Judging in Trial Courts: An Exploratory Study." *Journal of Politics* 39:368-398.

Sarat, Austin, and William L. F. Felstiner. 1986. "Law and Strategy in the Divorce Lawyer's Office." *Law and Society Review* 20:93-134.

Sarat, Austin, and Joel B. Grossman. 1975. "Courts and Conflict Resolution: Problems in the Mobilization of Adjudication." *American Political Science Review* 69:1200-1217.

Sarbin, Theodore. 1986. "The Narrative as a Root Metaphor for Psychology." In *Narrative Psychology,* edited by Theodore Sarbin. Westport, Conn.: Greenwood Press.

Sayrs, Lois W. 1989. *Pooled Time Series Analysis.* Newbury Park, Calif.: Sage Publications.

Schattschneider, E. E. 1960. *The Semisovereign People.* New York: Holt, Rinehart and Winston.

Scheingold, Stuart A. 1974. *The Politics of Rights: Lawyers, Public Policy, and Political Change.* New Haven, Conn.: Yale University Press.

Scheppele, Kim Lane. 1987. "The Re-Vision of Rape Law." *University of Chicago Law Review* 54:1095-1116.

___. 1988. "Facing Facts in Legal Interpretation." *Representations* 30:42.

Scheppele, Kim Lane, and Pauline Bart. 1983. "Through Women's Eyes: Defining Danger in the Wake of Sexual Assault." *Journal of Social Issues* 39:63-80.

Schlozman, Kay L., and John T. Tierney. 1986. *Organized Interests and American Democracy.* New York: Harper and Row.

Schrodt, Philip A. 1991. "Mathematical Modeling." In *Empirical Political Analysis,* edited by Jarol B. Manheim and Richard C. Rich. White Plains, N.Y.: Longman.

Schubert, Glendon A. 1959. *Quantitative Analysis of Judicial Behavior.* Glencoe, Ill.: Free Press.

___. 1960. *Constitutional Politics.* New York: Holt, Rinehart and Winston.

___. 1962. "Policy without Law: An Extension of the Certiorari Game." *Stanford Law Review* 14:284-327.

___. 1965. *The Judicial Mind.* Evanston, Ill.: Northwestern University Press.

Schulder, Diane, and Florynce Kennedy. 1971. *Abortion Rap.* New York: McGraw-Hill.

Schulhofer, Stephen J. 1984. "Is Plea Bargaining Inevitable?" *Harvard Law Review* 97:1037-1107.

Schultz, Terri. 1977. "Though Legal, Abortions Are Not Always Available." *New York Times,* January 2, sec. 4.

Schwartz, Alan. 1979. "The Case for Specific Performance." *Yale Law Journal* 89:271-306.

Schwartz, Bernard. 1983. *Super Chief.* New York: New York University Press.

___. 1990. *The Ascent of Pragmatism.* Reading, Mass.: Addison-Wesley.

___. 1994. *A History of the Supreme Court.* New York: Oxford University Press.

Schwartz, Gary T. 1993. "Tobacco Liability in the Courts." In *Smoking Policy: Law, Politics, and Culture,* edited by Robert L. Rabin and Stephen D. Sugarman. New York: Oxford University Press.

Schwartz, Herman. 1988. *Packing the Courts: The Conservative Campaign to Re-Write the Constitution.* New York: Charles Scribner's Sons.

Scigliano, Robert. 1971. *The Supreme Court and the Presidency.* New York: Free Press.

Segal, Jeffrey A. 1984. "Predicting Supreme Court Decisions Probabilistically: The Search and Seizure Cases 1962-1981." *American Political Science Review* 78:891-900.

___. 1985. "Measuring Change on the Supreme Court: Examining Alternative Models." *American Journal of Political Science* 29:461-479.

___. 1986. "Supreme Court Justices as Human Decision Makers: An Individual Level Analysis of Search and Seizure Cases." *Journal of Politics* 48:938-955.

___. 1987. "Senate Confirmation of Supreme Court Justices: Partisan and Institutional Politics." *Journal of Politics* 49:998-1015.

___. 1991. "Courts, Executives, and Legislatures." In *The American Courts,* edited by John B. Gates and Charles A. Johnson. Washington, D.C.: CQ Press.

Segal, Jeffrey A., and Albert D. Cover. 1989. "Ideological Values and the Votes of U.S. Supreme Court Justices." *American Political Science Review* 83:557-565.

Segal, Jeffrey A., and Harold J. Spaeth. 1993. *The Supreme Court and the Attitudinal Model.* Cambridge: Cambridge University Press.

___. 1994. "Preferences vs. Precedents: An Empirical Test of the Legal Model." Paper presented at the annual meeting of the American Political Science Association, New York.

Segal, Jeffrey A., Charles M. Cameron, and Albert D. Cover. 1992. "A Spatial Model of Roll Call Voting: Senators, Constituents, Presidents, and Interest Groups in Supreme Court Confirmations." *American Journal of Political Science* 36:96-121.

Segal, Jeffrey A., Lee Epstein, Harold J. Spaeth, and Charles Cameron. Forthcoming. "Ideological Values and the Votes of the Justices Revisited." *Journal of Politics.*

Sellin, T., and M. Wolfgang. 1964. *The Measurement of Delinquency.* New York: John Wiley and Sons.

Shafer, Byron. 1988. *Bifurcated Politics.* Cambridge, Mass.: Harvard University Press.

Shank, Roger. 1991. *Tell Me a Story.* New York: Charles Scribner's Sons.

Shapiro, Martin. 1964. *Law and Politics in the Supreme Court.* New York: Free Press.

___. 1970. "Decentralized Decision-Making in the Law of Torts." In *Political Decision-Making,* edited by S. Sidney Ulmer. New York: Van Nostrand Reinhold.

___. 1972. "From Public Law to Public Policy, or the 'Public' in 'Public Law.' " *PS* 5:410-418.

___. 1981. *Courts: A Comparative and Political Analysis.* Chicago: University of Chicago Press.

___. 1983. "Fathers and Sons: The Court, the Commentators, and the Search for Values." In *The Burger Court: The Counter-Revolution That Wasn't,* edited by Vincent Blasi. New Haven, Conn.: Yale University Press.

___. 1988. *Who Guards the Guardians?* Athens: University of Georgia Press.

___. 1990. "Interest Groups and Supreme Court Appointments." *Northwestern University Law Review* 84:935-961.

Shaw, David. 1981. "Media Coverage of the Courts: Improving but Still Not Adequate." *Judicature* 65:18-24.

Sheldon, Charles H., and Nicholas P. Lovrich, Jr. 1983. "Knowledge and Judicial Voting: The Oregon and Washington Experience." *Judicature* 67:234-245.

Sherry, Suzanna. 1987. "The Founders' Unwritten Constitution." *University of Chicago Law Review* 54:1127-1177.

___. 1989. "Women's Virtue." *Tulane Law Review* 63:1591-1598.

Sherwin, Richard. 1988. "Dialects and Dominance: A Study of Rhetorical Fields in the Law of Confessions" *University of Pennsylvania Law Review* 136:729-849.

Shogan, Robert. 1972. *A Question of Judgment: The Fortas Case and the Struggle for the Supreme Court.* Indianapolis, Ind.: Bobbs-Merrill.

Shribman, David. 1989. "Abortion-Issue Foes, Preaching to the Converted in No Uncertain Terms, Step Up Funding Pleas." *Wall Street Journal,* December 26, sec. A.

Silberman, Matthew. 1985. *The Civil Justice Process.* Orlando, Fla.: Academic Press.

Silbey, Susan, and Austin Sarat. 1989. "Dispute Processing in Law and Legal Scholarship: From Institutional Critique to the Reconstruction of the Juridical Subject." *Denver University Law Review* 66:437-498.

Silverstein, Mark, and Benjamin Ginsberg. 1987. "The Supreme Court and the New Politics of Judicial Power." *Political Science Quarterly* 102:371-388.

Singelais, Neil. 1985. "Yukica Gets Job Back." *Boston Globe,* December 21.

Slotnick, Elliot E. 1979. "The Changing Role of the Senate Judiciary Committee in Judicial Selection." *Judicature* 62:502-510.

___. 1991. "Television News and the Supreme Court: 'Game Day' Coverage of the Bakke Case." Paper presented at the annual meeting of the Midwest Political Science Association, Chicago.

Slotnick, Elliot E., and Jennifer A. Segal. 1992. "Television News and the Supreme Court." Paper presented at the annual meeting of the American Political Science Association, Chicago.

Slotnick, Elliot E., Jennifer A. Segal, and Lisa M. Campoli. 1994. "Television News and the Supreme Court: Correlates of Decisional Change." Paper presented at the annual meeting of the American Political Science Association, New York.

Smith, Eliot R., and Frederick D. Miller. 1978. "Limits on Perception of Cognitive Processes: A Reply to Nisbett and Wilson." *Psychological Review* 85:355-362.

Smith, Hedrick. 1988. *The Power Game: How Washington Works.* New York: Random House.

Smith, Rogers. 1985. *Liberalism and American Constitutional Law.* Cambridge, Mass.: Harvard University Press.

____. 1988. "Political Jurisprudence, the 'New Institutionalism,' and the Future of Public Law." *American Political Science Review* 82:89-108.

Smolowe, Jill. 1992. "Anita Hill's Legacy." *Time,* October 19.

Snell, Roger. 1991. "No Order in the Court." *Akron Beacon Journal,* November 7, sec. A.

Sniderman, Paul M., James M. Glaser, and Robert Griffin. 1990. "Information and Electoral Choice." In *Reasoning and Choice: Explorations in Political Psychology,* principal authors Paul M. Sniderman, Richard A. Brody, and Philip E. Tetlock. Cambridge: Cambridge University Press.

Sniderman, Paul M., W. Russell Neuman, Jack Citrin, Herbert McCloskey, and J. Merrill Shanks. 1975. "The Stability of Support for the Political System: The Impact of Watergate." *American Politics Quarterly* 34:437-457.

Solomon, Rayman L. 1984. "The Politics of Appointment and the Federal Courts' Role in Regulating America: U.S. Courts of Appeals Judgeships from T.R. to F.D.R." *American Bar Foundation Research Journal* 1984:284-343.

Songer, Donald R. 1982. "Consensual and Nonconsensual Decisions in Unanimous Opinions of the United States Courts of Appeals." *American Journal of Political Science* 26:225-239.

____. 1987. "The Impact of the Supreme Court on Trends in Economic Policy Making in the United States Courts of Appeals." *Journal of Politics* 49:830-841.

____. 1991. "The Circuit Courts of Appeals." In *The American Courts: A Critical Assessment,* edited by John Gates and Charles A. Johnson. Washington, D.C.: CQ Press.

Songer, Donald R., and Sue Davis. 1990. "The Impact of Party and Region on Voting Decision in the United States Courts of Appeals, 1955-1986." *Western Political Quarterly* 43:317-334.

Songer, Donald, and Susan Reid. 1989. "Policy Change on the U.S. Courts of Appeals: Exploring the Contribution of the Legal and Democratic Subcultures." Paper presented at the annual meeting of the American Political Science Association.

Songer, Donald R., and Reginald S. Sheehan. 1990. "Supreme Court Impact on Compliance and Outcomes: Miranda and New York Times in the United States Courts of Appeals." *Western Political Quarterly* 43:297-316.

____. 1992. "Who Wins on Appeal? Upperdogs and Underdogs in the United States Courts of Appeals." *American Journal of Political Science* 36:235-258.

Songer, Donald R., C. K. Rowland, and Robert A. Carp. 1984. "The Impact of the Supreme Court on Outcomes in the U.S. District Courts and the U.S. Courts of Appeals." Paper presented at the annual meeting of the American Political Science Association.

Songer, Donald R., Jeffrey A. Segal, and Charles M. Cameron. 1994. "The Hierarchy of Justice: Testing a Principal-Agent Theory of Supreme Court-Circuit Court Interactions." *American Journal of Political Science* 38:673-696.

Sorauf, Frank J. 1976. *The Wall of Separation: The Constitutional Politics of Church and State.* Princeton, N.J.: Princeton University Press.

Spaeth, Harold J. 1963. "Warren Court Attitudes toward Business." In *Judicial Decision Making,* edited by Glendon Schubert. New York: Free Press.

Spaeth, Harold J., and David J. Peterson. 1971. "The Analysis and Interpretation of Dimensionality: The Case of Civil Liberties Decision Making." *American Journal of Political Science* 15:415-441.

Spector, Malcolm, and John I. Kitsuse. 1977. *Constructing Social Problems.* New York: Aldine DeGruyter.

Spiller, Pablo T., and Rafael Gely. 1992. "Congressional Control of Judicial Independence: The Determinants of U.S. Supreme Court Labor-Relations Decisions, 1949-1988." *RAND Journal of Economics* 23:463-492.

Squire, Peverill, and Eric R. A. N. Smith. 1988. "The Effect of Partisan Information on Voters in Nonpartisan Elections." *Journal of Politics* 50:169-179.

Stanley, Harold W., and Richard G. Niemi. 1992. *Vital Statistics on American Politics.* Washington, D.C.: CQ Press.

Steele, John L. 1970. "Haynsworth v. the U.S. Senate (1969)." *Fortune* 81:90-94, 155-161.

Steinberg, Terry Nicole. 1991. "Rape on College Campuses: Reform through Title X." *Journal of College and University Law* 18:39-71.

Steiner, Gilbert Y., ed. 1983. *The Abortion Dispute and the American System.* Washington, D.C.: Brookings Institution.

Stewart, Richard. 1975. "The Reformation of American Administrative Law." *Harvard Law Review* 88:1669-1813.

Stidham, Ronald, and Robert A. Carp. 1982. "Trial Court Response to Supreme Court Policy Changes: Three Case Studies." *Law and Policy Quarterly* 4:215-234.

Stimson, James. 1985. "Regression in Space and Time: A Statistical Essay." *American Journal of Political Science* 29:914-947.

____. 1991. *Public Opinion in America.* Boulder, Colo.: Westview Press.

Stone, Deborah A. 1988. *Policy Paradox and Political Reason.* Glenview, Ill.: Scott, Foresman.

Stone, Rebecca, and Cynthia Waszak. 1992. "Adolescent Knowledge and Attitudes about Abortion." *Family Planning Perspectives* 24:52-57.

Stouffer, S. A., L. Guttman, E. A. Suchman, P. F. Lazarsfeld, S. A. Star, and J. A. Clausen. 1950. *Measurement and Prediction.* New York: John Wiley and Sons.

Strum, Charles. 1992. "Major Lawsuit on Smoking Is Dropped." *New York Times,* November 6, sec. B.

Stumpf, Harry P. 1988. *American Judicial Politics.* San Diego, Calif.: Harcourt Brace Jovanovich.

Sullivan, Ellen, Christopher Tietze, and Joy G. Dryfoos. 1977. "Legal Abortion in the United States, 1975-1976." *Family Planning Perspectives* 9:116.

Sunstein, Cass. 1993. *The Partial Constitution.* Cambridge, Mass.: Harvard University Press.

Swisher, Carl Brent. 1963. *Stephen J. Field: Craftsman of the Law.* Hamden, Conn.: Archon Books.

Taft, Bob. 1991. *Election Statistics for 1989-1990.* Columbus: Office of the Ohio Secretary of State.

___. 1993. *Ohio Election Statistics for 1991-1992.* Columbus: Office of the Ohio Secretary of State.

Tangri, Sandra, Martha Burt, and Leonor B. Johnson. 1982. "Sexual Harassment at Work: Three Explanatory Models." *Journal of Social Issues* 38:33-54.

Tarr, G. Alan. 1977. *Judicial Impact and State Supreme Courts.* Lexington, Mass.: Lexington Books.

Tarr, G. Alan, and Mary Cornelia Aldis Porter. 1988. *State Supreme Courts in State and Nation.* New Haven, Conn.: Yale University Press.

Tatalovich, Raymond, and Byron W. Daynes. 1981. *The Politics of Abortion.* New York: Praeger.

Tate, C. Neal. 1981. "Personal Attribute Models of Voting Behavior of U.S. Supreme Court Justices: Liberalism in Civil Liberties and Economics Decisions, 1946-1978." *American Political Science Review* 75:355-367.

Tate, C. Neal, and Roger Handberg. 1991. "Time Binding and Theory Building in Personal Attribute Models of Supreme Court Voting Behavior, 1916-88." *American Journal of Political Science* 35:460-480.

Thayer, James Bradley. 1901. *John Marshall.* Boston: Houghton, Mifflin.

Thomas, Pierre. 1994. "U.S. Marshals Dispatched to Guard Abortion Clinics." *Washington Post,* August 2, sec. A.

Tiberi, Todd. 1993. "Comment: Supreme Court Denials of Certiorari in Conflicts Cases: Percolation or Procrastination?" *University of Pittsburgh Law Review* 54:861-891.

Tobias, Paul H. 1988. "Current Trends in Employment Dismissal Law: The Plaintiff's Perspective." *Nebraska Law Review* 67:178-192.

Todd, A. L. 1965. *Justice on Trial: The Case of Louis D. Brandeis.* Chicago: University of Chicago Press.

Tolchin, Martin. 1977. "House Bars Medicaid Abortions and Funds for Enforcing Quotas." *New York Times,* June 18, sec. A.

Toledano, Ben C. 1990. "Judge Not: Memoirs of a Judicial Nominee." *National Review,* August 20.

Tomain, Joseph P. 1987. "Contracts." In *Encyclopedia of the American Judicial System,* edited by Robert J. Janosik. New York: Charles Scribner's Sons.

Toner, Robin. 1993. "Clinton Orders Reversal of Abortion Restrictions Left by Reagan and Bush." *New York Times,* January 23, sec. A.

Torrey, Morrison. 1991. "When Will We Be Believed? Rape Myths and the Idea of a Fair Trial in Rape Prosecutions." *University of California at Davis Law Review* 24:1013-1071.

Tribe, Laurence. 1978. *The Constitutional Protection of Individual Rights.* Mineola, N.Y.: Foundation Press.

___. 1985. *God Save This Honorable Court.* New York: Random House.

Twentieth Century Fund. 1988. *Judicial Roulette: The Report of the Twentieth Century Fund Task Force on the Appointment of Federal Judges.* New York: Twentieth Century Fund.

Twiss, Benjamin R. 1942. *Lawyers and the Constitution—How Laissez Faire Came to the Supreme Court.* Ithaca, N.Y.: Cornell University Press.

Ulmer, S. Sidney. 1960. "Supreme Court Behavior and Civil Rights." *Western Political Quarterly* 13:288-311.

___. 1972. "The Decision to Grant Certiorari as an Indicator to Decision 'On the Merits.' " *Polity* 4:429-447.

___. 1978. "Selecting Cases for Supreme Court Review: An Underdog Model." *American Political Science Review* 72:902-910.

___. 1984. "The Supreme Court's Certiorari Decisions: Conflict as a Predictive Variable." *American Political Science Review* 78:901-911.

Unger, Roberto. 1986. *The Critical Legal Studies Movement.* Cambridge, Mass.: Harvard University Press.

United States. *Bicentennial Committee of the Judicial Conference.* 1983. Judges of the United States. Washington, D.C.: Judicial Conference of the United States.

United States. Bureau of the Census. 1991. *Voting and Registration in the Election of November 1990.* Current Population Reports, Series P-20, no. 453. Washington, D.C.: U.S. Government Printing Office.

___. Various years. *Statistical Abstract of the United States.* Washington, D.C.: U.S. Government Printing Office.

United States. Congress. Senate. 1916. Committee on the Judiciary. *Hearings on the Nomination of Louis D. Brandeis to Be an Associate Justice of the United States before the Subcommittee of the Senate Committee on the Judiciary.* 65th Cong., 1st sess.

___. 1930. Committee on the Judiciary. *Hearings before the Subcommittee of the Senate Committee on the Judiciary on the Confirmation of the Honorable John J. Parker to Be an Associate Justice of the Supreme Court of the United States.* 71st Cong., 2d sess.

___. 1939. Committee on the Judiciary. *Hearings before the Senate Committee on the Judiciary on the Nomination of Felix Frankfurter to Be an Associate Justice of the Supreme Court of the United States.* 76th Cong., 1st sess.

___. 1958. Committee on the Judiciary. *Legislative History of the United States Circuit Courts of Appeals and the Judges Who Served during the Period from 1801 through March 1958.* 85th Cong., 2d sess.

___. 1968. Committee on the Judiciary. *Hearings before the Senate Committee on the Judiciary on the Nomination of Abe Fortas, of Tennessee, to Be Chief Justice of the United States and the Nomination of Homer Thornberry, of Texas, to Be Associate Justice of the Supreme Court of the United States.* 90th Cong., 2d sess.

___. 1969. Committee on the Judiciary. *Hearings before the Senate Committee on the Judiciary on the Nomination of Clement F. Haynsworth, Jr., of South Carolina, to Be an Associate Justice of the Supreme Court of the United States.* 91st Cong., 1st sess.

___. 1970a. Committee on the Judiciary. *Hearings before the Senate Committee on the Judiciary on the Nomination of George Harrold Carswell, of Florida, to Be an Associate Justice of the Supreme Court of the United States.* 91st Cong., 2d sess.

___. 1970b. *Congressional Record.* Daily ed. 91st Cong., 2d sess. April 23. S3746.

___. 1970c. *Congressional Record.* Daily ed. 91st Cong., 2d sess. February 24. S3501.

___. 1971. Committee on the Judiciary. *Hearings before the Senate Committee on the Judiciary on the Nomination of William H. Rehnquist, of Arizona, and Lewis F. Powell, Jr., of Virginia, to Be Associate Justices of the Supreme Court of the United States.* 92d Cong., 1st sess.

___. 1974. Committee on the Judiciary. *Hearings before the Subcommittee on Constitutional Amendments.* Vol. 2. 93d Cong., 2d sess.

___. 1976. Committee on the Judiciary. *Hearings before the Subcommittee on Constitutional Amendments.* Vol. 4. 94th Cong., 1st sess.

___. 1979. Committee on the Judiciary. *Selection and Confirmation of Federal Judges, Hearings before the Senate Judiciary Committee.* 96th Cong., 1st sess.

___. 1991. Committee on the Judiciary. *Hearings before the Senate Committee on the Judiciary on the Nomination of Clarence Thomas, to Be an Associate Justice of the Supreme Court of the United States.* 102d Cong., 2d sess.

United States. Merit System Board. 1988. Office of Merit Systems Review and Studies. *Sexual Harassment in the Federal Government: An Update.* Washington, D.C.: U.S. Government Printing Office.

The United States Courts: Their Jurisdiction and Work. 1989. Washington, D.C.: Administrative Office of the United States Courts.

Urofsky, Melvin I. 1988. *A March of Liberty.* New York: Knopf.

Utz, Pamela J. 1978. *Setting the Facts: Discretion and Negotiation in Criminal Court.* Lexington, Mass.: Lexington Books.

Van Alstyne, William W. 1973. "A Critical Guide to *Ex Parte* McCardle." *Arizona Law Review* 15:229-269.

Veronen, Lois T., Connie L. Best, and Dean G. Kilpatrick. 1979. "Treating Fear and Anxiety in Rape Victims: Implications for the Criminal Justice System." In *Perspectives on Victimology,* edited by William H. Parsonage. New York: Sage Books.

Vogel, David. 1989. *Fluctuating Fortunes.* New York: Basic Books.

Vose, Clement E. 1959. *Caucasians Only: The Supreme Court, the NAACP, and the Restrictive Covenant Cases.* Berkeley, Calif.: University of California Press.

___. 1972. *Constitutional Change.* Lexington, Mass.: Lexington Books.

Wahlbeck, Paul. 1994. "The Life of the Law: Judicial Politics and Legal Change." Paper presented at the annual meeting of the Midwest Political Science Association, Chicago.

Waits, Kathleen. 1985. "The Criminal Justice System's Response to Battering: Understanding the Problem, Forging the Solutions." *Washington University Law Review* 60:267-329.

Walker, Jack L. 1983. "The Origins and Maintenance of Interest Groups in America." *American Political Science Review* 77:390-406.

Walker, Leonore. 1979. *The Battered Woman.* New York: Harper and Row.

Walker, Samuel. 1990. *In Defense of American Liberties: A History of the ACLU.* New York: Oxford University Press.

Walker, Thomas G., and Lee Epstein. 1993. *The Supreme Court of the United States: An Introduction.* New York: St. Martin's Press.

Wanner, Craig. 1974. "The Public Ordering of Private Relations: Part One, Initiating Civil Cases in Urban Trial Courts." *Law and Society Review* 8:429-440.

___. 1975. "The Public Ordering of Private Relations: Part Two, Winning Civil Court Cases." *Law and Society Review* 9:293-306.

Want's Federal-State Court Directory. Various years. Washington, D.C.: Want Publishing.

Warren, Charles. 1926. *The Supreme Court in United States History.* Boston: Little, Brown.

___. 1939. *A History of the American Bar.* New York: Howard Fertig.

Wasby, Stephen L. 1970. *The Impact of the United States Supreme Court: Some Perspectives.* Homewood, Ill.: Dorsey Press.

Wasby, Stephen, and Joel B. Grossman. 1972. "The Senate and Supreme Court Nominations." *Duke Law Journal* 1971: 557-591.

Watson, Richard L. 1963. "The Defeat of Judge Parker: A Study in Pressure Groups and Politics." *Mississippi Valley Historical Review* 50:213-234.

Way, Frank H. 1968. "Survey Research on Judicial Decisions: The Prayer and Bible Reading Cases." *Western Political Quarterly* 21:189-205.

Wechsler, Herbert. 1959. "Toward Neutral Principles of Constitutional Law." *Harvard Law Review* 73:1-35.

Weinstock, Edward, Christopher Tietze, Frederick S. Jaffe, and Joy G. Dryfoos. 1975. "Legal Abortions in the United States Since the 1973 Supreme Court Decisions." *Family Planning Perspectives* 7:23-31.

Weisberg, Herbert. 1978. "Evaluating Theories of Congressional Roll-Call Voting." *American Journal of Political Science* 22:554-577.

Welch, Susan, and Timothy Bledsoe. 1986. "The Partisan Consequences of Nonpartisan Elections and the Changing Nature of Urban Politics." *American Journal of Political Science* 30:128-139.

Wells, Richard S., and Joel B. Grossman. 1966. "The Concept of Judicial Policy-Making: A Critique." *Journal of Public Law* 15:286-310.

Welsh, Wayne N. 1992. "The Dynamics of Jail Reform Litigation: A Comparative Analysis of Litigation in California Counties." *Law and Society Review* 26:591-625.

Westin, Alan. 1951. "The Supreme Court, the Populist Movement, and the Campaign of 1896." *Journal of Politics* 15:3-41.

Wheeler, Russell R., and Cynthia Harrison. 1989. *Creating the Federal Judicial System.* Washington, D.C.: Federal Judicial Center.

Wheeler, Stanton, Bliss Cartwright, Robert A. Kagan, and Lawrence M. Friedman. 1987. "Do the 'Haves' Come Out Ahead? Winning and Losing in State Supreme Courts, 1870-1970." *Law and Society Review* 21:403-445.

White, G. Edward. 1988. *The Marshall Court and Cultural Change, 1815-35.* Vols. 3 and 4 of History of the Supreme Court of the United States. New York: Macmillan.

White, Theodore H. 1961. *The Making of the President 1960.* New York: Pocket Books.

Who's Who in American Law. Various years. Wilmette, Ill.: Marquis.

Williams, Charles. 1988. "The Opinion of Anthony Kennedy: No Time for Ideology." *American Bar Association Journal* 74:56-61.

Williams, Joyce E., and Karen A. Holmes. 1981. *The Second Assault: Rape and Public Attitudes.* Westport, Conn.: Greenwood Press.

Williams, Roger M. 1979. "The Power of Fetal Politics." *Saturday Review,* June 9.

Williamson, John B., David A. Karp, John R. Dalphin, and Paul S. Gray. 1982. *The Research Craft.* Boston: Little, Brown.

Wilson, James Q. 1973. *Political Organizations.* New York: Basic Books.

Wines, Michael. 1982. "Administration Says It Merely Seeks a 'Better Way' to Enforce Civil Rights." *National Journal,* March 27.

Wisconsin Contracts Group. 1989. *Contracts: Law in Action.* Part B of *Contracts I.* Madison: University of Wisconsin Law School.

Witt, Elder. 1990. *Congressional Quarterly's Guide to the U.S. Supreme Court.* Washington, D.C.: Congressional Quarterly Inc.

Wittgenstein, Ludwig. 1976. *Philosophical Investigations.* 3d ed. Translated by G. E. M. Anscombe. Oxford: Blackwell.

Wold, John T., and John H. Culver. 1987. "The Defeat of the California Justices: The Campaign, the Electorate, and the Issue of Judicial Accountability." *Judicature* 70:348-355.

"A Woman's Right." 1973. *Evening Star* (Washington, D.C.), January 27, sec. A.

Wyszynski, James. 1989. "In Praise of Judicial Restraint: The Jurisprudence of Justice Antonin Scalia." *Detroit College of Law Review* 1989:117-162.

Yngvesson, Barbara. 1988. "Making Law at the Doorway: The Clerk, the Court, and the Construction of Community in a New England Town." *Law and Society Review* 22:409-448.

___. 1993. *Virtuous Citizens, Disruptive Subjects: Order and Complaint in a New England Court.* New York: Routledge.

Yngvesson, Barbara, and Lynn Mather. 1983. "Courts, Moots, and the Disputing Process." In *Empirical Theories about Courts,* edited by Keith O. Boyum and Lynn Mather. New York: Longman.

Yukica, Joe. 1986. "A Deal Is a Deal." In *1986 Summer Manual.* Altamonte Springs, Fla.: Special Editions Publishing.

Zaller, John, and Stanley Feldman. 1992. "A Simple Theory of the Survey Response: Answering Questions versus Revealing Preferences." *American Journal of Political Science* 36:579-616.

Zemans, Frances Kahn. 1982. "Framework for Analysis of Legal Mobilization: A Decision-Making Model." *American Bar Foundation Research Journal* 1982:989-1071.

___. 1983. "Legal Mobilization: The Neglected Role of the Law in the Political System." *American Political Science Review* 77:690-703.

Table of Cases

Demarest v. Manspeaker, 498 U.S. 184 (1991)

Doe v. Bolton, 410 U.S. 179 (1973)

Dombrowski v. Pfister, 380 U.S. 479 (1965)

Edwards v. Aguillard, 482 U.S. 578 (1987)

Eisenstadt v. Baird, 405 U.S. 438 (1972)

Employment Division, Department of Human Resources of Oregon v. Smith, 494 U.S. 872 (1990)

Engel v. Vitale, 370 U.S. 421 (1962)

Epperson v. Arkansas, 393 U.S. 97 (1968)

Everson v. Board of Education, 330 U.S. 1 (1947)

Firefighters v. Cleveland, 478 U.S. 501 (1986)

Firefighters v. Stotts, 467 U.S. 561 (1984)

Flast v. Cohen, 392 U.S. 83 (1968)

Freytag v. Commissioner of Internal Revenue, 501 U.S. 868 (1991)

Frothingham v. Mellon, 262 U.S. 447 (1923)

Fullilove v. Klutznick, 448 U.S. 448 (1980)

Furman v. Georgia, 408 U.S. 238 (1972)

Garcia v. San Antonio Metropolitan Transit Authority, 469 U.S. 578 (1985)

Georgia v. Stanton, 6 Wall. (73 U.S.) 50 (1868)

Gideon v. Wainwright, 372 U.S. 335 (1963)

Glidden Co. v. Zdanok, 370 U.S. 530 (1962)

Gollust v. Mendell, 501 U.S. 115 (1991)

Grand Rapids v. Ball, 473 U.S. 373 (1985)

Gregg v. Georgia, 428 U.S. 153 (1976)

Griswold v. Connecticut, 381 U.S. 479 (1965)

Harper v. Virginia State Board of Elections, 383 U.S. 663 (1966)

Harris v. McRae, 448 U.S. 297 (1980)

Hernandez v. Commissioner of Internal Revenue, 490 U.S. 680 (1989)

Humphrey's Executor v. United States, 295 U.S. 602 (1935)

In re Primus, 436 U.S. 412 (1978)

In re R.M.J., 455 U.S. 191 (1982)

In the Matter of Baby M, 525 A.2d 1128 (N.J.Super. Ch. 1987); 537 A.2d 1127 (N.J. 1988)

Johnson v. Transportation Agency, 480 U.S. 616 (1987)

Kaiser v. Weber, 443 U.S. 193 (1979)

Kiryas Joel Village School District v. Grumett, 114 S.Ct. 2481 (1994)

Korematsu v. United States, 323 U.S. 214 (1944)

Labine v. Vincent, 401 U.S. 532 (1971)

Lamb's Chapel v. Center Moriches Union Free School District, 113 S.Ct. 2141 (1993)

Larkin v. Grendel's Den, 459 U.S. 116 (1982)

Larson v. Valente, 456 U.S. 228 (1982)

Reed v. Shepard, 939 F.2d 484 (1991)

Regents v. Bakke, 438 U.S. 265 (1978)

Reynolds v. Sims, 377 U.S. 533 (1964)

Richmond v. Croson Co., 488 U.S. 469 (1989)

Roe v. Wade, 410 U.S. 113 (1973)

Roemer v. Maryland, 426 U.S. 736 (1976)

Roth v. United States, 354 U.S. 476 (1957)

Rust v. Sullivan, 500 U.S. 173 (1991)

Sable Communications v. FCC, 492 U.S. 115 (1989)

Schenck v. United States, 249 U.S. 47 (1919)

School District of Abington Township v. Schempp, 374 U.S. 203 (1963)

Scott v. Sandford, 60 U.S. (19 Howard) 393 (1857)

Shapero v. Kentucky State Bar Association, 486 U.S. 466 (1988)

Sherbert v. Verner, 374 U.S. 398 (1963)

Simmons v. State, 504 N.E.2d 575 (Ind. 1987)

South Carolina v. Gathers, 490 U.S. 805 (1989)

Stanford v. Kentucky, 492 U.S. 361 (1989)

State v. Frost, 577 A.2d 1282 (N.J.Super.Ct.App.Div. 1990)

Steelworkers v. Weber, 443 U.S. 193 (1979)

Stone v. Graham, 449 U.S. 39 (1980)

Strauder v. West Virginia, 100 U.S. 303 (1880)

Sullivan v. Stroop, 496 U.S. 478 (1990)

Swaggart Ministries v. California, 493 U.S. 378 (1990)

Texas Monthly v. Bullock, 489 U.S. 1 (1989)

Texas v. Johnson, 491 U.S. 397 (1989)

Thornburgh v. American College of Obstetricians and Gynecologists, 476 U.S. 747 (1986)

Thorton v. Caldor, 472 U.S. 703 (1985)

Tilton v. Richardson, 403 U.S. 672 (1971)

Toibb v. Radloff, 501 U.S. 157 (1991)

Twining v. New Jersey, 211 U.S. 78 (1908)

United States v. Darby Lumber, 312 U.S. 100 (1941)

United Mine Workers v. Red Jacket Consolidated Coal and Coke Company, 18 F.2d 839 (1927)

United States v. Carolene Products Co., 304 U.S. 144 (1938)

United States v. Paradise, 480 U.S. 149 (1987)

United States v. Vuitch, 402 U.S. 62 (1971)

United States v. Weber, 443 U.S. 193 (1979)

Valley Forge Christian College v. Americans United, 454 U.S. 464 (1982)

Virginia v. Bobbitt, Prince William County Circuit Court (Va.) CR 33821 (1993)

Index

Ginsburg, Ruth Bader, 59, 70
  abortion, 292, 401
  Establishment Clause (First Amendment), 106
  ideology, 258
Goetz, Bernard, 194
Goldberg, Arthur J., 293*n*
Goldstein, Leslie Friedman, 3
Gollust v. Mendel (1991), 298
Gompers, Samuel, 48
Goodman, Janice, 414
Government Accountability Project, 56
Governors
  elections, 20
  judges, 19
Graglia, Lino, 58
Graham, Robert, 58
Grand Rapids v. Ball (1985), 100, 101, 105, 110, 120
Grant, Ulysses, 324, 345*n*
Gray Panthers, 63
Great Depression, 255, 258, 314. *See also* New Deal; Roosevelt, Franklin D.
Gregg v. Georgia (1976), 122, 274*n*
Grier, Robert C., 329, 340, 345*n*
Griffin, Robert P., 50
Griswold v. Connecticut (1965), 278-280, 293*n*
Gun lobby, 54
Gunn, David, 406
Guttman, Louis, 309

Habeas corpus, 261, 315-316, 331, 332, 344*n*
Habeas Corpus Act of 1863, 325
Habeas Corpus Act of 1867, 335, 338, 339, 340, 341, 342
Haffey, J. Ross, 25
Hakman, Nathan, 111
Hamilton, Alexander, 396
Hand, Learned, 121
Harlan, John M., 49, 293*n*, 310
Harper v. Virginia State Board of Elections (1966), 276
Harris v. McRae (1980), 391. *See also* Abortion
Harvey, William, 57
Haynsworth, Clement, 49, 51-52
Hill, Anita, 59, 156-158, 161, 162
Holmes, Oliver Wendell, 229
Hoover, Herbert, 48
Horowitz, Michael, 57-58
House of Representatives, 20. *See also* Congress; Senate
Hughes, Charles Evans, 48
Humphrey's Executor v. United States (1935), 303

Hyde Amendment (1980), 391, 400-402, 415-416. *See also* Abortion

Illinois
  appellate courts, 203
  divorce, 186-187
  Supreme Court, 180-181
Illinois Committee for Medical Control of Abortion, 397
Immunities Clause, 283
In re Primus (1978), 388*n*
In re R.M.J. (1982), 388*n*
In the Matter of Baby M. (1987), 190-191, 194, 200
Indiana Supreme Court, 164-165
Inter-Circuit Tribunal, 270
Interest groups, 15. *See also* Lobbying
  Congress, 64-65
  conservative, 60-61
  corporate, 61
  growth of, 60
  information providers, 45
  judicial selection, 45-59
  liberal, 68-69
  Ohio, 29
  Senate, 64
  Supreme Court, 68, 72-80, 111-113

Jackson, Robert H., 95
Jacob, Herbert, 173
Jefferson, Thomas, 94
Jim Crow laws, 328
John Birch Society, 57
John Paul II (Pope), 194
Johnson, Andrew, 325, 327-329, 331-334, 339, 341, 343, 345*n*
Johnson, Charles, 22
Johnson, Frank, 173
Johnson, Lyndon B., 50, 397
Jones, Edith, 54
Jones, Stephanie Tubbs, 25, 27, 29-30, 35-36, 38-41
Judges, 15, 19, 241
  appellate courts, 232
  Congress, 210
  criminal defendants, 191
  election of, 19-20
  federal, 45, 123, 189-190
  Maine, 19
  memories of victims, 166-168
  Minnesota, 20
  nominations, 51
  partisanship, 21-22